PRACTICAL POSER® 8: THE OFFICIAL GUIDE

RICHARD SCHRAND

Course Technology PTR

A part of Cengage Learning

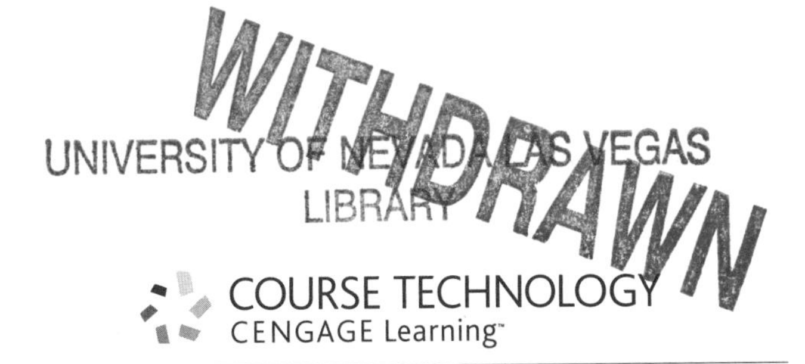

Australia, Brazil, Japan, Korea, Mexico, Singapore, Spain, United Kingdom, United States

Practical Poser® 8: The Official Guide
Richard Schrand

Publisher and General Manager, Course Technology PTR:
Stacy L. Hiquet

Associate Director of Marketing:
Sarah Panella

Manager of Editorial Services:
Heather Talbot

Marketing Manager:
Jordan Castellani

Acquisitions Editor:
Heather Hurley

Project Editor and Copy Editor:
Kim Benbow

Technical Reviewer:
Denise Tyler

Interior Layout:
Shawn Morningstar

Cover Designer:
Mike Tanamachi

DVD-ROM Producer:
Brandon Penticuff

Indexer:
Kelly Talbot

Proofreader:
Brad Crawford

Printed in the United States of America
1 2 3 4 5 6 7 12 11 10

Library of Congress Control Number: 2009933326

ISBN-13: 978-1-58450-697-3

ISBN-10: 1-58450-697-0

Course Technology
20 Channel Center Street
Boston, MA 02210
USA

Cengage Learning is a leading provider of customized learning solutions with office locations around the globe, including Singapore, the United Kingdom, Australia, Mexico, Brazil, and Japan. Locate your local office at: **international.cengage.com/region**

Cengage Learning products are represented in Canada by Nelson Education, Ltd.
For your lifelong learning solutions, visit **courseptr.com**
Visit our corporate website at **cengage.com**

To all my students past and present:
You persevered through what probably felt
like endless hours of tweaking poses, lights, and
camera positions until they were perfect.

Acknowledgments

There are times in life when a person can get away with taking full credit for a project. Authoring a book is not one of those times. There are so many people who are involved with the creation of a book, from the layout people to the editors and the big boss person—the one who hires and assigns the people who keep everything on track.

So I would like to thank (in no particular order) Kim Benbow, my editor, whose insight and knowledge have made this a better book. Denise Tyler, whose knowledge of Poser helped keep me on track and who allowed me to update her *Practical Poser 7* book. My thanks to everyone who worked on laying out the book and who took my ideas and turned them into reality. And to Heather Hurley, acquisitions editor extraordinaire, who, during SIGGRAPH 2009 in New Orleans, twisted my arm to write this book. (It still hurts, by the way!!!)

Okay. I'm kidding about the arm twisting. Really.

And then to all my friends, students, and family who continually asked, "Haven't you finished that dang thing yet?" All I can say is, "Yep. I have."

About the Author

Practical Poser 8: The Official Guide is the 14th book by **Richard Schrand**, and the second book he has written that covers this program. His other books include *Vue 6 Revealed* and *Vue 7: Beyond the Basics*, as well as books covering web design, Adobe Photoshop, video editing, and 3D modeling techniques. When not writing, he has been instrumental in helping to create two bachelor's degree programs for Nossi College of Art in Tennessee—one in graphic design and the other in video production.

Contents

Introduction

It's an interesting challenge I have been given: Update a book that is considered the epitome of Poser knowledge written by arguably one of the most respected Poser users there is—Denise Tyler. That's the conundrum I was faced with when first approached by the publisher of *Practical Poser 7*. So I did what any rational person in my position would do. I read the book and cogitated and cogitated, and then cogitated some more. Satisfied that I had sufficiently engulfed myself in the material, I re-read the book, and then thought about it some more. Then it finally came to me. I couldn't do it. I couldn't rewrite what is already a staple in many users' libraries. What I could do was carry the torch; I could add to and augment what was already there. This is Poser, after all. No matter the updates, there is still a comfortable familiarity with the program that has been meticulously retained by everyone involved in its production. By becoming involved with this book, there is almost a feeling of coming home. I have been involved with Poser since version 1. One of the first books I ever wrote was *Poser 4 Pro Pack fx and Design*, which was fairly well received and the first one produced covering the program. It's amazing how far Larry Weinberg's brainchild has come since then (see www.larryweinberg.com/gallery2/v/PoserHistory/).

Having started as an experiment in creating posing references for comic book artists, Poser has become a program that many artists use to assuage their artistic muse on a daily basis. I look back at my history with the program. I initially bought it due to curiosity. After I opened it and played around for a while, I decided that maybe I could use it with my new company. Back then, those first-generation models looked amazing, and there had to be some way for me to incorporate them in the layout work I was doing. Unfortunately, just about that time a local auto dealer put out a commercial with a 3D-generated giant that was so horrendously not good that it turned the entire community off of anything 3D. So I was limited to using Poser as a previsualization tool. And I still had to tell clients that, no, I wasn't using 3D for their ads. Oh, how times have changed.

As the program gained popularity with the general public, an entire support industry grew. Entire companies were created to supply professional-quality products, and individual artists began making content for the program—some free and some low cost. Entire websites emerged where Poser users could show their artwork or supply their original creations. From the most conservative to the most erotic, Poser created a phenomenon unheard of in the computing world. Yet there was, and still is, a stigma surrounding the program.

Some consider Poser a mere toy—something that isn't worthy of serious 3D artistic expression. Part of this could be equated to a purist mentality: "Unless I build and rig it myself, it ain't worth its weight in pixels." Or it could have been the 3D artists' difficulty with importing models into Maya, Max, LightWave 3D, or Cinema 4D. The latter problem was alleviated with Poser 8, the version of the program that will be covered in this book. With Poser 8, 3D artists are able to import the PZ3 (the native Poser format) or PZZ (the compressed Poser format) files into their modeling program of choice and have an extremely high-quality still or animated figure in their scene. This can now save hours of work while producing high-quality figure animations perfect for web, television, or movie productions. Poser, therefore, is much more than its humble beginnings would ever have indicated.

What About This Book's Content?

It is assumed that you have a strong working knowledge of Poser. While many introductory aspects are covered in the HTML files included on the accompanying DVD, you will be best served to review the Poser Reference Manual and the Poser Tutorial Manual that came with your software. In these pages, you will be taken further into the program, find out more about the new features, and discover just how powerful Poser 8 has become.

Nearly everything in Poser 8 has been upgraded. In many cases, these upgrades are under the hood. On the other hand, there are numerous changes that will immediately jump out at you. The first chapter will deal with the most apparent update, the graphical user interface (GUI). I then move to higher-level topics, mainly covering the features that you'll find in the Poser rooms. You'll learn how to prepare photographs so that you get the best results in the Face Room. You'll also learn how to create and save custom faces in the Face Room. You'll learn how to use the Hair Room to add hair to Poser clothing or props and how to pick up hair colors from underlying textures. You'll also learn how to work with the various types of Poser clothing and the differences between Conforming clothing, Dynamic clothing, and hybrid Conforming/Dynamic clothing. Finally, you'll learn how to decipher and build materials in the advanced Material Room.

Some of the most frequently asked questions involve creating and customizing Poser clothing. Although these are advanced-level skills that often require software other than Poser, it is a topic of great interest and need to Poser users; I will address this in the later chapters. First, you'll learn how to use magnets to create morphs in Poser. You'll also learn the steps involved to export and import morphs to and from an external morphing program. Through several chapters, you'll learn the procedures involved in modeling a simple piece of clothing, how to create UV maps for common clothing articles (shirts, skirts, and pants), how to assign materials in clothing, and how to group them correctly so that your models work properly in Poser. You'll also learn how to save different types of Poser content into the Poser libraries so that they also work properly. In addition, you'll learn what makes the Poser rendering engine work and how you can enhance your Poser renders so that they look their best.

Who Will Benefit from This Plethora of Information

As previously mentioned, a lot of information is going to be covered. A lot of thought went into how to present the content so you can easily find the feature you want to learn about when you are ready to learn it.

Practical Poser 8: The Official Guide, in conjunction with Poser's user manuals, will be invaluable learning tools. If you're an intermediate user you will find helpful tips and tricks that could take you to that next level. And, if you are an advanced user, this book will help you quickly discover how to use many of Poser's new features.

The Conventions

Being a cross-platform application—Poser is available for both the PC and the Mac—there are slight differences in the way the program is operated. If you have read any of my other books, you know that I bring up quick key commands whenever they are available. With Poser, the biggest difference is in how to accomplish those quick key commands. So throughout the book, quick key commands will be written using the following conventions: PC/Mac+x. For instance, to open an existing file, the quick key command would be Ctrl/Cmd+O. Continuing with the differences between Macs and PCs, when I talk about right-clicking, that pertains to both operating systems. Some people forget that Macs can use multi-button mouses (mice? meeses?) and have been able to for about a decade. But, if you don't have a multi-button mouse—first off, why not?!?—instead of right-clicking, hold down the Control (Ctrl) key on the Mac's keyboard.

Digging In

With all of this said, it's now time to dig in and begin working with Poser 8. There's a lot to explore and discover. The techniques that you learn in this book will help you get up to speed very quickly with the questions that Poser users ask most. I am also open to suggestions and additional questions that can be covered in future editions of this book, and I will watch the various forums in the online Poser communities for questions or comments from readers.

DVD-ROM Downloads

If you purchased an ebook version of this book, and the book had a companion DVD-ROM, we will mail you a copy of the disc. Please send ptrsupplements@cengage.com the title of the book, the ISBN, your name, address, and phone number. Thank you.

1 Everything Old Is New Again

In This Chapter:

- Poser's New Features
- Tutorial 1.1: Make the GUI Your Own
- Where Your Content Lives
- Tutorial 1.2: Searching for Content
- Tutorial 1.3: Saving Your Favorite Content
- Tutorial 1.4: Creating Runtime Folders on Your Hard Drive
- Tutorial 1.5: Adding a New Runtime Folder to the Poser Library

One thing that can be said about Poser is this: it has retained and honored its roots from the days when Kai Krause first designed its graphical user interface (GUI). Krause was one of the preeminent user interface designers back in the 1980s. According to Wikipedia, "Krause significantly broadened conventional notions of the graphical user interface by applying innovative design principles and providing realtime interaction for the user, neither of which were widely deployed in the 1980s because most users found them too oblique to learn and remember." Of course, these are now common elements in all GUIs on all operating systems—rounded corners, drop shadows, transparent backgrounds. Amazing how far we have come, isn't it?

Having founded MetaCreations, Inc., Krause put his visual stamp on not only Poser, but on Bryce and the popular Kai's Power Tools. Since its inception, Poser has kept the look and feel of Krause's interface, for both good and bad. One of the bad things: Poser was always a bit of a screen hog. Okay, maybe that was an understatement. You had control window upon control window, each of which overlapped the other, taking up screen real estate. They covered the workspace, and you had to constantly open and close windows or move them to the side so they'd be out of the way when accessing the controls you needed or to work with the figures. Poser's innovative look was also its hindrance to many users. Still, one could never deny how "cool" the program's interface looked.

With Poser 8, the interface has been updated and refined while retaining the feel and functionality that Poser users have grown to expect. The basic user interface has been streamlined and modernized with docked palettes and panels. You're able to move these into new locations and dock them as you like. You can even use multiple monitors to open the interface even further. In this chapter, I'll discuss some of the new features, and then build on those when moving into subsequent chapters.

Poser's New Features

Immediately upon opening the program, you will see that a lot of modifications that have been made to the Poser interface. There's a sense of newness blended with familiarity. To discover the plethora of changes, let's start with the GUI.

The New Graphical User Interface

With Poser 8, the look of the GUI has been modernized. However, even though it has been brought into the 21st century, the GUI has also remained true to Krause's design concepts. When you first open Poser 8, you will be greeted with the Pose Room shown in Figure 1.1, a more organized and accessible interface that at once looks familiar while showing off its cleaner layout. It's also worth noting that, depending on your screen resolution, the number of palettes or panels you see either increases or decreases. For example, you will see fewer panels at a resolution of 1024×768 than you will if your resolution is set to 1920×1600.

Windows have been organized and dock comfortably into one another. They have been given a more modern look that is familiar to most 3D and 2D artists. Controls can be undocked or moved and docked with other tools. They can be removed from the main interface entirely. So if you don't use a specific tool or control set very often, you can remove it to make room for other tools you use more regularly.

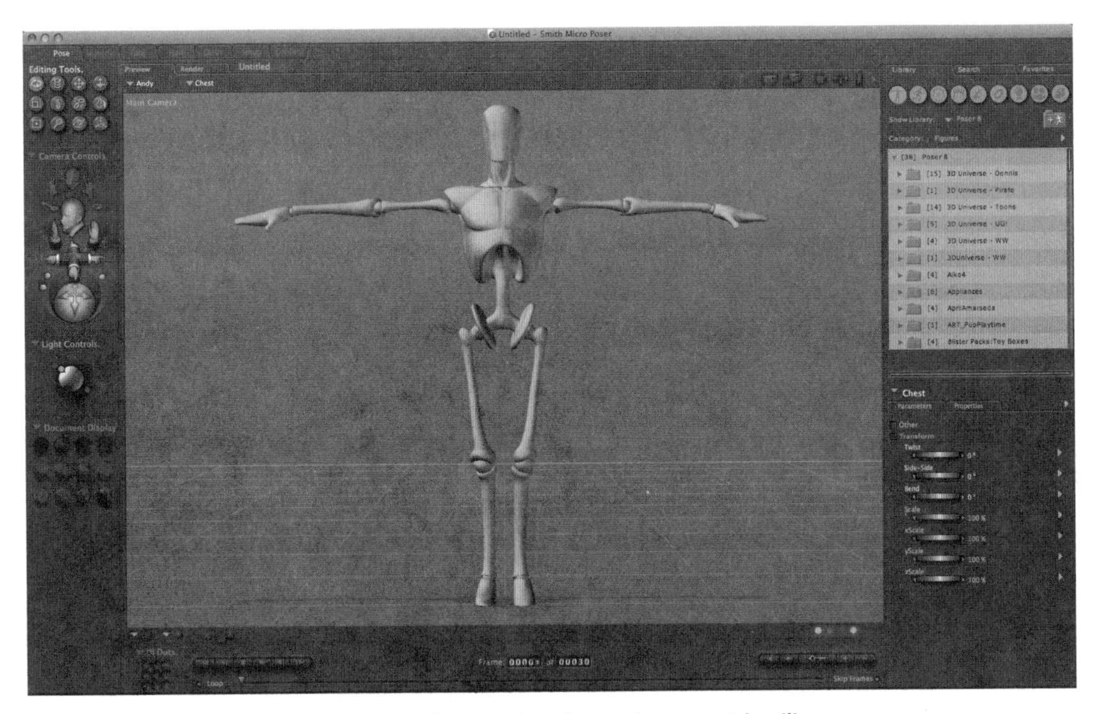

FIGURE 1.1 The new interface—cleaner yet familiar.

This is the same for each of the program's rooms: Material, Face, Hair, Cloth, Setup, and Content. Figure 1.2 shows each of these rooms and their new interface layout.

A subtle difference in the interface appearance comes from the icons for the various content directories—the folders where your models reside. Since the first version of the program, the directory icons were stacked vertically at the top of the Library panel. Now, as you see in Figure 1.3, they are positioned horizontally, giving more room to what's really important—access to the content itself.

Search Me

In addition to the new (yet not new) GUI, long-requested features have been added to help users speed up their workflow. If you are like most, you have gigabytes worth of content living on your main hard drive as well as on external drives. Unless you are completely and absolutely profoundly organized, your Runtime folder will often become unwieldy and finding the model you want will become a time-consuming chore. A new Search feature has been added so you can quickly and easily find that model you're looking for (see Figure 1.4).

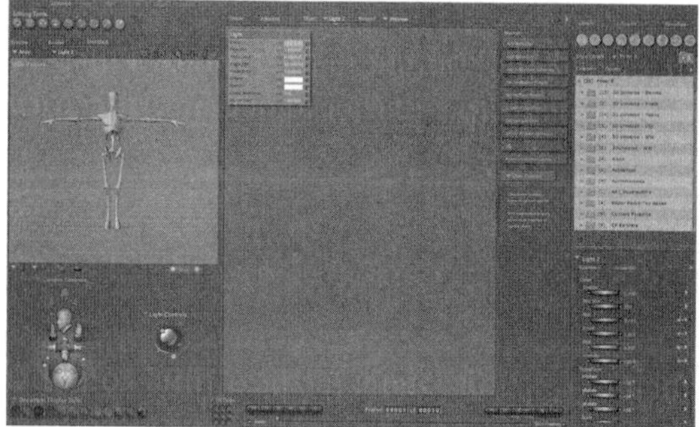

Material Room

Face Room

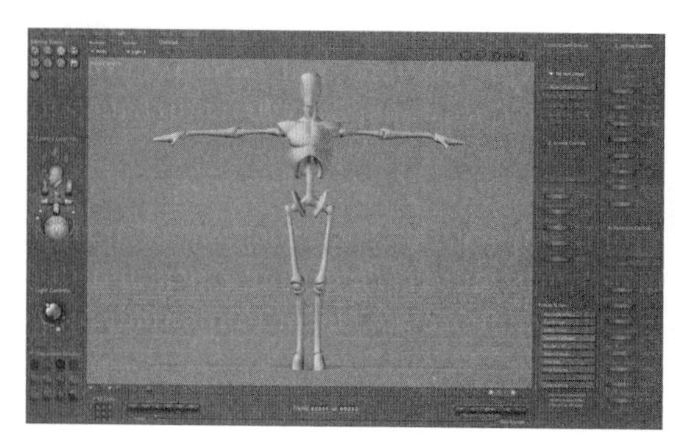

Hair Room

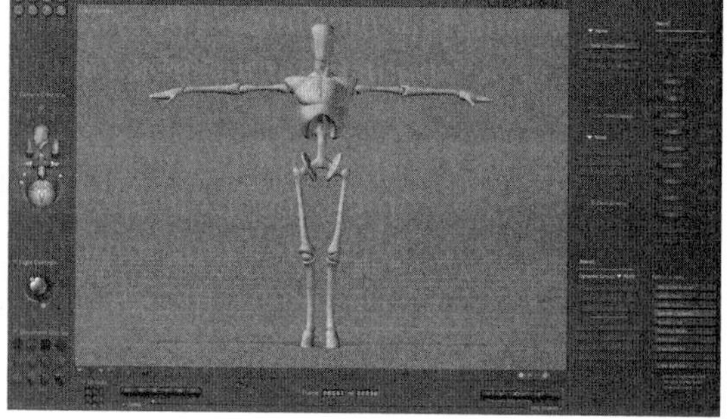

Cloth Room

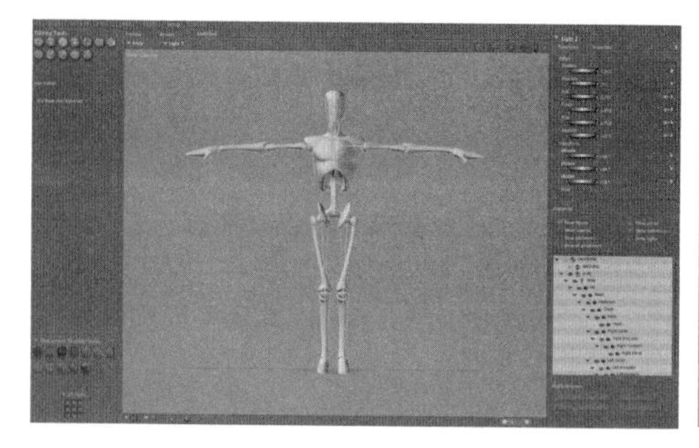

Setup Room

Content Room

FIGURE 1.2 The revised interfaces for the Material, Face, Hair, Cloth, Setup, and Content Rooms.

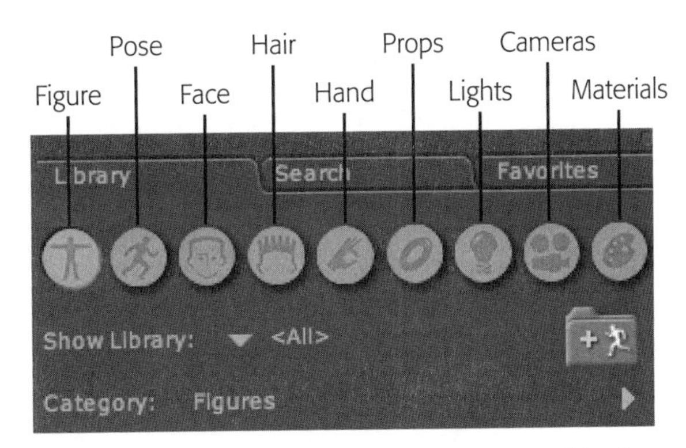

FIGURE 1.3 The content directory icons positioned horizontally.

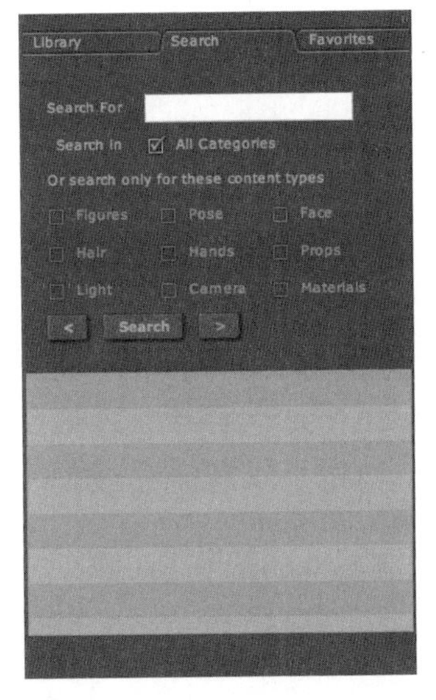

FIGURE 1.4 The Search panel.

BUT YOU'RE MY FAVORITE

If you're like me, there are models you use over and over and over again. Having to navigate through numerous folders can become a tedious process that just wastes unnecessary time. Welcome to the new Favorites panel (see Figure 1.5). Here, you can store links to your favorite models—those models you just can't create your images without. The Favorites can also be found inside the Runtime\Libraries\Collections folder.

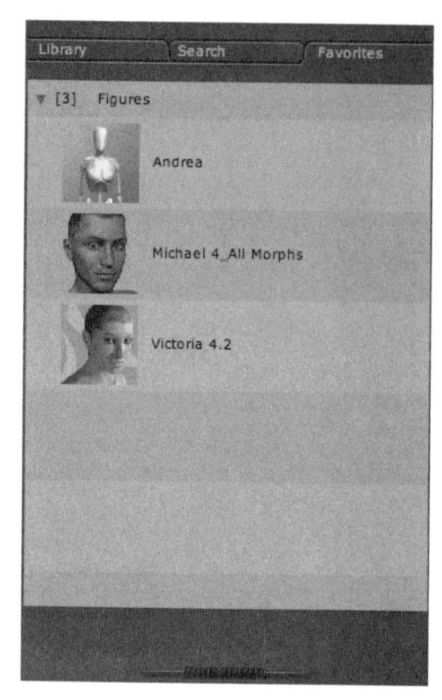

FIGURE 1.5 The Favorites panel.

Tutorial 1.1 Make the GUI Your Own

While this new look is welcome, it's not uncommon that you would want to set up the interface to work the way you do. While these control panels are set up in the same default positions they always have been, you might want to move them to some other location or remove some of the panels altogether. Here's how.

1. Notice the almost imperceptible dividing line between the panel sections. Move your cursor over that line, and the cursor will change into a grabber icon, indicating that you can click and drag to resize the panel group. On the positive side, you can increase the size of a window, and some palettes will move to accommodate this new configuration. On the other hand, you can actually expand a palette or panel in such a way as to cover up some of the other panels and their controls in the group. For instance, you can drag the Camera Controls panel upward and cover up half of the Editing Tools controls.

2. There is also a very small pop-up menu (officially called the Palette Docking Control Square) to the far right of the tabs in the various panel groups. Again, this can be very hard to see. But if you look closely, you will notice a small square indentation. Click on this square to open the submenu where you will see the following commands:
   - **Docked**: When this option is checked, as shown in Figure 1.6, the palette is docked with the other panels in the user interface. When you switch to this, it will put the control panel back in its last location.
   - **Floating**: Turns the panel into a floating window that can be positioned anywhere in the workspace, just as the windows did in earlier versions of the program.
   - **Drag-Docking Enabled**: With this feature enabled, you can drag a control panel away from the panel group and dock it anywhere else in the workspace. When you move a panel around like this, a bluish-purple overlay will appear when the panel is positioned where it can be re-docked (see Figure 1.7).
   - **Close**: Closes the panel. You will need to go back to Window > Panel Name to re-open the panel.

When you turn on Drag-Docking Enabled, you can undock and move any of the panels, not just the one that was clicked on to activate the command.

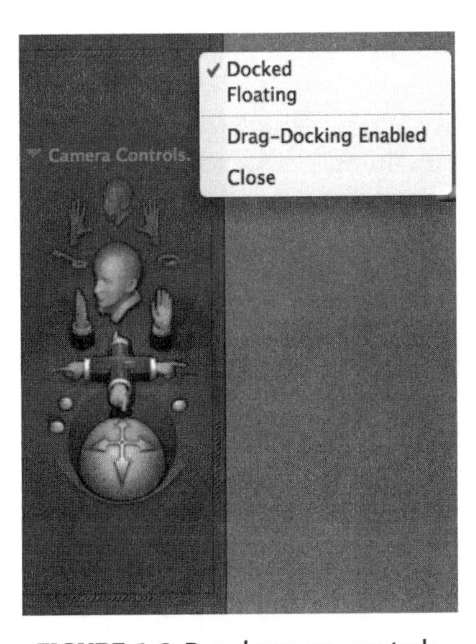

FIGURE 1.6 Panel pop-up controls.

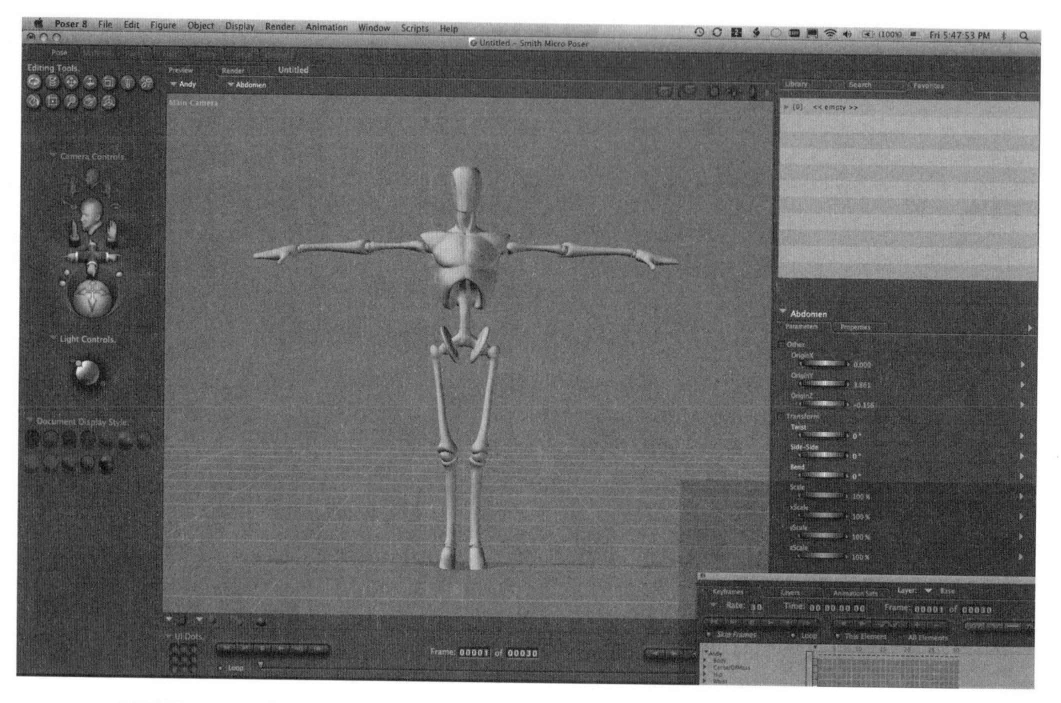

FIGURE 1.7 When you move a panel group over another panel group, a bluish highlight will appear to show the location where that panel will be docked.

3. Suppose you want to add a new panel to those already in place. Let's say that you do a lot of animations, so you're constantly opening the Animation Palette or moving it around as you are setting up those animations. It would be great to have that particular window always available to you. To do this, go to Window > Animation Palette. The palette will open above the workspace.
4. Click to open the panel options and choose Drag-Docking Enabled so you can drag the panel into the panel group you want.
5. Drag this panel underneath the Parameters panel. A bluish-tinted box will appear to show you where the panel will be docked (refer to Figure 1.7).
6. Once placed, the panel will be accessible without blocking out any other controls (see Figure 1.8).

NOTE

When you place one panel group with another, it can increase the overall panel width, reducing the size of the Preview window. Sometimes you can scale down the panel group, but most of the time you can't.

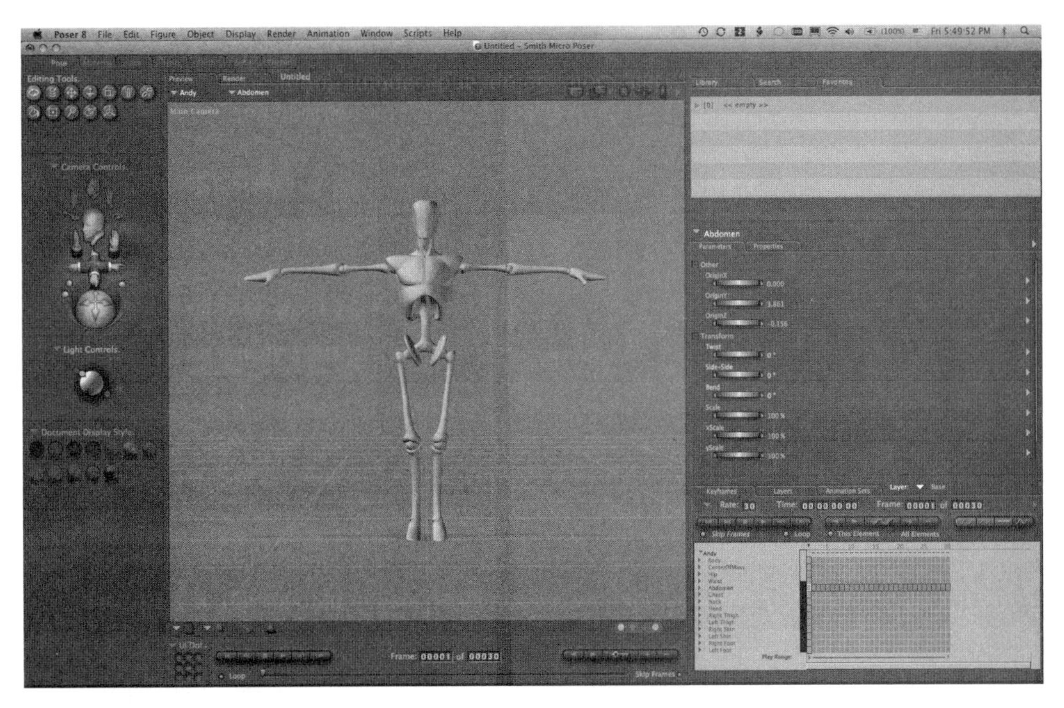

FIGURE 1.8 The Animation Sets panel docked with the Library and Parameters panels.

7. To undock the Animation Sets panel, move the cursor to the right of the window's tabs until the cursor turns into a hand icon. Click and drag the panel from the panel group and release. The panel will be floating above the rest of the GUI.

Another exciting aspect about the new interface is that you can set up panels for multiple monitors. The Animation palette, for instance, can be moved onto a second monitor in a dual monitor setup, thus adding more space for the main Pose Room window.

And remember, if you want to save your new interface layout, you need to go to Edit > Preferences and select Launch to Previous State; the next time you open Poser, your layout will be as you like it.

Where Your Content Lives

All physical Poser content files must reside beneath a master folder (file directory) named Runtime for Poser to properly display the content in the Library panel.

With Poser 8, you are able to define where your Runtime folder is created. It can be in its default location, or it can be in a location of your choosing. When you install the program for the first time, you will be asked where you want to place the Runtime folder (see Figure 1.9).

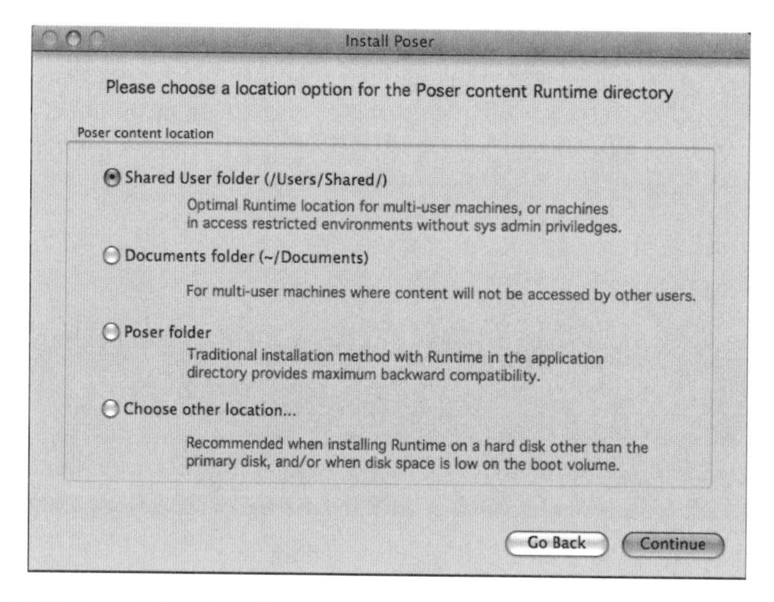

FIGURE 1.9 When installing Poser 8 for the first time, you can determine where you want the Runtime folder to be installed.

Historically, this folder has been installed inside the main Poser folder. (On the PC, it was located in the C:\Program Files\Curious Labs or e-Frontier\Poser 4 folder; on the Mac, this was located in the Applications\Poser(x) folder. If you have any questions about this, I would direct you to the Poser user manual for more information.

TUTORIAL 1.2 SEARCHING FOR CONTENT

Finding content was the challenge that Poser would often give to its long-time users, those who had downloaded and installed large amounts of figures, props, and other content. As mentioned earlier, the frustration many felt when trying to find that elusive file is now over (as long as you can remember the file name, that is).

1. Click on the Search tab next to the Library tab. Referring back to Figure 1.4, you can see the various controls at your disposal, including the Search For field and criteria for where you want Poser to look for the file in question. While it may seem to be a good idea to just keep All Categories checked, it can actually slow down the search response. If you know you're searching for a figure, then choose Figures so Poser will only search in that particular folder within the selected Runtime folder. In order to do this, deselect All Categories. The content types will highlight, and you can choose which folder or folders to search through.

Poser's Search option only searches in the selected (or active) Runtime library. It does not search your entire hard drive for content.

2. Type in **Andrea**. This is the name of one of the two new mannequin figures that come with Poser 8. Poser loads with Andy, the other mannequin, on the workspace.
3. Select Figures from the content types list.
4. Click Search to have the program search for the model. Within a few moments, the model will appear. There could be more than that one model in the list (the search engine is not infallible), but Andrea should be there.

When conducting a search, it is often faster to search for a folder than an individual file.

You can also view previous searches (or later searches if you have searched backward) by clicking on the left or right arrows that bracket the Search button (see Figure 1.10).

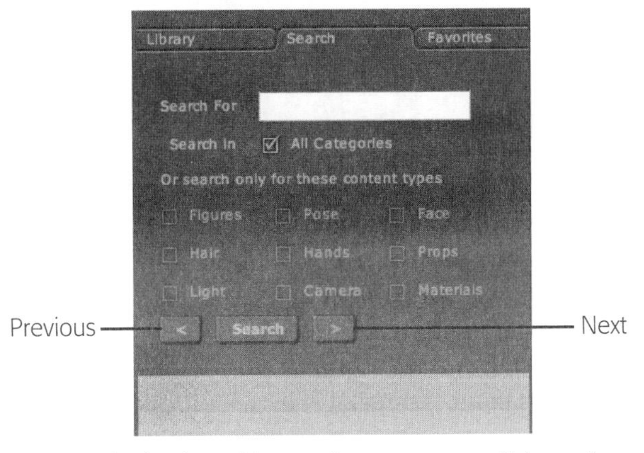

FIGURE 1.10 Use the back and forward arrows to scroll through your searches.

TUTORIAL 1.3 SAVING YOUR FAVORITE CONTENT

As I mentioned earlier, you probably have models you use over and over and over again. They might be the G2 figures that come with Poser, or Daz's Victoria 4, Michael 4, or any of the other Millennium figures. Maybe it's a prop you use over and over again. Or you have a specific MAT (Material) file you particularly like. Whatever the case, you can use the new Favorites tab to store and quickly retrieve often-used files.

1. One of my new favorites is the Andrea model searched for in the last section. So that's the first one I'll add to the Favorites panel. In the Library panel, go to the Figures category and open Poser 8\Additional Figures\Mannequins and click once on the Andrea figure (see Figure 1.11).

   Notice the difference in the way the Library panel displays content. While scrolling through the content, the thumbnail images are small. But when you click on a model, the thumbnail size increases, and you get a lot of information regarding that particular item, including the files' installation and modification dates and how large the model is.

NOTE

Immediately beneath the Library panel is a collapsed palette. Click on the handle icon and a menu will appear that gives you control over the size of the Library's icons as well as what features you want active in the Library panel.

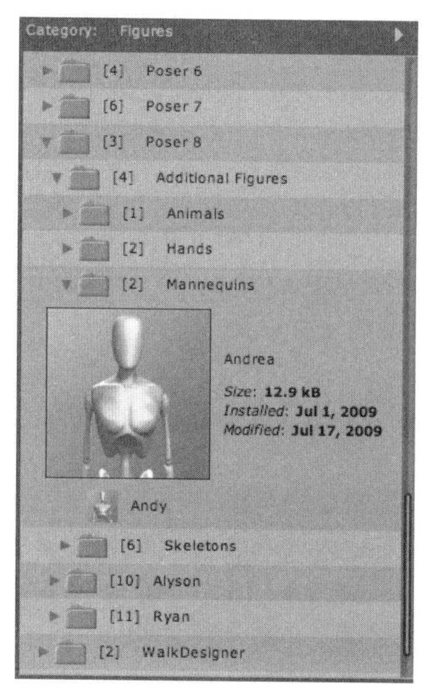

FIGURE 1.11 The new look for the way content is displayed in the Library panel.

2. Beneath the files listed is a series of buttons (see Figure 1.12). These buttons include the following:
   - **Change Figure**: Replaces the figure in the Preview window with the one selected in the list.
   - **Create New Figure**: Adds the selected model to the scene while keeping all other models in the workspace.
   - **Create New Folder**: Creates a new folder inside the current library category.
   - **Add to Library**: Adds the selected item in the workspace to the selected folder in the library.
   - **Remove From Library**: Removes the selected item from the Library list.
   - **Add to Favorites**: Adds the selected item in the Library panel to the Favorites list.

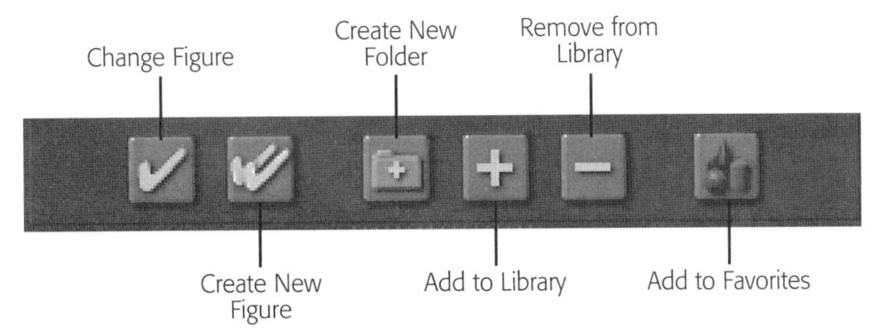

FIGURE 1.12 The control buttons at the bottom of the Library panel.

3. With the Andrea model selected, click the Add to Favorites button. A pop-up menu will appear to let you create a new folder in the Favorites panel or just add the model to the main area of the panel (see Figure 1.13). Select New Folder. A new window appears where you can name this folder. Title it Figures and click OK. It will look like nothing happened.
4. Switch to the Favorites tab. Now you have a Figures folder and inside that is the Andrea model.

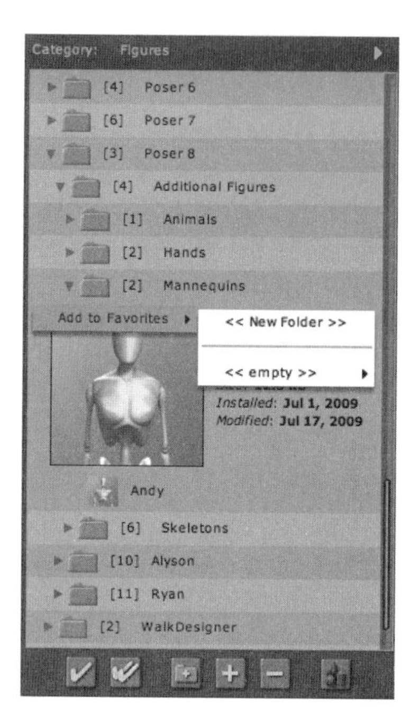

FIGURE 1.13 The Add to Favorites submenu lets you create a new folder or save your file in the top level of the Favorites panel.

When you restart Poser or any time you create a new scene, you can quickly add Andrea to your scene by going to the Favorites panel and doing one of two things:

- **Double-click on the model**: This is the other traditional method for adding models to the scene.
- **Click and drag the model onto the workspace**: That's right. Click on the model in the list and drag it to the workspace. This is the new way of adding content to your scenes. You'll be doing that a lot throughout the course of this book. It's a great way to add elements to the scene.

Now you can save all your favorite figures, props, materials, and poses for quick and easy access.

Tutorial 1.4 Creating Runtime Folders on Your Hard Drive

If you're like most Poser users, the first or even the second folder isn't enough to manage all of your files. Eventually, you'll find that several gigabytes of content are too cumbersome to maintain in one or even two folders. (Then again, there's the almost 25GB I have in my folder. Yes, I'm a glutton for punishment!) In the Poser world, several gigabytes of content are not uncommon! With the Poser 8 library's Add Library feature, you can create as many Runtime folders as you like. They can appear on any drive in your system, too.

You'll find it easier to locate items if you separate your several gigabytes of content into several smaller Runtime folders. For example, you might use one Runtime folder to store hair, another to store clothing for the Poser 7 female, another to store clothing for the Poser 7 male, and yet another for props and scenery.

To create multiple Runtime folders on a secondary drive—your D drive, for example—follow these steps:

1. Using Windows Explorer or the Finder on your Mac, locate the drive onto which you want to store your extra Poser content. Let's assume your secondary hard drive is drive D.
2. Create a folder that will store your additional Runtime folders. For example, you can call the folder Poser 8 Runtimes. (It helps to indicate the version number in case you have Runtime content from previous versions of Poser.)
3. Inside the new folder, create additional subfolders as needed. For example, if you want to create a folder that stores content for each of the third-party figures you use, you could create additional folders named James, Jessi, Kelvin, Koji, Miki, Olivia, and so on for each Poser figure that you own. You might also want other folders for items that you can use for any character, such as Hair or Scenery. Eventually, you'll have a folder structure that looks similar to Figure 1.14.

In addition to individual files, you can also select entire content folders.

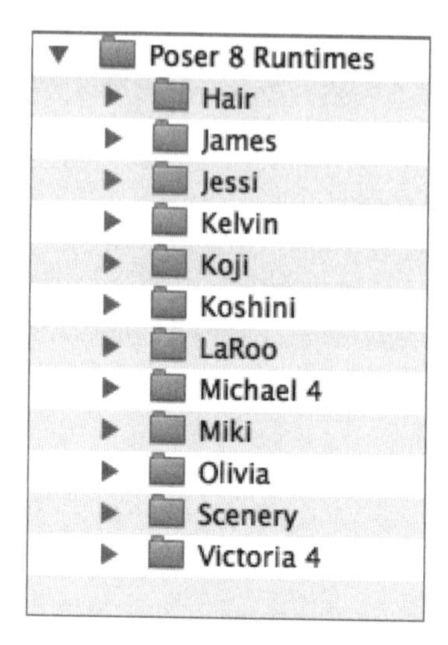

FIGURE 1.14 Create one or more folders to organize and store Poser content in categories that suit your needs.

TUTORIAL 1.5 ADDING A NEW RUNTIME FOLDER TO THE POSER LIBRARY

The second step in the process of creating additional Runtime folders is to make Poser 8 aware that they exist. Here is how you add new Runtime folders into the Poser Library Palette:

1. If the Poser Library Palette is hidden, click the bar at the right side of the interface to expand it.
2. If the Library Palette opens to display the library titles and not their contents, double-click any library category name (Figures, Cameras, and so on) to display the contents within it.
3. In previous versions of Poser, the first folder in any library was a special folder, the "up folder." This folder has now been replaced with the Add Library button just under the Content buttons (see Figure 1.15).
4. Navigate to the Runtime folder you created earlier and click OK (PC) or Choose (Mac).
5. Click OK to return to the Library panel. You should now see a new library folder, which is the folder you selected in Step 4.

6 Repeat Steps 4 through 6 for each additional Runtime folder that you want to add to your library.

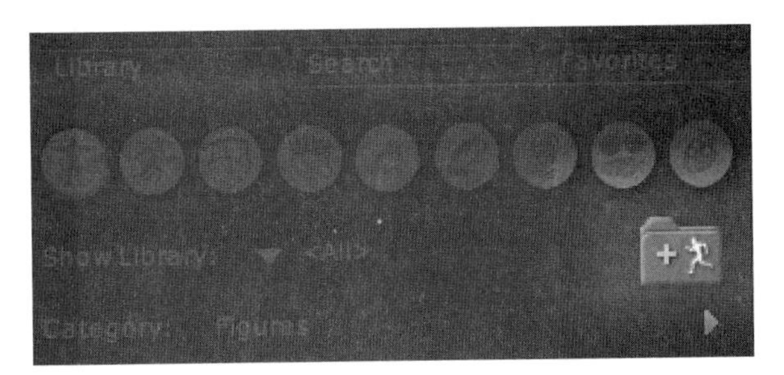

FIGURE 1.15 To get to the top-level (or root) library folder, click on the Add Library button.

If, for some reason, you want to remove a Runtime folder, select the folder in the list and a Remove Library button will appear to the right of the Add Library button. Click the Remove Library button, and the Runtime folder will no longer be part of the content list.

A Short Re-Pose

It's a great idea to take some time to get yourself organized when working in Poser. If you just updated to Poser 8, you will want to link to your previous Runtime folders and get used to the new GUI. Move the control panels to the location(s) you are most comfortable with. Remember, after you have moved the panels and set your workspace to your specifications, make sure to go to the Preferences window and set the Preferred State options.

2 Using Cameras

In This Chapter:

- Camera Overview
- Tutorial 2.1: Using and Selecting Multiple Camera Views
- Controlling What You See
- Tutorial 2.2: Creating and Saving Custom Head Cameras
- Tutorial 2.3: Creating Your Own Cameras
- Tutorial 2.4: Pointing and Parenting Cameras and Objects
- Tutorial 2.5: Using Depth of Field

"I've found it (photography) has little to do with the things you see and everything to do with the way you see them."

This quote from Elliott Erwitt (www.elliotterwitt.com), a photographer and television producer who is known for his photographs of abstract and absurd moments in real life, could not be more apropos to the world of 3D artistry. 3D art, in all reality, has little to do with the things we see because not many of us experience fantastic landscapes populated with hordes of dragons, scantily clad warrior princesses, or grungy space pirates fighting mutant aliens on strange barren planets. 3D art, however, has everything to do with how we actually see things. Even if you are creating a real world–style image, the outcome is a result of your personal experiences and point of view. There is nothing more personal than art.

But wait. Why quote a photographer when we're talking about the rendering of polygons and the manipulation of pixels? Well, nothing gets done in the 3D world without cameras. It's just a fact of digital life. When you open any 3D application, your initial view is through the Main Camera. Each render is based on how well you can manipulate the camera, how well you know optics, and then use that knowledge to define the final appearance of your render. Yes, lighting plays an integral part in the process, and that will be covered in Chapter 3. But, ultimately, the power of your image comes from the way in which you capture it. And that's down through the lens of that virtual camera.

When you first create a new Poser scene, Poser displays the contents through the Main Camera. There are several other cameras in Poser, and each of them has controls that are similar to real-world cameras; those controls and properties can be modified and saved for later use. In this chapter, you'll learn how to use Poser's cameras for different applications. You'll also learn how to save your own custom cameras, as well as how to point cameras and objects at each other.

Camera Overview

Poser comes with 13 different camera presets that can help you build and render scenes. In addition, the Object > Create Camera menu commands allow you to create your own custom revolving or Dolly Cameras. Cameras can help you accomplish other tasks as well. For example, you can use the orthogonal cameras (From Right, From Left, From Top, From Bottom, From Front, and From Back) to help you customize and position characters and objects, position magnets, and set up joints for character development. You can use the Left Hand Camera and Right Hand Camera options to help you pose a figure's hand to get the fingers just right.

What, exactly, does orthogonal mean? The formal definition is "having a set of mutually perpendicular axes; meeting at right angles." So an orthogonal element, such as Poser's cameras, is an element that describes its location based upon the point where the X/Y/Z coordinates meet in 3D space. Orthogonal cameras move along two of the three spatial axes, which vary depending on the camera view.

Part of the versatility and power of Poser is the ease with which you can switch between the available cameras. The two most obvious ways to change your current camera view are with the interactive Camera Controls area that appears within the Poser workspace, or with the Display > Camera menu options. Both methods are shown in Figure 2.1.

A third way to access a particular camera is to right-click on the view indicator at the top left of the Preview window and choose Camera View from the pop-up menu that appears.

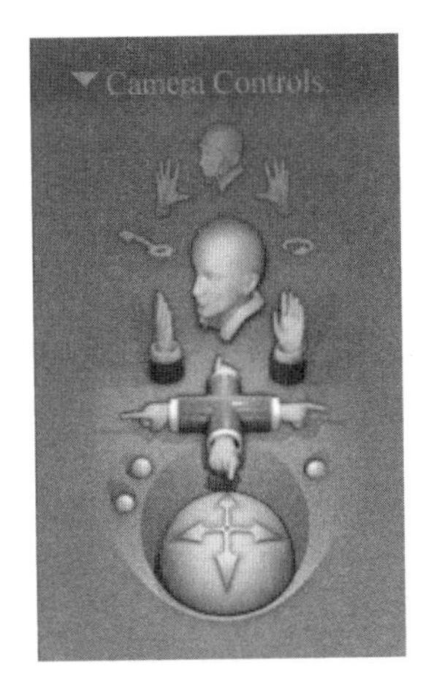

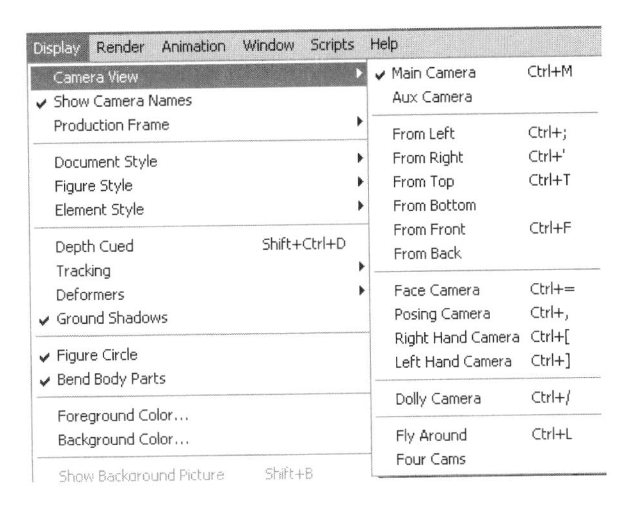

FIGURE 2.1 Use the camera selector in the interactive Camera Controls area (left), or the Display > Camera menu command (right) to choose a predefined camera view.

Poser's cameras are intended to help you accomplish many diverse tasks and accommodate a variety of personal work styles and needs. You can create final renders from any of the cameras in Poser.

The Main Camera (Ctrl/Cmd+M) and the Auxiliary Camera (no quick key command) work in a similar fashion; they rotate about the center of your scene. The focus of rotation can be changed but, by default, these cameras rotate around the center of the scene. Most people happily stick with the Main Camera to compose and render their final scene; however, other cameras are available.

- **Auxiliary Camera**: An excellent tool to compose your scene from different viewpoints without having to modify the position of the Main Camera or using up several Camera Dots.

Camera Dots allow you to store camera settings in the scene. You can store up to nine different camera configurations. These settings are stored in the program, not in the scene, which means that those camera settings will be available in every scene you create.

- **Posing Camera** (Ctrl/Cmd + ,): This rotates around the center figure's hip. If, for some reason, the center figure does not have a hip, the camera will rotate around the center of the body.

- **Face Camera** (Ctrl/Cmd + =): Specialized camera that helps you define facial expressions. It focuses on the center of the figure's head. This camera can also help you define and modify hair styles created in the Hair Room. If you're a content developer, to make this camera function correctly you must name the figure element head.
- **Left Hand Camera** (Ctrl/Cmd +]): Specialized camera that helps you define hand poses. It focuses on the center of the particular hand, letting you rotate around the element so you can refine its pose. If you're a content developer, to make this camera function correctly you must name the figure element lHand.
- **Right Hand Camera** (Ctrl/Cmd +[): Specialized camera that helps you define hand poses. It focuses on the center of the particular hand, letting you rotate around the element so you can refine its pose. If you're a content developer, to make this camera function correctly you must name the figure element rHand.
- **Dolly Camera** (Ctrl/Cmd + /): A unique camera in that it rotates around its own center, unlike the other perspective cameras that rotate around a point or object in your scene. This camera lets you easily duplicate that traditional Hollywood-style camera move in your animations.
- **Left** (Ctrl/Cmd + ;), **Right** (Ctrl/Cmd + '), **Front** (Ctrl/Cmd + F), **Top** (Ctrl/Cmd + T), **Bottom**, and **Back Cameras** (no quick key commands): These are the orthogonal cameras. They are extremely useful when you are setting up joint parameters, positioning magnets, placing objects in an exact relational position, and in other instances where a perspective view makes it difficult to determine the exact position of objects. An orthogonal camera uses a technique called *orthogonal projection* that shows the view without any perspective distortion (or lens anomalies).

To understand how the Posing Camera works, go to Display > Camera View > Posing Camera (or Ctrl/Cmd + ,). Next, open the Joint Editor window (Window > Joint Editor or Shift+Ctrl/Cmd+J). Select the hip on your figure, and change the X coordinate of the Center Point to .01. You will see the viewpoint of the camera track the center of the hip. The center point is displayed as a red + symbol located over the selected element. Note, however, that Poser can sometimes get confused if you try this with a scene that has one figure with a hip and one without.

To understand how the orthogonal cameras work, imagine holding a huge sheet of X-ray film in front of your camera, and then shooting parallel X-rays from the opposite side of your scene to expose an exact "image shadow" of your objects onto the film. The key here is that the X-rays are parallel. This means that objects are displayed at their actual sizes, regardless of how distant they are from the camera.

When you work with orthogonal cameras, you will probably find that having several up at once is a great help. You can divide your Preview window into several camera views to allow you to view left, right, top, and bottom for quick and accurate placement of objects with respect to each other. Tutorial 2.1 shows you how to accomplish this.

Tutorial 2.1 Using and Selecting Multiple Camera Views

Poser allows you to see more than one camera view at a time in your Preview window. This is handy when you are trying to position content in your scene; it can also be comfortable for many 3D modelers and animators because it turns the screen display into the more familiar multi-port view. You can select which camera will appear in each of the views. To configure the Preview window to display more than one camera, follow these steps:

1. Choose File > New to create a new scene in Poser. The default figure (Andy) appears in your scene. Adjust the camera view, if necessary, with the Camera Controls.

For some machines, having a default figure load when you start the program can slow the starting process. It also adds an extra step to your workflow because you have to remove the default figure from the scene before creating a new one. To alleviate this, delete Andy (or the default figure) from the workspace. Go to File > Option on the PC or Poser > Preferences on the Mac (Ctrl/Cmd+K), choose Launch to Preferred State, then click the Set Preferred State button. The next time you start Poser, you will get a blank workspace ready for your muse to take over.

2. Click the Port Setup menu in the lower-left corner of the Preview window, as circled in Figure 2.2. The Port Setup selections appear.
3. For this tutorial, choose Four Ports. This divides the document window into four equal parts. By default, the views are Front Camera and Top Camera in the top row and Right Camera and Main Camera in the bottom row.

As a reminder, you can place your cursor along the border between any two viewports to resize them in whatever manner you wish. The heights of the left and right sections can be adjusted independently of each other.

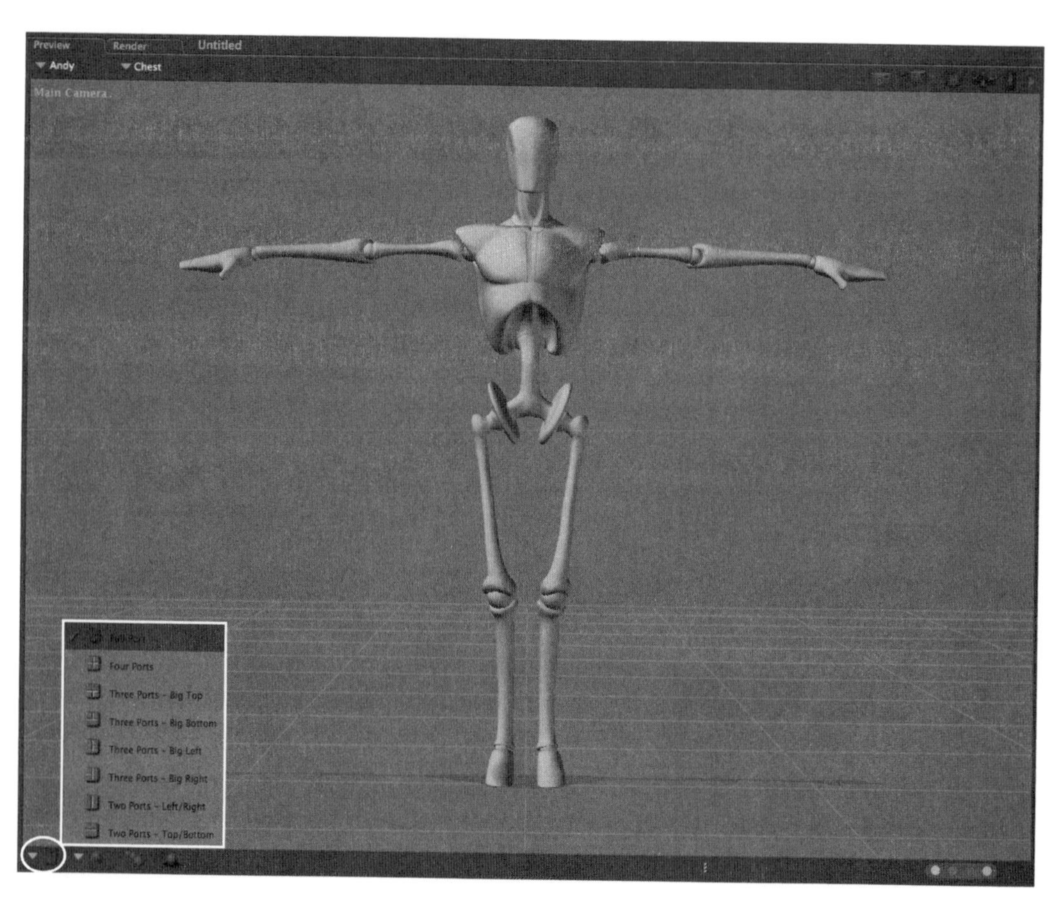

FIGURE 2.2 Use the Port Setup menu to choose the number of camera views to display. The Preview window will then change to reflect the camera layout you selected.

You can also choose the Display > Camera View > Four Cams menu command to display four camera views in the Preview window. To return to a single camera view, choose Full Port from the Document Window Layout menu.

4. If the camera names are not displayed in the ports in the Document window, choose Display > Show Camera Names to display them. To change the camera that is displayed in one of the camera ports, right-click on the camera name. Choose Camera View, and then drag right to open the menu shown in Figure 2.3. Then choose the camera that you want to display.

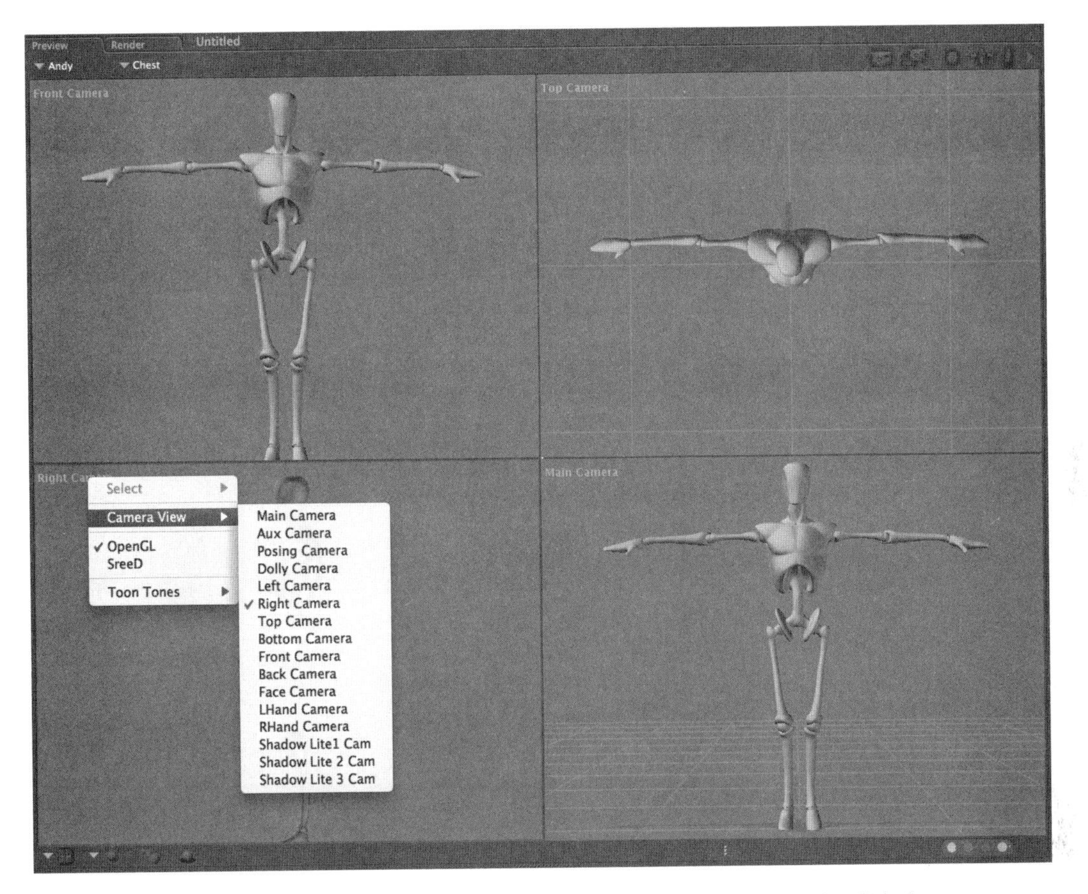

FIGURE 2.3 To change the camera that is displayed in a camera port, right-click the camera name to display the Camera View selection menu and select a camera from the list.

Controlling What You See

Now that you know what the cameras do and how they can work for you, it's time to actually work with them. This means looking at the various methods to control position, focal length, depth of field, and other features that will, when mastered, help you create your art exactly how you envision it.

Using the Camera Controls

The Camera Controls, shown in Figure 2.4, allow you to interactively select and position cameras for various purposes. By default, the Main Camera is selected.

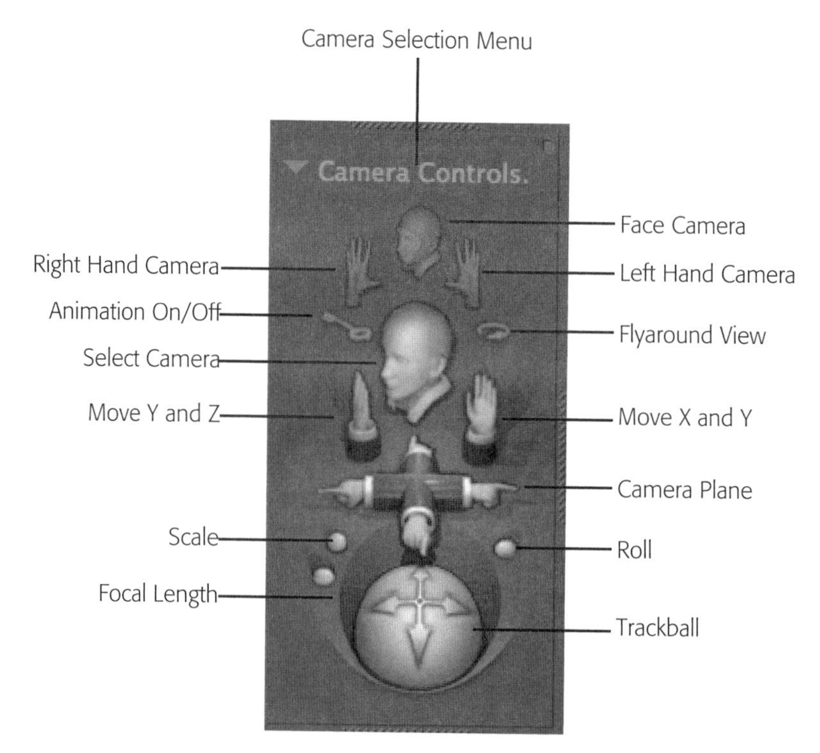

FIGURE 2.4 Camera Controls allow you to interactively select and position cameras.

The Camera Controls area makes the following functions available:

- **Camera Selection Menu:** Displays a list of cameras to choose from.
- **Face Camera:** This camera pivots around the currently selected figure's face, even as you zoom in, out, or rotate the camera view.
- **Right Hand** and **Left Hand Cameras:** These cameras pivot around the designated hand while zooming in or out or rotating the camera.
- **Animating On/Off:** Toggles the addition of camera keyframes to the animation timeline. To prevent the addition of camera keyframes while posing objects or body parts during animation, click the key icon to turn it red. This turns camera animation OFF. Click it again to resume camera animation.
- **Flyaround View:** Click this icon to get a 360-degree flyaround view of your scene. Click again to turn the flyaround view off.
- **Select Camera:** Click to cycle through the various camera views: Main, Top, Front, Left, Right, Face, Posing, Left Hand, Right Hand, Dolly, Back, Bottom, and Auxiliary.

- **Move Y and Z:** Click and drag left or right to move the camera along the Z (forward/backward) plane. Drag up or down to move the camera along the Y (up/down) plane.
- **Move X and Y:** Click and drag left or right to move the camera along the X (left/right) plane. Click and drag up or down to move the camera along the Y (up/down) plane.
- **Camera Plane:** Click and drag left or right to move the camera along the X (left/right) axis, or up or down to move the camera along the Z (forward or back) axis.
- **Scale:** This zooms into or out from the scene without affecting focal or perspective settings.
- **Roll:** Click and drag to roll the camera clockwise or counterclockwise.
- **Focal Length:** Click and drag toward the left to decrease the camera's focal length; click and drag toward the right to increase the focal length.
- **Trackball:** Drag the trackball to rotate the camera around its center; drag in the direction you want the camera to rotate.

Camera Parameters

The Parameters panel contains dials that allow you to set additional camera parameters, although many of the parameters are the same as those in the interactive Camera Controls area. To view the parameters and properties of a camera (as shown in Figure 2.5), select the camera from the menu at the top of the Parameters panel.

The parameters are as follows:

- **Focal:** Sets the camera's focal length. The default setting of the Main Camera is 55 millimeters (mm), which is great for landscape renders because this focal length results in a fairly wide field of view. Smaller focal lengths may produce a noticeable "fisheye" effect as more and more of the surrounding view is compressed into the camera's field of view.
- **Perspective:** The Perspective setting is usually calculated automatically by Poser and is the same as the Focal setting. You can change the perspective of your current camera and zoom in or out without affecting the physical location of your camera. Changing this setting from the automatically calculated default can be confusing, so unless you have a reason, it's probably best to leave it at its default.

- **Focus Distance:** This setting allows you to specify the distance at which objects will be most in focus. A focus indicator moves backward or forward through the scene to indicate where focus will occur. Objects that are farther away from the focal plane will be blurred.
- **fStop:** The fStop is a measure of the size of the lens aperture (the opening that allows light to come into the camera during an exposure). fStop settings determine the depth of field for your renders. The depth of field is a measure of how far in front of and how far behind your focus distance objects will remain in focus. A good rule of thumb about the relationship between fStop and depth of field is that the higher the fStop, the deeper (or longer) the field of focus. For a quick explanation with examples explaining depth of field, try the following online resources: www.dofmaster.com/dof_defined.html and www.azuswebworks.com/photography/dof.html.

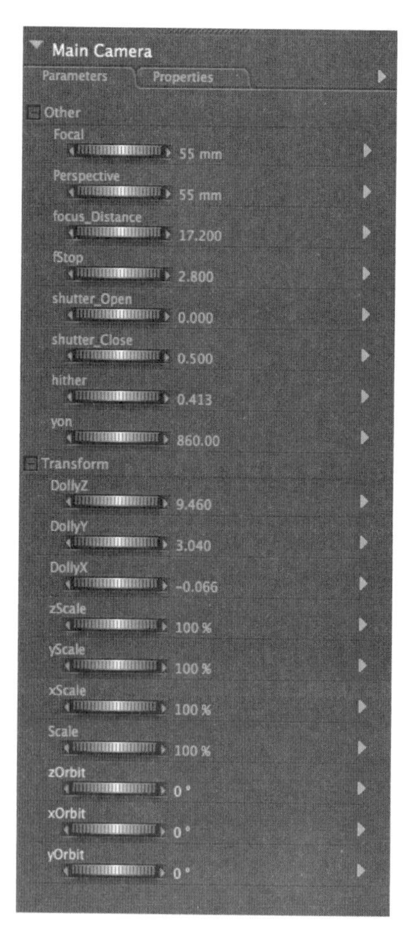

FIGURE 2.5 Poser camera parameters mimic settings found in real-world cameras.

- **Shutter_Open and Shutter_Close:** These two settings represent the point in an animation frame when the camera shutter opens and when the camera shutter closes. 0.0 represents the beginning of a frame, and 1.0 represents the end of a frame. The results of this setting are only visible when you activate 3D motion blur.
- **Hither:** This setting controls the location of the clipping plane, which is a specified distance from the camera that defines what objects are visible. Anything between the camera and the clipping plane will not appear in the Preview window. After you get past the clipping plane, you will see the objects in your scene. Figure 2.6 shows what happens if an object is too close to the Hither setting. If you see the front portions of your object disappear as if being dissected along the same plane, decrease the Hither setting until you can view the entire object.

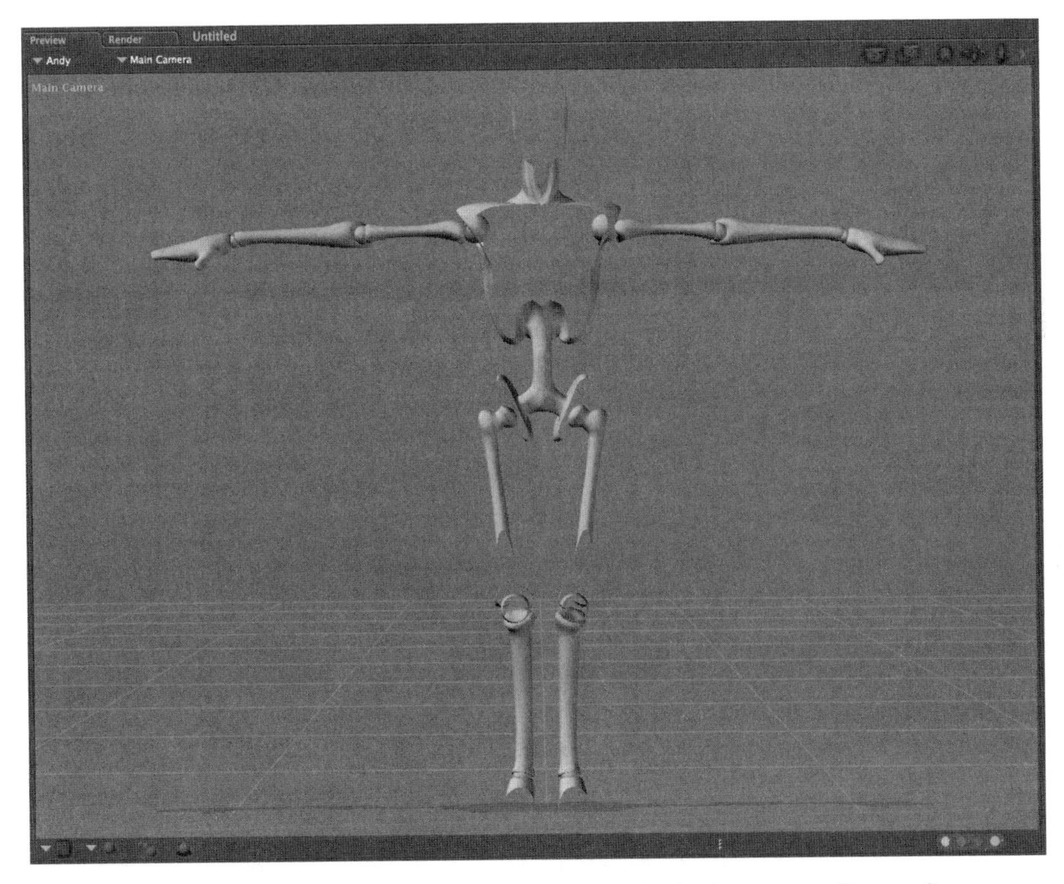

FIGURE 2.6 If your object is too close to the Hither setting, the front parts of it may disappear. Decrease the Hither setting if portions of an object appear to be cut away in the same plane.

- **Yon:** This setting works similarly to the Hither setting, except that it controls the far end of the clipping plane. Anything that lies beyond the Yon setting will not appear in your Preview window. This parameter only applies with Open GL hardware rendering.

Tutorials

With definitions in place and a good idea of what each camera control does, let's put the cameras to the test. Over the next few pages, you will work with various aspects of camera manipulation focusing on projects that Poser artists use most frequently.

Tutorial 2.2 Creating and Saving Custom Head Cameras

Although the Face Camera allows you to focus on the face, it is also helpful to look at the face from the front, left, and right sides without perspective distortion, especially when you are trying to create custom morphs for facial features and expressions, or when you are trying to refine features or fix seams in photorealistic textures. In this tutorial, you'll use some of the camera's Transform parameters to position and create useful head cameras.

The Transform parameters are very similar to those you see in any other object:

- **DollyX, DollyY, and DollyZ:** The Dolly settings move the camera left or right (X), up or down (Y), or forward and backward (Z).
- **xScale, yScale, and zScale:** The Scale settings scale the camera's width (X), height (Y), or depth (Z). In addition, the Scale setting increases or decreases the overall size of the camera.
- **xOrbit, yOrbit, and zOrbit:** The Orbit settings rotate the cameras forward to backward (X), around (Y), or side to side (Z).
- **Roll, Pitch, and Yaw:** These settings apply to the Dolly, Posing, Face, and Hand cameras and how they rotate around their own axes. Positive Roll settings turn the camera to its left (scene's right); positive Pitch settings make the camera pitch upward (scene appears to go downward); and positive Yaw settings tilt the camera to the left (scene appears to tilt right).

Although the process to make these cameras is somewhat similar for all Poser figures, you'll create a set of cameras for the figure of your choice here. These cameras will allow you to view your character's head from the front, back, left, and right when you add it to a Poser document from the library. To create and save the cameras, follow these steps:

1. Choose File > New to create a new scene. If you have not changed the Poser preferences, the default figure will appear in the scene. Delete it.
2. Add a different character from the Figures Library. In this example, let's use the new Ryan Casual, which you can find in the Figures/Poser/Ryan folder. Drag the figure onto the Preferences window.
3. Use the Figure > Use Inverse Kinematics menu command to turn off Inverse Kinematics on the right and left legs.
4. Choose Window > Joint Editor, and click the Zero Figure button in the Joint Editor to zero the position of your figure. Close the Joint Editor when you are finished.
5. Using one of the methods discussed earlier, switch to the Front Camera.
6. Use the drop-down menu at the top of the Parameters panel to display the parameters for the Front Camera, as shown in Figure 2.7.

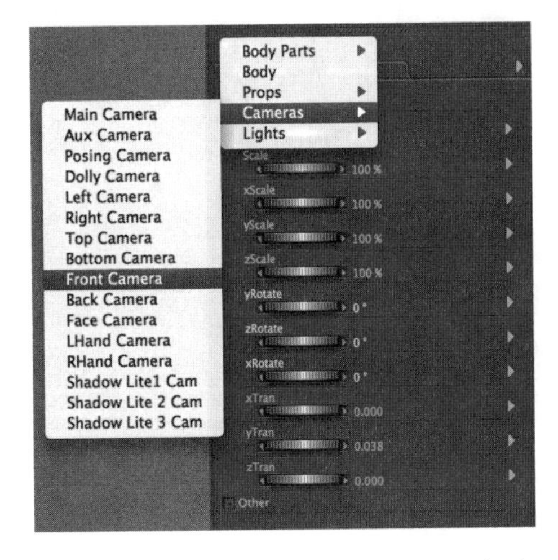

FIGURE 2.7 Use the drop-down menu in the Parameters panel to select the Front Camera.

7. Adjust the DollyY and Scale settings until you get a close-up of your character's head. To help you get started, use the following values:

   - DollyY = 31.485
   - Scale = 18%

   The DollyY control moves the camera up and down (along the Y axis) while Scale acts like a zoom control and, for all intents and purposes, moves the figure closer to the camera.

   With the camera parameters set, go ahead and save it so you can use it at any time in whatever scene you want.

8. Go to the Camera category (see Figure 2.8). You can do this in two ways:

   - Click the Category arrow at the far right of the Library panel, then select Camera > Poser 8 > Poser 8 from the pop-up menu.
   - Click the Camera Library button in the horizontal bar.

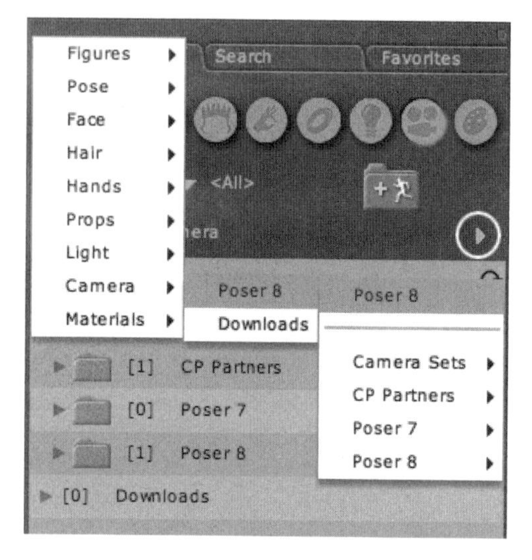

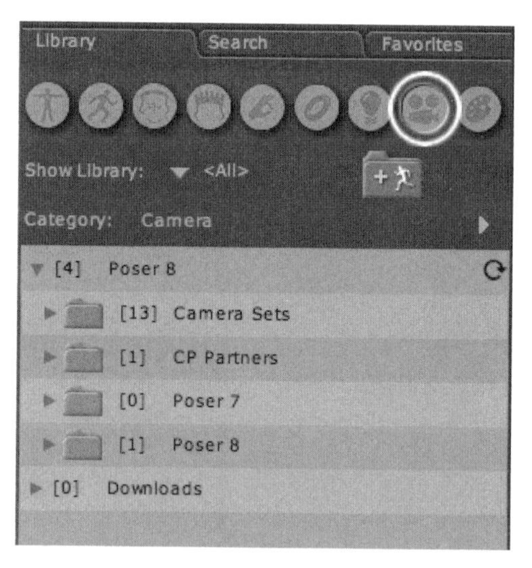

FIGURE 2.8 The two methods for accessing the Camera category (or any other category, for that matter). The displayed list of folders will look a bit different than in previous versions of the program.

You will also see that the default way in which Poser displays the folders in the Library panel is different. It is set to show all folders, so when changing to the Camera category, you will see both Poser 8 and Downloads. To change this, click on the Show Library pop-up menu (it is set to All) and choose Poser 8 (see Figure 2.9).

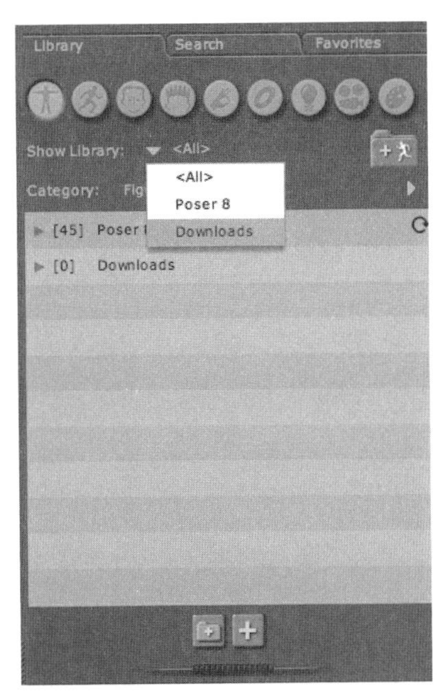

FIGURE 2.9 Determine what folders you want displayed by selecting an option from the Show Library pop-up menu.

There are definite advantages to reducing the number of folders displayed in the Library panel. If you have numerous Runtime folders, it could get very confusing figuring out which folder contains the model you are looking for. By changing the display to show only the Runtime folder you are working with, it cuts down on the clutter. On the other hand, by having multiple Runtime folders visible, you can search through them more efficiently in order to find out were a particular model is located.

9. Click the Create New Folder button at the bottom of the Library list (the folder with the + symbol on it). In the Folder Name dialog box, name this new folder. In this case, I went out on a limb and called it Ryan Head Cameras. Click OK to create the new folder.

When you create a new Library folder, you won't actually see a folder icon in the Library panel until you add content to it. Don't worry if all you see is a (0) File Name where the folder should be; the icon will appear later.

10. Make sure Ryan's head is selected by clicking on it once (or select it using any other method you're comfortable with). Click on the folder you just created to make sure it's active, then click the plus (+) button at the bottom of the Library list. This is the Add to Library button.
11. Enter **Ryan Head Front** (or a similar name for your character) for the camera set name. Then click the Select Subset button.
12. The Select Objects dialog box shown in Figure 2.10 displays all of the cameras you can choose from. In this case, you only need to select the Front Camera, which you used to create your current camera view. Check the Front Camera, and then choose OK to return to the previous window.

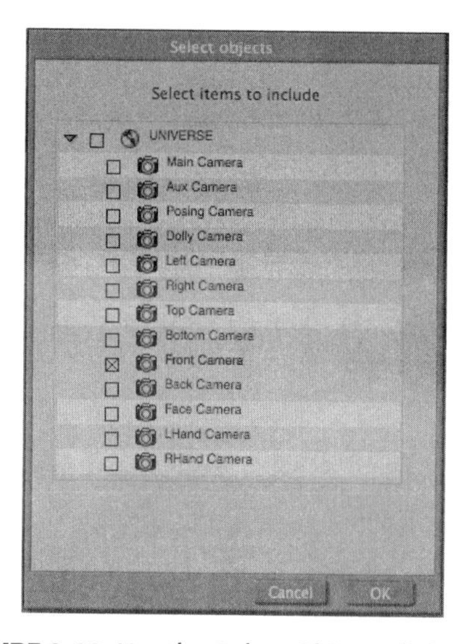

FIGURE 2.10 Use the Select Objects dialog box to select the camera that you want to save.

13. Choose OK again to display the Save Frames dialog box, which asks if you want to save a single-frame or multi-frame animation camera. Choose Single Frame, and click OK. The new camera appears in the library.
14. For the Left Camera, select Display > Camera View > From Left from the menu or choose Ctrl/Cmd + ;. Then from the Parameters panel, select the Left Camera from the drop-down menu. Be sure not to choose LHand Camera, which is different.
15. Set the DollyY parameter to the same value you used for the front camera (31.485 in this case). This will position it at the same height as the Front Camera. Then set the Scale to the same value you used for the Front Camera (18% in this case).

16. Adjust the DollyX setting until the head is centered in the Preview window (a setting of 1.000 works well for this).
17. Repeat Steps 7 through 10 to save the new camera as Ryan Head Left or a similar name for your character. Make sure you select the Left Camera from the Select Objects dialog box.
18. You can create Back and Right Head Cameras for your character as well. The Right Camera settings will be as follows:
    - DollyY = 31.845
    - DollyX = –1.000
    - Scale = 18%

    The Back Camera settings will be as follows:
    - DollyY = 31.485
    - Scale = 18%

When you're finished, your Ryan Head Cameras Library will look like that shown in Figure 2.11. You'll have a complete set of cameras that you can use while creating head morphs or for checking out head textures for your character.

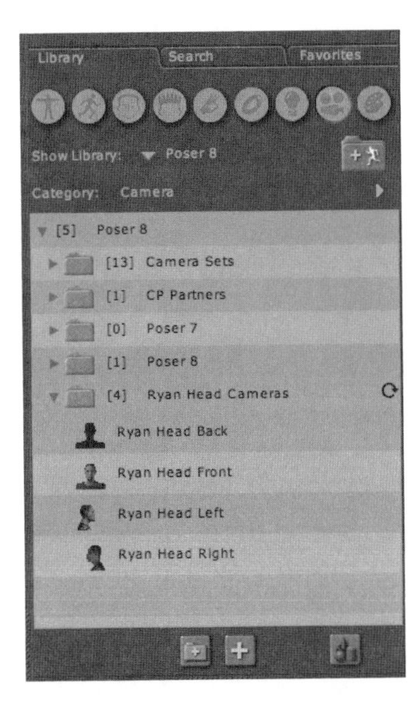

FIGURE 2.11 Four Head Cameras (Back, Front, Left, and Right) are created and saved for Ryan.

Refer to Appendix C, "Frequently Asked Questions," for information on how you can use Camera Dots to save cameras that you frequently use or how to memorize and restore one camera that gets saved with your Poser project.

Tutorial 2.3 Creating Your Own Cameras

Poser 8 enables you to create your own cameras and have them appear in the camera selection menus. That means you are no longer limited to using one of the 13 basic types of cameras that are installed with Poser. And there are two camera types you can choose from when creating you new cameras: Dolly or Revolving.

To create a new camera, follow these steps:

1. Choose Object > Create Camera, and choose either Dolly or Revolving from the expanded menu:
   - The center point of a Dolly Camera is the camera itself. That is, it rotates around its own axis. The view of the camera changes as you move the camera around in the scene. When you create a Dolly Camera, Poser names it Dolly Camera, followed by a number. Dolly Cameras accept Roll, Pitch, and Yaw transformations as well as DollyX, DollyY, and DollyZ translations.
   - The center point of a Revolving Camera is the center of the Poser workspace. When you move a Revolving Camera, you still look at the same part of the scene, but you look at it from a different angle. When you create a Revolving Camera, Poser names it Aux Camera, followed by a number. Revolving Cameras also accept Roll, Pitch, and Yaw transformations as well as DollyX, DollyY, and DollyZ translations.
2. To change the name of the camera, select the camera from the Actor list in the Properties panel. (It should automatically be selected right after you create the camera.) Enter a new name in the Name field as shown in Figure 2.12. Press Enter to set the new name for the camera.
3. Adjust the settings for the camera in the Parameters panel until you get the view you want in the Preview window.
4. By default, you're still viewing your scene through your new camera. Switch to another camera view in the Preview window and then switch back to the camera you just created by selecting it from the Camera View pop-up menu in that same window (see Figure 2.13).

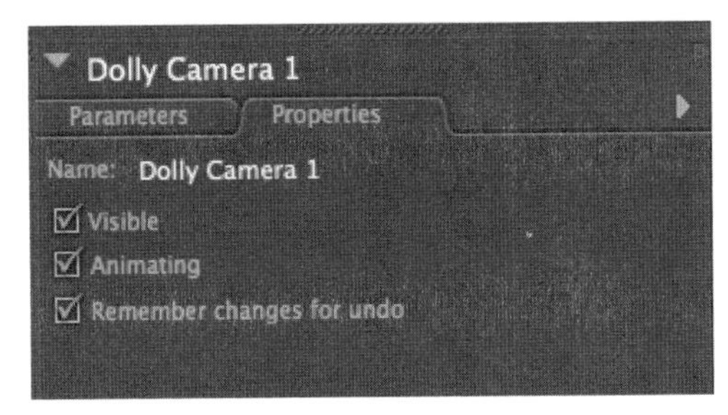

FIGURE 2.12 You can rename your custom cameras in the Properties panel.

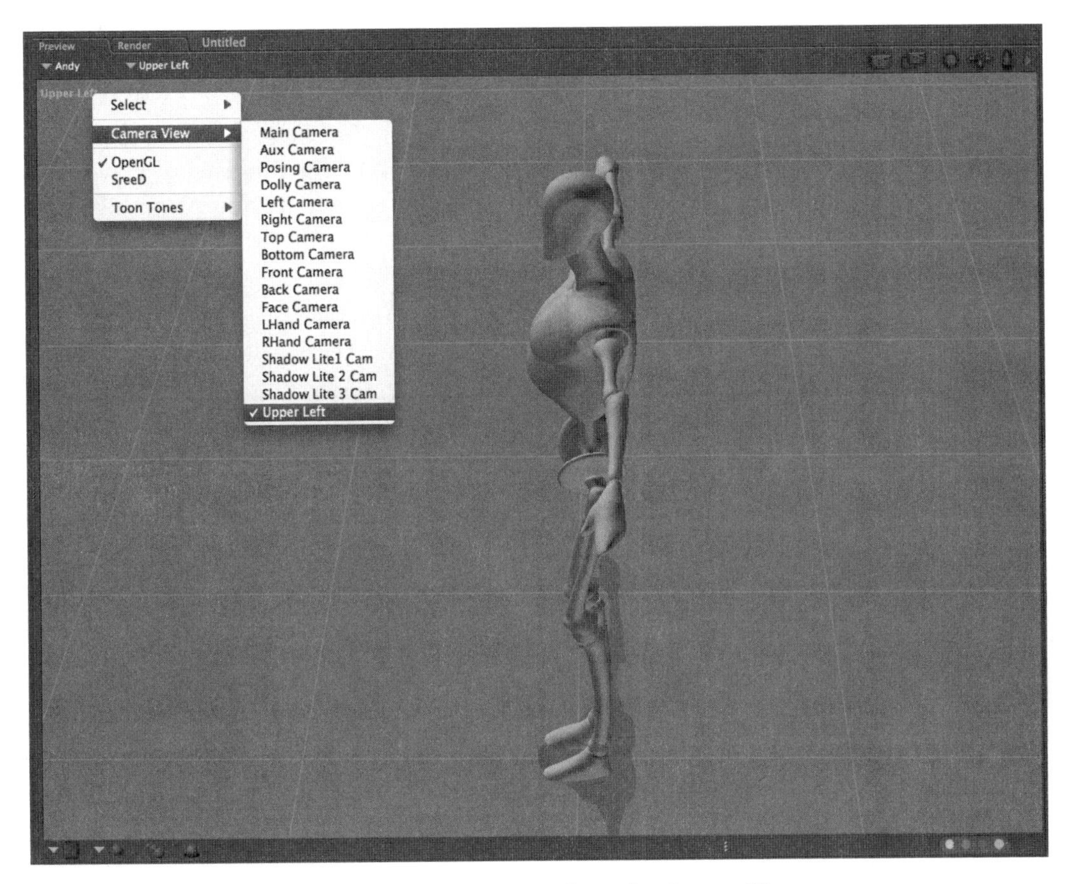

FIGURE 2.13 Select your custom camera from the Camera View pop-up menu after right-clicking the camera name in the Preview window.

Tutorial 2.4 Pointing and Parenting Cameras and Objects

Poser cameras can track any object in your scene; conversely, any item in your scene can follow the position of a camera. For example, let's say you create an animation in which your figure walks around the scene in a circle. You can set up the project so that the camera always points at the head of this figure. As a result, the figure remains centered in the camera view while it walks around the scene.

In a similar manner, you can also point objects toward a camera by using the Point At feature. For example, you can point the eyes of a character so that it is always looking at a camera. Posing the eyes of your figure helps to get rid of the "blank stare syndrome" that the default eye position is famous for creating in renders. Posed eyes help give your character life and personality.

As an alternative to using the Point At feature to pose eyes, you can also use the Up-Down and Side-Side parameter dials that appear for each eye in the Parameters panel. In fact, in most situations using Point At, you will also use Up-Down and Side-Side to control the strength of the Point At command. Point At can save you a lot of time and headaches by quickly positioning elements like eyes. All that's left is to tweak the settings to fine-tune the pose.

A common animation technique is to use what's called a null object *(an invisible piece of geometry) that model elements, such as the eyes, can point at. For instance, if you want to animate the collective eyes of a crowd of people to follow an off-screen object, you would use a null object and have all the eyes point at it. Then all you have to do is move the null and all the eyes will animate.*

To see how the Point At feature works, you will create a new scene and bring in another of the new figures that comes with Poser: Alyson. She is in the same Poser 8 master folder as Ryan. To point eyes at a camera, follow these steps:

1. Pose your figure—get everything but the eyes exactly the way you want it. I used a pose from the Alyson Standing folder. Then I took some time to give her a little friendlier expression.

You don't need to exactly duplicate the expression or the pose you see in the following images. Take some time and create an expression or a pose you like before moving to Step 2.

2. Choose the camera that you want to use for your final render. For this example, I moved the Main Camera closer to Alyson's face for a portrait render. (The Face Camera does not feature a Point At option, so it won't work in this instance.)
3. Click one eye to select it. You can see that the element is selected because its name will appear in two locations—immediately above the Preview window and at the top of the Parameters panel.
4. Go to Object > Point At. The Point At dialog box shown in Figure 2.14 appears. Notice that this dialog box allows you to point the eye at anything in your scene. You can point it at an object the character is holding, for example, or at another figure in the scene.
5. Choose the Main Camera, the one you selected in Step 2. Then click OK to apply the setting.

If you accidentally selected an item you don't want your selection to point at, go back to the Point At dialog box and click the None button at the bottom.

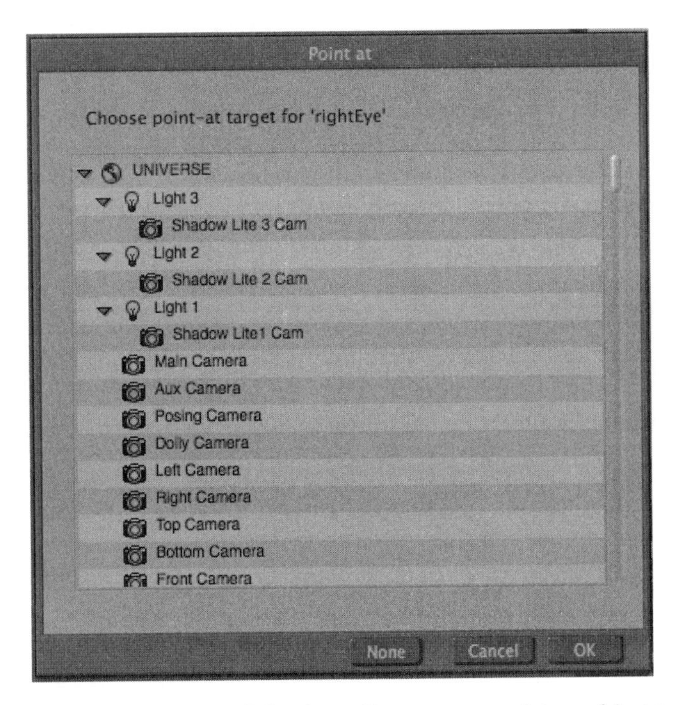

FIGURE 2.14 The Point At dialog box allows you to point an object toward any other figure, body part, object, light, or camera in your scene.

6. When you return to the Preview window, one eye should be pointing at your camera. Select the other eye, and repeat Steps 4 and 5 to point it at the same camera. Figure 2.15 shows the eyes before and after they are posed. Notice the difference it can make to an image.

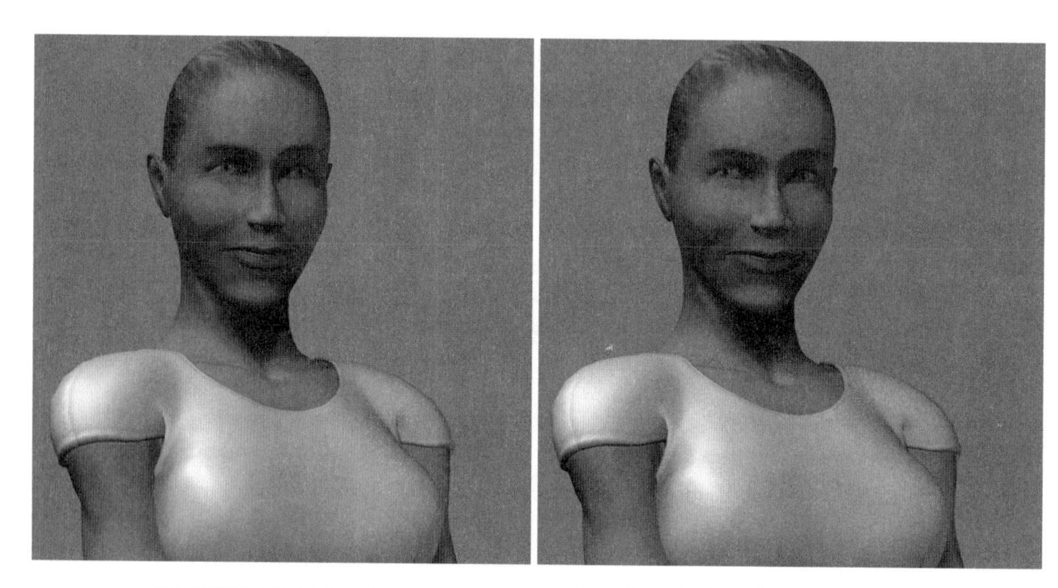

FIGURE 2.15 Before her eyes were posed, Sydney had a blank stare (left). After her eyes are pointed at the camera, she gains a little more personality (right).

NOTE

The Point At control in the Parameters panel will not appear until you have selected Object > Point At. Then it will appear at the very bottom of the Parameters panel in a new section called Other. Expand that section to see the Point At control dial.

7. Many times, the Point At feature will be extreme. With this example it isn't, but the eyes are a bit more turned than they need to be to truly "stare at the audience." The easy way to fix it is by changing the Point At intensity. With one of the eyes selected, go to the Parameters panel, and at the very bottom of the list is Point At. By default, it's set to 1.00, the full power. To reduce the Point At effect, use the dial and reduce the value until you are happy with the result. Here are the settings I used for Figure 2.16:
   - Right Eye = 0.375
   - Left Eye = 0.734

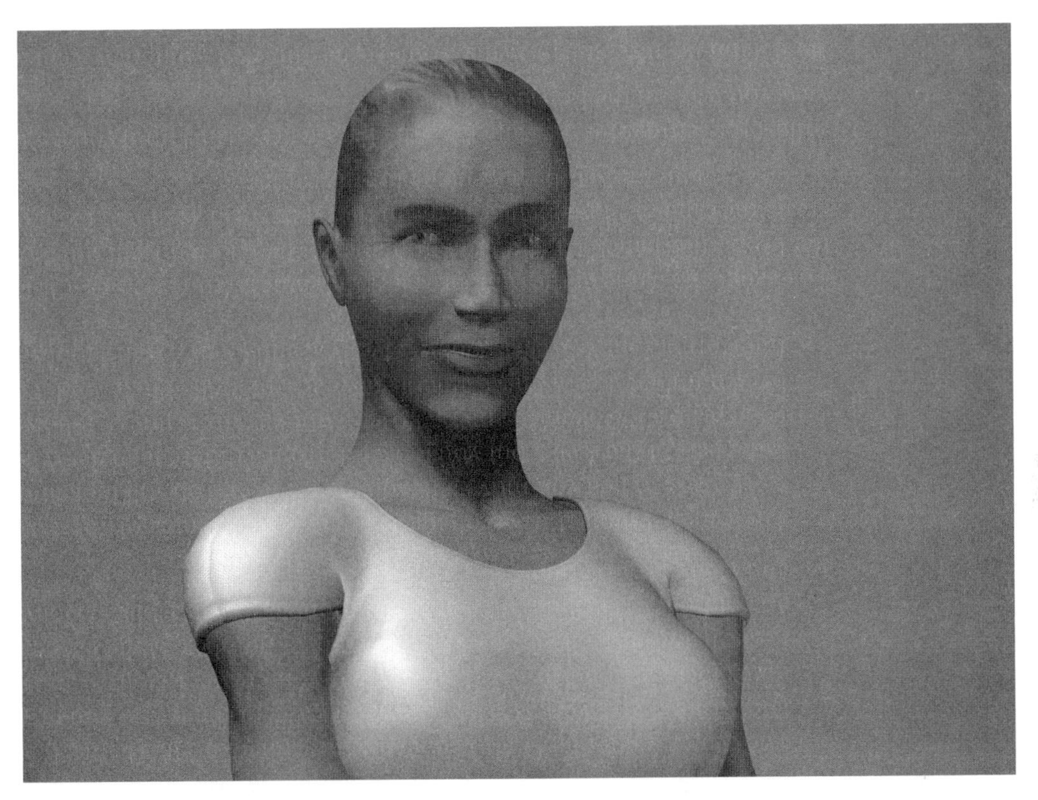

FIGURE 2.16 The eyes' Point At values have been lowered to give a more realistic appearance of looking at the viewer.

TUTORIAL 2.5 USING DEPTH OF FIELD

Depth of field (DOF) effects can be achieved quite easily with the FireFly render engine and with some simple settings on your camera. This process also makes use of a Python script written by Stefan Werner.

What is *depth of field*? It defines what area of an image will be in focus (most likely the subject) and what areas are out of focus (foreground and/or background elements in the scene). For some images, such as landscapes, a large DOF may be appropriate, while for others, such as portraits, a small DOF may be more effective. In cinematography, a large DOF is often called *deep focus*, and a small DOF is often called *shallow focus*.

The camera's focal length, fStop, and focus distance all play a part in determining the areas of your scene that will be in focus and the areas that will fade with depth. Smaller fStop values create a smaller area that is in focus.

1. Create a new scene. For this tutorial, I'm going to use Andy the mannequin with his Android face in view for the world to see. Use whatever figure you would like, but no matter which you choose, go to Edit > Duplicate "figure name" and make two copies. You will probably need to turn off Inverse Kinematics before moving the figures. Figure 2.17 shows the setup from four camera views. The Main Camera's focal length has been set to 80 mm for the scene.

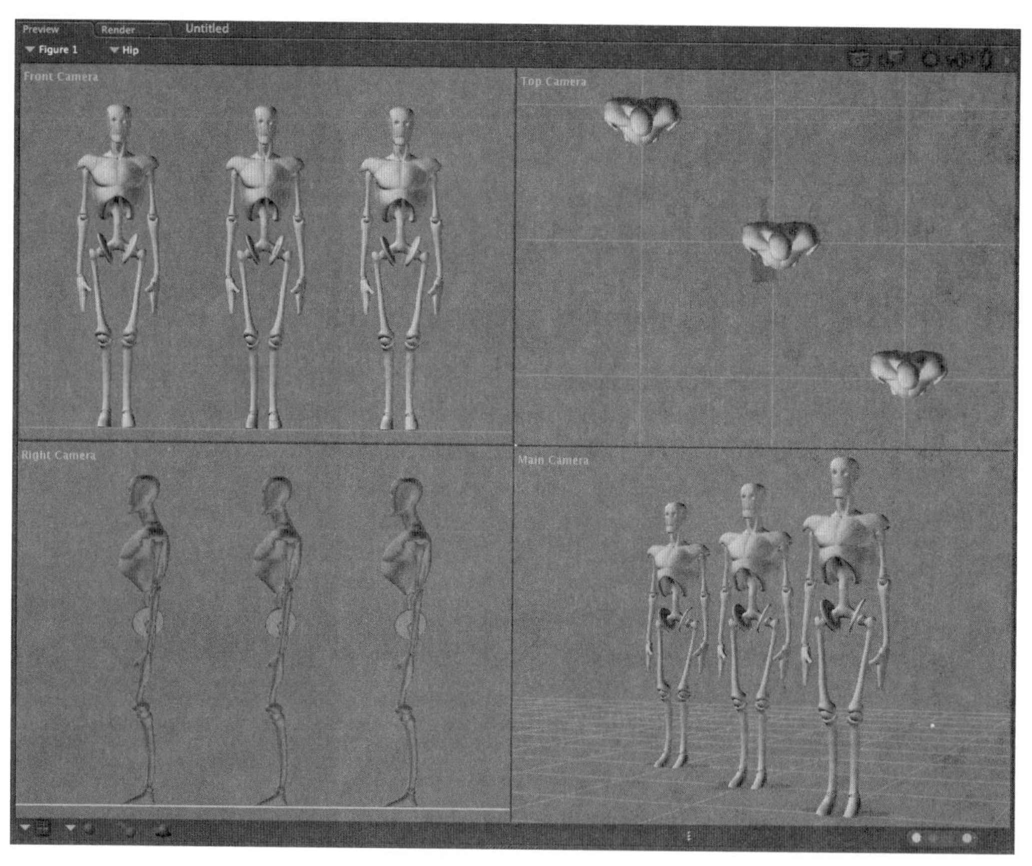

FIGURE 2.17 Three figures are added to the scene for the depth of field example.

2. Use the Edit > General Preferences menu command to open the General Preferences dialog box. Click the Interface tab, and verify that the Display Units setting is set to Feet.
3. Choose Window > Python Scripts to open the Python Scripts dialog box.

4. Click to select the figure that you want to be the focus of the scene. For this example, I select the middle figure.
5. From the main Python Scripts menu, click the Render/IO button. Then click the Calc DoF Focal Distance button. After the script runs, you will see a pop-up window that has a number in it. The number represents the distance, in feet, from the current camera to your currently selected object.
6. Copy the number onto your clipboard (Ctrl/Cmd+C) or write it down in a safe location. Make sure it's secure. Make sure there are no kids around who can run up, grab this number, and run away like gazelles. (Can you tell I've had something like that happen to me?) Actually, in all seriousness, I would advise keeping this window open until you're finished plugging the number into the appropriate field (see Step 8).
7. Use the pop-up selector menu in the Parameters panel to select the current camera. In this example, I select the Main Camera, as shown in Figure 2.18.

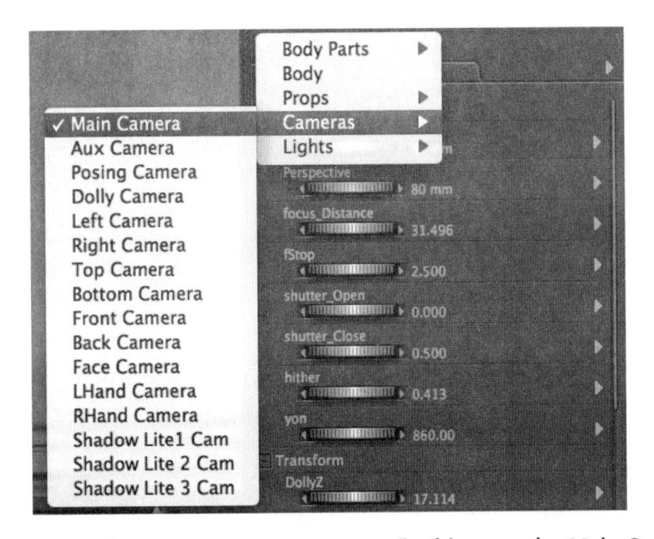

FIGURE 2.18 Choose your current camera (in this case, the Main Camera) from the pop-up menu at the top of the Parameters panel.

8. Enter or paste the number generated by the Python script into the Focus_Distance field.
9. At this point, you'll need to decide how strong you want your depth of field effects. Enter a small value for the camera's fStop parameter if you want a smaller area to stay in focus. Enter a larger value in the fStop parameter to keep a larger area in focus.

10. To see the DOF results, you have to use the FireFly renderer and configure the Render Options dialog box to use depth of field. To do so, choose Render > Render Settings to open the Render Settings dialog box.
11. In the FireFly tab of the Render Settings dialog box, first apply the Final Render settings from the Auto Settings options. Just drag the slider until it's aligned with Final or until it's all the way to the right.

    Then, click the Manual Settings button, as shown in Figure 2.19. Increase the Pixel Samples setting to reduce blotchiness in the render. I will start with a value of 5 for this example.

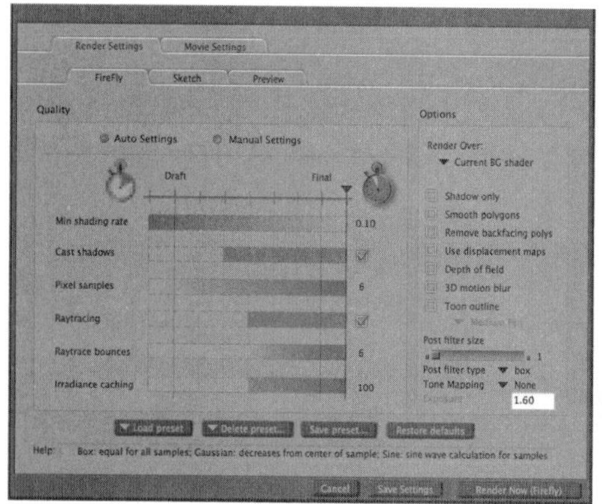

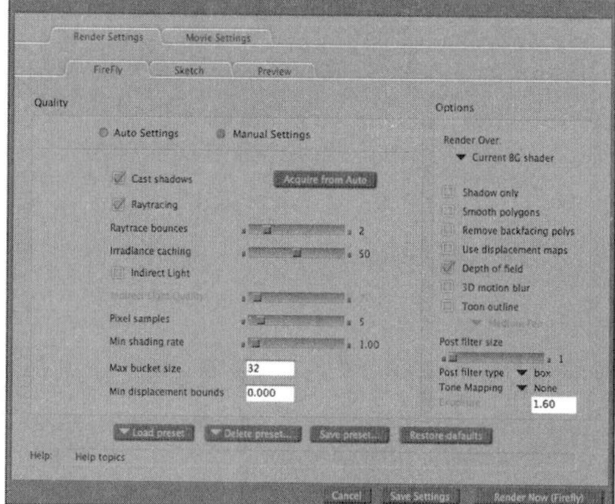

FIGURE 2.19 The Auto Settings and the Manual Settings options.

12. Check the Depth of Field box in the Options area of the Manual Settings screen.
13. You can click the Save Settings button so you can render the scene at a later time using these settings, but if you're like me, instant gratification is the name of the game. So, just click Render Now to render the scene. Figure 2.20 shows an example of a render that uses depth of field.

If you like the way the scene looks, re-open the Render Settings dialog box. All your settings will still be there, and you can click the Save Settings button to save the settings.

When you render a scene using the Depth of Field option, your renders will take much longer!

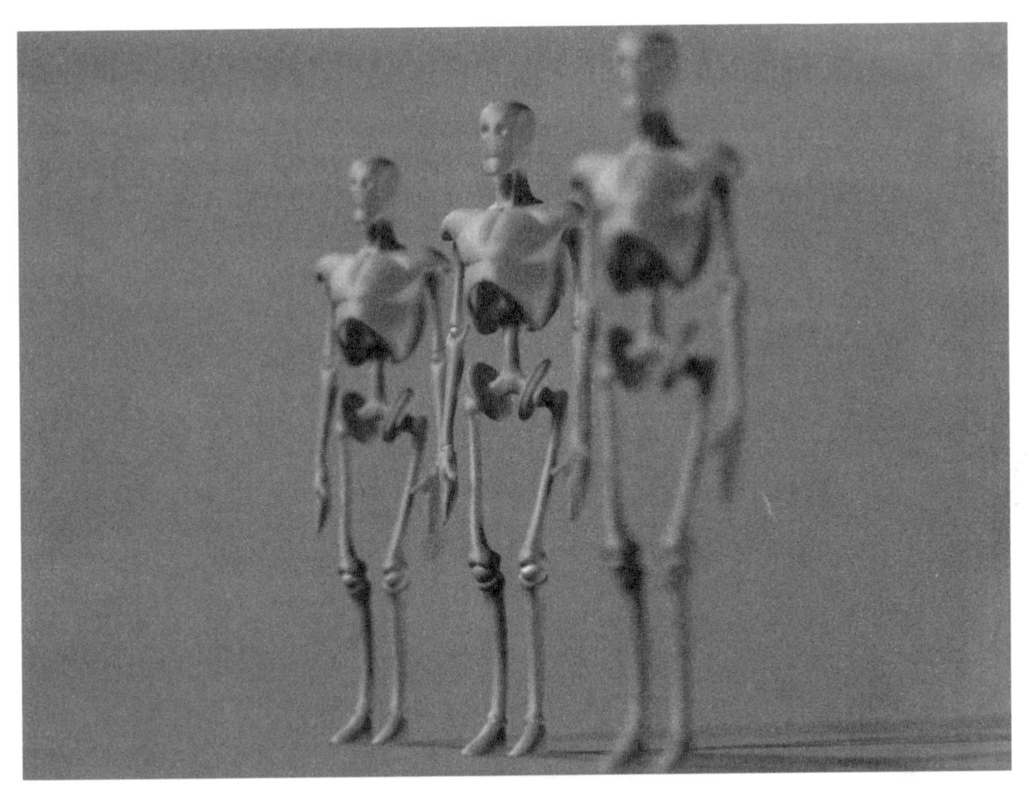

FIGURE 2.20 Interesting results can be achieved using depth of field.

A Short Re-Pose

And there you have it: The basic method used to work with cameras. At this point, you should make changes to the parameters for the selected camera and perform some test renders to see what happens. Also, practice creating new cameras and save them into the Cameras Library. The more you're able to have in place before moving ahead, the better. Because, hopefully, as you wend your way through these pages, the spigot for your creative juices will be opened, and the ideas will flow in a steady stream.

Remember, the final outcome of your work is dependent upon how well you can manipulate the cameras. But, the camera, like our eyes, can only respond based upon the amount of light entering the lens. So the second part of creating a great-looking image is to get comfortable with Poser's lights. That's next. So when you're ready, flip the page and begin the next part of your Poser journey.

3 Mastering Lights and Shadows

In This Chapter:

- An Illuminating Exploration of Light(ing)
- Casting Shadows
- Light Parameters and Properties
- Tutorial 3.1: The Three-Point Lighting Scheme
- Tutorial 3.2: Creating the Key Light
- Tutorial 3.3: Adding a Fill Light
- Tutorial 3.4: Adding the Back Light
- Tutorial 3.5: Saving the Light Set
- Tutorial 3.6: Setting the Scene
- Tutorial 3.7: Creating Highlights for Eyes
- Tutorial 3.8: Adding a Photographic Background
- Tutorial 3.9: Matching the Render Dimensions to the Photo
- Tutorial 3.10: Using the Ground Plane to Line Up the Scene
- Tutorial 3.11: Creating and Placing the Image-Based Light

"The principal person in a picture is light."

—Edouard Maneti

Ask any accomplished 3D artist, and they will tell you that the single most important thing that can make or break a render is lighting! Poor lighting will leave a render looking washed out, muddy, uninteresting. It can leave the most well-conceived and designed layout looking unfinished and pedestrian. Lighting is the descriptive prose of an image. Claude Monet stated, "For me, a landscape does not exist in its own right, since its appearance changes at every moment; but the surrounding atmosphere brings it to life—the light and the air which vary continually.

For me, it is only the surrounding atmosphere which gives subjects their true value." And that is very, very true. Look at a mountain range at different times of the day, and it will take on different personas. The play of light on a given object gives it an ever-changing character.

In other words, embrace the light.

An Illuminating Exploration of Light(ing)

Lighting adds realism and texture to a scene in ways that can't be accomplished with models or textures alone. Even detailed models and meticulously crafted textures will look mediocre if you don't pay attention to the way you light your scene. Poor lighting choices can make a render look dull and lifeless. Carefully planned lighting can make an image or scene come alive. The advanced lighting and shadow features in Poser 8 enable you to achieve lighting effects comparable to what you would expect from more expensive software. However, before getting into that, let's look at what types of lighting are available and how you can affect the environment by controlling the lights' properties.

Light Types

The four types of lights in Poser 8 are infinite lights, spotlights, point lights, and image-based lights. Each of these light types shares similar properties, such as color, angle, intensity, and a few other parameters. However, each type distributes light in a different way. Figure 3.1 shows a comparison of the four types of lights. All lights are configured to illuminate the figure's head.

In addition, Poser 8 introduces a new lighting type: indirect lighting (IDL). With IDL, you don't need as many lights to light your scene. The Indirect Lighting feature will be discussed in greater detail in Chapter 16, "Rendering Options and Techniques."

- **Infinite lights** are like sunlight. They provide a more even lighting from the point at which they are placed. These are the default lights in your scene and are best used as a base light from which you can build the lighting scheme for your scene.
- **Spotlights** shine light from a single point of origin and cast their light in a cone shape. Spotlights are similar to lights used by photographers or in stage productions. You can control the angle and distance of the cone, allowing you to create lighting effects, such as street lamps, candlelight, or the light from a crackling fire. Use the Angle End setting to adjust the size of the area that will be illuminated; higher values light larger areas, whereas lower values light smaller areas.

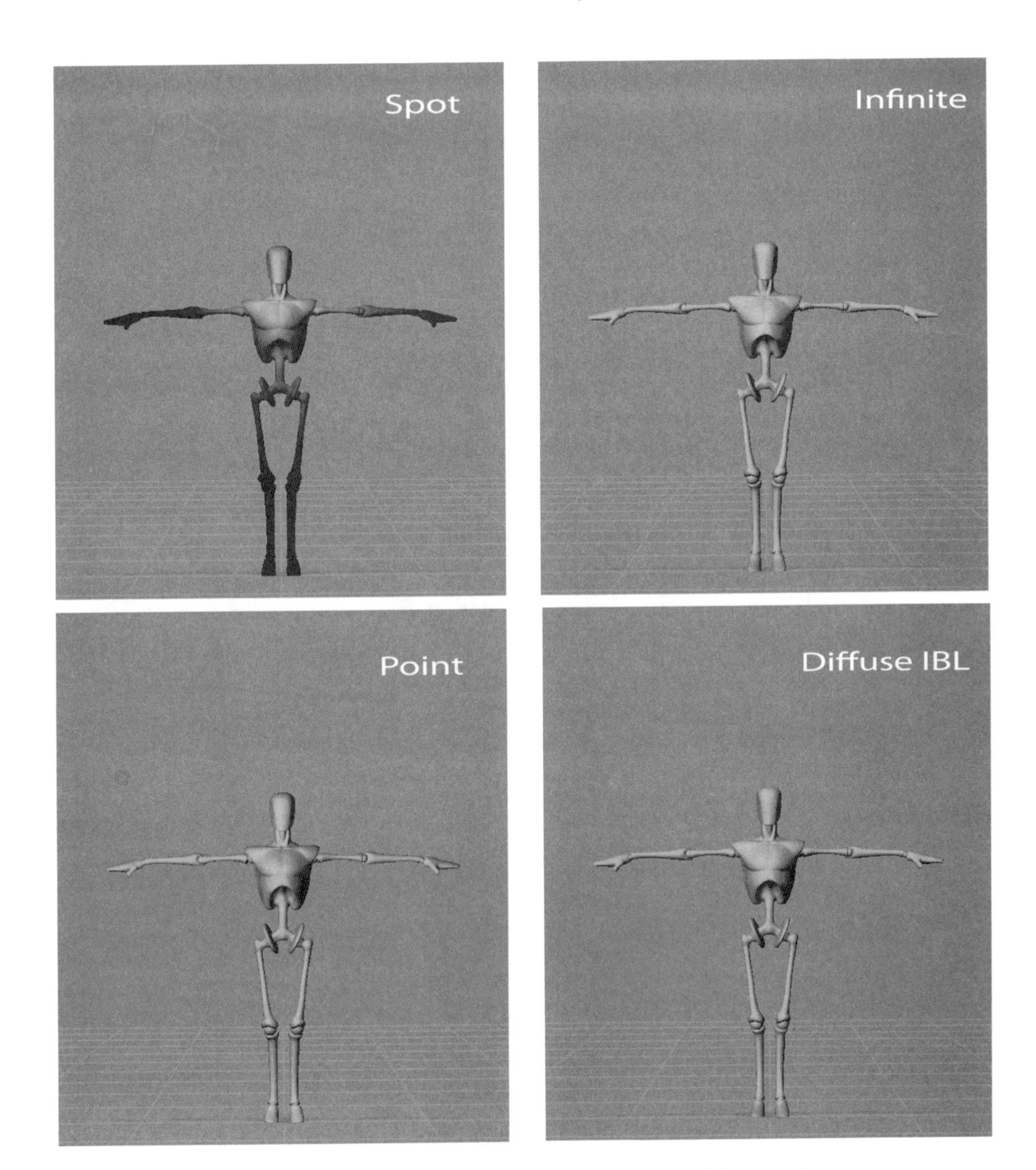

FIGURE 3.1 The four types of lights in Poser 8: infinite lights, spotlights, point lights, and image-based lights.

- **Point lights**, introduced in Poser 6, are *omnidirectional* (meaning that they shine light in all directions from a central point). Point lights are also called *global lights*. A soft point light in your scene can prevent total darkness in your render and give your scene a minimum threshold of ambient light. Take care not to make point lights too bright because they can wash out your scene and make it appear flat. Because point lights cast light in all directions throughout the scene, it might take a long time to calculate depth map shadows. For that reason, these lights cast raytrace shadows only.
- **Diffuse IBL (image-based lighting)** was introduced in Poser 6. These lights simulate many colors in a single light. The colors and placement of the light in your scene are derived from an image or movie that you specify. The end result makes your render appear as if your character is actually a part of the original image or movie, making it a great choice for work that requires photorealism. Image-based lighting is diffuse-only, meaning that if you want specular highlights in your scene (such as eye glints or highlights in hair), you will need additional lighting that is not image-based. This is the feature that allows you to use high dynamic range imagery (HDRI) for an even more realistic appearance.

Reviewing the Light Controls

The basic lighting control is one of the more iconic elements in the Poser interface. In that small package comes a wealth of control for adding and manipulating lights in your scene. As a review, let's look at what controls are at your disposal. You can refer to Figure 3.2 as you read through this section.

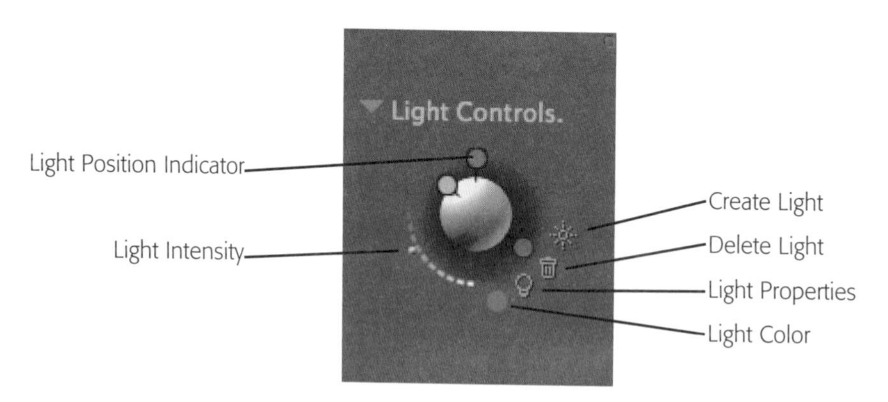

FIGURE 3.2 The Light Controls panel.

- **Create Light:** Click to create a new light, which is configured as a spotlight by default. New lights generally appear above and to the right of the Preview window (left side facing you).
- **Delete Light:** Deletes the currently selected light. Verify that you have selected the correct light before you delete it, as this action is not reversible.
- **Light Properties:** Displays the properties of the currently selected light in the Properties panel.
- **Light Colors:** Click the Light Color icon to open a color picker, and select a new color for the light.
- **Light Intensity:** Adjusts the brightness of the light from 0 to 100%. You can increase the setting to greater than 100% to create very bright lights. You can also enter negative values for interesting shadow effects.
- **Light Position Indicator:** Click and drag to position the light in your scene. The center of the globe represents the center of your camera view. As you rotate the camera, the positions of the lights move according to where they are with respect to your scene and the current camera view.

You can also add lights by going to Object > Create Light, and then selecting the light type.

If you find you have too many lights or some unneeded lights in your scene, you have two ways of deleting them. You can click on the trash can icon in the Light Controls panel or go to Figure > Delete Figure. (A light, when selected, is considered a figure in your scene.) If you want to start all over, instead of deleting each light individually, you can use a Python script that comes with Poser. Go to Scripts > Utility > Delete Lights. All the lights in your scene will be removed, and you can then start fresh.

Casting Shadows

Unlike the real world where lights, no matter how many, combine to cumulatively affect our environment, we have full control over how the lights interact with our scenes. It's a power trip of über-proportions because you control the way they cast shadows (if at all), what a light will affect, and how heavy that affect will be. The most common practice is for one light to cast a shadow—not necessarily the main light, either—while the rest just enhance the scene. There are two reasons for this.

One, by having only one light cast shadows the scene looks more natural, and people can focus on the image rather than where the light sources are; and two, by having fewer lights creating shadows, the render time is dramatically decreased.

Shadowy Confluences

Bet you didn't know there are different types of shadows, did you? Yep. There are. And Poser allows you to control what shadow type you use in your scene. Is the image high contrast, harsh, with lots of lights and darks defining its personality, or is the lighting soft and natural? It's totally up to you.

There are three types of shadows Poser's lights can cast:

- **Depth Map Shadows:** When you use depth map shadows, Poser generates a shadow map for each light that uses them. By default, the shadow map for each light is 256 by 256 pixels. You can increase the shadow map size if the shadows look pixilated. Larger sizes produce more defined and accurate shadows but also use more resources. (Remember, doubling your shadow map size will add four times the number of pixels that need to be calculated for the map and increase render times.) You can also control the amount of blur on depth map shadows with controls in the Properties panel associated with the light. Depth map shadows are the best option when you want shadows with softer edges and faster render times in general.
- **Raytrace Shadows:** Raytrace shadows are typically very sharp and also very accurate with respect to the original shapes of the object meshes. They are calculated during the render, rather than before the render as is the case with depth map shadows. Render times are significantly increased when using raytrace shadows. For the best results, use the FireFly render with quality settings at least halfway, as shown in Figure 3.3. Raytrace shadows will not render when FireFly is set to draft render mode.
- **Ambient Occlusion (AO):** AO adds additional contrast to images by reducing the amount of ambient light in the shadows, making them appear darker. This option is typically used with IBL but can also be used with the other light types.

Shadow maps and ambient occlusion often confuse a lot of people, even those who have used Poser or other 3D applications for some time. This information will become important as you read through this and subsequent chapters, as well as when you start building more intricate scenes.

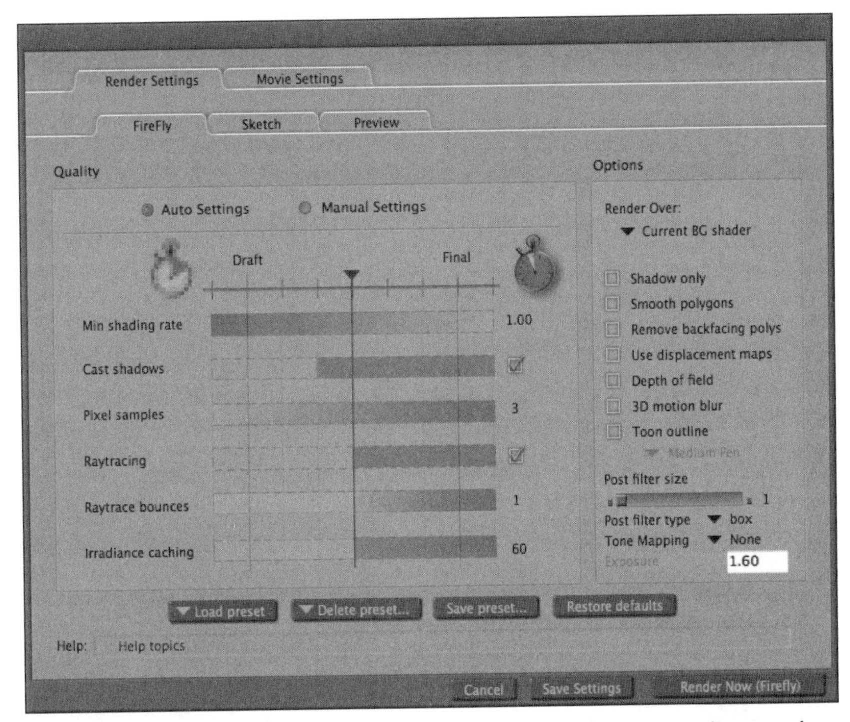

FIGURE 3.3 When using raytraced lights, set the FireFly render quality to at least the halfway point if you also want to calculate raytrace shadows.

- **A shadow map** is basically a depth map of the scene as viewed from the light's point of view. The purpose of a shadow depth map is to tell the render engine how far the effect of the light goes and which surfaces are in front of others from the light's perspective. At render time, the shadow map for each light is consulted to see if the spot on the currently calculating ray/object is receiving light from the light source or if it is in the shadow of another object or another part of itself.
- **Ambient Occlusion** is a measure of the amount of ambient light received by a point on the surface of an object surface. It simulates a huge dome light that surrounds the entire scene. If a surface point is under or behind another object (for example, a spot behind your figure's ear), that point needs to be much darker than the top-most object (such as the top of your figure's head). The occlusion map is used to darken the ambient levels at render time where appropriate. This subtle and potent lighting effect adds quite a bit of realism to renders without the addition of many diffuse lights in your scene. Although ambient occlusion calculations take up render time, they are not nearly as costly as using dozens of individually calculated light sources.

Light Parameters and Properties

Everything that has been discussed so far—from shadow maps to lighting and shadow types—is controlled using the Properties and Parameters panels. Before actually setting up some lights, let's break down these two panels so you can get more comfortable and work more efficiently when making lighting modifications. Refer to Figure 3.4 as you read through this section.

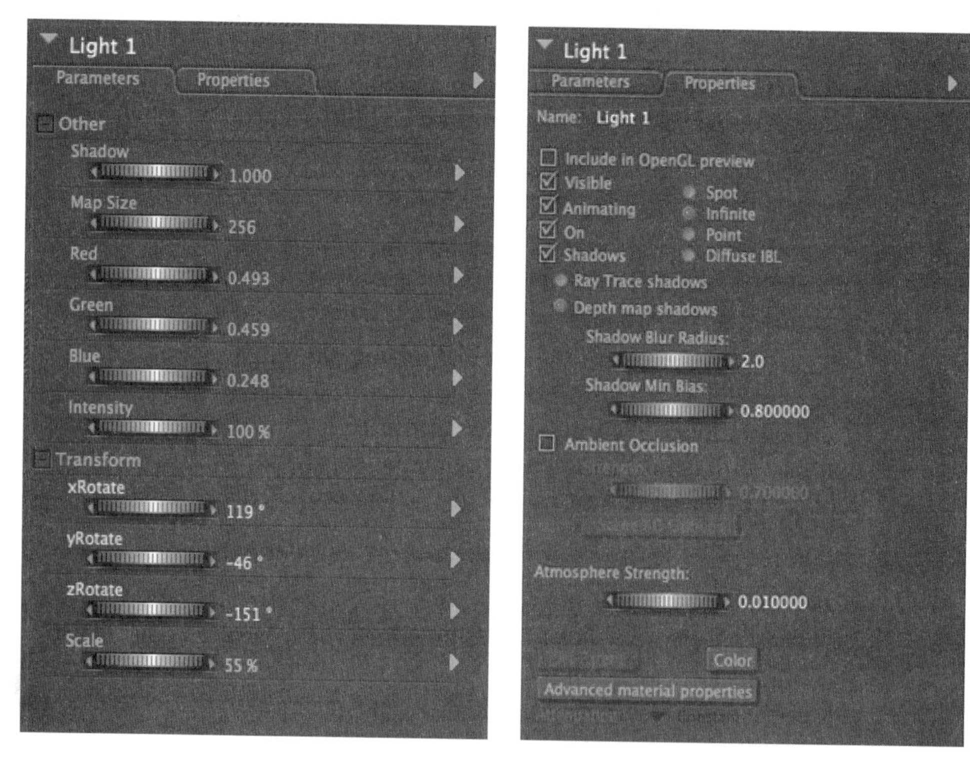

FIGURE 3.4 The light's Parameters and Properties panels.

Parameters:

- **Spotlight:** If your light is a spotlight, then specific controls will appear. If it is any other type of light, no controls will appear in this section.
- **Shadow:** Sets the strength of the shadow that is projected by the light. A value of 1 indicates 100% shadow strength. A value of 0 disables the shadow. Intermediate values make the shadow lighter or darker.

- **Map Size:** Defines the size of the depth map shadow for the associated light. The default is 256, which fits the shadow for the associated light into a 256 × 256-pixel square. Low values can result in shadows with very rough, pixilated edges; higher values create sharper shadows but also consume more system resources and rendering time.
- **Red, Green, and Blue:** Defines the amounts of red, green, and blue that are mixed to create the light color. When all three values are set to 1, the resulting "color" will be white (or Red, Green, and Blue values of 255, 255, 255). Color values are also automatically set when you choose a light color from the Light Controls color selector.
- **Intensity:** Sets the strength of the light. The default intensity setting is 100%. Lower values create a dimmer light and higher values create a brighter light. Values above 100% and negative values can also be used.

Properties:

- **Name:** Change the name of the light. Highly recommended if you have a large number of lights in your scenes. Many light sets that you download or that come with models you might have purchased usually have a large number of light types assigned to do specific chores in the scene. Using descriptive naming conventions can help you quickly find and modify the lights in your scene.
- **Include in OpenGL Preview:** Poser supports previewing up to eight lights in the scene. If you have more, only eight will be used. This control lets you define which lights are seen in the Preview window.
- **Visible:** Check to display the light indicator in the Document window. Uncheck this option to hide the light indicator.
- **Animating:** On by default, this option creates a keyframe when you make changes to a light in any frame but the first frame. This allows you to animate light properties such as color, position, rotation, or intensity. Uncheck this option if you want your light to remain the same throughout an entire animation.
- **On:** When unchecked, turns the light off so that it no longer shines light.
- **Shadows:** Check this option if you want your light to cast shadows. It takes longer to render scenes in which multiple lights cast shadows. If you choose to cast shadows, select one of the types of shadows introduced earlier (such as Raytrace Shadows or Depth Map Shadows).
- **Spot/Infinite/Point/Diffuse IBL:** Use this to change the light type. So, even if you started out thinking you wanted a point light, you can come here to change it into a diffuse IBL or spotlight.

- **Ambient Occlusion:** Check this to turn this feature on for that particular light.
- **Atmosphere Strength:** Used in conjunction with the Root Atmosphere Node in the Materials panel, this control lets you set the strength of volumetric effects in your scene.

TUTORIALS

It's time to put words into practice by creating some different lighting schemes. These projects will also include working with the camera, so the materials you went through in Chapter 2 are going to come into play as well.

NOTE

You will use base models that come with Poser for each of these projects. That way no one will feel left out if they don't have a particular model. There are, however, free models supplied by DAZ 3D on the enclosed DVD, and if you want to use them, you are more than free to do so.

TUTORIAL 3.1 THE THREE-POINT LIGHTING SCHEME

The three-point lighting setup is the most basic and versatile lighting scheme for still-life and portrait photography. As its name implies, it uses three lights—a key light, fill light, and a back light. Each plays a specific role in lighting the scene.

For this project, let's start by using the Andy character, the default mannequin that loads when Poser 8 opens. Andy also needs a face. Select the head and, in the Parameters panel, set Facial Features to 1.000. This will give ol' Andy a human-like face, almost like Robin Williams' robot character in the movie *Bicentennial Man.* But I digress.

Pose Andy in the following manner:

Head:

- **Twist:** –15
- **Side-Side:** –3
- **Bend:** 5

Neck:

- **Twist:** –19

Chest:

- **Side-Side:** 4

Next move the arms so they are down by his side using the method you are most comfortable with. They won't be seen in this shot.

Now set the Main Camera as follows:

- **DollyZ:** –4.042
- **DollyY:** 5.356
- **DollyX:** –0.264
- **xOrbit:** –10
- **yOrbit:** –32

Your Preview window should now look like what you see in Figure 3.5.

Now go to Scripts > Utility > Delete Lights. You're starting without any lights in the scene and will create them as you need them. When you select this Python script, you'll be told that it can't be undone. Click OK, because you don't want those lights in the first place. Yours will be much better!

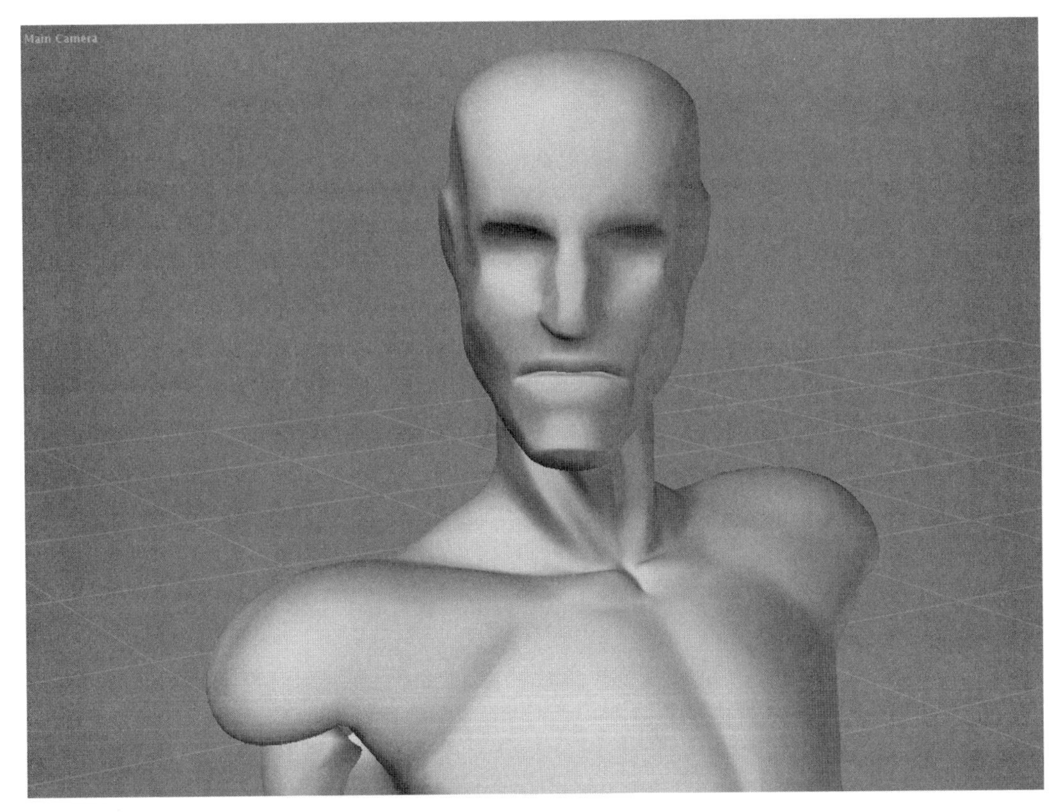

FIGURE 3.5 I'm ready for my close-up, Mr. DeMille!

Tutorial 3.2 Creating the Key Light

The key light is the main light in the scene. It will also define the shadows on the subject. The key light typically appears anywhere between 15 and 45 degrees to the left or right of the camera and 15 to 45 degrees higher than the camera. The lighting of a key light should appear similar to the lighting you want in your final scene, except that the shadows will be darker and have very harsh contrast. The most obvious choice to use for a key light is a spotlight.

1. Because you have removed all the lights in the scene, the only control you have in the Light Controls panel is the Create Light icon (see Figure 3.6). Click this icon to create a new light, which, by default, should be placed at approximately the 10 o'clock position on the panel's Light Position Indicator. This light, again by default, will be a spotlight.

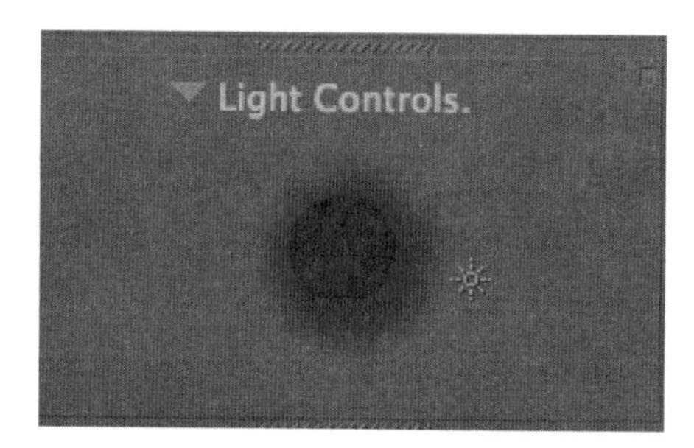

FIGURE 3.6 A total eclipse of the Light Controls panel.

2. At this point, you don't need to worry about any kind of exact positioning. Nope. This is going to be purely visual. Click on the Light Position Indicator and move it until it's in the upper-left section of the globe. Figure 3.7 shows the new position for the light.

   What you have accomplished here is to position the light approximately 45 degrees off your camera. If you moved the light to the center of the globe icon, the light would be placed directly in front of (or behind) the scene's figure.

3. Because Andy is fairly tall—he is an android, you know—the light is pointing more toward his chest than his head. With the light still selected, fix that by using the Object > Point At menu command and from the list, select the Head (see Figure 3.8). Now the light is pointing exactly as you want it. In addition, if we move the light later on, this will keep the light pointing at Andy's head as you move the light.

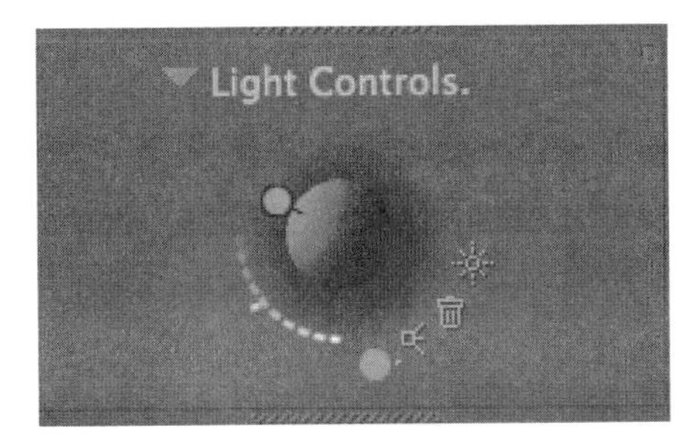

FIGURE 3.7 The approximate position for the key light.

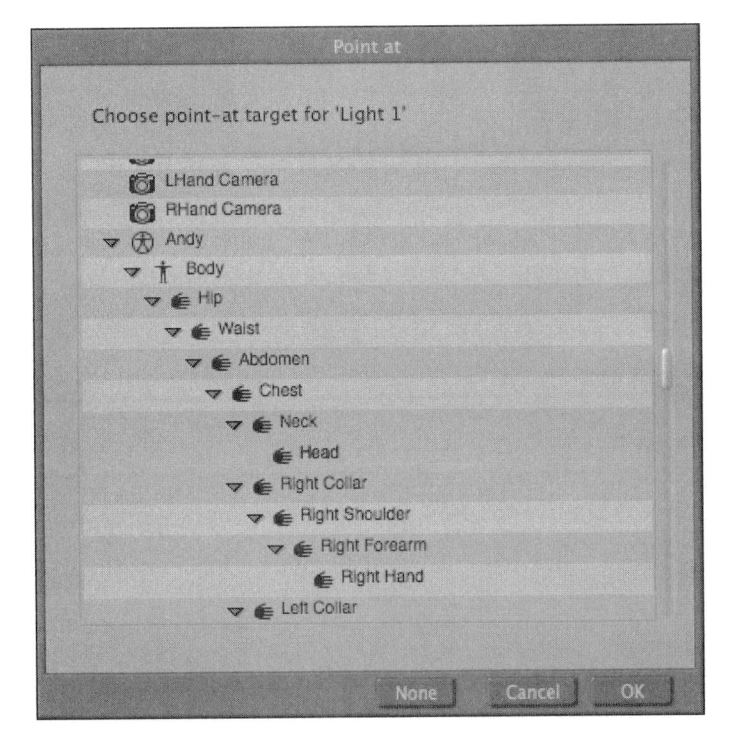

FIGURE 3.8 Select Head from the Point At list.

It's a good idea to save your file often. While it doesn't happen a lot, like any program, Poser can crash—at the worst possible moment, too. So I would suggest you use Ctrl/Cmd+S every other step or so.

4. White and gray lights are neutral-color lights that don't affect the colors in the materials of the objects you are rendering. When the Red, Green, and Blue values are each set to 1, the light is pure white or gray, depending on the Intensity setting. Set the Red, Green, and Blue parameters to 1, and set the Intensity of the light to 100%.

   There is another way to accomplish this task. (You knew that was coming, didn't you.) You can use what's called a *wacro*: the Set Up Light Style wacro to be specific. Go to the Material Room and click the Set Up Light Style wacro button at the right side of the window. Select White Only after the Choose a Light Style dialog appears, then click OK. The current light will turn white.

Another way to get to the Material Room is, with the light selected, open the Properties panel and click the Advanced Material Properties button at the bottom.

5. Before continuing, let's rename this light. Light 1 really doesn't tell you anything, and if this were a scene where you had a dozen lights, remembering what light is doing what job would be rather difficult. Click on the Properties tab and rename Light 1 to Key Light.

Using the Point At command can save you a lot of time and energy as you continue building your scene(s). When you need a light to continuously illuminate a specific part of your model, you can use Point At so that you don't need to keep repositioning that particular light each time you move the model. And by adding color to the light, you can dramatically alter the overall look of the model's colors; so by starting with neutral colors, you can focus your attention on the scene-creation process before getting more detailed.

Tutorial 3.3 Adding a Fill Light

The fill light softens the contrast of the key light and makes more of the subject visible. The fill light usually comes from the opposite side of your key light (for example, if your key light is on the left, your fill light is on the right). Because they are typically used to add ambient color in your scene, fill lights are sometimes tinted to use a color that is predominant in the scene (such as blue for moonlight or yellow for sunlight). Fills are usually about one-eighth to one-half as bright as the key light, depending upon how much shadow contrast you want in your final image. Spotlights can be used for fill lights, but point lights are the most common. Shadows are optional. In addition, fill lights are sometimes created as diffuse-only lights so that they do not add additional specular highlights to the scene in areas that are supposed to be in shadow.

Here's how to add a fill light to your scene:

1. Create a new light.
2. Move this new light to the opposite side of the positioning globe, creating what is called an *asymmetrical lighting setup*. Figure 3.9 shows the light's position and its effect on Andy. As you move the light around, you'll see the shadows change, so use your own judgment when placing the light. This, ultimately, is your picture and not mine.

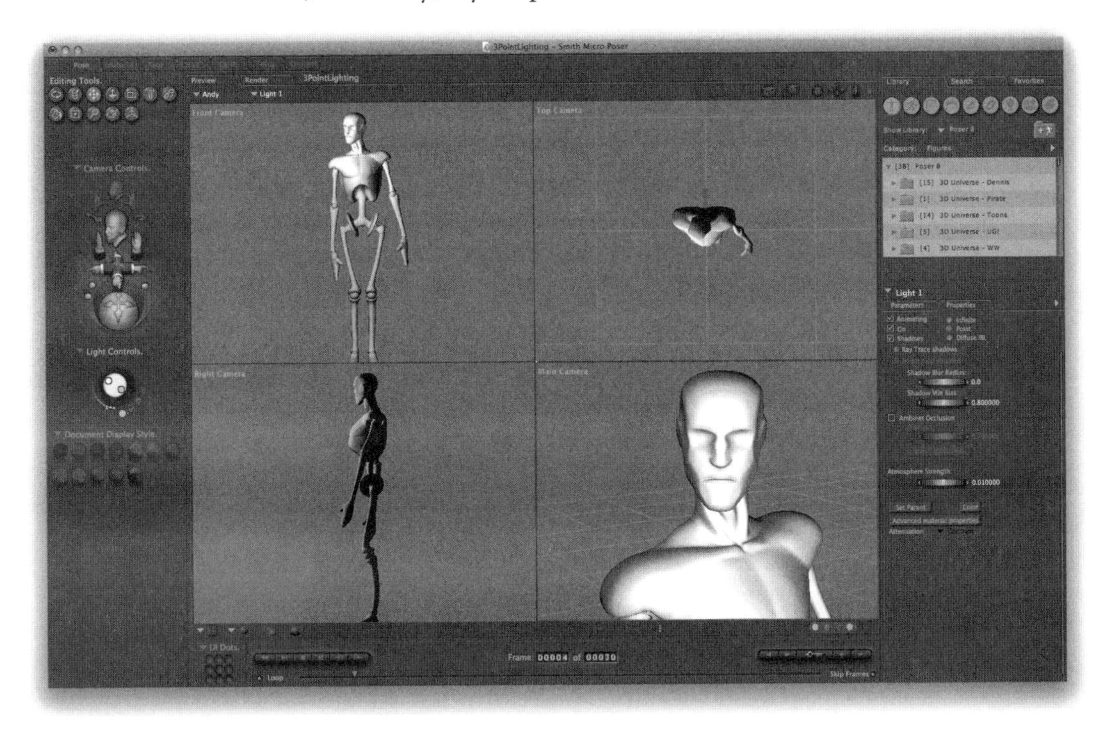

FIGURE 3.9 The fill light positioned in the scene.

3. In the Properties panel, change the fill light to Diffuse IBL. Then change to the Parameters panel and set the light Intensity setting to 20% for now. (This will probably change after Step 5.)

Diffuse IBL lights are most often used in conjunction with an image (hence, the term image-based lighting*). I will discuss how to add an image to the scene later in the chapter.*

4. Take a moment to change the light's name to Fill Light.

5. Most of the time, you're going to want to add a shade of a prominent color in the scene to add continuity to its appearance. Since Andy is the only model in this scene, you can come up with your own color for the light. For the image I'm creating, I used the following RGB settings:
   - **Red:** .686
   - **Green:** 0.776
   - **Blue:** 1

With this new color, 20% won't affect the model as much as you'd probably like. So change it to 35%, and you will see after rendering the file that Andy is definitely feeling a bit blue. Hmmm. He's kinda looking like Dr. Manhattan from *Watchmen.*

TUTORIAL 3.4 ADDING THE BACK LIGHT

The back light appears above and behind the subject and usually directly opposite the camera. The purpose of the back light is to separate the subject from the background by creating a rim of light around the top or side. A spotlight or point light is good for a back light, and shadows are usually turned off because back lights are intended for highlights only. This highlighting effectively separates the subject from the background.

1. When setting up a back light, it's best to turn off any other lights in your scene. Nice and easy in this case. All you have to do is turn off two lights—the key light and the fill light. Select each light in the Properties panel and click the On selector. This will turn the light off and throw Andy into darkness (see Figure 3.10).
2. Create a third light for the scene. Go ahead and change the name to Back Light before moving ahead. Also, while you're there, turn off the shadows as well.
3. Set the light to point at Andy's head, just as you did with the key light.
4. In the Parameters panel, change the color of the new light to white (Red, Green, and Blue values set to 1). Set the Intensity to 125%. This will create a light that is slightly brighter than the others and will bring the highlights out when the light is behind the figure.
5. In the Light Controls area, move the Back Light indicator to the top and slightly behind the globe. It is easier to see the effect of the back light if you have a dark background color. You can also adjust the Angle End and Dist End settings of the light to increase the effect of the back light. Watch the Preview window until you get a backlighting effect that you are happy with. Figure 3.11 shows an example.

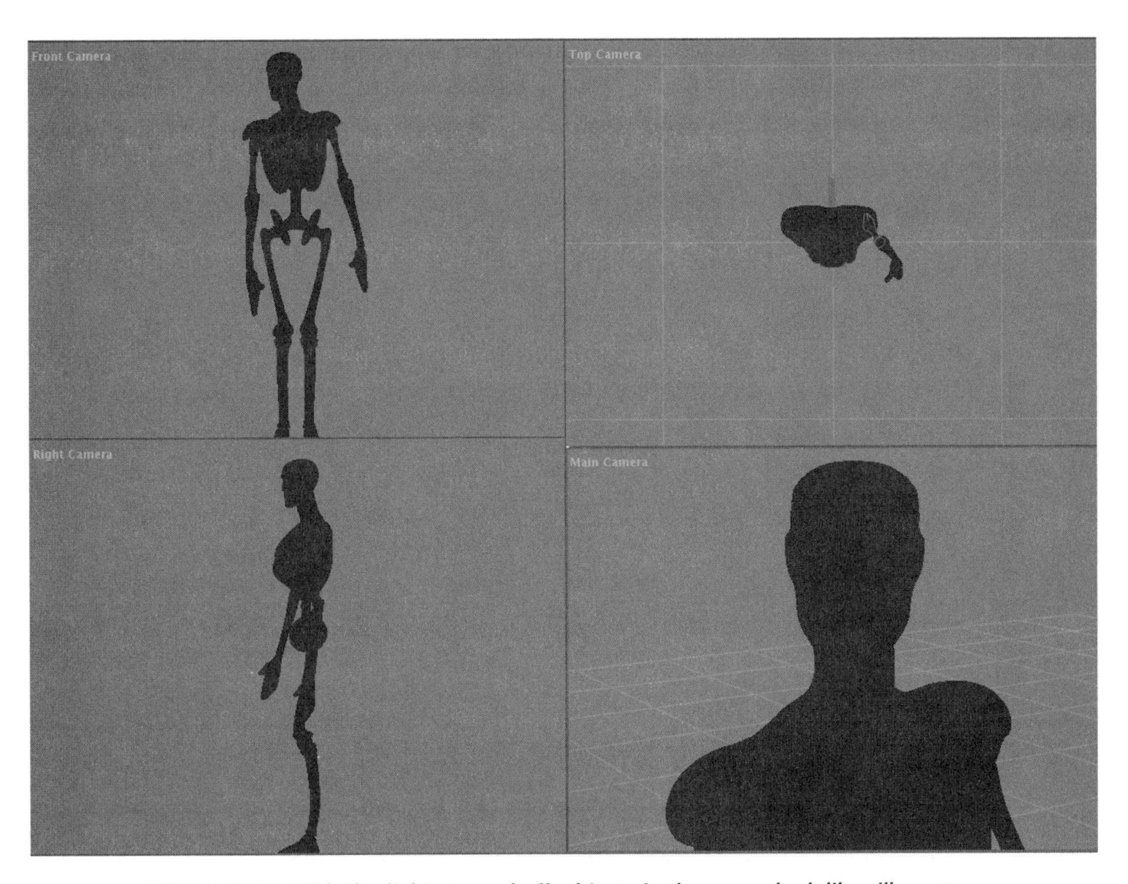

FIGURE 3.10 With the lights turned off, objects in the scene look like silhouettes. But this helps in the process of setting up back lights.

To change the background color, go to Display > Background Color and change the color to whatever you want.

6. In the Properties panel, turn off Shadows if that is turned on.
7. While you're in the Properties panel, choose Key Light from the top menu to turn it back on. Do the same for the fill light.
8. Render your result to check the final lighting. Make adjustments to your settings and tweak the light positions until you get the effect you want. Figure 3.12 shows the final result.

FIGURE 3.11 Adjust the position of the back light until you get a highlight that is acceptable.

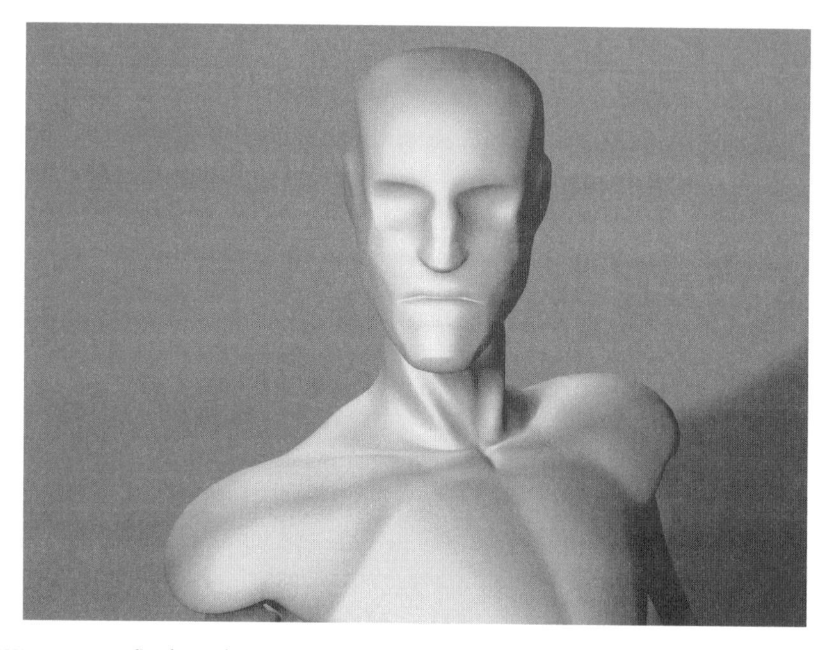

FIGURE 3.12 A final rendered portrait of Andy using the three-point lighting technique.

This is pretty good. Andy's pretty well lit. But what about those highlights? How will these lights translate to a humanoid figure? Save this file, and let's replace Andy with Ryan Casual so that the latter is in the exact location as the former.

9. Go to the Figures category and choose Poser 8 > Ryan > Ryan Casual, and then click the single check mark button under the Figures list. This is the Change Figure button. When you click on this, the Change Figure dialog will appear. For now, leave all selections unchecked and click OK. In the next window, leave Keep Current Proportions unchecked and click OK. Ryan will be placed into the scene exactly where Andy was.
10. Notice that Ryan looks dark; the lights aren't affecting the figure. That's because I broke the Point At links. Remember, I had the lights pointing at Andy's head, but Andy's not there any more. To make the lights affect Ryan, select each light and set Point At to Ryan's head.

When you replace one model with another, the new model will retain the name of the original model. So Ryan Casual will continue to have the name Andy. It's a little bug that will hopefully be fixed in later versions of Poser.

11. Take a few moments to pose him. In my case, I set Point At to each eyeball, having them point at the Main Camera. He's going to be a dangerous dude in the little story I set up in my mind. All he needs are a few scars, and he'll be set to go.
12. Render the scene. Figure 3.13 shows the rendered Ryan, along with the P8 Ryan Hair 1 hair model added to his head.
13. His skin color is a bit pale because of the white light. Change the Key Light color to the following settings, and then re-render. This light shade of pink is just enough to pull out some red in the skin. (Save this file for later use.)
    - **Red:** 1.000
    - **Green:** .867
    - **Blue:** .933

With the lights in place (and before moving on to Tutorial 3.5), save this scene as lightingSetup.pz3. You will come back to it later in this chapter.

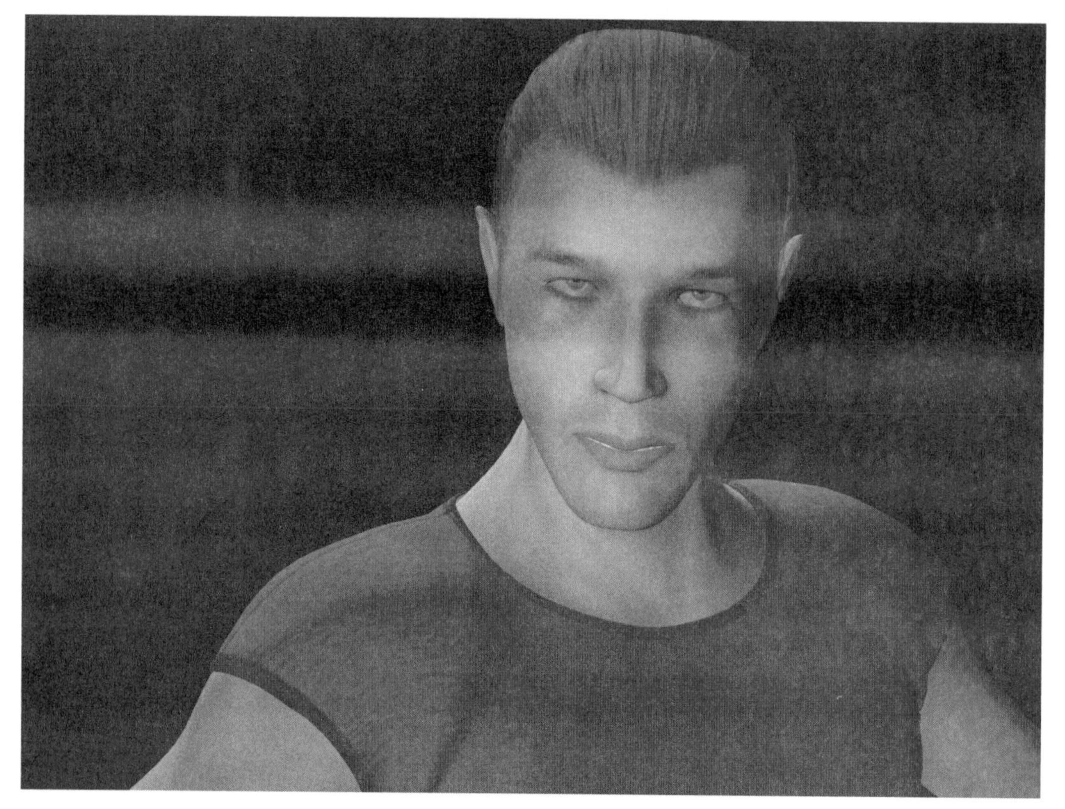

FIGURE 3.13 A rendered Ryan using the three-point lighting scheme. The background was changed to black to enhance the back lighting.

Tutorial 3.5 Saving the Light Set

This light set is one of a kind. Well, okay, it's a one-of-a-kind light set equal to the number of you who are reading and following along. I keep seeing the equation LS = R x B (Light Sets = Readers x Books), but that's neither here nor there. Since you took all this time to create this set, why not save it for later use in any other portrait scene you want to create. This process is identical to saving your cameras (which you learned how to do in Chapter 2).

1. In the Library palette, select the Lights runtime folder.
2. Click the Create New Folder button and title the folder Portraits.
3. With the new folder highlighted, click the Add to Library button. Name this 3 Point Lighting, and click Select Subset.

4. Select the three lights from the list and click OK.
5. Choose Single Frame from the Save Frames window.

Your light set is saved and ready to be added to any scene you want.

Adjusting Lights and Shadows

Wouldn't it be great if you could actually see what a light sees? Well, guess what. You can. Each light you create has a camera associated with it. These are called shadow light cameras. They allow you to look into your scene through the light, exactly as the light "sees" it. It's almost as if you have a little spy cam inside the light that you can access at any time so you can fine-tune your lights. Figure 3.14 shows the shadow light cameras in the Cameras list. These are also represented in the Camera View selector in the Preview window.

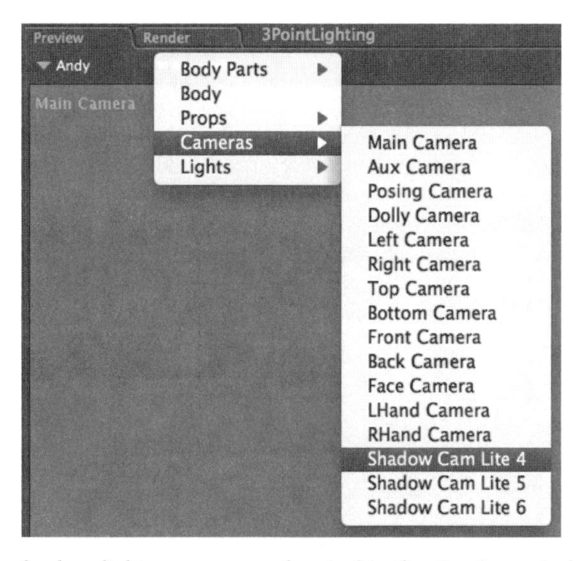

FIGURE 3.14 The shadow light cameras are located in the Preview window pop-up menu.

When might you need the ability to look through your lights into the scene? I'm glad you asked. One reason is if you are creating eye lights. Eye lights are used to get rid of shadows around the eyes that might be created by the eyebrows or hair. You can also use them to create eye highlights. In either case, the light would be pretty thin, and it would be extremely hard to focus the light without looking through it. Another reason for using shadow light cameras is to see exactly where an object's shadow would fall.

Included on the DVD (in the Chapter 3 folder) is a face file titled Pleasant.fc2. It's located in the Alyson_Original folder, which you can place directly in the Runtime \Library\Faces\lPoser 8 folder.

Tutorial 3.6 Setting the Scene

With the lighting scheme created in Tutorial 3.1, let's use the shadow light cameras to refine the scene's lighting.

1. If you need to, open the three-point lighting scene you created in the previous tutorials (lightingSetup.pz3). Yep. Good ol' Andy the Mannequin/ Android is back for more. But not for long. Select him and delete him from the scene.
2. Add the Alyson Casual model (Figures category > Poser 8 > Alyson > Alyson Casual).
3. Go to Poses > Poser 8 > Alyson > Standing > Thinking and add the preset pose to the Alyson model. If you installed the Pleasant.fc2 file into the Faces folder, add that to the figure's head.
4. Now let's set up the camera. Using the Main Camera, set the following parameters. You can also refer to Figure 3.15 to make sure your numbers match the ones I have set up.
   - Hither = .413
   - Yon = 860
   - DollyZ = –6.443
   - DollyY = 4.938
   - DollyX = 0.661
   - zOrbit = 9 degrees
   - xOrbit = 2 degrees
   - yOrbit = –45 degrees
5. If necessary, select each of the three lights (Key, Fill, and Back) and have them point at Alyson's head. Make sure you save this file before moving to the next tutorial.

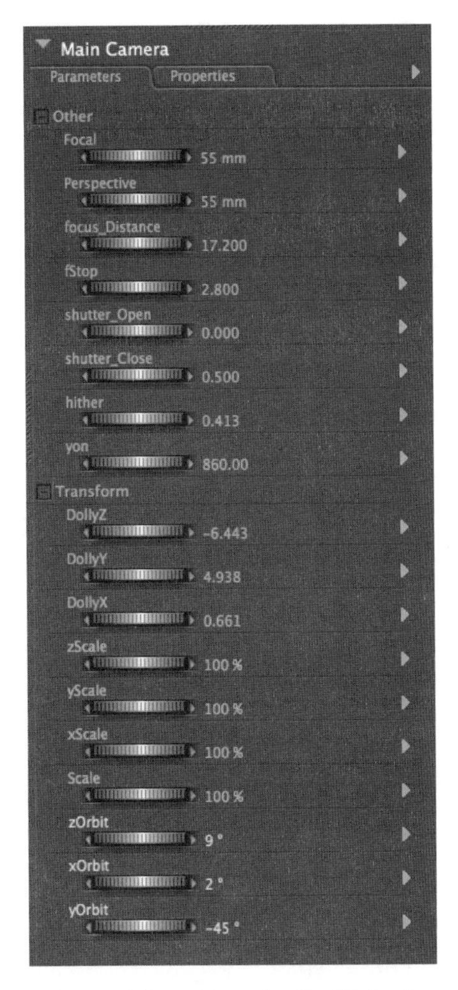

FIGURE 3.15 The settings for the Main Camera.

TUTORIAL 3.7 CREATING HIGHLIGHTS FOR EYES

A quick render shows a fairly well-lit portrait (see Figure 3.16), but when you break it down a little bit, it's not complete. If you look closely at a lot of portraits—not the fashion-shoot type but a true portrait sitting—the eyes will often have a subtle highlighting to bring them out. That's what you're about to create.

FIGURE 3.16 The portrait you set up in Tutorial 3.6.

1. Create a new light called eyeLight_R and turn off shadows. This will remain a spotlight so its focus can be controlled.
2. In the Properties panel, select Cameras and the last Shadow Cam Lite in the list. In the same manner in which you changed the name of the lights, change Shadow Cam Lite to eyeLightCam. You will want to do this with all the other shadow lights as well, naming them for their corresponding light's name.
3. Select eyeLight_R again. Go to Object > Point At and choose rightEye from the list (see Figure 3.17). Now as you move the light around, the eyeLight camera will always point at Alyson's eye. This will save you a lot of work.
4. As you begin this process, switching to the quad view (four viewports) will be very helpful. Change one of the viewports to the eyeLightCam so you can see exactly what the light is seeing. You'll also notice that the light's icon has a camera attached to it. That's the Shadow Cam Lite in all its glory.

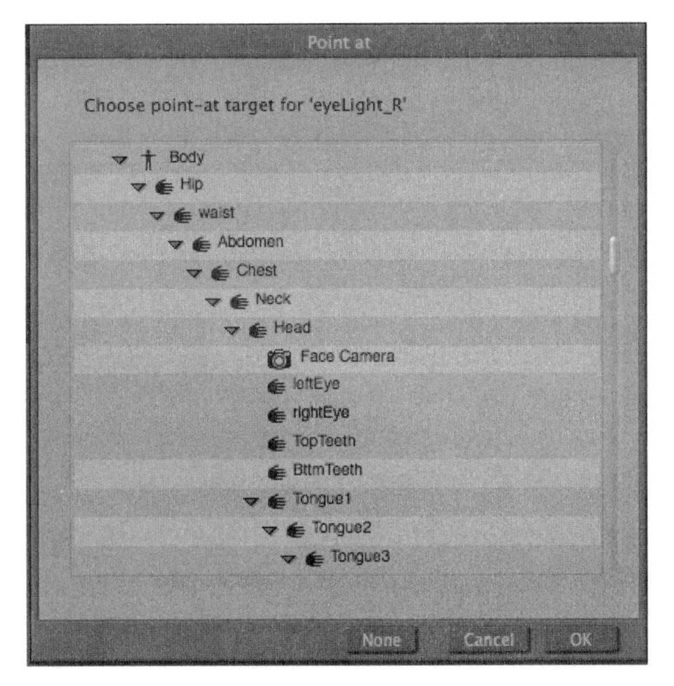

FIGURE 3.17 Select the right eye from the Point At list.

5. Select Cameras > eyeLightCam in the Parameters panel. Its controls will appear. Use the xTran and yTran controls to move the light until it's facing Alyson's right eye. Refer to Figure 3.18 to help you with the positioning.
6. Select Lights > eyeLight_R and change the light's settings to the following:
   - **Angle End:** 3
   - **Distance End:** 10
   - **Intensity:** 88%
7. The light's color becomes very important. You need something that isn't too harsh but that looks natural against the skin tone. In my case, I chose the following color for the light:
   - **Red:** 115
   - **Green:** 116
   - **Blue:** 179

FIGURE 3.18 The eyeLightCam is pointed to face Alyson's right eye.

8. Repeat Steps 1 through 5, this time calling the light eyeLight_L and the Shadow Cam Lite eyeLightLeft. Point it at the left eye and set it so it matches the parameters of the right eye light. Figure 3.19 shows the positioning for the renders I created. Also, since the light colors are randomly generated, change the color of eyeLight_L to the same color as eyeLight_R.

Figure 3.20 shows a comparison between the render without the eye lights (left) and with the eye lights.

Using Photographs and Image-Based Lighting

One of the most exciting features in all of 3D lighting is image-based lighting (IBL). IBL simulates the ambient colors in a photograph or movie and lights your scene in a way that makes your Poser content appear as if it is part of the environment.

An IBL setup gets its light information from a light probe that projects a photograph or movie onto a sphere to determine how the light will surround the content in your scene. In most cases, it makes sense to use the same image for your background and for the light probe. Figure 3.21 shows an example of a light probe.

FIGURE 3.19 The positioning for the eyeLight_L light.

FIGURE 3.20 There is a big difference in the visual interest of the portrait with eye lights added to the scene.

FIGURE 3.21 Light probes for IBLs use photographs or movies that are projected onto a sphere to determine the color and intensity of the light hitting the object in your scene.

Poser is also able to use HDRI (high dynamic range imaging) formats as light probes. Although you can use a regular photograph as an image probe, you will get more accurate results with a spherical light probe. There are a couple of utilities that can help you make more accurate light probes. One such utility is HDR Shop, a PC-only program that, at the time of this writing, is free for noncommercial use. You can download a copy from the Institute of Creative Technologies at www.ict.usc.edu/graphics/HDRShop/. However, if you have money to burn, there is Genetica Pro (www.spiralgraphics.biz). An alternative is Flexify, which is a reasonably priced Photoshop-compatible plug-in available for purchase from Flaming Pear Software (www.flamingpear.com/flexify.html). When using Flexify, you might want to combine it with Topaz Adjust from Topaz Labs (www.topazlabs.com/adjust). There is a free demo of Topaz Adjust on the attached CD-Rom. Make sure to read the ReadMe file in order to activate the demo.

NOTE

An HDR file is located in the Chapter 3 folder on the DVD. It's titled derelictBarn.hdr and will be used as part of Tutorial 3.8. I have also included a TIF file created in Photoshop that you can use to practice creating light probes or HDR (or radiance) image files.

It is important to note that IBLs are diffuse-only. That is, they don't add highlights to an image. As a result, it's good practice to use other lights in addition to an IBL—for example, you can position a second light in approximately the same position as an IBL and use it for the specular highlights.

When using a standard three-point lighting arrangement with a photographic background, it seems a natural choice to use an IBL as a fill light so that you capture the ambient colors from the photograph or movie. If you use an IBL for your fill light, you might consider using the key light to generate the predominant light in the scene (such as sunlight in an outdoor scene, or a streetlight or the moon in a night scene).

Poser also has a feature that helps achieve even more realism when using photos for a background. By default, the Ground plane in Poser is set up as a shadow catcher. When set as a shadow catcher, the Ground plane itself is invisible, but it captures the shadows as if the ground were solid. This allows you to apply realistic shadows to photographic backgrounds. If you align the default Ground plane so that the perspective is the same as your photograph or movie, the Ground plane will render a pretty decent low-cast shadow over the photographic background. It is a quick and simple solution if you don't have time to do any post-processing work in programs like Photoshop, Paint Shop Pro, or CorelDraw.

To use the default Ground plane as the floor in your scene, go to the Material Room and select the Ground plane from the Object menu (Props > GROUND). Near the bottom of the Poser Surface window, uncheck the Shadow Catch Only option. This allows you to see the Ground plane. To add a texture to the Ground plane, click the Diffuse_Color node button and choose the node you want to attach (such as a 2D Textures > Image Map node). You'll learn more about materials in Chapter 4, "Creating Materials."

Tutorial 3.8 Adding a Photographic Background

Now that you have a firm grasp on HDRI and image-based lighting, it's time to explore exactly what photographic images can do to add realism to your renders. In this tutorial, you will add an image that has been saved as an HDRI file and use it to illuminate your scene.

Before starting, create a new scene and add any human model to the workspace. For this project, I'm using DAZ 3D's Michael 4 character. But any character model will work for this. If you have the Michael 4 character, I have included a pose file (Stroll.pz2) for your use. It's in the Runtime folder inside the Chapter 3 folder on the DVD.

1. Choose File > Import > Background Picture. When the Open dialog box appears, open the derelictBarn.tif image file you downloaded from the DVD. Poser tells you that the width/height ratio of the background image is different from your Preview window. Click Yes to force the window to match the image. Figure 3.22 shows the derelictBarn.tif file in the background.

FIGURE 3.22 The background image has been loaded into the Preview window.

If for some reason your Preview window no longer displays the entire photo, select Window > Document Window Size. Then click the Match Background button, and choose OK to complete the change.

If you want to remove the background image, go to Display > Clear Background Image. It will immediately remove the picture from the scene and return your aspect ratio to its original settings.

2. Another way you can add an image is to go into the Material Room. Choose Background from the Object menu. The Color channel of the Background Palette will be attached to a BG Picture node. Alternatively, you can use a background color of your choice (specified in the BG Color node), solid black (Black node), or a background movie (BG Movie).

Adding a background image to the scene and forcing the Poser file to match the width/height of that image is the first step in preparing your scene. You want to make sure that the actual render dimensions match your workspace, which will be accomplished in Tutorial 3.9.

Tutorial 3.9 Matching the Render Dimensions to the Photo

When you work on your scenes (especially making modifications to the lighting), you'll probably find that you need a lot of test renders. The usual process is tweak, render, tweak, render, tweak, and render again—and again and again—until you get it right. To render the entire photo in your scene, you'll have to set up the render dimensions so that they match the dimensions of your Preview window. Follow these steps:

1. Choose Render > Render Dimensions from the menu or use Shift+Ctrl/Cmd+Y. The Render Dimensions dialog box appears, as shown in Figure 3.23.

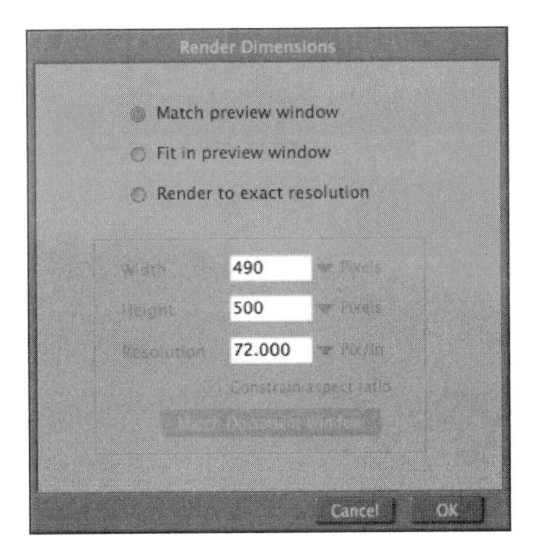

FIGURE 3.23 Use the Render Dimensions dialog box to define the size of your test and final renders.

2. Choose one of the following options:
   - If you want your test renders to remain the same size as the Preview window, choose the Match Preview Window option.
   - To render an image that is larger or smaller than the Preview window, first select the Render to Exact Resolution option. Make sure that the Constrain Aspect Ratio box is checked so that you maintain the required width-to-height ratio to display the photo properly. Then enter the desired width or height in either the Width or Height field. The other dimension should change accordingly to keep the photo at its proper aspect ratio.

When rendering a scene that uses a background photo, it is recommended that you set the FireFly renderer to Final quality. You'll learn more about rendering in Chapter 16, "Rendering Options and Techniques."

TUTORIAL 3.10 USING THE GROUND PLANE TO LINE UP THE SCENE

This image has an area set where you can comfortably place your figure so that he's walking in the scene. But you have to line up the character so he looks like he's part of it. The grid making up the Ground plane will work perfectly for this.

1. If you do not see the grid (for the default Ground plane) superimposed over the image, select Display > Guides > Ground Plane. It will also make it easier to see Michael's feet if you turn off the ground shadows (choose Display > Ground Shadows to uncheck them).
2. Use the Camera Plane controls (the control with hands pointing in four directions) to move the figure to the right side of the image. You can also hold down the spacebar and click and drag within the Preview window to pan or tilt the camera.
3. Use the camera Trackball control to turn the Main Camera so that your figure is walking toward the left side of your screen and so that the perspective of the Ground plane matches the perspective in the photo. Figure 3.24 shows a good placement for the camera angle and position.

TUTORIAL 3.11 CREATING AND PLACING THE IMAGE-BASED LIGHT

Now, let's light this scene. If you do a test render, things look pretty good. But, remember, you can use image-based lighting to control the color and quality of the light to make your figure look like he's actually being lit by the image itself.

FIGURE 3.24 Position the camera so that James appears to be walking across the rocks and so that the perspective of the Ground plane matches that of the photograph.

You'll go into the Material Room to do this. But first, get rid of the lights so you can start with a blank slate.

1. Choose Window > Python Scripts, and use the Utility Funcs > Delete All Lights script to delete the default light set from your scene.
2. Use the Create Light icon in the Light Controls panel to create a new spotlight. Change the color of the light to white.
3. Click the Material tab to enter the Material Room. In the Wacros panel at the right, click the IBL button. The Texture Manager dialog box appears, as shown in Figure 3.25.

FIGURE 3.25 The Texture Manager dialog box asks you to choose a texture for your IBL light scheme.

4. The Texture Manager dialog box asks you to choose a texture for the image map. At this prompt, you will choose the image that you will use for the light probe. Click the Browse button and locate the derelictBarnA.hdr file.
5. After you return to the Texture Manager dialog box, click OK to exit. You'll be asked if you want to activate Ambient Occlusion for this light. This is a feature that prevents light from affecting recessed areas, making shadows appear darker. Choose Yes to return to the Material Room.
6. Go back to the Pose Room and render the scene. In the case of an IBL, it won't matter where you position the light indicator around your scene. The light probe image determines how the scene is lit. Figure 3.26 shows an example of what your scene might look like at this point.
7. After you render the image, you may decide that you want to add some highlights and shadows because IBLs are diffuse-only. Click the Create Light icon in the Light Controls to create a second light for the scene.
8. Look closely at the photograph and notice the direction that the sunlight is coming from. In this case, the sun is coming from the front left. That's where the second light will be positioned.
9. Choose Object > Point At and point the light at your figure's left shoulder.
10. Set the yTran setting to about 7. This raises the light well above the figure's head.
11. To move the light back slightly and toward your right, make the following adjustments:
    - **xTran (left-to-right):** 1.573
    - **zTran (front-to-back):** 5.318
12. Render the scene again to check the shadows and highlights. Figure 3.27 shows the final result.

FIGURE 3.26 After rendering your image with the IBL, the scene looks pretty good! But, it can use a little more fine-tuning.

You might want to make sure the ground is set as a Shadow Catcher if Michael appears to be "floating." This way, shadows will appear under the character in a natural manner.

FIGURE 3.27 The second light has added depth to the highlights and shadow in the image.

A Short Re-Pose

Lighting, as you learned in this chapter, is a complex process. There are no shortcuts or magic steps that will make one light set work for every scene. You must use trial and error built upon a strong knowledge base to bring your scenes to life. There's more information in Appendix C, "Frequently Asked Questions," to help you go even further. But, suffice it to say, this will not be the last time you touch lights while working through this book.

So now it's time to move on. You'll leave lighting behind and begin learning how to bring your figures to life using another method—materials. Yes, my friends, it's time for (drum roll, please) the Material Room.

4 Creating Materials

In This Chapter:

- Meet the Material Room
- The Simple View
- Tutorial 4.1: Adding Diffuse Color
- Tutorial 4.2: Adding Specular Highlights
- Tutorial 4.3: Adding Ambient Maps to a Material
- Tutorial 4.4: Working with Reflection Maps
- Tutorial 4.5: Adding a Bump Map
- Tutorial 4.6: Working with Transparency Maps
- The Advanced View and a Discussion of Nodes
- Tutorial 4.7: Working in the Advanced View

"There are no absolutes in painting. All is measured by that relative term quality. *It is in this search for quality that the artist is, of necessity, the eternal student."*

—Rex Brandt

Creating materials for Poser characters can be a very lucrative enterprise. Lots of money is spent on textures for clothing, props, and figures to enhance the Poser products. People are always looking for high-quality textures to make their models stand out from the rest. And artists are creating amazing textures using Poser's Material Room as well as with Photoshop, Paint Shop Pro, and other image manipulation programs or a combination thereof. Of course, this isn't to say that the moment you begin creating your own materials you will end up earning tens of thousands of dollars and be able to quit your day job. While this has happened for a few, the majority of digital artists make enough to simply augment their income while having a lot of fun doing it.

With that in mind, this chapter delves into Poser's Material Room using both the Simple and the Advanced views. You'll learn about the various types of maps—texture, bump, displacement, reflection, and transparency—in order to build procedural shaders. These can be created quickly and easily even though the Material Room might appear a bit daunting when you first enter it. But, by the end of this chapter, you will have gotten a good grasp on the controls and will be well on your way to building complex materials.

What is this thing called a procedural shader? Those things with the high-falutin' name create materials based on mathematical equations, much like vector art. Because procedural shaders use math to define elements within the texture, the materials are resolution-independent and can be scaled to whatever size is needed to fit on a 3D model. So that cube primitive you put into your scene then scaled to 10,000 percent of its size will have the same clean, precise texture as its non-scaled counterpart.

Meet the Material Room

Before you start working in the Material Room, you'll need to become familiar with the controls at your disposal. You can get to the Material Room two different ways—by clicking on the Material Room tab at the top of the workspace, or by going to Render > Materials. Either way, if this is the first time you have opened the Material Room or if you have opened this room but haven't changed the default workspace, your Material Room screen will look like Figure 4.1. You can use this image as a reference as we look at what each of the controls does.

- **Editing Tools** (1): These are the same editing tools you find in the Pose Room, with the addition of the Eyedropper tool. The Eyedropper is found on the far right of the Editing toolbar. Select this tool and click any object or any part of an object to load or edit the material used on the selected part.
- **Preview window** (2), **Camera Controls** (3), **Light Controls** (4), **UI Dots** (5), **and the Document Display Style toolbar** (6): Each of these does the exact same thing as it does in the Pose Room.
- **Material Room interface mode tabs** (7): These tabs allow you to switch between the Simple and Advanced material editing view formats.
- **Object list menu** (8): The Object list menu allows you to select an object in the current scene. You can also select the Background, Atmosphere, and Lights options.

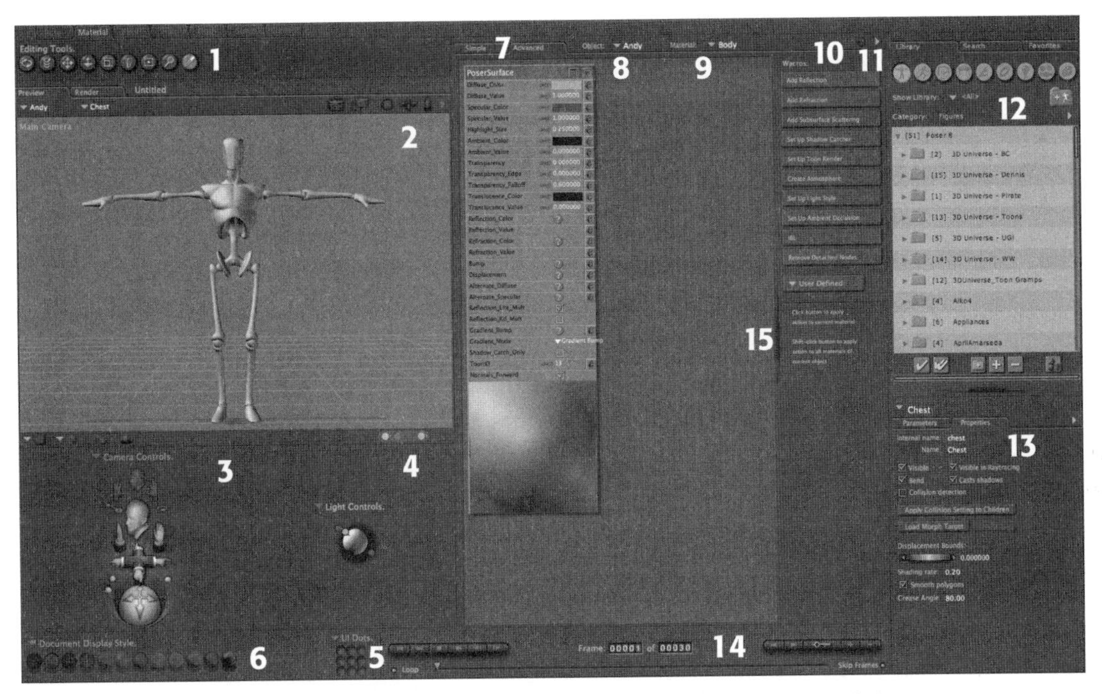

FIGURE 4.1 The Material Room interface showing the Advanced view.

- **Material group list menu (9)**: The Material group list menu allows you to select any of the materials that are associated with the current object. The current object appears in the Object list menu. Figure 4.2 shows the expanded list for the Ryan character.
- **Wacros drawer (10)**: Wacros are Python scripts created to work specifically with materials. Several predefined wacros cover the most common Material Room tasks. You can create your own wacro scripts and make them available in the User Defined pop-up menu by placing them in the Poser 8\Runtime\Python\poserScripts\Wacros\UserDefined folder within your Poser 8 installation. This area of your screen is a *drawer*, which means that you can "close" the drawer to hide its contents by clicking on the drawer handle (15). Click the handle again to toggle the drawer open.
- **Node Options pop-up menu (11)**: This menu, as shown in Figure 4.3, only appears in the Advanced material view, where you can click the Node Options menu icon, right-click anywhere within the Advanced view tab, or right-click anywhere within a node. The Node Options menu allows you the options to Cut, Copy, Paste, Delete, Apply to All, Select All, and Invert Selection. Some options on the menu act upon the currently selected node.

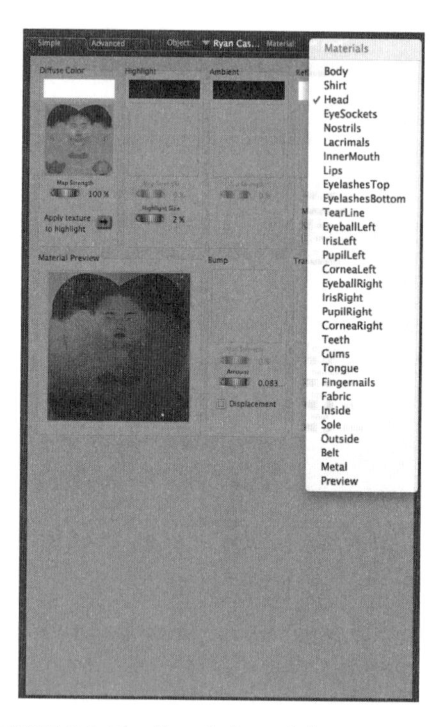

FIGURE 4.2 The list of all model parts as seen through the Material group list menu.

- **Library Palette (12) and the Parameters/Properties panels (13):** These are the same as their counterparts in the Pose Room.
- **Animation Drawer (14):** This serves the same function as it does in the Pose Room.

Python scripts should be installed in the default Poser Runtime folder. If you install them in the Downloads folder or in another external runtime folder, they may generate errors.

The Simple view of the Material Room is the perfect place to whet your creative whistle while learning how to create materials for your models. You can use the next section to hone your already burgeoning skills. Once you've gotten the hang of it, the Advanced view of the Material Room won't look quite so menacing. If you're comfortable in the Simple view, then you can skip ahead to the section "The Advanced View and a Discussion of Nodes" later in this chapter.

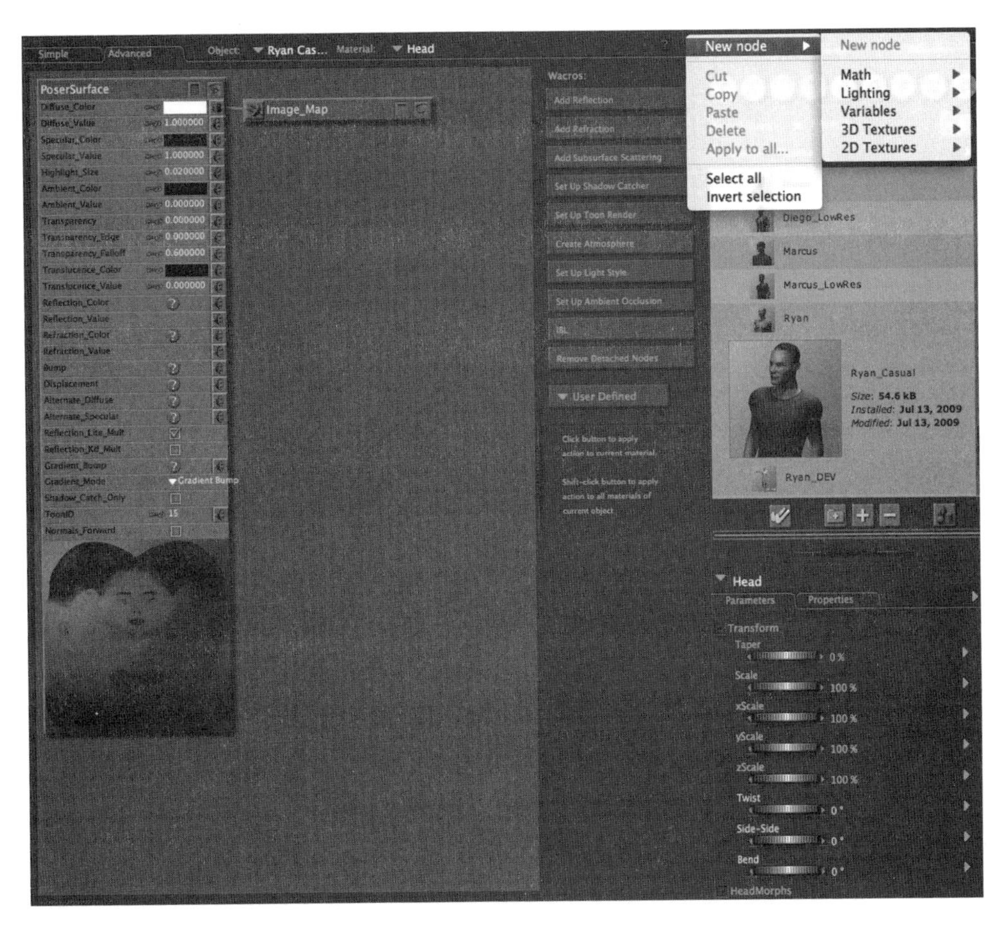

FIGURE 4.3 The Node Options menu in the Advanced view.

THE SIMPLE VIEW

The Simple view of the Material Room, shown in Figure 4.4, allows you to quickly assign colors or texture maps for the most common types of materials and material settings used in Poser. Those who are familiar with Poser Pro Pack and earlier versions of Poser will find the Simple view to be somewhat easier to use than the Advanced view. Here, you can assign texture maps and pertinent settings for diffuse color, highlight, ambient, reflection, bump, and transparency maps, as well as view a preview of the texture as you make your changes. The Material Preview pane shows what your material looks like with the current parameter settings.

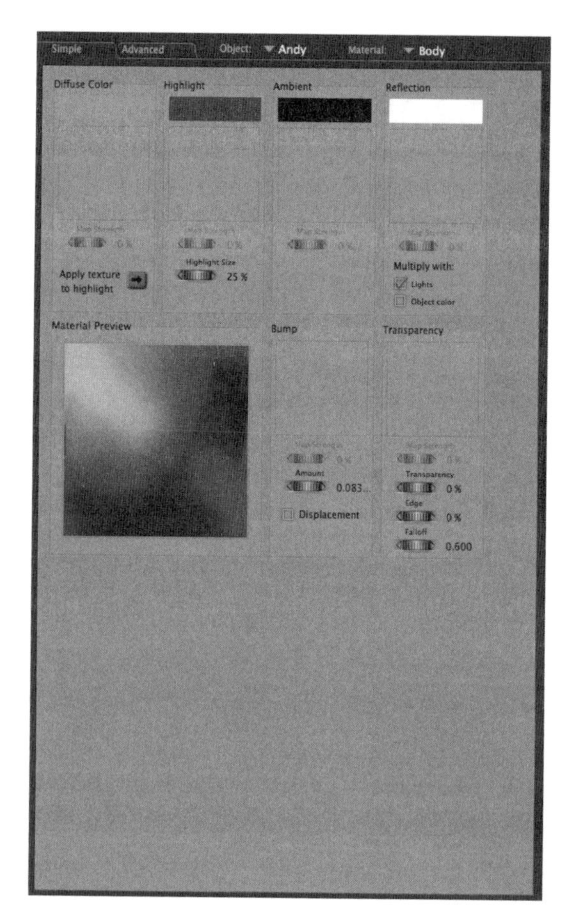

FIGURE 4.4 The Material Room Simple view interface.

If you should happen to see a tiny yellow caution symbol, this is an alert to adjust the associated setting in the Advanced view. The quickest way to do this is to click on the caution symbol. You will automatically be taken to the Material Room Advanced controls.

So, let's work with image maps. To assign an image map to one of the channels in the Simple view, click the Diffuse Color thumbnail preview area (the large gray square area) to open the Texture Manager dialog box (see Figure 4.5). Once this dialog opens, you can select a new image file, a previously used image file, or a movie clip.

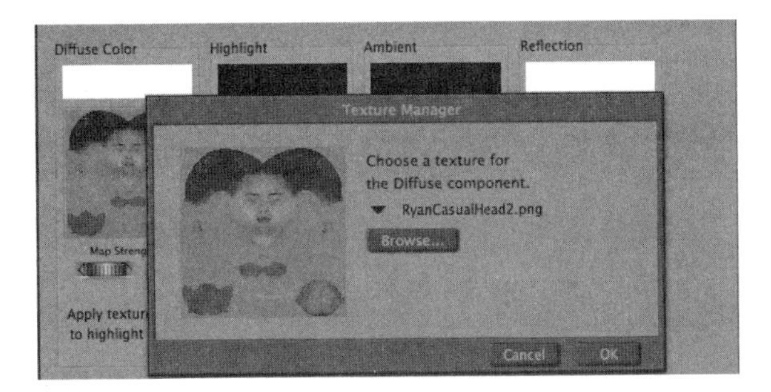

FIGURE 4.5 Click the thumbnail preview area to quickly access the Texture Manager dialog box.

With all of this information wrinkling your brain, I'm sure many of you are saying, "Okay! Enough already! Let's start using this Material Room thingie." That's exactly what you're going to do. Right now.

TUTORIALS

Now you are going to use various texture maps created in an image editing program and assign them to the Ryan character. These texture maps started out as the RyanCasualShirt.jpg texture map that loads with the Ryan_Casual figure. I opened the file in Photoshop and used it as the base for this project. You can find the image maps used in these tutorials in the Chapter 4 folder on the DVD.

TUTORIAL 4.1 ADDING DIFFUSE COLOR

The Diffuse Color section of the Simple view (see Figure 4.6) is used to set an object's primary color before any procedurals or modifiers are added to the mix. This diffuse color can be anything from a uniform color (red, green, blue, persimmon, and so on), or it can be based on an image that is mapped onto the object's surface—that infamous texture or image map. In addition, the diffuse channel can be made from a procedural calculation. In this case, you will use an image map.

You can also add a color tint when using a texture map or procedural, in which case your entire image map will be shifted into the direction of the applied color tint. If you do not want to tint your image map, leave the diffuse color set to white. If you do want to add a tint, then merely click on the color slot and use the color picker to set a color.

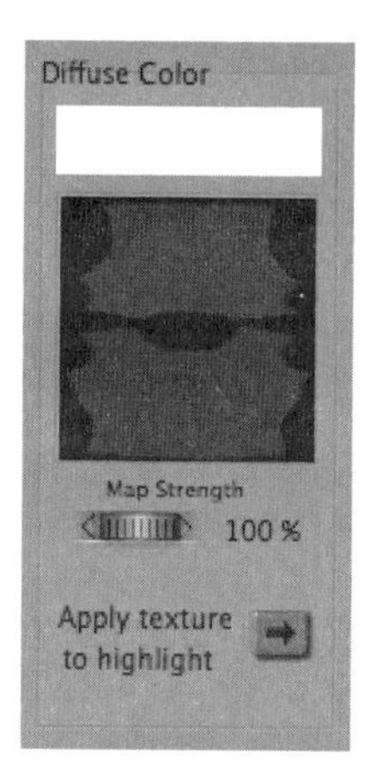

FIGURE 4.6 The Diffuse Color channel defines the main color of the object.

KNOW YOUR TEXTURE MAPS

The texture you will be building will use various texture maps that combine to create a complex image. If you aren't sure what each texture input is, here's a quick set of definitions to help you along.

- **Diffuse Color texture map:** Applies color to the object.
- **Highlight/Specular map:** Determines the color of specular highlights in the object.
- **Reflection map:** Determines the appearance or shape of highlights in the object.
- **Bump map:** Adds bumpiness and texture to the object. This is a simulation, with the bumpy appearance caused by the texture itself. The mesh of the object is not affected in any way.
- **Transparency map:** Determines which areas of a texture are opaque and which are transparent, and also prevents shininess in transparent areas.
- **Mask map:** Determines the areas that should receive stronger highlights.
- **Displacement map:** Adds additional shape to the geometry by actually warping the mesh.
- **Mask 2 map:** Determines areas that will receive additional specular highlights.

Before starting, drag the Project_01 folder from the Chapter 4 folder on the book's DVD to your desktop or to any folder where the files will be easy to access. Also, if necessary, replace whatever figure might be in your workspace with the Ryan_Casual figure. Remember, with Poser 8, you can now drag the figure onto the workspace. The Ryan_Casual figure comes with a really interesting shirt style. Not sure where it came from, but I know no one in my area would be caught wearing that style of t-shirt! But, that's neither here nor there. Let's add a new texture to the shirt—one that shows the pride you have in owning this book.

1. In the Simple view section of the Material Room, click the Diffuse Color thumbnail preview square. The Texture Manager dialog opens to prompt you to choose another texture. You can refer back to Figure 4.5 if necessary.
2. Because the Body is the active element of the model, you will want to change this to the shirt. Using the Materials pop-up menu, select Shirt from the list (see Figure 4.7).

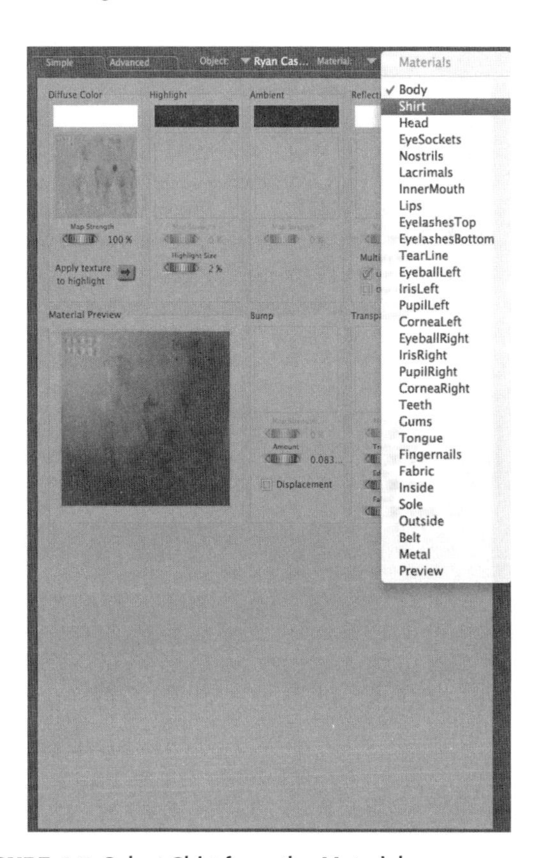

FIGURE 4.7 Select Shirt from the Materials pop-up menu.

3. Click the Browse button, then navigate to the folder that contains the image map you want to use. Textures are typically stored in the Runtime\Textures folder, but you don't have to place them there in order to use them. The texture you are going to use is Ryan_PoserBookShirt.png. Once you have found it, highlight the texture file and click Open to return to the Texture Manager dialog box.
4. Click OK in the Texture Manager dialog, and you will see the material updated in the preview area. You can also click Cmd/Ctrl+R to render the scene. Figure 4.8 shows the image map applied to Ryan's t-shirt.

You will notice that, in the initial rendering, the new texture looks fuzzy or soft. The quality isn't that good. This is because you haven't changed the Render settings to a higher quality render. So it is common as you work on a file for the test renders to look soft.

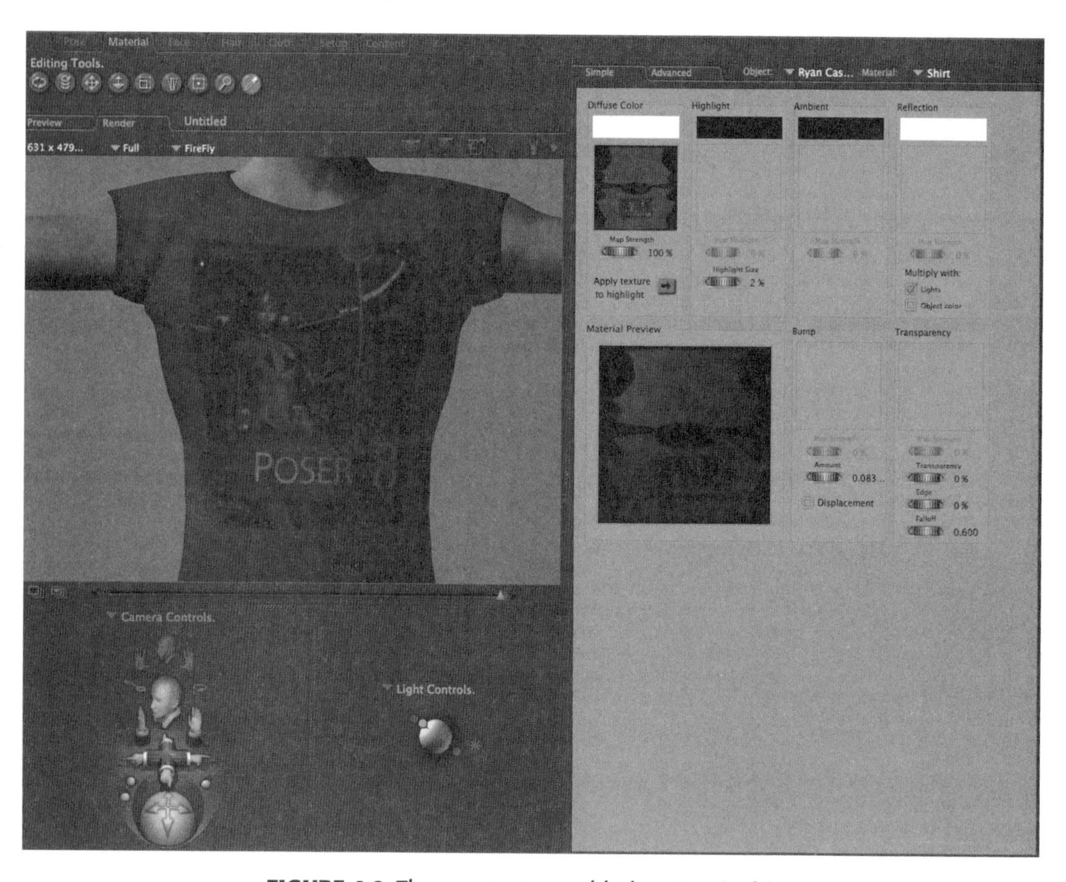

FIGURE 4.8 The new texture added to Ryan's shirt.

Tutorial 4.2 Adding Specular Highlights

Highlights are the areas of your material where the majority of the light's frequencies reflect straight into the camera. They are particularly important for adding realism to eyes, glass, and other shiny materials. Highlights are usually white, but you can tie them into an image map or a procedural material if you prefer to create more complicated highlight effects. You'll learn more about this in the steps that follow.

Many times, the easiest way to add highlights to a material is by using the same image map. This often gives the most realistic look to the material and can be done very quickly by clicking the Apply Texture to Highlight button at the bottom of the Diffuse Color channel controls. When you click this button, Poser copies the texture map from that channel to the Highlight channel, saving you from having to manually look for the file again. This will work in most instances, but not necessarily for all. When it comes to this shirt and this tutorial, I'll discuss adding highlights in two different ways—by using the texture map to create highlights and by using a different image map to create the highlights. First, the original map.

1. Again, choose Shirt from the Material pop-up menu.
2. Click the Apply Texture to Highlight button located in the Diffuse Color section. The Ryan_PoserBookShirt.png file will appear in the Highlight thumbnail preview area.
3. In order to see the highlight, you will need to change the highlight color from black to white. I'm going extreme here. With white the highlights will be very prominent, but you can use shades of gray or other colors to tone the highlights down or create interesting color washes. Here, you'll use white as I just stated. In the Highlight section, change the color by clicking on the color chip and selecting white in the color picker.
4. By default, the Highlight area's Map Strength dial will be set to 100%, which is where you want it. For Highlight Size, the value is determined by how you want the highlights to look on your model. In this case, change this value to 100% and then render. Figure 4.9 shows a comparison between the shirt without a highlight map and with it. There is a marked difference in the realism of the image when highlights are added to the texture.

What if you wanted a specific area to have a highlight on your material? Let's say the book cover on the shirt was made from a shinier material than the shirt itself. You would need to use a specially created image map to do this—a specular map.

Specular maps are grayscale images where white defines shiny areas and black defines the non-shiny surfaces. Shades of gray give different levels of shininess to the surface.

1. Making sure you have Shirt selected in the Materials pop-up, click on the thumbnail image area of the Highlight section.
2. Navigate to the Project_01> Extra _Maps folder and select the Ryan_PoserBookShirtSpecular.png file. You will see that this is a grayscale image. Many times specular, bump, highlight, and displacement maps use gray values from black to white to do their magic.
3. Once the image map is added, set the Highlight Size to 55%.
4. Render the file, and you will see the added highlight on the shirt's artwork (see Figure 4.10).

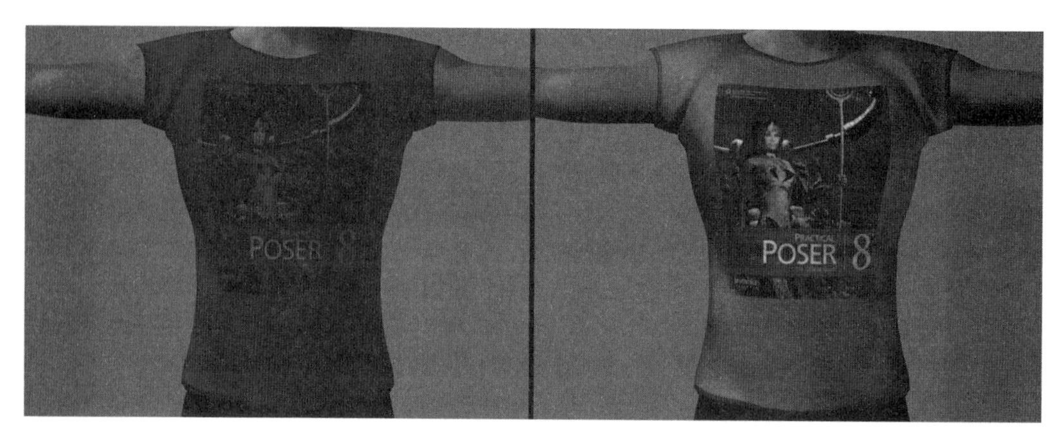

FIGURE 4.9 The rendered shirt without highlights (left) and with highlights added (right).

You would really want to tweak the Highlight Size value to make the texture look better, but you get the idea. By using a specialized map, you can add more interest and more detail to your materials.

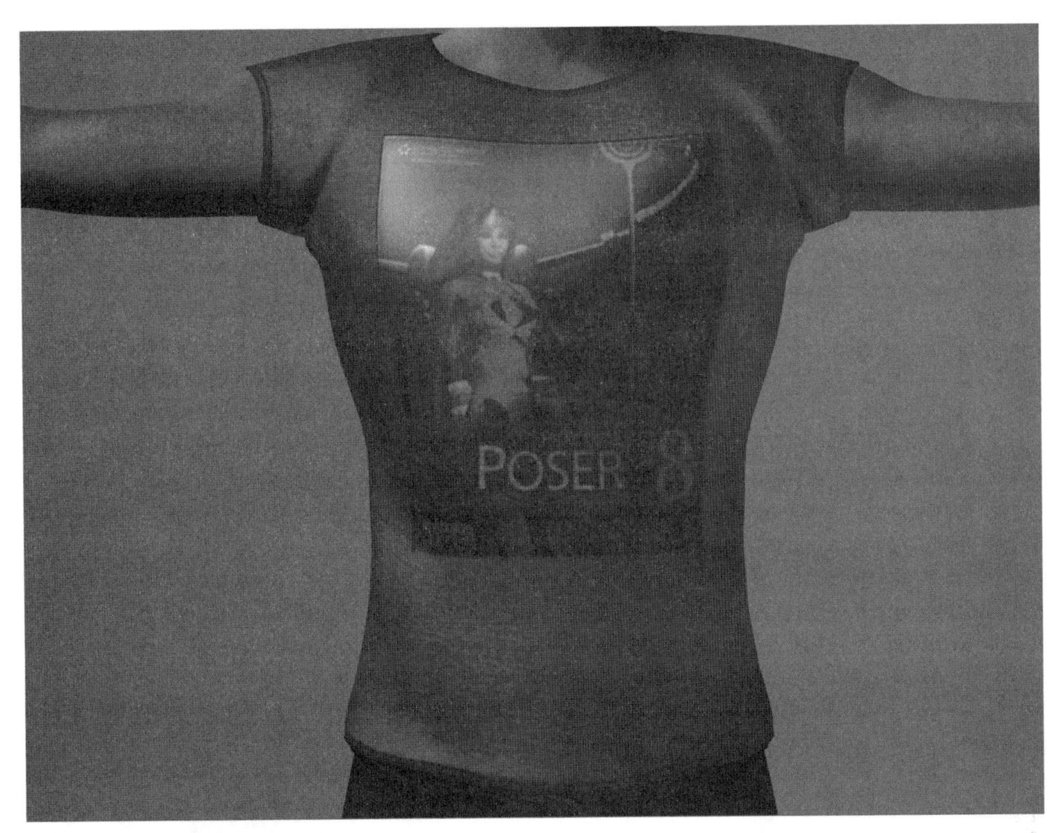

FIGURE 4.10 A highlight has been added to the material by using an original image map rather than by duplicating the diffuse map.

TUTORIAL 4.3 ADDING AMBIENT MAPS TO A MATERIAL

The Ambient section of the Material Room Simple view simulates the overall lighting condition in an environment. This control is a little different in that it isn't affected by the other color properties.

What, exactly, is ambient light? It is light that comes from all directions. It is a natural "fill" light. *Ambient light* is the light that exists in indoor or outdoor environments before any additional lighting is added. The relative intensity of ambient light, along with any fill lights added to the scene, is known as the *lighting ratio* and is important for calculating the contrast in your image. Basically, when you turn out the lights in a room so that there are no other light sources, it is the ambient light that you are using to see the room. Based upon lighting conditions—a heavily overcast day or a bright sunny day—the look of the area changes because that color making up the ambient light is interacting with the objects around you.

Now, let's apply this concept to materials in Poser. Ambient color is essentially emitted from an object when it's added to a material. Even if you delete all of the lights, an ambient color other than black will cause an object to appear self-illuminating. However, it doesn't actually illuminate the scene (see Figure 4.11). If you set the ambient color too bright, you will lose all the shadowed areas of the object and create an overall flattening effect on the materials applied. You can combine color with a texture map in the Ambient section to cause that element to stand out in your scene.

1. Making sure Shirt is selected in the Materials pop-up, click on the Ambient section image preview and add the Ryan_PoserBookShirt.png file.
2. Click on the color chip at the top of the Ambient section and select a yellow color. It doesn't matter what the shade of yellow is; just use one you like.

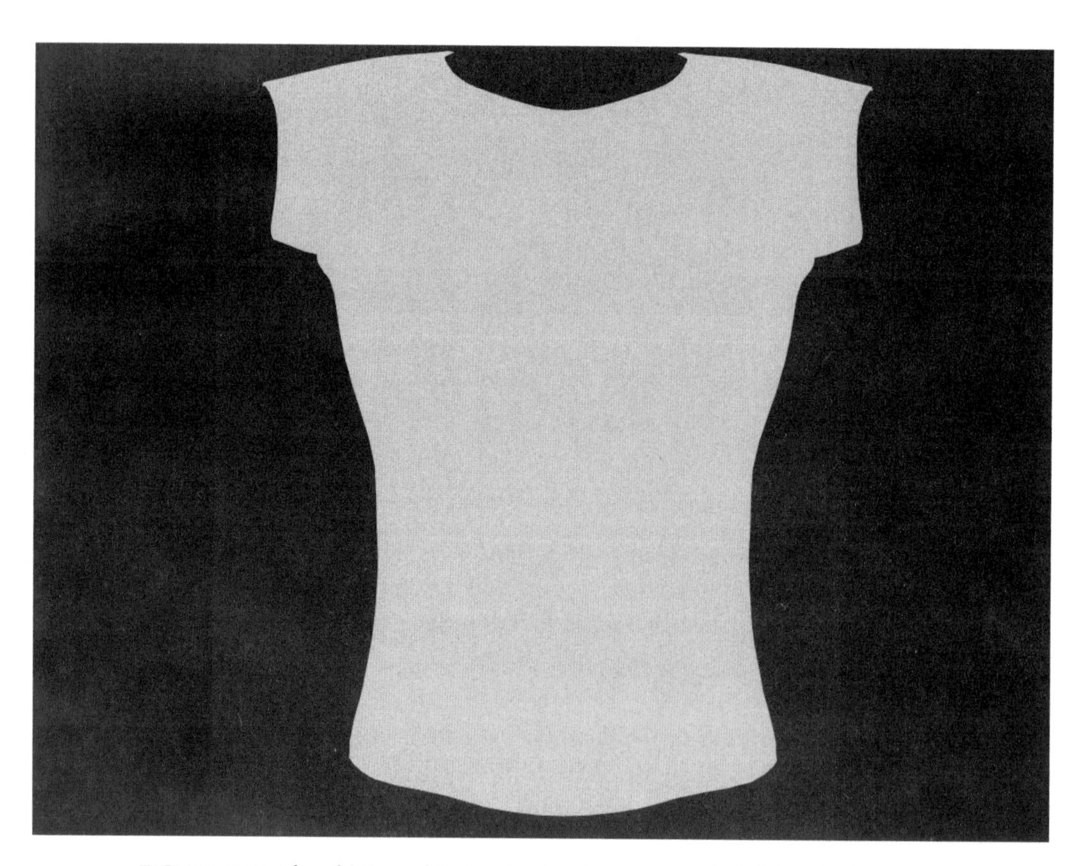

FIGURE 4.11 The shirt's ambient color has been set and all lights in the scene have been turned off. Also the background color has been turned to black. The shirt appears to glow, but does not illuminate the scene.

3. Make sure Map Strength is set to 100%. This will allow the image map to be the main material, while the color chip will add a wash over the entire object. If you lessened the Map Strength value, then you would get a very washed out look to the material, eventually reaching the point where the image map could not be seen at all.
4. Now go to the Parameters panel and choose Lights 1, 2, and 3 in whatever order you want and set their Intensity values to 0%.
5. Render the scene. All you will see is the shirt with a yellowish cast to it, as shown in Figure 4.12.

Now that you have tried the Ambient section of the Material Room Simple view, undo everything you have done. Return the light values to 100%, remove the image map, and reset the Ambient color to black.

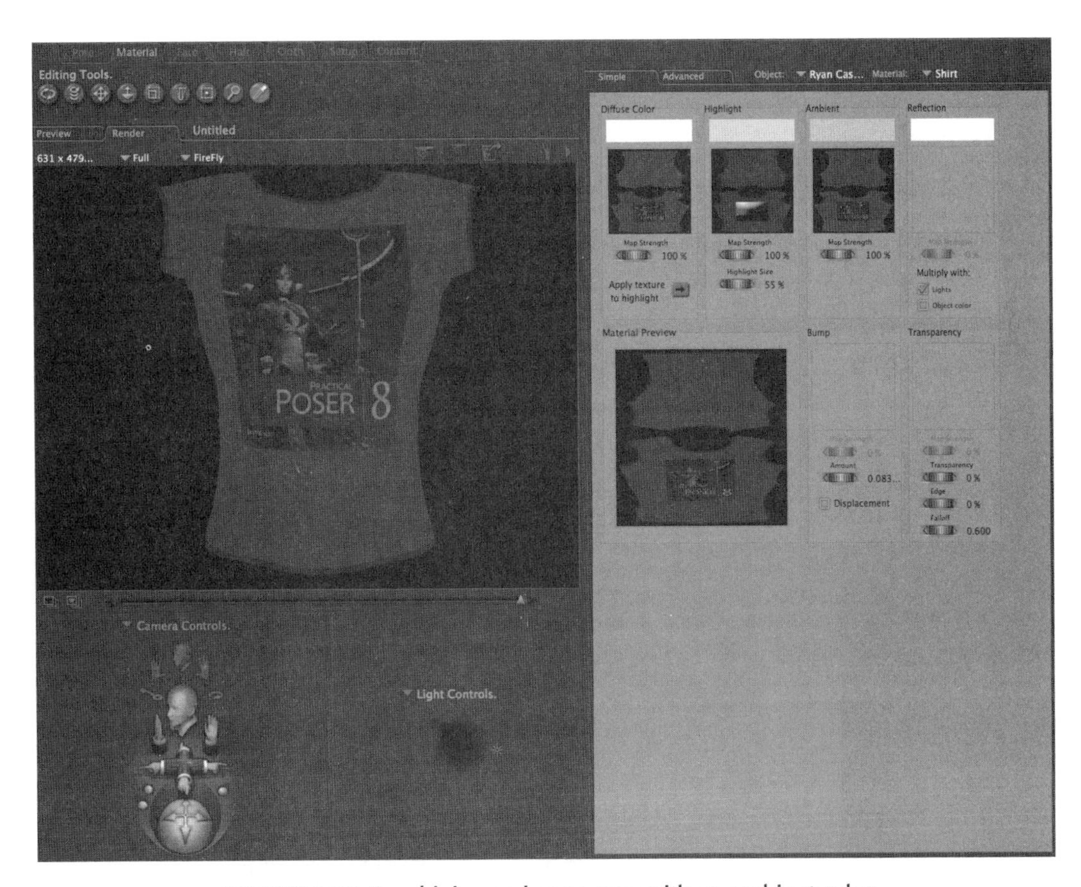

FIGURE 4.12 Combining an image map with an ambient color can make the object stand out from the rest of the scene.

In order to remove a texture from a material section, click on the material thumbnail preview, click on the image's name, and then select No Texture from the pop-up menu.

TUTORIAL 4.4 WORKING WITH REFLECTION MAPS

What is most useful in many circumstances is reflections. When it comes to eyes or metallic surfaces or glass and plastic, the realism of your render can be greatly enhanced by adding a reflection. The Reflection section in the Simple view gives you two ways to configure the reflective quality of your material. You can choose between a spherical map or raytrace reflections. The former takes advantage of image maps to create the reflection and renders quickly, while the latter will take longer to render.

You can change the tint of your reflection by selecting a color or image (or procedural calculation) in addition to your main reflective element. You also have an option called Multiply with Lights, which creates reflection effects that will be darker where there is no light. The Multiply with Object Color option tints the reflection effect with the current diffuse color.

It's difficult to get the reflections set to a specific area (such as the image section of the t-shirt) because the image map assigned to the material is turned into a spherical map. Namely, it is turned into a sphere to cover a 360-degree radius. But it's definitely not impossible. However, where the reflection map is really going to stand out is on metal. So you're going to do two things in this tutorial. First, you'll look at how a reflection map is applied to a primitive object, in this case, a sphere; and second, you'll add it to Ryan to bring out some details in the metal object in the texture.

Before starting, save your Ryan file. You'll come back to it momentarily.

1. Create a new file. If you have the Andy figure, load it with new scenes, delete him, and then go to Props > Primitives in the Library panel and select Hi Res Ball. Once in the scene, scale the ball to 500% and use Ctrl/Cmd+D to reposition the object on the ground plane. Ctrl/Cmd+D "drops" the selected model onto the ground plane, but in this case, the quick key command raises the ball model so that the ball is sitting on top of the ground.
2. Click the Material tab and add a diffuse color to the object by clicking on the color chip in the Diffuse Color section. In my case, I used a metallic gray.
3. Add the metalMat.png file from the Project_01 folder as the image map.

4. Set the Map Strength to 50%. When you render, you will see a brushed metal-like surface, as shown in Figure 4.13. Not very metal-ish, is it?

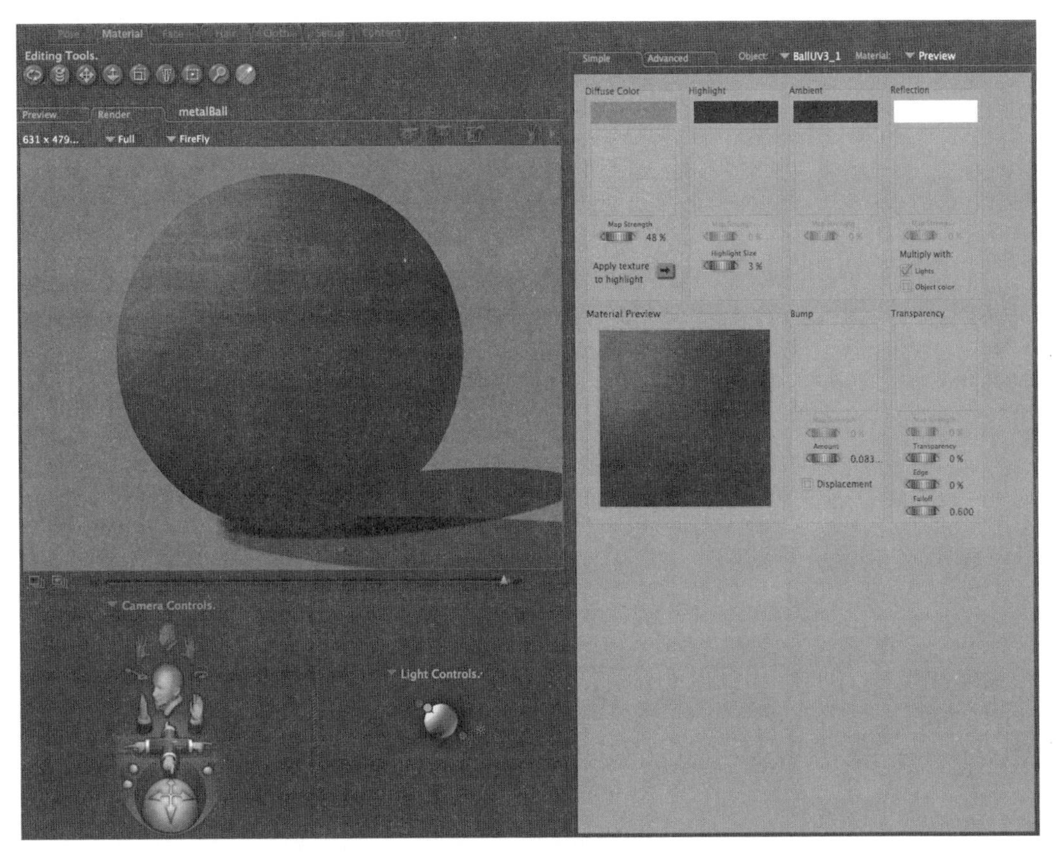

FIGURE 4.13 A brushed metallic surface created using both a diffuse color and an image map assigned to the Diffuse Color channel.

5. Set the Highlight color to a gray color and the Highlight Size to 2. This will reduce the size of the points of light reflecting off the surface of the metal ball.
6. Now go to the Reflection section and click on its thumbnail preview square. Choose Spherical Map from the Choose Reflection Type dialog and click OK. This will open the Texture Manager window and, from here, select reflectionMap.png from the Project_01 folder. When you render the scene, the sphere will look very similar to what you see in Figure 4.14.

FIGURE 4.14 The reflection map assigned to the sphere object.

Now that you see how a simple pattern in black and white can literally be turned into a pattern that adds an extra semblance of realism to your model, let's see how you can use it for good ol' Ryan. Figure 4.15 shows the belt buckle and the metal elements before any changes are made.

1. Open the Ryan file you saved a few minutes ago.
2. Zoom in so you can see the figure's belt buckle. This figure has a number of metal pieces on him, so you're going to add some reflection maps to help make them look better.
3. Go into the Material Room and, from the Materials pop-up, select Metal. It's located down at the bottom of the list.

FIGURE 4.15 The metal elements before the reflection settings are changed.

4. Before adding the reflection map, let's add a basic reflective quality to the metal pieces. Click on the Reflection section's thumbnail preview and select Ray Trace reflections from the list, then render your scene. This adds some basic reflective qualities to the metal elements that will make the reflections maps look more dynamic.
5. Click on the thumbnail preview again and select Spherical Map from the list. Navigate to the Project_01 folder and choose buckleReflection.png. Click Open and then OK.

Practice by changing the Map Strength as well as by turning on and off Multiply with Lights and Multiply with Object Color. Figure 4.16 shows the metal elements with the buckleReflection.png image assigned, Map Strength at 75%, and both Multiply with Lights and Object Color turned on.

FIGURE 4.16 The reflection with the Map Strength at 75% and both the Multiply with Lights and Object Color options turned on.

Tutorial 4.5 Adding a Bump Map

Adding bump maps can drastically alter the way a viewer perceives the reality of your overall material. Most objects have some sort of chaos to their surface—even glass, plastic, and other seemingly smooth objects. When you add a bump map to your object, it gives the appearance of high and low points without actually changing the geometry of your model. By clicking on Displacement in the Bump section of the Simple view, you are telling Poser to actually alter the geometry of the shape, with the high and low points actually warping the mesh. Figure 4.17 shows the same metal ball from Tutorial 4.4 with the metalMat.png assigned as the bump. As you can see in the left-hand image, the ball looks very bumpy. But look closer. The edges of the ball are perfectly smooth. So the bump map is merely giving the impression of height, whereas when I turned on displacement (the right-hand image), the metal ball's mesh has been altered.

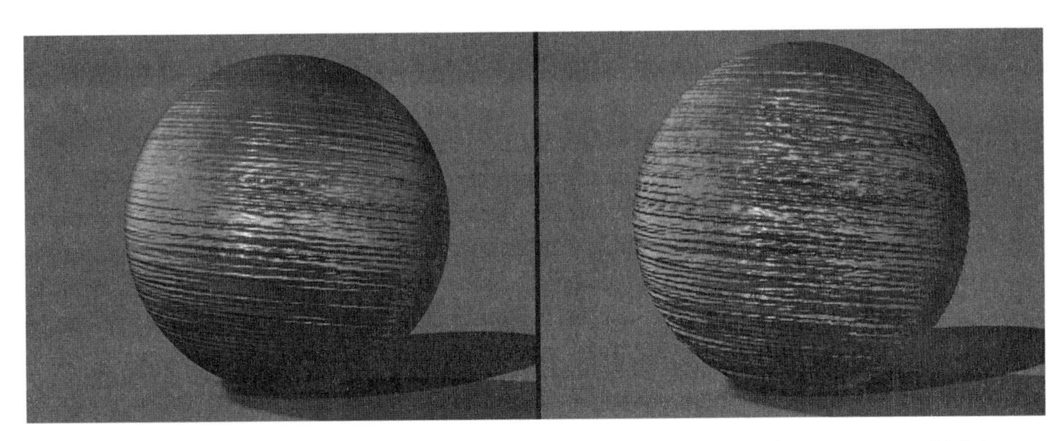

FIGURE 4.17 A comparison between a bump map (left) and a displacement map (right).

In order to see your displacement maps in the render, you need to go to Render > Render Settings (Ctrl/Cmd+Y) and turn on the Use Displacement Maps option.

When using the Displacement option, you control the strength of the displacement by clicking on Manual Settings in the Render Settings window (Render > Render Settings or Ctrl/Cmd+R) and changing the Min Displacement Bounds value to something other than the default 0. A setting between .02 and .05 is a good starting point.

Let's see. You have made a new shirt material and made the belt buckle look more realistic. Howzabout adding some interest to the belt itself?

1. Make sure Belt is selected from the Materials pop-up menu.
2. Click on the thumbnail image of the Diffuse Color channel and add the beltMaterial.png file in the Chapter04 folder on the DVD. This will add a clothlike pattern to the belt.
3. Set the Diffuse Color to somewhere between 25% and 35% gray. You will probably need to click on the red/green/blue square (the color picker) to go into the other color selection modes. Select RGB and change the values to 152/152/152.
4. Click on the thumbnail preview area of the Bump section and select the same image: beltMaterial.png.

5. Turn on the Displacement option.
6. In the Render Settings window, turn on Use Displacement Maps. See the previous Note if you don't know how to do this.

When you render your scene, it will look something close to what you see in Figure 4.18.

FIGURE 4.18 The belt now has a texture and displacement map assigned to it.

Also, if you copy the Diffuse Color material to the Highlight section, you can get a belt that has more of a leather look to it (see Figure 4.19). Experiment a little bit until you get something you like.

FIGURE 4.19 With highlights, the belt can look more leather-like.

TUTORIAL 4.6 WORKING WITH TRANSPARENCY MAPS

And now you're at the final section of the Material Room Simple view—Transparency. As you may know, transparencies are determined using shades of gray, with black being totally transparent and white being totally opaque. There are three options associated with the Transparency setting—Transparency, Edge, and Falloff.

- **Transparency:** Creates a transparent region based upon black values in an assigned image or in a texture. Black will be totally transparent, white is opaque, and shades of gray create semi-transparent areas.
- **Edge:** This parameter determines how transparent the edge of the object will be. A high Edge value makes the edges of the object more transparent.

- **Falloff:** This parameter sets the rate at which the transparency becomes more opaque as you approach the edge(s) of an object. A smaller value produces a sharper edge, while a higher value creates a more gradual transition.

If you set the Edge and Transparency values to the same number, there would be no effect because they would cancel each other out.

For this project, you will assign a transparency map to Ryan's shirt. The transparency map (Ryan_PoserShirtTransparency.tif) is located in the Chapter04 folder on the DVD. You will add the transparency map to the shirt, which will ultimately look a bit strange because the Ryan model does not have a body underneath the shirt. At the end of this short tutorial, you will also discover how to fix this problem.

To reduce the number of polygons making up a model, portions of an underlying mesh (like Ryan's body that would be underneath the shirt and pants) are removed. This can cut down on the time needed for a computer's processor to calculate the geometry in order to render it.

1. Select Shirt from the Materials pop-up menu.
2. In the Transparency section, click the thumbnail image area and then navigate to the Ryan_PoserShirtTransparency.tif file.
3. If you render now, the shirt will be semi-transparent because of the Falloff and Edge settings. (These two settings create a blurring effect on the mesh, affecting the way in which the transparency is assigned to the model, and in this case blending the white and black values in the transparency map, creating a semi-transparency.) You don't want this; you want the shirt to be opaque and the hole in the side to be a...well...a hole in the side.
4. Change the Edge and Falloff settings to 0 and then re-render. The edges of the black regions of the transparency map image are no longer blurred, and the hole you wanted to create is now well defined. Your image should look like Figure 4.20.

When rendered, this file is a bit disconcerting because Ryan has no body! That's right, Ryan ain't got no body. Sounds a bit like part of the lyrics to an old David Lee Roth song, doesn't it? Here's how to fix that.

5. Add the Ryan figure (that's the one without clothes) to the scene. As long as you haven't moved Ryan_Casual, Ryan will be placed in the same spot as his dressed counterpart.

FIGURE 4.20 The transparency map assigned to Ryan's shirt.

6. Open the Hierarchy Editor (Window > Hierarchy Editor) and turn off the visibility for all of Ryan's body parts, except for his waist and abdomen. Make sure you do this to Ryan, not Ryan_Casual.

You might want to save the abdomen and waist as a separate model so you can use it over and over again.

7. Choose either Ryan's waist or abdomen to make it the active model, then go to Figure > Set Figure Parent. You want to make it so the bare abdomen moves with its corresponding element on the Ryan_Casual model. So, in the Figure Parent window, choose Shirt and then Abdomen or Waist, whichever is the corresponding part you chose on Ryan. Now when you render the scene, Ryan will have a body showing through the hole in the shirt (see Figure 4.21).

FIGURE 4.21 Ryan now has a waist showing through the shirt.

The Advanced View and a Discussion of Nodes

The Advanced view of the Material Room is like a huge collection of pipes and control points that can be connected in an infinite number of ways to create the material you want. Unfortunately, that's exactly what makes the Material Room seem so overwhelming at first.

The Advanced view is really where you take advantage of the power of Poser's material capabilities, many of which work in conjunction with the FireFly rendering engine. When you open the Advanced view, you'll immediately notice that there are more parameters jammed into a smaller space. The left side of the Advanced view window displays the PoserSurface panel, which is a list of materials and their root nodes.

A *node* is a building block used in the creation of a material. Nodes have specific types of inputs, internal parameters, formulas, and outputs, depending upon what type of node they are. The various nodes, when joined together, create a material that is also known as a *procedural shader* (also interchangeably referred to as a *material shader*, or more simply as a *shader*). All shaders start with a root node. The basic anatomy of nodes is shown in Figure 4.22, where you see the various components that can make up a node.

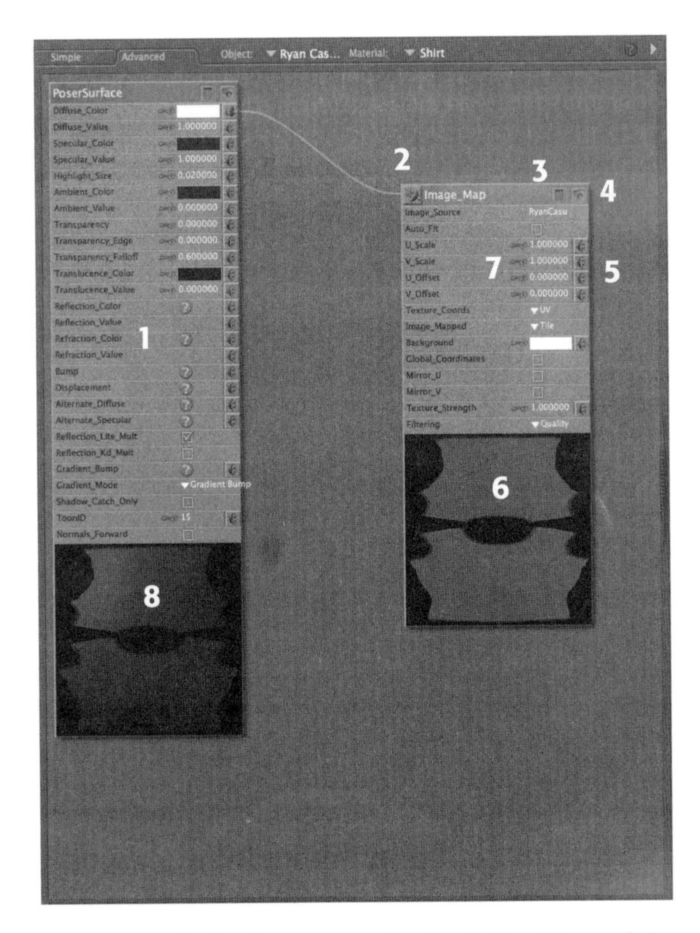

FIGURE 4.22 The basic anatomy of nodes in the Advanced view.

Each of these items serves the following purposes:

- **PoserSurface panel (1):** This is also referred to as the root node. This panel is the central gathering point for each material shader's root node. It accepts input from various components (colors, settings, and other nodes) to define and create the current material. A root node has no node outputs to connect to other nodes; instead, its "output" is the material shader itself. The panel shows a preview of the material in its PoserSurface preview pane (8) in real time—a handy feature when editing nodes and making changes to parameter values.

- **Output (2):** Each node (except the root node) has at least one output connector. The output value is based on the functionality of the node, the input(s) fed into it, and the values of the parameters used in its calculations. Outputs are depicted by the male half of a two-pronged electrical plug.
- **Parameter view toggle (3):** This toggles the display of the node's parameter value area.
- **Output preview toggle (4):** Toggles the display of the node's Output preview pane (6).
- **Input(s) (5):** All nodes have at least one input connection, although not all nodes require external inputs to function. Inputs are depicted by the female half of a two-pronged electrical plug.
- **Output preview pane (6):** Displays a preview of the node's current output.
- **Animation toggle (7):** Toggles animation on and off for the selected parameter. The animation toggle icon is a small key.
- **PoserSurface preview pane (8):** This pane shows a real-time display of the material with the current node and parameter configuration.

Depending on what object you have selected in the Advanced view, the root node may have other nodes attached to it. For example, Figure 4.23 shows three connections from the PoserSurface panel (Diffuse Color and Specular Color, plus Transparency) with connections to different Image Map nodes (Image Map and Image Map 3). A shader's root node mixes together all of the material modifiers that are "plugged in" to it. A material modifier can be a static value, an image, a color, an algorithm, another node, or any combination of these. There are four different types of root nodes that accommodate the various items that can use shaders. The most common node is a material root node, but you'll also find three additional nodes that include specific properties for backgrounds, hair, and lights.

Here's an analogy: Think of the Advanced view as a cookie factory. Raw ingredients (the various types of nodes) are brought into the system and mixed via several input pipes (the inputs and outputs of the nodes). Spices and chemicals are added to change the flavor (the parameters within the nodes and the operations they perform). Finally, it all comes together to be baked in the oven (the root node, which combines everything). The final result is your wonderful-tasting cookie (the resulting material, as shown in the PoserSurface panel).

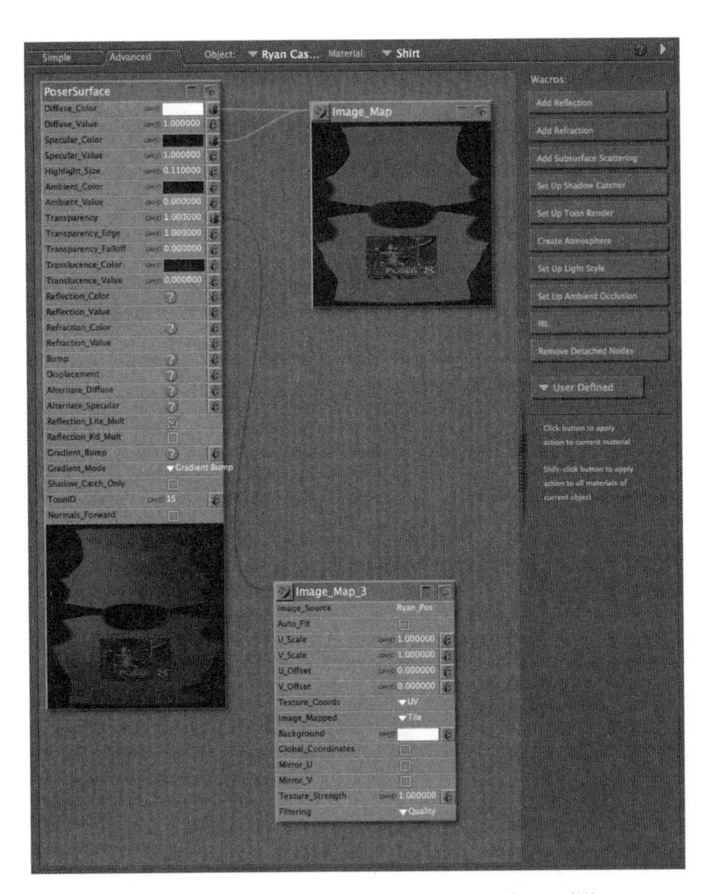

FIGURE 4.23 Two material nodes attached to three different root nodes in the Material Room Advanced view.

Nodes are versatile "black boxes" that act upon the input fed into them, and then output something else as a result of their unique actions. To connect a node to the root node, you click on the little plug icon on the right side of the PoserSurface panel. From there, choose New Node to display the submenu shown in Figure 4.24.

There are five major types of nodes: Math, Lighting, Variables, 3D Textures, and 2D Textures. Within each major node category, there are several nodes that behave in different ways. Here is a brief description of each node and what it represents.

- **Math nodes:** These perform mathematical calculations and transformations based on the values of their inputs. The Math node choices are Blender, Edge Blend, Component, Math Functions, Color Math, User Defined, Simple Color, Color Ramp, and HSV.

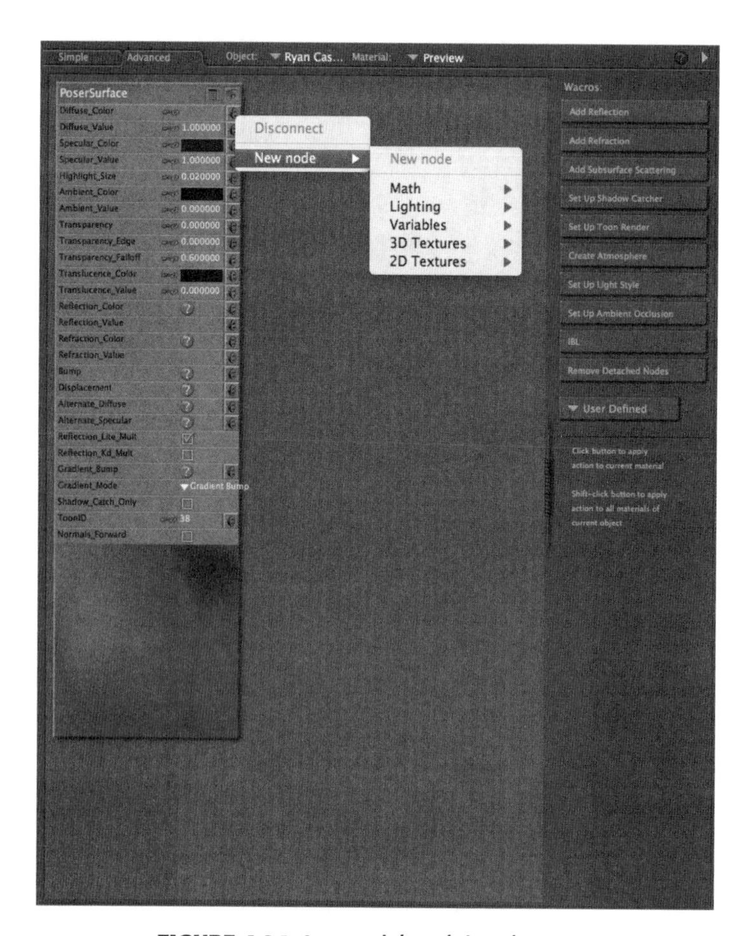

FIGURE 4.24 A material node's submenu.

- **Lighting nodes:** These work with lighting properties. Each of the five categories (Specular, Diffuse, Special, Ray Trace, and Environment Map) has a submenu of additional choices. Some interesting lighting nodes gather light from environmental inputs, such as the probe-light (in the Diffuse subcategory) and gather (in the Ray Trace subcategory) nodes.
- **Variable nodes:** These return values based on the current point on an object being rendered. These nodes have very cryptic variable names, such as N, P, frame_number, u, v, Du, Dv, dPdv, dPdu, dNdv, and dNdu. Their purpose is to look at various values that are being returned at any given point in time. For example, the N node returns the value of the normal at the current point on an object, the frame_number node returns the current frame number, and the v node returns the coordinate in space of the current point on the current object.

- **3D Texture nodes:** These are math-based (or often fractal-based) and create output that is calculated for all three spatial dimensions (X, Y, and Z). Many of these nodes can be used to simulate natural materials. Nodes included in this category are Fractal Aum, fBm, Turbulence, Noise, Cellular, Clouds, Spots, Marble, Granite, Wood, and Wave3d.
- **2D Texture nodes:** These produce output based on 2D transformations (X and Y). You can use these nodes to create 2D patterns, such as Wave2d, Brick, Tile, and Weave. Two additional 2D textures, Image Map and Movie, allow you to choose image maps or animated AVI or MOV files as textures.

Using Nodes

The variety and complexity of nodes can be overwhelming when you are trying to select the right node to develop a certain type of material, but after a little bit of practice, you'll get the hang of which groups of nodes work best for your tastes.

A node's output can be used as input for any number of other nodes. Wherever you see a plug icon on the right side of a root node or a regular node, it indicates that you can plug the output of another node in to affect that parameter. For example, you can feed two images into a Subtract node (a subcategory of the Math nodes) and use the resulting output image to create the diffuse color of your material. It is common practice to use the same output to drive several parameters, and it often helps make the materials and environments more believable. In real life, we often find that many properties of materials both affect and are dependent upon each other.

Now that you know a bit about the anatomy of a node, let's examine how you actually handle them:

- **Parameter values:** Nodes typically accept several parameter types. The most common are numbers, colors, image files, and outputs from other nodes. To edit parameter values, click on the number you want to edit and either type the new value in the number field or use the dial to change the current value. When the parameter is an image file (such as in the Image Map node), click the name of the image source and use the drop-down menu to browse your hard drive for the image file you need or select an image that you have already used from the history list. When the parameter is a color, click the color block to open up the Poser color picker. If you would rather use the RGB color picker, just click on the rainbow icon at the top right of the Poser color picker.

- **Selecting nodes:** Click any blank area within the node you want to select. You can select multiple nodes by holding the Shift key while selecting or by using the Node Options pop-up menu to choose Select All Nodes or Invert Selection.
- **Arranging nodes:** The position of a node in your view window will have no effect on its operation. In fact, your material may become so complex that your nodes will "disappear" underneath your Wacros drawer. If this happens, just use the Advanced view scrollbar along the bottom to scroll to those hidden nodes. You may find that you need to rearrange the nodes to get a better idea of how they are interconnected. To move a node, select and drag it to where you want it while holding down your left mouse button.
- **Creating new nodes:** To create a node, use the Options menu and progress through the submenus to find the specific type of node you want to create. Clicking on a node's input (or output) icon will also open the Options menu, except, in this case, the only available menu choice will be to make a new node. An alternate way to access the Options menu is to click a node's input (or output) icon and drag to create a wire. When you release the mouse, the Options menu will open with the option to create a new node. These methods will only work when clicking on empty input and output icons. Just adding a new node won't do any good until you link it to something.
- **Deleting nodes:** To delete a node, select it and press the Delete key. Alternatively, you can right-click on the node and use the Options menu to delete the node.
- **Linking nodes:** You can click the output icon of one node and drag it to the input icon of the node you want to connect it to. Conversely, you can start with the input icon and drag to an output of another node to connect those two nodes. After your nodes are connected successfully, you will see "wires" linking one node to the other.
- **Moving links:** To move a link to another node, just grab the end you want to move with your mouse, drag it to where you want it to go, and then release it. If you want to leave that end unconnected, just drop it anywhere in the Advanced view window.
- **Many-to-many links:** Remember, you can connect the input and output of a node to as many other inputs and outputs of other nodes as you need! However, an output can only go into another node's input.
- **Deleting links:** To delete a link, just click on the end you want to disconnect and drag it to anywhere in the Advanced window. You can also click on the end of the link you want to delete and use the Options menu to disconnect that end of the link.

- **Animating node parameters:** To toggle animation on or off, click the animation toggle icon (the key) for the parameter you want to animate.
- **Node "Window Shades":** When you start working with many nodes in your materials, you might want to minimize the nodes you are not currently focusing on. You can "roll up" a node into a smaller display in a few different ways (see Figure 4.25). You can toggle the display of the Output preview by clicking on the Output preview toggle icon, the eye icon in the upper right of the node. You can also toggle the display of the node parameters by clicking on the window icon just to the left of the eye icon.

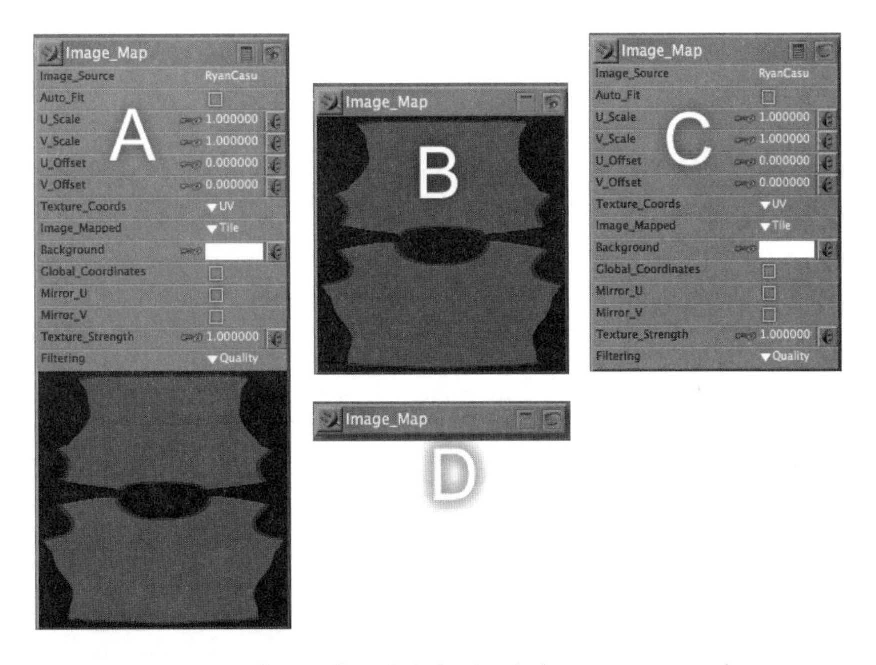

FIGURE 4.25 Nodes can be minimized to help save screen real estate. The various Node views are Full View (A), Parameters Hidden (B), Output Preview Hidden (C), Parameters and Output Preview Hidden (D).

TUTORIAL 4.7 WORKING IN THE ADVANCED VIEW

The Advanced view allows you to connect nodes to other nodes, including the Alternate Diffuse channel, which provides additional enhancements to the normal Diffuse channel. (You'll also notice an Alternate Specular channel that accomplishes the same thing for the Highlight or Specular channel, as you'll discover in a bit.) When you attach an input to the Alternate Diffuse channel, the two inputs blend, based on your settings, to result in a material with more depth.

One way to use the Alternate Diffuse channel is to make modifications to the appearance of the diffuse texture without taking it into an image editor. By making texture modifications in the Material Room, you open up a wider variety of results that can be achieved with one set of image maps.

For this section, you will use the Belt texture so you can enhance its appearance.

You will want to close the Wacros section of the Advanced view as you work through this tutorial. Otherwise, you will run out of room to work efficiently.

1. From the Advanced view of the Material Room, choose Belt from the Materials pop-up menu.
2. Click on the plug icon to the right of the Diffuse Color channel and choose New Node > Math > Blender (see Figure 4.26). By selecting this new node, the original connection will be broken.
3. Connect both Input 1 and Input 2 to the Image Map node that is attached to the Specular Color channel. Why do this? You just effectively hooked the Diffuse Color channel back to the image you just disconnected it from. By reassigning the image map to the two input channels, you now have more control over the look of the diffuse color. You can blend colors to give an entirely different look, or you can use gray values to enhance or remove detail from the texture.
4. In this case, you're going to add some color to the belt. Instead of being pure black, you're going to set a color closer to the shirt color, as if the shirt were being reflected slightly in the belt's material. Click on the Input 1 color chip, switch to the RGB color mode, and set the following values: R=181, Green=110, Blue=0. When you do a preview render, Ryan's belt will have a brown cast to it.
5. Next, go to the Alternate Diffuse channel and repeat step 2.

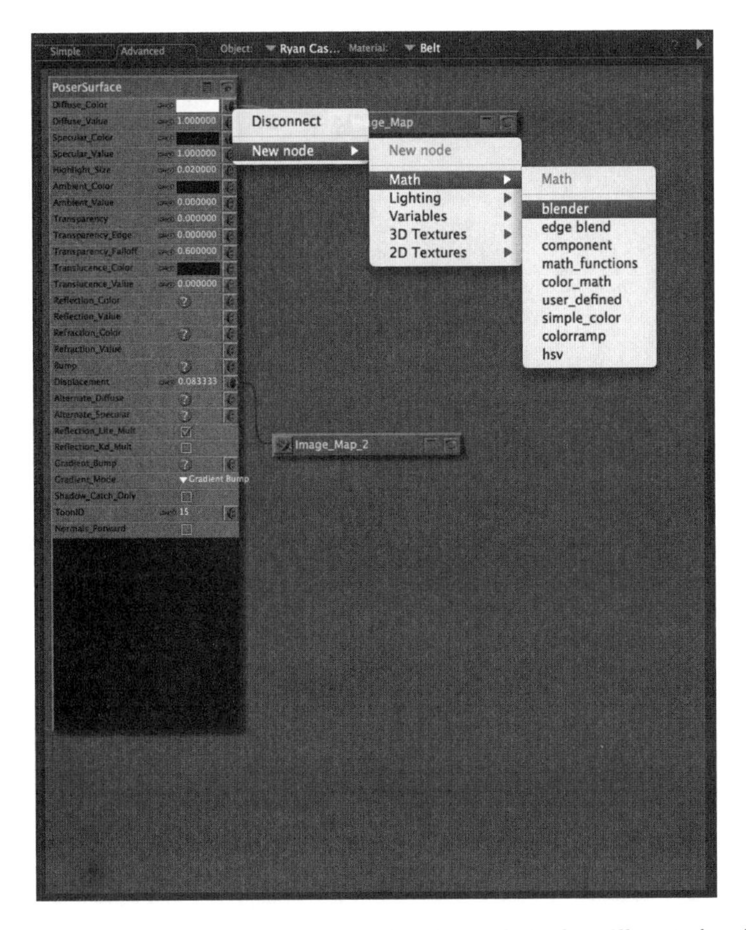

FIGURE 4.26 Creating a connection to the Blender node in the Diffuse Color channel.

6. Link Input 1 of the Blender 2 Node to the Diffuse Color channel for the Blender node. Do this by dragging the connector from Input 1 to the Blender node itself. Figure 4.27 shows this connection, which has temporarily ruined the look of the belt. The belt is too brown and the color is too flat as well as too brown. But that's about to be fixed.
7. Right-click in any blank area of the Advanced view window and, from the pop-up menu, select New Node > 2D Textures > Image Map. By clicking in a blank area of the workspace, you can create a free-standing node that can be connected to anything. This is just another way to create a new node in the Advanced view of the Material Room.

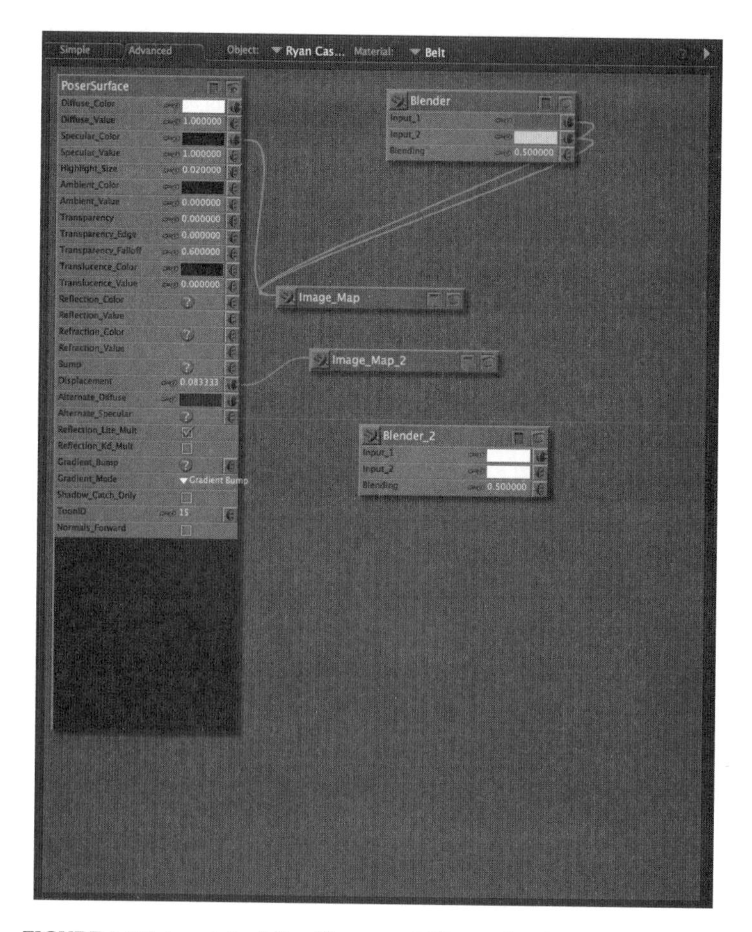

FIGURE 4.27 Input 1 of the Alternate Diffuse Blender node is linked to the Blender node of the Diffuse Color channel.

8. In this new node, click on the word None in the Image Source row. Using the familiar Texture Manager dialog, select the buckleReflection.png image file you've been using. At this stage, nothing happens because this node isn't attached to anything; it's free-floating, waiting for a reason to exist. So let's give it one.
9. Link Input 2 of the Alternate Diffuse channel's Blender node to the Image Map node (see Figure 4.28 for reference). In the PoserSurface preview pane (at the bottom left of the PoserSurface pane) you will see the effect of the reflection image on the material.

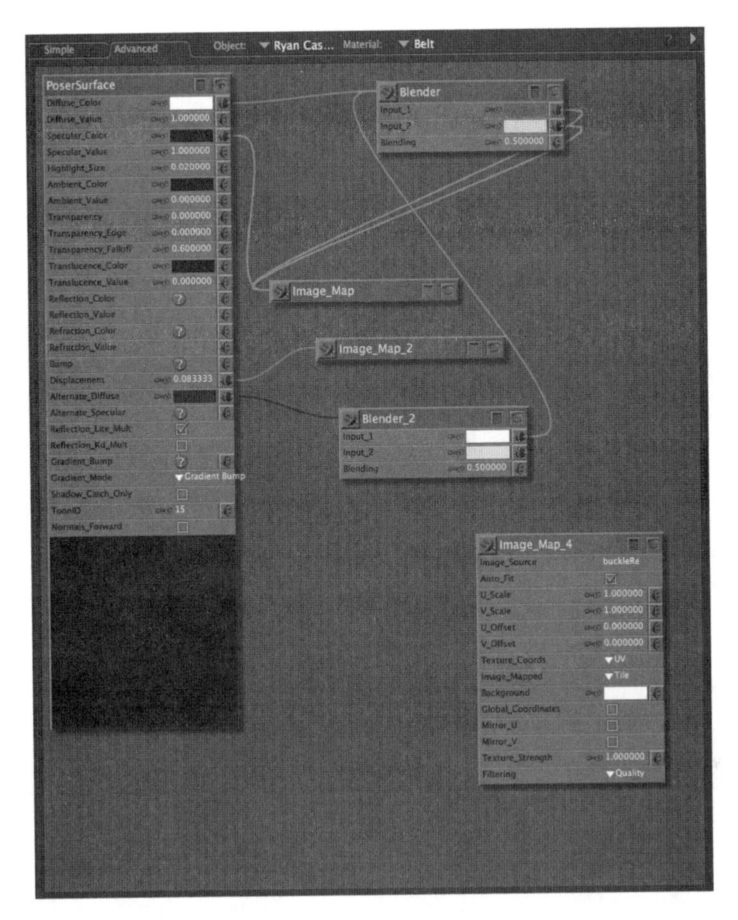

FIGURE 4.28 The Image Map node is linked to the Input 2 channel of the Alternate Diffuse's Blender node.

10. Now let's add another node, this time to the Alternate Specular channel. Click on the plug icon and choose New Node > 2D Textures > Image Map, then assign the reflectionMap.png image file. If you do a preview render, you will see that the two reflection maps are actually working pretty well, but you're losing some detail in those reflections. Let's fix that.
11. Click on the color chip for Input 2 of the Alternate Diffuse node and, using the RGB color window, set the color to Red=181, Green=110, Blue=39. This will give a slight brownish cast to the edges of the blended reflections.

12. You can now set a grayscale value to both the Alternate Diffuse and Alternate Specular channels to control the brightness of the reflective belt surface. Figure 4.29 shows the Advanced view of the Material Room and all of the connected nodes.

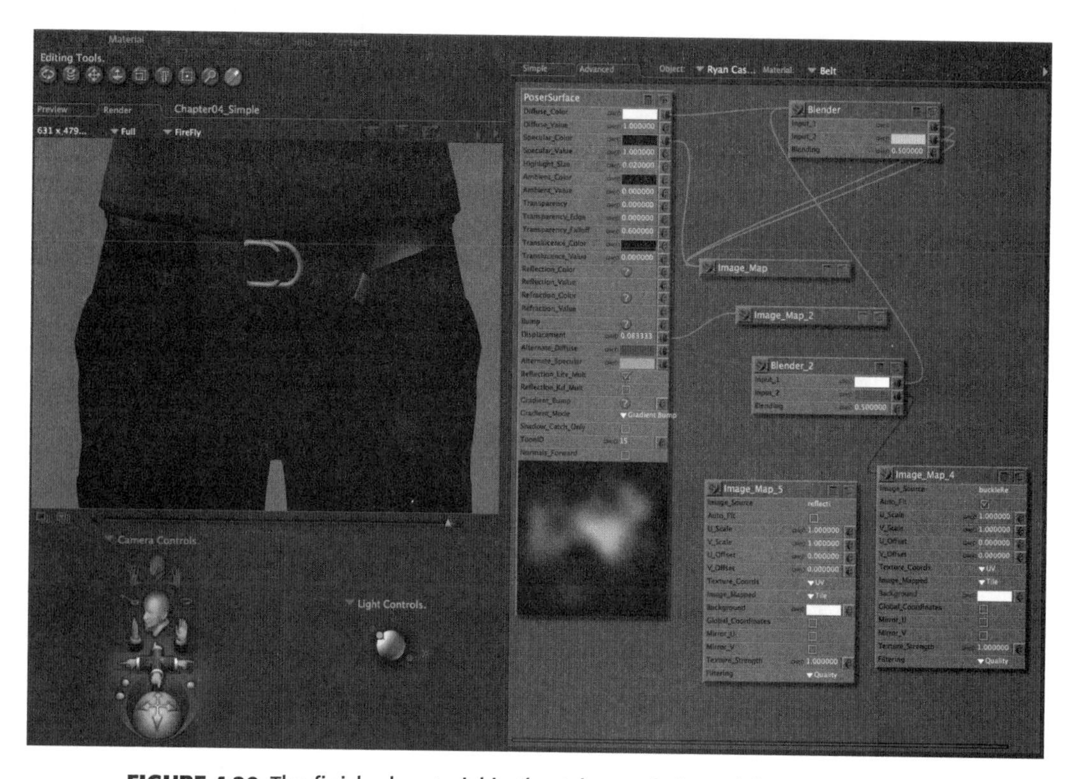

FIGURE 4.29 The finished material in the Advanced view of the Material Room.

There is now a nice highlight that goes from the dark belt color into a brownish color that looks like a reflection from the shirt that then blends into white. Of course, you can also change the color of the Alternate Specular node to give a deeper shade of the appropriate color for your scene, or just add a darker shade of gray to mute the white highlights a bit.

A Short Re-Pose

Between both the Simple and Advanced views of the Material Room, you have the power to create virtually any material you can imagine. In many cases, old pros of Poser might shun the Simple view because of its simplicity and lack of controls, but it is a great place to build the foundation of your materials. You can then go to the Advanced view to enhance that base texture to fit your needs.

But you might be saying to yourself, "Hey! He went through that awfully fast." And you would be right. There are entire books out there that deal entirely with creating textures, and almost all of them go into great detail regarding node-based texturing. The nodes in Poser's Advanced view are the same as in most other 3D applications, although the interface will be different. So if you want to travel further into the complexities of texture creation, you might want to look into texture-specific books on the market and use those to work in Poser's Advanced view of the Material Room. It will be well worth your while.

You're now going to explore another area of Poser that seems to confuse people more than many other aspect of the program—the Face Room. So after you're finished practicing with nodes, move on to Chapter 5.

5 Creating Custom Faces

In This Chapter:

- Face Room Overview
- Tutorial 5.1: Creating Texture Guides
- Tutorial 5.2: Preparing Your Photos
- Tutorial 5.3: Matching Ethnic Textures to the Body
- Tutorial 5.4: Saving Multiple Faces in One Figure
- Tutorial 5.5: Like Putty in Your Virtual Hands

"I think your whole life shows in your face, and you should be proud of that."

—Lauren Bacall

It's also said that a picture is worth a thousand words. And in addition to those two quotes, you can say that two photos are worth a million faces. With the use of both front and side views, you can create skin textures derived from the photo of a boyfriend or girlfriend, wife, husband, brother, sister, or that stranger with an interesting face sitting at the bus stop drinking a mocha latte. You can then use these photos to modify the facial features of your models and literally create a digital doppelganger. In this chapter, you will be learning how to do both—use photos for textures and as templates.

You can create custom faces in Poser in many ways. The most obvious method is to use the Face Room, introduced in Poser 5. This room allows you to customize the faces of the Poser G2 male and female characters, along with additional figures developed by e frontier. By importing front and side photos of a person, users can create a wide variety of characters. In fact, through the many facial morphs available in the Face Room, the range of characters that you can create is virtually limitless.

Here's a full list: Poser 8's Alyson and Ryan, Poser 5's Don and Judy, Poser 6's James and Jessi, Miki 1, and the G2 figures of James, Jessi, Kelvin, Koji, Simon, and Sydney. The Apollo Maximus character, a free, open source model available at antonkisieldesigns.com, is also compatible with the Face Room. There is also a Runtime\Heads directory where you will find configuration files for all the supported figures.

And because a wide variety of third-party figures are also available for use in Poser, you'll learn about a handy feature that works for any figure that contains morphs. With the Randomize Morphs Python script, you can create unique faces for other Poser-compatible figures.

Face Room Overview

The main areas of the Face Room are shown in Figure 5.1. Each of these areas serves a specific purpose and helps you achieve a wide range of characters for your Poser scenes. The following sections give a brief overview of the Photo Lineup area, texture variation, face sculpting, Texture Preview, Action buttons, and Face Shaping Tool.

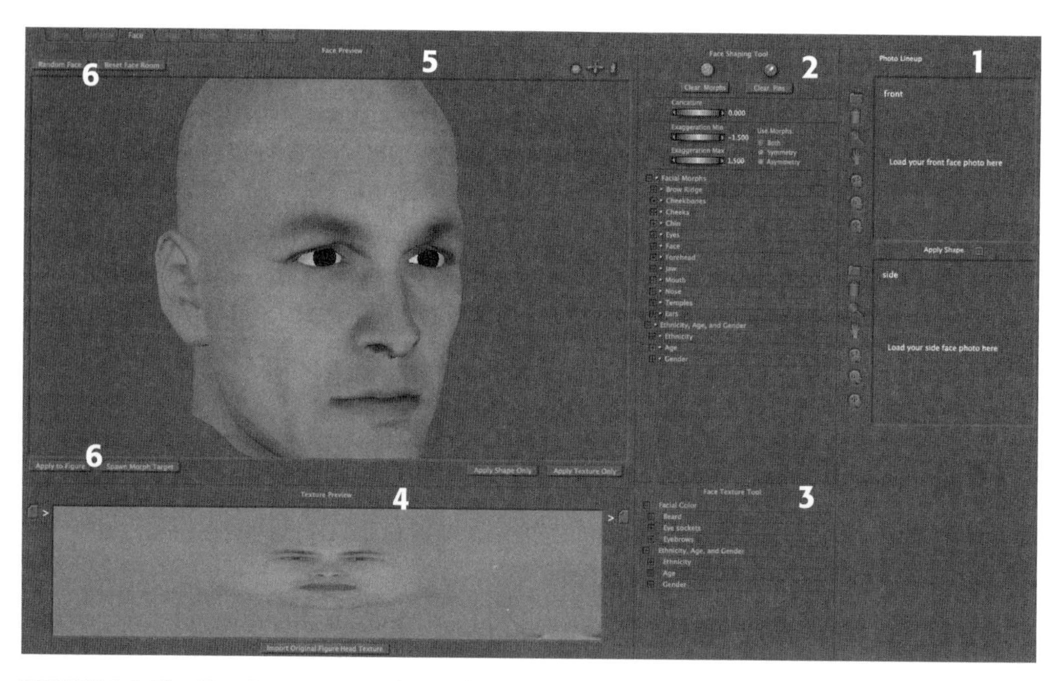

FIGURE 5.1 The Face Room areas: Photo Lineup (1), Face Shaping Tool (2), Face Texture Tool (3), Texture Preview (4), Face Preview (5), and the Action buttons (6).

The Photo Lineup area, perhaps the most challenging part of the Face Room, is shown in Figure 5.2. Use this area to import front and side photos of the same person and to create a face texture for your character. As you work with the facial outlines and feature points in the Face Room, you will get the best results in the Photo Lineup area if you take your time, save often, and make changes in baby steps.

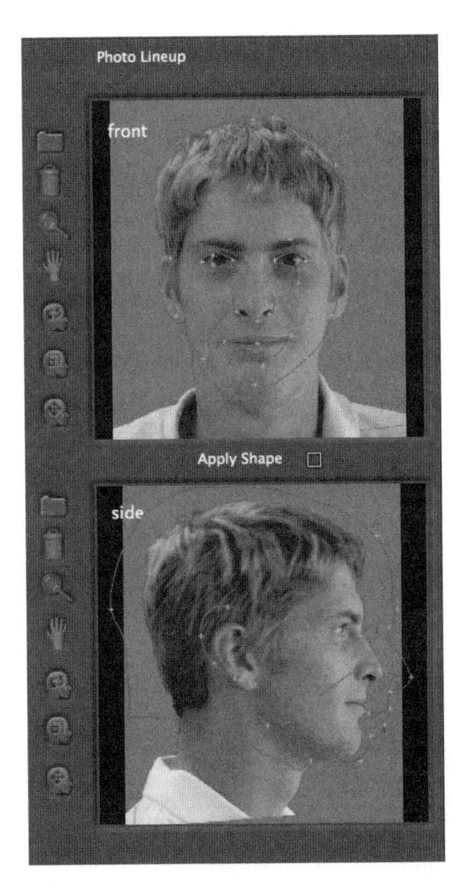

FIGURE 5.2 The Photo Lineup area is used to create the texture using a front- and side-view photo.

Most people new to the Face Room try to use the Photo Lineup area to both morph and texture the head to look like the photos they are using. However, when you keep the Apply Shape option checked while you adjust the red outline and green feature points, you quickly end up with a severely distorted head (see Figure 5.3), and you need to start all over again. The best approach is to leave the Apply Shape option unchecked, and use the Photo Lineup area strictly for texture generation.

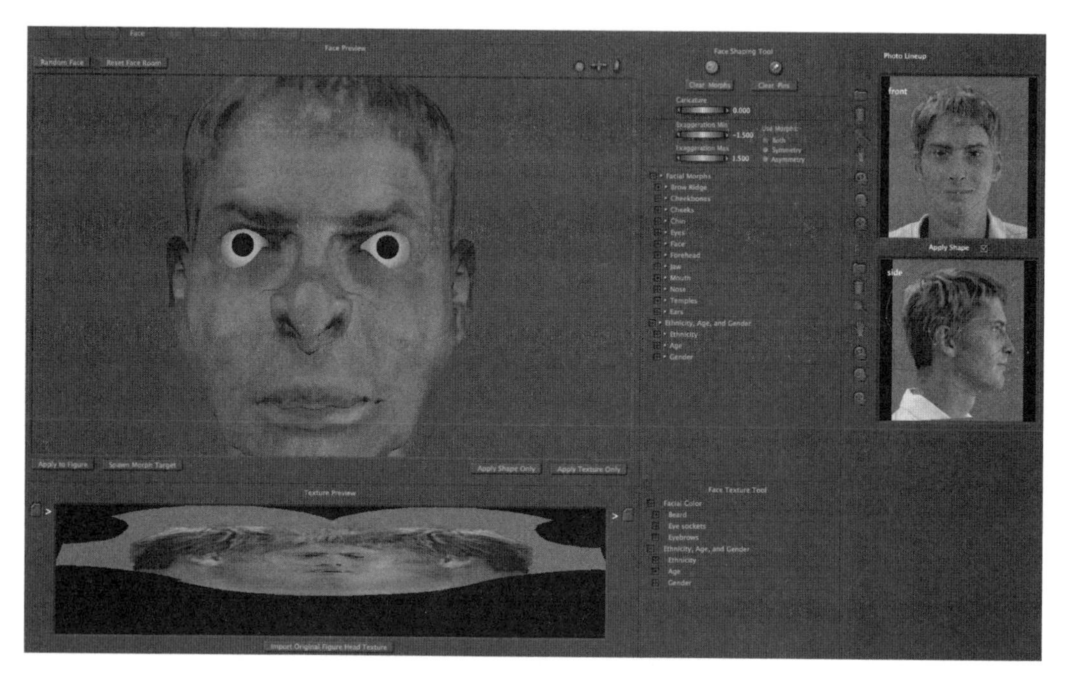

FIGURE 5.3 With Apply Shape active, you can quickly distort your model. (Boy, am I going to hear about this one!)

Face Shaping Tools

The Face Shaping Tool allows you to visually sculpt, or create, morphs on your Face Room head. Click the Morph Putty icon (1) in the Face Shaping Tool area, shown in Figure 5.4. Then click on the 3D Face Preview in the area you want to morph (2). A green dot appears. Move the dot to reshape the morphs until you are satisfied.

Rather than sculpting the morphs by dragging with your mouse, you can dial in a face using the many Facial Morphs dials (3) available in the Face Shaping Tool. You can control the minimum and maximum range of all dials by the values you enter in the Exaggeration Min and Exaggeration Max (4) settings in the Face Shaping Tool.

The Facial Morphs dials are arranged in the following categories. A value of zero means that the morph has no effect. Negative values morph the feature toward one end of the spectrum, whereas positive values morph the feature more toward the other end. The morphs in the following list add asymmetry to the face, which can make your character look more realistic and natural.

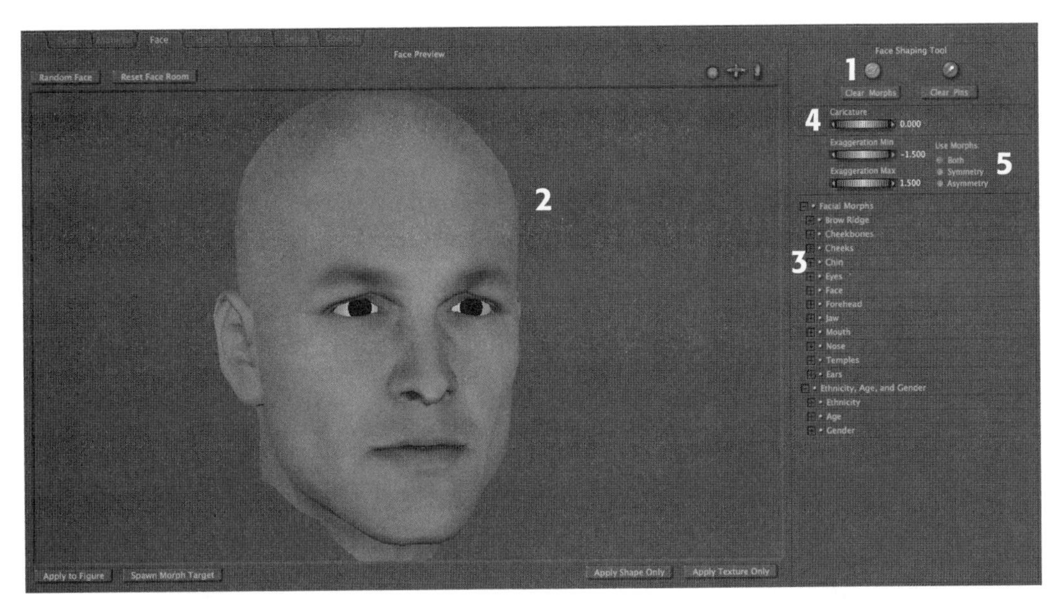

FIGURE 5.4 Use the Morph Putty tool to visually sculpt your head shape.

The asymmetrical morphs are removed from use when you select the Symmetry option (5) in the Face Shaping Tool.

- **Bridge (subcategory of Nose):** Shallow/Deep, Short/Long, Transverse Shift.
- **Brow Ridge:** High/Low, Inner-Up/Down, Outer-Up/Down, Forward Axis Twist.
- **Cheekbones:** High/Low, Shallow/Pronounced, Thin/Wide, Protrusion Asymmetry.
- **Cheeks:** Concave/Convex, Round/Gaunt.
- **Chin:** Forward/Backward, Pronounced/Recessed, Retracted/Jutting, Shallow/Deep, Small/Large, Short/Tall, Thin/Wide, Chin Axis Twist, Forward Axis Twist, Transverse Shift.
- **Ears:** Up/Down, Back/Front, Short/Long, Thin/Wide, Vertical Shear, Forward Axis Shear.
- **Eyes:** Up/Down, Small/Large, Tilt Inward/Outward, Together/Apart, Height Disparity, Transverse Shift.
- **Face:** Brow-Nose-Chin Ratio, Forehead-Sellion-Nose Ratio, Light/Heavy, Round/Gaunt, Thin/Wide, Coronal Bend, Coronal Shear, Vertical Axis Twist.
- **Forehead:** Small/Large, Short/Tall, Tilt Forward/Back, Forward Axis Twist.

- **Jaw:** Retracted/Jutting, Wide/Thin, Jaw-Neck Slope High/Low, Concave/Convex.
- **Lips (subcategory of Mouth):** Deflated/Inflated, Large/Small, Puckered/Retracted.
- **Mouth:** Drawn/Pursed, Happy/Sad, High/Low, Protruding/Relaxed, Tilt Up/Down, Underbite/Overbite, Mouth-Chin Distance Short/Long, Corners Transverse Shift, Forward Axis Twist, Transverse Shift, Twist and Shift.
- **Nose:** Up/Down, Flat/Pointed, Short/Long, Tilt Up/Down, Frontal Axis Twist, Tip Transverse Shift, Transverse Shift, Vertical Axis Twist.
- **Nostrils (subcategory of Nose):** Tilt Up/Down, Small/Large, Thin/Wide, Frontal Axis Twist, Transverse Shift.
- **Sellion (subcategory of Nose):** Up/Down, Shallow/Deep, Thin/Wide, Transverse Shift.
- **Temples:** Thin/Wide.
- **Age:** Younger/Older.
- **Ethnicity:** Less/more African, less/more European, less/more South East Asian, less/more East Indian.
- **Gender:** Male/Female.

Take a few moments and try playing with the various morph dials. As you'll see, these controls work exactly the same as the Parameters panel dials in the Pose Room. To apply them to the model, click the Apply to Figure button under the Face Preview.

Texture Preview

The Texture Preview area (see Figure 5.5) provides a two-dimensional, flattened preview of your texture, just like a UV map. The preview is a bit misleading, however, because the Face Room generates square texture maps with one exception: when you import textures for the Poser figures that have rectangular textures and then make texture variation modifications to them, the texture is exported at the same size as the original texture.

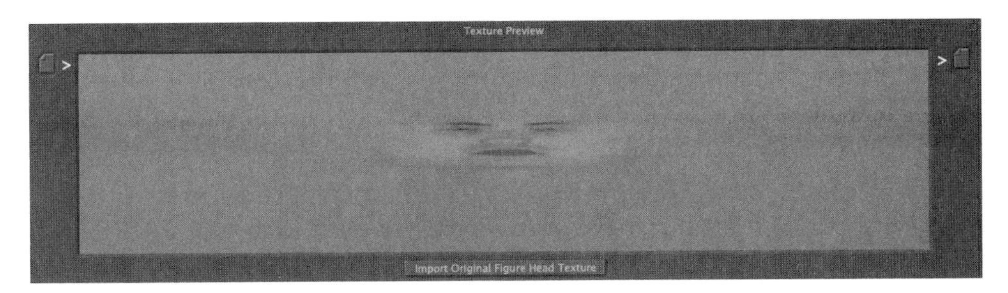

FIGURE 5.5 The Texture Preview area.

How to Use Third-Party Textures

You may have third-party textures that you want to use on your Face Room–compatible figures. It can be helpful to use those face textures while you create a character morph in the Face Room. To import a third-party head texture into the Face Room, click the Import icon (the page icon on the left of the Texture Preview area shown in Figure 5.5). Locate the face texture that you want to use, and click Open to return to the Face Room. Your third-party head texture should now appear on the head. You are now ready to create your character morph with the Face Shaping Tool.

The Import Original Figure Head Texture button will not load a third-party texture. It loads the texture that is assigned to the model you are using. You will learn more about this button later in the chapter.

More Notes About Face Room Textures

Because they are created "on the fly," Face Room textures aren't as perfect as those meticulously created by hand. They contain smudges and may be slightly misaligned from the physical geometry of the features. For example, you might notice when you close the figure's eyes that there are unwanted smears on the eyelids. It's important to be aware that Face Room textures contain these undesirable artifacts; however, they still make a great starting point. You can always use the original photos to improve the Face Room texture in an image editing program after you create this base texture.

By default, Poser stores the Face Room textures in PNG format in the Runtime\Textures\Faceroom folder. The file name is based on the date and time that you applied the texture to the figure.

Action Buttons

The Action buttons shown in Figure 5.6 are used to apply the shape of the head, the texture, or both to the currently selected figure in the Pose Room.

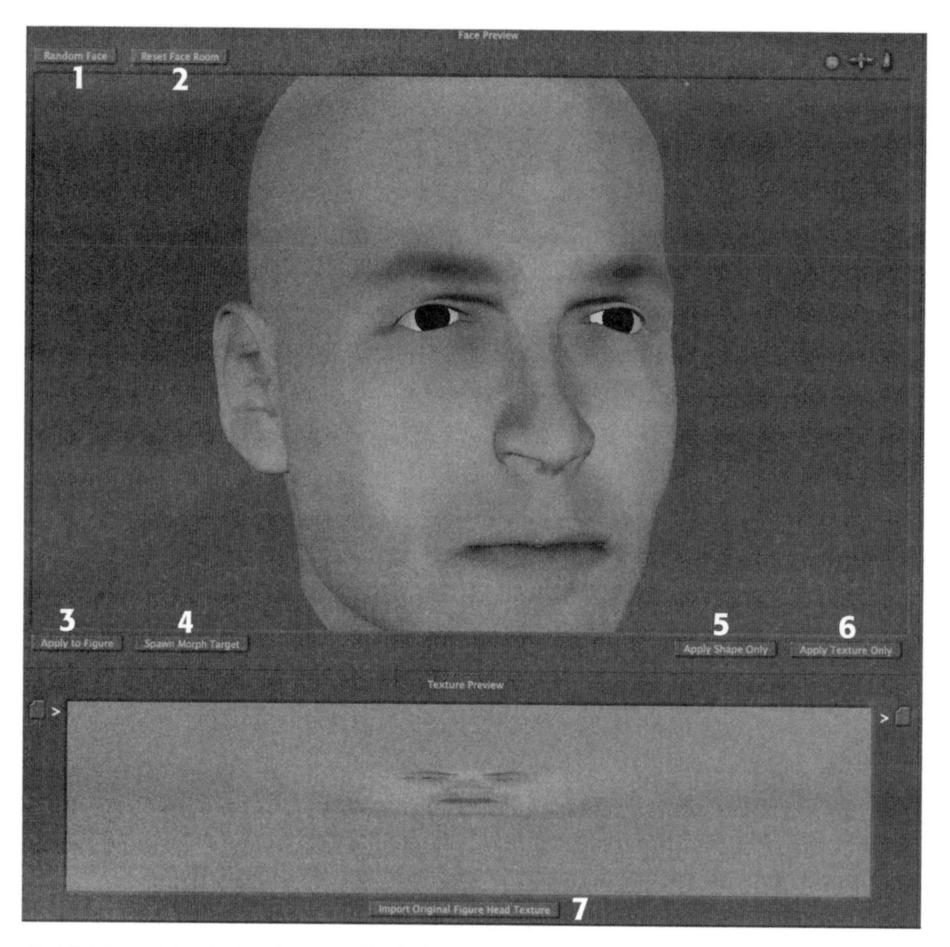

FIGURE 5.6 The Action buttons flank the Face Preview and Texture Preview windows.

If you only have one figure in the Pose Room, the changes will apply automatically. If you have multiple figures, make sure you have the correct figure selected as the current figure before you use these buttons.

Each Action button is described in the following list:

- **Random Face (1):** Poser generates a new face and texture for the model.
- **Reset Face Room (2):** Reverts back to the default face and texture. This will cause you to lose any changes you might have made. You would need to use Spawn Morph Target prior to resetting your face if you want to retain what you have done.
- **Apply to Figure (3):** Click this button to apply the head shape and texture to the currently selected figure. This option replaces the character's default head with the head you created in the Face Room. If the new texture has sufficient resolution to be larger than 512 x 512, Poser asks if you want to change the texture resolution. Click No to keep the texture at that size, or click Yes to create a larger texture of the dimensions stated in the dialog box. After Poser generates the texture, you may be informed that the face color is different from the figure color. Click No to apply the face texture exactly as you see it in the Face Room. (This will probably require that you create or alter the body texture yourself.) If you click Yes, Poser will create a blend between the Face Room texture and the body texture through the use of an alpha mask.
- **Spawn Morph Target (4):** Adds morph dials for the head, left eye, and right eye to the figure that is currently selected in the Pose Room. When set to 1, the morph dials duplicate the face created in the Face Room.
- **Apply Shape Only (5):** Applies the shape, but not the texture, to the figure that is currently selected in the Pose Room.
- **Apply Texture Only (6):** Applies the texture, but not the face, to the figure that is currently selected in the Pose Room.
- **Import Original Figure Head Texture (7):** Applies the head texture from the figure that is currently selected in the Pose Room onto the head in the Face Shaping Tool area.

TUTORIAL 5.1 CREATING TEXTURE GUIDES

The Photo Lineup area of the Face Room allows you to move feature points to match photos. This can often be a very tricky endeavor because head shapes vary from person to person. Differences in gender, age, race, height, and weight can make the shape of the head entirely different from the default figure you are using. As a result, if you try to move the feature points to match your photographs, you can end up with areas in your texture that are stretched or distorted.

You can compromise by preparing the photos so that they somewhat match the shape of the head in the photos that you are using. To start that process, you create texture guides that will help you place the photos correctly.

When I talk about texture guides, I am talking about creating basic renders that can be brought in to programs such as Adobe Photoshop, Adobe Fireworks, Paint Shop Pro, or any other image editing program. These guides could also be called "templates"; however, the term could become confused with regular texture templates, so I'll be using the term "guide" instead.

The following steps were used to create the head guides for Simon G2. Similar steps can be used to create texture guides for any figure that is compatible with the Face Room.

1. With Simon G2 selected, go to Window > Document Window Size. The Preview Dimensions dialog appears (see Figure 5.7) where you first need to click the Float Palette button. With the new GUI, the Preview panel is docked, and thus locked. Making it a floating panel unlocks the dimensions. Now enter equal values in the Width and Height fields to create a square document. In this example, a value of 500 is entered in both fields. Choose OK to change the document size to the desired window size.

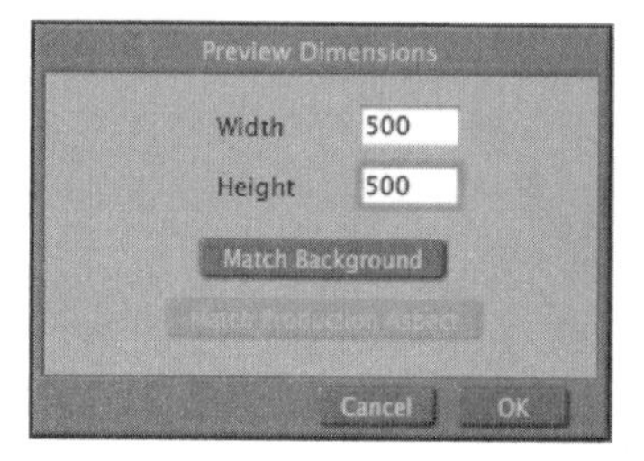

FIGURE 5.7 Click the Float Palette button in order to resize the document window.

2. Now, you need to configure the render settings so that you render the image at the same aspect ratio. To create a texture guide that measures 2048 × 2048 pixels, choose Render > Render Dimensions. The Render Dimensions dialog box appears. First select the Render to Exact Resolution option. Then make sure that the Constrain Aspect Ratio box is checked. Next, click the Match Document Window button. The values in the Width and Height fields should change to match the dimensions of your document window.

Square textures are more efficient with memory than rectangular ones, and it also helps to create textures that are divisible by a power of 2. Recommended sizes for textures are 512 × 512, 1024 × 1024, and 2048 × 2048. (Poser will not go higher than 4000 × 4000.)

3. Now, enter 2048 in either the Width or Height fields. The other value should automatically change to match. Click OK to set the new values.
4. The goal is to create texture guides from the front and left sides, so you'll need to create a Front Camera view and a Left Camera view for your renders (discussed in Chapter 2, "Using Cameras"). Set up your cameras as shown in Figure 5.8.

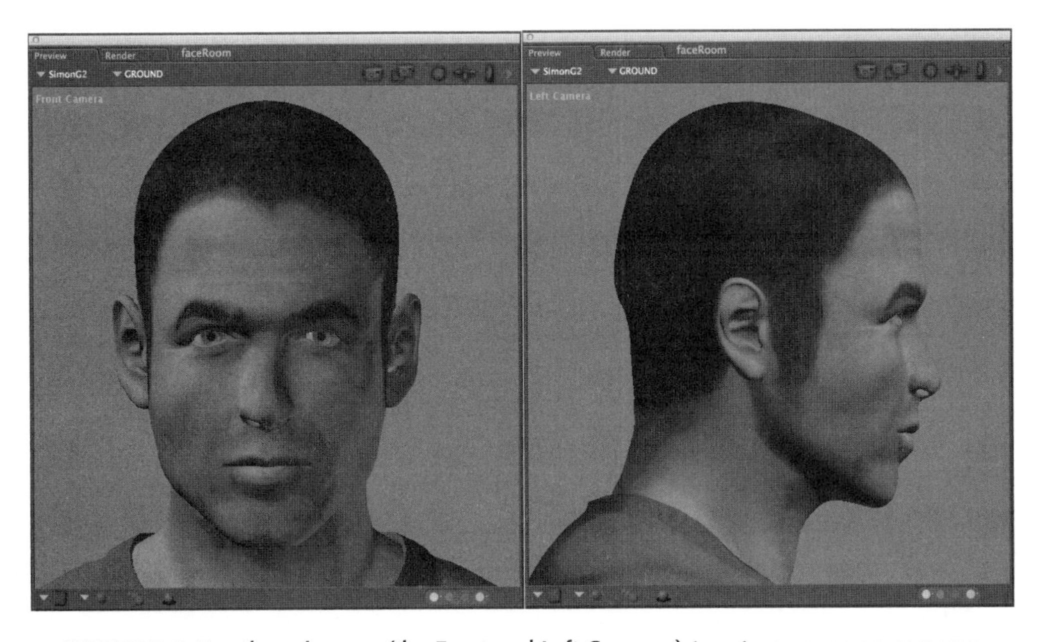

FIGURE 5.8 Use these images (the Front and Left Cameras) to set up your own cameras.

5. Because you've already set your document window size and render settings, it's time to render your first texture guide. Choose Render > Render. Default render settings are fine for this purpose. Save the front image to your hard drive in TIF format.
6. Repeat Step 6 with the Left Camera, and render the left guide. Now you can use the guides to prepare your photos.

TUTORIAL 5.2 PREPARING YOUR PHOTOS

Now that the guides—or templates, if you will—are completed, it's time to prepare your photographs for use in the Face Room. Starting with this tutorial, I will be using photographs that are available to you in the Chapter05 folder on the DVD. The set titled Front.jpg and Side.jpg are smaller images, while the Front1.jpg and Side1.jpg are full size and compatible with the next tutorial. In this tutorial, though, I will use the smaller images. I will also be using Photoshop as the image editing program.

1. Open the Front and Side texture guides that you created in Tutorial 5.1.
2. Duplicate the render of your guide onto a new layer. This new layer will allow you to adjust the transparency of the guide so that you can see your texture work beneath it. Set the transparency of the layer to 40%.
3. Open the front view of the photo that you want to use in the Face Room. Paste a copy of the photo into the first image you opened, in between the base layer and the partially transparent copy.

High-resolution photographs, such as those found at www.3d.sk, billed as Human Photo References for 3D Artists and Game Developers, will give you the best results. However, a paid subscription is required in order to download their products. The best idea is to just get a good camera (at least 5 megapixels) and take pictures of a family member or close friend for your textures.

4. Place the photograph onto the same document as the guide and name it Head_Mstr. This will automatically create a new layer. You need to change the opacity of this layer so you can see the guide underneath. Then scale the photograph so that the outline of the head stays slightly inside the photo. Figure 5.9 shows an example in Photoshop CS4.

Some people advise duplicating the background layer (the base layer) of the guide file. There is nothing wrong with doing this as, for some people, it might be easier to do the alignment with the guide layer above the photograph.

5. You will be blending this photograph layer with modified layers created from the same photo. The easiest way to accomplish this is to reset the photo's opacity to 100% (you have already positioned it where you need it to be), and then, using whichever selection tool you like, select the eyes and eyebrows, leaving enough room to resize this selection. Remember, this selection will also be covering the underlying photograph (Head_Mstr).

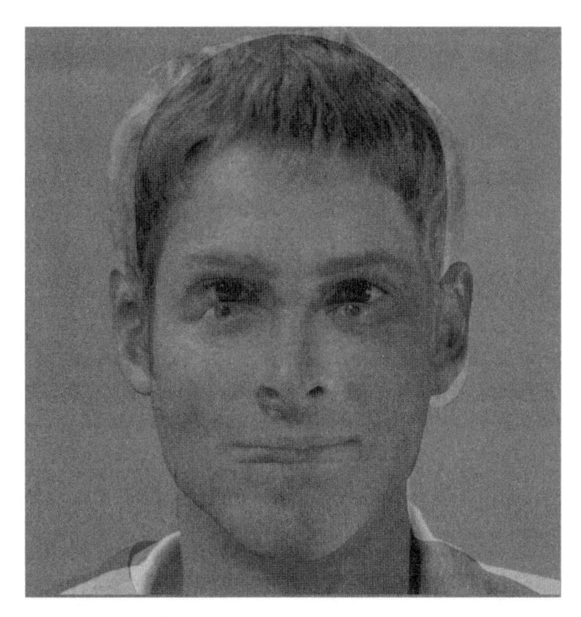

FIGURE 5.9 The photograph is placed over the guide, and its opacity is reduced to show both layers.

6. Copy and paste this selection (placing it automatically onto a new layer). Turn off the visibility of the Head_Mstr copy layer, then change the opacity so you can see the guide. Scale (if necessary) and use the Warp tool to fit the eyes to the guide layer's eyes. Figure 5.10 shows the eyes and eyebrows in place over the guide layer.
7. Rename this layer Eyes, and then blur the edges so they blend with the photograph better. I will leave the method of blurring up to you.
8. Repeat Steps 6 and 7 for the nose and the mouth, naming the layers respectively. Figure 5.11 shows the re-worked photograph along with the original.
9. You might need to use the Clone Stamp and/or the Healing Brush (or their equivalents if you're not using Photoshop) to clean up areas if they don't blend into the original images. In addition, you might want to use the Clone Stamp to get rid of the nostrils (that dark, shadowy area); let the lighting add that shadowiness because all that will happen is the dark sections will bleed into the face texture.

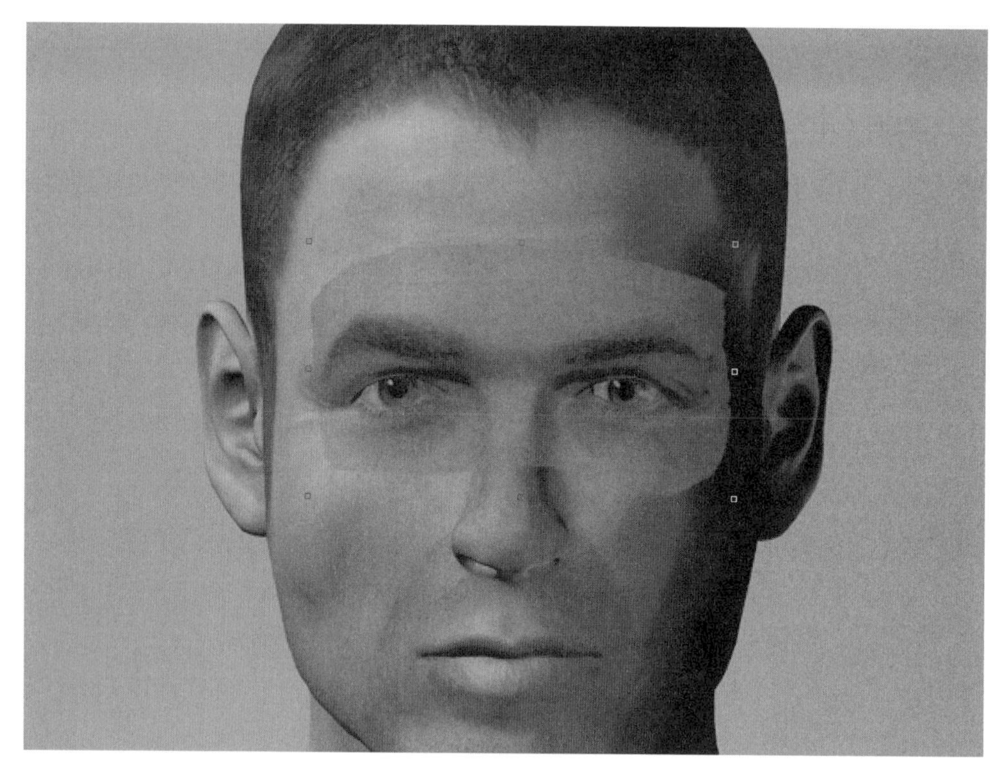

FIGURE 5.10 The eyes and brows have been scaled and warped to match the eyes and brows in the guide layer.

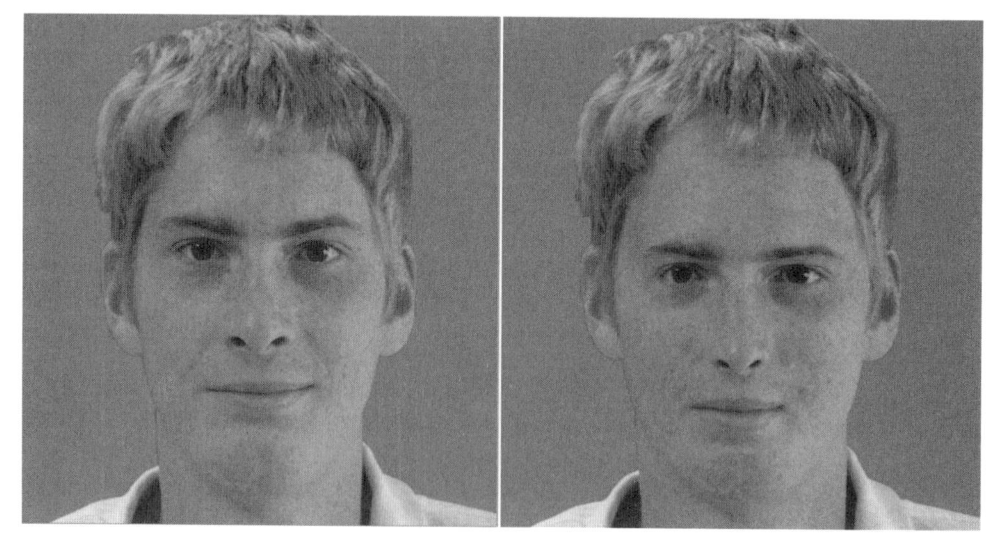

FIGURE 5.11 The original photograph (left) and its modified almost-doppelganger (right).

10. Save this image as either a TIF, PNG, BMP, or PCX file. You could also save the file as a GIF or JPG, but both of those formats are *lossy*—they throw away some file information—and aren't recommended for high-quality work. The GIF file format only supports 256 colors (of the 16.7 million available), and the JPG format throws away information it says it doesn't need in order to simply look good on a screen.
11. Now for the side view. This view is probably the most critical when it comes to avoiding distortion in the final texture. Most distortion comes from the head being tilted differently from the Poser figure. You will use the Side.jpg image as the guide to properly align the angle of the photograph. As you did with the front photo, scale the side view photo to size and then rotate it. Figure 5.12 shows the finished setup.

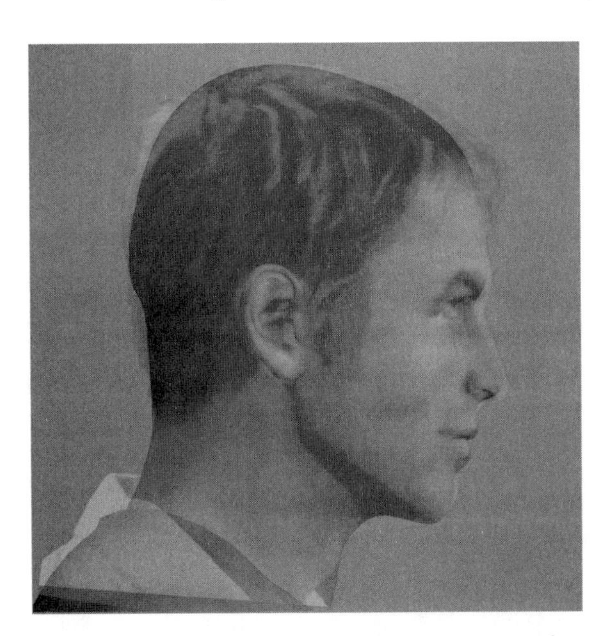

FIGURE 5.12 The scaled and rotated photograph shown over the guide image.

12. Using the same techniques as in Steps 6, 7, and 9, modify the photograph to fit as closely as possible with the guide layer. You might need to include the ear this time, lining up key areas with the model's ear.
13. Save the side image in the format of your choosing, preferably in a lossless format.

14. Import the revised photographs into the front and side views in the Face Room's Photo Lineup. You will probably see that the altered photographs make it much easier to create your new face texture with a minimal amount of resizing and moving of feature points. Only move the feature points when you need to refine the texture placement on the 3D model in the Face Preview area. Figure 5.13 shows an example of a finished texture after some points have been adjusted.

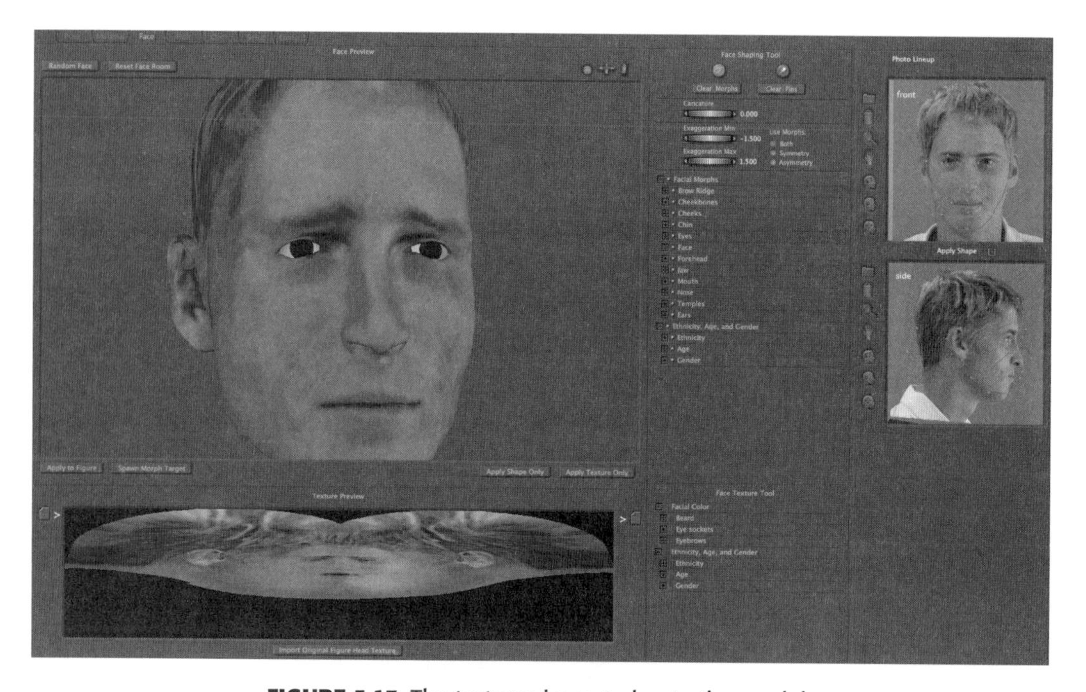

FIGURE 5.13 The textures imported onto the model.

As you can see, you're going to want to be careful with the small details of your photographs. In the case of the Side.jpg photo, the subject has hair over his ear, so that is being added to the image. You would have to clone this out so that it doesn't show up on the ear because, as you can see, the hair does not look realistic as part of a texture. I'm also a big fan of removing shading from the source photo; those shadowy areas inside the ear should be lightened because the lights in the scene will create their own shadows on the model.

MATCHING THE HEAD AND BODY

If you are using photographs to create a face texture, you have two options in matching the head texture to the body texture. When you save or try to apply the head texture to the figure in the Pose Room, Poser asks if you want to change the head texture to match the body texture. If you choose Yes, Poser blends your head texture to the body texture by adding a graduated alpha (transparency) edge over the image. This is a good option if you have a body texture that is close in color to the photographs you are using for your figure. If your new texture is too far off, you might have to create an original body texture using photographs of the same person that you used in the Face Room, or by bringing both texture maps into your graphics editing program and make adjustments to the color of the body texture. Even if your texture is far off in color, having Poser blend the head texture down into the body texture may be a good way to get a baseline color and texture area to use when adjusting the rest of the body texture color.

VARIATIONS ON A THEME

The Face Texture Tool, shown in Figure 5.14, applies color and shading changes so you can modify the ethnicity, sex, or age of the face texture. You can also use this area to darken eyebrows or create the appearance of a beard.

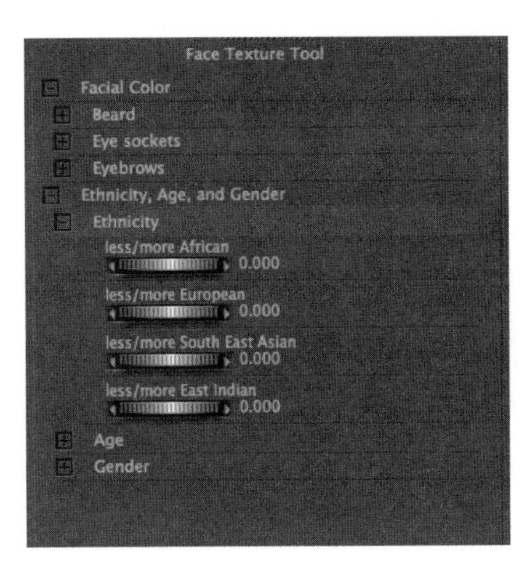

FIGURE 5.14 The Face Texture Tool area of the Face Room.

If you have one or more light-skinned textures that you like but want to create darker-skinned ethnic characters, there are a number of approaches you can take.

One way to darken skin is to use the Material Room to adjust the procedural shaders. Try darkening the diffuse color for the face and body textures by the same amount. Try gray or a tinted gray color to keep from introducing additional colors to the skin tone.

When using Poser 6 figures, an alternative to the manual approach is to purchase the Poser 6 Character Realism kit or the Unimesh Realism Kit by face_off. These are available for the Mac or PC at the Renderosity.com marketplace. The Poser 6 Character Realism kit allows you to lighten or darken textures while adding other realistic features, such as sheen, bump, and skin imperfections.

However, in the following tutorial you will learn how to use the Face Texture Tool and be introduced to the Face Shaping Tool without the benefit of third-party extensions.

TUTORIAL 5.3 MATCHING ETHNIC TEXTURES TO THE BODY

To create an ethnic variation of a texture, let's use the Poser 6\James\JamesCasual model. Add the figure to a new scene, turn off inverse kinematics, and then zero the figure. Once you have done that, go into the Face Room.

1. Beneath the Texture Preview area, click on the Import Original Figure Head Texture button, and the head texture that James is using in the Pose Room will be imported.
2. In the Face Texture Tool area, expand the Ethnicity, Age, and Gender option, and then expand the Ethnicity option. Set the Less/More African texture variation setting to 1.000.
3. In the Face Shaping Tool area (shown at the right in Figure 5.12), expand the Ethnicity, Age, and Gender morph category, and then expand the Ethnicity morph category. Set the Less/More African morph value to 0.500. Your character should now look like the one shown in Figure 5.15.
4. Immediately under the Face Preview area, click the Apply Shape Only button to add the face morph to James. Do not click the Apply to Figure button or else the head shape and the texture will automatically be applied to the figure. You only want the features applied at this point.

When you click the Apply Shape Only or the Apply to Figure button, you will not automatically be taken back to the Pose Room. To see your changes applied to the actual figure, click on the Pose tab.

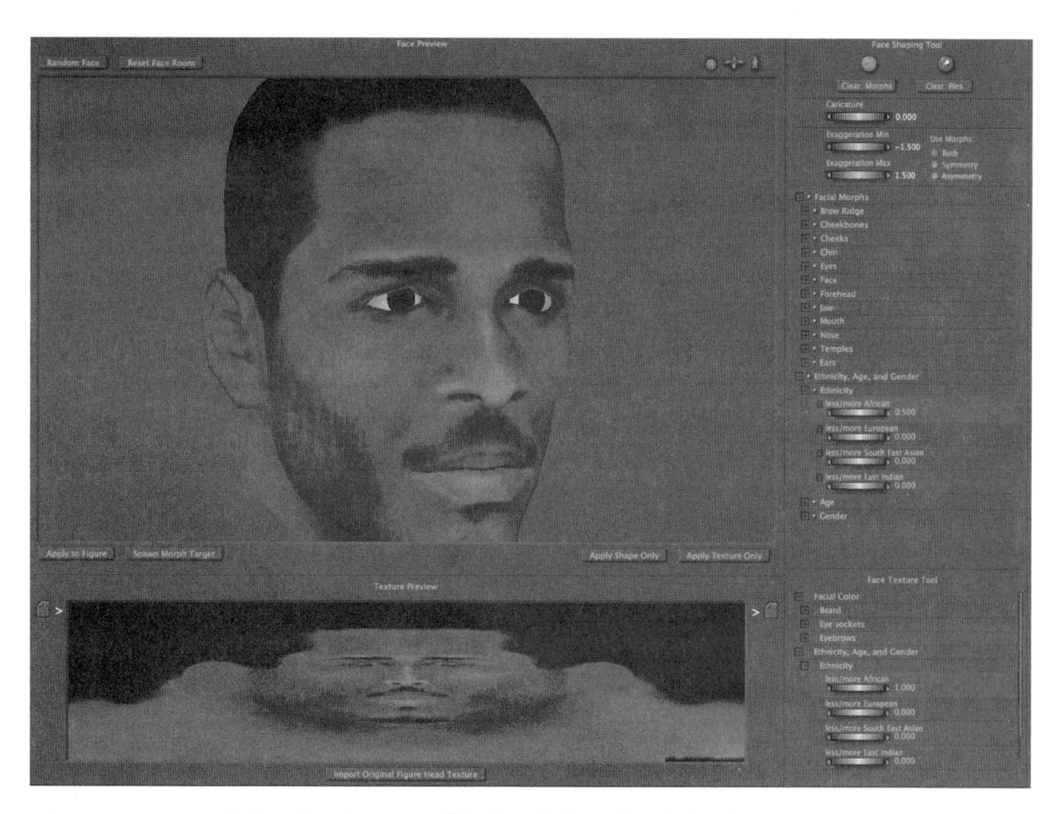

FIGURE 5.15 James's face has been modified, and the color of the skin texture has been changed.

5. If you try to apply the head texture to James at this point, Poser automatically generates an alpha map that blends the head texture with the current body texture. Unfortunately, this won't look quite right with an ethnic texture. The way around it is to save the ethnic texture into a separate file and manually apply it to the head in the Material Room. To begin this process, click the Save icon that appears at the right of the Texture Preview area (shown in Figure 5.16). Poser asks if you want to change the resolution of the texture. Choose Yes to save the texture at 1024 x 1024. Choose the folder to which you want to save the texture and name it JamesEthnicHead. If you intend to add to or improve the texture in your image editor, save the texture in a lossless format, such as TIF. If you will use this texture as the final version, you can save it as a JPG file with 100% quality.

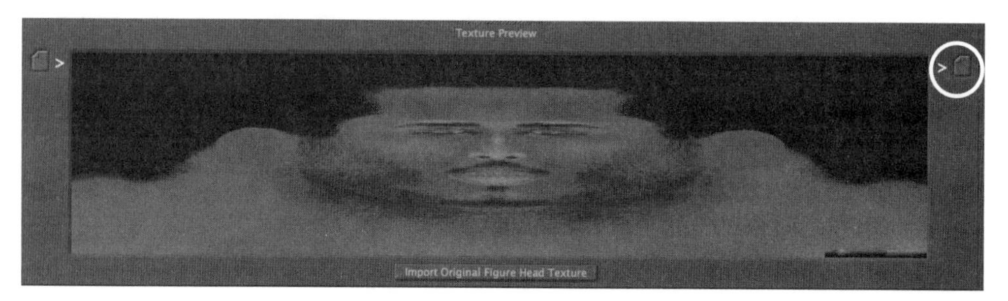

FIGURE 5.16 The texture Save button.

NOTE

Mac users: When you export the image file, there is a glitch in the Save feature. The file you export more than likely will be blank. But—and here's the good news—the file has actually been saved in the Runtime\Textures\Faceroom folder in the main Poser folder. Hopefully, the rendering problem will be fixed by the time you read this, but it's been an issue since Poser 7, so I'm not sure it will be.

NOTE

If you are saving in the TIF format, make sure to turn compression off. You cannot import a compressed file into Poser.

6. Click the Material tab to enter the Material Room. Select James as the current figure and the head as the current actor.
7. In the Image Map node, click the Image Source name field, then locate and select the ethnic face texture that you saved in Step 5 (or go to the Textures\Face Room folder to access the texture), and click OK to apply it.
8. Now select James's body as the current material. In the PoserSurface Diffuse Color root node, click the white color swatch (which is white by default).
9. After the Poser color selector window appears, click the tricolored square in the upper-right corner to open the RGB color picker. Set the RGB color values to 150, 150, and 150 to create a medium shade of gray. The face and body colors should now match.

TUTORIAL 5.4 SAVING MULTIPLE FACES IN ONE FIGURE

Many Poser users like to save one single figure that contains all of their characters. You can use the Face Room to generate a head morph and then apply it to your figure as a morph. You can then save the figure to the library after you add the morph. When it's time to create another morph, start with this custom character.

To illustrate this process, I will generate some custom faces with the Random Face button. I'll be using the Simon G2 figure, but you can use whichever compatible figure you prefer. Make sure you turn off inverse kinematics and zero the figure after placing it into a new scene.

1. Change to the Face Camera so that you can see your figure's face as you create the new characters. Brighten the default lighting, if necessary, so that you can see the facial features more clearly.
2. Click the Face tab to enter the Face Room.
3. Click the Import Original Figure Head Texture button. The default face texture for your figure appears on your Face Room head.
4. It will help create more realistic faces if you set the Caricature value in the Face Shaping Tool to a negative number. For purposes of this tutorial, set the Caricature value at –1.750. This will help create faces that are more realistic than those created with the setting at its default of 0. Leave the Exaggeration Min and Exaggeration Max settings at their defaults of –1.5 and 1.5, respectively.
5. Click the Random Face button until you get a face that you like. Figure 5.17 shows an example of a nice morph created in this manner.
6. To transfer the face to the figure in the Pose Room, click the Spawn Morph Target button immediately underneath the Face Preview. This is a little tricky initially because it appears as if nothing happens. If you click the Spawn Morph Target button again, you'll actually create a second, duplicate morph. So resist that urge.
7. Go to the Pose Room where you will see absolutely no difference in your character's head. Ah, but wait! Select the head and open the Parameters panel if necessary. Scroll down to the bottom, and you should see a new category named Morph, along with a new morph named Head, as shown in Figure 5.18. This is the head that you created in the Face Room. Click the arrow that appears at the right of the morph, and choose Settings to rename the dial to a name that you will recognize the next time you load the character.

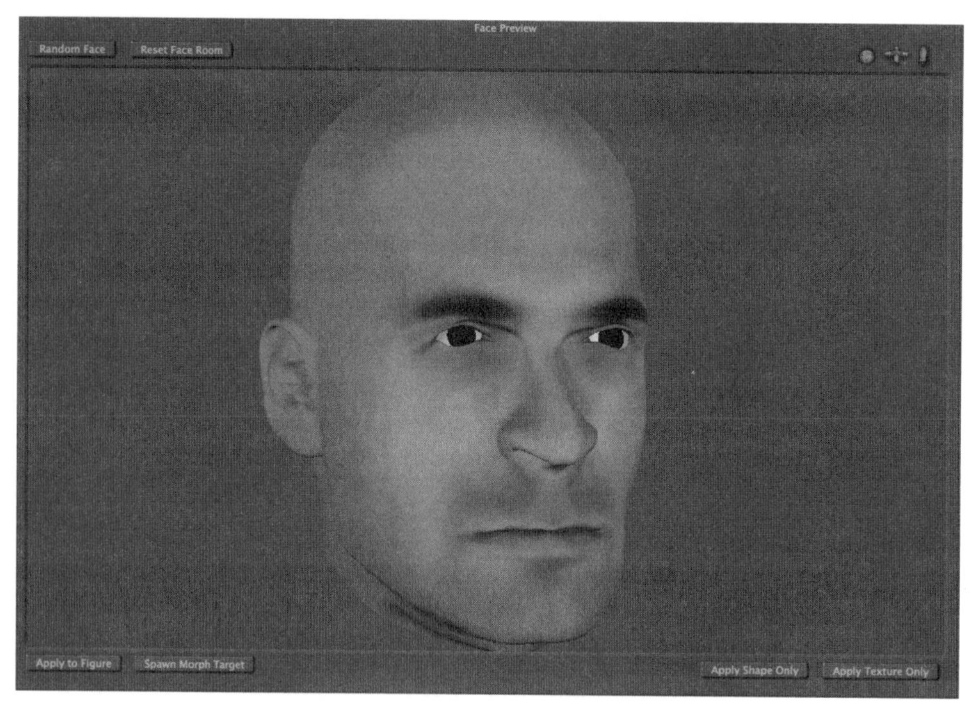

FIGURE 5.17 An interesting, randomly generated face.

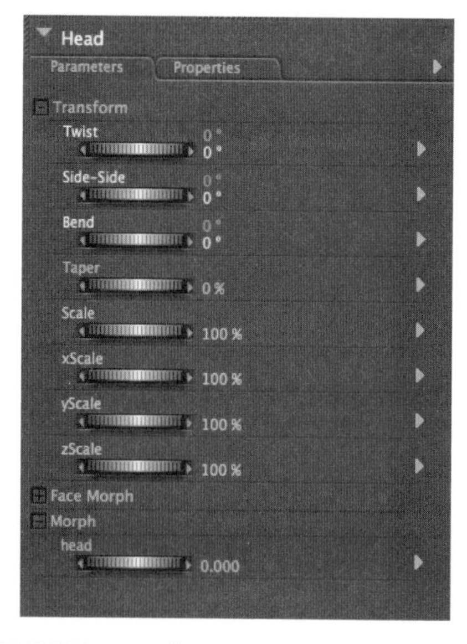

FIGURE 5.18 The new morph, Head, has been added to the head's parameters.

8. The eyes also have a Face Room morph associated with them. Click the right eye to select it. In its Parameter panel, you'll notice a new morph named RightEye. This is the eye morph that is associated with your first Face Room morph. Rename this dial the same as you did the head. Repeat this step for the left eye. If you dial the face, left eye, and right eye morphs to 1, the face should appear as it did in the Face Room.

Don't forget to dial the face, left eye, and right eye morphs back to 0 when you want to use another morph, or you may get unexpected results from the combination of the two morphs.

9. Repeat Steps 7 through 11 for additional characters, if desired.
10. When your morphs are all created and renamed, locate the Figures Library to which you want to save your custom figures. Click the Add to Library icon and enter a name for your multi-character figure, then click OK. A thumbnail appears in the library. Every time you want to add custom morphs, load this figure into the library, and then resave it after you are finished.

TUTORIAL 5.5 LIKE PUTTY IN YOUR VIRTUAL HANDS

Let's try one more modification, only this time, instead of using the Random Face button, let's use the Morph Putty tool mentioned earlier in the chapter. Make sure both eyes and the head are reset to 0, and then go back in to the Face Room.

1. By default, the Morph Putty tool is active. As mentioned earlier, place the cursor over the part of the head you want to modify and then click. This will set a "pin," which you will see as a green dot. Do this between Simon's eyes, as shown in Figure 5.19.
2. While still holding the mouse button down, drag downward to create a heavy alien-like brow, as shown in Figure 5.20.
3. Click on the left corner of the mouth and drag inward to make his mouth much smaller.
4. Click on the inside corners of the eyes and drag away from the nose, making them smaller as well.
5. Now click in the middle of his forehead and drag upward to increase the size of his noggin. Figure 5.21 shows the final result.
6. Click Spawn Morph Target and repeat the morph-naming steps shown in the last tutorial. Figure 5.22 shows the rendered head.

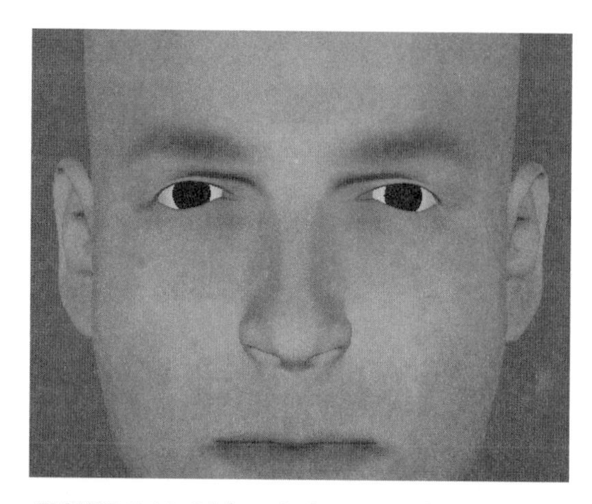

FIGURE 5.19 Stick a pin between Simon's eyes.

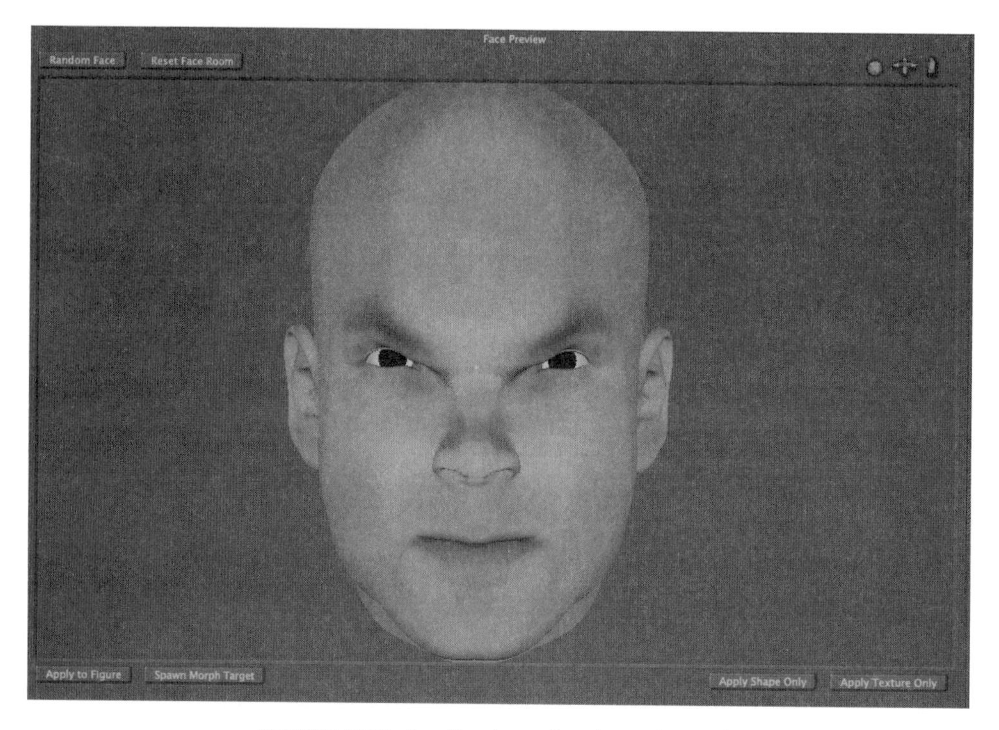

FIGURE 5.20 An alien brow has been formed.

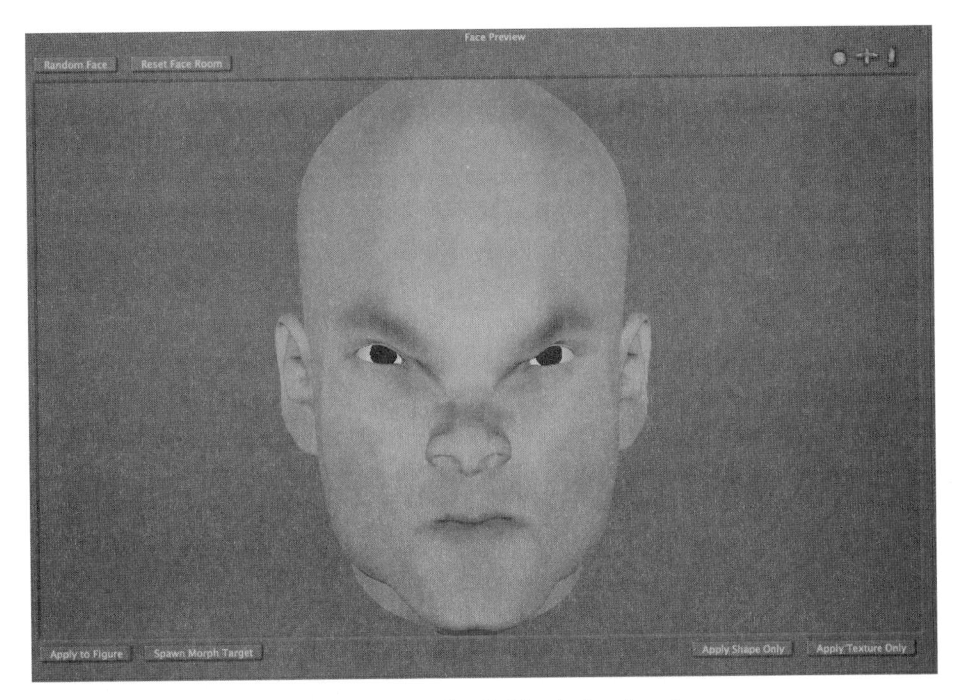

FIGURE 5.21 The finished alien head.

FIGURE 5.22 There are aliens among us.

A Short Re-Pose

Poser allows you to customize your figures in a number of ways. Through the Face Room, you can create several different characters of varying ethnicities that are based on the Poser 7 male and female (Simon and Sydney), the Poser 6 male and female (James and Jessi), or the Poser 5 male and female (Judy and Don), if you want to go back that far into the annals of Poser-dom. Of course, with the third-party figures like DAZ3D's Victoria and Michael models, you have a myriad of morphs at your disposal.

Next, you're going on a hair-raising adventure. (Sorry, I just had to say that.) Actually, there's nothing scary about what's coming up next. You're heading into the Hair Room with a look at the Dynamic Hair feature and how it can help you add realism to your renders.

6 Working With Hair

In This Chapter:

- Hair in All Its Forms
- Strand Hair
- Tutorial 6.1 Getting Stranded
- Tutorial 6.2 Creating and Using Skullcaps
- Tutorial 6.3 Stylin' the Growth Groups
- Tutorial 6.4 Hair Color

"Life is an endless struggle full of frustrations and challenges, but eventually you find a hair stylist you like."

—Author unknown

One of the first things anybody purchases after getting a new model is hair. There are so many hairstyles for the various poser models, you would think you're looking at a stylist's book at the hairdresser. And, as follows in the real world, there are more hairstyles for the women than for the men. It seems that a female's flowing tresses are much more important than what grows up top on the male models.

In this chapter, you're going to briefly work with Prop and Conforming hair. These are the most basic hair types and, if you've worked with Poser for more than a couple of hours, you have worked with these types of hair models. Where you're really going to spend some time is in the Hair Room, learning how to make sense of what is often seen as a room too complex and, therefore, never used.

Hair in All Its Forms

Hair props were first introduced way, way back in Poser 3 and were stored in the Hair Library—the location where they still reside. Prop hair uses the HR2 or HRZ extension when saved into the Hair Library and is made up of polygons, just like the other figures and props stored in your program. If you happen to store every hair model, Conforming or Prop, it can definitely become a challenge to find the one you're actually looking for because, if you look at Figure 6.1, you'll see that the first two hair element icons look exactly alike. Even after you have used the hair in your scene, you may not be able to visually distinguish between Prop and Conforming hair. The easy way to figure out which you have added to your scene is to find where the hair model's name appears in the drop-down menus at the top of the Preview window. If it appears in the Props submenu, then you have a prop; if it appears in the Figures submenu, you have a conforming hairstyle.

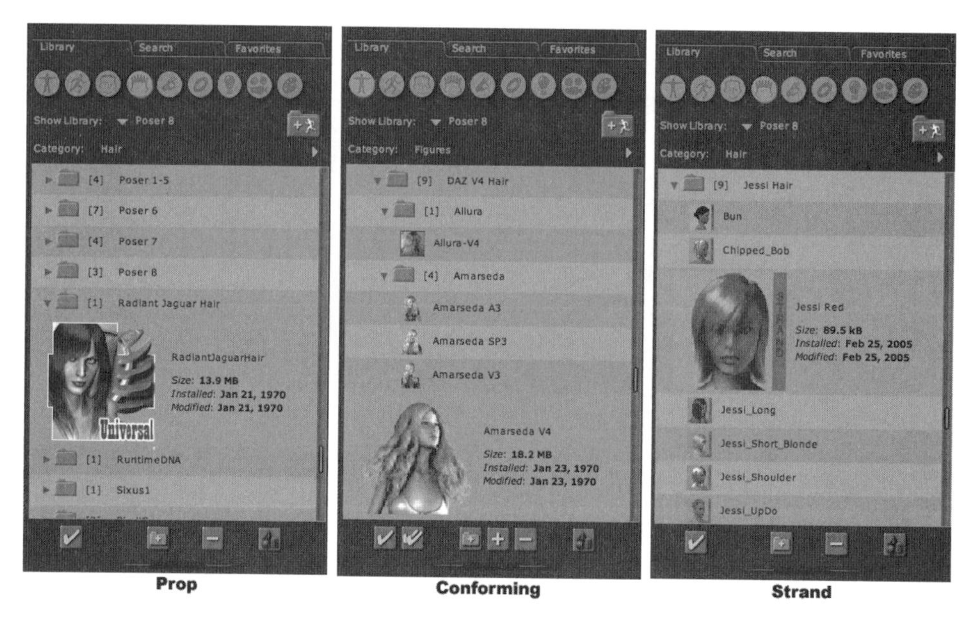

FIGURE 6.1 The three different hair types: Prop (left), Conforming (middle), and Strand (right).

It is not uncommon to purchase a Conforming or Prop hair model and have presets for various versions of the figure it's created for. For instance, if you purchase a hair model for the Victoria 4 character, you might very well receive morph files Victoria 3, Aiko 3, Stephanie Petite 3, and Victoria 4—much more bang(s) for the buck.

So what's the big deal about the differences between Conforming and Prop hair? If they're virtually indistinguishable other than how to select them on the workspace, why even bother trying to determine which is which? The biggest difference is that Prop hair often plays nicer with others. Huh? Prop hair can be more easily repositioned along the xTran, yTran, and zTran and scaled using the x-, y-, and zScale dials to fit numerous models in your library. So in many ways, Prop hair is more useful in a wider range of images. You're not stuck using a specific model because a particular hair model is set to conform to it.

It's easiest to reposition and scale the Prop hair while your figure is in the "zero pose" before you make any changes to the pose of your figure; otherwise, it can be quite time-consuming to match the angles of the head to the hair. To zero the pose, with the character selected, go to Window > Joint Editor and, at the bottom of this panel, click the Zero Pose button. It doesn't matter which part of the model is selected.

Many of the hair models come with built-in morphs that allow for a wide range of posing. Some, like the P8 Alyson Hair2 model located in the Hair\Poser 8\Alyson folder can be converted to a Beehive hairstyle with the twist of a dial (see Figure 6.2). You need to be careful about taking many of these models to their extremes (a setting of 1.00 to 1.500 for the Beehive, for instance) because anomalies in the transparency maps and the textures can occur. You can see one of those anomalies in Figure 6.2 in the Beehive where portions of the shadows lose their realism. This is why many people opt to paint the hair onto a model and completely forego the hair models. However, this isn't the best solution in many cases and, as long as you know limitations, you can use many of the very high-quality hair models on the market to make some very sophisticated scenes.

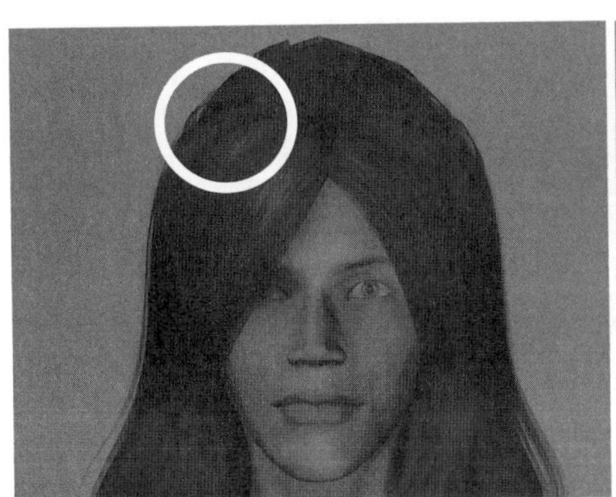
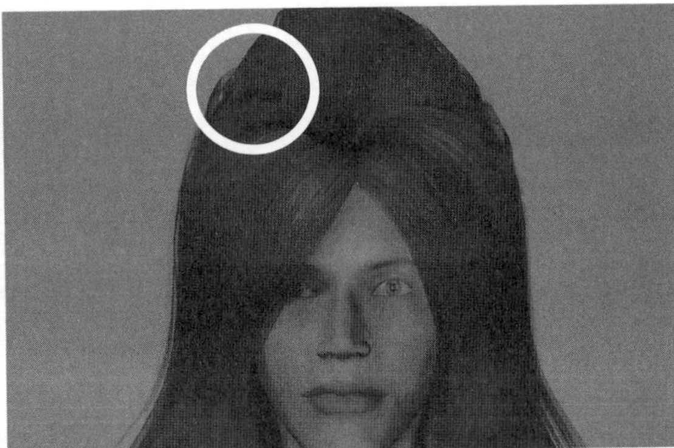

FIGURE 6.2 Alyson's hair is morphed into a beehive, causing sections of the shadows to lose their realism.

Strand Hair

Strand hair, also referred to as Dynamic hair, was introduced in Poser 5. Unlike the other two hair elements, which, again, are based on polygons and geometry, Dynamic hair is strand-based. What this means is that Dynamic hair is actually made up of hair strands that "grow" from the prop called *skullcaps* or *follicle sets.* Although you can grow hair directly on a figure's head, skullcaps or follicle sets are necessary to create hair that you can use more than once or to create hair that you can share with or distribute to others.

Dynamic hair has advantages and disadvantages over the geometry-based hair that you have already become familiar with. The key advantage is that Dynamic hair can respond to changes in position, movement, and wind forces. Instead of creating morphs that make the hair move, you use controls in the Hair Room to calculate how the hair responds to those forces. You can also "style" (bend and shape) individual guide hairs to create complex hairstyles for your figure without ever having to adjust polygons in a 3D-modeling application.

As an alternative to Dynamic hair, you can also take some Prop hair models into the Cloth Room and clothify *them. Clothified Prop hair will respond to changes in position, movement, and wind. Although Dynamic hair might behave more realistically, clothified Prop hair will calculate faster and be easier on system resources. Clothifying clothing and other objects is discussed in Chapter 7, "Working with Clothing."*

The main disadvantage of Dynamic hair is that all of the calculations and rendering consume a lot of processor resources. If your computer is barely above minimum recommended system specs, you may prefer Prop or Conforming hair because it requires fewer resources.

Many people say that to effectively use the Hair Room, some background in hair styling is a plus. I tend to agree, though I'm not a hair stylist. I'm just lucky to know how to comb my hair so I don't look like I have bed head all day. So creating a strand-based hairstyle is not exactly my proverbial cup of tea. Has that kept me out of the Hair Room? Nope. Not in the least. And it shouldn't keep you out either.

There are two considerations you will face when entering the Hair Room: will this hairstyle only be used on this particular model in this particular image, or will it be something you will want to use over and over again? If the former, then you can create Dynamic hair directly on the model; if the latter, you will want to create a skullcap that will then conform to or be a prop for your model(s). Let's first add hair to a single model, then you'll move on to making and saving a skullcap.

Before beginning, create a new scene and add the Ryan character to it. Not Ryan_Casual, just plain ol' Ryan. Because this particular model is naked (or *nekkid*, as is said in my part of the country) and looks like an unclothed Ken doll, I will work from the Face Camera so no one is offended. I also changed the focal length of the Face Camera to 55mm rather than its default 95mm.

Now that the scene is set up and the camera is chosen, let's take a quick tour of the workspace. First, you'll see that the Hair Room is divided into various sections. And, as with the rest of Poser 8's interface, the Hair Room has experienced a makeover as well; but if you are familiar with the controls from previous versions, you won't really see anything new here; the controls are just presented in an updated manner. Refer to Figure 6.3 as you move through the following sections.

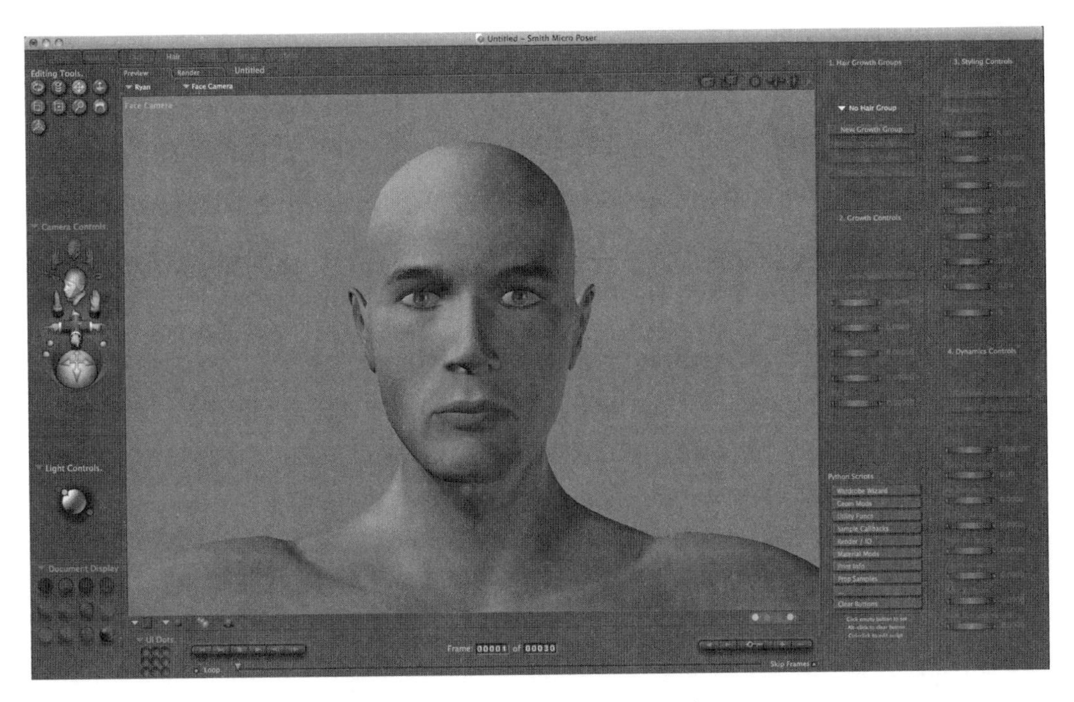

FIGURE 6.3 The Hair Room interface.

Section 1: Hair Growth Groups

Before you can grow hair on an object, you have to create hair growth groups that define which polygons in the object will grow hair. A hair object can contain several growth groups, and each group can be a different length or have different properties, such as curliness or how it responds to gravity. Make sure you have selected the correct object on which to grow hair. Click the New Growth Group button and assign a growth group name for the area you want to affect. To specify the polygons in the group, click the Edit Growth Group button, and use the Group Editor to select the polygons. Continue in this manner until you have finished creating one or more growth groups.

The Growth Group section is probably the one area where you want to take the most time. And you will quickly find that time will be well worth the effort in order to set up the hair groups correctly. Figure 6.4 shows a basic breakdown of growth groups and placement for hair. As you can see, there are four sections: the bangs (1), two sections along the side of the head (2 and 3), and the back (4). This makes for easier styling and is similar to the way hair is added to doll heads.

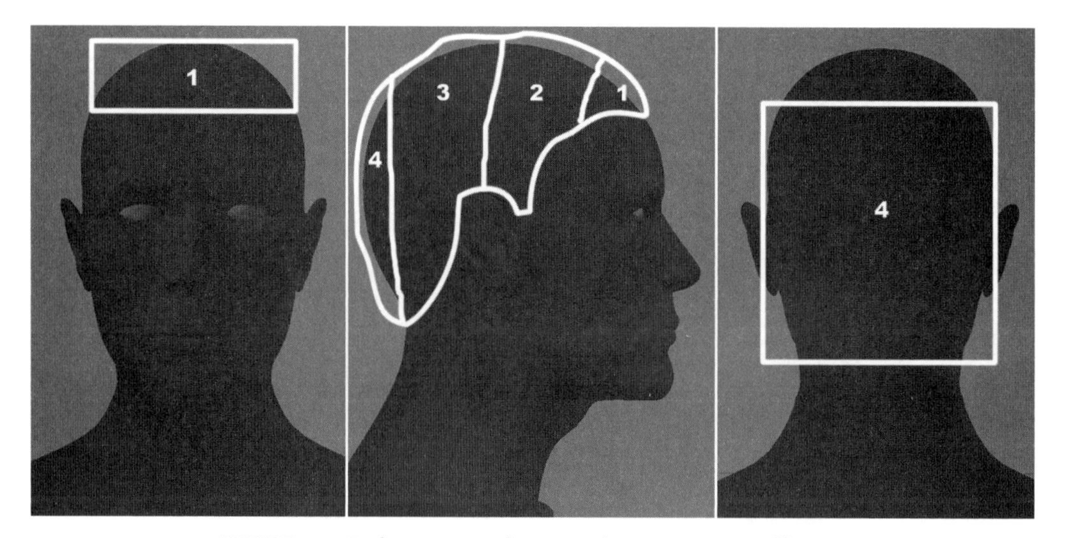

FIGURE 6.4 To best set up the Growth Groups, you will want to think about sections like those you see here.

SECTION 2: GROWTH CONTROLS

Select the group that you want to grow hair on from the Current Group menu in the Growth Group section. Then click the Grow Guide Hairs button in the Growth Controls section to grow a starting group of hair. Use the dials or number settings in the Growth Controls area to specify the Length and Length Variance settings (or "shagginess") of the hair. The Pull Back, Pull Down, and Pull Side controls are not intended for styling. Instead, they define the base properties of the hair. For example, hair on the sides of a male head normally pulls back. A buzz cut doesn't pull down at all; it goes straight up, so the Pull Down setting is a negative value. Long hair has more weight in real life, so it should be set to pull down.

SECTION 3: STYLING CONTROLS

The Styling Controls area offers tools that help you select, deselect, move, twist, and curl hair. This is where the real styling takes place. Click the Style Hairs button to open the Hair Style Tool panel, shown in Figure 6.5. The options are outlined in the following list.

- **Select Hairs:** Selects the hairs you will work with as you click and drag across the hairs in the Growth Group.
- **Translate Hairs:** Let's you interactively move the hairs forward, backward, up, and/or down.
- **Curl Hairs:** Twists the selected hair into curls.
- **Scale Hairs:** Lengthens or shortens the hairs as you drag.
- **Deselect Hairs**: As it states, this will deselect the hairs as you drag across them.
- **Translate Hairs In/Out:** Moves the hair forward, back, toward, away from the figure. If you aren't careful, you can literally translate the hairs into the model itself.
- **Twist Hairs:** Twists the hairs into clumps. Good for braids or more complex hair styles.
- **Constrain Length:** Keeps the hairs at the same length as you make changes, or when turned off, causes the hairs' length to change as you manipulate them.
- **Falloff (Tip/Root):** Determines how much of the length of the hair is affected by the changes you are making. Closer to the tip, only the vertices near the hair tips will be affected; closer to the root, the more length will be affected by your changes.
- **Lengthen:** Will increase or decrease the length of the selected hairs.
- **Clear Selection:** Quickly deselects the selected hairs.

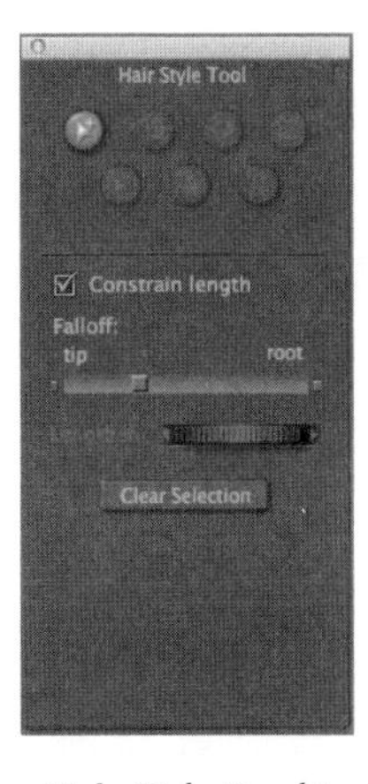

FIGURE 6.5 Use the controls in the Hair Style Tool to translate, curl, scale, or twist hairs.

Section 4: Dynamics Controls

The Dynamics Controls area contains settings that define how hair moves during animation, when objects collide against it, or when affected by wind forces. These settings are most important when you are using Dynamic hair in an animation. However, they are also useful when you want to render a still image of hair while it is in motion, such as when a long-haired woman turns her head quickly. There are eight Dynamics controls:

- **Gravity:** Controls how much or how little the hair is affected by gravity. Higher values weigh hair down more, and negative values cause hair to "float" (which is great for underwater or space scenes).
- **Spring Strength:** Defines how much hair bounces when in motion. (Higher values are more bouncy.)
- **Air Damping:** Defines how much or how little the hair reacts to wind. (Higher values blow more easily.)
- **Spring Damping:** Defines how stretchy the hair is. (Lower values allow the hair to bounce longer.)
- **Bend Resistance:** Controls how much or how little the hair is allowed to fold or bend.
- **Position Force:** Controls how much or how little the hair reacts to dynamic forces. (Higher values cause the hair to remain stiffer and more resistant to movement, collision, and wind.)
- **Root Stiffness:** Controls the stiffness of the root of the hair (the hair closest to the head).
- **Root Stiffness Falloff:** Controls how near or far from the head the stiffness range extends.

The Dynamic Controls area also includes a Do Collisions check box. When this option is checked, dynamic calculations will take longer, but they will also prevent the hair from intersecting with body parts or other objects that have collision detection enabled. To enable collision detection on a body part or object, select the part or object you want the hair to collide with. Then check the Collision detection box in the Properties panel, as shown in Figure 6.6. In fact, I would advise setting this first, before ever heading to the Hair Room.

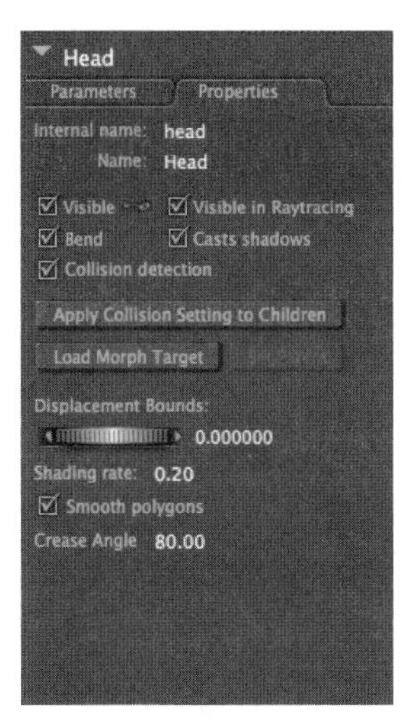

FIGURE 6.6 The Collision Detection check box is located in the Properties panel for the main model.

TUTORIAL 6.1 GETTING STRANDED

Now that you have Ryan on the workspace, have selected his head, have turned on Collision Detection in the Properties panel, and have switched to the Face Camera, let's go to the Hair Room and make him hairy. You'll begin by creating the hair growth groups.

1. Enter the Hair Room and double-check that you have Ryan's head selected. You need to have something selected in order to activate the Hair Growth Groups controls.
2. To create the hair groups, click once on the New Growth Group button in Section 1. A window will open asking you to name this particular growth group. Name the group whatever makes sense for you, and then click OK. All the controls in Sections 1 and 2 of the Hair Room will become active.
3. Click the Edit Growth Group button in Section 1. This will open the Group Editor panel (see Figure 6.7) and turn the figure on the main workspace gray so you can more easily see the polygons you select. The Group Editor panel is used in many of the rooms, including the Cloth, Material, Set Up and, of course, Hair Room. You need to be very aware of what you're doing within this panel because you can actually make a permanent change to the model and inadvertently mess it up.

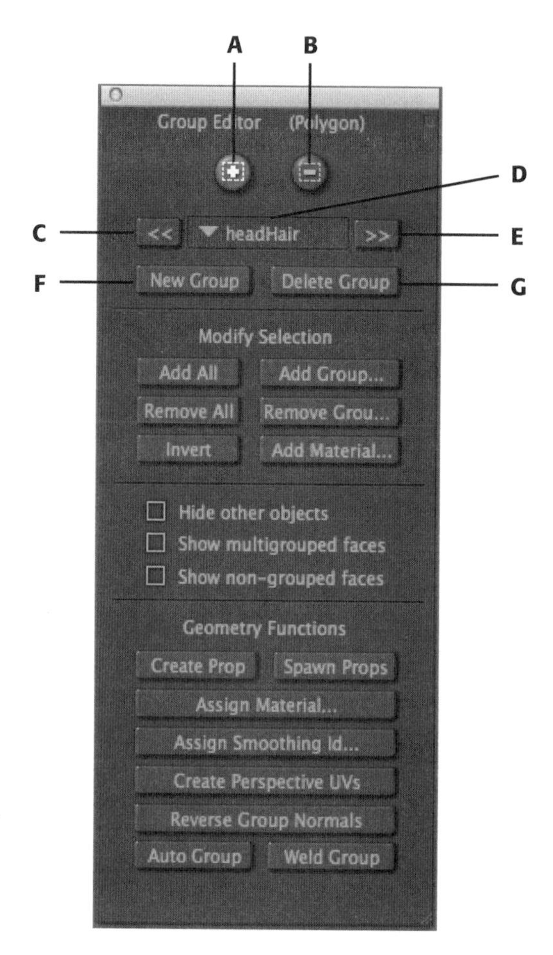

FIGURE 6.7 The Group Editor panel.

Referring to Figure 6.7, let's take a moment to look at these controls.

Group Editor Area

- **Select button (A):** When activated, allows you to select polygons on your model.
- **Deselect button (B):** When activated, allows you to deselect selected polygons on your model.
- **Previous (C) and Next (E) buttons:** Allows you to quickly change to another growth group.

- **Current Group drop-down menu (D):** Allows you to select a specific growth group from the list.
- **New Group button (F):** Allows you to create a new growth group by clicking on this button.
- **Delete Group button (G):** Clicking on this will delete the currently selected growth group.

Modify Selection Area

- **Add All button:** When selected, all the currently selected object's polygons are added to the active group.
- **Add Group button:** When selected, the current group can be added to other groups making up your growth group. This effectively creates a subgroup within that growth group set.
- **Remove All button:** When selected, this will remove the polygons from the selected group.
- **Remove Group button:** When selected, this removes the currently selected group and places the polygons into the main growth group. This works in conjunction with the Add Group button.
- **Invert button:** When selected, it inverts the selection so the currently selected polygons are deselected and the currently unselected polygons become selected.
- **Add Material button:** Clicking on this will create a material group that is assigned only to the selected polygons.

Hide/Show Area

- **Hide Other Objects:** When selected, all non-selected objects in your scene will be hidden. If you have a complex image with a lot of props and items assigned to the selected object, this can make the view much easier to work with.
- **Show Multigrouped Faces:** When selected, you will see all the polygons making up a group. If, for instance, you have created a model in a 3D modeling application and grouped the polygons, selecting Show Multigrouped Faces will show all the polygons in that group.
- **Show Non-Grouped Faces:** When selected, this will show all the polygons that are not part of any group.

Geometry Functions Area

- **Create Prop:** Does exactly as it states. When selected, this will create a new prop from the selected polygons. A screen will appear where you can name the prop that has been generated.
- **Spawn Props:** When selected, creates props for all of the object's growth groups.
- **Assign Material:** When selected, this creates a new material class for the selected polygons. A material class is a defined area where a new material can be placed.
- **Assign Smoothing ID:** When selected, this allows you to define smoothing groups so, when assigning the smooth polygons feature when rendering, these polygons will be smoothed into the surrounding polygons. Refer to Chapter 16, "Rendering Options and Techniques," for more information on smoothing the polygons.
- **Create Perspective UVs:** When selected, this assigns (or maps) UV coordinates to the specific polygons in the group. This is especially helpful when you need to place a specific image map section onto a corresponding section of your model.
- **Reverse Group Normals:** When selected, this reverses the *normals* (the way the polygons face). This is often good for environmental mapping.
- **Auto Group:** This is used when you are ready to take a model into the Setup Room (see Chapter 13, "Joint Parameters and Dependencies") to create a custom Poser figure.
- **Weld Group:** This is used if you want to rename or rework predefined groups that have already had a bone structure applied so you can change their setup in the Setup Room.

4. With the Select button active, select the forehead polygons as shown in Figure 6.8.

It can often be difficult to select polygons if your Preview window is set up to display in the Smooth or Texture Shaded modes. To more precisely select the polygons you want, change to Smooth Lined mode. After you have chosen the polygons and grown some hair, you might want to change back to Smooth or Texture Shaded so that the polygons are no longer visible.

5. Click the Grow Guide Hairs button in Section 2, Growth Controls. A set of strands will sprout from the selected polygons (see Figure 6.9).

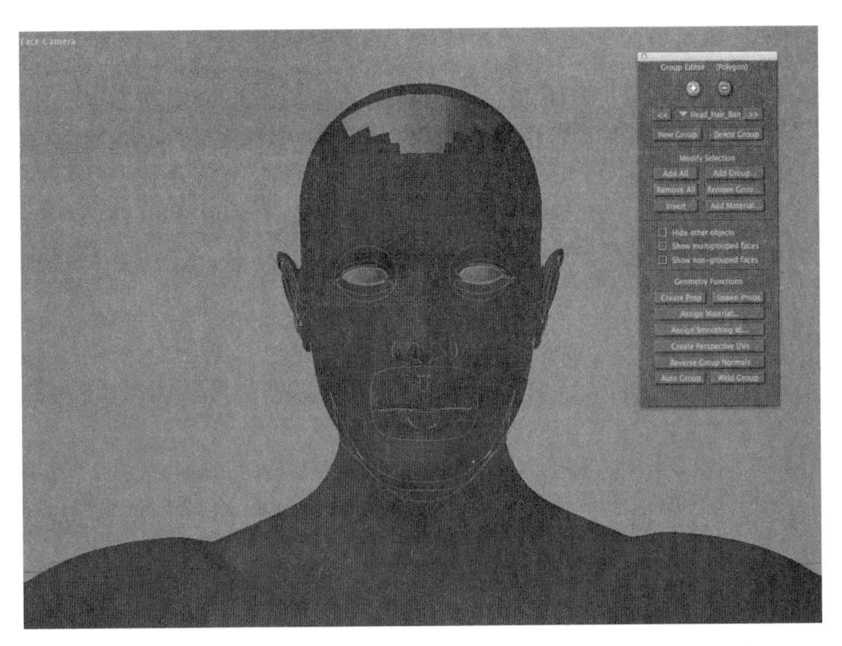

FIGURE 6.8 The selected forehead polygons that will become the Bangs hair group.

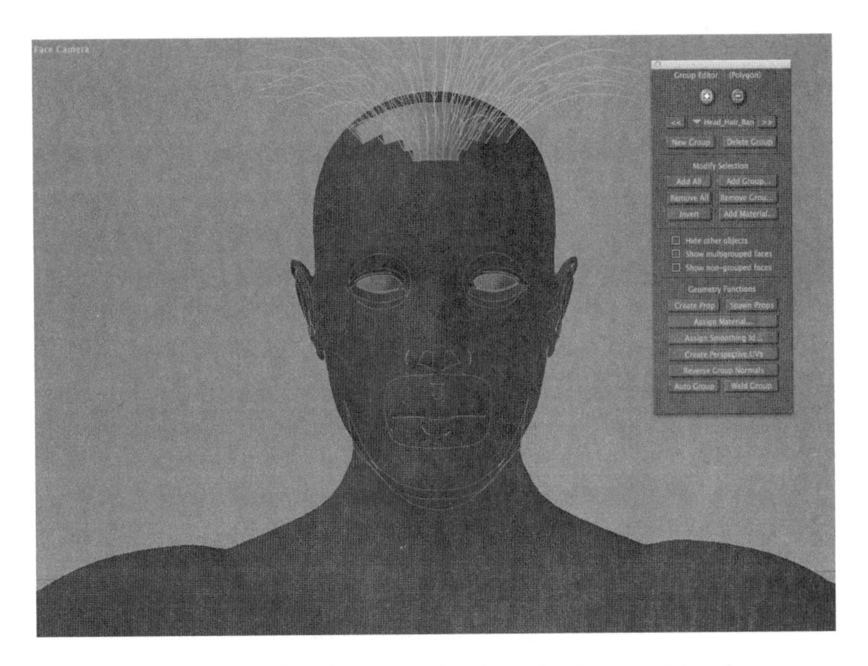

FIGURE 6.9 Strands of hair sprouting from the head—wild and crazy and totally not what you'll end up with.

6. Change the Hair Length value to .15, and then change Pull Down to .00030. Use whichever method you're most comfortable with when changing parameters—by moving the dial or by clicking on the number to activate the numeric field and typing in a new value. After changing the values, the strands will appear to curl downward and will be much shorter. If you'd like, you can do a quick render to see what you have at this point, but that render will not be anywhere close to what you're going to end up with. In fact, I'm sure Ryan would be very upset to look like he's loosing that much hair! Normally, I add hair like this so that, as I'm selecting polygons for the different growth groups, I know where those polygons need to be selected. You will see why this is important as you move through Steps 7 and 8.

You can click and drag across the model to select multiple polygons at one time. A square bounding box will appear when you do this, showing which sections of the model will be selected.

Remember to use the Deselect Polygon button to remove unwanted polygons from the selection. In addition, you can hold down the Ctrl key and click on the polygons you want to deselect, or you can also use the click-and-drag method to deselect multiple polygons.

7. Create a new growth group (click the New Growth Group button in the Hair Growth Groups area, not the New Group button in the Group Editor panel). I named it Head_Hair_FrontSideR because I'm only selecting the right front side of the head. Refer to Figure 6.10 for polygon selection for this group.
8. Add strands of hair as you did in Step 6, using the same numerics for right now. The numbers will be changed later in this tutorial.
9. Repeat Steps 7 and 8 to create the following growth groups:
   - Head_Hair_BackSideR
   - Head_Hair_Back
   - Head_Hair_BackSideL
   - Head_Hair_FrontSideL

   Refer to figure 6.11 for a composite of the different growth group head sections to help you in the creation of your growth groups. Don't worry about slight overlaps; those will actually benefit you when growing the hair. Also, watch out for stray selected polygons around the ears. You don't want hair growing out of them unless you're creating a really, really old character.

FIGURE 6.10 The growth group polygons for the front-right side of Ryan's head.

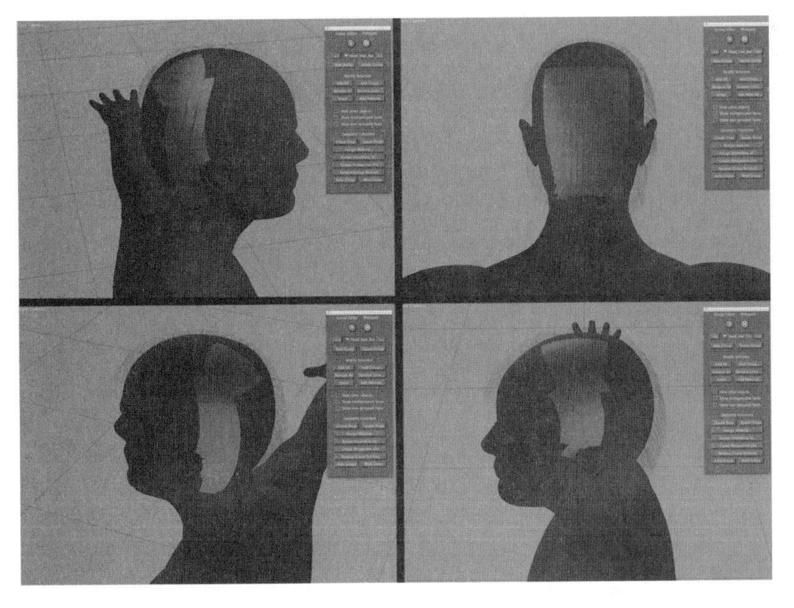

FIGURE 6.11 The different growth groups assigned to the different head areas. When rendered, the strands of hair will slightly overlap so that you don't have gaps or bald spots.

And there you have it, the base for your hairy head. Save this file as RyanHair before moving on to the next tutorial.

Tutorial 6.2 Creating and Using Skullcaps

You have now created a basic hair setup by defining separate areas of the model's head and then adding hair to those sections. This setup is assigned to this model only. While you have controls to create a prop, there is no way of grouping these six separate regions (Bangs, FrontSideR, FrontSideL, BackSideR, BackSideL, and Back) into one large skullcap. You can select each of them and create a separate skullcap for each head section (or skull segment, if you will) but that would be very inefficient to work with. Let's take a few moments to define an area that can be used as a skullcap, and then export it as a prop for use on different instances of the Ryan model.

When you create a skullcap, you cannot redistribute that file or make money off of it. This is because the polygons that have been created are extracted from a copyright-protected model. The only way you can make a skullcap that can be redistributed (either for free or for a fee) is to model your own skullcap in a modeling program such as Cinema 4D, Maya, or 3D Studio Max to name a few.

1. Create a new file, remove Andy, and add Ryan. (I'm starting to feel like those two models are old friends who come over, watch the big game with me, and join me to quaff a few drinks on a quiet Saturday evening. Kinda sad, isn't it?!)

I have included a new face file on the DVD. It's located in the Chapter06\Runtime\Libraries\Face\Poser 8\Ryan_Originals folder and is named Clarence.fc2. I am using this face for this tutorial and, if you want, you can use it as well.

2. Set the camera the same way you did in Tutorial 6.1 and go into the Hair Room.
3. With Ryan's head selected, click New Growth Group and name it Ryan_HairGoup.
4. Select Edit Growth Group and add the model's entire head and scalp as you see in Figure 6.12. Try to match both sides of the head as closely as possible. Remember to rotate around the model, making sure you don't have any unwanted polygons selected.

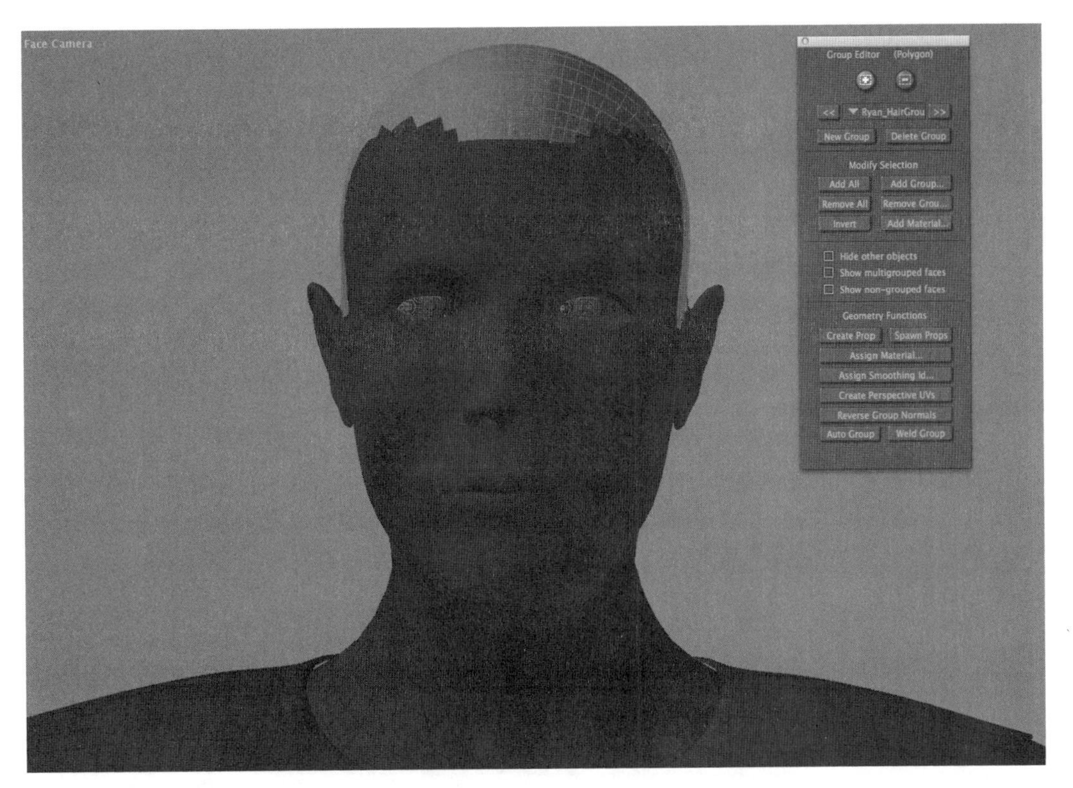

FIGURE 6.12 The selected polygons for the skullcap.

5. Once everything is selected, click the Create Prop button. A dialog opens asking you to name this prop. I named mine Ryan_Skullcap. After clicking OK, the new skullcap will appear outlined on Ryan's head and will also be a selection in the Props drop-down menu.
6. At this point, I will usually go back into the Pose Room, remove the model itself, and then save the skullcap to a folder inside the Props folder. So, in the Pose room, select the Ryan model and delete him, leaving the skullcap hovering in space (see Figure 6.13).
7. Select the Poser 8 folder inside the Props folder and create a Skullcaps folder. With the latter folder selected, add the skullcap, naming it Ryan_Skullcap. Now your skullcap is saved and ready to add to your figure at any time.

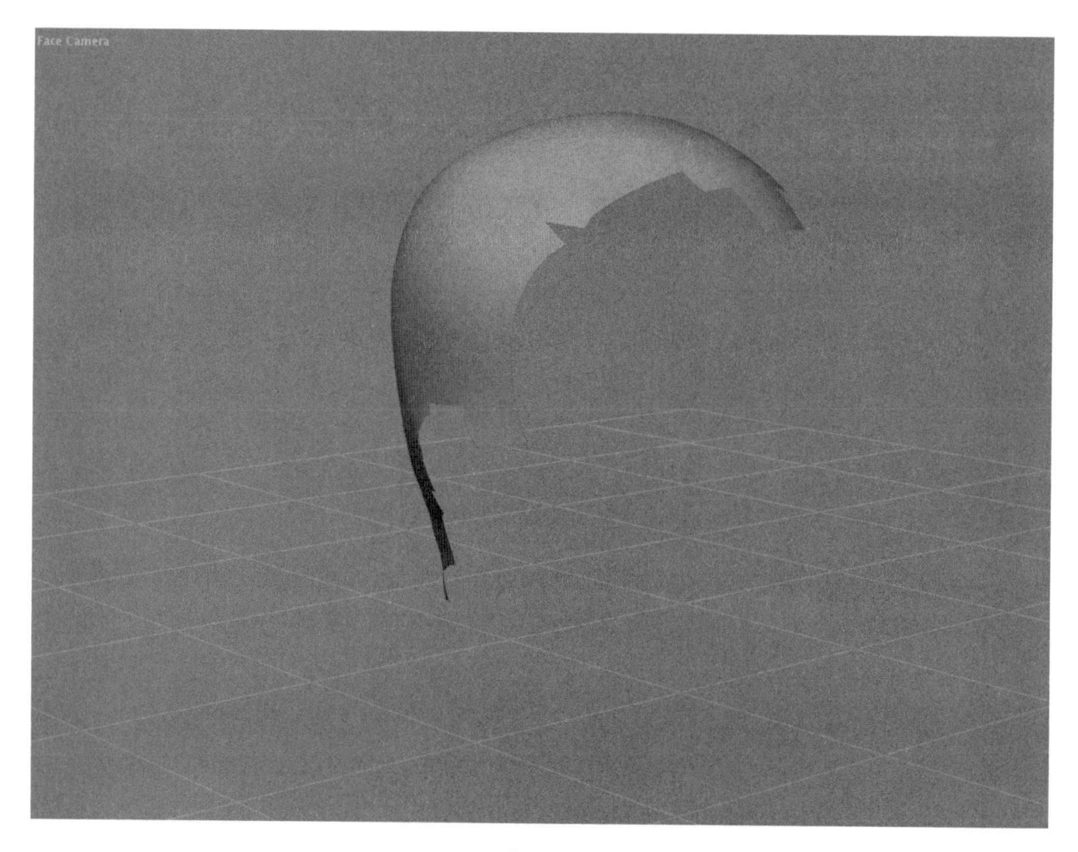

FIGURE 6.13 The finished skullcap.

But wait! That's just one big ol' skullcap without any areas defined like they were in Tutorial 6.1. And you are right. You can take the skullcap into the Hair Room, divide it into different sections as you did in the last tutorial, re-save that prop and, when you add it into your scenes, select the groups and add the hair to them.

TUTORIAL 6.3 STYLIN' THE GROWTH GROUPS

Let's return to tutorials gone by—Tutorial 6.1, that is—and continue the tour of the Hair Room controls. You have set the hairs for the different sections of Ryan's head, but you haven't styled those hairs yet. Let's look at how you do that.

1. Re-open RyanHair and go back to the Hair Room.
2. Select the Head_Hair_Bangs growth group, and then click the Grow Guide Hairs button. In this instance, it makes sense to have the hair combed back, and one of the easiest ways of accomplishing that is to use the Pull Down and Pull Back controls. Using these controls is not always the best, but it will work for this instance.
3. Change the Pull Back and Pull Down values to the following:
   - Pull Back = 0.00210
   - Pull Down = –0.00005

   Figure 6.14 shows the hairs sweeping back across Ryan's head. You can also use the Pull Side control to have the hair sweep to either side of Ryan's face. But for this, I'll just have it sweep back.

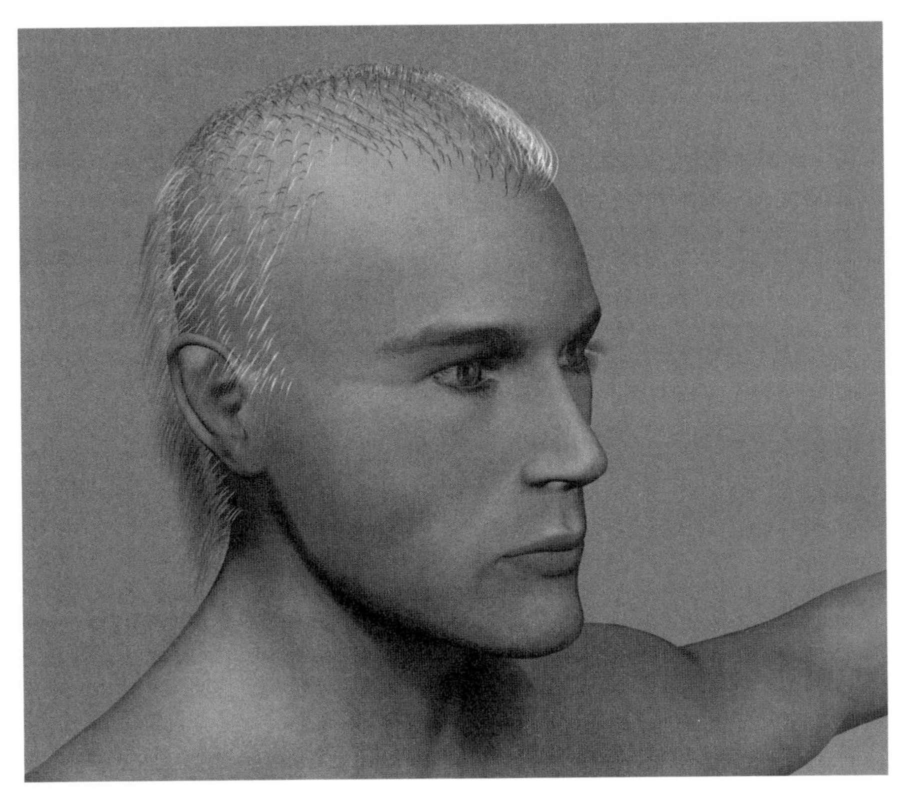

FIGURE 6.14 Ryan's thin hair is swept back using the Pull Back and Pull Down controls.

4. Select Head_Hair_FrontSideR. This time, you're going to work with Section 3 of the screen, Styling Controls. Here is a breakdown of the various commands at your disposal:
   - **Style Hairs:** This opens the Hair Style Tool panel (refer to Figure 6.5), which allows you to interactively make changes to the hairs.
   - **Show Populated:** When active, this shows both the guide hairs and the hair as it will look when populated. It doesn't increase refresh time as you work with the growth group.
   - **Hair Density:** Changes the number of hairs making up the growth group. It makes the hair more lush or more thin. The more hairs you add, the longer the render time can become.
   - **Tip Width:** Controls the width of the hairs at their tips. Usually, you will want to keep this number smaller than the one for Root Width.
   - **Root Width:** Controls how wide the root of the hair is as it comes out from the skullcap or the object.
   - **Clumpiness:** Groups the hairs, creating clumps. This is great for creating dreadlocks or other hair styles where the hair is closely grouped.
   - **Kink Strength:** Controls how wavy the hair is. Higher values make the hair more wavy.
   - **Kink Scale:** Controls how intense the waves of the hair are. Higher values, again, create more drastic waves.
   - **Kink Delay:** Controls when the waviness will begin from the root. The higher the value, the farther away from the root the waviness will start to appear.
   - **Verts Per Hair:** Controls how many vertices each hair has. The higher the value, the smoother the hair will appear, but it also increases render and refresh times since the hairs are more complex.
5. With that explained, activate Show Populated so you can see the actual hairs on Ryan's head.
6. Next, increase Hair Density to 900. You will see the numbers immediately above this control change to reflect how many hairs are now being generated in this growth group.
7. Click the Style Hairs button to open the Hair Style Tool panel (refer to Figure 6.5).

8. Let's use the Hair Style Tool tools to make some changes to the Head_Hair_FrontSideR growth group. First, click the Select Hairs button and then click and drag across the sideburn area of the selection. Those hairs are way too long and wild, so you'll need to fix them. When you drag across the hairs with the Select Hairs tool, you will see small selection indicators appear where the vertices are (see Figure 6.15). Those are the control points. If you don't have all the control points selected that you want, merely click and drag across the hairs again to add to the selection.
9. First, let's shorten the hairs. If you want to create sideburns, I would suggest you create more growth groups and populate them appropriately. The hairs you're working with now might work as sideburns for a female model (that loose, wispy hair falling in front of the ear), but they won't necessarily work for this macho guy. So turn the Lengthen dial to the left to scale these selected hairs.
10. Use the Translate tool to move the hairs toward Ryan's head, then click Clear Selection to deselect those hairs.
11. If your hairs are like mine (on the model, that is, not on you personally), you have some sticking through the ears. Select those, then shorten and translate them as well. This hair section should look something like you see in Figure 6.16.

Do not be afraid to rotate the view or zoom in and out so you can get a better idea of what you are doing. You want to constantly change your view to make sure everything is as you want it.

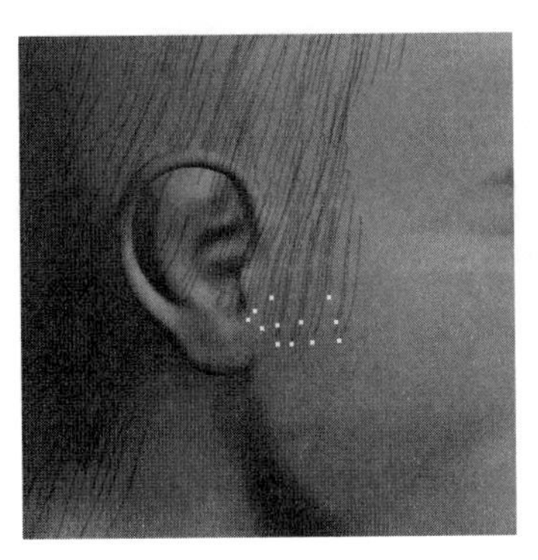

FIGURE 6.15 The vertices of the selected hairs are highlighted with small yellow squares.

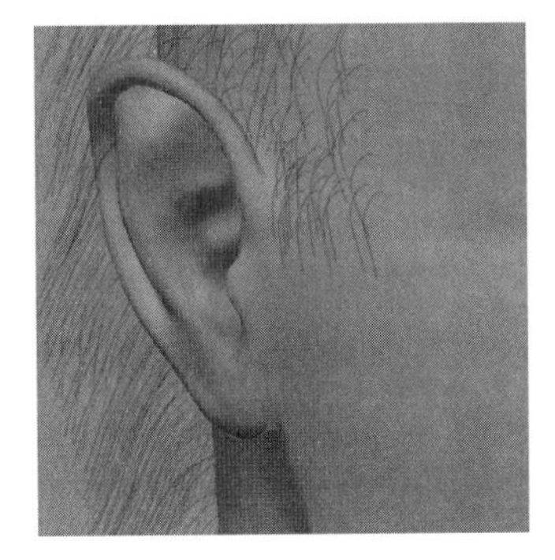

FIGURE 6.16 The translated hairs no longer grow out of Ryan's ear.

12. Click Clear Selection.
13. Select the rest of the hairs in this growth group (see Figure 6.17). Use the Translate tool to sweep them backward. When you finish, do a quick render, and your hairs should look close to what you see in Figure 6.18. Repeat this process for the rest of the hair groups before moving to the next project.

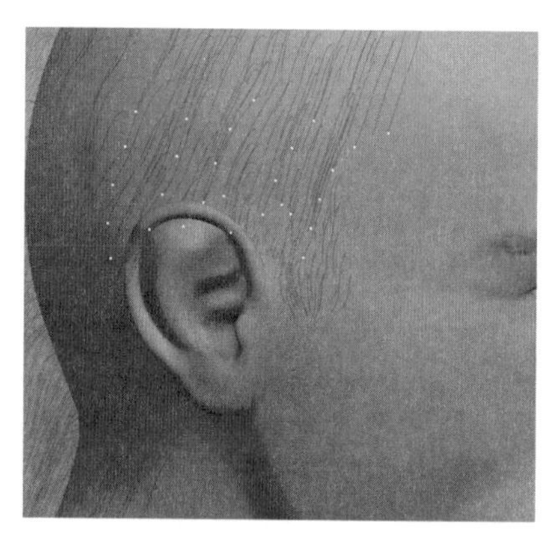

FIGURE 6.17 The selected hairs that will be swept back along the side of Ryan's head.

FIGURE 6.18 The swept back and styled hair.

TUTORIAL 6.4 HAIR COLOR

The default color of the hairs created in Poser's Hair Room is a yellow/gold. It's okay for some situations, but you will more than likely want to have more variety in hair color. Brunettes, redheads, even little blue-haired men or women are possible. Here's how.

1. With the Ryan model you worked with in Tutorial 6.3 still open, go to the Material Room.
2. In the Objects pop-up menu, you will see each of the growth groups listed. Select Props > Head_Hair_Bangs and the Alternate Diffuse node will change to reflect the colors assigned to the hairs. This node contains three very important channels (see Figure 6.19): Root Color, Tip Color, and Specular Color. Each of these combined help you create a realistic look to your hair. This node is also connected to a Noise node, which helps determine how the Root and Tip Color channels interact along the follicle(s).

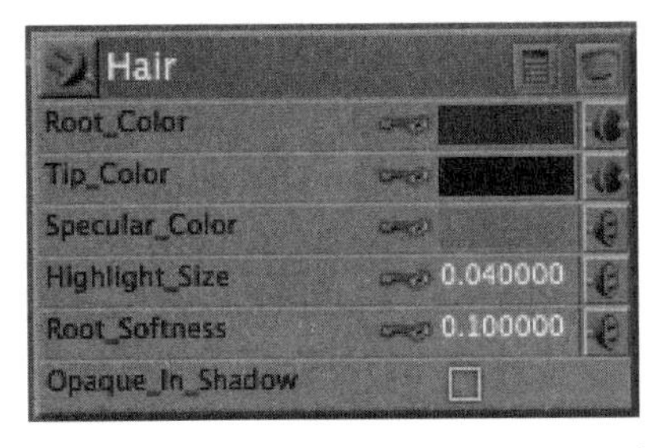

FIGURE 6.19 The Hair node assigned to the Alternate Diffuse channel.

NOTE

You will want to be careful when modifying the Specular Color channel because even the slightest difference in the node can make a drastic difference in the appearance of the hair.

3. Change the colors for each of the growth groups to the following:
   - Root_Color: Red=44, Green=0, Blue=6
   - Tip_Color: Red=25, Green=2, Blue=8

These two colors will change Ryan's hair from that default yellow/gold to a dark brunette (see Figure 6.20). Try different color combinations for more interesting and creative looks.

FIGURE 6.20 Ryan with dark hair.

It's interesting to note that for some reason the root color needs to be lighter than the tip color, something that has no basis in reality. Normally, the root color would be darker and any highlights would be created with a lighter tip color. While there is no formal reason for the color anomaly, as long as you know this is how hair coloring works, you can assign lighter shades to the root and darker to the tip to make the hair look the way you want.

You should also try giving Ryan a beard, mustache, goatee, or other types of facial hair, as well as some chest hair, to see how different settings can affect the look of the hair on your figures.

The final thing to do is activate Do Collisions in the Dynamics Controls section. You already set up Collision Detection for Ryan's head, so Do Collisions will recognize those polygons and not cut into them. There is one problem, though—with this many hairs, it's going to take a long, long time to render. To help speed up the dynamics calculation time, go to the animation controls and set the animation to 1 frame by clicking once on 30 and typing in 1. When you click on the Calculate Dynamics button, the Draping window will appear showing you how much time is left until the draping process is complete.

A Short Re-Pose

While hair on a figure is the first thought when using the Hair Room, there are so many other things you can create. From the fletching on arrows to horses' tails to grass and plants to feathers. Literally, anything that is thin and (usually) grown can be created in the Hair Room. Just use your creativity, and you'll soon be creating everything from sea anemones to flowers, pine trees, and the aforementioned grass and feathers. Also, practice with the Dynamics Controls for the growth group to add even more realism via gravity and air resistance.

After you have worked in the Hair Room for a while, flip the page to go to Chapter 7 where you'll explore working with cloth. (You can't always have naked Poser people populating your scenes, now can you?)

7 Working With Clothing

In This Chapter:

- Types of Poser Clothing
- Common Clothing Problems
- Using the Cloth Room
- Tutorial 7.1: Preparing the Scene
- Tutorial 7.2: Making Multiple Simulations
- Tutorial 7.3: Calculating the Simulations
- Tutorial 7.4: Constraining Parts of the Cloth

"Our clothes are too much a part of us for most of us ever to be entirely indifferent to their condition: it is as though the fabric were indeed a natural extension of the body, or even of the soul."

—Quentin Bell

Mark Twain also said, "Clothes make the man. Naked people have little or no influence on society." However, it could be argued that the Victoria model, in all her numeric incarnations, is one of those "people" who have tremendous influence on Poser society with or without clothing (or wearing as little as possible when going into battle).

Types of Poser Clothing

There are three types of clothing you can use in Poser: Conforming, Prop, and Dynamic. Conforming and Prop are the most common types and ones that you have used in one way or another since you first opened Poser. Dynamic clothing, while it is most realistic because of the way it fall and flows with the model it's attached to, is both revered and misunderstood. So a good portion of this chapter will deal with dynamics. You will also discover how to overcome one of the banes associated with Conforming and Prop clothing: poke-through.

When it comes to Dynamic clothing, what is often confusing is the need to create an animation to have the clothes fall properly in place, even if you only want to create a still image. By having the clothing drape around the figure via multiple frames, the way in which the clothing interacts with the model is enhanced, as is the realism. (In the section "Using the Cloth Room," you will make clothing that looks and flows naturally on various figures.)

There are two types of categories when it comes to accessories (such as earrings, bracelets, necklaces, and other pieces of jewelry): props and Smart props. The differences are explained in the following list.

- **Standard props** initially appear in your scene in their default "as modeled" position. Generally, this is in the exact center of the stage. If you already have other content located in the center of the stage, there is a chance that you won't be able to see that the prop was properly loaded into your scene. It is much easier to attach a prop to a figure when the figure is in its zero (or default) pose. It takes more time to place a prop on a figure that is already posed because you have to translate and rotate it precisely to position it correctly. You'll have to manually position a standard prop with the editing tools or with the Tran and Rotate dials in the Parameters panel. After that, you'll need to parent the prop to the figure by selecting the prop and choosing Object > Change Parent. Make sure you attach the prop to the appropriate body part (such as the head for a hat or earrings, or the hand for a ring or a sword). Afterward, whenever you move the parent body part, the prop should move as well.
- **Smart props** already know what they are supposed to be attached, or parented, to. Basically, a Smart prop is a standard prop that was saved to the library after it was attached to the appropriate body part. When you load a Smart hat, for example, it finds the head and positions itself at or near the correct position and at the same angle of the figure's head. Figure 7.1 shows an example of Smart props. Alyson's earrings automatically find their way to the correct places when you add them to the figure.

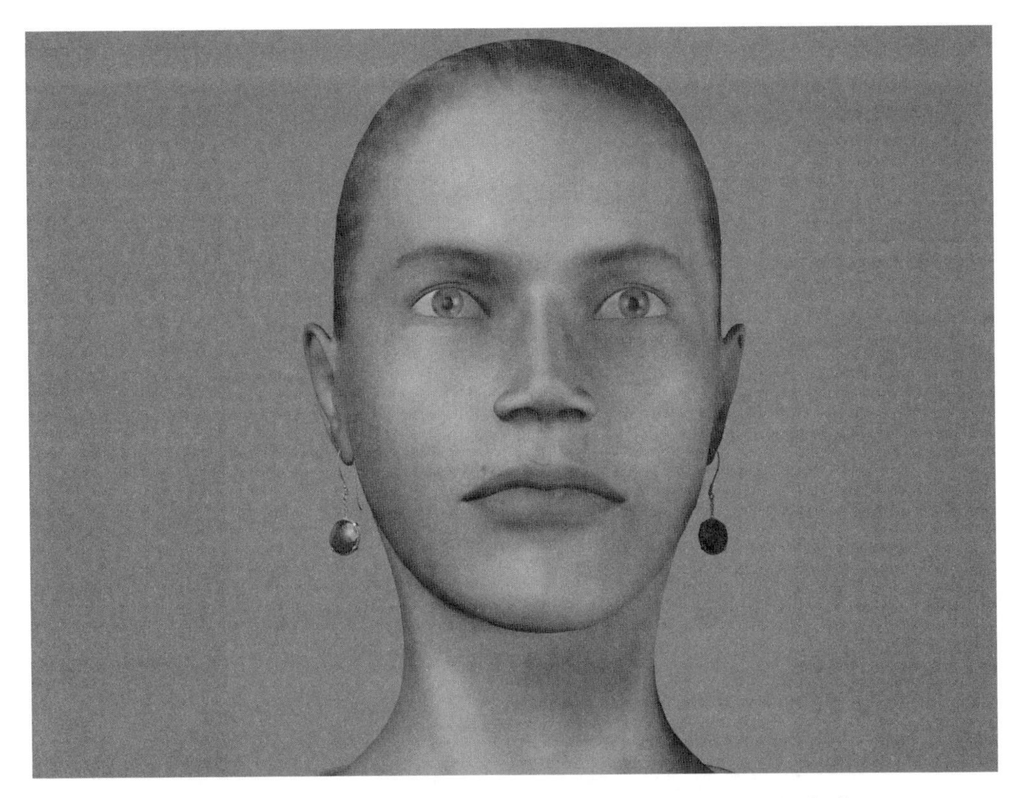

FIGURE 7.1 The earrings on Alyson are Smart props, automatically positioning themselves when brought into the scene.

Common Clothing Problems

Let's say you've added clothing to your figures, and something doesn't seem right. Body parts stick out. The clothing doesn't pose correctly, or it doesn't pose at all. Sometimes you add items from the library, and you don't see clothing at all! What's going on, and how do you fix it? The following sections anticipate some of the more common problems that Poser users face and explain how to prevent them.

Clothing Doesn't Conform Correctly

We have all faced it. We go to the closet, pick out our favorite shirt or pants, put them on and...they don't fit any more! Somehow, our waistlines have expanded or, on the good side, that diet has worked and the clothes are too big. Maybe we just grabbed the wrong item and we accidentally put on our spouse's clothes. Well, with Poser clothing, especially Conforming clothing, this can happen in its digital correlation.

Basically, for Conforming clothing to work properly, you have to use clothing that was built for the figure that wears it. This is because each figure has its own body shape, along with unique joint parameters that tell Poser how to bend and blend the body parts when you pose them.

If clothing is made for a different figure than the one you're working with, it may not be enough to rescale the clothing so that it fits around the figure correctly. To work properly, Conforming clothing must also use joint parameters that are extremely close, if not identical, to the figure that wears it.

It isn't always easy to determine if you have the right clothing, especially because several Poser figures have been released in multiple versions. For example, DAZ3D Victoria 1 and 2 share the same basic body shape and joint parameters, but Victoria 3 is built a bit differently. And Victoria 4 is built on a whole new mesh and configuration. So, putting the V4 version of an outfit on an earlier version of the model results in a poor fit and subsequent poke-through (see Figure 7.2). Because the joints on the two figures are different and the scale of the two models are different, poke-through is most evident in extreme poses.

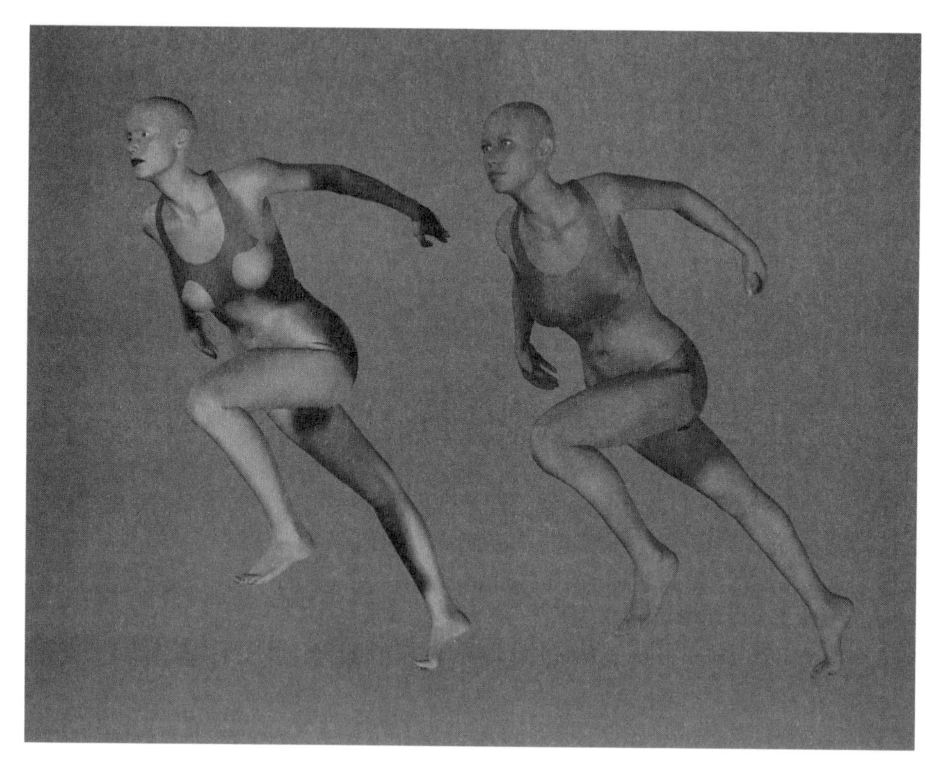

FIGURE 7.2 Victoria 4 (right) and Victoria 3 (left) wearing the same clothing items. There's a lot of poke-through, causing Victoria 3 to have very little dignity.

If your clothing doesn't seem to conform properly, here are some things that you can check:

- **Use clothing that is made for the figures:** Pay attention to the figures that you are using, and select clothing made for those figures. At the same time, be aware that there may be other "generations" of a figure that use different clothing parameters.
- **You accidentally posed the clothing and not the figure:** You're not alone with this mistake. When you work with Conforming clothing, it's all too easy to apply a pose to the clothing instead of to the original figure. If you catch it right away, you can undo the operation with the Edit > Undo menu command. You can also reconform the clothing to the character with the Figure > Conform To menu command. A third option is to open the Joint Editor (Window > Joint Editor), select the clothing that is not posed correctly, and click the Zero Figure button to get the clothing back to its default state. Then apply the pose to the human figure.
- **The arms and legs bend when conformed:** You're certain you are using the right clothing, but when you conform it to the figure, the arms and legs bend. This is a common symptom when clothing is saved in a nonzero pose. Select the clothing and zero the pose with the Joint Editor as mentioned in the previous list entry. Then choose Edit > Memorize > Figure. Resave the new memorized version to your Figures Library under a new name, and use your fixed version in place of the original.

Fixing Poke-Through

Even when you put the right clothing on the right character, there will be times when you see skin poking through. If you frequent the Poser communities, you'll probably notice that tight-fitting clothing is quite common. Although it's obvious that one of the reasons is because people like to create images of beautiful women in sexy clothing (a mild understatement in Poserdom), another reason is because tight-fitting clothing is easier to create and use than looser-fitting clothing, which requires adjustments in the joint parameters—not an easy task!

Speaking of clinging clothing (I love alliterations!), Figure 7.3 shows Victoria 4 in the V4 bodysuit in one of the standard poses that comes with the model. As you can see, that clingy material doesn't fare well with her thighs or (to a much lesser extent) with her breasts. This is a perfect example of what can happen with clothing and something that, if you have used Poser for more than a few hours, you have more than likely experienced yourself.

FIGURE 7.3 Some dramatic poke-through issues with the Victoria 4 model in one of the standard poses.

One solution is to fix problem areas after you render, using an image editor to blend or clone surrounding areas over the skin that shows through. But this can be rather time-consuming. Imagine taking the image from Figure 7.3 into Photoshop or Paint Shop Pro or any other image editor and fixing it in post-production (or *post*, as it's often referred to). You would have to take time to match the pattern in the bodysuit material, get into the small nooks and crannies between V4's fingers, and really take time to fix the image in a credible manner. Instead, you can address some poke-through issues before you render your scene:

- Select the body part that is poking through the clothing. Open the Properties panel, and uncheck the Visible box to hide the offending body part, as shown in Figure 7.4. Repeat this for each body part that is poking through the clothing. While this works very well, it's rather tedious having to go to the pop-up menu, select the body part, and then turn off its visibility.

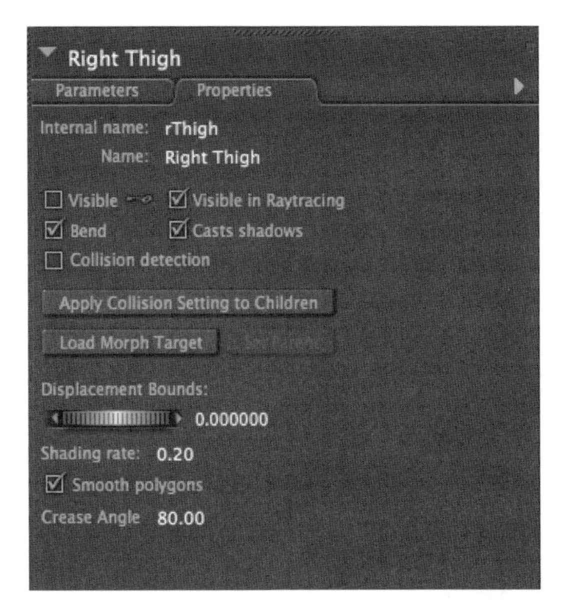

FIGURE 7.4 After selecting the body part, visibility has been turned off in the Parameters panel.

- Go to Window > Hierarchy Editor, scroll down the list of elements in your scene, and then uncheck the parts you don't want to see in the render. Figure 7.5 shows the Hierarchy panel and the Left Thigh element turned off.
- Sometimes a body part is only partially covered by clothing, so you won't have the option of hiding it. In cases like these, select one of the problem sections in the clothing or the body selection itself. Check the Parameters panel for morphs that loosen the clothing in the offending body part, and use them to adjust the clothing.
- Another option to address partially covered body parts is to do two renders (one with the body part visible and another with the body part invisible), and then composite the two images in your favorite graphics editor. If you decide to use this method, you can also take advantage of Poser 8's Area Render feature and only re-render that small section of your scene as needed.
- For clothing that does not have sizing or adjusting morphs, use the xScale, yScale, or zScale dials in the Parameters panel to scale the body part down, scale the clothing part up, or do a combination of both.
- Use magnets or the morphing tools to alter the shape of the clothing so that it fits better. These tools can shape and morph any object in Poser. You'll learn more about them in Chapter 8, "Creating Custom Morphs."

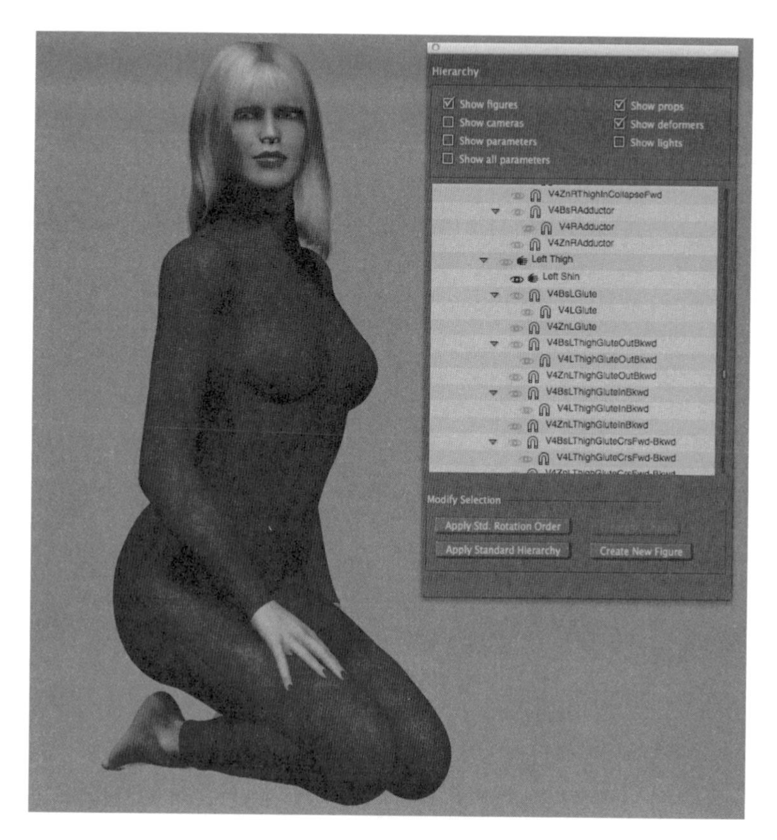

FIGURE 7.5 Using the Hierarchy Editor, you can turn the visibility of unneeded body parts on or off.

Some of the new models (such as Victoria 4's bodysuit) take advantage of the new Magnetize Pose feature. In the case of the bodysuit model, you will find a folder titled Magnetize Clothing inside your Victoria 4 folder (Pose\DAZ's Victoria 4\Magnetize Clothing). When you select Magnetize to V4 from the list, the clothing will automatically be reworked to fit the Victoria 4 model.

When Body Shapes Are Different

Many Poser figures offer morphs that change the overall body shape. Busty, buxom women and muscular, heroic men pervade the Poser art galleries; but when you try to create and dress one of your own, the figure bursts out of its clothing like the Incredible Hulk going through his metamorphosis without those miraculously stretchable pants. The morphed figure of Michael 4 in Figure 7.6 shows you an example of this.

FIGURE 7.6 DAZ3D's Michael 4 has gotten a bit too big for his britches.

The ability to create your own characters is part of the fun of Poser. But what fun is it if they don't fit into their clothing? Certainly, there must be a solution—actually, there are several.

- If you are using DAZ3D figures (Michael, Victoria, Stephanie Petite, David, Aiko, and others), many DAZ original Conforming clothing products include most, if not all, of the morphs that the figures include. Other merchants that make clothing for DAZ3D figures include morphs that are compatible with only the most popular body morphs. When body morphs are included, a complete morph list usually appears on the DAZ3D product information pages. Use the same morph settings in the clothing as you did when you created your character.

- When Conforming clothing does not contain body-shaping morphs, you can use utilities like The Tailor (available at www.daz3d.com for PC only) or the Wardrobe Wizard, which is now included in Poser 8. It is accessible in the Scripts drop-down menu at the top of the Poser screen. The Tailor allows you to alter clothing made for a particular figure so that it fits a morphed version of the same figure. Wardrobe Wizard is a Python script that converts clothing from one Poser figure to fit another. This utility supports clothing conversion between many of the popular Poser figures and boasts excellent support and frequent updates.

PhilC's Wardrobe Wizard (at www.philc.net) gives you the ability to interactively repurpose clothing models for use on multiple Poser figures. So you can take clothing made for Victoria 4 and rework it to fit Jessie, Aiko, or other figures. Phil created a very good tutorial for working with Wardrobe Wizard, located at www.philc.net/WW2_help.php. Though Wardrobe Wizard is now built in to Poser 8, there is a standalone version that allows you to make changes to the clothing models without having to open Poser itself.

- If you're a do-it-yourself type of person, you can use Poser's magnets or an external 3D modeling program to morph Conforming clothing so that it fits your custom figure.
- Use Dynamic clothing and the power of the Cloth Room to morph the clothing for you. Dynamic clothing is very easy to morph so that it fits custom figures. A full explanation of the process is included in Chapter 11 of the Poser Tutorial Manual.

Posing Skirts

Before Dynamic clothing was introduced in Poser 5, one of the Holy Grails of Poser was the development of skirts and long robes that moved and posed realistically. Although Dynamic clothing fills that void quite admirably, the quest for the ultimate Conforming skirt still exists. In fact, of all the types of Conforming clothing that you can use in Poser, the most difficult to develop and use are dresses, skirts, and robes.

The difficulties are due, in part, to the technicalities involved in making Poser objects. When dividing the human character into body part groups, the right and left legs are separated by the hip. To pose automatically with a figure, the clothing must be divided in the same manner. This means that skirts, dresses, and other long robe-like garments have to be divided that way as well.

For dresses and similar clothing, you will often find right and left thighs serving as the legs of the skirt, and a full-length hip section separates the two sides. Because of this, the skirt has no shins, so it doesn't bend at the knees. Additionally, the center hip section remains fairly rigid and serves as the blending zone between the two legs. As Figure 7.7 shows, this design makes it difficult to achieve sitting poses in all but very short skirts. The middle hip section of the dress has a tendency to stretch and distort the texture when legs are moved sideways, forward, or backward.

FIGURE 7.7 Long Conforming skirts can present problems when modified to a sitting position.

As a result of these limitations, long dresses and skirts usually look their best with standing poses, and even then, mostly in poses where legs are not spread too far from their original, straight position. Most long clothing now comes with control handles that give much more control over posing the dress or robe.

Using Body Handles

As early as 2000, even before the release of Poser 5 and Dynamic clothing, there was discussion in the Poser community about different ways to approach the morphing and posing of figures and clothing. Developers on the Poser technical boards began discussing the possibility of using phantom or ghost body parts (parts that are not actually visible on the body or clothing but exist in the underlying hierarchy structure) to pose and otherwise manipulate clothing and figures. The challenge was developing them in such a way that the "average Joe" would be able to use them without too much difficulty.

As a result of the discussion regarding ghost parts, body handles were introduced during the first quarter of 2002. This ingenious method of posing figures adds extra ghost parts to the figure's standard hierarchy. For example, in addition to the upper body parts, the abdomen, and the hip, a dress might have another extra part named "skirt." To pose the skirt, you drag a little piece of geometry called a *body handle*, which is typically shaped like a cone or a sphere. These body handles allow the user the freedom to work with clothing that poses in part with the character and in part by manual interaction.

Although body handles can be used in long hair, beards, and extra clothing parts, you see them used most often in long dresses, robes, and other flowing clothing. The solution for dresses is to make the skirt as one group—the hip, or a different group named "skirt" (or something similar). The body handle appears centered beneath the figure, generally below ground level.

Figure 7.8 shows the DAZ Morphing Fantasy Dress for Victoria 4. By dragging the cone-shaped handles surrounding the skirt portion of the dress, you can make small changes to the position of the dress to better fit whatever pose you put V4 in.

FIGURE 7.8 Body handles help you adjust the position of long clothing.

After you pose the clothing with the body handles, you will typically find morphs that will improve the flow of the clothing. For example, in the DAZ3D Morphing Fantasy Dress, several morphs appear in the body that widen, loosen, flare, twist, and otherwise style the pose of the dress. Figure 7.9 shows an example of some of the morphs in use.

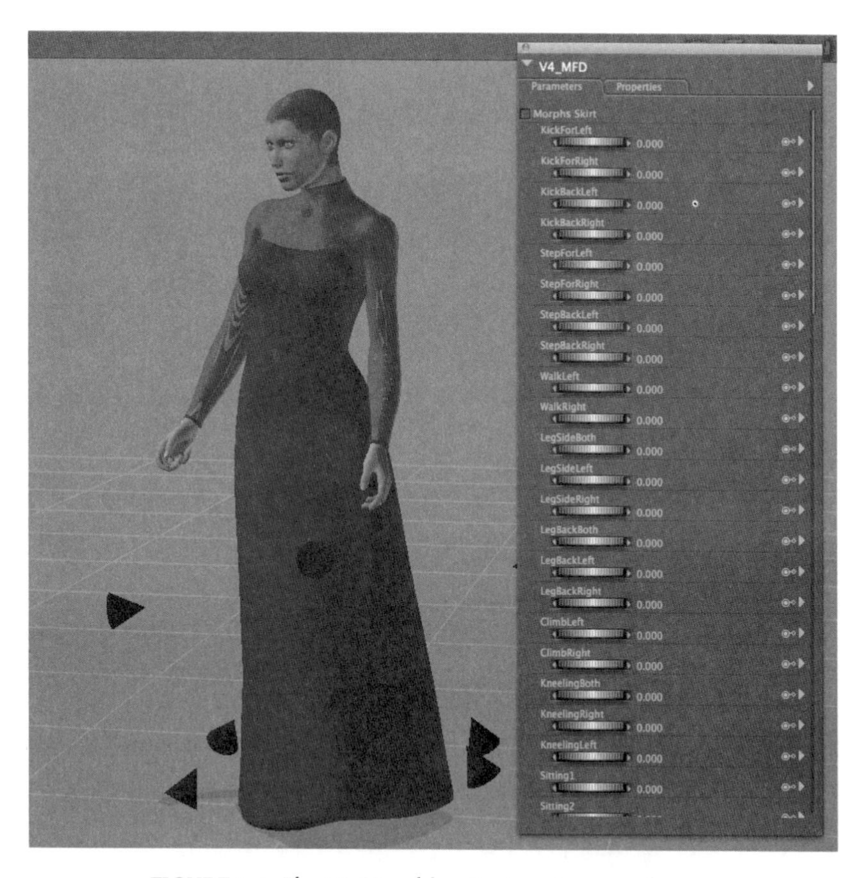

FIGURE 7.9 The V4 Morphing Fantasy Dress and some of the skirt morphs in the Parameters panel.

Posing Shoes

Shoes come in all shapes and sizes, ranging from sandals to thigh-high boots. For the most part, shoes conform to the feet in much the same way as other Conforming clothing. As long as shoes are relatively flat, there isn't a lot of extra work involved to pose them.

The exception to this is shoes that have high heels. Because clothing is typically modeled around figures that are in their default pose, high heels look extremely strange when you first put them on your figure. The position of the shoes on the feet makes it look like your character has just stepped on a banana peel and is about to slip and fall. The heels are usually below ground level and appear to be poking through the floor. Figure 7.10 shows an example of high-heeled shoes that are added to a foot in its default pose.

FIGURE 7.10 High-heeled shoes look pretty unnatural on default-posed feet.

The solution to posing the feet is pretty obvious. You'll need to angle the front of the feet downward and possibly (but not all the time) angle the toes upward. While doing so, you also have to make sure that the shoes are landing properly on your floor or the ground. Figure 7.11 shows a properly posed foot and shoe.

Clothing and MAT Files Don't Load Correctly

Just as a reminder , if you ever have trouble loading clothing models, make sure you're actually using a figure or prop and not a pose. Pose files often show previews of the material on the item it is assigned to and can sometimes get confusing if you are just starting out with Poser or if you are in a hurry—which is what happens to me a lot!

In addition, if you don't see the MAT (MATerial) files appear on the model, make sure you have the correct model selected for the specific MAT file. One of the easiest mistakes to make is when you're working in the Material Room and you accidentally select the wrong folder. Most figure models have the same name for their materials (Head, Torso, Hip, and so on). But if you choose the wrong folder, you could choose a file with the same name, and then the material won't fit because the model's mesh is different (see Figure 7.12).

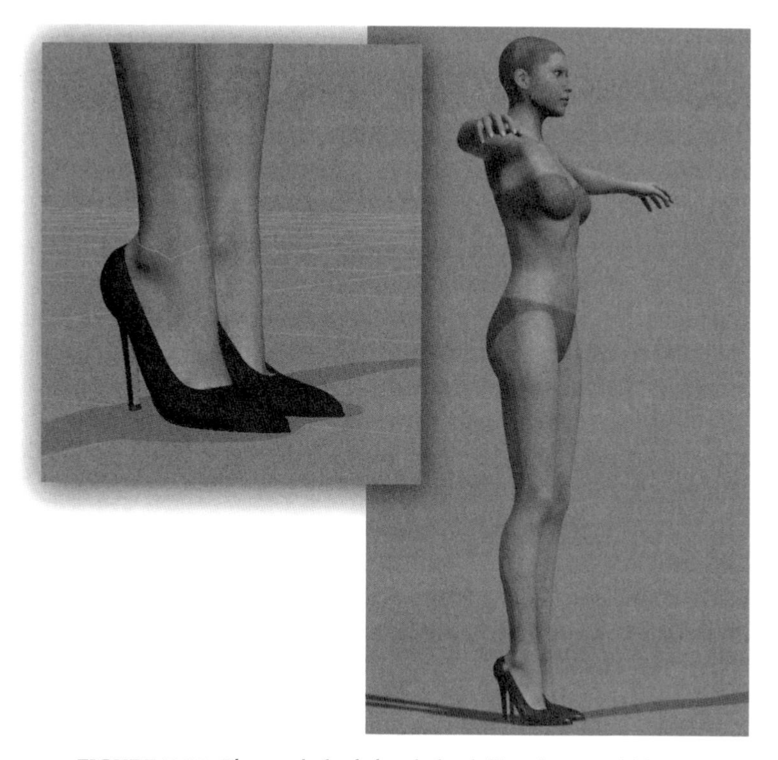

FIGURE 7.11 Those six-inch heels look like they could hurt!

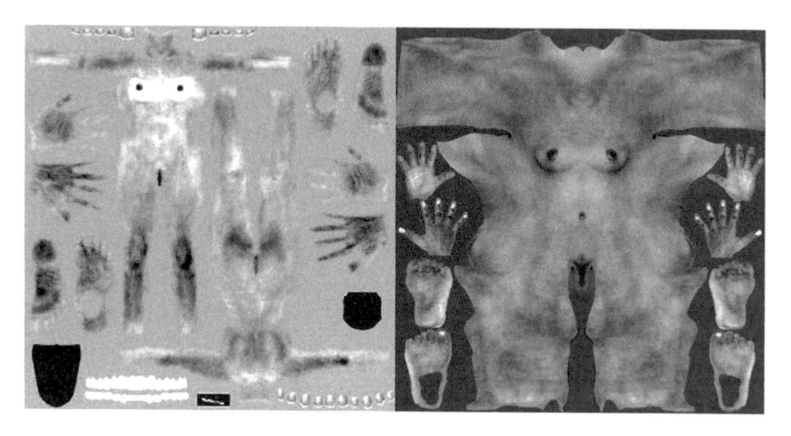

FIGURE 7.12 Two MAT files, each for a different figure. You can see the difference in size and location of the body parts.

Using the Cloth Room

Now that I've covered some of the common problems that can occur when using Conforming clothing, you'll learn a bit more about Dynamic clothing and the Cloth Room. Dynamic clothing works a bit differently from Conforming clothing. The main differences between Conforming clothing and Dynamic clothing appear in Table 7.1.

TABLE 7.1 Conforming and Dynamic Clothing Comparison Chart

Conforming Clothing	Dynamic Clothing
Able to handle complex geometry, such as multilayered clothing or overlapping faces more easily than Dynamic clothing.	More particular about clothing construction. Avoid overlapping or self-intersecting geometry or hems that fold.
Clothing geometry is divided into body part groups that are named the same as the figure for which they are created. The body part groups should match those of the underlying figure as closely as possible.	If clothing geometry contains more than one group, the boundaries between the groups must be welded. You can also use the Group Editor in the Cloth Room to create cloth groups that give areas of the clothing different Dynamic properties that simulate different types of cloth.
To attach the clothing to the figure, select the clothing item and choose Figure > Conform To. Select the name of the character as the object to conform to.	To attach the clothing to the figure, select the clothing item and choose Object > Change Parent. Generally, you select the character's hip or body as the parent, but items like scarves or hats are better parented to the head.
After conforming the object, the clothing poses automatically when you pose the character.	After assigning the parent, you must create a simulation in the Cloth Room to pose the clothing.
Morphs may be necessary to make the clothing move more realistically in an animation.	Cloth simulations make the clothing move realistically in an animation.

The Cloth Room is shown in Figure 7.13. This is where you change static clothing props into clothing that can move and animate with more realism than Conforming clothing. You accomplish this by working through the four main areas of the Cloth Room: the Cloth Simulation area (1), the Cloth area (2), the Cloth Groups area (3), and the Dynamics Controls area (4).

FIGURE 7.13 The Cloth Room and its control sections.

Each area of the Cloth Room serves a specific purpose. For example, in the Cloth Simulations area, you can assign a name and additional parameters for your cloth simulation. You can specify parameters, such as the frame numbers, through which the simulation takes place, whether or not you want to drape the cloth before calculations start, as well as additional cloth collision options.

Use the Cloth Objects section to choose the item to turn into cloth and to specify the objects that will cause the clothing to react when the cloth collides against them. You can choose any body parts on your figure, other cloth objects, or other props in your scene. Remember, however, that you should keep the number of collision objects as low as possible to conserve resources. The more items you select, the longer calculations will take, and the more resources will be used.

The Cloth Groups area contains several buttons that help you divide your clothing object into several types of cloth groups.

- **Dynamic Group:** Gives you the ability to create more than one type of clothing in your object. By default, all polygons in your clothing are assigned to one cloth group, and they all behave the same. If you create additional Dynamic groups, you can assign different properties to the vertices that are included in the new Dynamic group.
- **Choreographed Groups:** Respond to keyframed animation.
- **Constrained Groups:** Help keep vertices in place in relation to your figure. (For example, they will keep the strap of a dress in place if your figure drops her shoulder.)
- **Soft Decorated Groups:** Used for items like pockets or other flexible decorations that are not attached to the main clothing article. This prevents the pockets from falling off the clothing.
- **Rigid Decorated Groups:** Used for items like buttons, cuff links, jewelry, or other rigid objects that are a part of the clothing but not attached to the geometry.

Finally, the Dynamics Controls area contains several parameters that help you define the behavior of the cloth.

Creating and Saving Dynamic Clothing

Although the Cloth Room is relatively easy to use, it is very resource-intensive. Chances are, you might need to use more than one article of Dynamic clothing in a scene. If resources are scarce, make sure you pay attention to the polygon counts in your Dynamic clothing, especially if you are going to use more than one piece of Dynamic clothing in each scene. Remember that each piece of clothing will require a separate simulation. You can either calculate all simulations at the same time or calculate each simulation individually.

It is also easier to use pieces of clothing that were designed to work together. For example, if you have a shirt, pants, vest, and coat that were purchased in the same set, chances are very good that they were designed in layers. In other words, if you put the shirt on, it tucks under the pants, the vest goes over the pants and shirt, and the coat goes over all other clothing without the previous layers poking through.

If you randomly pick clothing that was not designed to work together, you may need to adjust the scale of each layer of clothing or use magnets to reshape the clothing so that the underlying layers do not poke through the layer or layers that are above them.

And remember those durn ol' poke-through issues discussed earlier in the chapter? Well, if you don't deal with them before you calculate the simulations, you may get error messages that the simulations have failed. This is because Poser expects the cloth to remain outside of the figure, so when clothing intersects the geometry of the figure, calculations can go out of bounds.

Tutorial 7.1 Preparing the Scene

The pieces of clothing that you'll use in this tutorial were designed to work together. You'll add a top, skirt, and jacket to Jessi before you create the simulations. You'll begin this tutorial by importing each clothing article.

1. Before you open Poser, locate the JessiTop.obj, JessiSkirt.obj, and JessiJacket.obj and the related JPG files in the ChapterFiles\Chapter07 folder on the DVD that accompanies this book. Copy these files to the location of your choice. I would suggest making a folder on your desktop and storing the files there.
2. Load Jessi or JessiHiRes into a blank Poser scene. I have imported the latter.
3. Use the Figure > Use Inverse Kinematics command to turn IK off on each leg, and use the Joint Editor to zero the pose of Jessi. The Zero Pose button will not zero the xTran, yTran, or zTran dials in the Parameters panel, so you may need to adjust those settings manually (see Figure 7.14).

The Jessi figures are located in the Figures > Poser 6 > Jessi folder.

4. Click the Cloth tab to enter the Cloth Room. If the Room Help window appears, close it.
5. Choose File > Import > Wavefront OBJ. The Import Options dialog box shown in Figure 7.15 appears. Uncheck all of the options to import the OBJ file at the scale and position at which it was created. Click OK to continue.
6. When the Import: Wavefront OBJ dialog box appears, navigate to the folder you created, and select JessiTop.obj. Click Open to import the object. If, for some reason, the clothing does not get placed correctly on the model, you'll need to go to Window > Parameter Dials. Move the clothing into place before moving to the next step. The reason this would happen is if you hit Cmd/Ctrl+D to move the figure to sit on the Ground plane more accurately. If you didn't change Jessi's position, the clothing will fit just fine.
7. With the top selected, choose Object > Change Parent. The Object Parent dialog box appears.

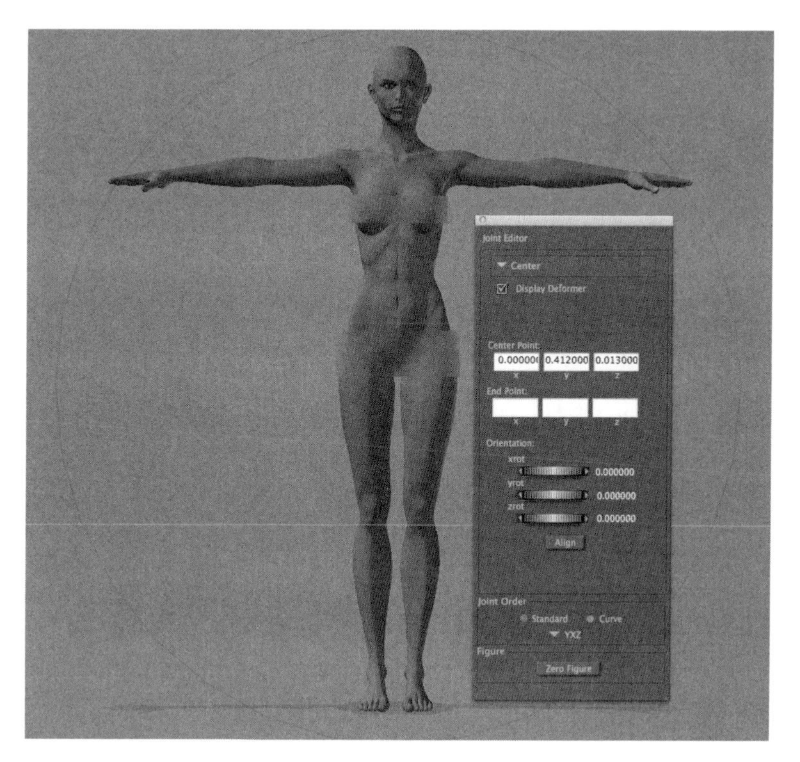

FIGURE 7.14 The JessiHiRes file with the xTran, yTran, and zTran dials set to 0.

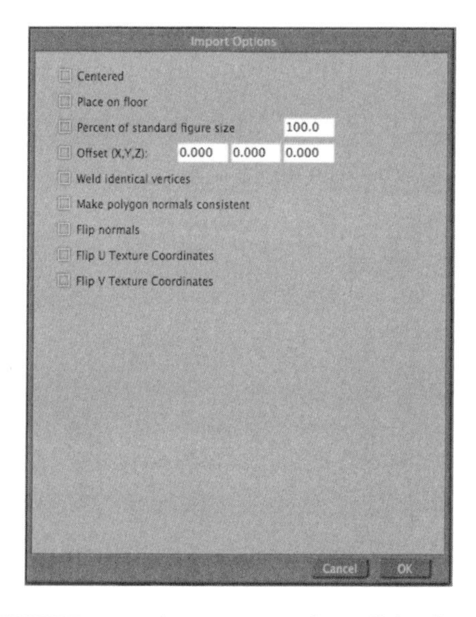

FIGURE 7.15 The Import Options dialog box.

8. Select Jessi's hip as the parent for the top, as shown in Figure 7.16. Choose OK to continue. Why choose the hip rather than her body? When you zeroed the figure, the zero point became the common point along the model. By choosing the hip for all the clothing objects, they clothify around a common point on the model so they fall correctly on the character's extremities.
9. Repeat Steps 6 through 8 to import JessiSkirt.obj from the same location as the top. Again select Jessi's hip as the parent to the skirt.
10. Repeat Steps 6 through 8 to import JessiJacket.obj from the same location as the top. Once more, Jessi's hip will be the parent to the jacket. Figure 7.17 shows Jessi more modestly dressed and ready to have her clothes clothified.

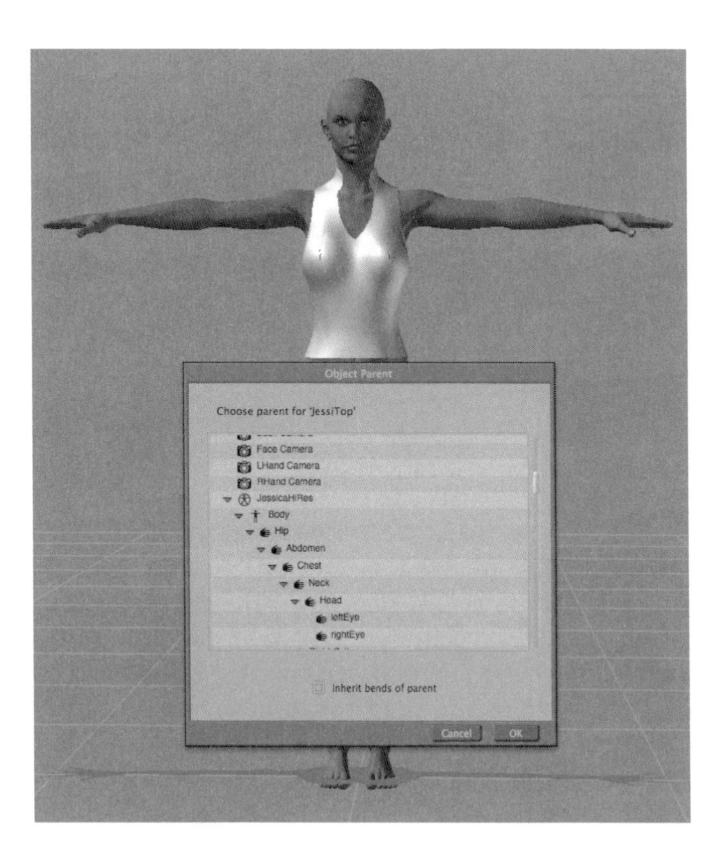

FIGURE 7.16 Jessi's hip element selected in the Object Parent dialog box.

FIGURE 7.17 Jessi's clothes are ready to be clothified.

TUTORIAL 7.2 MAKING MULTIPLE SIMULATIONS

When you have more than one layer of Dynamic clothing on a figure, you should always create the simulations for the underlying layers first, and then follow with each subsequent layer until you reach the top-most layers. Think of the way that you dress and the order in which you put on your clothing. In this tutorial, I'm going to assume that you put your shirt on before your pants or your skirt and that you put the jacket on over both. I feel pretty safe in that last assumption; the shirt, pants, or skirt—that's a whole other matter that's really none of my business.

In the case of the clothing that you now have on Jessi, you will create the simulation for the top first and set it to collide with Jessi's torso. Then you will create the simulation for the skirt and set it to collide with Jessi's lower body and the shirt.

Finally, you will set up the simulation for the jacket and have it collide with some of Jessi's body parts as well as the top and the skirt. If you don't choose the previous layers of clothing as collision objects, the layers above them will act as if the underlying layers aren't even there, and, chances are, will end up intersecting the layers below.

So, go into the Cloth Room (if you're not there already), select the top, and let's get started.

1. Go to the Animation Drawer at the bottom of the workspace and change the first frame to Frame 15. You do this by clicking in the left numeric field and typing in 15. Then place Jessi into a new pose. You can always go to the Pose Room and select a pose from Jessi's Poses folder, or you can just create one of your own by opening the Parameter panel. If you are unsure how to do this, refer to the book *Poser 8 Revealed: The Official Guide* (Cengage Learning, 2009) or the Poser Tutorial Manual.
2. Click the New Simulation button in the Cloth Simulations area of the Cloth Room. The Simulation Settings dialog box appears.
3. Enter **JessiTop** in the Simulation Name field.
4. The default settings create a simulation that starts at Frame 1 and ends at Frame 30 (the default length of a Poser animation). Leave these settings at their defaults.
5. Set the Cloth Draping value to 10 frames (see Figure 7.18). This allows the top to settle on the figure's body before the Dynamic Controls calculations begin. Then click OK to exit the Simulation Settings dialog.
6. Next, click the Clothify button in the Cloth Objects area of the Cloth Room.
7. If necessary, select JessiTop from the Cloth Objects drop-down list, and then click the Clothify button. (Of course, you don't have to do this step if JessiTop is showing in the menu.) After you turn the object into cloth, the buttons in the Cloth Groups and Dynamics Controls areas will be enabled.
8. Before you leave the Cloth Objects section, you have to tell Poser which object(s) the top should collide against. If you do not choose any collision objects, the clothing will fall to the ground. Generally, you want the clothing to collide with the smallest number of body parts possible because it will save on system resources by reducing the number of calculations that have to take place. Click the Collide Against button to open the Cloth Collision Objects dialog box shown in Figure 7.19.

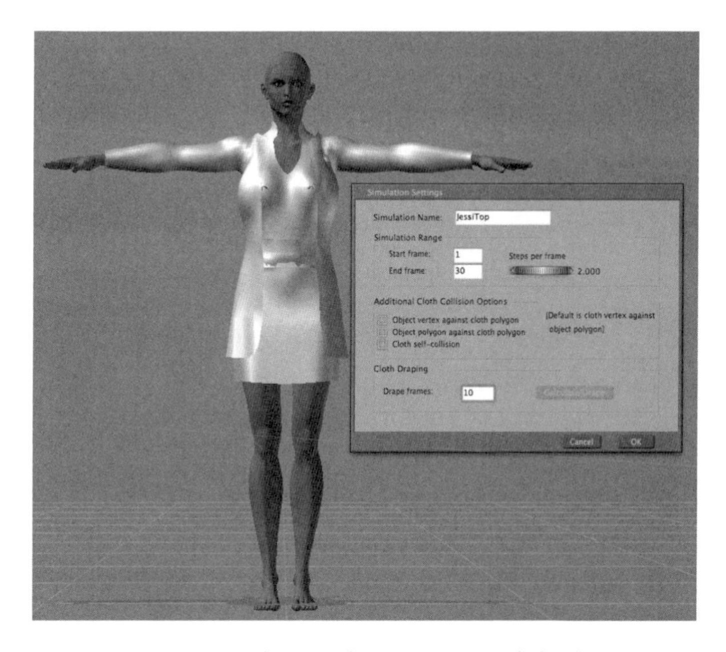

FIGURE 7.18 The Simulations Settings dialog box.

FIGURE 7.19 Dynamic clothing must collide against your character's body, other clothing articles, or other objects that it might come into contact with.

9. To select collision objects, click the Add/Remove button in the Cloth Collision Objects dialog box. The Select Objects dialog box opens.
10. Select any body parts, clothing, or other objects that you expect will come into contact with Jessi's top. Select the hip, abdomen, chest, neck, right collar, and left collar. Figure 7.20 shows a portion of the selected parts.

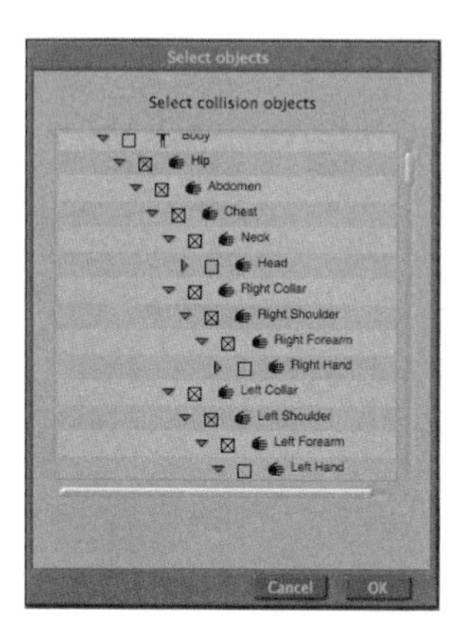

FIGURE 7.20 The suggested body parts the shirt will collide against.

11. Click OK to return to the Cloth Collision Objects dialog box. The various collision controls are now active. So, what do those things do? I'll take a moment to review them.

- **Collision Offset:** This determines how far away from the object the material is colliding against will begin affecting that material.
- **Collision Depth:** This determines how close to the collision object the cloth object must be before it is affected.
- **Static Friction:** This determines the amount of friction that is created when the cloth object collides against the collision object(s). This allows for more realistic movement because of the drag that is generated.
- **Dynamic Friction:** This determines the amount of friction created when the cloth object moves across a collision object.
- **Start Draping From Zero Pose:** Important to have active when you are creating Dynamic cloth. By starting from the zero pose (which you set up in Tutorial 7.1), the draping of the cloth will be accomplished correctly.
- **Ignore Head/Hand/Feet Collisions:** Does what it implies. When active, the cloth object will not collide against those particular elements.

Now that you know what those controls are, you're going to ignore them. OK, not ignore them; just leave them set to their defaults. So click OK to assign the collision objects and return to the Cloth Room.

12. The next layer above the top is the skirt. This piece of clothing must be set to collide against some of Jessi's body parts but must also collide with the top. To begin, click the New Simulation button again. Name the simulation **JessiSkirt**, and set the Drape Frames value to 10.
13. Click the Clothify button. (Or select JessiSkirt as the object to clothify, and then click the Clothify button.)
14. Click the Collide Against button. When the Cloth Collision Objects dialog box opens, click the Add/Remove button to open the Select Objects dialog box.
15. Select Jessi's hip and abdomen, as well as the right and left thighs. Then scroll down to the bottom of the Select Collision Objects list and check JessiTop. Click OK to return to the Cloth Collision Objects dialog box, and click OK again to return to the Cloth Room.
16. The final layer is the jacket, which must be set to collide against Jessi's arms, along with the top and the skirt. Once again, click the New Simulation button. Name the simulation **JessiJacket**, and set the Drape Frames to 10. Click OK to create the simulation.
17. Click the Clothify button. (Or select JessiJacket as the object to clothify, and then click the Clothify button.)
18. Click the Collide Against button. When the Cloth Collision Objects dialog box opens, click the Add/Remove button to open the Select Objects dialog box.
19. Select Jessi's chest, neck, right collar, right shoulder, right forearm, left collar, left shoulder, and left forearm. Then, scroll down to the bottom of the Select Objects dialog box and check JessiTop and JessiSkirt. Click OK to return to the Cloth Collision objects dialog box, and click OK again to return to the Cloth Room.

Now everything is in place to begin the simulation, which is the subject of Tutorial 7.3 in the next section.

Calculating Simulations

There are three different ways that you can approach multiple simulations. You can calculate all cloth simulations, all hair simulations, or all cloth and hair simulations.

If you only want one Dynamic group, then you can skip Dynamics Controls of the Cloth Room altogether. If, however, you want to make multiple groups, then you will need to work through this area.

Let's take a few moments to look at the various controls in the Cloth Groups and Dynamics Controls areas. First, I'll cover the Cloth Groups section, which has four types of groups:

- **Dynamic**: Made up of the entire object. This is the default grouping, created when you create your Dynamic cloth object.
- **Choreographed:** An empty one is also created when you make your Dynamic cloth object. Choreographed vertices can be excluded from the cloth simulation or can be keyframed.
- **Constrained:** Allows you to define specific vertices that are not affected by the clothifying. This is good for sections that need to stay with the mesh, such as the straps of bathing suits. An empty Constrained group is created when you clothify.
- **Decorated:** There are two flavors of the Decorated group, Soft and Rigid. Decorations are things like pockets or knots in ties. They are elements that move with the underlying object, such as the shirt color in the case of a tie. Soft decorations can bend and flex, while Rigid decorations don't. An example for the latter would be pins or buttons.

When you click on the New Dynamic Group button, you get the chance to name the new group. Then, you would click on Edit Dynamic Group to begin adding or removing vertices. Just like working in the Hair Room, you select points along the model's surface (the vertices) that will or won't be affected by the simulation. Figure 7.21 shows what the Group Editor panel looks like.

The Dynamic Controls area is where the magic truly happens. This section lets you control the physics of the cloth as it interacts with itself and with the atmosphere. What's nice is that the Poser programmers did all that high-falutin' math stuff so you don't have to. Following is a breakdown of how each of the Dynamic Controls functions so you can more accurately build a realistic cloth simulation.

- **Calculate Simulation:** Determines how the cloth will fall in each frame based on what has been assigned in the other sections and begins simulating the clothification process. (Yes, I know *clothification* is not really a word, but maybe if I'm really persistent it will become one.)

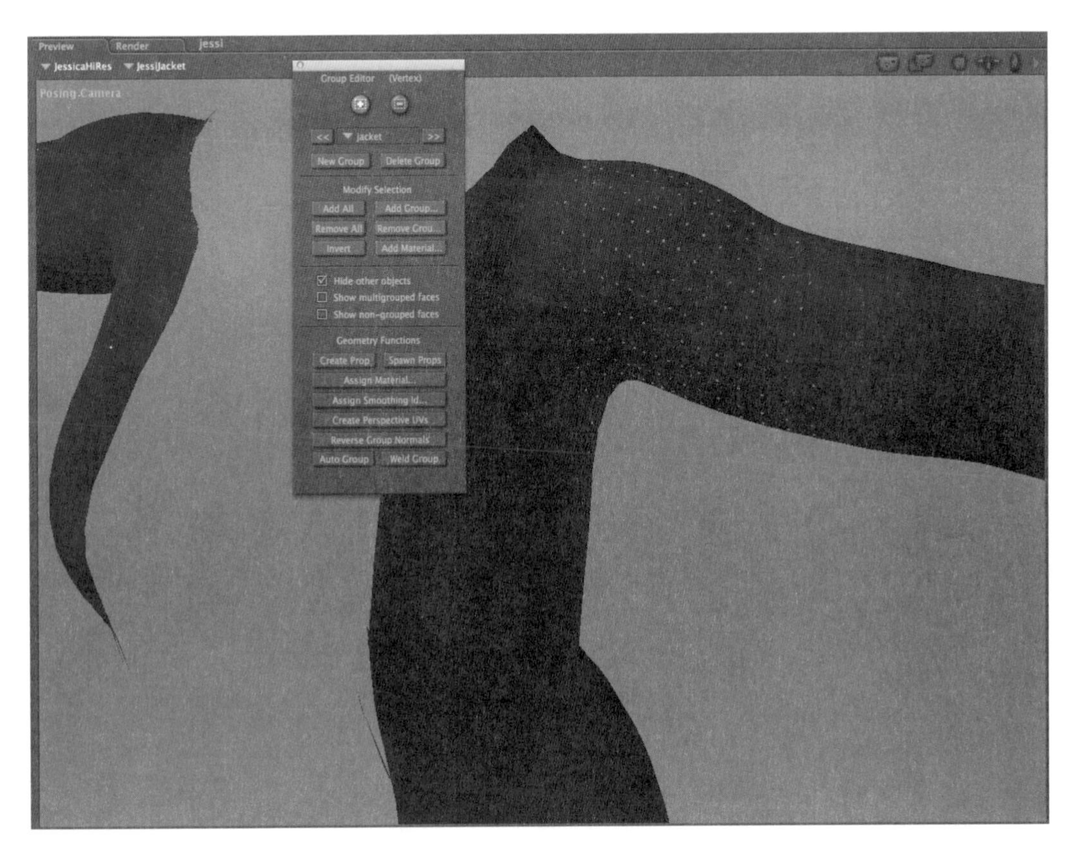

FIGURE 7.21 The Group Editor panel shows the vertices that make up the group's objects, allowing you to make changes to what is and isn't affected in the cloth simulation.

- **Play Simulation:** Lets you review the simulation to make sure the elements do what you want them to do.
- **Collision Friction:** This ignores both Static and Dynamic Friction and goes with the cloth's Dynamic settings instead.
- **Fold Resistance:** Controls how the material folds. A higher number makes the material more stiff, thus not folding as easily.
- **Shear Resistance:** Controls how the material will move from side to side. A higher value makes the material more stiff, causing it to move less.
- **Stretch Damping:** Determines how quickly the cloth slides over its collision object over time. A higher number causes the material to slow down faster, which means lower numbers let the material glide farther.

- **Cloth Density:** How heavy the cloth is. For instance, burlap is a very heavy material, while silk is very light.
- **Cloth Self-Friction:** Controls how easily the cloth moves over itself.
- **Static Friction:** This controls how sensitive a material is to outside material it is resting against (silk on a concrete block, for instance) and how fast it will move across that surface from a standing start.
- **Dynamic Friction:** While Static Friction deals with how material moves from a resting state, Dynamic Friction controls how materials will interact as they rub against each other.
- **Air Damping:** Determines how the material will move through air. The higher the value, the thicker the air and the less the material will move or sway.
- **Clear Simulation:** Erases the current simulation, allowing you to assign new dynamics and settings.
- **Reset:** Resets all the parameters in the Dynamics Controls area.

TUTORIAL 7.3 CALCULATING THE SIMULATIONS

The next step is to configure the Dynamic properties of each item of clothing, and then calculate the simulations. The main purpose for this tutorial is to show you how to perform Dynamic calculations when there are multiple simulations in one scene.

So, let's get simulating! You'll create individual simulations for the skirt and top. The jacket will be covered in Tutorial 7.4.

1. Select JessiTop from the Cloth Simulations area pop-up menu. This makes that particular Dynamic cloth object active.
2. Click Calculate Simulation in the Dynamics Controls area. Within a few moments, the simulation will begin. You'll see the program running through the frames of your animation and the cloth settling more naturally against Jessi's body.
3. Select JessiSkirt and repeat Step 2. Figure 7.22 shows Jessi in my scene with the skirt and shirt clothified.

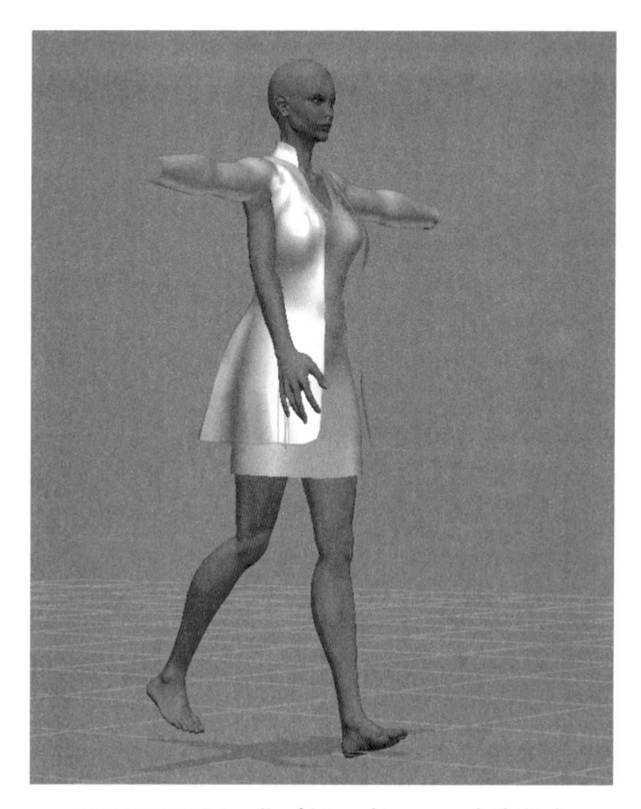

FIGURE 7.22 Jessi's skirt and top are clothified.

TUTORIAL 7.4 CONSTRAINING PARTS OF THE CLOTH

If you did the jacket simulation right now, you would find that the collar softens too much and literally folds down too far on the shoulder. This can be fixed by making a Choreographed Dynamic Group. I'm going to make sure the collar stays in place while the rest of the jacket clothifies.

1. Select JessiJacket from the Cloth Simulations area pop-up menu.
2. Click on Edit Constrained Group in the Cloth Groups section.
3. When the Group Editor panel opens, drag across the edge of the collar. You might want to activate Hide Other Objects so you can more easily work with the jacket. Figure 7.23 shows the selected vertices in the jacket's collar.
4. Now that you've told Poser to keep the collar where it is, it's time to clothify the jacket. Close the Group Editor panel and then click on the Calculate Simulation button to watch the magic happen. Figure 7.24 shows the final clothified scene.

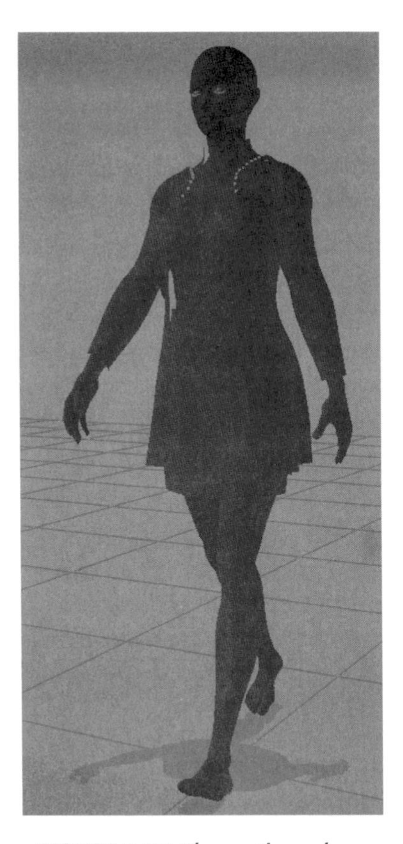

FIGURE 7.23 The vertices along the collar's edges are selected.

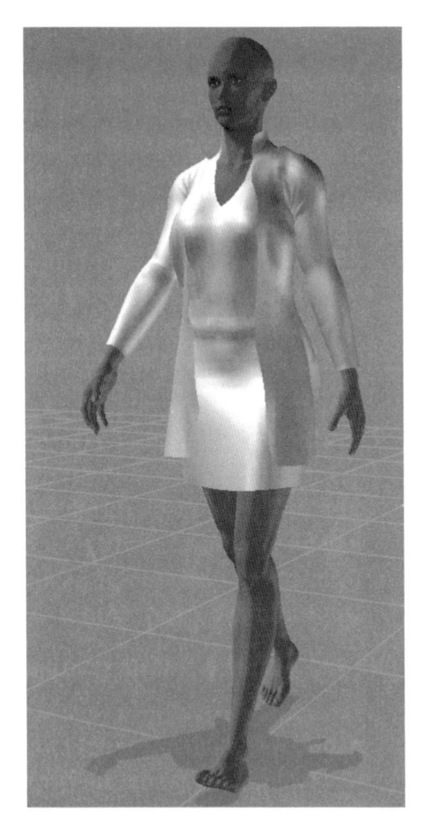

FIGURE 7.24 The jacket's collar stays in place while the rest of the jacket is clothified.

A Short Re-Pose

So there you have it—common problems with Conforming and Prop clothing solved. You've discovered what those crazy blue triangles are used for in some of the clothing items. The controls in the Cloth Room have been made clear (or at least less muddy). You've clothified a suit. You've constrained vertices. You've done all kinds of fun stuff. But it's not over yet. There's more fun coming your way and some more methods for fixing those dag-nabbed nagging poke-throughs. Yep, this means you're going to work with magnets and Poser 8's enhanced morphing features.

CRUCIFORM
Artist: Bjorn Malmberg

NEW WORLD
Utilizing Poser's Sketch renderer.

POCAHONTAS SAVES JOHN SMITH
Artist: Ron Brower

IBL LIGHTING

A comparison of the same scene rendered without IBL (left) and with IBL (right). Notice the details that appear in the shadowed areas when IBL is active during the render.

TRIBUTE TO LOVECRAFT

Post-production work done in Adobe Photoshop.

THE FLAPPER

Post-production work done in Adobe Photoshop.

JOB FAIR

Incorporates Movement Of Mass (M.O.M.) Crowd Generator available at http://market.renderosity.com/mod/bcs/index.php?ViewProduct=71815.

PORTRAIT 1
Artist: Richard Schrand

PORTRAIT 2
Artist: Richard Schrand

MOUNTAIN GUARD
Artist: Bjorn Malmberg

8 Creating Custom Morphs

In This Chapter:

- What Are Morphs?
- The Anatomy of a Morph
- Tutorial 8.1: Creating Morphs with Poser Magnets
- Tutorial 8.2: Saving a Magnet
- Tutorial 8.3: Mirroring a Magnet
- Tutorial 8.4: Spawning Morph Targets
- Tutorial 8.5: Creating the Partial Body Morph (PBM)
- Tutorial 8.6: Creating the Full Body Morph (FBM)
- The Morphing Tools
- Tutorial 8.7: Creating Face Morphs
- Tutorial 8.8: Fixing Poke-Throughs
- Distributing Morphs
- Avoiding Problems

"Everyone is like a butterfly; they start out ugly and awkward and then morph into beautiful graceful butterflies that everyone loves."

—Drew Barrymore

It might seem strange to quote Drew Barrymore in a chapter about morphs, but in this case, what she says is rather apropos, especially in the Poser world. Throughout our lives, we morph into an amalgam of experiences, creating the unique individuals we are. It's said that the only constant in life is change, and change is what I'm going to talk about in this chapter—changes through morphs and magnets. Here you will learn what morphs are, how to create them, and how to manage the morphs you have. You'll also learn about external binary morphs, which save morphs in an external compressed file, separate from the character file.

WHAT ARE MORPHS?

Morphs are used in Poser to alter the shape of a Poser object. For example, if you want to open a character's mouth, close the character's eyes, or change the character's shape, you turn a dial to make that happen. You are using morphs to accomplish those tasks. In the case of the Poser 8 figures as well as Victoria 4 or Michael 4 from DAZ3D or RuntimeDNA's LaRoo2 product, the models are packed with morphs; so many, in fact, you can literally create anything from photorealistic to cartoon-like with a few tweaks of the dial. Figure 8.1 shows Michael 4 and a small portion of the face morphs that you can work with.

When you move a body part with a bone, it always bends, twists, or turns around the same center point. The basic shape of the body part doesn't change much, except around that center point. Morphs, on the other hand, can affect one or all of the vertices in an object. For example, if you want to make your figure smile, puff up his or her cheeks, raise his or her eyebrows, or even gain or lose weight, you use one or more morphs to do it.

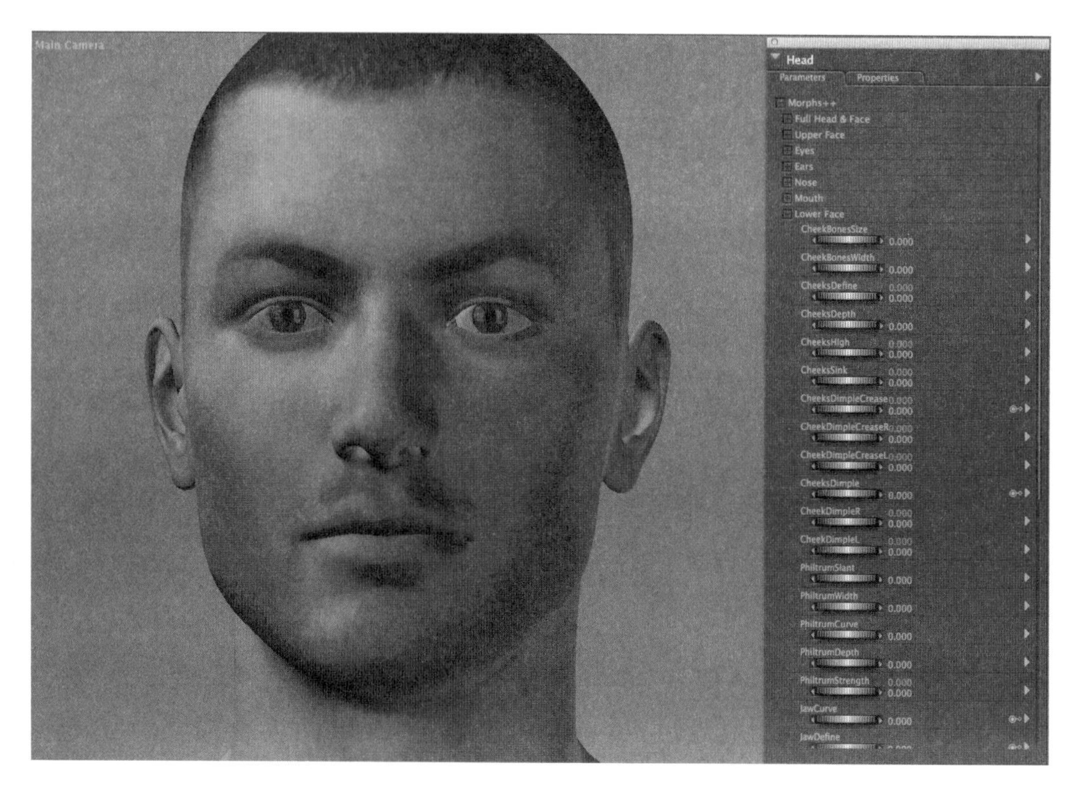

FIGURE 8.1 Figures such as DAZ3D's Michael 4 come with accessory morph packs that help you create whatever character you would like.

At its most basic—and this is something I can say with confidence that you have done since the first day you opened Poser—you adjust the dials in the Parameters panel or with the Face Shaping Tool in the Face Room (refer to Chapter 5) to make changes to your character's pose, body shape, or facial features. I'm going to take this a bit further in this chapter, so just bear with me for a few more paragraphs. First, in order to comfortably work with morphs, it's good to know what goes into making a morph. I'm a big fan of knowing a little something about everything I'm interested in, from its history to the parts that make it up. This way, even if I don't go into a specific area of design (creating morph packs for resale, for instance), I want to know how it's accomplished so I have a better understanding of why the morphs are set up as they are.

The Anatomy of a Morph

When you create a morph in Poser, or import a morph target that was created in an external program, Poser compares the starting shape (or the source shape) to the ending shape (or the target shape). When you save the morphed character to the library, the library file includes the delta information for each morph. That is, the library file stores information that describes how far each vertex in the morph moved, and from where and to where it moved.

Let's say, for example, that you see a dial that changes the size of the eyeballs on a character. When you increase the setting on the morph dial, the entire eye gets larger, as shown on the left eye in Figure 8.2. If each eye contains 200 vertices, the morph information adds 200 extra lines of information to your library file for each eye because you are changing the position of every vertex in the eyeball.

On the other hand, let's say there is another dial that only affects the vertices in the pupil of the eye. In this case, let's say that the dial only moves 20 of those 200 vertices. Poser doesn't store the morph information for all 200 vertices for that morph. Instead, it only stores the information for the 20 vertices that change the size of the pupil.

If the figure or clothing doesn't have a morph that will accomplish what you want your Poser content to do, you have to create the morph yourself. There are several programs you can use to create morphs for Poser content. One method is to use Poser magnets, which help you deform the polygons in an object by pushing, pulling, twisting, moving, translating, or rotating them.

After you wrap your head around the three basic parts of a magnet, it's not too difficult to create morphs with them. In fact, some very popular Poser morph artists create their morphs strictly with Poser magnets! One such artist is Capsces, whose character morph packs enhance many popular third-party Poser figures with entirely new levels of caricature and realism.

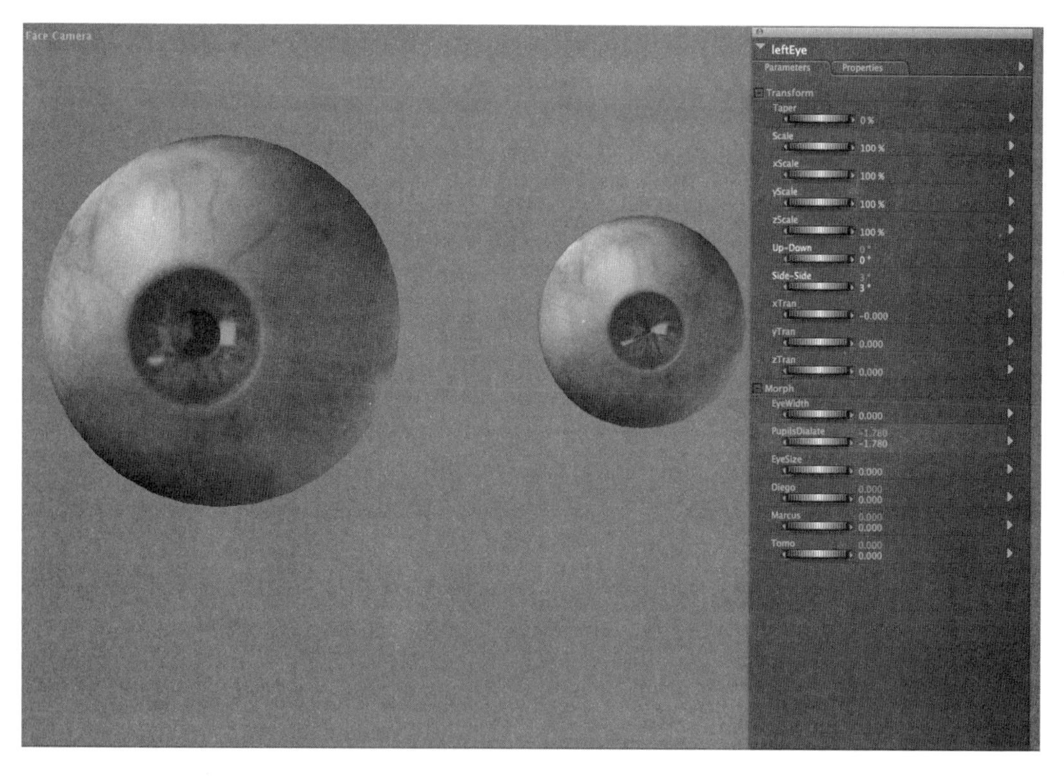

FIGURE 8.2 Morphs can affect all vertices in an object (image left) or just a portion of the vertices, like in the pupil (image right).

A magnet has three parts: the magnet base, the magnet zone, and the magnet. These parts are shown in Figure 8.3.

- **Magnet base:** This is the bar-shaped rectangle that appears at the base of the magnet. The center of the magnet base defines the operating point of the magnet. Dials in the Parameters panel allow you to scale the base, which changes the overall size of the magnet prop without affecting the geometry. If the magnet is too large or too small to work with, you can change the scale of the base to change the size of the magnet. Parameter dials also allow you to rotate and translate the position of the magnet base. The magnet base can actually be positioned at some distance from the object being deformed, and then you can translate the magnet. If you then move the base, you won't see any change in the deformation the magnet produces.
- **Magnet zone:** This is the spherical outline that indicates the area where the magnet will affect the object. The magnet will have the most effect in the center of the falloff zone (which initially appears as the outline of a sphere). The effect

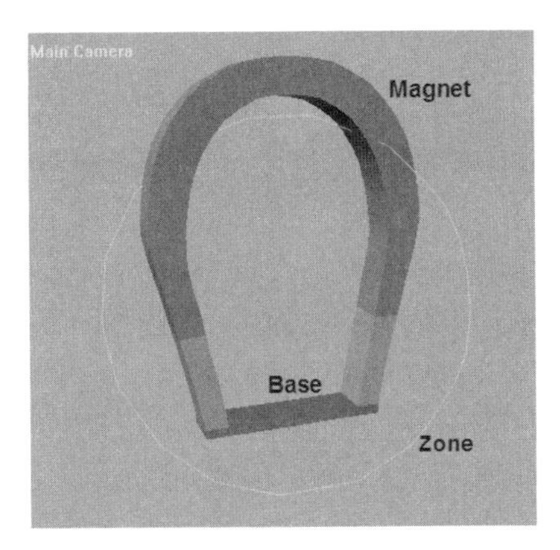

FIGURE 8.3 The three parts of a magnet: the base, zone, and the magnet itself.

of the magnet gradually falls off as it reaches the outer edge of the zone. You adjust the shape of the magnet zone by increasing or decreasing the xScale, yScale, or zScale values of the magnet zone. You can also change the shape of the magnet zone using the Magnet Zone Falloff graph. Select the magnet zone, open the Properties panel, and click the Edit Falloff Graph to open the Graph Editor. You can adjust the curve to have more or less effect in different areas of the magnet zone. When you enlarge the size of the magnet zone, you affect more polygons in the object you want to morph. Reduce the size of the magnet zone to affect fewer polygons. You can also translate or rotate the magnet zone on the x (left/right), y (up/down), or z (forward/backward) axis to position the magnet base away from the center point of the magnet zone.

- **Magnet:** This is the element that actually moves the polygons in the object. The polygons that move are determined by the area defined by the magnet zone. You translate, rotate, or scale the magnet to move the polygons in the object. After you move the magnet, you can make changes to the placement of the magnet zone or magnet base until you achieve the desired shape of your morph.

TUTORIAL 8.1 CREATING MORPHS WITH POSER MAGNETS

You will better understand the function of each magnet part if you use it yourself. In this tutorial, you'll create a morph for Ryan Casual's face. The morph will change the shape of his cheeks. Actually, you'll use two magnets to create the morph, one on each side of the face. To create the face morph for Ryan Casual, follow these steps:

1. After creating a new scene, add Ryan Casual from the Figures > Poser 8 library. Turn off Inverse Kinematics, and use the Joint Editor or the Zero All Python script to zero his pose.

You will find that it's often a good idea to turn off Inverse Kinematics and to zero out the figure when you first start working with it. If you get tired of constantly repeating the actions in Step 1, merely perform the actions, and then save the figure into the folder of your choice. Load that model each time you want to use it, and the settings will be as you saved them so you won't have to constantly turn off Inverse Kinematics or zero the figure again.

2. Select the Face Camera, and, if it isn't already, change the display mode to Texture Shaded.
3. Click Ryan Casual's head to select it as the current actor. Then choose Object > Create Magnet. Your scene should look similar to Figure 8.4. In my warped way of looking at things, Ryan now appears to be wearing a very plain Easter Bonnet. But I digress.

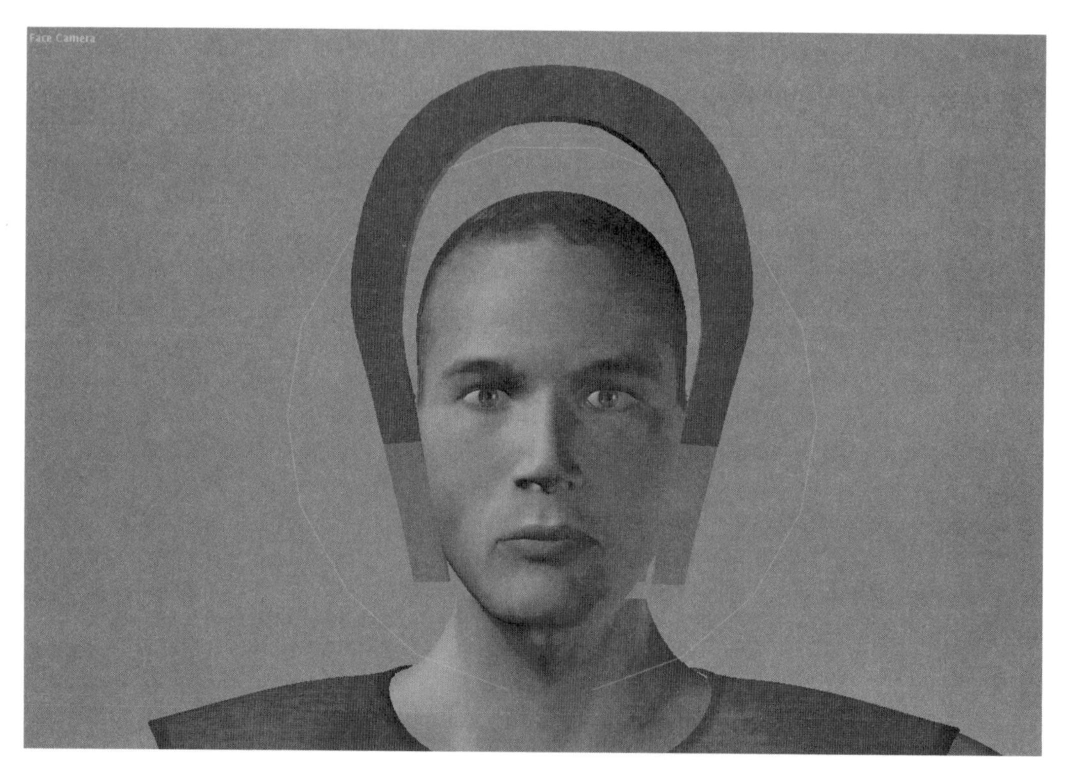

FIGURE 8.4 A magnet is created for Ryan Casual's head.

4. The first thing you notice is that the magnet zone automatically encloses and is centered around the selected body part, and the magnet base appears near the base of the head or, in this case, is cutting through his wattle. You want to affect one of the cheeks with this magnet, so let's start by moving the magnet base right and upward toward the right cheek. Click the magnet base to make it the current object, then make the following adjustments:
   - xTran: –0.181
   - yTran: 5.631
   - zTran: .212
5. Because part of the magnet is buried inside his head, you can also rotate the magnet base so that you can see the magnet better. You'll also make the magnet a little smaller. Scale the magnet base to 7%, and adjust the zRotate value to 90 degrees. Your magnet should now look like the one shown in Figure 8.5.

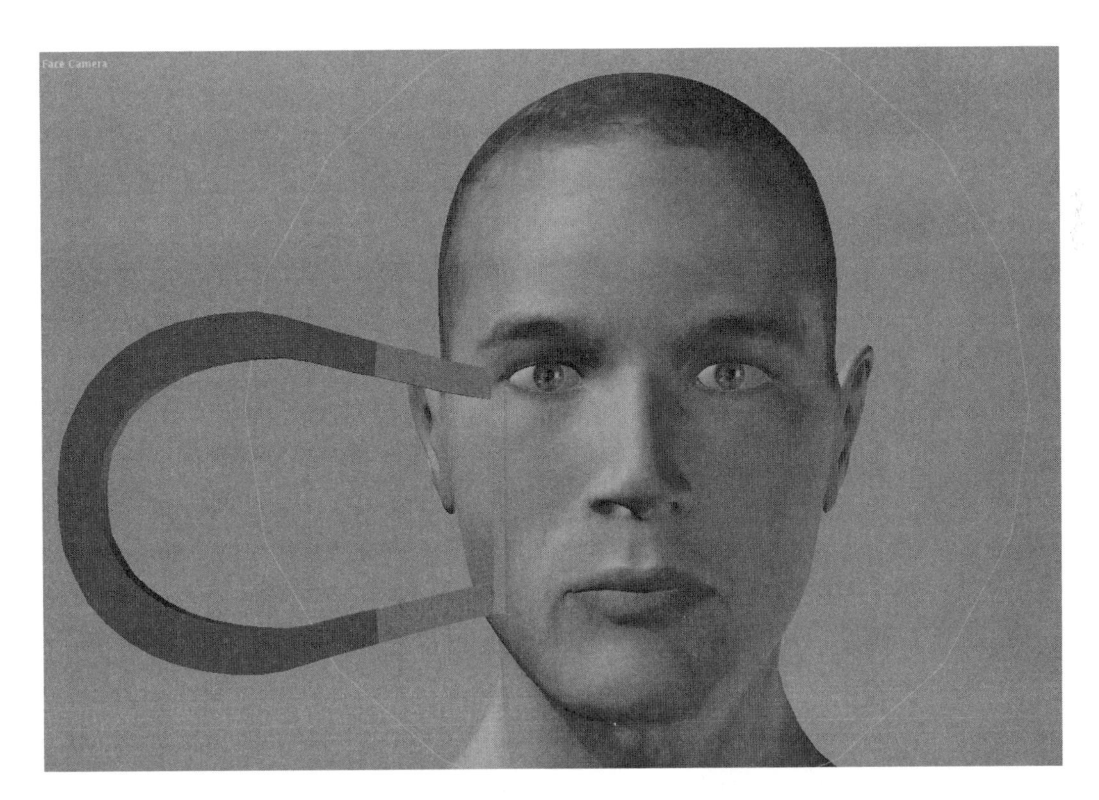

FIGURE 8.5 The repositioned, scaled, and rotated magnet. It no longer looks like Ryan is wearing a bonnet.

Notice in Step 5 that instead of scaling and rotating the magnet (which would move the polygons in Ryan's face), I scaled and rotated the magnet base to change the size and rotation of the magnet itself. Always change the magnet base when you need to reposition or scale the magnets without affecting geometry.

6. If you move the magnet at this point to morph the cheeks, the magnet will change the polygons in the entire head. This is because the magnet zone currently surrounds the entire head. You need to move the magnet zone forward, toward the front of the face, and decrease its size so that it only affects the right cheek. To begin, click the magnet zone (the white outline around the head) to make it the current object. The Parameters panel will show Mag Zone 1 as the current object.
7. Some Poser users find it easier to work with magnet zones when they can view them in three dimensions. You can change the display of the magnet zone to Wireframe to help you visualize the area that it affects. With the magnet zone selected, choose Display > Element Style > Wireframe. The magnet zone turns into a wireframe ellipsoid.
8. Adjust the camera so that you see Ryan Casual's head toward the side (or use the Head Cameras that you created in Chapter 2, "Using Cameras.")
9. You're going to change all scale settings; zRotation values; and x, y, and zTran values for the magnet zone. You want to create an elliptical magnet zone that will enhance and raise Ryan's right cheekbone. To modify the magnet zone, select Magnet Zone from the Props list in the Parameters panel, then use the following settings:

   - Scale: 3%
   - yScale: 40%
   - xScale: 81%
   - zScale: 56%
   - yRotate: 11°
   - xRotate: 73°
   - zRotate: –6°
   - xTran: –0.162
   - yTran: 5.632
   - zTran: 0.224

10. Now that you have changed the shape of the magnet zone, you can move the magnet to examine how it affects the right cheek. You will scale the cheekbone so that it is a little bit larger, and also pull the faces forward (zTran) and to the right (xTran). After you select and set the Magnet values in the Parameters panel as follows, your cheek magnet should look like the one shown in Figure 8.6.

    - Scale: 80%
    - yRotate: –8°
    - xTran: –0.212
    - yTran: 0.363
    - zTran: 0.733

FIGURE 8.6 The new magnet makes the right cheekbone dramatically more pronounced.

Tutorial 8.2 Saving a Magnet

Time to make a decision. You could leave Ryan's cheek swollen like this and create a texture that looks like he's been in a fight. But, hey, that's not what this chapter is about. You're here to create magnets so you can better modify your models. This means that you have two options to make Ryan's other cheek as pronounced as his right cheek. The first option is to save the magnet to the library, mirror some settings after flipping the magnet to the other side of his head, and make him cheeky on both sides, or you can create a new magnet from scratch and type in all those numbers again.

I don't know about you, but I prefer the first method. So that's what I'll do. If you want to create a new one from scratch, follow the steps again in Tutorial 8.1 and change the magnet's settings. Since you're going to save the existing magnet, you'll need to create a new folder in the Props library where you can store it. I'm calling my folder Ryan_Magnets, but you can call yours whatever you'd like.

1. Click on the folder you created to make sure it's the active folder. Since it's empty, it won't open to reveal its contents, but there will be a small curved arrow to the right of the folder name indicating that the folder is active.
2. Click the magnet in your Preview window, and then click the Add to Library icon at the bottom of the Library panel. The New Set dialog box appears.
3. Click the Select Subset button to open the Select Objects dialog box. Check Mag Base 1, Mag 1, and Mag Zone 1, as shown in Figure 8.7.
4. Click OK to return to the New Set dialog box. Assign a name to the magnet, such as Ryan_RightCheek. Click OK to save the magnet to the library.

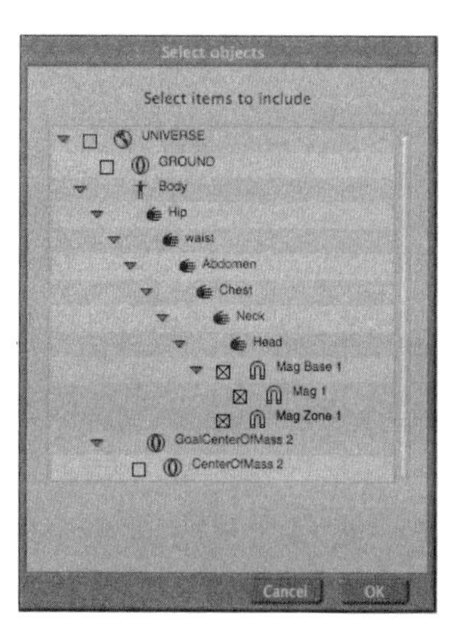

FIGURE 8.7 When saving the magnet to your library, select all three magnet components in the Select Objects dialog box.

TUTORIAL 8.3 MIRRORING A MAGNET

With the magnet saved, you can now begin the process of adding another magnet that will do exactly the same thing to the left cheek. You'll do that with the existing magnet in your scene.

1. Click the magnet base. Change the xTran setting from its negative value to the positive value. For instance, if the xTran is –0.181, change it to +0.181. This places the base on the opposite side, in the same relative position.
2. Adjust the zRotate value from 90 degrees to –90 degrees. This flips the magnet in the other direction. Your magnet should now look like the one shown in Figure 8.8.
3. But wait a minute. Look at his poor right cheek. It's now concave. That's because the magnet and the base were moved, but the zone remained in place. You have to change the magnet zone so that it flips the other way and Ryan's right cheek returns to normal. Click the magnet zone to select it as the current object.

FIGURE 8.8 Ryan has turned the other cheek, with the magnet having been rotated to the other side of his face.

4. To rotate the magnet in the opposite direction, and change the zRotate value from –6 to 6 degrees, once again changing the negative value to a positive value. The ellipse rotates in the opposite direction.
5. Change the xTran value from –0.162 to 0.162 (changing the negative number to a positive number).
6. Now click the magnet. Change the xTran value from –0.212 to 0.212. Your magnet should now be a mirror opposite of the one you created for the right cheek.
7. Using the steps as described in Tutorial 8.2, save the magnet to the library as Ryan_LeftCheek.
8. Finally, add the Ryan_RightCheek magnet to the scene, and you have a new, cheeky look for your character (see Figure 8.9).

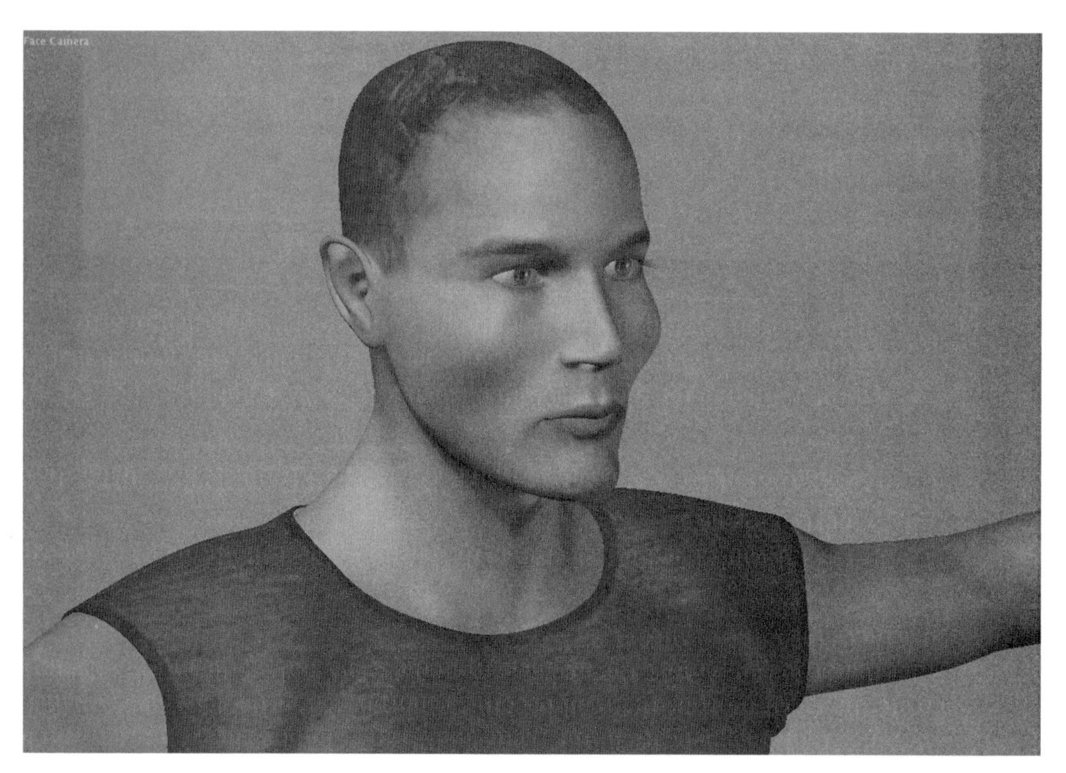

FIGURE 8.9 Ryan with his new set of cheeks. I'm not sure this will make any issue of *Plastic Surgery Successes Monthly*, though.

TUTORIAL 8.4 SPAWNING MORPH TARGETS

After you change the shape of a body part with a magnet, you have to "spawn" a morph target. Basically, spawning is a process that takes the shape of the magnetized part and turns it into a morph dial. Afterward, you can delete the magnet or magnets, and set the morph dial to 1 to achieve the same shape as created by the magnets.

Since both magnets are in the scene and Ryan's chubby cheeks are set, you'll create the facial morphs that will become a morph dial in the Parameters panel. After that, you can remove the magnets from the scene and set the morph dial to 1 to achieve the same results.

1. Click Ryan's head to select it as the current object. Both magnets appear next to the face.
2. Choose Object > Spawn Morph Target. The Morph Name dialog box appears.
3. Enter a name for the morph dial (such as Cheeks_Chubby). Click OK to save the morph to the Parameters panel. You should see the morph dial in the Morph section of your Parameters panel, as shown in Figure 8.10.

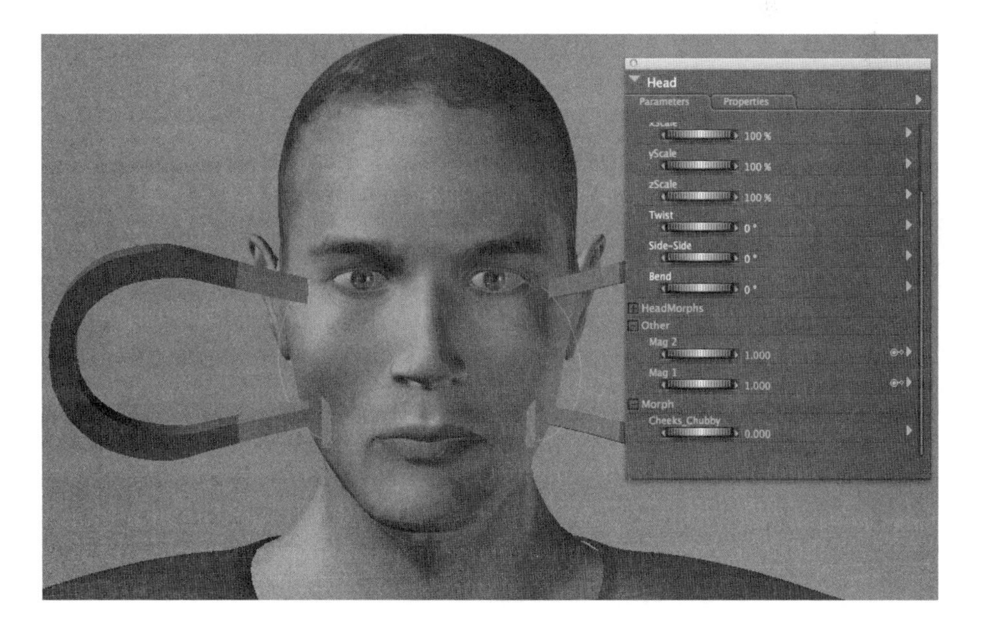

FIGURE 8.10 The Cheeks_Chubby morph dial was spawned into the Parameters panel.

4. Click one of the magnets, and press the Delete key to delete it. Click OK to confirm that you want to delete the magnet.
5. Click the head to make the second magnet visible, and then click the second magnet to select it. Press the Delete key, and then choose OK to confirm that you want to delete the magnet.
6. Click the head to select it as the current object. Then set the dial for your new morph target to 1. You should see the head morph, as shown in Figure 8.11.

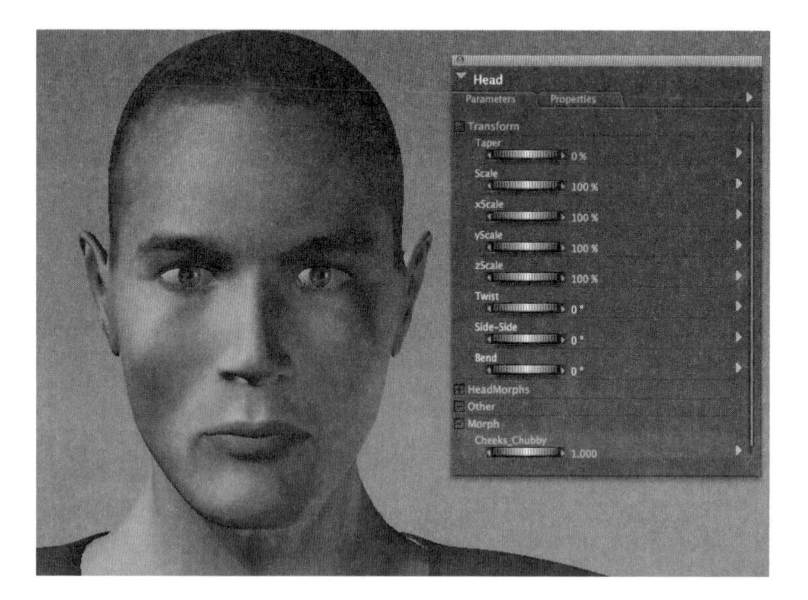

FIGURE 8.11 The morph dial now controls Ryan's cheeks.

7. The problem you have at this point is that the dials can be dialed up to extremely high numbers and can completely mess up Ryan's handsome face. You can control just how strong the morph can be, both positively and negatively, by setting limits. To do that, click on the arrow to the right of the Morph dial (see Figure 8.12). In the resulting pop-up menu, select Settings.

FIGURE 8.12 The arrow shown here will give you access to various options that will control how your morphs react.

8. Figure 8.13 shows the Edit Parameter Dial dialog. Set the Min Limit to 0, which will restrict the morph from going below 0, and set the Max Limit to 1.000000, which will keep you from taking the morph higher than 1.

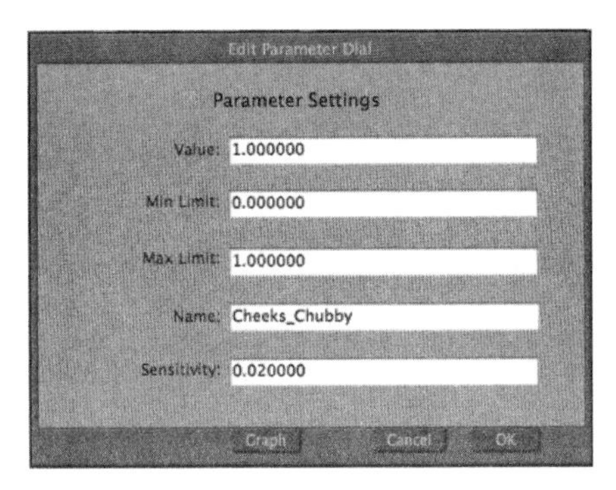

FIGURE 8.13 Limits have been set so you can't overdo a morph.

9. Taking this one step further, click on the right arrow again and select Split Morph. You'll get a warning message that this will split the morph into left and right channels, which is what you want. After clicking OK, you will have two more morph channels: Cheeks_Chubby_r and Cheeks_Chubby_l. Now you can control each cheek separately. Once again, though, you will have to set limits for the morphs, or else you could get something that looks like Figure 8.14.

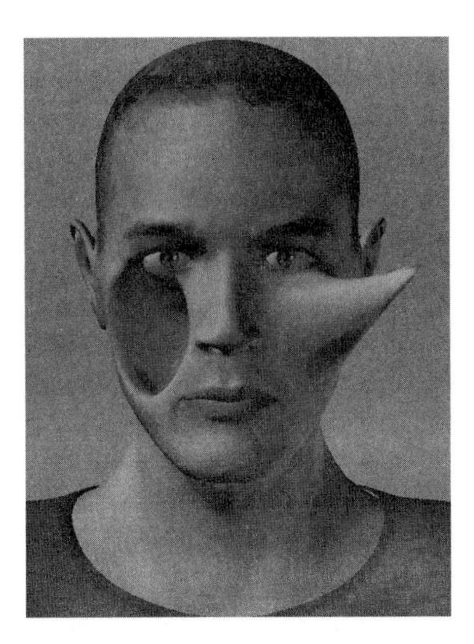

FIGURE 8.14 Without limits, you can really mess up poor Ryan's features.

With the limits set, you can now save your figure and the file for later use. I overwrote the original Ryan_Casual file, replacing it with this one. That way, my morphs will appear the next time I load him and work with his head.

By overwriting the file, you would completely replace the original. If you think you would ever want to use the non-modified original model, save the one you modify as a new model. This way you won't have to reinstall the original Poser 8 content.

TUTORIAL 8.5 CREATING THE PARTIAL BODY MORPH (PBM)

Now that you know how to create and spawn a morph that affects a particular part of the body, let's explore how to affect multiple body parts with a single magnet. For this project, you'll continue to modify Ryan (the poor guy!), giving him a pot belly. The guy's been sitting on the couch too long; that's all there is to it. Here, you will start with one body part, the abdomen, and then add more to the list of body parts that the magnet will affect.

1. Go to the Main Camera view so you can see Ryan's entire torso.
2. Click on his waist to make it the active element.
3. Choose Object > Create Magnet. Note that the magnet initially appears inside Ryan so that you cannot see it. You should, however, see Mag 1 displayed in the Parameters panel, and you'll also see a small magnet zone that surrounds the abdomen, as shown in Figure 8.15.
4. Click the magnet base to select it, or choose Mag Base 1 from the menu in the Parameters panel. Adjust the zTran value to 0.6 to bring the magnet outside of the abdomen.
5. Set the xRotate value for the magnet base to 90 degrees to rotate the magnet. Note, however, that this step is not necessary. You are only rotating the magnet base to make the stomach area a bit more visible. Rotating the magnet base also affects the orientation of the X, Y, and Z axes, so it can be confusing if you rotate the magnets too often. I will explain later when you move the magnet how the base rotation affects the orientation.
6. Right now, the magnet will only affect Ryan's waist. To add a second part, click the magnet to select it as the current object. Then select the Properties panel, and click the Add Element to Deform button. The Select Objects dialog box appears.
7. Select the hip from the Select Objects dialog and click OK. You return to the Poser document.

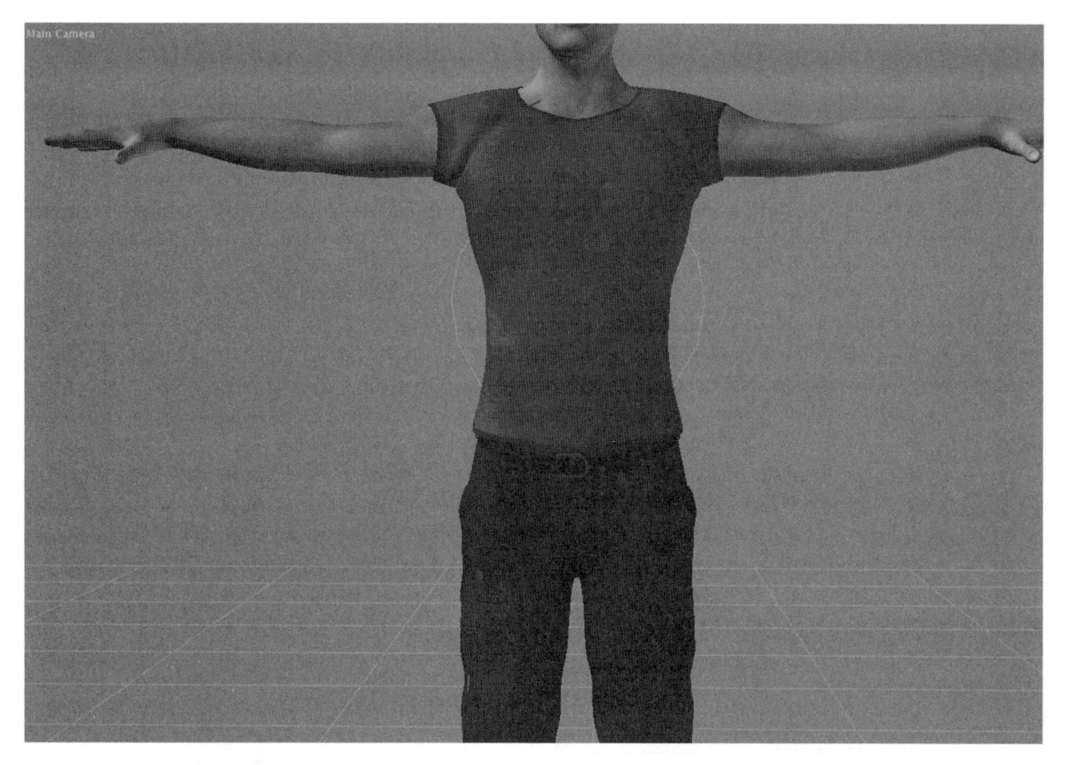

FIGURE 8.15 The magnet for the waist is embedded inside the body. All you can see to verify that the magnet has been added is the magnet zone circle.

8. Repeat Steps 6 and 7 to add the abdomen, right thigh, and right buttock, as well as the left buttock and left thigh, to the magnet. Your magnet will now control multiple body parts. Unfortunately, you cannot choose more than one part at a time in the Select Objects dialog, so you have to re-open the dialog box for each element you want to add.
9. Click the Parameters panel, and make the following changes to the magnet zone. These changes will make the magnet zone narrower, moving it forward on the z axis so that it only affects Ryan's front area:
   - Scale: 11%
   - xScale: 109%
   - yScale: 161%
   - zScale: 70%
   - yTran: 3.734
   - zTran: 0.561

10. Now click the magnet to select it, and you'll see how it affects Ryan's belly. Change xScale to 115%, xRotate to –13, yTran to 3.233, and zTran to 0.851 to make his belly wider and make it stick out more. Also, remember when you rotated the magnet base earlier? Because of this, the yTran parameter moves the magnet forward and backward instead of up and down as it normally would. When you're done, Ryan should have a big belly, as shown in Figure 8.16.

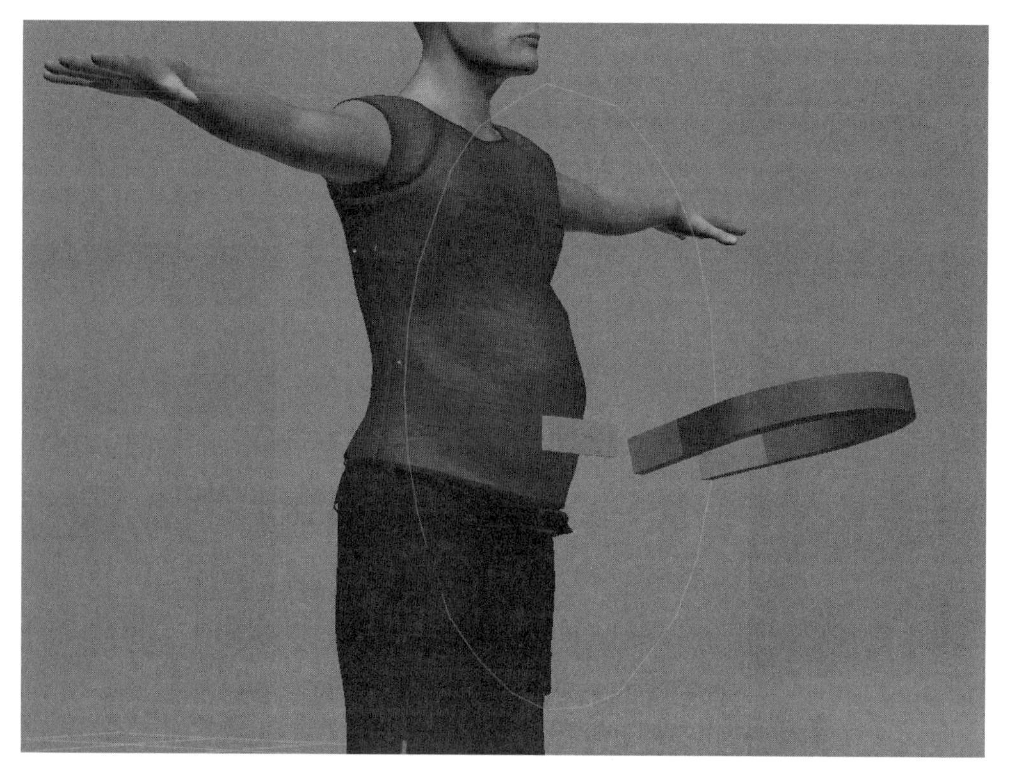

FIGURE 8.16 Here's Ryan with a good ol' jelly belly.

11. Before you delete the magnet, you have to spawn morphs for each of the body parts affected by the magnet. On the Ryan model itself, select each of those parts in turn. Choose Object > Spawn Morph Target. Name the morph target for each of the body parts as PBMBigBelly. The prefix PBM (which stands for partial body morph) reminds you that it is one of several partial body morphs that are to be combined into a final shape.
12. Save your magnet to the library, if desired, as described in Tutorial 8.2. Then delete the magnet. Your morphs are complete.

At this point, I would go through each of the PBMs you just made and set minimum and maximum limits. You can, of course, set the minimum limit to a negative number (–1.000000) if you want.

TUTORIAL 8.6 CREATING THE FULL BODY MORPH (FBM)

PBMs are great. Their one problem, though, is having to change the values of various body parts to create the particular look you want. This can be a little tedious. What about making a morph that affects all those body parts at one time? Now that would be a time saver! That's what you'll do now. You will create a full body morph (FBM) from the PBMs you made in Tutorial 8.5. Life is good.

1. Continuing from the previous tutorials, click Ryan Casual's abdomen and set the PBMBigBelly morph dial to 1.
2. Repeat Step 1 for the other body parts that are part of the PBMs. Ryan should now look like what's shown in Figure 8.17.

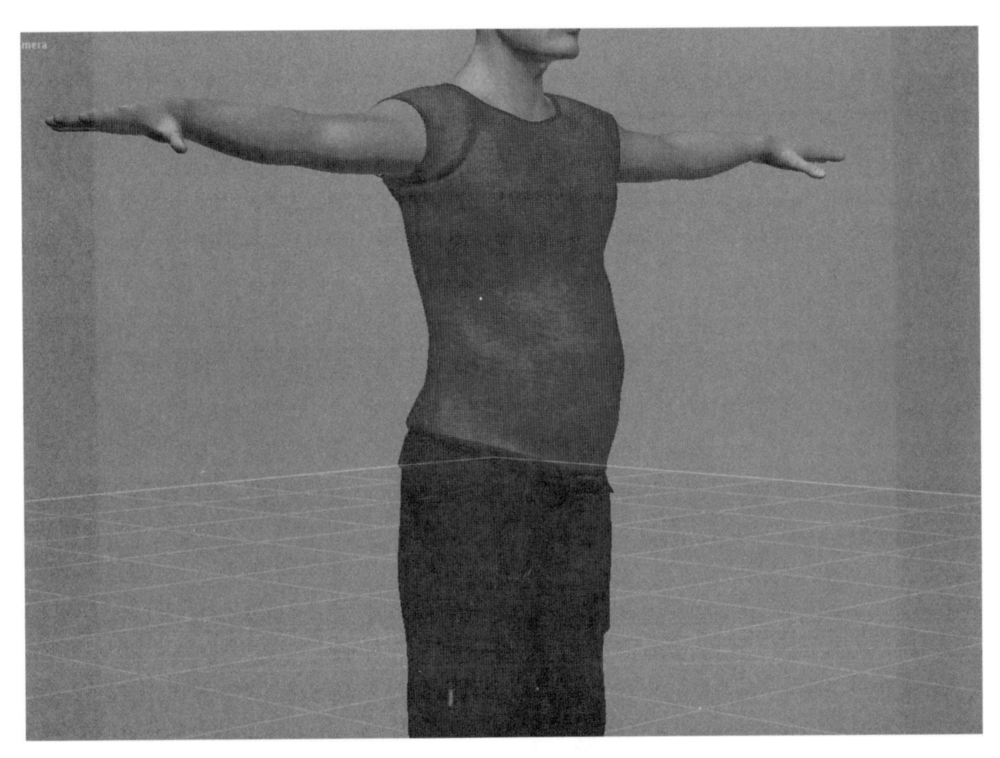

FIGURE 8.17 Ryan's belly is ready for an FBM (which not only stands for a full body morph but also a full body makeover!)

3. Before you create your full body morph, make sure that there are no other morphs that are dialed in anywhere else on your figure, other than the ones you want to include in the full body morph. For example, if you are creating a full body morph to make a big belly and only a big belly, make sure that you don't have any extra muscles dialed in anywhere else on the chest, arms, or legs. Otherwise, every time you use your big belly morph, you'll also get muscles thrown in to the mix.

You can also zero out the figure by using the Wardrobe Wizard. When you open the wizard's controls, click the Utilities button, then Morphs > Zero All Morphs. Once you have created the FBMs, you can use the Wardrobe Wizard to once again set the dials back to 0. This can save a lot of time compared to checking all the different morph dials.

4. Choose Figure > Create Full Body Morph. The Morph Name dialog box appears.
5. Enter BigBelly for the morph name, and choose OK.
6. Now, go through each of the individual body parts to set all PBMBigBelly morphs to zero (0). Ryan Casual should return to his default shape.
7. Now, with Ryan Casual selected, choose Body from the Current Actor selection menu in the Parameters panel.
8. You should see your BigBelly full body morph in the section named Other. When you dial this morph to 1, you'll see all of the individual body parts morph together at the same time to create your big belly, as shown in Figure 8.18. Your full body morph is now complete.
9. You might also want to set the limits to –1.000000 and 1.000000.
10. Locate the Figures Library into which you want to save your morphed figure. Click the Add to Library button to add your new morphed character to the library, assigning a name of your choosing.

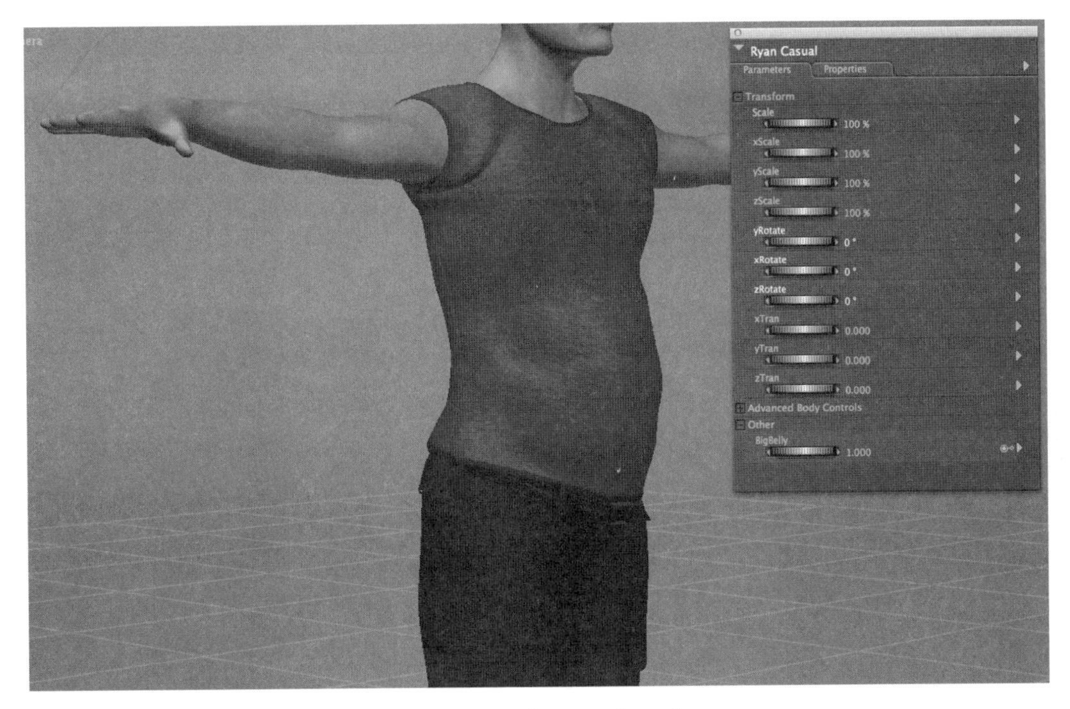

FIGURE 8.18 The FBM in action.

THE MORPHING TOOLS

When you activate the Morphing Tool (click the Morphing Tool button in the Editing Tools, as shown in Figure 8.19), a new panel will appear.

This Morphing Tool panel is divided into two tabs, Create and Combine. The Create tab, shown in Figure 8.20, contains tools that allow you to push, pull, smooth, or restore vertices to their original positions. In other words, you can create your own custom morphs by moving vertices and polygons around with a tool that is similar to a paintbrush.

There are five sections in the Create tab. The controls in these sections serve the following functions:

- **Push, Pull, Smooth, and Restore:** Select one of these options to determine how the Morphing Tool will affect your geometry. Push moves the vertices inward (like a dimple) toward the direction that you push the tool. Pull moves the vertices outward (like a bump) toward the direction that you pull. Smooth evens out the irregularities in the morph, creating softer transitions between high and low areas. Restore gradually removes the morph in the areas that you use the tool.

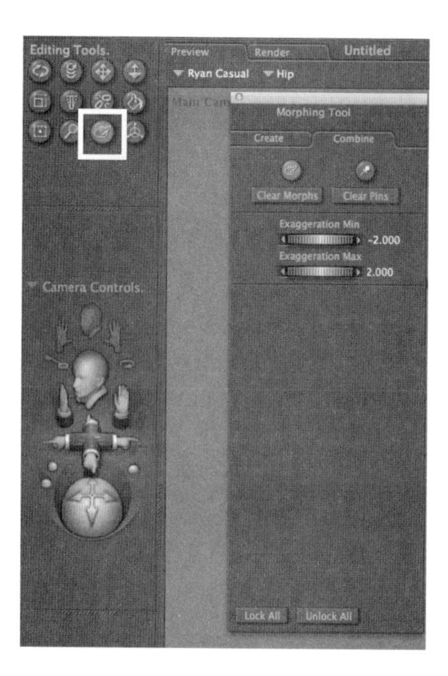

FIGURE 8.19 Clicking on the Morphing Tool opens the Morphing Tool panel.

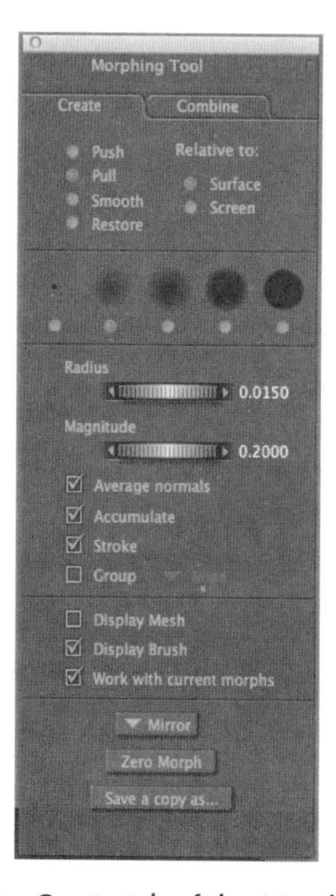

FIGURE 8.20 The Create tab of the Morphing Tool panel.

- **Relative To:** Select one of these options to determine the point of reference that relates to the changes in the morph. Choose Surface (the default) to create changes based on the direction at which the surface normals of the polygons are facing. Choose Screen to move the vertices toward the current view relative to the screen.
- **Brush styles:** The five brush shape icons display how the Morphing Tool will affect the area that you morph. Choose the first option button to move one vertex at a time. The remaining options affect the area that you define by the radius setting, but each option has a different falloff rate. The second brush shape affects the vertices in the middle of the brush but gradually falls off to having no effect in the outer areas. Each successive brush falls off more rapidly until the last brush shape, which has no falloff at all and will affect all vertices equally.
- **Radius:** This setting defines the area that will be affected by the Morphing Tool. If you have the Display Brush feature enabled (as described later), you can see the effect of the Radius value setting and how large the affected area will be. Decrease the value to affect a smaller area, and increase the value to affect a larger area.
- **Magnitude:** This setting determines the strength of the Morphing Tool. Reduce this value to obtain finer control over the response of the brush. Higher values will create results that are more dramatic but not as easy to control.
- **Accumulate:** Check this option to make changes to the mesh for as often as a single brushstroke passes over the same polygons. Uncheck this option to make changes to the mesh when the brush passes over polygons only once.
- **Stroke:** Check this option to allow mouse movements to adjust the degree of the morph in the area on which you first clicked the brush. Uncheck this option to allow the brush to affect areas outside the initial area you clicked upon. This latter option allows you to paint morphs on your geometry very freely.
- **Group:** Check this option to specify the groups the Morphing Tool will affect. Enable this option to display a list of all polygon groups that exist for the current actor, and then select a group to work on.
- **Display Mesh:** Check this option to display the wireframe mesh as a guide while you create your morphs.
- **Display Brush:** By default, Poser displays the area that the Morphing Tool will affect as a multicolored circular area, with the red part of the circle having the most effect and the green area of the circle having the least effect. An example is shown in Figure 8.21. If you find the display distracting, check this option to hide it while you work on your morphs.
- **Work with Current Morphs:** Check this option if you want to create a morph that works in combination with other morph settings. Set the existing morphs as desired, and then use the Morphing Tool to customize the morphs further.

When you set the previous morphs back to zero, you will then see only the custom morph that you created yourself. If you want to create a totally original morph, leave this option unchecked and use a combination of magnets and the Morphing Tool to create your morphs.

- **Mirror:** Select an option from the Mirror menu to mirror the effects of a morph on one side of a group to the opposite side. Note that this option does not affect multiple groups; the affects of the morph are only mirrored in the current group you are working on. The +x to –x option mirrors morphs on the left side to the right side. The –x to +x option mirrors morphs on the right side to the left side. The +y to –y option mirrors morphs on the top side to the bottom side. The –y to +y option mirrors morphs on the bottom side to the top side. The +z to –z option mirrors morphs on the front side to the back side. The –z to +z option mirrors morphs on the back side to the front side.
- **Zero Morph:** Click this button to remove all changes made by the Morphing Tool in the current group.

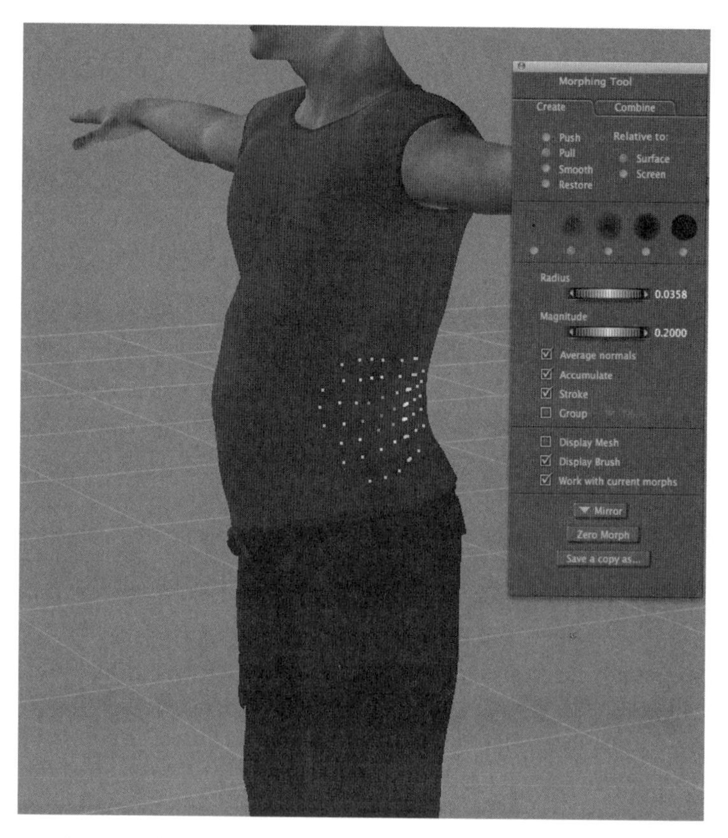

FIGURE 8.21 The area that will be affected is displayed as multicolored dots by default.

- **Save a Copy As:** Click this button to save a copy of the morph under a name of your choosing. A dialog box prompts you to enter a name for the morph. The new morph dial appears in the Parameters panel when you select the body part from which the morph was created. Note that if you created the morph with the Work with Current Morphs box selected, the morph saved with this option will only include the changes that you made with the Morphing Tool. If you want to combine morphs made with magnets along with morphs made with the Morphing Tool, choose Object > Spawn Morph Target instead.

Tutorial 8.7 Creating Face Morphs

One of the first things you can do with the new Morphing Tool is enhance existing or create new face morphs to build totally original characters. The morph brush helps you push or pull vertices around to reshape the features of your character. In this tutorial, you'll learn how you can define a few facial morphs and add new morph dials for the face. This example will use Ryan again, but you can use any figure you would like.

1. Once you have loaded the character, switch to the Face Camera.
2. Activate the Morphing Tool if it isn't still active and make sure you have the Create tab selected.
3. In the Morphing Tool panel, choose Pull, Relative To Surface, and select the second brush shape option. These are actually the default settings, so unless you changed the controls while reading the last section, the defaults should already be selected.
4. Verify that the Display Brush option is selected, and adjust the Radius value until you get a brush size that is appropriate to morph Ryan's cheek. I am using a setting of 0.0122 in this example.

When you place your cursor over a part of the model, you can move to the controls while still seeing the area you are affecting. This way, you can change brush sizes and interactively see the area of the model that will be affected.

5. Adjust the Magnitude setting until the brush responds to your liking. Too high of a value makes the morph brush work too easily. Lower values give you finer control of the brush effect. Test the setting by making adjustments to the face with the Morphing Tool, and click the Zero Morph button to restore the face to its original shape before you continue finding a setting you like. In this example, I used a setting of 0.174.

6. Uncheck the Accumulate option, and check the Stroke option. This allows you to work anywhere on the face with the morphing brush.
7. Make some changes to the left side Ryan's face. In this example, I made changes to his cheek and into his jaw just under his lower lip to simulate a swollen area where he might have a tooth problem. You may need to use a combination of Push, Pull, Smooth, and Restore to get the shape you want. An example of the change I made is shown in Figure 8.22.
8. Fortunately, there is an easy way to make the morph symmetrical on the other side of the face. You can use the Mirror feature to create an identical morph on the right side of Ryan's face (see Figure 8.23). To do so, click the Mirror button in the lower section of the Morphing Tool. Because you want to mirror the left side (+x) to the right side (–x), choose the +x to –x option.

You can mirror a morph on the right side of the face to the left side of the face. But the left and right sides of the morph must be contained in the same group that you are currently working on. However, if you create a morph for the left collar and want to mirror it to the right collar, you'll have to first use the Group Editor to create a group that includes both of those parts. Morph one side of the group, and then mirror the morph to the other side.

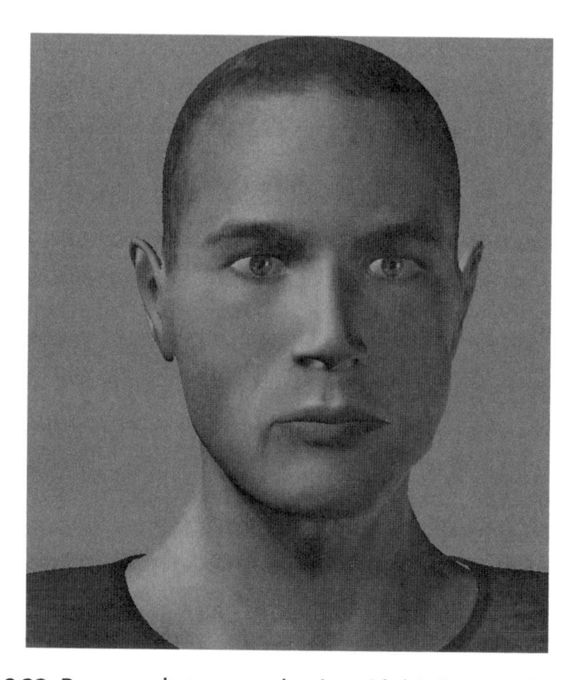

FIGURE 8.22 Ryan needs to see a dentist with his face swollen like this.

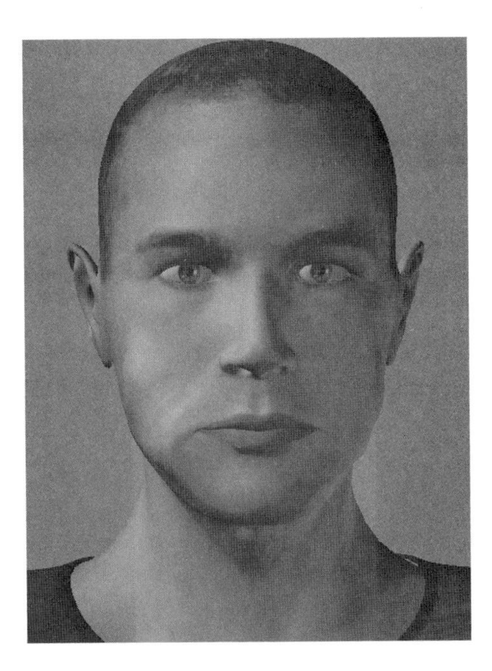

FIGURE 8.23 Now Ryan is looking a bit like Marlon Brando in *The Godfather*, thanks to the Mirror feature.

Another option for mirroring morphs is to purchase Poser Tool Box from www.philc.net. This reasonably priced, very ingenious set of Python scripts includes many utilities that enhance the use of Poser. Among them is a Mirror Morph script that will mirror morphs from one side of a figure to another.

9. Finally, after you complete your original morph, click the Save a Copy As button at the bottom of the Morphing Tool. Poser will prompt you to add a name for your new morph in the same manner you have in all the previous tutorials.
10. If you want to continue making unique morphs, click the Zero Morph button in the Morphing Tool to start from an unmorphed head. You can continue making as many morphs as you like in this manner.
11. After you complete your morphing session, don't forget to save your new character to the Figures Library. Simply navigate to the library of your choice, and click the Add to Library button at the bottom of the Library panel. Poser will prompt you to enter a name for your new figure, and then you should see a thumbnail appear in the Figures Library.

TUTORIAL 8.8 FIXING POKE-THROUGHS

Another handy use for the new morphing features is to help eliminate poke-throughs in clothing when you pose your figure. Figure 8.24 shows an arm muscle that is poking through a sleeve. The Morphing Tool is much easier and quicker to use than magnets for fixing these types of problems. You'll also find the tool to be a very effective solution for fitting clothing to body shapes that are different from the default body shape.

FIGURE 8.24 Diego's upper arm is poking through the sleeve of his jacket.

The following steps work really well when you are trying to adjust poke-through in clothing:

1. Add your figure and clothing to your scene, and conform the clothing to the figure. In this case, I used the Diego character, which is located in the Figures\Poser 8\Ryan folder. (He's a variation of the Ryan character.) The clothing is located in the Props\Poser 8\Ryan\P6 James WW Conversion folder. The pose I'm using can be found in the Poses\Poser 8\Ryan\Standing folder.

Even though you selected the Diego character, you will see Ryan as the name in the figure's list. That's because Diego was built from the Ryan character, and the name was not changed. You can change it by selecting the body, open the Properties panel, click on the model's name to activate the text field, and type in the new name. After that, the new name will appear in the figures list.

2. Examine the figure for poke-through issues. In the example shown in Figure 8.24, you see the arm poking through his right sleeve.

As you learned in Chapter 7, Poser 8 figures have Magnet deformers just as the Victoria 4 model clothing models do. These deformers can be found in the Poses\Poser 8\Ryan or Alyson\Specialty folder.

3. Before you open the Morphing Tool, click the offending body part that is poking through the clothing. In this case, click Diego's right shoulder.
4. Choose Figure > Lock Figure. This prevents accidental morphing of Diego's body while you work on the clothing morph.
5. Now, click the Morphing Tool icon to open the Morphing Tool.
6. Make sure that you have Pull selected as the morphing mode. Select the type of brush you want to use, and adjust the Radius and Magnitude values of the tool to get the results you desire.
7. Check Accumulate and Stroke so that you can build up the morph as you work.
8. Start the stroke on a section of the shirt where the arm is not poking through the sleeve, and then work your way in toward the area that is poking through. You will eventually "brush away" the poke-through of the arm as you pull the sleeve out over the arm. Figure 8.25 shows the result of this procedure.

FIGURE 8.25 The fixed sleeve after the morph has been applied.

Distributing Morphs

Morphs can be distributed in a number of different ways, and the method you use depends on the user's license of the figure that you created the morphs for. Remember, these models are copyrighted, and you can't just give them out to anyone. You need to read through the End User License Agreements (EULAs) and all pertinent information that comes with the models to know what you can and cannot do when considering distribution of original morphs.

Here are some other considerations you need to take into account when distributing your morph sets:

- By default, Poser saves morph data for objects as external binary morph files. These files have a PMD extension and are saved in the same library as the original character file. The only drawback to this option is that PMD files are compatible only with Poser 6, 7, and 8. If you want to create morphs that are compatible with earlier versions of Poser, you should disable this feature so that Poser saves the morph data within the CR2 file. To do so, choose Edit > General Preferences (on the Mac choose Poser > Preferences), and click the Misc tab. Uncheck the Use External Binary Morph Targets box, as shown in Figure 8.26.

Many models have copyright restrictions on the CR2 files, meaning you cannot redistribute the CR2s without the permission of the copyright holder. This includes DAZ3D content as well. If you are hoping to sell your modifications, you will need to set up INJ/REM files and distribute those.

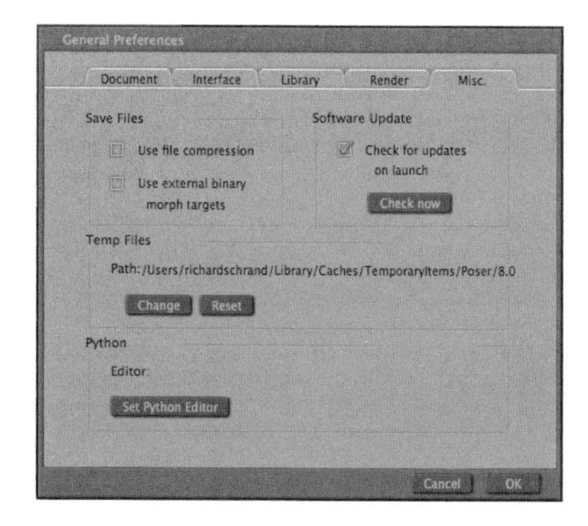

FIGURE 8.26 Uncheck the Use External Binary Morph Targets box to create morphs for earlier versions of Poser.

- If you want to distribute morphs with your own original clothing, you can save the morph data within the CR2 library file. To do this, make sure you uncheck the Use External Binary Morph Targets box and also that you do not use file compression when saving your files to the library. Your morphs will be saved, along with the clothing, in an editable CR2 file.
- Many characters (most notably the DAZ3D Unimesh figures, such as Michael 4 and Victoria 4, Aiko 4, The Girl 4, and so on) are furnished with separate face and body morphs. The base character file has morph channels within it that are ready to accept "injected" morphs. The morph data is furnished separately, and library files are included in the Pose Library to inject or remove the morph data from the model. Utilities such as Injection Magic and Injection Pose Builder are available at DAZ3D to help you prepare injection morphs such as these.

There are also some tutorials available at DAZ3D's Tutorial Arcana (www.daz3d.com/support/tutorial/index.php?cat=6) regarding creating injection morphs by hand or with the previously mentioned utilities.

Avoiding Problems

Many things can go wrong when you create morphs. For example, the software you use to create the morphs might place the vertices in a different order when you save the geometry. Or you can accidentally move the geometry, and when you apply it to your figure, the geometry might fly off in a different direction than you intended. To avoid these problems, here are a few things to keep in mind:

- Don't move the position of the figure after you import it into your modeling program. For example, if the figure comes into your modeling program with its feet above or below ground level, don't translate the position. It will affect the ending position of your morphs.
- Many modeling programs cannot handle the extremely small scale used in Poser, If you are using a program such as Maya, Cinema 4D, 3D Studio Max, Carrera, or Hexagon, go into the Preferences of both Poser and your modeler and set the scale to the same units (feet, inches, miles, and so on). If that doesn't work as you expect, you'll need utilities to scale the figures up for morphing, and then scale the figure back down by the equivalent amount for importing into Poser. Because procedures vary from 3D program to 3D program, it's a good idea to touch base with others who use the same modeling software that you use. Chances are, they have figured out the best approaches for your software and can help you through the process.
- When using an external program for morphing, don't make any changes to the construction of the geometry—that is, don't weld vertices, don't add or remove vertices, and don't subdivide any vertices. Doing so will make your morphs incompatible with the original figure.
- When you try to import a morph target into Poser, you might get a message that says, "Target geometry has wrong number of vertices." First check to make sure you have selected the right body part to add the morph to. Then make sure that the morph target you are importing was created for that body part. If the body parts are the same, you may have inadvertently added or removed vertices during the process of creating the morph. One way to verify this is to open the morphed version in UVMapper Professional and compare the number of vertices in the original with those in the morphed part.

- Sometimes the morph target appears to apply itself correctly. But when you dial the morph in, the body part looks all wrinkled and jumbled. This is because your morphing software reordered the vertices. If this happens, delete the morph from the Parameters panel. Then when you re-import the morph, check the Attempt Vertex Order Correction box in the Load Morph Target dialog box. This may resolve the problem. If it doesn't, UVMapper Professional also has the capability to re-order vertices, and you may be able to fix the morph that way.

A Short Re-Pose

So there you have it. A run-through of the morphing procedures—from creating and saving morphs and magnets to using morphs to fix those frustrating poke-throughs. What wasn't discussed was the way in which you can use magnets in animations to simulate all kinds of things, including some alien entity crawling under the characters skin. But, from what was covered in this chapter, you're ready to begin modifying your characters with original morphs of your own design. As you get better at it, you should think about offering them for free and, eventually, for a price on the various websites that cater to the Poser user, like Renderosity.com, RuntimeDNA.com, PoserAddicts.com, and others.

9 Creating Your Own Textures

In This Chapter:

- Textures and Copyrights
- Creating Clothing Textures
- Tutorial 9.1: Making a Reflection Map in Photoshop
- Tutorial 9.2: Creating a Realistic Tattoo
- Tutorial 9.3: Adding Personality to Skin Textures

"The true worth of a man is not to be found in man himself, but in the colours and textures that come alive in others."

—Albert Schweitzer

You have spent time in both the Simple and Advanced views of the Material Room (way, way back in Chapter 4) in order to combine several type of image maps. There are hundreds upon hundreds of textures available for free or for sale to enhance the models in your collection. But even with all that, you will more than likely have a vision for a particular look that just isn't available through online communities. This means you have to create that texture yourself. It's not as scary as it might sound. You can build upon the existing textures in your library, adding elements that bring your vision to life. In the case of DAZ3D's Victoria or Michael 4, there are Merchant Resource Kits for sale that give you the layered base textures you can use as an underpinning for the final texture you want to build. No matter how you build the textures, though, if you are using an existing texture as you base, there are some legal issues you must be aware of.

Textures and Copyrights

Because Poser content is distributed digitally, it is all too easy to reuse elements created by others in your own projects. If you purchase the content, you have the right to modify it for your own use. For example, if you purchase a clothing texture but want to change the color or add some extra detail to it yourself, you can use your customized version for your own renders. When you distribute all or part of it (either for free or for sale), you are entering the danger zone. Several scandals have been brought to the attention of the online Poser community. In some cases, the scandals could have been avoided with a better understanding of copyright laws and ethical standards. Ignorance of these laws does not serve as an excuse.

Copyrights are, literally, the right to copy something. The original creator of the object or the material is usually the holder of the copyright, unless ownership was transferred legally by contract or other written permission. Basically, if you don't own the copyright for something, you can't use or redistribute it, in whole or in part, unless you obtain permission from the person or persons who hold the copyright.

The safest and best rule of thumb is, if you didn't make it yourself, don't use it without permission from the original copyright holder. If there is any reason to question who the original copyright holder is, the rule of thumb is, when in doubt, leave it out. This means that you cannot copy the hand of one model onto another, edit the underlying mesh or geometry of a model, or take someone's texture map file and change some colors on it, and then redistribute any of it without explicit permission from each of the original copyright holders. Here are some resources you can use to learn more about copyright law:

- www.copyright.gov/
- www.chillingeffects.org/
- http://darkwing.uoregon.edu/~csundt/copyweb/#Useful

In addition, the Copyright Laws and Ethical Standards forum at Renderosity.com addresses specific questions that Poser content creators have regarding copyright and ethical issues. Free membership is required to access the forums. Once there, point your browser to www.renderosity.com/mod/forumpro/showforum.php?forum_id=12395.

When you reach the point of wanting to build your own image maps, you need to make sure you have the right tools. This might sound like a no-brainer comment, but the right tools often mean getting a higher-end type of program to work in. Adobe Photoshop, as well as Corel's Paint Shop Pro, Painter, and Draw are a few.

There is also GIMP, a free alternative that is available for both the PC and Mac. There are others, but these are some of the most popular. The main thing when building textures is to have a program that works with layers and to save that layered file before saving the flattened image that is used in Poser.

A layered file serves a couple of purposes. First, if you want to make any changes to color or position, you can do it quickly and easily without having to start from scratch. Second, and maybe most important, that layered file serves as proof that a texture is yours in case someone disputes ownership at a later time. In addition, all files have a creation date and time embedded in them. In this day and age, protecting yourself should be a top priority.

MAP TYPES

The type of maps you create will match the input nodes you worked with in Chapter 4 and can all be added using an input node in the Advanced view of the Material Room. These maps are shown in Figures 9.1 and 9.2.

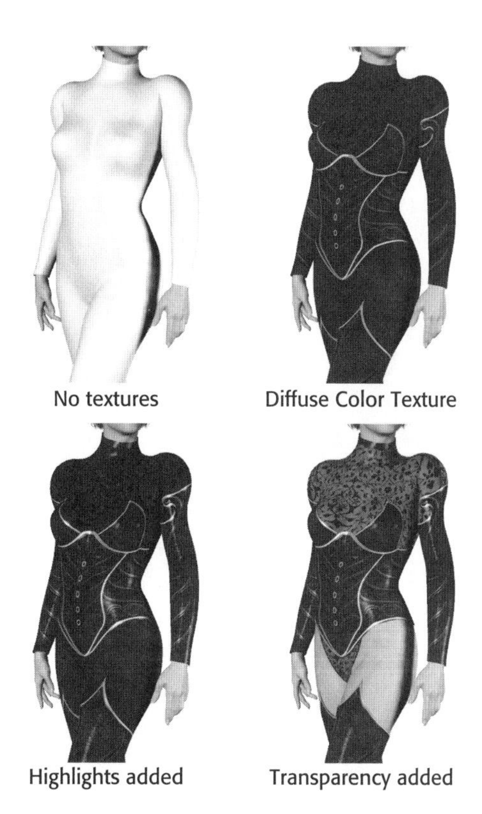

FIGURE 9.1 The effect of the various image map channels when assigned to a model.

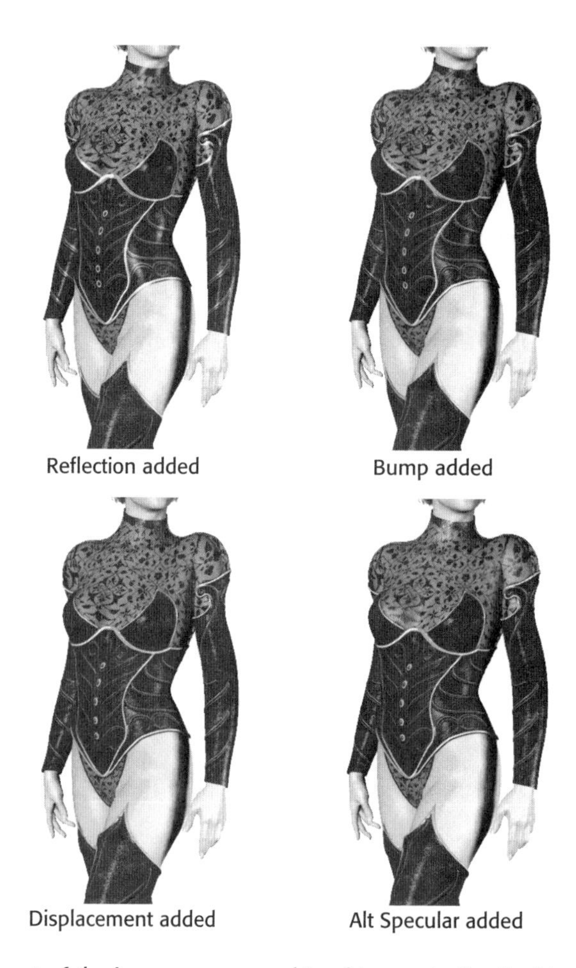

FIGURE 9.2 The rest of the image maps combined to create the final look for the outfit.

The images used in this section of the chapter are from Ana Winson's The Bootie texture created for Victoria 3. Ana is known as Arien on many of the Poser discussion boards.

- **Diffuse:** The map that will define the color(s) on the figure.
- **Specular**: Controls the shininess of the material and controlling highlights.
- **Transparency**: Creates transparent and semi-transparent areas on the object.
- **Reflection**: As it states, it adds a reflection to the surface of the object. Using an image map to create a reflection will cut down on render time.

- **Bump**: Creates the illusion of high and low points on an object.
- **Displacement:** The same as the bump map, only this warps the mesh, actually creating high and low points on the object.

The Alt Specular map shown in Figure 9.2 is an addition that enhances the specularity in the lacy area of the garment. This is a more specialized map and is not used for every texture.

Poser uses pre-defined UV texture templates. You'll learn how to create your own UV maps in Chapter 11. In this chapter, you'll draw on UV templates that come with the models.

Texture Considerations

There are some basic considerations when creating any texture, whether it's a skin texture or for clothing.

- **Repeating patterns:** Most textures consist of some sort of repeating pattern. That pattern can be seamless (such as plaids or stripes, or the actual material, such as burlap or denim) or chaotic, such as pores on the skin.
- **Shadows and highlights:** In most cases, you should leave shadows or highlights off of the diffuse map. The lighting in the scene will add those for you. By trying to paint these elements onto your diffuse map, you will often create competing shadows and highlights that ruin your work.
- **Height and depth:** These relate to shadows and highlights. If you're going with a bump map only, then adding some shadows and highlights to show height in areas such as buttons will be necessary. If on the other hand, you are using a displacement map, the scene's lighting will take care of all highlights and shadows in your image.
- **Scaling:** In some ways, this is a no-brainer. If patterns are too large, you've lost your semblance of reality. If too small, you've made something that loses its details due to miniaturization.
- **Resolution:** Unlike print where your document needs to be 300dpi, the resolution of an image map is 72dpi. However, the resolution is based upon the width and height of the file. A high-resolution image is commonly between 2,500 × 2,500 pixels and 4,000 × 4,000 pixels.

Creating Clothing Textures

Now let's look at how Ana Winson created The Bootie texture for Victoria 3. This section will feature Adobe Photoshop, since creating textures based on the model's template(s) has to be done in an image editing program.

First, Ana created a template for The Bootie, measuring 2500 by 2500 pixels. Higher resolution templates allow you to create detailed textures that can later be downsized if necessary.

Working in Photoshop, a layer of white fill is placed above the template layer and turned off while developing the textures. After the textures are done, the white fill layer can be turned on to cover the template and provide the background for the texture.

Next, a new layer is created, in which all areas of the clothing are filled with a dark gray solid color with a slight bit of noise. This serves as a base for the clothing texture. The solid color extends slightly beyond the borders of the clothing to avoid the possibility of seams showing up at render time. After scanning some lace and cleaning up transparent areas, a layer of black lace is placed above the gray fill. The lace layer is then duplicated and a slight bevel is added to give the lace some extra highlights and dimension.

Four layers of dark gray seams are added above the lace to place seams around the collar, panties, and arm lace. Finally, another layer adds a lighter, varied shade of gray leather over portions of the arms. Figure 9.3 shows the progress so far.

Similar details are added to the corset and legs. First, two layers add leather to the corset area and bust, allowing the bust covers to be shown or hidden depending on the look desired for the outfit. A central plate is added in a new layer over the center of the corset. Above that, layers of dark gray leather are added for a busk (the area of the corset that contains the clasps) and busk shadow. Graceful curves are added over the leather to provide detailed cutouts. Finally, a layer of gems and gem insets is added to give further detail to the busk at the center of the corset. Figure 9.4 shows these new layers on the corset.

Finally, additional trim and details are added to the clothing in several layers. First, a couple of adjustment layers darken the color of the leather areas on the sleeves, legs, and corset to give them a richer appearance. Additional cutouts are added to the leather on the legs and sleeves, and a beveled duplicate of the cutouts adds additional dimension. Curved lines are added to form a metallic border around the leather corset, sleeves, and legs, and then beveled to add dimension to the trim. Figure 9.5 shows these additions.

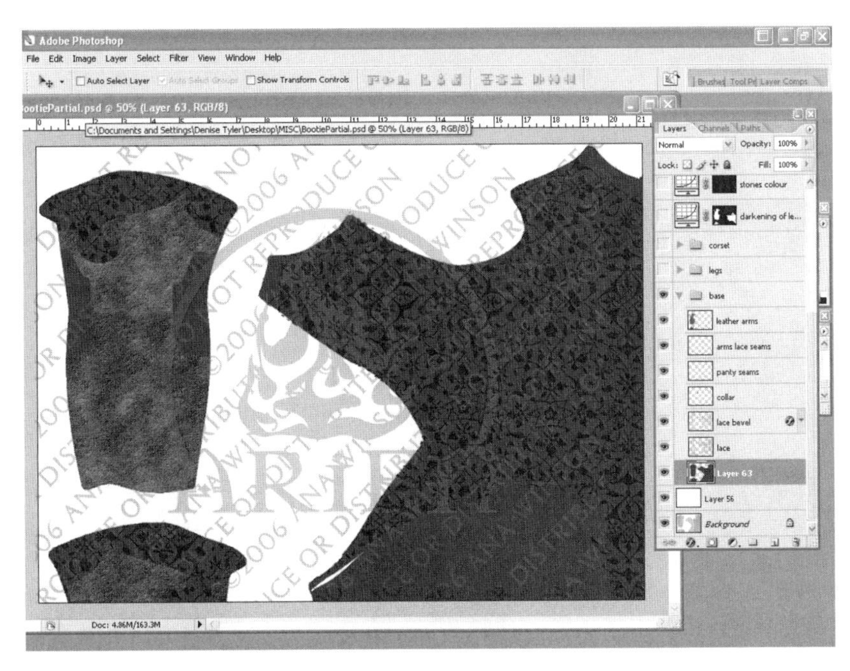

FIGURE 9.3 The Bootie texture is made up of several layers: a gray fill, two lace layers, seams on the collar, panties and arms, and leather areas on the sleeves.

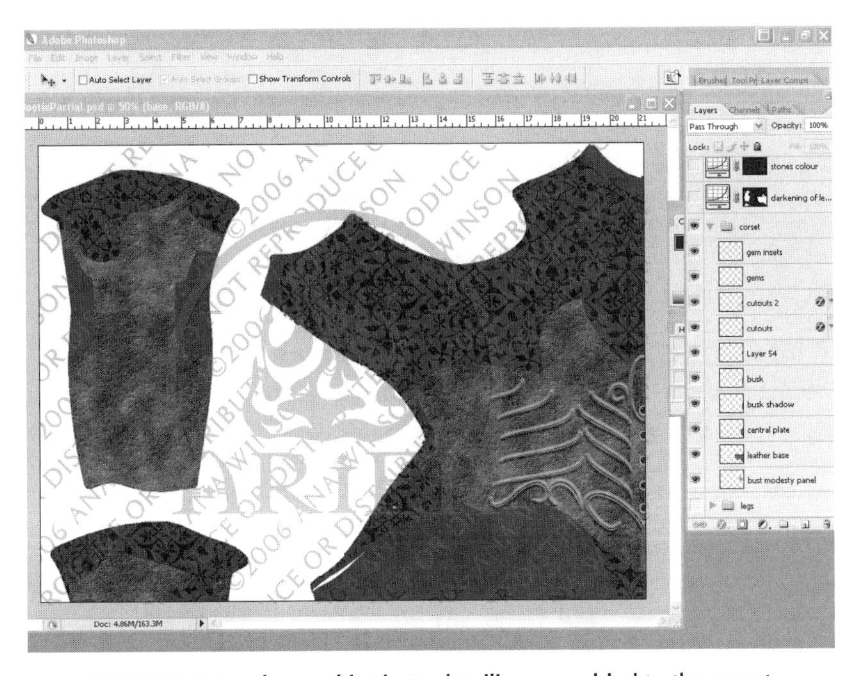

FIGURE 9.4 Leather and intricate detailing are added to the corset.

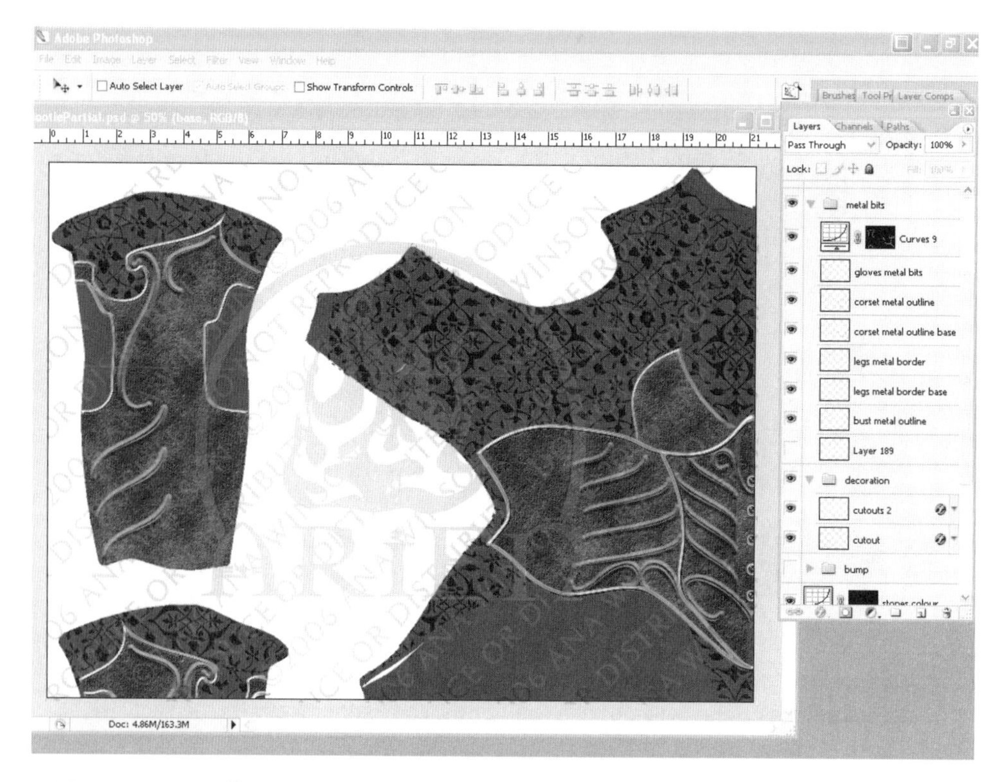

FIGURE 9.5 Metallic trim and additional details are added to the corset, sleeves and legs.

To finish the detailing on the corset, several layers are used to build up eyelets and lacing on the back of the corset. Care is taken to line up the lacing across the back seam so that the laces match up perfectly—a process that is well worth the effort. Figure 9.6 shows the detail on the lacing and eyelets.

Specular Maps

Specular maps control the color and amount of highlights in a material shader. Images that define specular color can be color or grayscale. Darker values will produce softer highlights, and lighter values will produce brighter highlights. If you are using colored specular maps, desaturated colors will produce milder highlights, whereas saturated colors create very hot highlights.

When you develop your diffuse texture in layers, you can reuse some of the layers to create additional maps for your material shader. Such is the case with the specular map that Ana created for The Bootie. Here's how she approached the specular map.

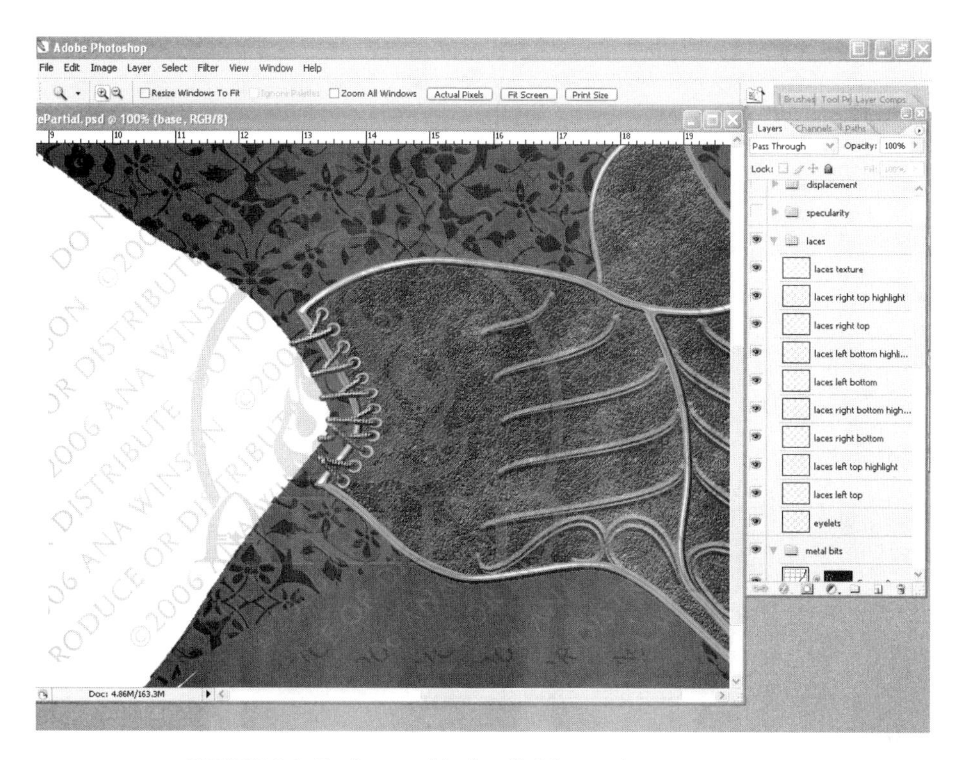

FIGURE 9.6 Eyelets and lacing finish out the texture map.

Ana starts with a black background, which represents areas that do not receive specular highlights. Next, she creates a new layer and fills all areas in the clothing that will not be transparent with solid white. By reducing the opacity of this layer to 30 percent, she is able to determine an appropriate base level for the highlights in the clothing. A new layer is created, and the leather areas on the corset, legs, and sleeves are selected and filled with a grayscale cloud pattern. Noise is added to the cloud pattern to give it a bumpy feel. Progress thus far is shown in Figure 9.7.

Next, Ana duplicates the cutouts on the arms, corset, and legs, and moves them to a new layer above the previous specular layers. She then adds bright white borders around the leather on these areas so that the metallic trim on the leather receives the most specular highlights. An adjustment layer then brightens the underlying layers a bit. Figure 9.8 shows the progress to this point.

A new layer is added, and white highlights are hand painted in areas of the corset, arm, and leg leather. A band of light gray is added around the neck so that it receives more highlights than the lace. Finally, to complete the specular map, the eyelets are lightened to receive more highlights, and the laces are darkened to receive little to no highlights. The finished specular map is shown in Figure 9.9.

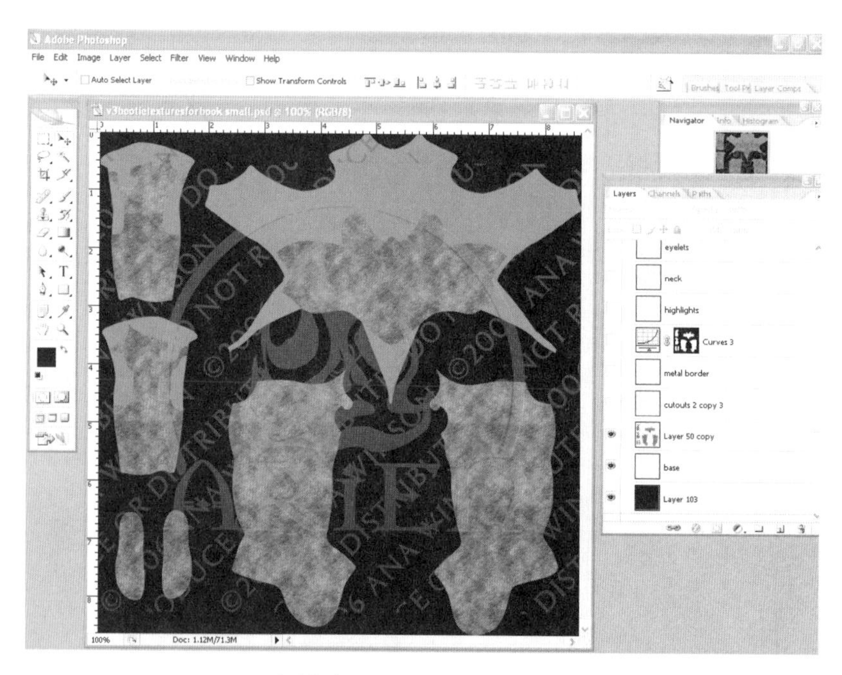

FIGURE 9.7 Highlights are created using shades of gray.

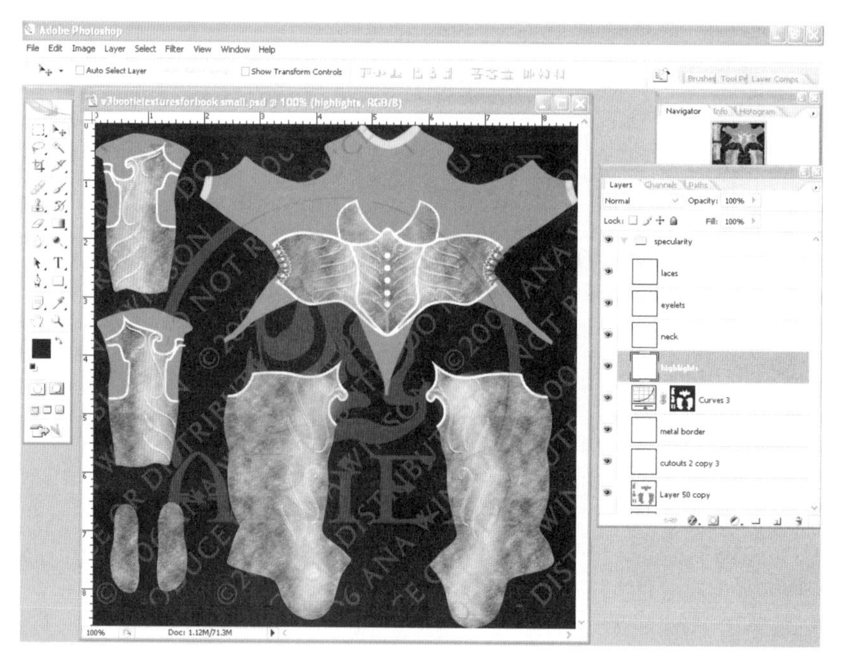

FIGURE 9.8 Lighter shades of gray are added to the arms, corset, legs, and metallic trim.

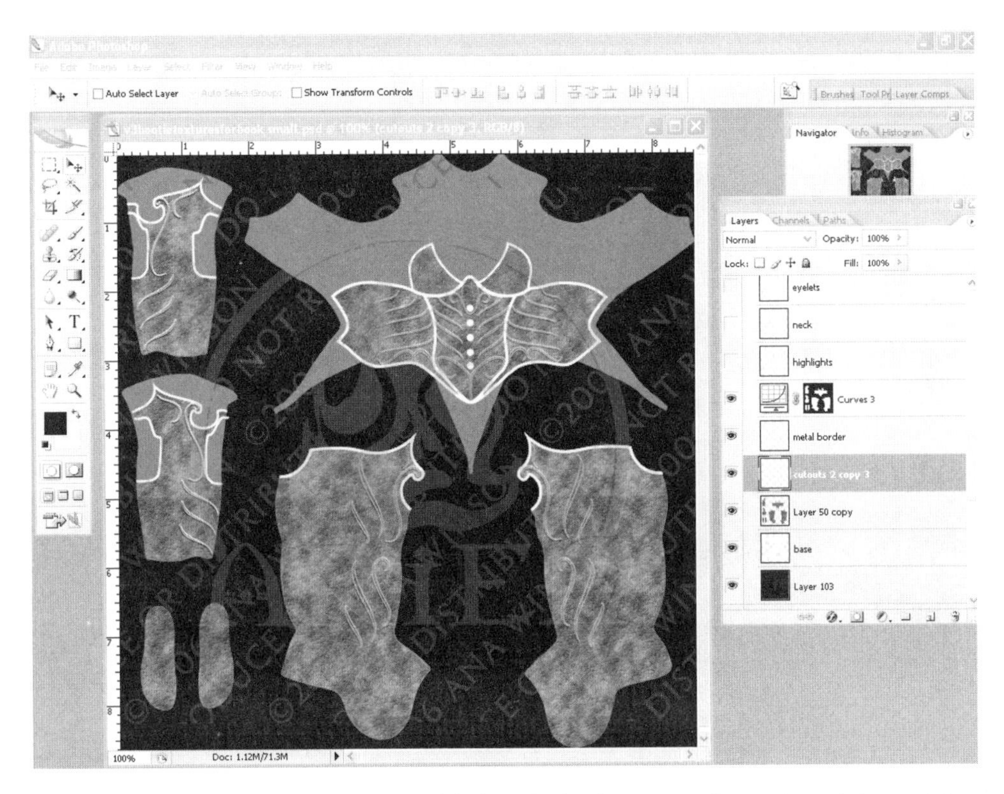

FIGURE 9.9 The final highlights are added to the leather areas, the neck, and the eyelets.

Transparency Maps

Transparency maps determine which portions of an object's surface are transparent and which are opaque. Because transparency maps only use the brightness values of an image and ignore the color data, they are usually grayscale images.

Transparency maps typically start against a pure black (Red 0, Green 0, Blue 0) background. Where black appears in the transparency map, the clothing will be invisible. All white areas in the transparency map will be fully opaque. Darker shades of gray will be more transparent, and lighter shades of gray will be more opaque.

To create the transparency map shown in Figure 9.10, Ana starts with a pure black layer. She then duplicates the lace layer and fills it with white, making portions of the lace opaque. The leather areas on the sleeves, corset, and legs are duplicated and filled with white to make them opaque. White areas are added to create seams in the panties, bodice, and sleeves. Finally, a border of white is added to make the neckband opaque, as is a layer of white that makes the lacing opaque.

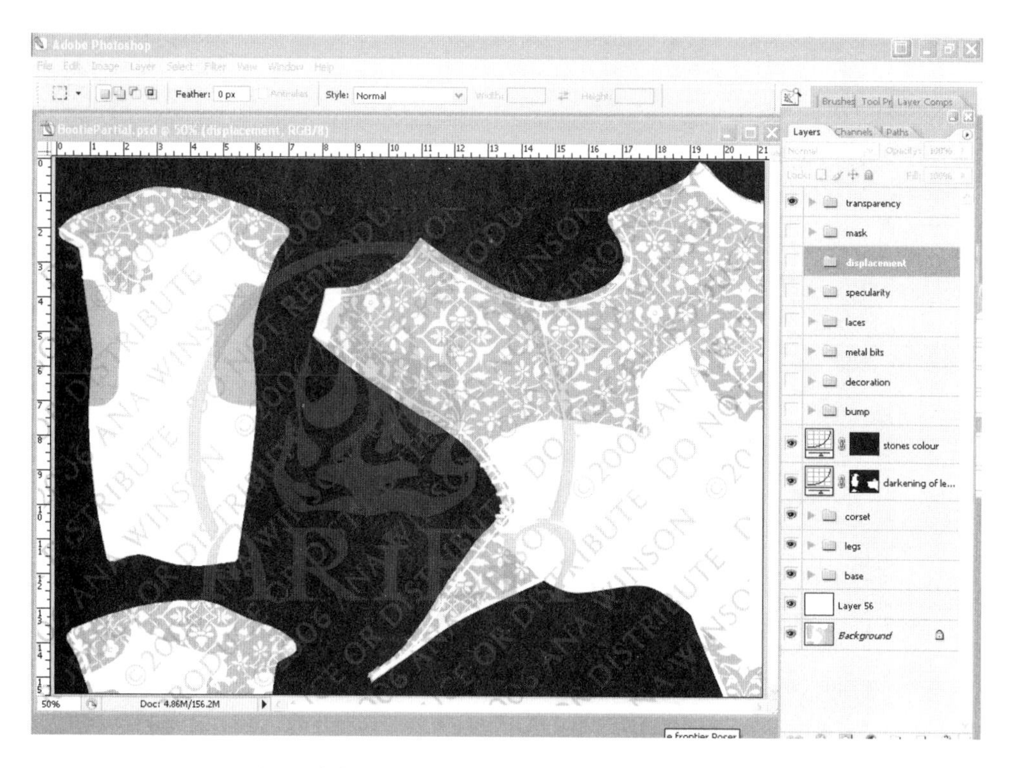

FIGURE 9.10 Using a light gray creates a partial transparency in the leg material.

Raytraced Reflections and Reflecting Maps

When reflections appear in objects, they typically reflect their surrounding environment. To that end, Poser allows two different ways to incorporate reflections in your Poser scene: raytraced reflections and reflection maps.

Raytraced reflections simulate how the elements of your scene might appear if projected onto an imaginary hemisphere that surrounds your scene. The reflections are then bounced back onto your Poser content during render time. You create raytraced reflections in the Advanced view of the Material Room.

Raytraced reflections do take some time to render, so the option of using reflection maps can sometimes decrease your rendering time considerably. Reflection maps can create believable reflections where you don't have to reflect elements in your scene. Typically, a reflection map is a photograph of some "real world" elements that is *spherized.* To create the reflection map for The Bootie, Ana took a photograph from inside a window looking outward. She then increased the contrast to increase the difference between the light and dark areas. Finally, she ran the image through a spherize filter, giving the reflection map the appearance of looking at something through a metallic ball. Figure 9.11 shows a similar type of reflection map and the results it achieves on the Poser mannequin.

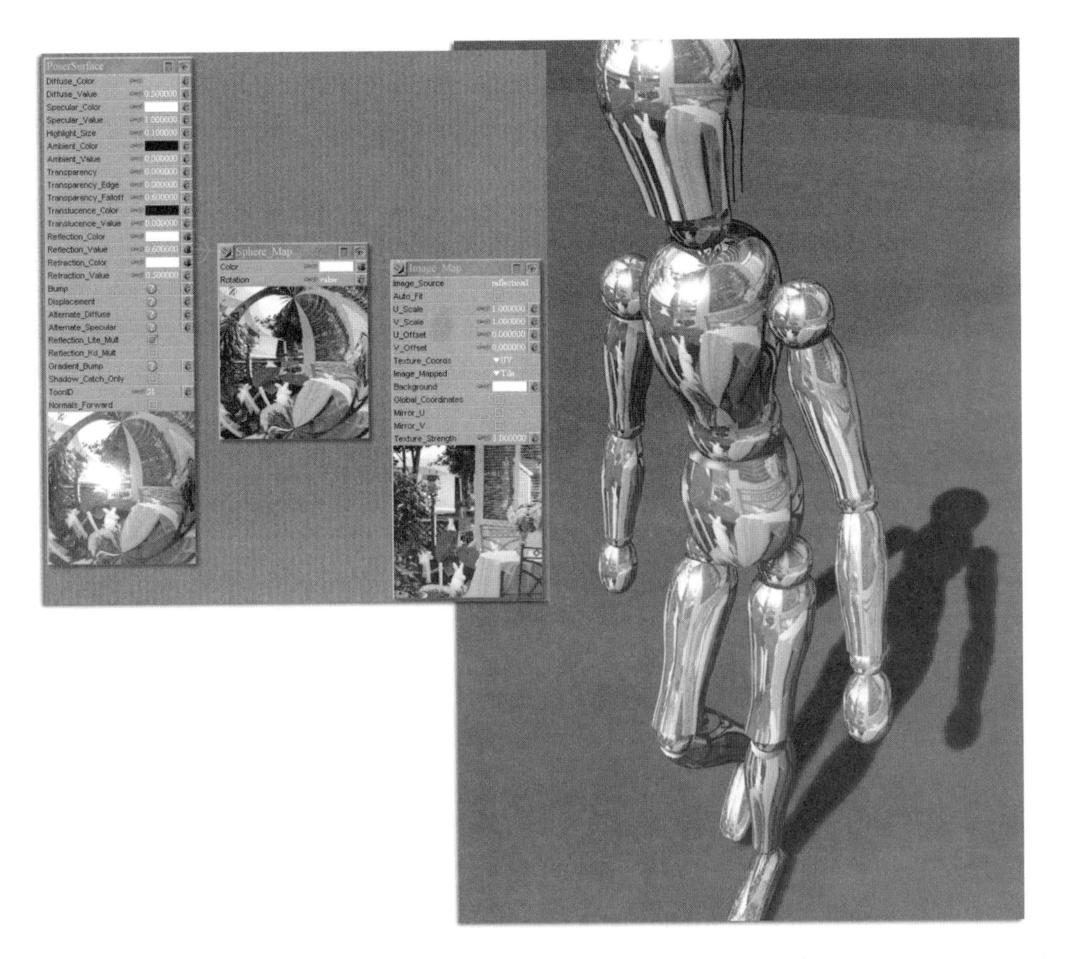

FIGURE 9.11 Reflection maps are frequently created by reflecting real-world environments onto an object.

TUTORIAL 9.1 MAKING A REFLECTION MAP IN PHOTOSHOP

In addition to the raytraced reflections, image maps can be used to create realistic reflections as well. And those maps don't have to be photorealistic to add that realism to an object. You added a reflection map to the belt and metallic pieces in Chapter 4, and in this tutorial you will see how I made those maps. I will be using Adobe Photoshop CS4 for this project, but you can use other image editing programs to create the same type of image.

The main thing to remember about a generic reflection map is that it doesn't have to be overly detailed. You can see that in those Chapter 4 files included on the DVD.

1. In Photoshop, create a file that is 1024 pixels by 1024 pixels. Color mode should be set to grayscale, and make the file 72dpi.
2. Fill this Background layer with black, and then create a new layer.
3. Change the Foreground color to Black and the Background color to White. White will become the specular value, and black will be flat. Shades of gray will provide varying specular intensity.

NOTE

Remember, you're dealing with Adobe Photoshop in this tutorial, so if you're using a different program, you will need to translate this information to fit with your particular program's features.

4. Once the colors are set, go to Filter > Render > Clouds. Clouds uses a fractal generator to create random cloud-like patterns using the foreground and background colors. These fractals are resolution-independent, just like vector files, so you can increase their size without loss of quality. If you aren't happy with the pattern, you can either go to Filter > Clouds (the first option in the list) or press Cmd/Ctrl+F to generate a new pattern. Basically, you want a fairly good smattering of black throughout the image.
5. Open the Levels window (Image > Adjustments > Levels or Cmd/Ctrl+L) and click on the Black point eye dropper. Use Figure 9.12 for reference if you aren't sure where this and the next item are located. Move your cursor over a medium gray portion of your image and click. That medium gray color will become black. Repeat this process with the White point eye dropper, selecting the brighter areas of the image until you get something that looks like what you see in Figure 9.13.

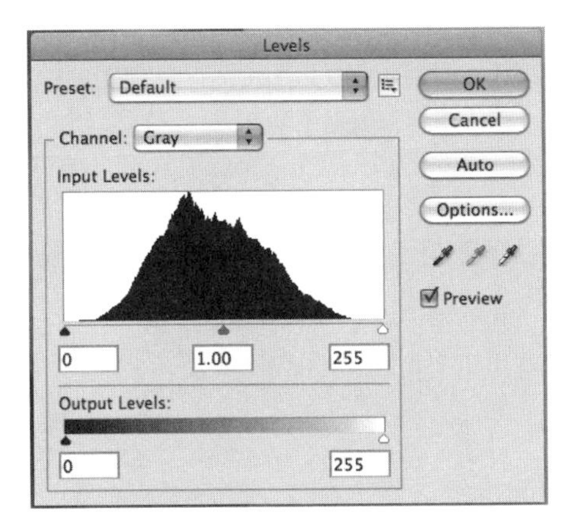

FIGURE 9.12 Use the Black and White point eye droppers to set new saturation levels in your image.

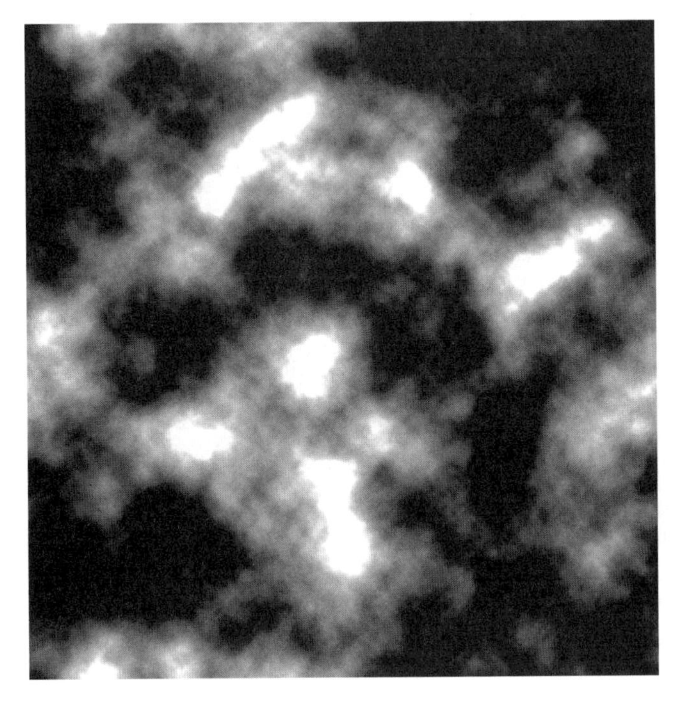

FIGURE 9.13 The re-saturated cloud image.

6. Go to Edit > Transform > Scale or select the Move tool and turn on Show Transform Controls in the Options bar. Either way, you will get control handles around the clouds layer. Scale this image down so you have about a 1/4-inch border around the clouds layer (see Figure 9.14).

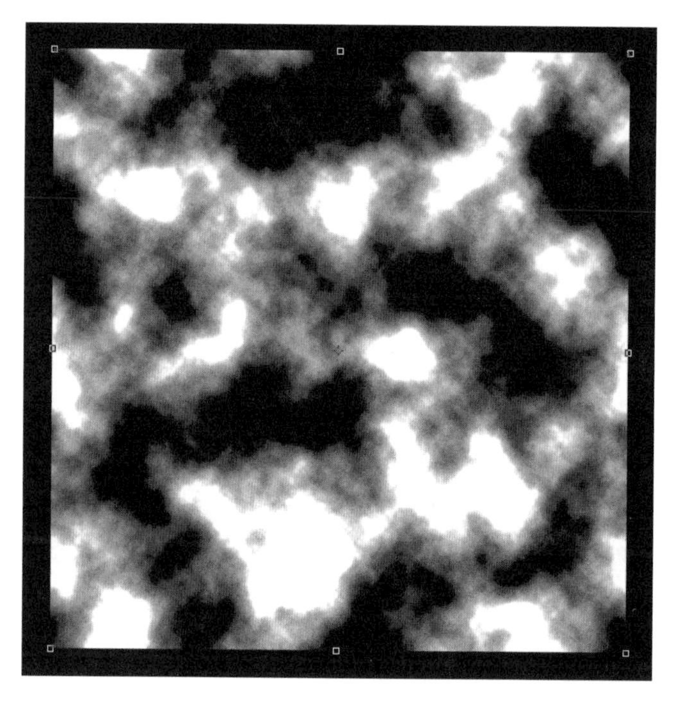

FIGURE 9.14 Scale the clouds layer so there is an approximate 1/4-inch border.

7. Go to Filter > Blur > Gaussian Blur and blur the image until all the details are gone, and you are left with flowing shapes. If you want, you can change the opacity of the layer to bring the brightness of the whites down a bit.

The reason you added the border before blurring the clouds layer is so that you have a seamless reflection map. Also, if you blurred the clouds layer with it all the way to the edge, you would have straight edges when you reduced the size of the layer. Now you can add your reflection map to a folder of your choice within Poser and use it whenever you want. The map I made is available in the Chapter 9 folder on the DVD.

Bump Maps

Bump maps are usually grayscale images. Light (white) values create areas that appear more raised from the original surface of the mesh, and dark (black) areas appear more indented or recessed from the surface. This effect is most apparent where the surface of the object is perpendicular to the camera and falls off as you get to the edges of the object. For this reason, bump maps are great for objects that are farther away or for objects whose edges are not prominent or are hidden behind other objects.

For the bump map, Ana starts with a black background. On a new layer, she selects all non-transparent areas in the clothing and fills the selection with a middle gray that has some noise added to it for texture. The noise adds to the bumpiness of the base bump map. Over the base noise layer, she selects the leather areas on the corset, sleeves, and legs, and fills them with a varied gray base with a slight leather appearance. The areas of the lacing and eyelets are made lighter to raise them from the leather area of the corset. Figure 9.15 shows the initial progress.

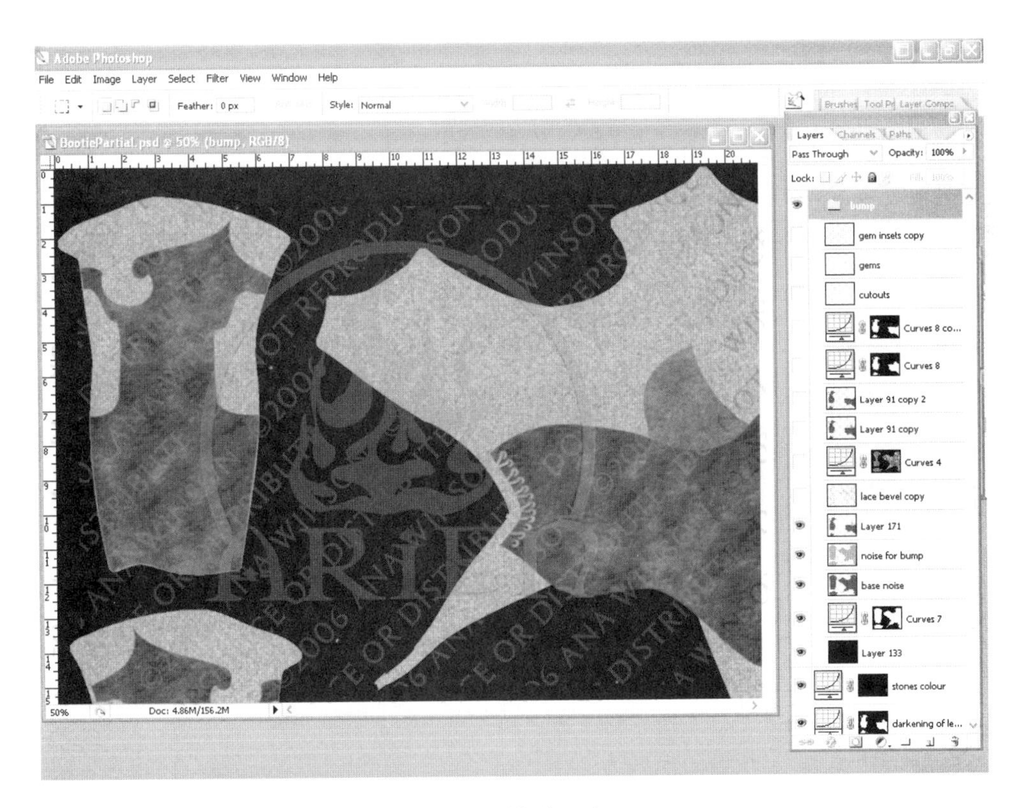

FIGURE 9.15 A noise layer is added to the non-transparent areas.

Next, Ana duplicates the beveled lace from the diffuse map and places it above the previous layers. She uses an adjustment curve to lighten the lace so that it brings the details forward in the bump map. Next, the leather areas are again superimposed over the lace and lightened so that they do not recede into the texture as much. These additional steps are shown in Figure 9.16.

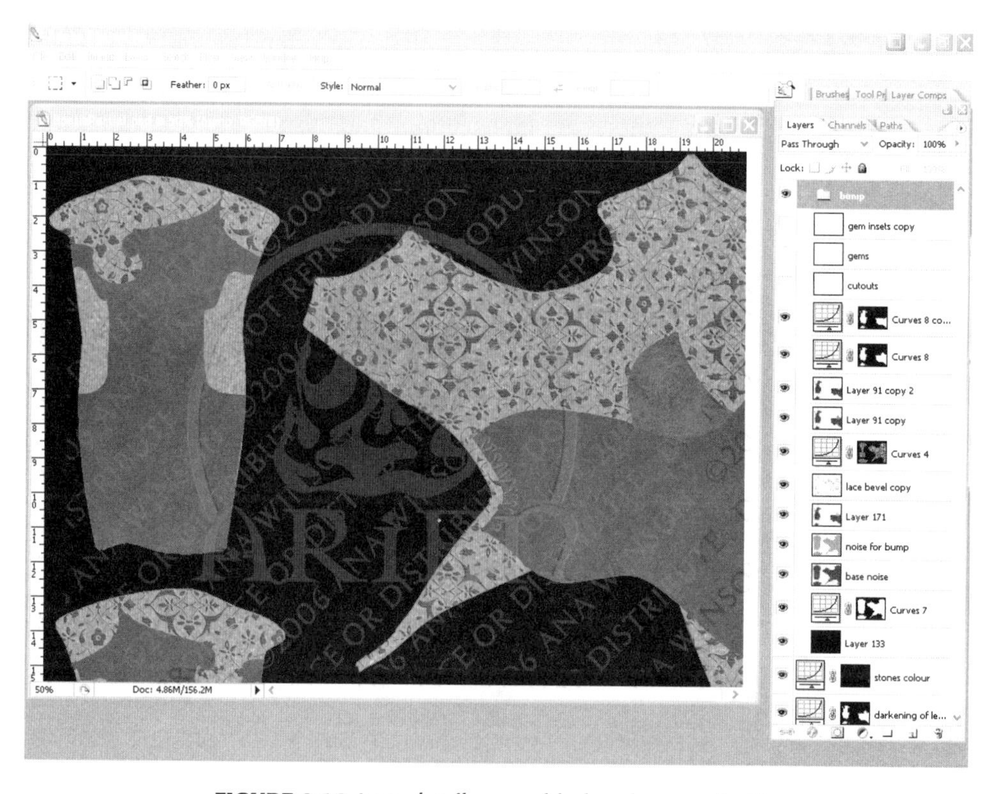

FIGURE 9.16 Lace details are added and covered with the leather areas in the corset, sleeve, and legs.

To complete the bump map, all of the intricate details are added in the lightest colors so that they are raised higher to add more detail. The cutouts on the corset, arms, and legs are added, as are some lighter areas that raise the gems and gem insets. The metallic trim areas around the lacing eyelets, corset, sleeves, and legs are the brightest areas of the bump map, causing these areas to be raised the farthest. Figure 9.17 shows the finished bump map.

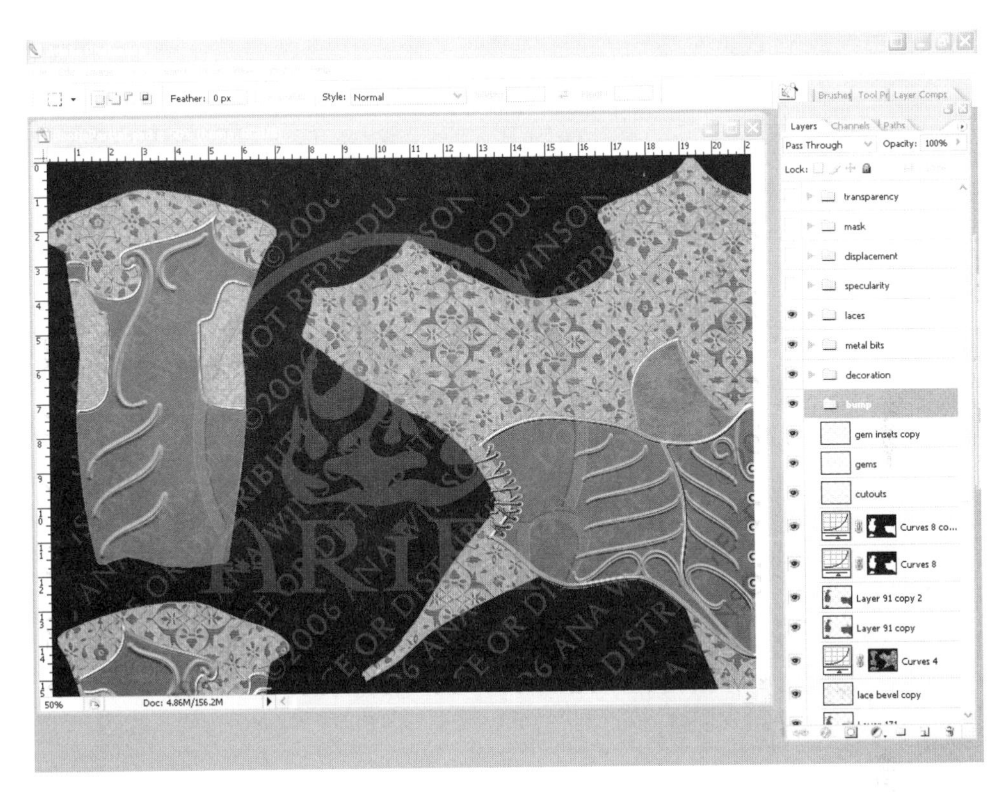

FIGURE 9.17 Decorations and metal trim are added to the brightest layers of the bump map.

Displacement Maps

To create her displacement map, Ana once again begins with a solid black layer. Next, she duplicates a copy of the lace layer and places it above the black base. A third layer adds deep shadows at the seams of the garment. Next, lighter gray seams are added around the panties, and the leather on the corset, arms, and legs is filled with a solid gray value that is similar to the lightest color in the lace. Figure 9.18 shows the progress thus far.

A slightly lighter shade of gray is added around the center of the corset to raise its level slightly. Next, the cutouts on the arms, legs, and corset are duplicated and brightened to raise the detail outward from the base leather on the sleeves. Figure 9.19 shows this next level of displacement, which really adds a lot of detail and dimension to the leather areas.

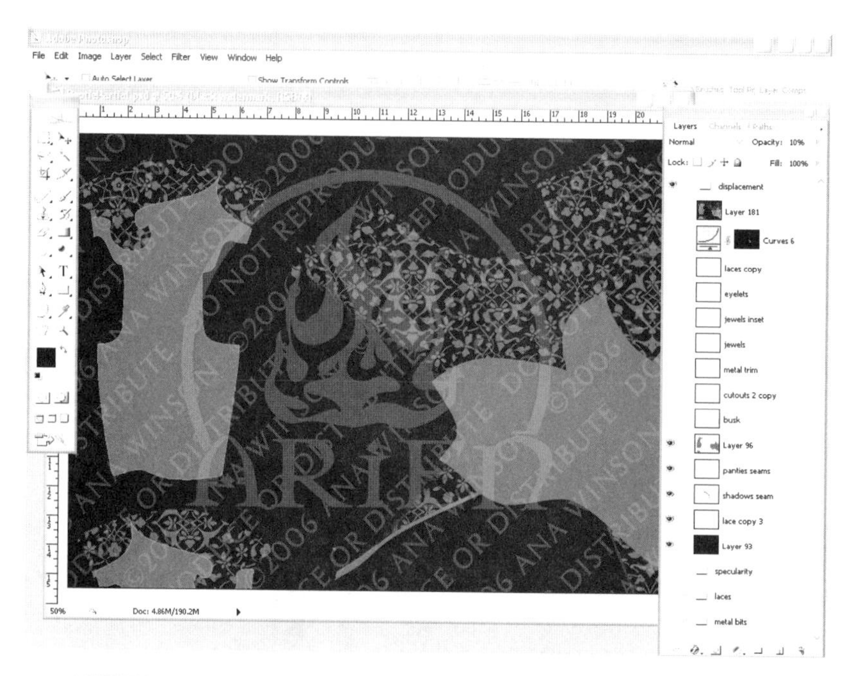

FIGURE 9.18 Deep gray provides the least amount of displacement for the lace and leather areas of the corset.

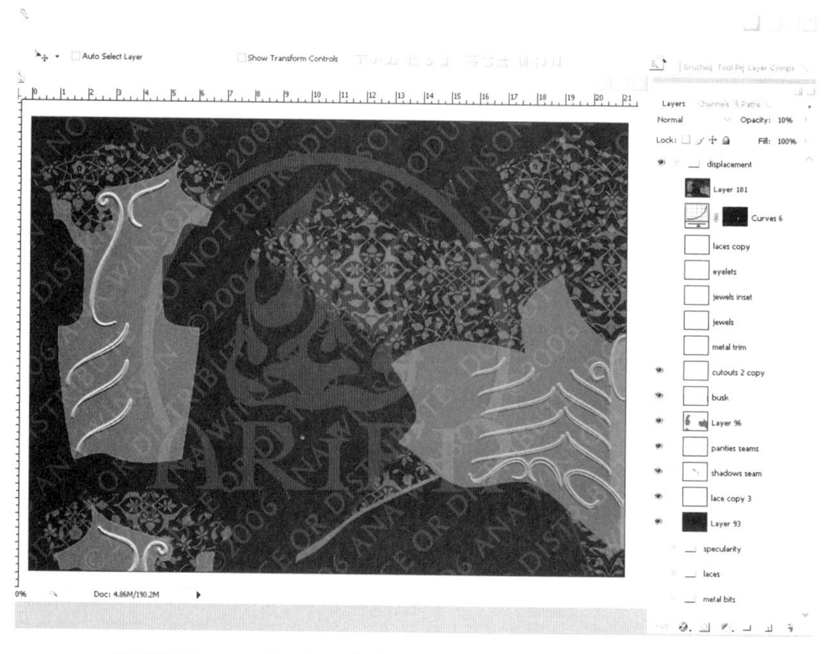

FIGURE 9.19 The detailed cutouts on the leather portions of the clothing get a greater level of displacement.

To complete the displacement details, Ana adds a light gray border around the edges of the leather, where the metallic trim appears in the texture map. Light gray areas are also added to raise the jewels, jewel insets, eyelets, and laces on the corset.

The last step is very important for displacement. When there are stark transitions between light and dark, the displacement will leave very sharp edges instead of soft transitions. Ana adds an adjustment curve that blurs and softens the edges of all the displacement layers so that the displacement effects transition smoothly from one level of displacement to another. A portion of the final displacement map is shown in Figure 9.20.

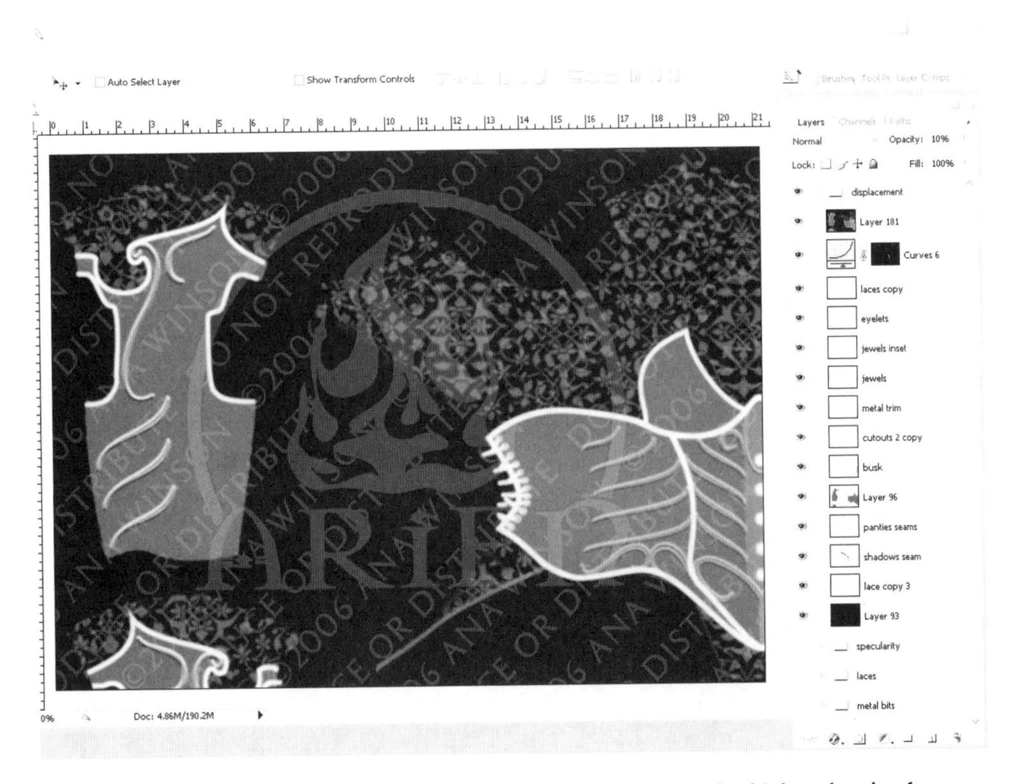

FIGURE 9.20 The metallic trip, eyelets, and laces receive the highest levels of displacement, while an adjustment layer adds smoothness to the transitions.

As you learned in Chapter 4, there are a few settings in the FireFly renderer that must be enabled for displacement maps to work: the Min Displacement Bounds setting (in Manual Settings) has to be at least as high as the displacement value that you enter in the Displacement setting in the root node. Also, make sure you enable (check) the Use Displacement Maps option.

TUTORIAL 9.2 CREATING A REALISTIC TATTOO

After looking at clothing and seeing how Ana Winson went about creating the maps that made up The Bootie texture, let's turn to skin textures. There are many skin textures on the market, and many of them have tattoos; but in most cases the tattoos appear to be merely plopped on top of the texture and don't exactly look natural. How can you make a tattoo look like it is actually ink injected into the skin?

NOTE

The artwork I am using for the tattoo is free and can be downloaded from Vector Graphics at www.vectorgraphics.info/vector-clipart.php?cat=tattoos2.

1. From Photoshop (or whatever image editing program you are using), open the RyanBody.png texture file located in the Runtime > Textures > Poser 8 > Ryan folder. After doing that, go to File > Place and place the Tattoo103.eps file onto the template.
2. Rename the tattoo layer Tattoo_Base.
3. Scale the tattoo and move it into position on the upper arm. Use Figure 9.21 as a guide to the size, location, and rotation of the tattoo image.

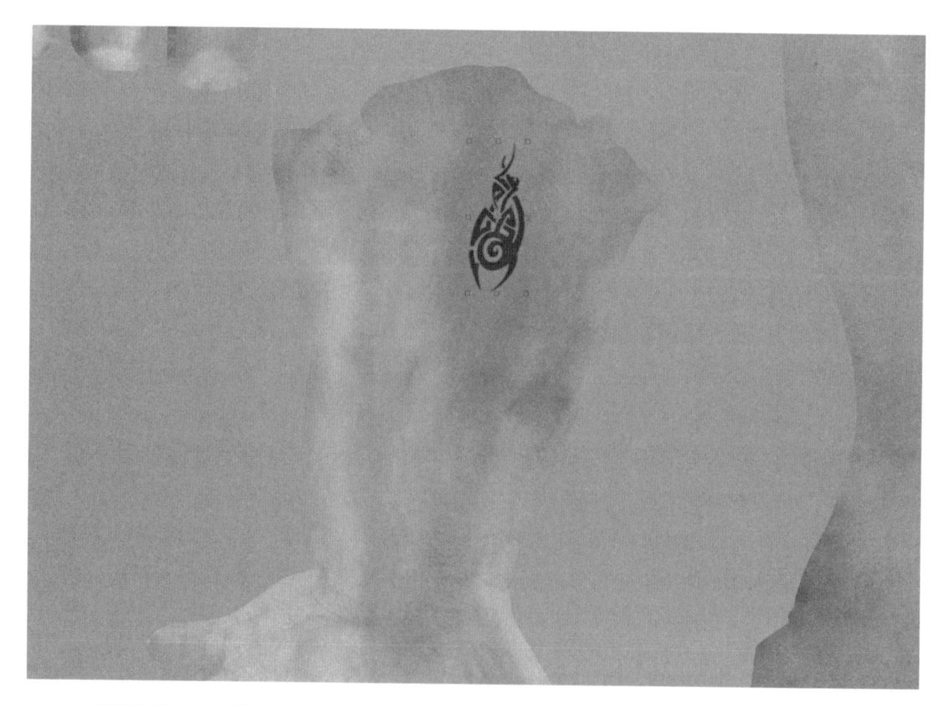

FIGURE 9.21 The tattoo rotated, scaled, and positioned on Ryan's left arm.

4. Go to Filter > Blur > Gaussian Blur and change the setting to 2. This will blur the tattoo, giving the initial appearance of the ink spreading slightly under the skin.
5. Change the Blend mode to Darken, and reduce the Opacity to 33% (see Figure 9.22).

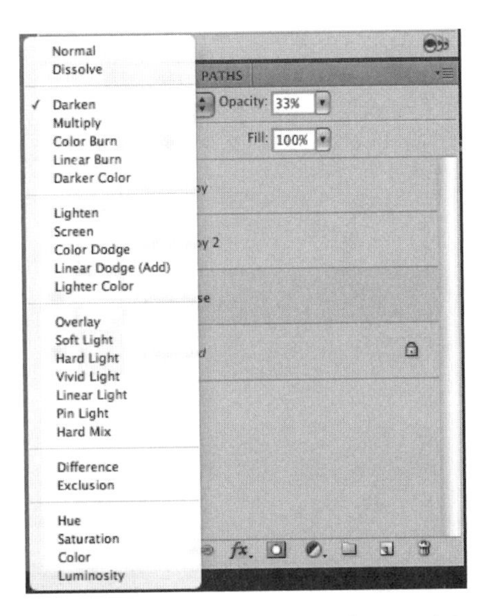

FIGURE 9.22 The Blend mode is set to Darken and Opacity to 33%.

6. Duplicate the Tattoo_Base layer, change the Blend mode to Overlay, and the Opacity to 80%. This will darken the tattoo and turn it to a maroon-like color. Title this layer Tattoo_Overlay.
7. Duplicate the Tattoo_Overlay layer, change the Blend mode to Soft Light, and the Opacity to 64%. Title this Tattoo_SL. This darkens the tattoo while adding a little more red to the edges.
8. Save the file as RyanBody_Tattoo.png.
9. In Poser, go to the Material Room, select Ryan in the Object list and Body from the Material list. Replace the RyanBody.png file with your new tattoo image. When you render the scene, the tattoo on Ryan's left arm will look very natural (see Figure 9.23).

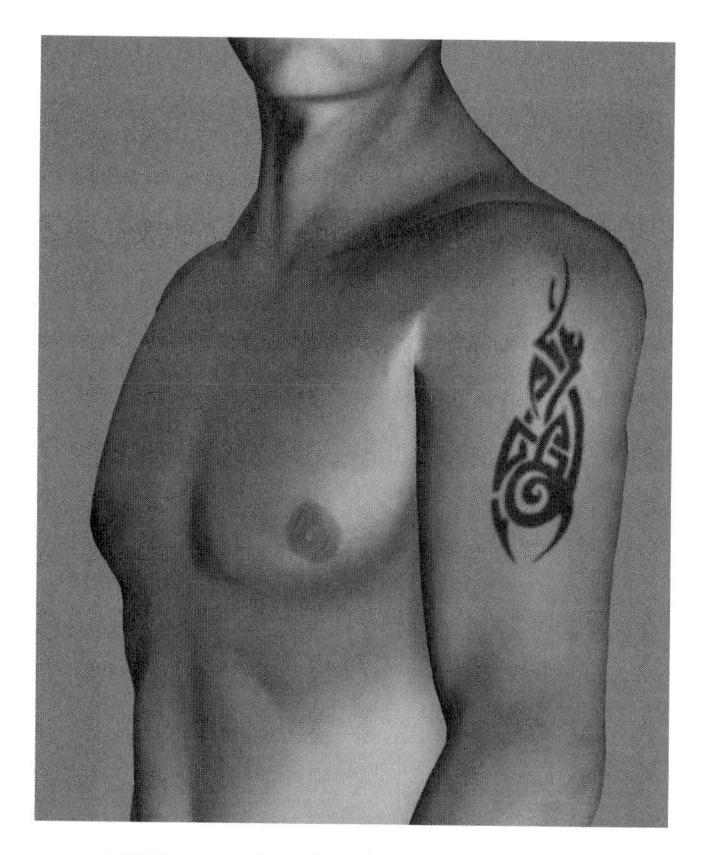

FIGURE 9.23 The finished tattoo on Ryan's arm.

Tutorial 9.3 Adding Personality to Skin Textures

The tattoo was fairly simple in that it only involved one texture node. What about a texture that involves multiple nodes? I knew you were going to ask, so, as people like me are wont to say, your wish(es) are my command. And, you'll use the same texture map you just put the tattoo on.

This time, you'll do one of those tattoos that are raised on the arm that seem to have become very popular over the past few years. This will be tribal band—or in this case, a Celtic band—around Ryan's right arm.

1. Download Tattoo131.eps from the Vector Graphics website.
2. In Photoshop, go to File > Place, and then scale and rotate the band so it looks like Figure 9.24.

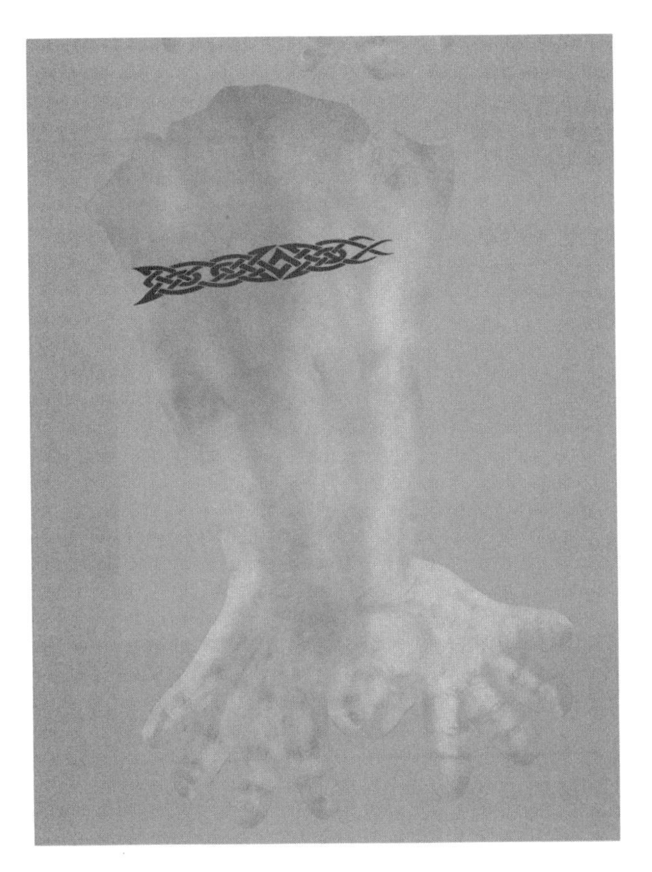

FIGURE 9.24 The band tattoo in position.

3. Set the Blend mode for this band layer to Screen and the Opacity to 50%. This will make a very light band encircling Ryan's arm. Save this file as RyanBody_TattDiff.png. (The name stands for Tattoo Diffuse.)
4. Create two more copies of this tattoo layer, and then blur both of them with the Gaussian Blur filter. You want just enough of a blur to create a softening effect to the band, allowing the skin to look stretched when the displacement map is added.
5. Duplicate the Tattoo131 layer, and then right-click on this new layer and select Rasterize from the menu. When you placed the EPS file, it was brought in as a Smart Object. You don't want it to be a Smart Object but rather a regular pixel-based image. Once converted, press Cmd/Ctrl+I to invert the layer. The black will become white, which is what you need in order to raise the tattoo on the arm.

NOTE

To learn more about Smart Objects in Photoshop, go to Help > Photoshop Help and then search for Smart Objects.

6. Open the Layer Styles window by clicking on the fx button at the bottom of the Layers window. Select Bevel and Emboss, then make the following setting changes:
   - **Style:** Inner Bevel
   - **Size:** 10 pixels
   - **Angle:** 141°
   - **Shadow Mode** > **Opacity:** 100%
7. The tattoo is too sharp for what you want to accomplish. So select Filter > Blur > Gaussian Blur and change the setting to anywhere between 3.5 and 4 pixels. Figure 9.25 shows the tattoo layer that is about to become the displacement map.
8. Next, duplicate the beveled layer, and in the Edit > Fill window make sure you have Preserve Transparency active and fill the layer with 50% gray. Set the Opacity to 19%. This gives just enough gray to the white sections of the displacement to soften them more naturally.
9. Add a layer under the displacement layers and fill it with black. Figure 9.26 shows the layers and their order.
10. Turn off the visibility of the top three layers (Black, tattoo131_displacement, tattoo131_dispGray) and save the remaining visible layers as Armband.png.

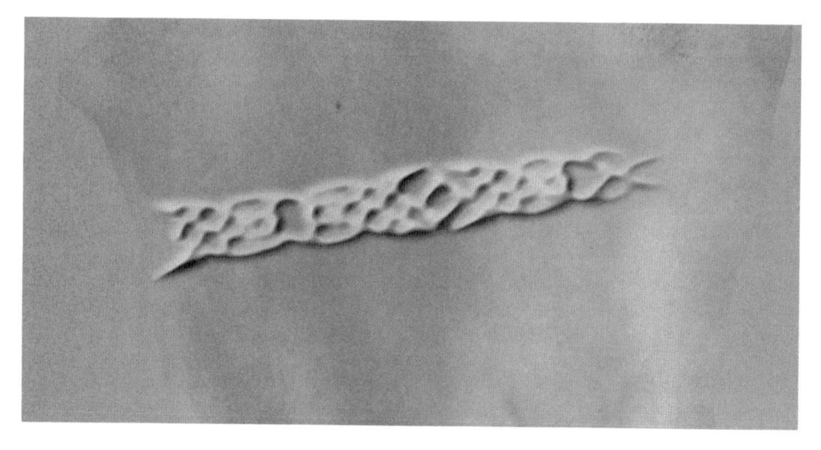

FIGURE 9.25 The tattoo prepared as a displacement object.

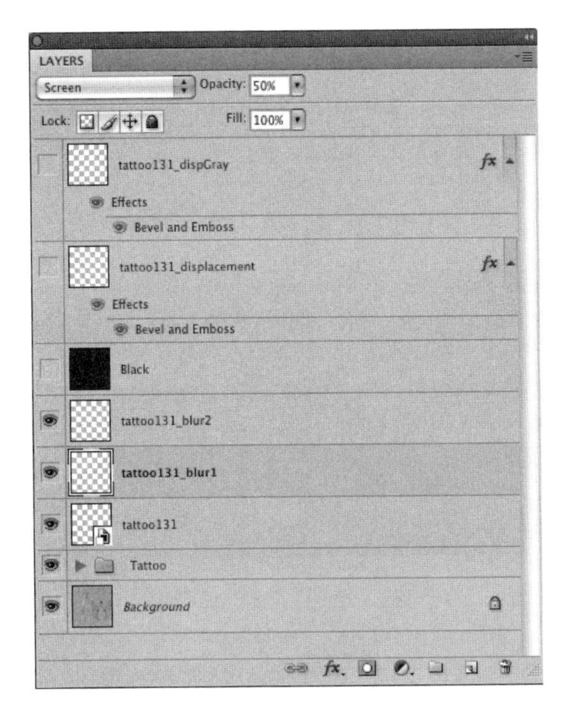

FIGURE 9.26 The order of the layers with their content names to help you put your file together.

11. Turn on the visibility of three layers you turned off in Step 9 and save the file as Armband_disp.png.
12. In Poser's Material Room, select Ryan's body and, in the Diffuse section, change the image file to Armband.png.
13. Go down the list to Displacement. Click on the plug, choose New > 2D Textures > Image_Map, and add the Armband_disp.png file.
14. Next to Displacement in the PoserSurface node list, change the value to 0.00855.
15. Go to Render > Render Settings and make the following changes.
    - **Auto Settings:** Set to Final
    - **Use Displacement Maps:** On
16. Render your file, and it will look very much like what you see in Figure 9.27.

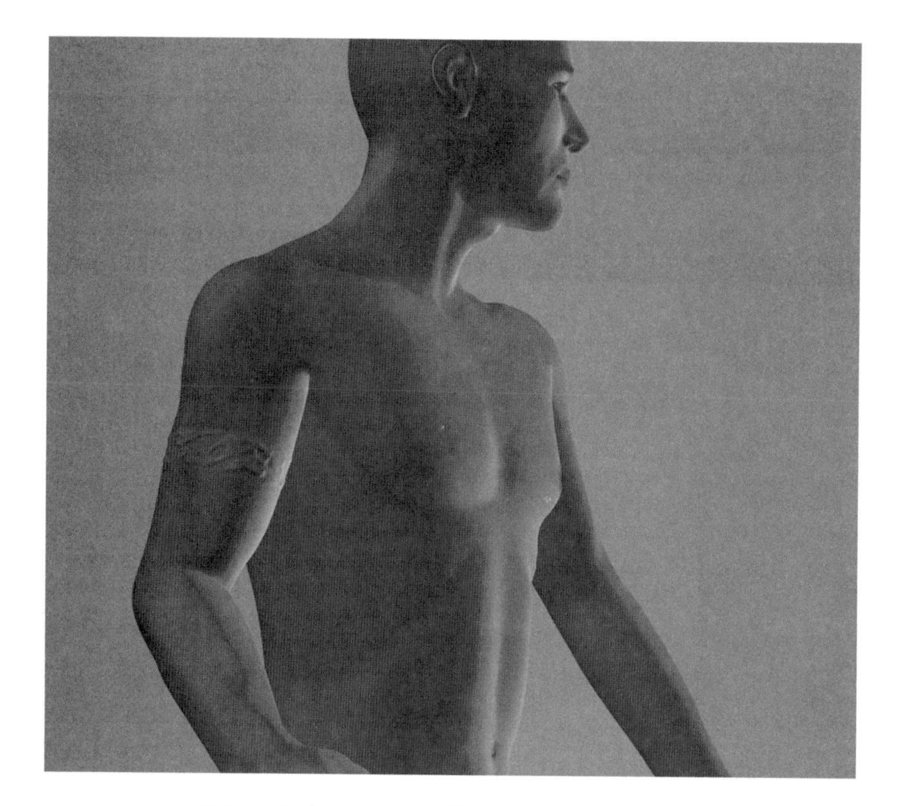

FIGURE 9.27 The rendered file with a raised band tattoo.

The displacement map is too strong, but I gave numbers that would best show how the displacement works. You should change the setting to best fit your vision of what a tatt like this would look like.

A Short Re-Pose

Now that you have worked with textures and modified existing UV maps, you're set to start experimenting and building your own textures—either for your own use or to sell. There are entire books that cover texture creation and how to make photorealistic materials from scratch. That didn't fall under the scope of this chapter, but you got an introduction and some knowledge of what to look for and what techniques to use to create specific looks in your texture files.

In the next chapter, you'll take it a little farther, learning how to create your own UV maps so that, if you begin creating content for Poser, you can create the texture maps as well.

10 UV Mapping

In This Chapter:

- The What and Why of UV Mapping
- Using UVMapper Professional
- Tutorial 10.1: Using UVMapper to Map a Skirt
- Tutorial 10.2: Using UVMapper to Map Pants
- Tutorial 10.3: Using UVMapper to Map a Shirt
- Making Templates
- UV Mapping with Maxon's Body Paint 4/4.5
- Tutorial 10.4: Importing a Poser OBJ File into Body Paint
- Tutorial 10.5: UV Mapping a Shirt Using Body Paint

"I've been researching the plants and looking at their heights, time, color, texture, and foliage."

—Cindy Gehm

You just spent time making textures using pre-defined texture maps. These are the most common maps most people will work with. But, what if you get into—or are already into—creating 3D models for Poser? The need to create templates like the ones you have worked with becomes very important. Actually, in order to map a texture onto an object correctly, you need to create a UV map. Some 3D applications give you the ability to "unfold" your mesh and create a template. Others don't.

A UV map is, more or less, a flattened representation of the surface of a 3D object. Without some way of mapping textures and other properties on the surface of an object, the entire surface of the object could only be one color or one material.

If poorly mapped, the UV map can make textures appear distorted. In this chapter, you'll learn about various types of UV maps that you can generate and how to break an object down into its basic shapes so that distortion and stretching are minimized when you map textures onto it.

The What and Why of UV Mapping

To begin, what, exactly does the UV in UV maps stand for? Untethered vertices? Uncooperative vermin? Uncool vehicles? Nope. The U represents the X axis (horizontal) and the V represents the Y axis (vertical). So why not just go with X and Y and call it what it is: XY Mapping? It comes from history, actually. You have the base X (horizontal), Y (vertical), and Z or Zed (depth) coordinates—that's common knowledge. W, though, is used to describe the *roll* of the object, or the forward/backward in the texture map. For most texturing, W has been removed and is, in most circles, forgotten. But, UVW plays off of the X/Y/Z coordinate system. You had XYZ Cartesian coordinates to represent width/height/depth, so, to keep with the alphabetic order, you got UVW. Programs like Cinema4D still use the term UVW in their mapping system.

So, what does UV (or UVW) mapping do? Basically, a UV map "flattens" the surface of a 3D object so that you can create a texture for it in a 2D paint program, such as Photoshop. To explain UV maps in simple terms, imagine peeling an orange and then smashing the peel flat onto the surface of the table. The peel of the orange would need to be cut in several places to accommodate being flattened out. The important thing is that, if you wanted to, you could pin the peel back onto the surface of the orange and all the seams would line up perfectly—you could wrap the orange back up in its peel. Another way to think of it is to imagine taking a map of the world and wrapping it around a sphere. If you have a map that is flat and rectangular, the poles appear to be as wide as the equator. But the Earth is truly a sphere, and the equator is wider than the poles, so to wrap a flat world map around a sphere, you would have to reduce the width of the texture toward the top and bottom of each side to make it fit without wrinkling.

UV maps work on the same principle. When you create a UV map, you are "unfolding" your 3D object onto a flat plane. Along with telling the software what shape your object is, you are also determining which axis to orient the texture map to—in other words, whether you are looking at the object from the top, side, or front.

That is what a UV map does. It basically tells your 3D software that the pixels in one portion of a flat 2D texture are applied to one or more specific polygons in the 3D model. So, to wrap the Earth texture around the sphere properly, you have to create a UV map that says, "Wrap a rectangular texture around this object in a spherical fashion, and place the top-left corner of the image at this point of the 3D model."

Types of UV Maps

Most modeling or UV mapping software allows you to create at least four common types of UV maps:

- **Spherical:** Best for globes and other objects that are shaped like a sphere.
- **Planar:** Best for flat objects, such as a door, a tabletop, or a mirror. A playing card is also a good example of planar mapping. If you flipped the card over, you'd see a mirror image of the map that is projected on the front.
- **Box:** A natural for box-shaped objects that require a different texture or orientation on each side.
- **Cylindrical:** Good for cans, sleeves, and many types of clothing. Cylindrical mapping can also include mapping for solid ends (also known as *end caps*) when needed.

If you take the time to use the right type of mapping on each object or each portion of an object, you can avoid stretching and distortion. Sometimes the right mapping isn't obvious, especially with organic shapes, so you have to experiment with what works best. With careful study, you can break any object into one or more of these different shapes.

Before we get on with the tutorials, it will help you to see how the different types of mapping look on different shapes. It is important to note that the results of the various types of mapping also vary depending on which axis you orient the mapping to. With that in mind, the examples shown in Figures 10.1 through 10.3 show objects oriented as they would normally appear: top up, bottom down, and with front facing toward the viewer at a slight angle.

Figure 10.1 shows how a sphere looks when mapped with each of the different mapping types. In this example, both spherical (top left) and cylindrical (bottom right) mapping do an adequate job of mapping the sphere with minimal distortion. On the other hand, planar mapping (top right) creates distortion on the sides, and box mapping (bottom left) creates too many seams.

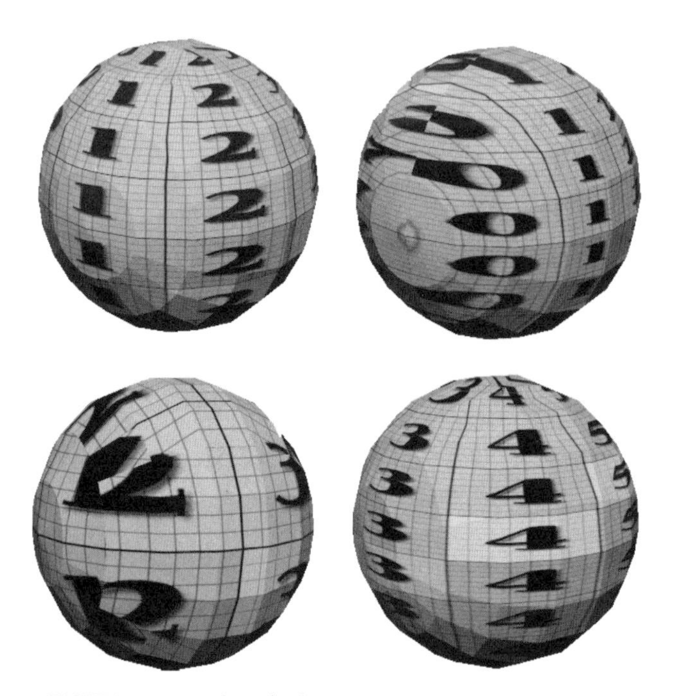

FIGURE 10.1 Going clockwise from upper left, a sample of spherical, planar, box, and cylindrical mapping.

In Figure 10.2, you see a cube that is mapped with the various mapping types. The most natural choice for a cube is box mapping, shown at the bottom left. Spherical mapping (top left) distorts the map on all sides, and cylindrical mapping (bottom right) distorts the top and bottom. Planar mapping would map opposite sides perfectly, although the back side would be mirrored when it faced the camera, and the remaining four sides would be distorted. You can map each individual side of a box with planar mapping, but you would have to change the orientation of the planar map for each side. Box mapping does this for you automatically.

Figure 10.3 shows how the various types of mapping affect something that is cylindrical in shape. The natural choice is cylindrical (bottom right) if the object is open at either end. If closed at both ends, as a can of soup would be before you opened it, some UV mapping programs give you the option to include the end caps in the UV map. In that case, the end caps would be mapped in flat, or planar, mode.

Continuing with the cylinder examples, note that spherical mapping (top left in Figure 10.3) can also be used to successfully map a cylinder. The tops and bottoms of the cylinder will be mapped so that the texture meets in the center of the flat plane. Planar mapping (top right) will cause distortion at the sides and top, and box mapping (bottom left) will create unwanted seams.

FIGURE 10.2 Going clockwise from the upper left, the effects of box, spherical, planar, cylindrical, and box mapping on a cube.

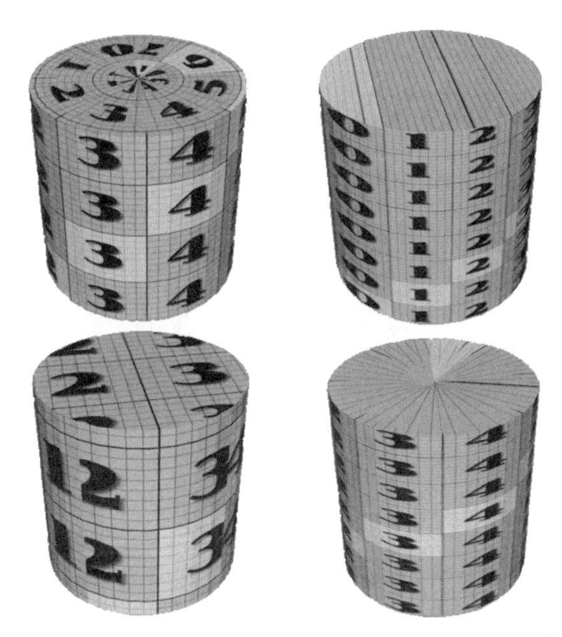

FIGURE 10.3 Although cylindrical mapping (bottom right) is a logical choice for objects that are cylindrically shaped, spherical mapping (top left) also works very well.

Using UVMapper Professional

With the basics out of the way, let's take a look at how you can actually apply this information. The tutorials in this section use UVMapper Professional (www.uvmapper.com), a demo of which is included in the Freebies\Software_Demos\UV_Mapper folder on the DVD that accompanies this book. UVMapper Professional is a PC-only program. If you are using a Mac, then you can download UVMapper Classic from the same site. Even though the last update was in 2006, the Mac version of UVMapper seems to be working just fine with v10.6.1 (Snow Leopard), which is what is installed on my computers. UVMapper Professional (UVMP) was, as of this writing, updated in 2008, with UVMapper Classic for Windows having been updated in 2009.

If you are using the demo version of UVMapper Professional, you will not be able to save your models, so mapped versions of the models used in this chapter are included on the DVD in the Chapter 10 folder.

UVMapper Classic for the Mac does not have all the features discussed in this chapter, and I have not been able to find a program like UVMP for the Mac with those same features.

Tutorial 10.1 Using UVMapper to Map a Skirt

In order to get used to creating UV maps, let's start with something simple—a skirt. As you prepare to create a UV map, you need to think about the main types of mapping that you have (spherical, planar, box, and cylindrical) and which will work best for the particular model you are mapping. (UVMapper also creates polar mapping, but the needs for this type of mapping aren't as common as the others.) Of these types of shapes, a skirt most closely resembles a cylinder, so that's the mapping type that will be assigned.

1. Open UVMapper Professional. Choose File > Open Model, and locate the Tutorials\Chapter10 folder on the DVD that accompanies this book. Choose skirt.obj, and click Open.
2. UVMapper displays the statistics of the object. Click OK to continue. A 3D version of the skirt appears in the Perspective view on the right side of the screen. Initially, the left side is blank, indicating that the object does not have any UV information.

3. Choose Texture > Checker > Color. This puts a checkered pattern with numbers in the Texture view on the left. This helps you position objects so that seams match and also helps you determine whether the texture map is facing in the right direction.
4. Because the skirt most resembles a cylinder in shape, choose Map > Cylindrical. The Cylindrical Mapping dialog box shown in Figure 10.4 appears.

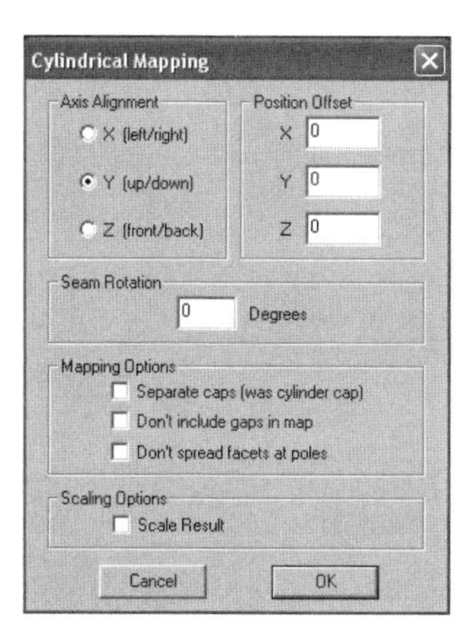

FIGURE 10.4 The Cylindrical Mapping dialog box, with the Y axis selected.

5. In the case of the skirt, you want the UV mapping to map the skirt along the Y (up/down) axis, which is selected by default. Also note the Seam Rotation setting. When set at 0, the seam appears in the back of the garment, which is what you want. Accept the remaining default settings, and click OK.
6. Observe the left and right sides of the UV map. You may notice that the seam didn't break evenly along the same line of polygons. One way you can fix this is to select polygons from one side and move them to the other. You'll find it easier to perform this task if you turn the checkered texture off, so choose Texture > Clear. Answer Yes when UVMapper asks if you really want to clear the background.
7. Use the Magnifier tool and the Hand tool to move in closer to the left side of the texture area.
8. With the Selection tool, select the polygons that you want to move to the other side of the skirt. Figure 10.5 shows the polygons selected.

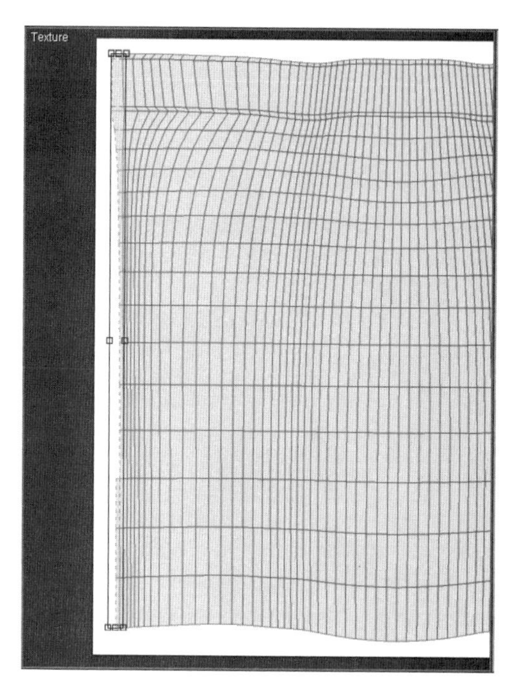

FIGURE 10.5 A portion of the skirt's polygons are selected in preparation for moving to the other side.

9. Pick the Hand tool, and pan the Texture view down to see the remaining polygons if you couldn't get them all in the first round. Shift-click to add the additional polygons to the selection if necessary. You can also Alt-click to remove polygons from the selection.
10. Use the Magnifier tool to zoom out until you can see the entire texture again. Or use the View > Reset View menu command.
11. Press the Shift key while you use the right arrow key to move the selected polygons to the right side. When the polygons get close to where you want them, use the right arrow or left arrow keys (without pressing the Shift key) to nudge them into place one pixel at a time. If necessary, zoom in closer with the Magnifier tool to position them immediately next to the existing polygons. Figure 10.6 shows proper placement.
12. To stitch the moved polygons back into the skirt, you need to switch to Vertex Selection mode. To do so, choose Select > Select Method > By Vertex.

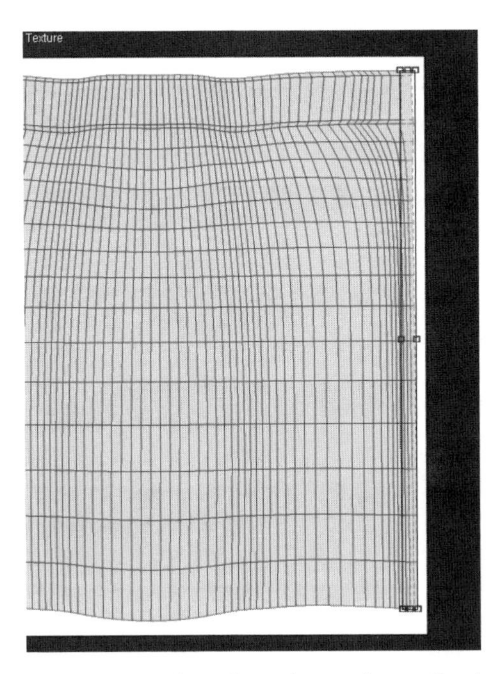

FIGURE 10.6 Place the polygons immediately adjacent to those on the other side.

13. Zoom out until you see the entire right side of the skirt. Use the Rectangular Selection tool to draw a selection around the polygons on the right side, making sure that you enclose all of the polygons you moved plus some additional for good measure. The selected vertices turn red.
14. To stitch them together, choose Tools > UVs > Stitch. When UVMapper asks if you really want to stitch the vertices together, choose Yes.
15. If desired, choose Texture > Checker > Color to view the final result before you save the new skirt. (Remember that you cannot save with the demo version of UVMapper Professional.)
16. If you have the full version of UVMapper Professional, choose File > Save Model. Leave all options unchecked, and choose OK to save the model with its UV information. A mapped version of the skirt appears on the DVD in Tutorials\Chapter 10 as skirt-mapped.obj. Figure 10.7 shows the final result of the UV maps.

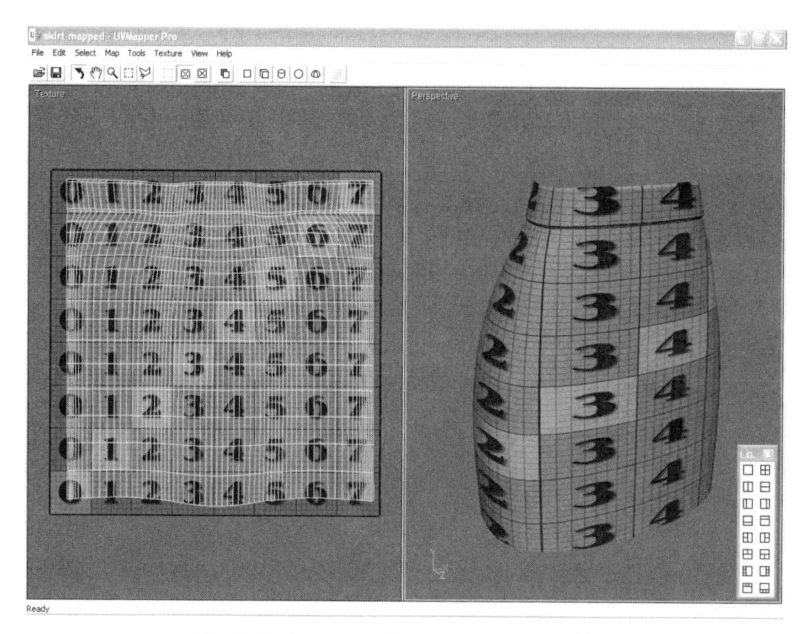

FIGURE 10.7 The final map for the skirt.

TUTORIAL 10.2 USING UVMAPPER TO MAP PANTS

As you can probably guess, mapping pants is a bit more difficult than mapping a skirt. This tutorial will show you how to break down the parts that make up a model in order to create a proper map.

When you look at a pair of pants, you see two separate cylinders joined together at the top center. That is also the best way to approach mapping—divide the pants in half with one cylinder in each half. After the division, you unfold each of the cylinders to flatten them, and then stitch them back together again.

As you start this project, open the pants.obj model in UVMapper Professional.

1. After opening the pants.obj model, UVMapper displays the statistics of the object. Click OK to continue. A 3D version of the pants appears in the Perspective view on the right side of the screen. Initially, the left side is blank, indicating that the object does not have any UV information.
2. Turn off the display of the background texture. It will help you see things more easily until you get to the final stage. To do so, choose Texture > Clear.
3. The best way to start with pants is to first map them in planar mode without separating the front and back. To do so, choose Map > Planar. The Planar Mapping dialog box appears (see Figure 10.8).

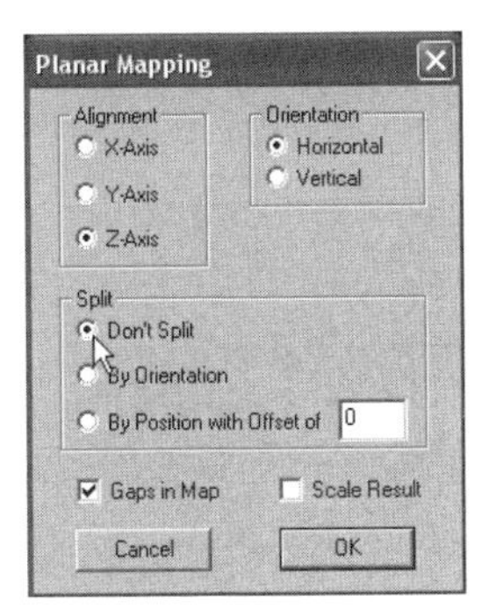

FIGURE 10.8 Keep the pants as a whole when you begin to map them.

4. By default, UVMapper Professional does planar mapping on the z axis and by orientation. These two options together split the clothing article between the front and back sides. You don't want to split the clothing right now, so choose Don't Split (as shown in Figure 10.8). Click OK to continue.
5. If you are continuing from the previous tutorial, you'll need to change to Facet Selection mode. To do so, choose Select > Select Method > By Facet.

In the last tutorial, you worked in Vertex Selection mode. This allowed you to select points along the unwrapped mesh and modify the texture map in order for the texture not to stretch along the surface of the object. When you choose the By Facet mode, UVMapper selects the actual faces of the unwrapped mesh so you can either modify the entire mesh object or specific faces of the mesh. In this tutorial, you will be selecting specific faces of the mesh.

6. With the Rectangular Selection tool, select the entire left side of the pants to the center seam. Make sure that you select all of the polygons on the inside of the leg. The easiest way to do this is to start with the selection on the left side of the pants and drag to the center until the selection box is exactly over the center line of the pants.
7. With the selection still active, choose Map > Cylindrical. The Cylindrical Mapping dialog box appears. Accept the default Y (up/down) for the Axis Alignment option, and continue with the next step.
8. By default, cylindrical mapping places the seam toward the back when you are mapping to the y axis. You want the seam to fall on the inside of the leg. To do this, enter **90 degrees** in the Seam Rotation field. Then click OK to exit the dialog box. UVMapper Professional maps the pants leg in a cylindrical fashion.

9. You'll notice that some of the facets in the bottom of the leg are flipped around the wrong way and create a tear in the leg. To fix that, use the Polygonal Selection tool to select the lower half of the pants, making sure that you start the selection above where the distortion begins. An example is shown in Figure 10.9.

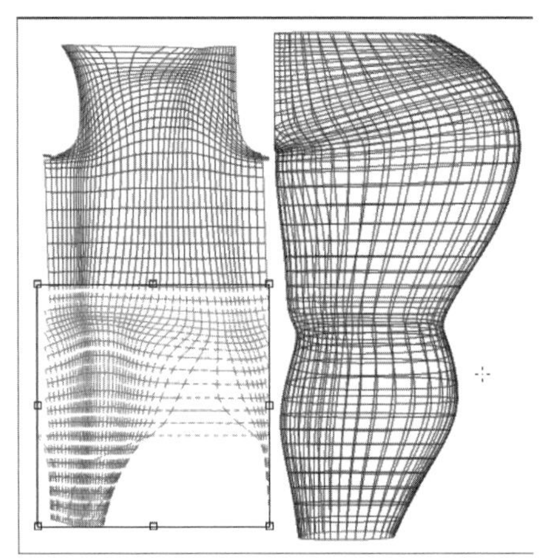

FIGURE 10.9 Select the lower portion of the pants to fix the distortions.

10. With the selection of the lower half of the pants leg in its original position, choose Map > Cylindrical again. The settings should remain from the previous time you used them. Click OK to exit the dialog box.
11. Now, choose Vertex Selection mode (Select > Select Method > By Vertex). Make a selection that includes the area where you broke the connection between the upper and lower portions of the pants, as shown in Figure 10.10. Then stitch them together (Tools > UVs > Stitch). Select the other half, and stitch them together as well.

If you select the entire width of the leg to stitch the vertices together, UVMapper will stitch them together at the seam. This makes the UV map hard to read. Selecting half at the time prevents this from occurring.

12. Now, return to Facet Selection mode (Select > Select Method > By Facet). Select the other leg, and choose Map > Cylindrical again. This time, enter **270 degrees** in the Seam Rotation field so that the seam appears on the inside of this leg. Then choose OK.

13. Remap and stitch the lower portion as you did in Steps 10 through 12. If the width of the lower section is different from that of the upper section after you remap it, drag the selection from any side to resize them to match the upper section. Then stitch them together, one half at a time, in Vertex Selection mode. The final result should look similar to Figure 10.11.

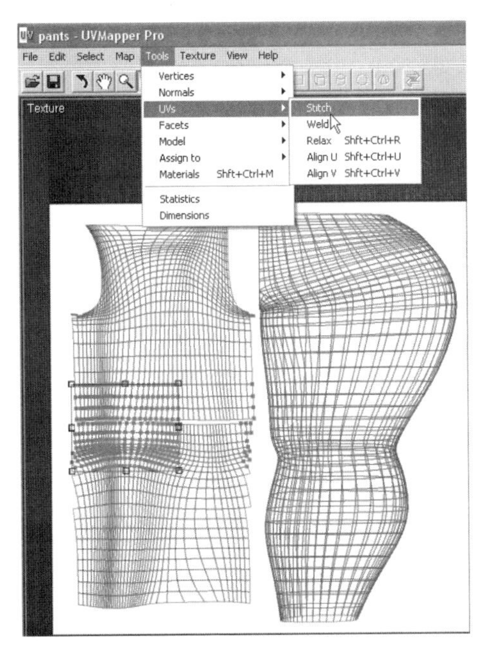

FIGURE 10.10 After remapping the lower portion of the pants, stitch the upper and lower legs back together.

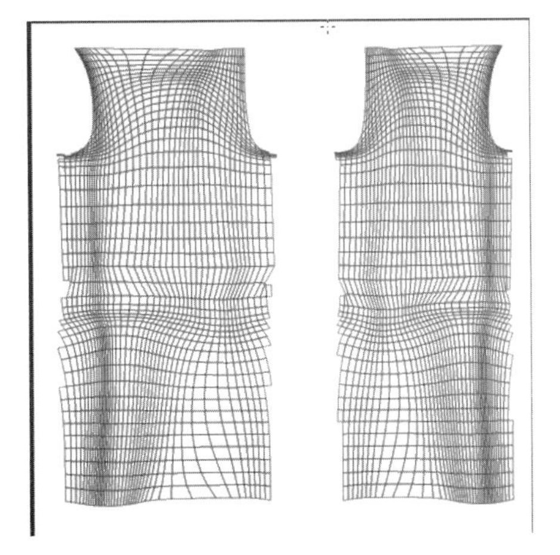

FIGURE 10.11 Both sides of the pants are mapped in a cylindrical fashion.

14. The final problem that you have to tackle is cleaning up the seams so that the break falls along the same column of polygons. First, switch back to Facet Selection mode (Select > Select Method > By Facet).
15. Let's add a little more space between the two sections of pants. Select the left half, and hold the Shift key while pressing the left arrow key once or twice to move the section toward the left edge of the work area.
16. Use the Polygon Selection tool to click just above the first two rows of polygons on the left side of the pants. As you work your way down, remain in the same column of polygons while you follow it down to the bottom of the pants. Then click outside of the selection to work your way back up to the top, as shown in Figure 10.12. Double-click the Polygon tool to end the selection.

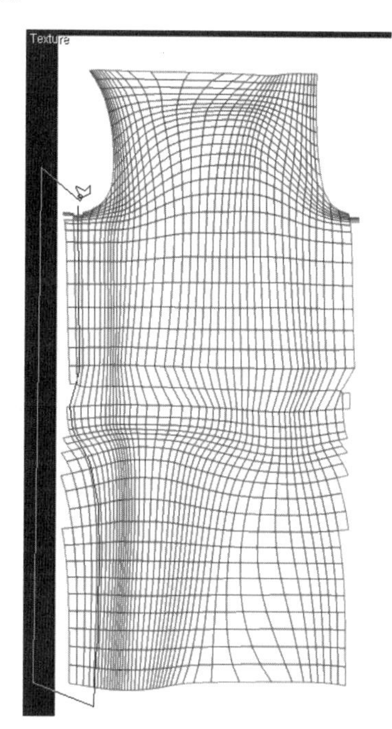

FIGURE 10.12 Select the polygons that you want to move to the other side of the pants leg.

17. Press the Shift key while you use the right arrow to move the selected polygons to the other side of the pants leg. When you get close to the target spot, release the Shift key, and use only the arrow key to nudge the selection into place. Position them as close as you can without overlapping any of the polygons (note that some may not match up exactly, but this is okay).

18. Switch to Vertex Selection mode (Select > Select Method > By Vertex). Use the Selection tool to make a selection large enough to enclose the polygons you moved and the polygons you want to attach them to.
19. Choose Tools > UVs > Stitch. Answer Yes to the confirmation dialog box.
20. Repeat Steps 15 through 20 for the other leg, except that you will move polygons from the right side of the leg to the left side. When you are finished, both legs should look as shown in Figure 10.13.

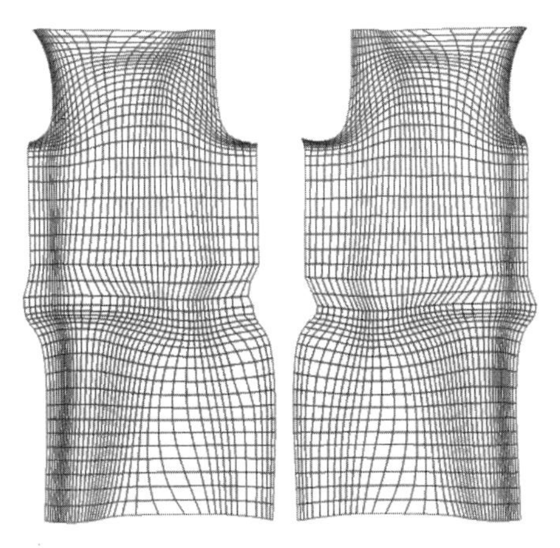

FIGURE 10.13 The legs have been cleaned and stitched.

If your legs are different sizes, select one of the legs with the Rectangular Selection tool, and then drag the left or right side to change the width accordingly.

21. Choose Texture > Checker > Color to check the final result in the mapping. A final version appears on the DVD in Tutorials\Chapter10 as pants-mapped.obj (if you are unable to save your model with the demo version).

If desired, you can use UVMapper Professional's Relax feature to even out the spacing between the polygons. To do so, first choose Edge Selection mode (Select > Select Method > By Edge). Select both sections of pants, and the edge vertices should turn blue. Then choose Tools > UVs > Relax. Leave the settings at their defaults, and click the Apply button one or more times until you are satisfied with the results. Watch the checkerboard texture on the 3D preview while you relax the vertices.

TUTORIAL 10.3 USING UVMAPPER TO MAP A SHIRT

Shirts present even more of a challenge than pants, especially for those who are new to UV mapping. Basically, the best way to UV map a shirt is with a combination of planar and cylindrical mapping. Again, as I brought up in the last tutorial, if you visualize the object into its different elements prior to unwrapping it, you will have a good idea of how you need to go about the process. Break it into pieces in the position where seams would occur. In the case of the shirt, the sleeves would become separate from the torso, and the front of the shirt would be detached from the back.

1. After opening tshirt.obj, UVMapper displays the statistics of the object. Click OK to continue. A 3D version of the shirt appears in the Perspective view on the right side of the screen. Initially, the left side is blank, indicating that the object does not have any UV information.
2. If necessary, remove the checkerboard background from the Texture view (Texture > Clear). Also verify that you are in Facet Selection mode (Select > Select Method > By Facet).
3. To begin, you will planar map the shirt so that you can remove the sleeves and map them separately. Choose Map > Planar. When the Planar Mapping dialog box appears, choose the Z-Axis Alignment option (which divides the shirt into front and back) and the By Orientation Split option (which splits the sides so that front appears on the left and back appears on the right). Then click OK to create the map.
4. Now use the Rectangular Selection tool to select the first row of polygons for each sleeve in both views, and then Shift-click to add additional selections to the set. Your selection should look that shown in Figure 10.14.
5. Press the zero (0) key on your keyboard. This expands the selection by one row of polygons. Press 0 nine additional times until you have selected all of the vertices in the sleeves.
6. Position the cursor inside the selection area so that the Selection tool changes into an arrow. Drag the sleeve polygons above the work area temporarily.
7. Now select both sections of the shirt and choose Map > Cylindrical. Accept the default of Y (up/down). All other options should be unchecked or set to zero. Click OK to map the shirt.
8. You can easily leave the shirt this way except for one reason that will become obvious if you turn on the Color texture checker (Texture > Checker > Color). The polygons distort the mapping at the top of the shoulders because they are too close together. However, it's a lot easier to select the

front of the shirt while the shirt is in Cylindrical mode. Use the Polygonal Selection tool to select the front portion of the shirt, dividing it along the center of each armhole. Figure 10.15 shows an example of the selection.

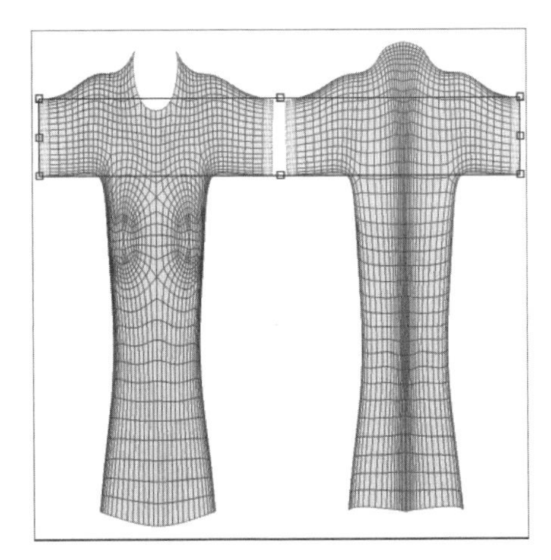

FIGURE 10.14 The first row of vertices is selected in both sleeves.

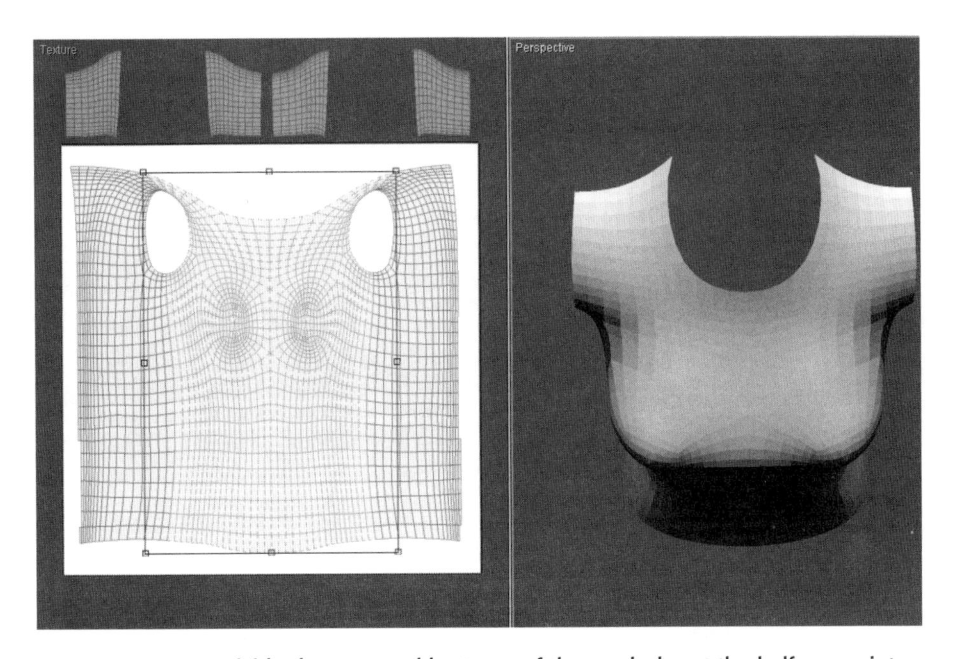

FIGURE 10.15 Divide the tops and bottoms of the armholes at the halfway point.

If necessary, you can also select polygons in the 3D Perspective view. Use the Rectangular Selection tool, and Shift-click to add polygons to the existing selection. You only need to include a small portion of the polygon to add it to the selection. If you mistakenly add polygons to the selection that you do not want, Alt-click to remove them from the selection.

9. With the front of the shirt selected, choose Map > Planar. Choose Don't Split to prevent UVMapper Professional from separating the side polygons into the back section of the shirt.
10. Press the forward slash (/) key on your number pad to halve the size of the front of the shirt so that you have more room to work on the other two sections.
11. Select one of the back sections, and choose Map > Planar. Accept the previous settings, and choose OK. Divide it in half with the / key on the number pad. Then select the entire section, and choose Select > Rotate > Flip Horizontal so that the side with the sleeve opening faces the front sleeve opening.
12. Repeat Step 11 for the other back section.
13. Select one section at a time, and move them in closer together if necessary. Space and size the three sections similarly to those shown in Figure 10.16. You can also move the sleeves back on to the work area now.

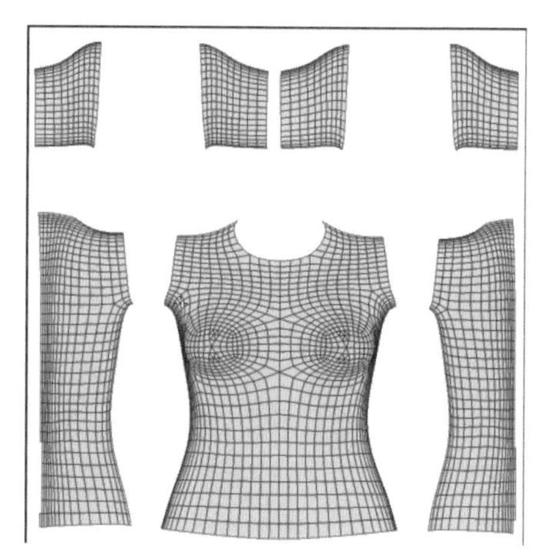

FIGURE 10.16 Scale and position the three sections of the shirt at the bottom of the UV map area.

14. Change to Vertex Selection mode (Select > Select Method > By Vertex). Use the Rectangular Selection tool to enclose the vertices between the left side and the front of the shirt, starting from the underarm and continuing to the bottom. Then choose Tools > UVs > Stitch to join them.
15. Similarly, enclose the vertices between the right side and the front of the shirt. Then choose Tools > UVs > Stitch to join them. The result should look like what's shown in Figure 10.17.

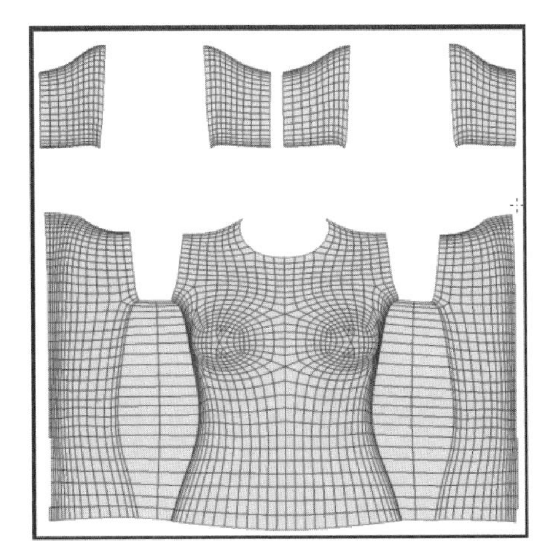

FIGURE 10.17 Stitch the front and sides together at the seams.

16. If you turn on the Color texture checker at this point (Texture > Checker > Color), you'll see that the sides look very distorted. This will result in stretching with any texture you apply to the shirt. UVMapper Professional allows you to relax vertices to eliminate stretching. But first, you have to hide the parts that you don't want to relax. After you return to Facet Selection mode (Select > Select Method > By Facet), select the sleeves. Then press the left bracket ([ ) key to hide them.
17. Choose the Edge Selection mode (Select > Select Method > By Edge). Draw a selection around all three shirt sections. The outer vertices will turn blue, indicating that they are selected.
18. Choose Tools > UVs > Relax. When the Relax UVs dialog box appears, accept the default choices. Click the Apply button one or more times while watching the texture change in Perspective view. Choose OK to apply the changes when you are satisfied with the mapping on the sides of the shirt. Figure 10.18 shows the result.

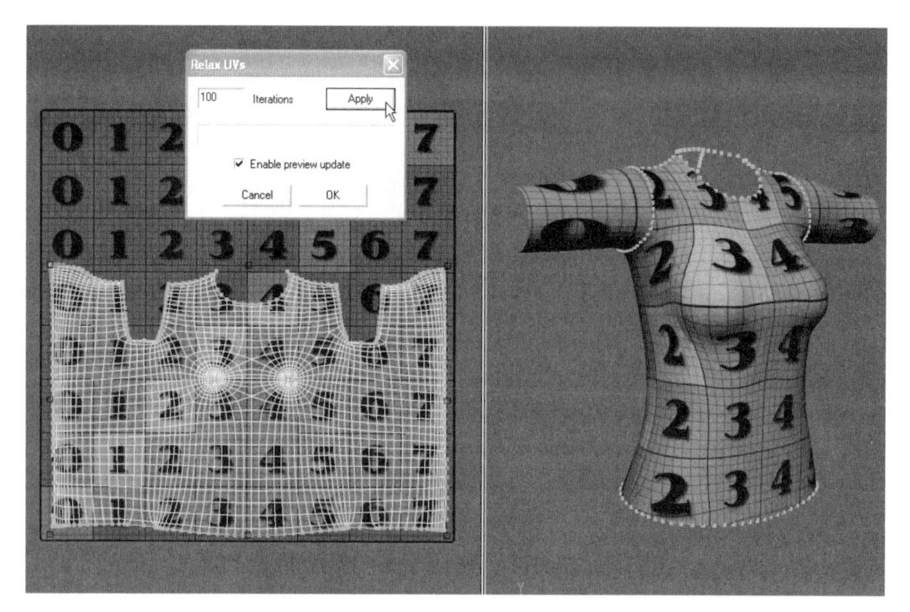

FIGURE 10.18 Relax the UV mapping until you are satisfied with the appearance of the sides of the shirt.

19. Return to Facet Selection mode (Select > Select Method > By Facet). Press the right bracket key ( ]) to unhide the sleeves. You need to join them at the top. First, select the two sleeves at the left of the screen (the front sleeves). Choose Select > Rotate > 180 degrees to rotate them so that they match up properly with the appropriate sleeve back. Then position the sleeve fronts above the sleeve backs.
20. Switch to Vertex Selection mode (Select > Select Method > By Vertex), and draw a selection that encloses the vertices you want to join on the sleeves. Then choose Tools > UVs > Stitch to connect them. Figure 10.19 shows the result.
21. The final step is to relax the sleeves and position them in their final place on the map. Make sure you hide the front of the shirt first to prevent it from relaxing further. First, return to Facet Selection mode (Select > Select Method > By Facet). Select the front and back of the shirt, and hide it with the [key.
22. Return to Edge Selection mode (Select > Select Method > By Edge). Select both sleeves. Then use the Relax feature (Tools > UVs > Relax), clicking the Apply button one or more times until the top edges are blended better.

FIGURE 10.19 The sleeves are joined at the top.

23. Press] to unhide the remainder of the shirt. Return to Facet Selection mode, then rotate and position the sleeves with the Select > Rotate command, and position them as shown in Figure 10.20.

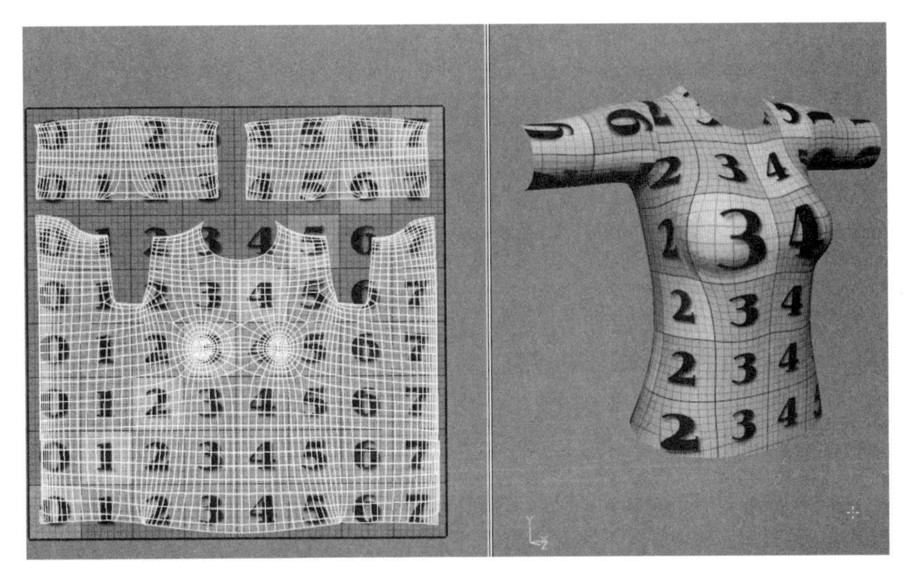

FIGURE 10.20 The finished shirt.

Making Templates

UVMapper Professional colors the template based on the way it is displayed in Texture view. By default, the template is black and white (white background with black lines). You can also color the templates based on how they are assigned by material, group, or region. For example, if your object is made of different materials, and you want to represent the materials with different colors in your template, choose Map > Color > By Material. You can also color the map by group (such as the body part groups that you use in Poser) or by region (for example, if you want to save the items on the head as one region and the remainder of the body as another region). You'll learn more about assigning groups and materials in Chapter 11, "Groups and Materials for Models."

It's fairly easy to save a template. After you save your model, just choose File > Save Template in UVMapper Professional. The BMP Export Options dialog box appears. The options are as follows:

- **Width and Height:** Enter the desired width and height for the template. Although the dimensions do not have to be square, many programs (including Poser) use resources more efficiently when textures are 512, 1024, 2048, or 4096 pixels in width and height.
- **RGB Color, Antialiased:** Choose this option if you want your template to be recognized as a high-color or true-color image, with antialiased edges to smooth jagged edges on diagonal lines.
- **RGB Color:** Choose this for full-color templates that are not antialiased.
- **256 Color:** Choose this option to create a 256-color image that creates a smaller file size. Even though you can create high-color or 256-color images for your templates, you'll find that the template only contains 16 colors. The color selections determine how your image editor sees the template.
- **Flip Texture Map Vertically:** Check this option to flip the texture vertically (up and down).
- **Flip Texture Map Horizontally:** Check this option to flip the texture map horizontally (right to left).
- **Include Hidden Facets:** When checked, also includes any facets that might be hidden from view by using the [key. This is handy when you need to create templates for models that require two or more texture maps.
- **Include Labels:** If your texture map is colored by group, material, or region, you can include labels on the texture map that show the names of the groups, materials, or regions by their color.

If you are working on a Mac, you will not have any of the preceding options in the Export Texture Options dialog. The only controls you will have are for file format (PDF or TIFF) and to set the width and height of the exported map.

After you make your selections, click OK to create the texture map. You can then open the map in an image editor, such as Photoshop, to paint a texture using the map as a guide.

UV Mapping with Maxon's Body Paint 4/4.5

Maxon's Body Paint has become a favorite in the 3D community because of its relative ease of use and high-end interactive painting capabilities. Body Paint comes as both a stand-alone program and as a plug-in to Maxon's Cinema4D modeling program.

The UV mapping features are easy to use and full-featured. One of the nicest things about Body Paint is you're not limited to just painting on one OBJ file; you can import, paint, and make UV maps for multiple OBJs at one time. Another difference is the Relax UV feature creates mapping that is more uniform in appearance.

There is a fully functional demo version of Body Paint 4.5 on the book's DVD. Or you can go to www.maxon.net to download this or Cinema4D demos before starting this section.

Again, an entire book could be written about using Body Paint, and I certainly don't have that much space or time to cover detailed projects in this book. So I will do a quick walkthrough of a simple project where you will import an OBJ file, create the UV map, paint on the object, and export it for use in Poser.

Tutorial 10.4 Importing a Poser OBJ File into Body Paint

Importing an OBJ file into Cinema4D and Body Paint is a straightforward proposition.

I will be using Cinema4D 11.5 and Body Paint 4.5 for this tutorial. My version of C4D has the Body Paint (BP) module. What's important to note is, when you're in the BP module, there is no difference between what you see in this tutorial and the actual Body Paint program. If you are using Body Paint, refer to the manual regarding importing an OBJ file before moving to Step 3.

1. In Cinema4D, go to File > Open. Navigate to the tshirt.obj file.
2. After selecting the file, you will see the dialog box shown in Figure 10.21. The scale of the Poser OBJ is extremely small in comparison to the Body Paint units, so you're going to have to increase the OBJ's size. Set Scale to 1000 and click OK. The shirt will appear in the main workspace (see Figure 10.22).

NOTE

If you own an earlier version of Cinema 4D and Body Paint (v. 11 or earlier), there is a plug-in for C4D that allows for an easy import and export of OBJ files. It's called Riptide, and can be downloaded for free at Spanki's Prop Show (http://skinprops.com/riptide.php).

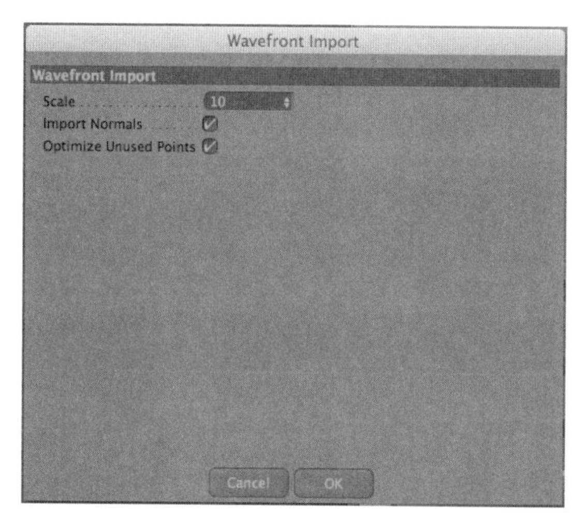

FIGURE 10.21 The scale of the OBJ needs to be changed in order to match Body Paint's scale.

3. Next, click on the 3D Setup Wizard button (see Figure 10.23). This will convert the OBJ file into a paintable mesh. You're going to be asked to make some choices during this process. Figure 10.24 shows the screens that appear as you walk through the paint setup process.

   When you go through these screens, unless there is a reason to do it, do not change any of the default settings. For this tutorial, the only thing you might want to change is in the second screen—uncheck Single Material Mode. Then just click Next through the rest of the screens and close out of the 3D Setup Wizard.

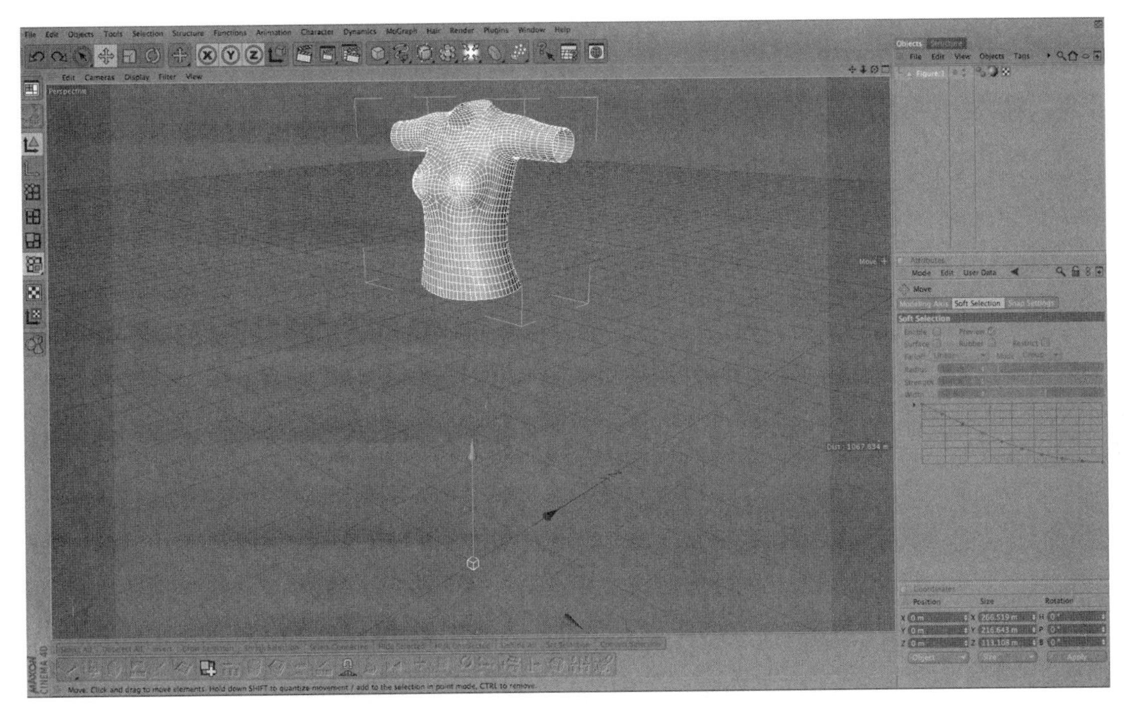

FIGURE 10.22 The tshirt.obj file opened in Body Paint.

FIGURE 10.23 The Body Paint 3D Setup Wizard button looks like a paint brush with three stars in a semi-circle.

4. At the top of the window, there are two tabs: View and Texture. View is the default where you see the mesh. Texture is where you see the generated UV (or UVW) map. When you click on the Texture tab, you will get a blank screen. In order to see the UV map, go to UV Mesh > Show UV Mesh, and you'll see what is shown in Figure 10.25.

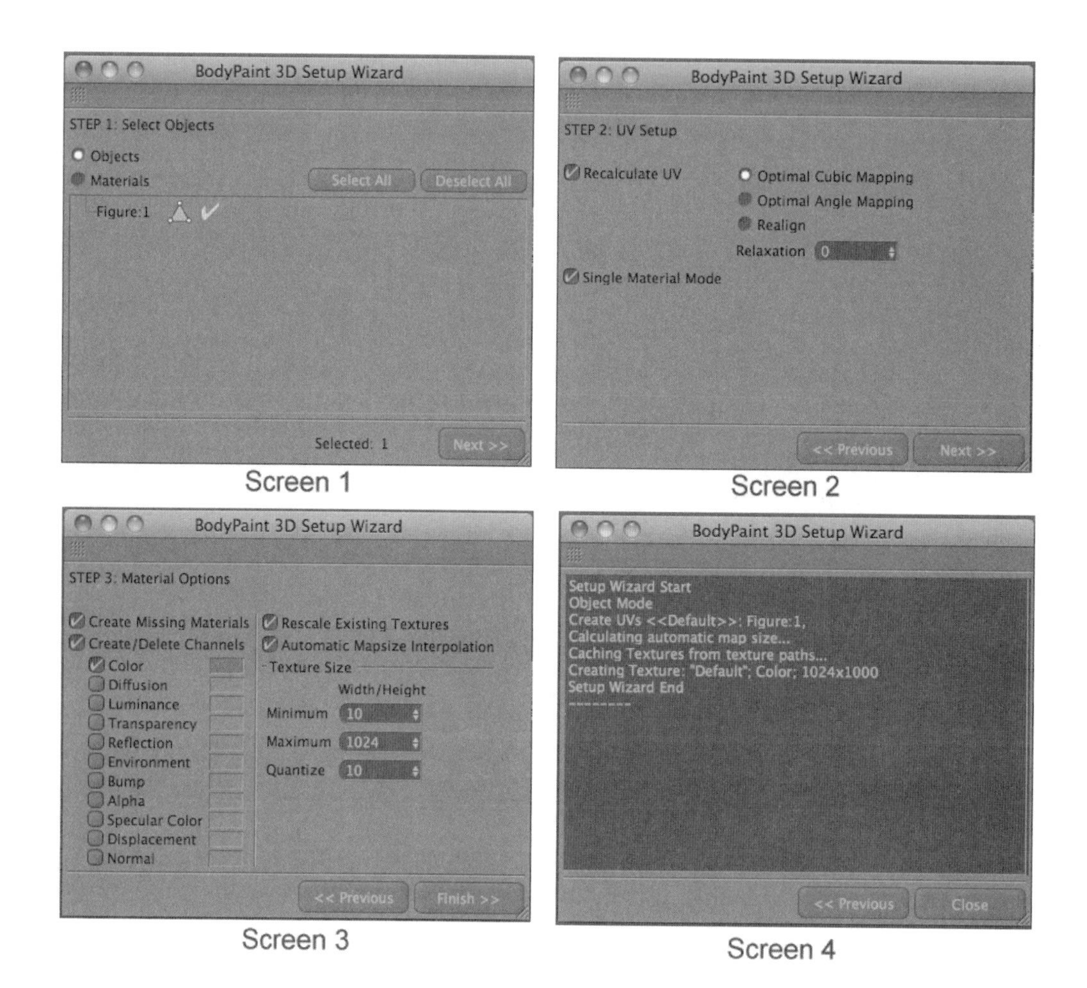

FIGURE 10.24 The 3D Setup Wizard screens that turn your OBJ into a paintable mesh.

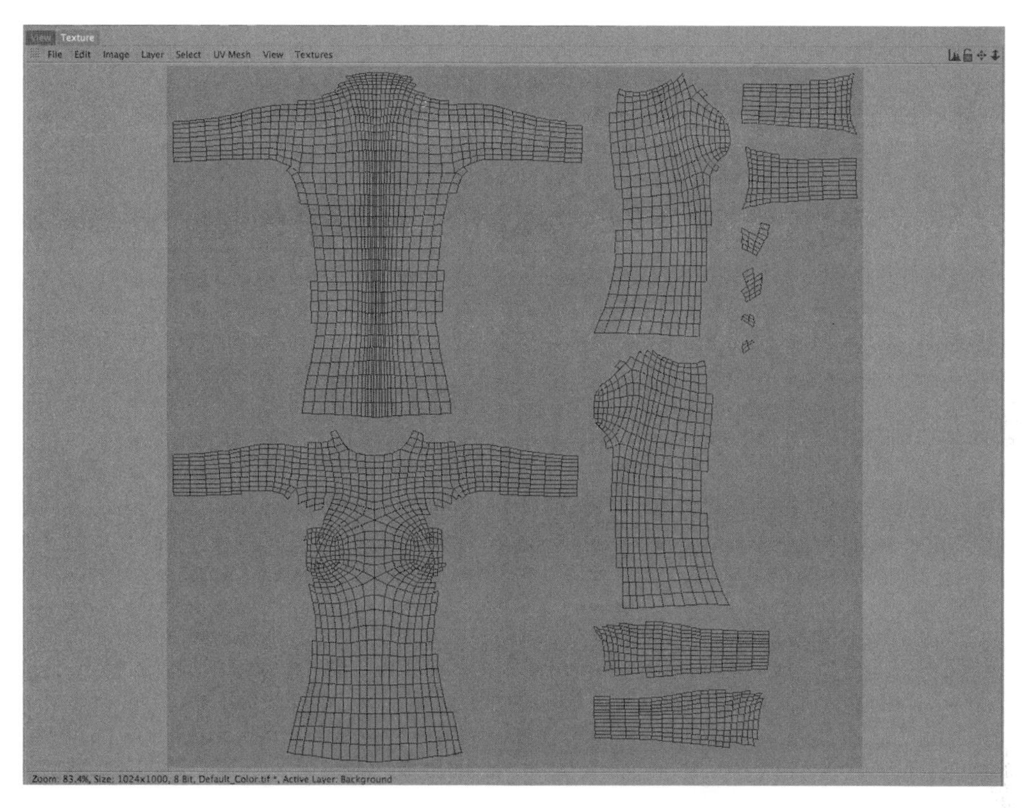

FIGURE 10.25 The generated UV map inside of the Body Paint module in Cinema4D.

TUTORIAL 10.5 UV MAPPING A SHIRT USING BODY PAINT

With the UV map created, it's time to use it to create a texture for the tshirt.obj file. You have the choice of painting directly on the mesh or on the UV map.

1. Switch to BP UV Edit mode (see Figure 10.26). The screen will change to show both the model and the UV mesh (see Figure 10.27).
2. At the top of the screen, go to Select > Select All. All of the polygons making up the mesh will be highlighted.
3. In the lower-right section of the workspace, make sure to select the UV Mapping tab and then the UV Commands button (refer to Figure 10.27). Select Start Interactive Mapping, and you will immediately see the mapping of the t-shirt change. That's because Body Paint will superimpose a flat projection across the front and back (see Figure 10.28).

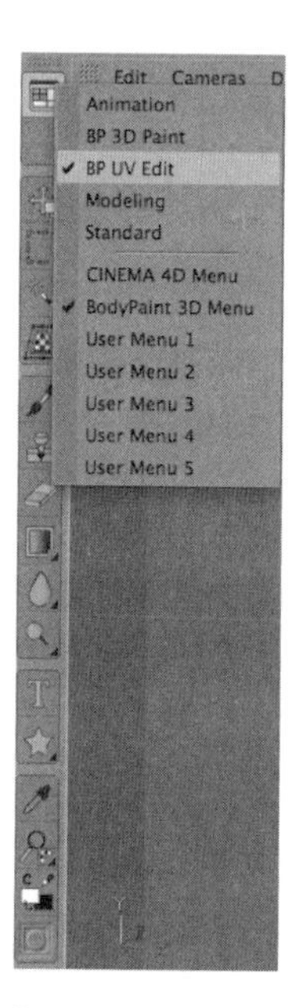

FIGURE 10.26 Switch to BP UV Edit mode in Cinema 4D.

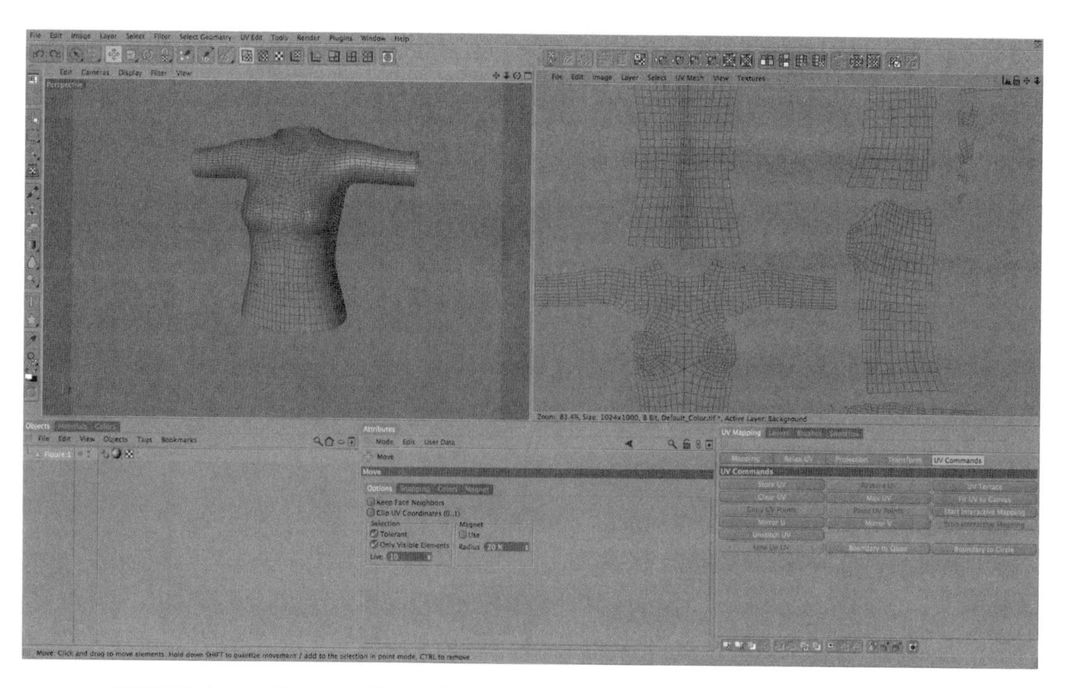

FIGURE 10.27 The UV Edit workspace showing the shirt model and the UV map.

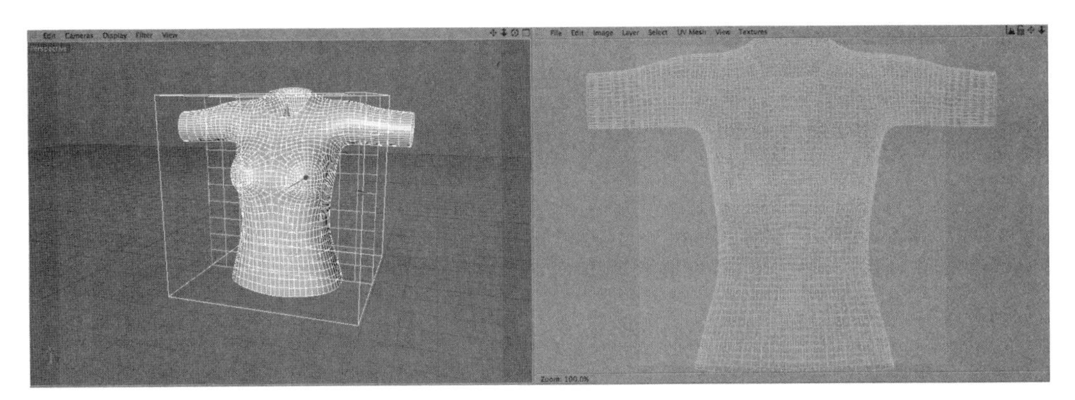

FIGURE 10.28 The t-shirt with a flat projection superimposed across the model.

4. What you want to do is separate the sleeves from the remainder of the shirt. Click on the shortened double-arrow at the top of the UVW window and zoom out until you can see the entire UV map. Or you can go to View > Fit to Screen in the menus immediately above the UV map window.
5. In order to select the sleeves, you now need to exit the interactive mode. Click the Stop Interactive Mapping button in the UV Mapping tools area.
6. Right-click in the UV map window and choose Select Geometry > Deselect All from the menu.
7. Choose the Live Selection tool from the horizontal tool bar at the top of the screen. You can tell what tool you are choosing by rolling the cursor over the tool and looking at the lower left of the window. The tool's name will be displayed there. You could also go to Tools > UV Tools > Live Selection Tool.
8. With the Live Selection tool active, paint the 11 rows of polygons that make up the left sleeve (see Figure 10.29). You can do this in either the Perspective or UV map view, although it will probably be easier to do in the Perspective view. You'll need to hold the Shift key in order to add to your selection.
9. Use the Move tool to move the sleeve off the UV texture map.
10. Repeat Steps 8 and 9 on the right sleeve. After you're finished, the UV map will look like the one in Figure 10.30.
11. Choose the Rectangle Selection tool from the toolbar, or go to Tools > UV Tools > Rectangle Selection menu command. Draw a selection around the body of the shirt.

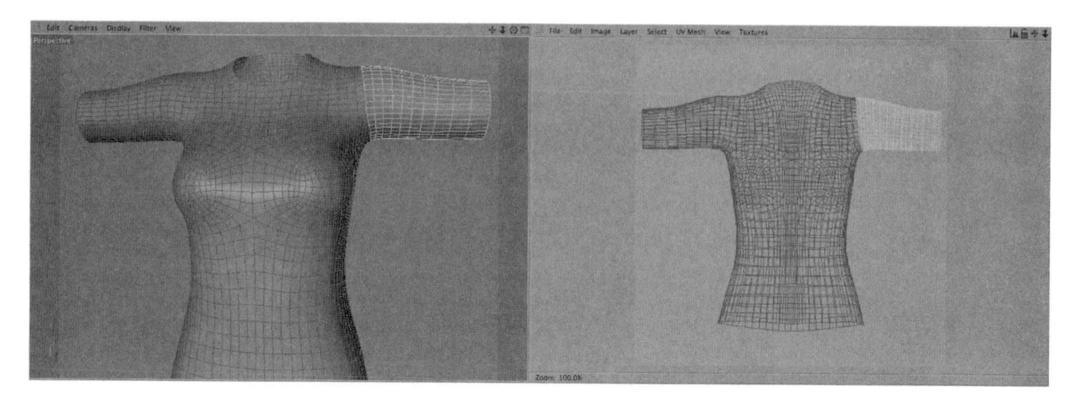

FIGURE 10.29 On the left sleeve, 11 rows of polygons have been selected.

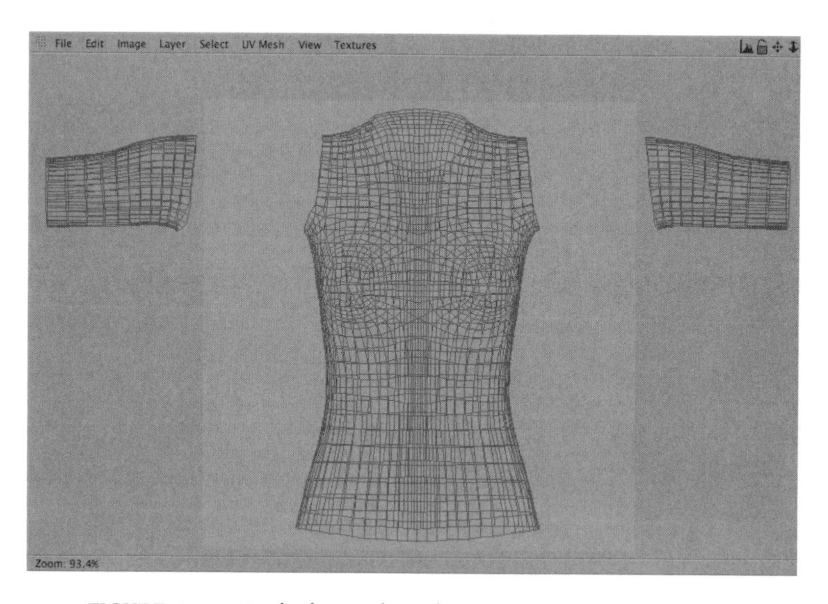

FIGURE 10.30 Both sleeves have been moved off the UV map.

12. Choose Start Interactive Mapping from the UV Mapping controls once again.
13. In the Attributes tab (the middle control window), choose Cylindrical for the Projection option (see Figure 10.31). The seam (the green line seen in the Perspective view) initially appears at the side of the shirt. This works because you're separating front and back.

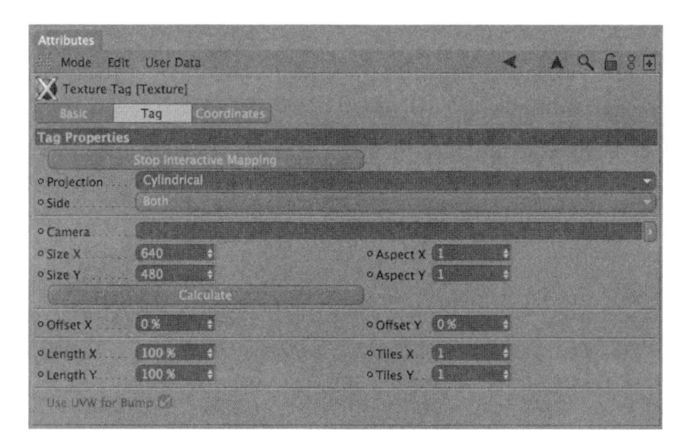

FIGURE 10.31 The Attributes tab with Projection set to Cylindrical.

14. Choose Stop Interactive Mapping, and then select the Polygon Selection tool. Separate the front part of the shirt from the back part. When you select the polygons, keep in mind that half of the sleeve hole should be in the front and half should be in the back.
15. If necessary, use the Live Selection tool to refine the selection in the Perspective view. Use the Shift key with the tool to add polygons to the selection, or use the Ctrl key with the tool to remove polygons. An example of the completed front selection is shown in Figure 10.32.
16. Use the Move tool to move those polygons off the canvas.
17. Select the polygons for the back of the shirt (the polygons that remain in the UV mapping area) with the Rectangle Selection tool.

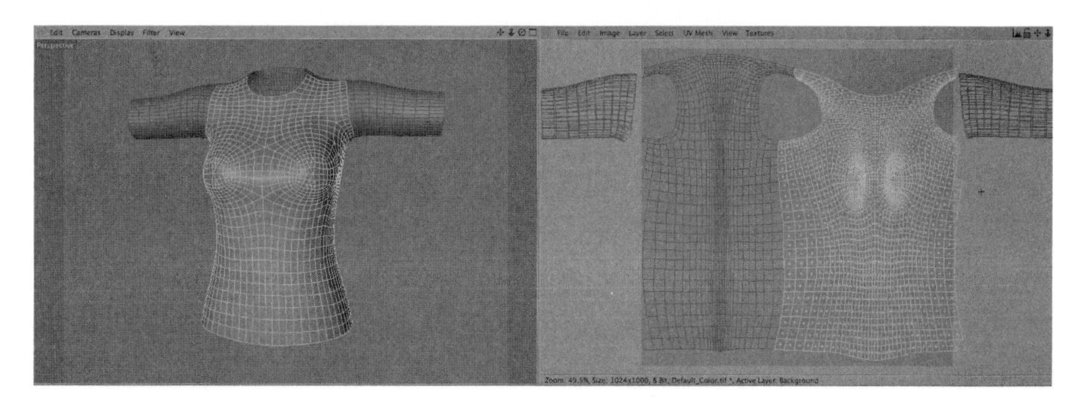

FIGURE 10.32 The front polygons have been selected for the shirt.

18. Click the UV Mapping tab, click Projection, and choose Flat from the selector. The polygons for the back of the shirt will flatten and fill the UV mapping area. Move them off of the canvas.
19. Select the polygons for the front of the shirt with the Rectangle Selection tool. Again, use Flat Projection on these polygons, and move them off the canvas.
20. Select the sleeve that appears on the left side in the UV mapping view. Choose Start Interactive Mapping from the UV Mapping tab.
21. In the Attributes tab, click the Coordinates button, and then enter **90** degrees in the B field. This rotates the cylinder so that the seam is on the bottom of the sleeve. You should see the sleeve flatten out perfectly, as shown in Figure 10.33.

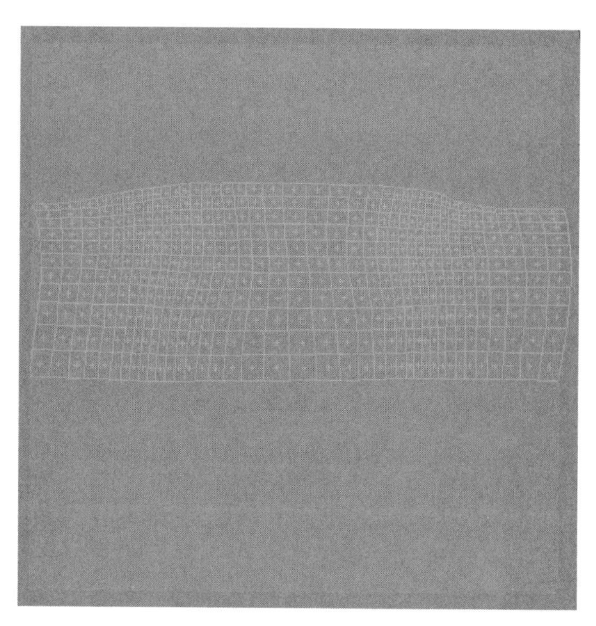

FIGURE 10.33 The first sleeved mapped in a cylinder projection rotated 90 degrees.

22. Choose Stop Interactive Mapping from the UV Mapping tab, and move the sleeve off the canvas with the Move tool.
23. Select the other sleeve with the Rectangle Selection tool. Again, choose Start Interactive Mapping. The second sleeve should automatically use the same properties as the other sleeve.

24. So that both sleeves have the cuffs on the bottom in the texture map, you'll need to rotate the present sleeve by 180 degrees. Enter **180** degrees in the H field (see Figure 10.34). Now both sleeves are facing the same direction on the map.

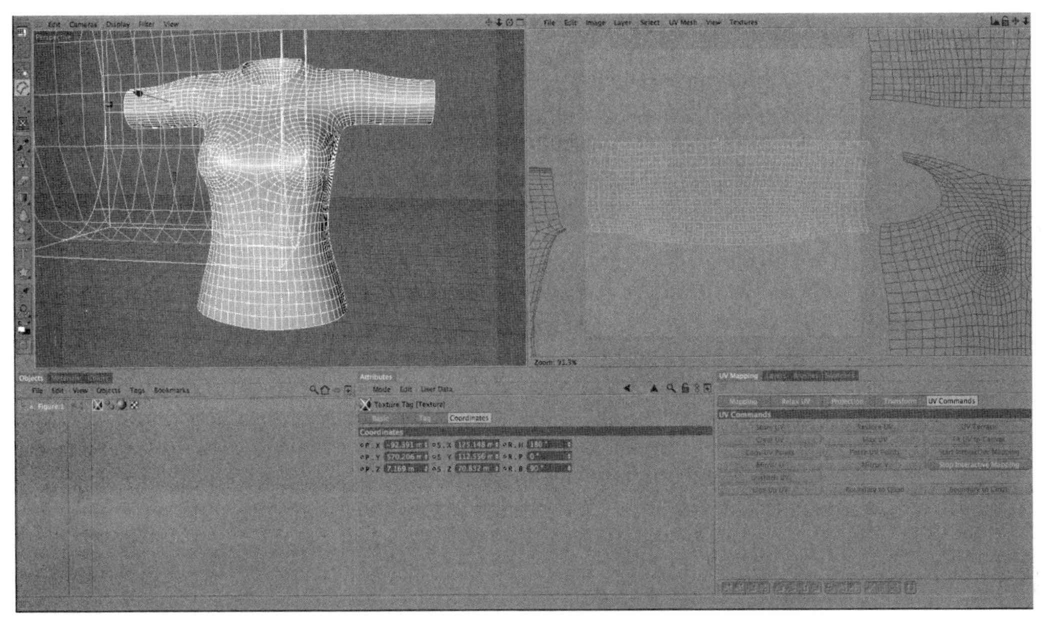

FIGURE 10.34 The right sleeve is rotated into position using the H field.

25. Choose Stop Interactive Mapping, and move the second sleeve next to the first one off the canvas.
26. Now you need to relax the front and back of the shirt so that the textures don't stretch. Select the back of the shirt with the Rectangle Selection tool.
27. Click the UV Mapping tab, and then select Relax UV. Uncheck Pin Border Points and Pin To Neighbors. Then click the Apply button three times.
28. Repeat Step 26 for the front of the shirt. Your mapping should now look similar to Figure 10.35.
29. Finally, use the Scale tool and the Move tool in the toolbar to position and size the various parts so that they are arranged neatly. Select all of the polygons with the Rectangular Selection tool. Then choose UV Commands > Fit UV to Canvas from the UV Mapping tab. Your final mapping should look similar to Figure 10.36.

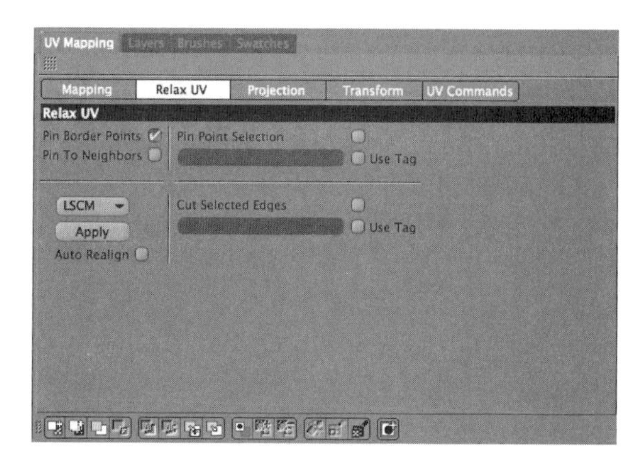

FIGURE 10.35 The front and back sections have been relaxed using the Relax UV command.

FIGURE 10.36 The final UV map.

30. At this point, choose File > Save. The Save File dialog box will prompt you for a location and file name. Note that this file will be saved in Cinema 4D format, which is not compatible with Poser. However, it is a good idea to save the Body Paint project file in case you have to make revisions in the future. Click Save after you select a folder and enter a file name.

From here, you would begin painting in Body Paint, working with your UV map and layers to generate the texture you would like. You can also go back into the BP 3D Paint section, go to Texture, increase its size to fit in the window, and then do a screen capture to save the UV map for use in other programs (such as Photoshop).

Of course, the main reason to import a model into Body Paint is to paint on it, and then use that painted file in your scenes. As would be expected, that would require taking the shirt back into Poser. This means the OBJ file has to be exported and saved for use in Poser. Just go to File > Export > Wavefront OBJ and save the file for use in Poser. Remember, though, you increased its size from 1 to 1000 when you started, so you will have to scale the OBJ file back down. However, when I'm working on files like this, I don't scale them up. I zoom in (massively at times) to keep the object to scale. You can, however, also keep the scaled file and then scale it back down when brought into Poser. There are myriad ways you can do this; it all comes down to your comfort level and how you like to work.

A Short Re-Pose

UV mapping is an extremely important part of the modeling process. Without a good UV map, you will have massive difficulties designing great textures that bring your work to life. When care is taken in creating UV maps, you can eliminate stretching and distortion on your model, and by breaking down the objects into their basic shapes (spheres, planes, boxes, or cylinders), you can map complex objects with ease.

In the next chapter, you will do just that—work with complex models that were modified in Poser. So our little sojourn from Poser has now gone full circle.

11 Groups and Materials for Models

In This Chapter:

- About Group Names
- Decompressing an OBZ File
- Using Poser's Group Editor
- Tutorial 11.1: Assigning Groups and Materials
- Saving Grouped Objects for Later Use
- Tutorial 11.2: Exporting an OBJ File from Poser
- Using Auto Group Editor to Map Grouped Models
- Tutorial 11.3: Grouping with the Auto Group Editor
- Using UVMapper with Grouped Objects
- Tutorial 11.4: Groups and Materials in UVMapper Professional

"Art never improves, but the material of art is never quite the same."

—T.S. Eliot

Time to end the texturing trifecta with a look at considerations faced when you model your own clothing, such as a floor-length skirt. This goes beyond the UV mapping; you actually need to break the polygons down in order to match specific areas of the body of the model to which it's being assigned. You can select polygons from the waist to the miniskirt length and assign them to a material named Mini. You can then select the polygons that start at just after Mini and go to approximately the knees. These you could call, appropriately enough, Knee. Then you select polys from knee level to mid-calf and call the new material MidCalf. Finally, take the rest of the polys from MidCalf to floor and call this material Full. By dividing this hypothetical skirt into several materials, you can make one or more layers invisible to vary the length of the skirt and give more power to the model.

In addition, when you model clothing, you'll need to know ahead of time whether you want the clothing to be Dynamic clothing (for the Cloth Room) or Conforming clothing that poses automatically with your figure. If you decide to make Conforming clothing, you will need to divide your model into body part groups that coincide with the groups in your human figure.

Most 3D modeling programs allow you to assign materials and groups to 3D objects during the modeling process, and it is generally easiest to perform these tasks at that time. If you have obtained models that need groups or materials assigned, or if you prefer to use other methods to accomplish these tasks, this chapter will introduce you to other alternatives.

About Group Names

If you are creating Dynamic clothing, you do not need to create predefined polygon groups. Instead, you use the Group Editor in the Cloth Room to assign vertices to one or more cloth groups. This process is explained in detail in Chapter 11 of the Poser Tutorial Manual.

Conforming clothing, on the other hand, works much differently. For Conforming clothing to conform to a human figure, you have to divide the clothing model into body part groups that coincide with those on the model that they cover. For example, if you are creating a shirt, you'll probably need to create groups such as chest, abdomen, lCollar, rCollar, lShldr, and rShldr (the last four being the required names for left and right collars and shoulders). The polygons in the clothing groups should be named the same and match the area of the corresponding polygons in the figure's groups as closely as possible. The reason for the "l" and "r" nomenclature is to allow Poser to perform its Figure > Symmetry commands. Although you could start right and left group names with a letter other than r or l and pose the figure, the Symmetry commands would not work.

The group names that you normally see for human figures in Poser menus and lists have names such as Left Forearm, Right Collar, and Left Shoulder. However, there are also shorter internal group names that Poser references in its CR2 Character Library files. Internal group names can contain capital letters, but they must always begin with a small letter to work properly. You can see a group's internal name when you click a body part and view the associated properties in the Properties panel. For example, you see Marcus's Right Collar in Figure 11.1, where it has an internal name of rCollar.

The Marcus character is a derivative of the Ryan model. He is located, by default, in the Figures\Poser 8\Ryan folder.

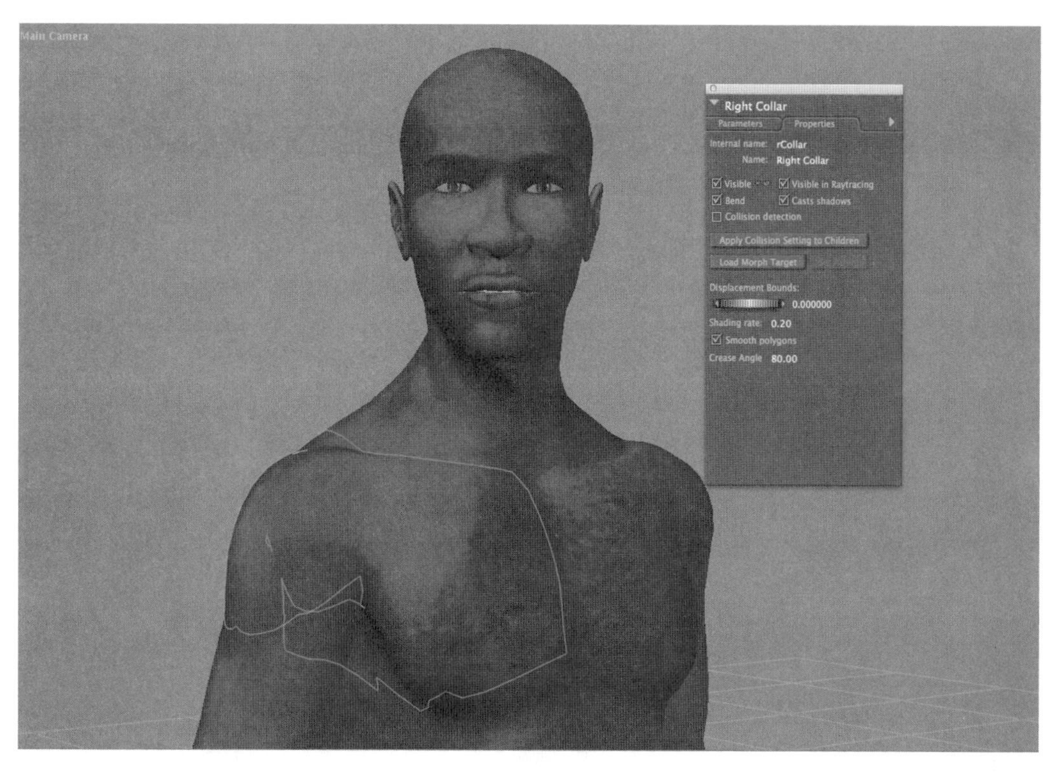

FIGURE 11.1 Each body part has an internal name referenced in the Properties panel.

For Conforming clothing to automatically pose the same as the figure that wears it, you have to create groups in the clothing that are named exactly the same as those in the figure. For the most part, all Poser figures use similar group names. There are minor exceptions, which will be mentioned when applicable.

It is important to understand how the polygons in a standard Poser figure are grouped. Just as the center of gravity of your own body is found at hip level, the same is true of a Poser human figure. The hip is the central part of the figure and the point at which all of the hierarchical chains begin. The hip is the first parent in the hierarchy.

As you work your way from the hip to the feet, each subsequent level is a child of the body part that preceded it. For example, the hip is the parent of the thigh, which in turn is the parent of the shin, which is in turn the parent of the foot. Working your way backward up the chain, the left foot is a child of the left shin, which is in turn a child of the left thigh, which is in turn a child of the hip.

Figure 11.2 shows internal group names for Jessi. Many Poser figures use the same grouping that Jessi uses. Starting with the hierarchical chain that runs from the hip to the head and eyes, the internal group names are hip, abdomen, chest, neck, and head. The rightEye and leftEye parts are both children of the head. Other figures may have a second neck part, named upperNeck, which falls between the neck and head. There are sometimes differences in the way that the chest and collar sections are grouped. In Jessi, the chest group contains the breasts. In other figures, you may see the breasts as part of the right and left collar sections.

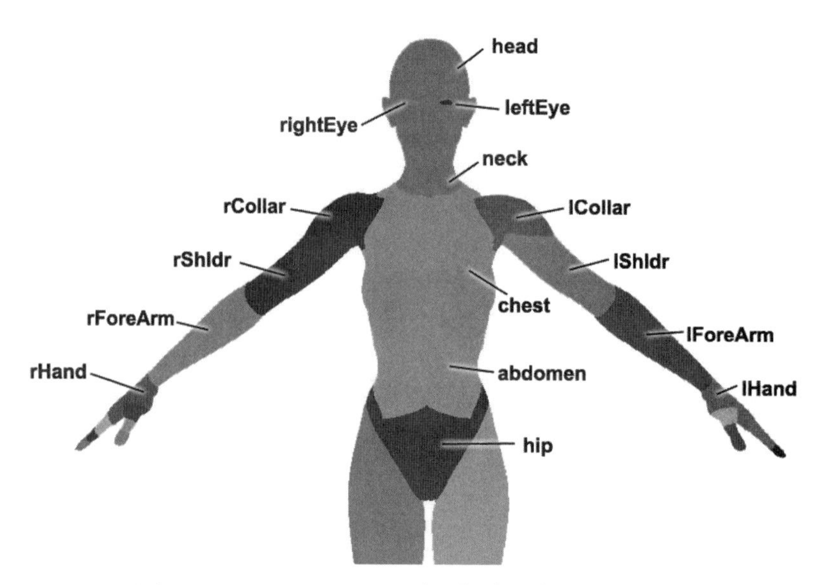

FIGURE 11.2 Group names for the head, torso, and arms.

The right and left collar and arm sections connect from the chest. Each arm has parts with similar internal names, except that the internal names for the right arm parts begin with a lowercase "r," and the left arm parts begin with a lowercase "l." Starting from the chest and working downward, the right arm group names are rCollar, rShldr, rForeArm, and rHand. Left arm parts are named the same, with the exception of the "l" prefix.

Finally, you reach the fingers, which are shown in Figure 11.3. Each hand branches out into five fingers, each of which is divided into three sections. The section closest to the base of the hand is number 1, the middle section is number 2, and the last section (with the fingernail) is number 3. As for the names of the fingers, the right hand finger groups are named rThumb1, rThumb2, rThumb3, rIndex1, rIndex2, rIndex3, rMid1, rMid2, rMid3, rRing1, rRing2, rRing3, rPinky1, rPinky2, and rPinky3. The fingers on the left hand are named the same, with the exception that "l" is the first letter instead of "r."

The Poser 8 figures also have a few extra body parts that can help you pose them more naturally. These include the Waist, positioned appropriately enough between the abdomen and the hip, as well as extra joints in the fingers. These extra joints are labeled rThumb0, lIndex0, and so on. These extra joints allow for more natural hand poses.

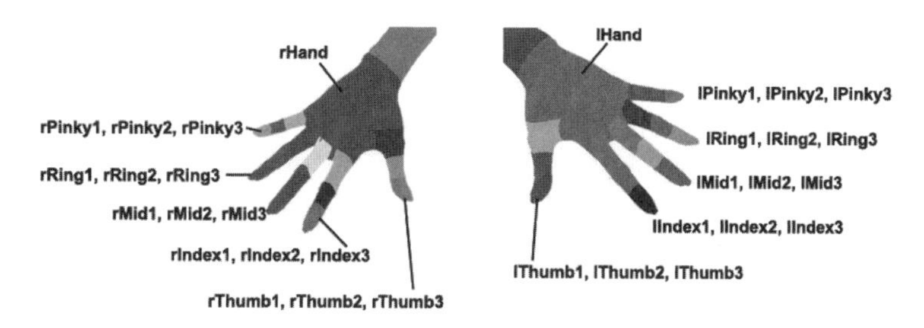

FIGURE 11.3 The left and right hand and finger group names.

The groups for the legs and feet of Jessi are shown in Figure 11.4. Starting from the hip, the right leg is divided into rButtock, rThigh, rShin, and rFoot. Other figures may also have a rButtock or lButtock section appearing between the hip and the corresponding thigh.

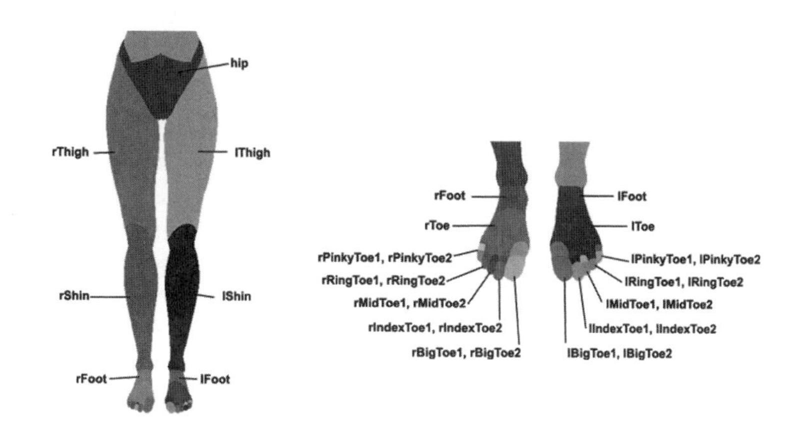

FIGURE 11.4 Leg, foot, and toe group names.

Next, you come to the toes, where there are also differences between figures. Jessi has articulated toes, meaning that each toe can be posed individually, just like the fingers in the hands. You will not find this feature in all Poser figures. When toes are not articulated, you will see groups in the right foot named rFoot and rToe and groups in the left foot named lFoot and lToe. The toe sections move all five toes at the same time.

In the case of articulated toes, the rToe and lToe sections serve as common first joints for all five toes, respectively—in other words, the rToe and lToe sections are equivalent to the balls of the human feet. From that point, each toe branches out into two joints apiece. For the right foot, these sections are named rBigToe1, rBigToe2, rIndexToe1, rIndexToe2, rMidToe1, rMidToe2, rRingToe1, rRingToe2, rPinkyToe1, and rPinkyToe2. As with the fingers, the toe closest to the common section is part number 1, and the part with the toenail is the highest numbered part (2, in this case). Left foot sections are similarly named.

Decompressing an OBZ File

To create groups in your clothing, it helps to view the model underneath your clothing at the same time. For example, if you know where the polygons for the abdomen fall on the human figure, you can select the polygons in your clothing that overlap that area and assign those polygons to the abdomen group in the clothing. This allows you to create the clothing groups more accurately. Because Poser 8 furnishes its figures in OBZ format (a compressed version of the OBJ file), you will need to decompress it before you import the model into any utility that imports OBJ files. There are two ways to decompress an OBZ file into an OBJ file:

- Open the OBZ file in a utility that opens ZIP files, such as WinZip for the PC or its Mac equivalent. Then extract the OBJ file to a directory of your choice. Use this default model whenever you create or set up clothing or create morphs.
- Use the Python script furnished with Poser to decompress all compressed files in a specified folder. Choose Scripts > Utility > Uncompress Poser Files. A dialog box prompts you to select the directory under which to decompress the files. Make sure you check the option to Uncompress geometry files (obj). Also, if you check the Delete Original Files After Uncompressing option, you avoid having duplicate versions of the thumbnails in your library. After you select your path and options, click OK. Your OBJ file will be located in the same folder as the original OBZ file.

You can turn off automatic saving of compressed files in the General Preferences dialog box. Choose Edit > General Preferences, and click the Misc tab. Uncheck the Use File Compression option. Whenever you save library files or export geometry files, Poser will not use the compressed formats and instead will save them to the uncompressed, and editable, versions of the files.

Using Poser's Group Editor

Poser's Group Editor serves a variety of purposes and operates in two modes—Polygon mode and Vertex mode. While in Polygon mode, the Group Editor allows you to select polygons in an object and assign them to a material or to body part groups for conforming clothing. Polygon mode also allows you to add polygons to hair growth groups in the Hair Room. Alternately, the Group Editor switches to Vertex Selection mode to enable you to assign selected vertices to cloth groups while you are in the Cloth Room.

When you use the Group Editor to assign groups and materials to an object, you work in Polygon mode, as shown in Figure 11.5.

FIGURE 11.5 The Group Editor contains numerous buttons that help you assign groups and materials in an object.

When you select and assign polygons to groups, you will mainly use the following buttons:

- **New Group:** To create a group in the clothing, click the New Group button. The New GroupName dialog box prompts you to enter a name for the new group. Click OK to add the group. Use the Delete Group button to delete the currently selected group from your object.
- **Previous and Next:** These arrow buttons allow you to move through the list of groups in your current object. Click the down arrow in between the Previous and Next buttons to select a group from the menu.
- **Select and Deselect:** When the Select button is enabled, you add polygons or vertices to the currently selected group. When the Deselect button is enabled, you remove polygons or vertices from the currently selected group.
- **Add All:** The Add All button adds all polygons in an object to the current group. Several other buttons help you add or remove polygons from the currently selected group.

The Group Editor also offers an Auto Group feature that you can use in conjunction with the Setup Room to add clothing groups. This method will be discussed in more detail in Chapter 12,"From Modeler to the Poser Library."

Now that you know what controls are at your disposal in the Group Editor, let's look at how they help you in assigning materials.

TUTORIAL 11.1 ASSIGNING GROUPS AND MATERIALS

To use Poser's Group Editor to assign groups and materials, follow these steps:

1. Starting with an empty scene in Poser, add Jessi or JessiHiRes from the Figures\Poser 6\Jessi library. Turn Inverse Kinematics off, and zero the pose of the figure.
2. Choose File > Import > Wavefront OBJ.
3. The Import Options dialog box appears, as shown in Figure 11.6. For this example, you don't need to check any of the options because the geometry will import in the correct scale and in the correct location. These options will be discussed in more detail in Chapter 12. After you uncheck the options, choose OK to continue.
4. Locate the OBJ file you want to open. In this case, choose skirt-mapped.OBJ in the Tutorials\Chap11 folder on the DVD. The skirt appears in the scene.

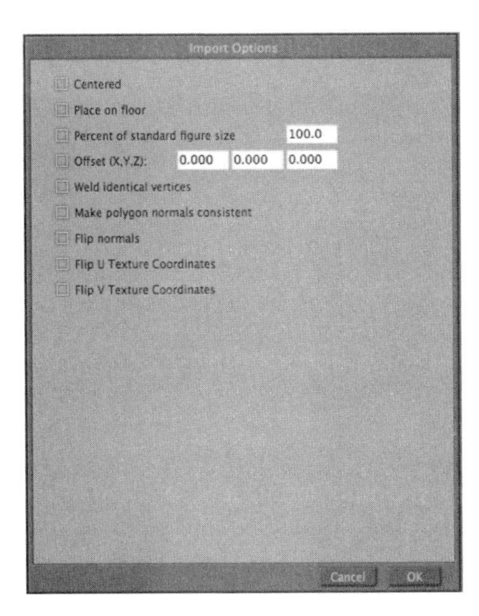

FIGURE 11.6 Uncheck all options in the Import Options dialog box.

5. The skirt will consist of two groups: abdomen and hip. To select polygons for the abdomen of the skirt, you will have to do two things: display the skirt in Wireframe mode and hide the abdomen of the human figure. To display the skirt in Wireframe mode, make sure that skirt-mapped.obj is selected as the current actor. Then choose Display > Element Style > Wireframe. The skirt changes to Wireframe display mode.
6. To hide Jessi's abdomen, first click her abdomen to make it the current object. Then open the Properties panel. Uncheck the Visible option, as shown in Figure 11.7. Now you'll be able to select the proper polygons on the dress to correspond with Jessi's abdomen.
7. From the Editing Tools, click the Grouping Tool icon to open the Group Editor.
8. The skirt has two groups that you will need to remove before you create the abdomen group. The groups are named Figure and 1. These groups were inadvertently added when saving the figure from an external modeling program and are not necessary to keep. Click the Delete Group button in the upper section of the Group Editor to delete each of these groups.
9. Now you'll create the new group for the abdomen. Click the New Group button in the Group Editor. When the New GroupName dialog box appears, enter **abdomen** (in lowercase letters) for the group name. Click OK to create the new group.

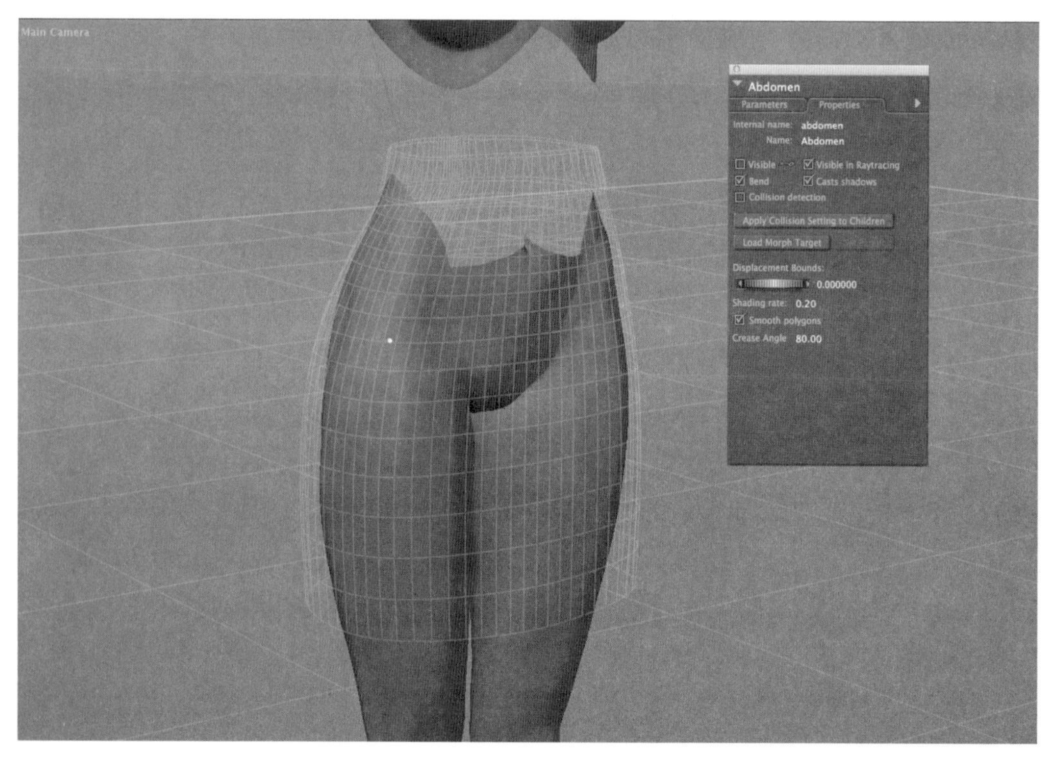

FIGURE 11.7 Hide the abdomen so you can see where to select polygons for the skirt.

10. Select polygons in the skirt that overlap Jessi's hidden abdomen. View the skirt from different camera angles to make sure that you include all polygons in the abdominal area. To select polygons, you can do one of the following:

    - Click to select a single polygon to add to the current group, or Ctrl/Option-click to remove a single polygon.
    - Draw a rectangular selection area to select multiple polygons to add to the group, or press the Ctrl/Option key while you draw a rectangular selection area around the polygons you want to remove.

11. After you select the polygons that cover the abdomen, choose Display > Element Style > Use Figure Style to turn the skirt solid again. This displays the selected polygons in red so that you can see them more clearly. Add or remove polygons from the selection to make the abdomen symmetrical. Figure 11.8 shows an example of the faces that are selected for the abdomen.

FIGURE 11.8 If necessary, switch from Wireframe display to Use Figure Style display mode to adjust the selection.

12. The remaining polygons will be assigned to the hip. To begin this process, click the New Group button. When the New GroupName dialog box appears, enter **hip** (in lowercase letters) for the group name. Click OK to create the new group.
13. Verify that the hip is selected as the current group. Then click the Add All button to add all of the skirt polygons to the hip group. All of the polygons in the skirt turn red.
14. At this point, the polygons in the upper part of the skirt have been assigned to two groups: the abdomen and the hip. Polygons can only be assigned to one group, so you must remove the abdomen polygons from the hip group. To do so, click the Remove Group button in the Group Editor. Select abdomen from the drop-down list in the Remove Group dialog box, and choose OK to remove the abdomen polygons from the hip group. Your skirt should look similar to that shown in Figure 11.9.

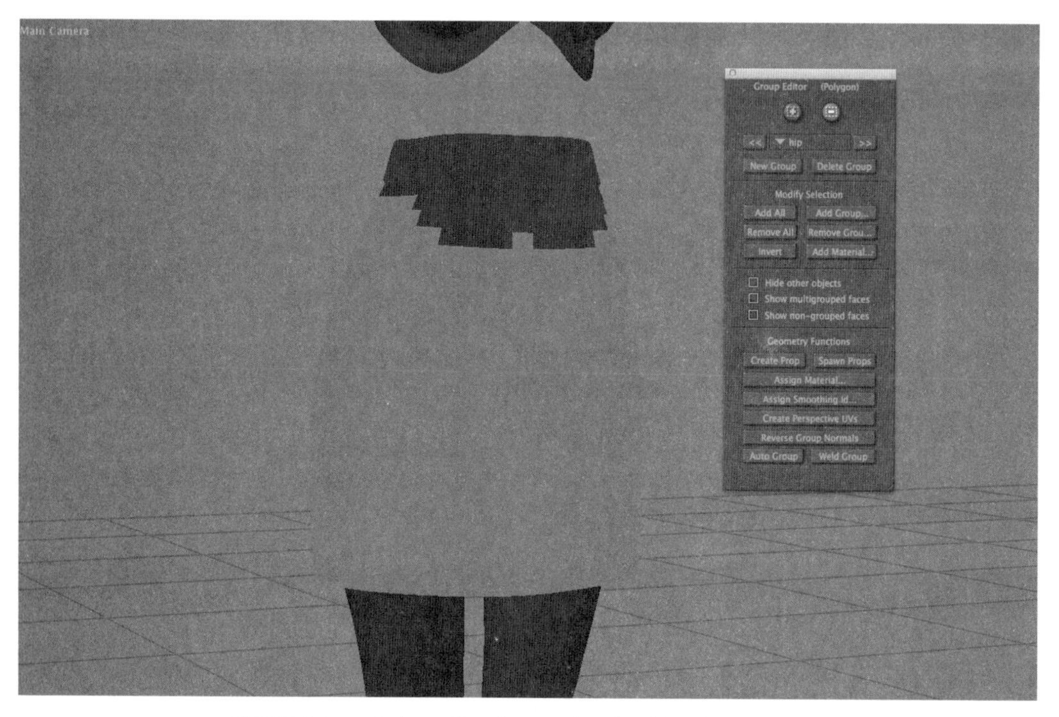

FIGURE 11.9 Select all polygons for the hip, then remove the polygons that are assigned to the abdomen.

15. The Group Editor also allows you to assign polygons to materials on a group-by-group basis. To assign the currently selected group (which should still be the hip section) to a material named Skirt, click the Assign Material button that appears in the Geometry Functions section in the bottom portion of the Group Editor. The Assign Material dialog box opens.
16. Enter **Skirt** for a material name, and click OK.
17. Return to the Group Editor, and select the abdomen group. Click the Assign Material button again. When the Assign Material dialog box appears, click the Materials button, and choose Skirt from the drop-down menu. Then click OK to assign the abdomen polygons to the Skirt material. Your groups and materials are now complete for the object.
18. Before you export your object, verify that all polygons are correctly assigned to their groups. Then, use the Weld Group button in the Group Editor to weld each group. This prevents your geometry from splitting apart at the group seams when imported into other 3D software such as UVMapper Pro or ZBrush.
19. Save the object, as described in Tutorial 11.2.

Saving Grouped Objects for Later Use

Once you have set up your groups, assigning names and materials to the different parts, you will want to save your work for later use. In this next tutorial, you will learn how to export the file so you can work with it in Poser as well as in programs like UVMapper.

Tutorial 11.2 Exporting an OBJ File from Poser

After you assign groups and materials, in Poser you'll need to save the OBJ file with its new information. The most logical place to save the file is in the final location that will be referenced in the Poser library file. Because most Poser users are accustomed to finding the original OBJ files in the Geometries folders, it is particularly important to locate the OBJ files in a folder beneath the Poser 8\Runtime\Geometries folder if you intend to distribute your models.

To export an OBJ file from Poser, follow these steps:

1. From Poser 8, choose File > Export > Wavefront OBJ. The Export Range dialog box appears.
2. Poser prompts you to select a range of frames for export. The only reason you choose Multi Frame Export is if you have morphed or animated the OBJ file, which is not true in this case. Keep the default selection (Single Frame), and choose OK to continue.
3. The Select Objects dialog box appears. Initially, all objects are checked. To uncheck all items, click the UNIVERSE item that appears at the top of the list. This will clear all of the other selections in the dialog box. After all items are unchecked, scroll to the bottom of the list and check the clothing object that you want to export, as shown in Figure 11.10.
4. Click OK to continue. The Export Options dialog box appears, as shown in Figure 11.11.
5. Because you are exporting an object that will be used for Conforming clothing, you need to check two options: Include Body Part Names in Polygon Groups and Weld Body Part Seams. Click OK to continue with the exporting process.
6. The Export as Wavefront OBJ dialog box appears. Create or navigate to the folder that will store your final object. For purposes of this tutorial, use a path called Poser 8\Runtime\Geometries\PP7Projects, and name the object **JessiSkirt.obj**. Click Save to complete the process.

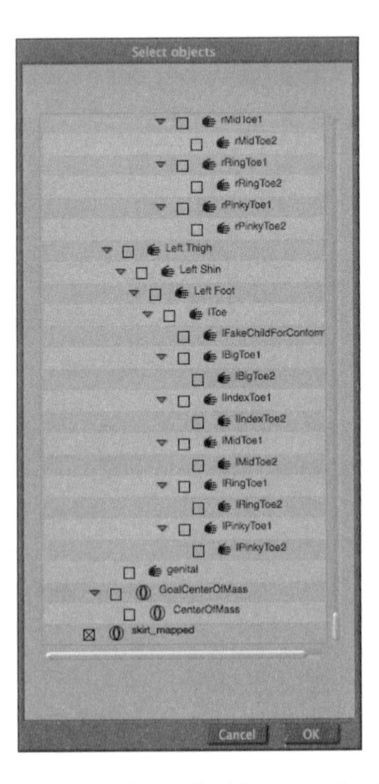

FIGURE 11.10 Deselect all objects in the Hierarchy Editor except for the clothing object.

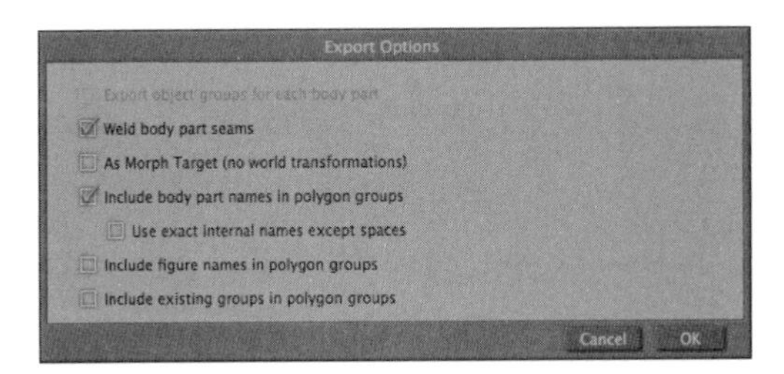

FIGURE 11.11 Make sure you include the existing groups and weld body part seams when you export the object from Poser.

When you export geometry from Poser, the options you select vary depending on the purpose of the object. For this example, check the options as follows:

- Normally, you would leave Include Body Part Names in Polygon Groups, Use Exact Internal Names Except Spaces, and Include Figure Names in Polygon Groups unchecked. These options affect the names of the groups or can remove the grouping information from your model. In this case, however, leaving Include Body Part Names in Polygon Groups is preferred, as mentioned in Step 5.

- Check the Include Existing Groups in Polygon Groups option when the OBJ contains groups for Conforming hair or clothing. If left unchecked, the object will export with only one group. You do not need to check this option if you are exporting geometry for Dynamic clothing or props because they typically do not contain more than one group.
- Check the Weld Body Part Seams option only if you are converting Conforming clothing (which contains groups) into Dynamic clothing (which does not necessarily have to contain groups). If you don't weld the groups at their seams, the Dynamic clothing will split apart at the group seams during dynamic calculations.
- Check As Morph Target (No World Transformations) when it is important to reference the original position, scaling, and rotation of the geometry that you are exporting. This is particularly important when you are exporting an object for the purpose of creating morphs.

After you save the OBJ file under its final name and location, it's always a good idea to perform a final check in UVMapper Professional. Select each group, one at a time, and hide its faces to make sure that the group looks symmetrical and that it doesn't contain any stray faces or holes. Also, check the group list and the material list to make sure that there are no unwanted or erroneous groups and materials in the object that can create confusion later on.

Using Auto Group Editor to Map Grouped Models

This next section deals with a program that is PC-only, so if you're working on a Mac, this section is pretty well moot. Also, this is a third-party product that is for sale and is not included with Poser. Auto Group Editor is a utility that makes it easier to add body part groups to your clothing model. The main reason for covering this utility is because it displays each body part group in a different color, which makes it very easy to determine where each group starts and ends.

NOTE

If you are interested in Auto Group Editor, you can learn more by going to www.renderosity.com/mod/bcs/index.php?ViewProduct=21081.

Auto Group Editor allows you to import a human figure as a CR2 (Poser Figure Library character) or an OBJ file. Each group on the original figure appears in a different color so that you can easily see where you need to create the corresponding groups on your clothing. When you import your clothing model, you can display it in Wireframe mode while you use the colored groups of the underlying figure to create equivalent groups in the clothing.

A nice feature of Auto Group Editor is that it allows you to create symmetrical selections and then assign the right and left sections individually.

Although Auto Group Editor does make it easy to create and assign polygons to groups for conforming clothing, it cannot assign materials. You will need to assign materials with another utility or in your modeling program.

TUTORIAL 11.3 GROUPING WITH THE AUTO GROUP EDITOR

To create clothing groups in Auto Group Editor, proceed as follows:

1. From Auto Group Editor, choose File > Load Source Figure. Use the Open dialog box to locate the uncompressed OBJ file for your character. In this example, after uncompressing the OBZ file for Jessi, you can find the OBJ file in the same folder (Runtime\Libraries\Character\Jessi folder). Select the OBJ file, and click Open to import the figure.
2. Choose File > Load Clothing Object. Locate the clothing object that you want to assign groups to. For this example, locate the tshirt-mapped.obj file in the Tutorials\Chap11 folder on the DVD that accompanies this book. Click Open to import the clothing object. Your project should look like what's shown in Figure 11.12.
3. Now you need to transfer some group names to the shirt. Notice that the bottom section of the Group Controls panel (in the left section of your screen) displays the name of all groups in the figure. Beneath the Groups list are several buttons. First, click the None button to deselect all of the group names in the figure. This will hide all of the figure groups.
4. Now, click the Upper button to select all of the groups in the upper torso and arms. In addition to those groups, check the neck and hip groups to add them to the selection.
5. To transfer the selected groups to the upper pane, which will be the groups for the T-shirt, click the Transfer Groups button at the bottom of the Group Controls panel. The group names should now appear in the top pane of the Group Controls panel.
6. It is easier to assign groups to your geometry when the clothing is in Wireframe display mode. This allows you to view the groups in the original model. To display the clothing in Wireframe, click the Transparent option beneath the upper pane of the Group Controls panel. Your project should now look like what's shown in Figure 11.13.

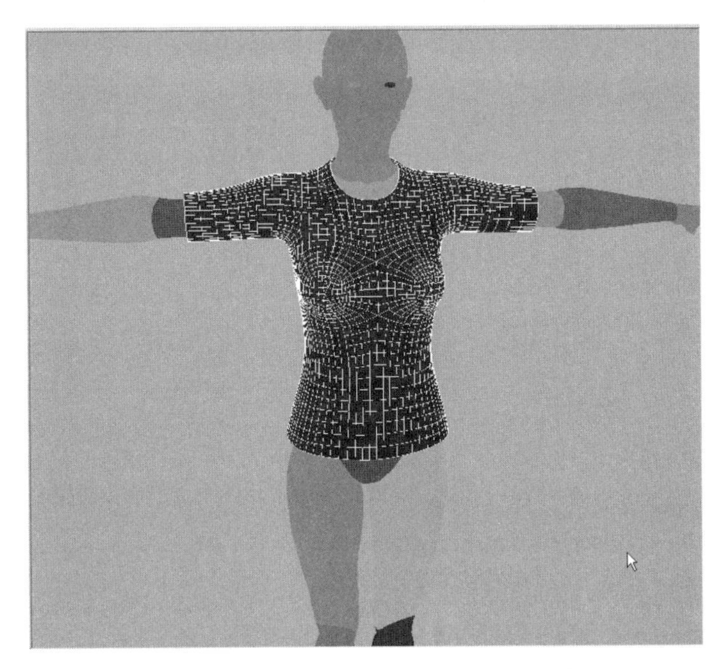

FIGURE 11.12 Import the geometry for the figure and the clothing you want to group.

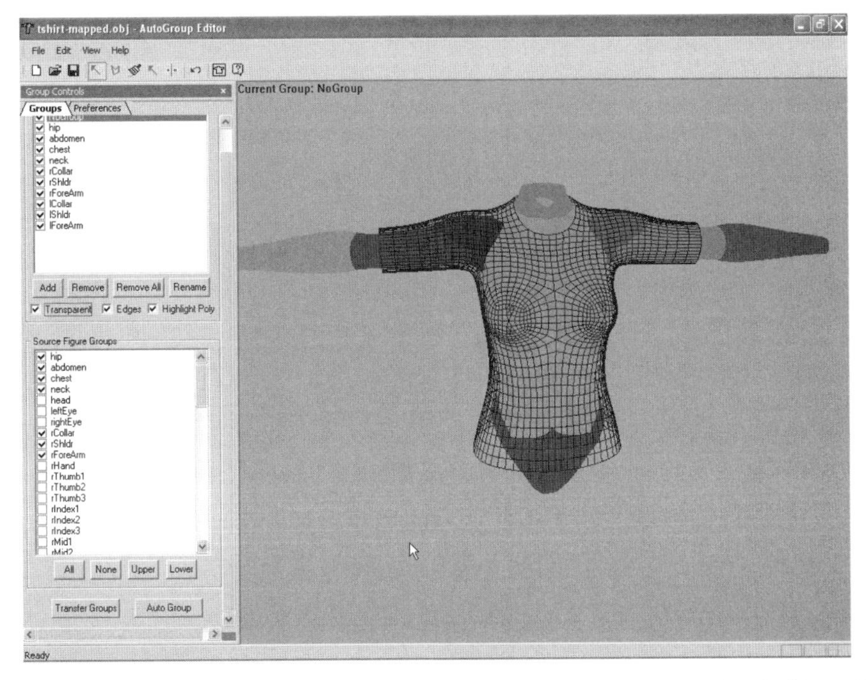

FIGURE 11.13 Transfer the appropriate group names from the figure to the clothing object.

7. Groups should always be symmetrical, providing that the mesh itself is symmetrical; that is, the right side and left side always contain the same number of polygons. To create symmetrical selections in Auto Group Editor, first click the Symmetrical Selection icon. As you select polygons, Auto Group Editor automatically creates symmetrical selections if this option is activated.

   Auto Group Editor also makes use of a three-button mouse to perform some features. If you need to pan, move, or rotate the model while you are selecting polygons, use the following options:

   - Select polygons with the left mouse button.
   - Shift-click the left mouse button to deselect polygons.
   - Click and drag the middle mouse button or wheel to rotate the view.
   - Shift-click and drag the middle mouse button to pan the view up, down, right, or left.
   - Ctrl-click and drag the middle mouse button to zoom in and out.

8. Select polygons in the chest group until your selection looks similar to that shown in Figure 11.14. Use the selection tools as follows:

   - The Normal Selection tool allows you to select all polygons in a rectangular area.
   - The Polygon Selection tool allows you to select all polygons in an irregularly shaped area.
   - The Paint Selection tool allows you to select polygons by "painting" over them.

9. With the selection made, verify that the chest is highlighted in the top section of the Group Controls panel. Then right-click over the selected polygons in the graphic view, and choose Assign Left Select to Group. This assigns the left side of the selection to the chest group in the T-shirt. Right-click again, and choose Assign Right Select to Group.
10. Uncheck the chest group in the upper pane of the Group Controls panel. This hides the polygons that you just assigned to the chest and protects them from being selected further.

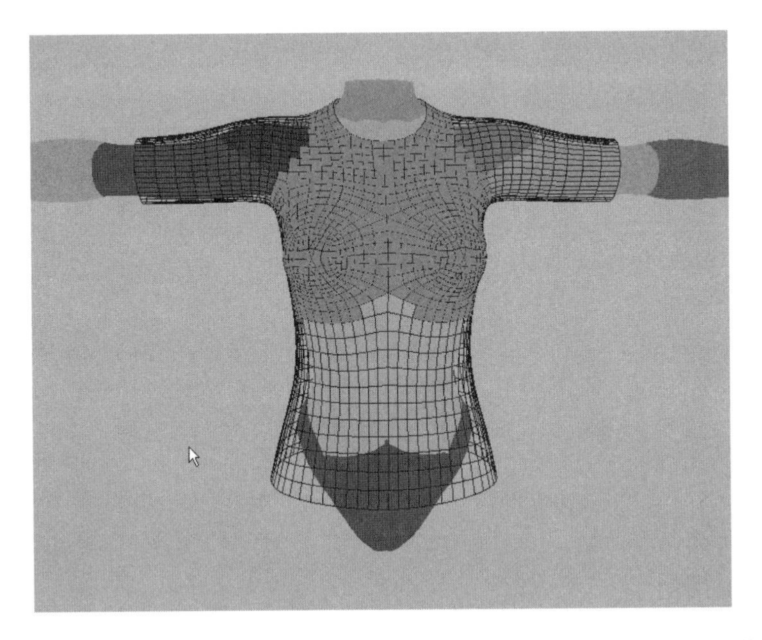

FIGURE 11.14 A symmetrical selection of polygons for the chest group is ready to be assigned.

11. Use the selection tools to select the polygons for the left or right collar. For Jessi, these are the polygons that separate the chest from the upper arm. As you select the polygons for one side, the polygons for the other side are automatically selected to create symmetrical groups.
12. To assign the right section of polygons to the right collar, verify that the rCollar group is selected in the top pane of the Group Controls panel. Then, right-click over the selected polygons, and choose Assign Right Select to Group. Uncheck the rCollar group in the upper section of the Group Controls panel.
13. In a similar manner, highlight the lCollar group in the Group Controls panel. Right-click over the remaining selection of polygons, and choose Assign Left Select to Group. Uncheck the lCollar group in the upper pane of the Group Controls panel.
14. Repeat Steps 12 and 13 to assign polygons for the right and left shoulder sections (named rShldr and lShldr).
15. Select polygons for the abdomen, and assign right and left selections to the abdomen group.

16. All remaining polygons at the bottom of the T-shirt should be added to the hip group.
17. After you assign all polygons in the T-shirt to appropriate groups, you can save your model. Choose File > Save Clothing Object (as shown in Figure 11.15) to save over the previous version of the clothing, or choose File > Save Clothing Object As to save the grouped model to a location that you specify.

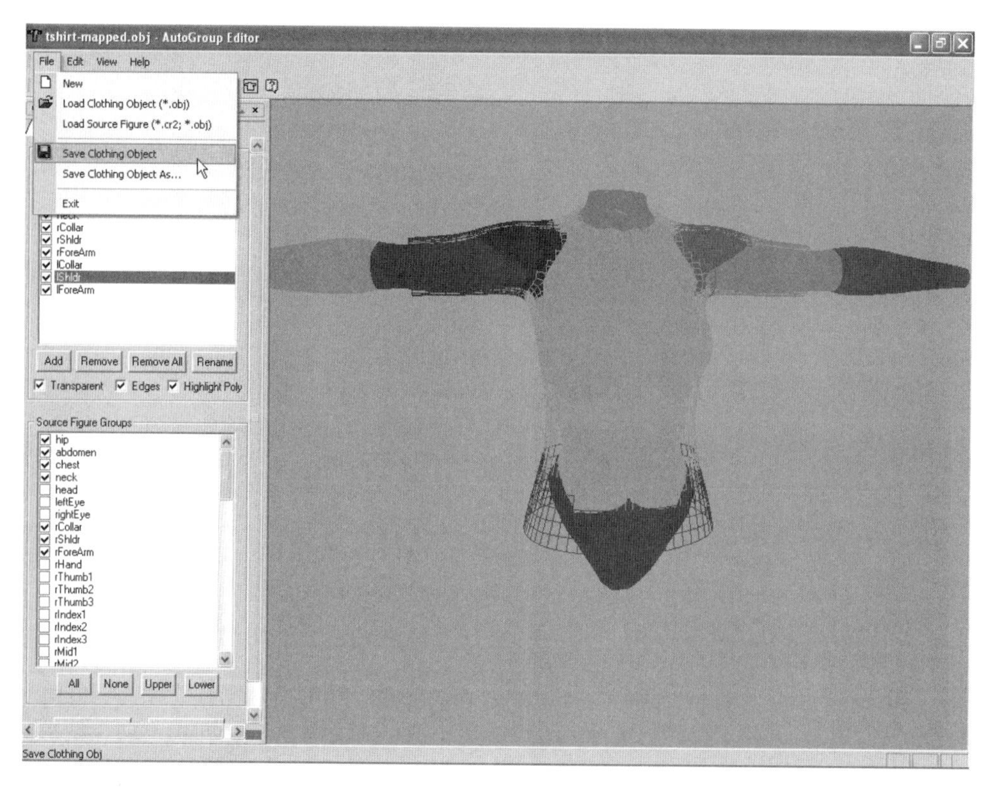

FIGURE 11.15 After you assign all polygons, use the Save Clothing Object or Save Clothing Object As command to save the grouped clothing object.

Although you can save OBJ files to the same folder in which your library files are located, you most often find OBJ geometry files in the Runtime\Geometries folders. A suitable location and file name for this T-shirt, for example, might be Runtime\Geometries\CustomFolder\Jessi\t-shirt.obj, where CustomFolder is an optional name for a folder that you assign to clothing objects that you create yourself.

Using UVMapper with Grouped Objects

You have already seen how UVMapper Professional and UVMapper Classic can help you in creating UV maps so you can design new materials for your models. The Professional version can also help you in grouping, too.

Unlike Auto Group Editor, you cannot use the human figure as a guide while you select polygons for your groups. Secondly, UVMapper doesn't have an option to create symmetrical selections, so you have to keep track of the groups visually. The easiest way to do this is to hide faces as you assign them to groups. The following tutorial gives you some ideas for how you can overcome these situations.

Tutorial 11.4 Groups and Materials in UVMapper Professional

For this tutorial, you will need UVMapper Professional. UVMapper Classic for Mac or PC will not work. In this tutorial, you will assign groups and materials to the pants by following these steps:

1. From UVMapper Professional, choose File > Open Model. Locate the pants-mapped.obj file in the Tutorials\Chap11 folder on the DVD that accompanies this book. Click Open to import the pants.
2. Use the Rectangular Selection tool to select the first row of each pants section. Make sure that all polygons in the top row are selected. Then press the zero (0) key on your keyboard to increase the selection by two rows. Your selection should look similar to that shown in Figure 11.16.
3. Choose Tools > Assign To > Group. When the Assign Selection Group dialog box appears, enter **abdomen** and click OK. Answer Yes when UVMapper Professional asks if you want to create the new group.
4. With the abdomen polygons still selected, choose Select > Display > Hide, or use the left bracket ([ ) shortcut key to hide the selected polygons.
5. Select the bottom row of polygons on the left leg facing you (this is actually the right leg of the pants). Press the zero (0) key on your keyboard 14 more times to make a total of 15 rows selected.
6. Choose Tools > Assign To > Group. Enter **rShin** to assign these polygons to the right shin of the pants. Then hide the selected faces with the [keyboard shortcut or the Select > Display > Hide menu command.
7. Repeat Steps 5 and 6 for the same rows on the opposite leg. Assign these polygons to the lShin group and hide them from view.

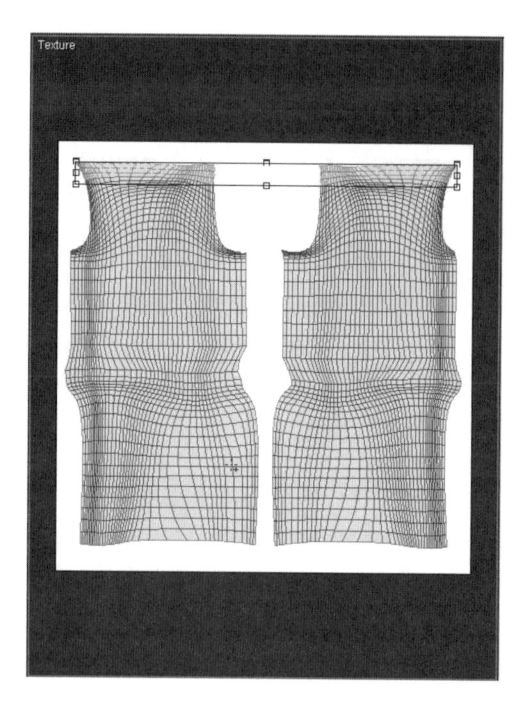

FIGURE 11.16 Assign the first three rows of the pants to the abdomen group.

8. If you look at the way Jessi's body is actually grouped, you'll see that the fronts of her shins are about three polygons higher than the back of her shins. To reproduce that in the pants, use the Polygon Selection tool to select three rows of polygons on the leg on your right (the left leg of the pants), and extend the selection inward by 20 columns. Your selection should look similar to that shown in Figure 11.17. Use the Tools > Assign To > Group menu command to assign this selection to the lShin group of polygons.
9. Repeat Step 8 to assign three rows by 20 columns of polygons on the opposite leg to the rShin group.
10. Deselect all polygons (Select > Deselect), and then use the right bracket ( ]) shortcut or choose Select > Display > Show to unhide all of the previously hidden polygons.
11. Use the Rectangular Selection tool to select the top row of polygons on each side of the pants. Then extend the selection by pressing the zero (0) key 14 more times. The selection should look like what's shown in Figure 11.18.

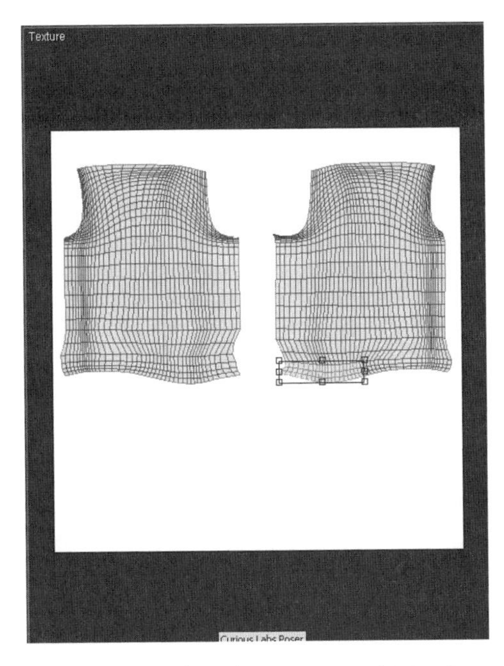

FIGURE 11.17 Select three rows and 20 columns.

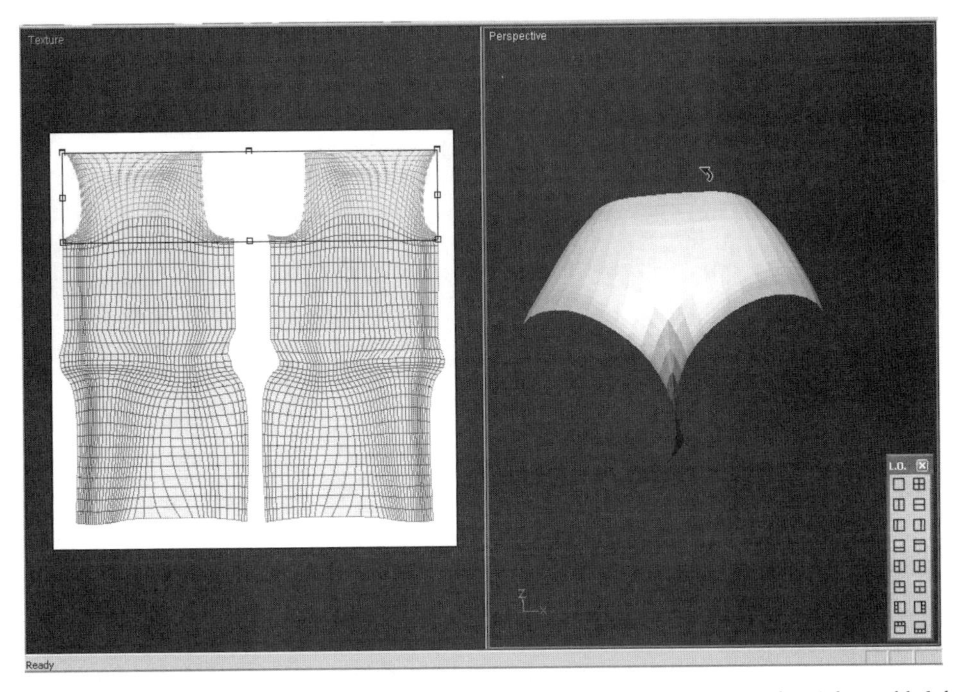

FIGURE 11.18 Make sure that the hip group includes polygons that separate the right and left legs.

12. Choose Select > Display > Hide Unselected. This hides the polygons in the remainder of the pants.
13. Now, choose Select > Select By > Group. When the Select By Group dialog box appears, highlight abdomen, and then choose OK.
14. Hide the abdomen polygons with the Select > Display > Hide menu command or by using the [shortcut.
15. Use the Rectangular Selection tool to select the polygons that remain in the Texture view. Then choose Tools > Assign To > Group. Assign these polygons to a new group named hip.
16. With all polygons deselected, choose Select > Display > Show or use the] shortcut to unhide all faces. Now you need to unhide all of the polygons that have already been assigned.
17. Choose Select > Select By > Group. When the Select By Group dialog box appears, highlight abdomen, hip, lShin, and rShin. Choose OK to select the polygons, and then hide them with the [shortcut.
18. Use the Rectangular Selection tool to select the polygons on the left side of the Texture view (the right side of the pants). Then choose Tools > Assign To > Group. Assign these polygons to a new group named rThigh.
19. Now use the Rectangular Selection tool to select the polygons on the right side of the Texture view (the left side of the pants). Then choose Tools > Assign To > Group. Assign these polygons to a new group named lThigh. All of the polygons in the pants should now be assigned to groups.
20. It's actually a very similar process to assign materials in UVMapper Professional. After you select the polygons you want to assign, you use the Tools > Assign To > Material menu command to create a material for the clothing. For purposes of this tutorial, you will assign all polygons to a material named Pants (material names can begin with capital letters, if desired, and do not have strict conventions like group names do). If you desire, you can optionally create more than one material zone in the pants. For example, you can select the upper portion of the pants and create a material named Shorts, and then add the remaining polygons to a material named Pants.
21. With all groups and materials assigned, it's time to save the OBJ file. Choose File > Save Model. When the OBJ Export Option dialog box appears, leave only one option checked, Don't Export Normals, as shown in Figure 11.19. This is extra information that Poser doesn't use, and it adds unnecessary file size to the object. Click OK to save the object to the folder that you will use as the final destination for your Poser clothing. For example, you can

save the object to the Runtime\Geometries\YourFolderName\Jessi folder, and name the file object pants.obj. Further information about file locations will be covered in Chapter 12.

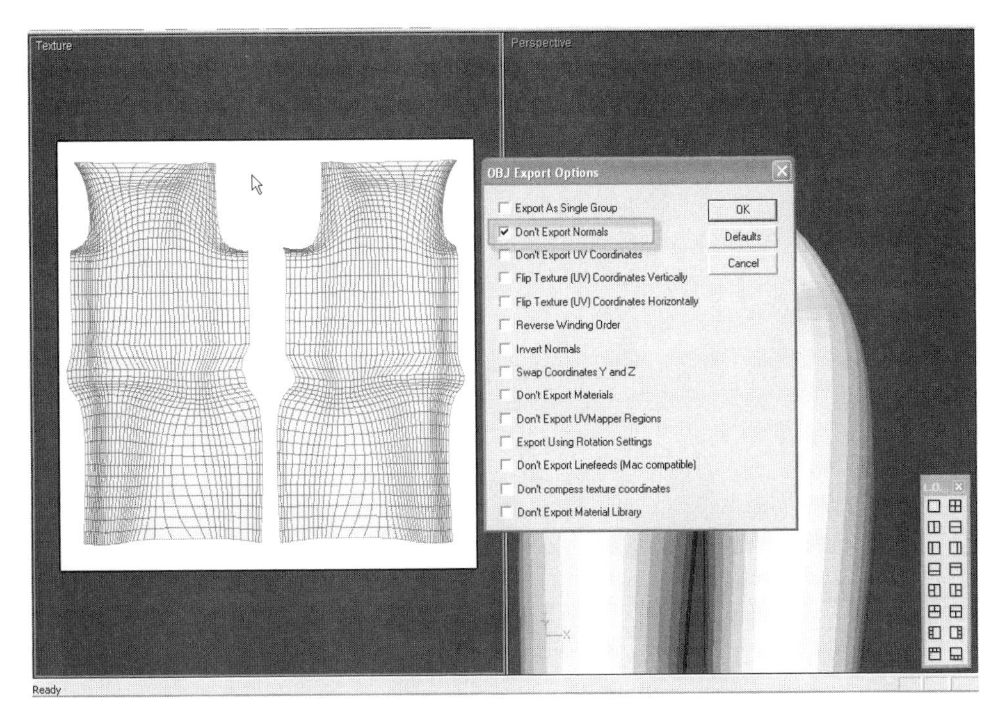

FIGURE 11.19 When you save the OBJ file, do not include normals information.

A SHORT RE-POSE

When an object contains multiple materials, you can use different textures or transparency settings on the different parts of the object. To make an object posable, as in the case of Conforming clothing, the object should contain groups that define the posable parts of the object.

You're not through, though. Nope. Not by a long shot. You now have to add this new content to your libraries, and there are different processes depending on which type of model you're adding. In the next chapter, you'll discover how to tell Poser what type of file you're importing and how Poser can tell the difference between props, Smart Props, Dynamic, and Conforming clothing.

12 From Modeler to the Poser Library

In This Chapter:

- Importing OBJ Files
- Tutorial 12.1: Removing Embedded Geometry from Props
- Tutorial 12.2: Fixing OBJ and Texture Paths
- Anatomy of a Smart Prop
- Tutorial 12.3: Creating Smart Props
- Creating Conforming Clothing
- Tutorial 12.4: Using a Donor CR2
- Tutorial 12.5: Using the Setup Room

"Technology, like art, is a soaring exercise of the human imagination."

—Daniel Bell

Objects modeled in a 3D program can serve many purposes in Poser, and you'll hear these 3D objects referred to by many content names. The objects that you model can be saved to the library as props, Smart props, articulated props, Dynamic clothing, Conforming clothing, Dynamic hair, Conforming hair, and figures. The differences among these types of content are based upon the steps you complete before and during the time that you save them to the library.

In this chapter, you'll learn what distinguishes one type of content from another, how you prepare them for Poser, where to locate your content files, and how you save them to the library. This chapter will also address some of the edits that you must make to the files before you share them with others.

The procedures covered in this chapter are typical for creating objects that are compatible with Poser 7 and 8 only. If you want to create content that is compatible with previous versions of Poser, there are many other factors and procedures to consider. For example, Poser 5, 6, and 7 have the capability to use procedural shaders, Dynamic clothing, and Dynamic hair that cannot be used in earlier versions.

There are also supplementary files that users of older versions of Poser expect as a convenience, such as pose files that automatically apply material or morph changes to an object (MAT or MOR poses, respectively). Poser 8 provides solutions that help make it easier for users to share morphs or apply materials to their items.

In the past few chapters, you have covered quite a bit of ground, and you should understand that with practice comes perfection. Although I have tried to show procedures that take you beyond the basics, I also expect that you will approach Poser with your own methods and innovations from this point on. Nevertheless, I have set the groundwork from modeling to UV mapping to group and material assignment, so you now have the knowledge you need to create content for Poser.

Here's a brief overview of what should be done before you complete the tasks covered in this chapter:

- Model your object in a 3D program. Most of the objects made for Poser are built with rectangular (four-sided) polygons and a minimal number of triangular (three-sided) polygons.
- Create UV maps for your geometry using your modeling program or a third-party utility, such as UVMapper Professional. This is a process that prepares your model so that it can accept textures. It also "flattens" your 3D object onto a 2D plane so that you can create realistic textures for your models using an image editing program.
- Assign the polygons in your object to one or more materials using your modeling software, Poser's Group Editor, or a third-party utility.
- If you are creating an original posable character, Conforming clothing, Conforming hair, or posable props that require groups and bones, use Poser's Group Editor, UVMapper Professional, Auto Group Editor, or any other similar method to create the necessary groups in your model. You'll learn later in this chapter how to associate those groups with bones that cause the object to become posable.

After completing all of the preceding tasks, you can bring your content into Poser, apply the materials, and save your content to the library. The tutorials in this chapter will take you the rest of the way!

IMPORTING OBJ FILES

This sounds like a very basic section. I'm not going to tell how to import an OBJ. You know that. This section is going to look at those selections that pop up when you're doing the importing. To many, those selections could just as well be written in Greek, so this section of the chapter will merely deal with explaining those controls.

Here is what the options in the Import Options dialog box control. Refer to Figure 12.1 for this section.

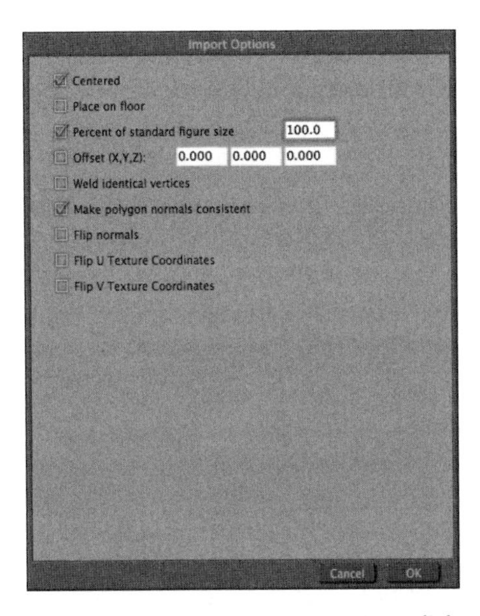

FIGURE 12.1 The oft-seen Import Options dialog box.

- **Centered:** The object will be placed in the exact center of the scene (X = 0, Y = 0, Z = 0). This is a good option to choose if you are not sure where the object will be needed in the scene.
- **Place on Floor:** Drops the lowest point of the object onto the Ground plane or at the Y = 0 point if the Ground plane has been removed.
- **Percent of Standard Figure Size:** Poser uses scaling units that are much smaller than other 3D software applications. If you model content in another 3D application that uses different scaling (which, again, most every program does), your objects will probably import at a much larger size than you want. When you select this option, your object will be sized in relation to the standard height of a human figure. Enter a numerical value to rescale your object in

relation to Poser's standard figure height (which is around six feet, give or take a few inches). So if you want your object to be three feet high, for instance, select this option and enter a value of 50%.

In most cases, content that is created specifically for Poser is scaled correctly for use in Poser. On occasion, you'll find some wonderful content created in other 3D software. After you import the content into Poser, you quickly see that the content is substantially larger than the content you use in Poser. In fact, you may not be able to see it because it is too large, or it appears above or below the view of the camera.

One way to resolve this issue is to check the first three options in the Import Options dialog box so that your object appears in the center of the stage, on the floor, and approximately 100% of figure size. You can then use the Scale dials in the Parameters panel to scale the model appropriately. After the object appears to be the correct size, choose Figure > Drop to Floor so that the object rests on the floor.

Next, export it from Poser, checking only the Include Groups in Polygon Groups option if your object has body part groups. Otherwise, you do not need to check any options.

When you reimport this new object into Poser, it should appear in the center of the stage, at the correct scale, and on the floor, just as you exported it. You can then complete the process of saving the object to the library.

- **Offset (X, Y, Z):** Choose this option to offset your object from its default position or from the center position when used in conjunction with the Centered option. Enter a positive or negative number (in Poser units) for the amount of offset from the zero coordinate for the x, y, or z axis.
- **Weld Identical Vertices:** Choose this option if your geometry is split into separate groups or contains many common vertices in the same location. This option welds the identical vertices back together.

Objects that are made of right angles, such as boxes, may give better results if their common vertices are left unwelded. This is because Poser can smooth polygons at render time. If you weld the sides of a box together, you may end up with a bloated balloon-like box if you try to smooth polygons. To prevent this from happening, you will need to add a tiny row of polygons at each edge so that if polygon smoothing is selected, only the tiny polygons will be affected and the large portions of each side remain flat. When converting Conforming clothing to Dynamic clothing, it is recommended that you select this option when you reimport the OBJ file.

- **Make Polygon Normals Consistent:** 3D objects are made of faces that can be one-sided (visible from one angle, but invisible from its opposite side when facing the camera). The direction of the normals defines which side of a one-sided face is visible and which is not. If your object appears with transparent areas in it, the cause may be flipped normals, meaning the polygon is facing away from the camera. If you reimport the object with this option active, it will probably alleviate the problem of the amazing disappearing polygon(s) by forcing all polygon's normals to face the same direction.
- **Flip Normals:** Check this option if your object imports with all faces inside out so the front of the object is invisible. This will flip all normals so that the polygons face outward.
- **Flip U Texture Coordinates:** Use this selection if your textures appear to be mirrored horizontally when you render. You will need to reimport your object if this happens.
- **Flip V Texture Coordinates:** Use this selection if your textures appear to be mirrored vertically when you render. You will need to reimport your object if this happens.

Tutorial 12.1 Removing Embedded Geometry from Props

When you first save your prop to the library, Poser embeds the geometry information into the library file. This may seem to be advantageous because you would only have to keep track of one library file, rather than a library file and a geometry file. However, if you embed the geometry in the prop file, you won't be able to make new UV maps or regroup the object without destroying the prop file.

As a result, most content creators strip the geometry information out of the prop file and add some lines in the prop file that reference an external OBJ file in the Runtime > Geometries folder. This means you will have to open the prop file in a text editor and make the changes manually. If you follow the next set of procedures, the change should be relatively painless.

Hacking library files is not for the faint of heart. Always make a backup copy of the file you are editing before you make any changes. Keep the backup copy in a safe place in the event that you ever need the original file again!

This section uses the bench.obj file. It was opened in Poser and saved as a standard PP2 file. If you are unfamiliar with how to save a file as a Poser prop, refer to the book, Poser 8 Revealed *by Kelly Murdock (Cengage Learning, 2009) or to the Poser Reference Manual. The PP2 file along with the bench.obj file is located in the Chapter 12 folder on the DVD. Feel free to add a texture to the OBJ file or to use the bench.jpg file, which is also included on the DVD.*

To remove the embedded geometry from a prop file and reference an external OBJ file, follow these steps.

1. Create a backup copy of your prop file. For this example, copy the bench.pp2 file you have either created or pulled from the book's DVD, and save it as benchBAK.pp2.
2. Open bench.pp2 in a text editor that can save ASCII-compatible text files (such as Microsoft Word, WordPad, TextEdit, or Pages on the Mac).
3. At the beginning of the prop file, you will notice several lines that appear similar to those shown in Figure 12.2. These lines should remain untouched.

```
{

version
	{
	number 7
	}
prop bench
	{
```

FIGURE 12.2 The first few lines should remain untouched.

4. The custom geometry section begins with a line that reads `geomCustom`. Following that will be a few lines that tell the number of vertices for several different categories. Finally, there will be a slew of lines that begin with the letters `v`, `vt`, and `f`. All of these lines should be removed. Figure 12.3 shows the beginning and the ending sections of the custom geometry. Make sure you also remove only one ending brace that follows the lines that begin with `f`.
5. After you delete that custom geometry, the lines that remain at the top of the prop file should look like what's shown in Figure 12.4. The dotted line in the figure shows where the custom geometry existed and where you need to add a couple of lines of code.

```
geomCustom
{
      numbVerts 1008
      numbTVerts 984
      numbTSets 4008
      numbElems 1002
      numbSets 4008
      v -0.396000 0.193000 0.100000
      v 0.396000 0.193000 0.100000
      v 0.396000 0.193000 -0.100000
      v -0.396000 0.193000 -0.100000
      v -0.396000 0.213000 0.100000
      v 0.396000 0.213000 0.100000
```

This section will include many lines that begin with the letters v, vt, and f, until you see the end of these lines as shown below ...

```
      f 1008/979 845/980 841/981 1006/977
      f 992/963 1004/972 1007/983 998/982
      f 1004/972 1003/970 1008/979 1007/983
      f 1003/970 840/984 845/980 1008/979
}
```

FIGURE 12.3 Remove the custom geometry section that begins with `geomCustom` and ends with the curly brace following the `f` lines of code.

```
{

version
      {
      number 7
      }
prop bench
      {
......................................................
      }
      prop bench
      {
            name bench
            on
            bend 1
            dynamicsLock 1
            hidden 0
            addToMenu 1
            castsShadow 1
            includeInDepthCue 1
            useZBuffer 1
            parent UNIVERSE
            creaseAngle 80
            channels
            {
```

FIGURE 12.4 The beginning of the prop file after the custom geometry has been removed.

6. In the area designated by the dotted line in Figure 12.14, add the following lines of code:

   ```
   storageOffset 0 0.3487 0
    objFileGeom 0 0 :Runtime:Geometries:PracticalPoser7:
    Chap12:bench.obj
   ```

   This code provides a pointer to the location where you saved the OBJ geometry file. After you add this code, your altered prop file will look like Figure 12.5.

```
{
    version
    {
        number 7
    }
    prop bench
    {
        storageOffset 0 0.3487 0
        objFileGeom 0 0 :Runtime:Geometries:PracticalPoser6:Chap16:bench.obj

    }
    prop bench
    {
        name bench
        on
        bend 1
        dynamicsLock 1
        hidden 0
        addToMenu 1
        castsShadow 1
        includeInDepthCue 1
        useZBuffer 1
        parent UNIVERSE
        creaseAngle 80
        channels
        {
```

FIGURE 12.5 The embedded geometry section with a reference to the external geometry file.

Figure 12.5 also shows four lines that are highlighted with arrows. One of the lines contains the name of the object file (bench.obj). Make sure that the other three lines marked with the arrows name the prop the same as the object. For example, if your object is instead named benchseat.obj, the other three lines should read `prop benchseat` or `name benchseat` for the external call to the object to work correctly.

7. Save your edited prop file to the same location as previously saved, overwriting the version that contained the embedded geometry. The revision is now complete.

TUTORIAL 12.2 FIXING OBJ AND TEXTURE PATHS

When you save any type of content to the Poser libraries, Poser sometimes creates absolute path references to the geometry and texture map files. Absolute paths give a complete reference to a file. For example, if you loaded a texture from an external runtime file on your D drive, you might see a texture reference like D:\Runtime\Textures\Jessi Clothing\dress.jpg.

The path works fine on your computer, and it will also work fine if someone else creates exactly the same path on their own computer. But if someone else chooses to install files to a different location, error messages will appear when the user tries to load the product from the library. This is why you should always use relative paths to geometry and image files in the items that you save to the library. The path to the OBJ file or texture map must always begin with `:Runtime`, and use colons (:) rather than backslashes (\) as separators to maintain compatibility with Macintosh file structures.

To edit file paths, follow these steps.

1. Open your library file in a text editor that can save ASCII-compatible text files. Files that can include references to OBJ or image files can include items in your Figures, Props, and Hair Libraries. Also make sure that you open an uncompressed version (CR2, PP2, or HR2) rather than a compressed version that cannot be edited (CRZ, PPZ, or HRZ).
2. Use the Search feature of your image editor to search for OBJ or obj. A reference to an OBJ file usually occurs only twice in a figure's CR2 file (see Figure 12.6), once in a prop's PP2 file (see Figure 12.7), and once in a hair set's HR2 file (see Figure 12.8). If your path contains forward slashes or back slashes and does not start with `:Runtime` as shown in these figures, edit the file paths to use the proper syntax, as shown in these examples. Try to keep paths as brief as possible, and do not exceed 60 characters so as to maintain Mac compatibility.

```
{
version
      {
      number 5
      }
figureResFile :Runtime:Geometries:ArtyMotion:PetiteChou:PetiteChouDress.obj
actor BODY:1
      {
```

Several sections that begin with the word actor appear between the two OBJ references.

```
actor skirt:1
      {
      storageOffset 0 0 0
      geomHandlerGeom 13 skirt
      }
      figureResFile
:Runtime:Geometries:ArtyMotion:PetiteChou:PetiteChouDress.obj
actor BODY:1
      {
```

FIGURE 12.6 A figure file (CR2) includes two references to external geometry separated by several actor sections. If the path is long, it may wrap around to two lines. This has the same effect as chopping the text at the place where the text wrapped to the new line.

```
{

version
      {
      number 4.01
      }
prop EgyptianThroneClassic
      {
      storageOffset 0 0.3487 0
      objFileGeom 0 0
:Runtime:Geometries:Anton'sPeople:Treasures_Of_Egypt:EgyptianThroneClassic.obj
      }
```

FIGURE 12.7 A prop file (PP2) includes one reference to an external object.

```
{
version
	{
	number 4.0
	}
prop figureHair
	{
	storageOffset 0 0.34875 0
	objFileGeom 0 0 :Runtime:Geometries:3Dream:3DreamParadiseHair.obj
	}
```

FIGURE 12.8 A hair file (HR2) includes one reference to an external object.

3. In a similar manner, search for JPG or jpg in your library file. You'll see various types of references to JPG images in your library files that most often reference diffuse, bump, displacement, or specular maps. Figure 12.9 shows the correct syntax for an image map reference.

```
	}
node "image_map" "Image_Map"
	{
	name "Image_Map"
	pos 473 23
	nodeInput "Image_Source"
		{
		name "Image_Source"
		value 29 29 29
		parmR NO_PARM
		parmG NO_PARM
		parmB NO_PARM
		node NO_NODE
		file
":Runtime:Textures:ArtyMotion:Jessi:Immortals:JessiImDressTop.jpg"
		}
```

FIGURE 12. 9 Image map references should also begin with `:Runtime` and use colons rather than backslashes to denote the file path.

Verify that all paths to the images used as textures are correct and use the correct syntax. Just as the paths to the OBJ files should be relative and not absolute, the same is true of the paths to image files. They should begin with `:Runtime` and use colons instead of backslashes to trace the path hierarchy. Also keep in mind that there may be multiple images used in an object, and there can also be more than one material reference to a single image. For complete results, do a search through the entire file for the JPG or jpg file extension until your text editor informs you that it cannot find any additional instances of the extension. You should also do a search for any of the other image file types that Poser can use as an image map source. These file types include TIF, PSD, and BMP.

ANATOMY OF A SMART PROP

There is only one difference between a regular prop and a Smart prop. When you add a regular prop to a scene, it doesn't automatically attach itself to anything. On the other hand, when you add a smart prop to a scene, it automatically finds and attaches itself to the appropriate figure or body part.

To explain this a little bit further, let's say you are creating a scene in which a man is kneeling on the floor looking up at a woman who is sitting on a couch. She is looking down at her hand. You find a nice diamond ring in your Props Library, and you add it to the scene. You quickly learn how difficult it is to move the ring into position on a figure that is already posed. When you try to grab the ring, you accidentally move other items in the scene. If you try to use the xTran, yTran, and zTran dials in the Parameters panel, it takes a lot of time to move the prop into place.

If you save the ring to your library as a smart prop, it automatically finds its way to the woman's left ring finger when you add it to the scene. To save the engagement ring to the library, select the ring, choose the body part that is supposed to be its parent (the body part to which the ring will attach itself), and then save the prop to the library. If the procedure is completed correctly, the ring will always attach itself to the figure's left ring finger whenever you add it to a scene, regardless of how that figure is posed. Table 12.1 includes prop information at a glance. Before you save the smart prop to the library, use the Object > Change Figure Parent command to assign a parent to the prop.

TABLE 12.1 Prop Types and Their Locations

Content Type	Smart Props
File Extensions	PP2, PPZ (Compressed)
Path to Geometry Files	:Runtime:Geometries:(Folder Name)
Path to Texture Files	:Runtime:Texture:(Folder Name)
Path to Library Files	:Runtime:Props:(Folder Name)

Tutorial 12.3 Creating Smart Props

To create a Smart prop for the ring, follow these steps:

1. Locate the ring.obj file in the Tutorials > Chap12 folder on the book's DVD.
2. Create a folder named PracticalPoser8 in the Downloads > Runtime > Geometries > folder. Copy the ring.obj file to this new folder.
3. Locate the ring.jpg texture file in the Tutorials\Chap12 folder on the CD. Create a folder named PracticalPoser8 in the Downloads\Runtime\Textures folder and copy the ring.jpg image to it.
4. Create a new scene in Poser, and add Jessi to the scene. Turn off Inverse Kinematics, and use the Joint Editor to zero her pose. Also, open the Parameters window, and verify that the xTran, yTran, and zTran dials on the hip and body are set at zero as well.

NOTE

Jessi is installed with the Legacy Content option, so if this model is not available, you can go back and install the Legacy Content from the installation disk.

5. Choose File > Import > Wavefront OBJ. To import the ring in the same position in which it was modeled, leave all options in the Import Options dialog unchecked, as shown in Figure 12.10. Click OK to continue.

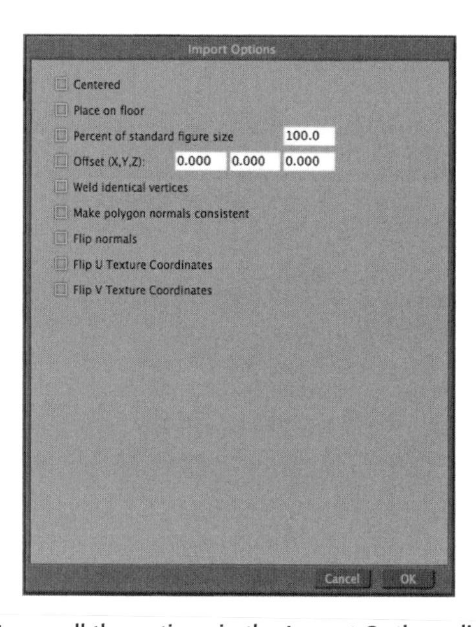

FIGURE 12.10 Leave all the options in the Import Options dialog unchecked.

6. The Import: Wavefront OBJ dialog box appears. Navigate to the PracticalPoser8 folder you created, and select the ring.obj. Click Open to continue. The ring should be positioned on Jessi's left ring finger when it appears in the scene.
7. Choose Display > Document Style > Texture Shaded, or click the Texture Shaded (last) icon in the Document Display Style controls, which is located by default to the left of the Preview window. The textures appear on the figures in the scene.
8. Choose Display > Camera View > Left Hand Camera, or click the Left Hand Cam icon in the Camera Controls. This focuses your current view on the left hand, where you can see the ring. Adjust the camera as necessary to get a good view of the ring on the hand. This prepares the camera view for the image that you will see in the library thumbnail. Figure 12.11 shows an example.
9. Adjust the lighting as necessary to get a good view of the ring. In addition, you may want to turn the display of shadows off before you save your ring to the library. Choose Display > Ground Shadows to uncheck the option if necessary.

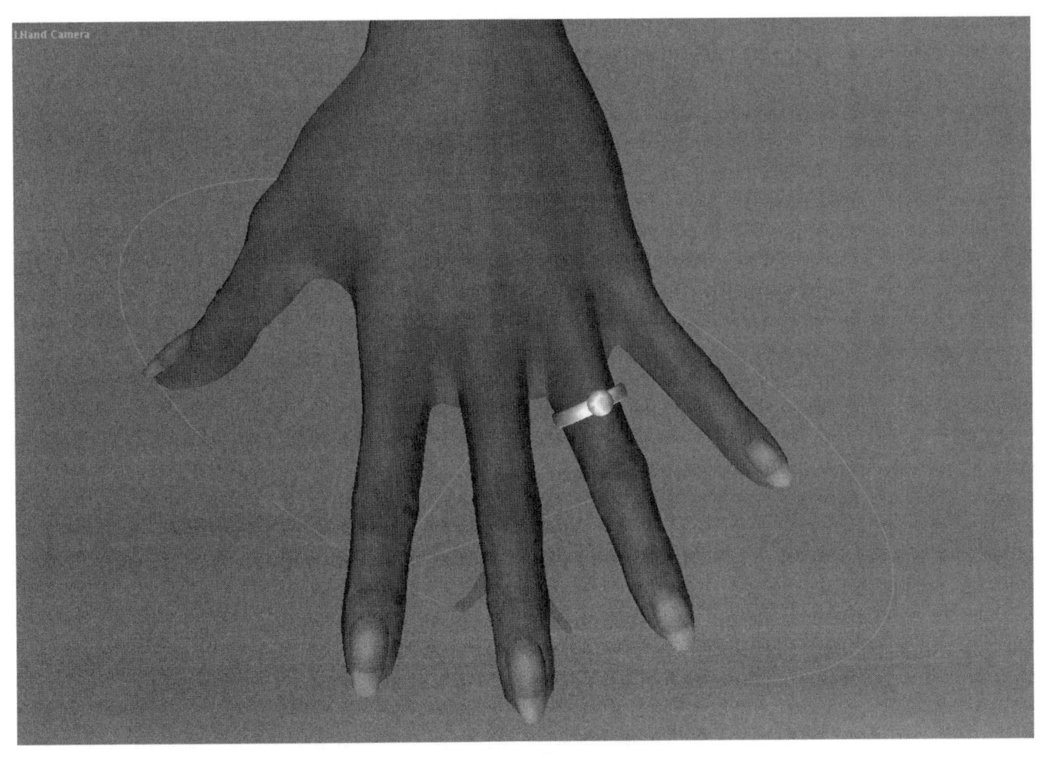

FIGURE 12.11 Adjust the Left Hand Camera for a better view of the ring.

10. You might notice that the diamond on the ring does not appear to be faceted. This is due to the Smoothing feature of Poser, which softens rough edges on low-resolution geometry to make it appear as though it is higher in resolution. However, in cases when you want faceted geometry, you can adjust the Crease Angle setting in the Properties panel. Any geometry that is below the setting will be smoothed. Any geometry that is above the crease angle setting will be faceted. For the ring, reduce the Crease Angle setting from 80 (the default) to 15 degrees, as shown in Figure 12.12. After you make this adjustment, you will see a faceted gemstone on the ring.

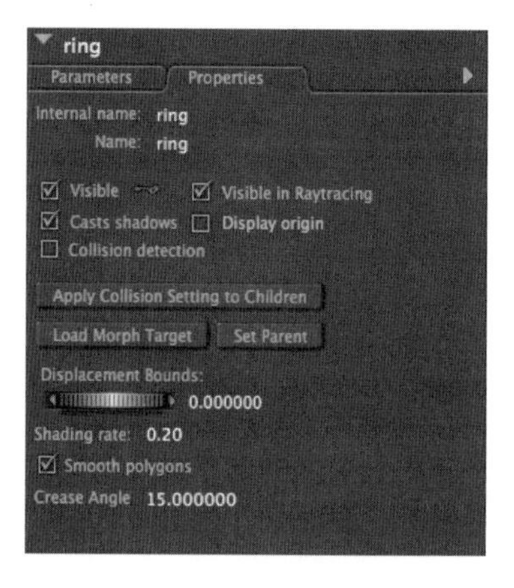

FIGURE 12.12 By reducing the Crease Angle value in the Properties panel, you restore the facets in the gemstone.

With Poser 8, the text/numeric fields in the Properties panel are not automatically active. By default, they look as if they are not even modifiable. Merely click on the text or number to activate the field.

11. Click the Material tab to go to the Material Room. Select the Simple view tab if necessary.
12. From the Object menu at the top of the Simple view, select Ring as the current object. The default material selection will be Gem.
13. Click the square that appears underneath the Diffuse Color rectangle. Locate the ring.jpg texture map in the PracticalPoser8 folder, and select it for the texture for the gem. The gem displays the texture and now should look more like a diamond.

14. Select Ring from the Material drop-down menu, and again select the ring.jpg texture map. The ring turns silver.
15. Click the Add Reflection wacro in the Material Room to add a raytrace reflection to the ring band. Your material settings should now look as shown in Figure 12.13.

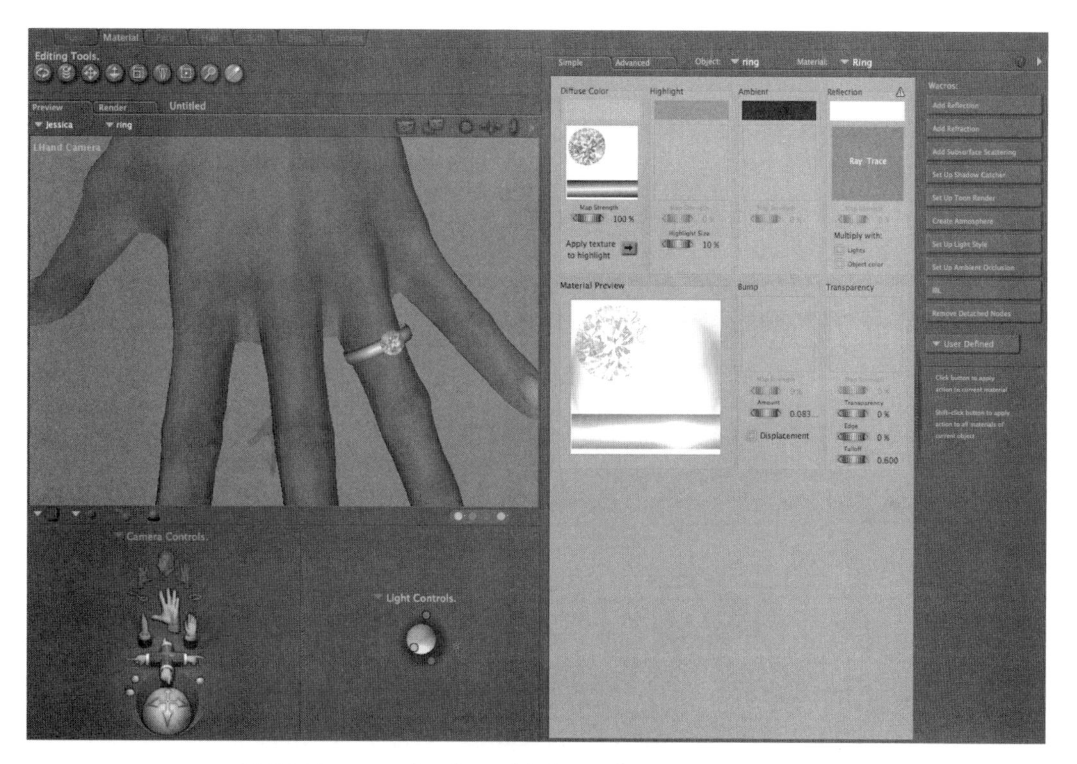

FIGURE 12.13 The ring with the Reflection wacro added.

16. Click the Pose tab to return to the Pose Room. To attach the ring to Jessi's finger, select the ring by clicking on it or by choosing it from the Current Actor menu in the Preview window.
17. Click the Set Parent button in the Properties panel. The Object Parent dialog box opens.
18. Scroll down the list and choose lRing1 as the parent for the ring, as shown in Figure 12.14. The ring should now be attached to Jessi's finger.

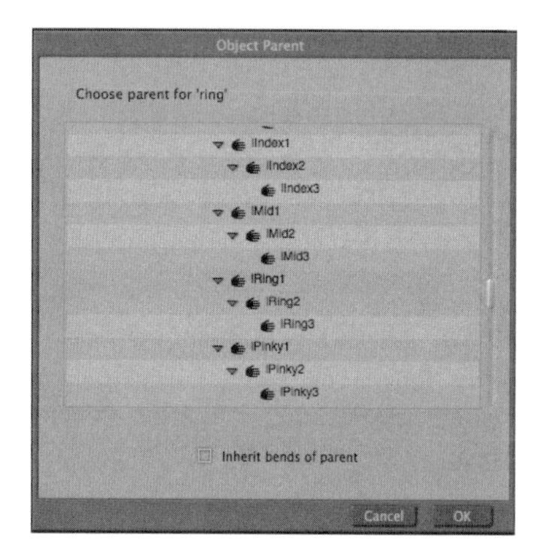

FIGURE 12.14 The lRing1 element is chosen to be the parent of the ring.

19. Locate the folder in the Props library that you want to use to store the ring. I suggest creating a folder titled PracticalPoser8 to store the prop files. Verify that the ring is selected as the current object, and then click the Add to Library icon at the bottom of the Library window. The New Set dialog box opens.
20. Enter **Diamond Ring** as the name for the prop. Do not click the Select Subset button. Instead, click OK to continue.
21. The dialog box shown in Figure 12.15 informs you that the prop has a parent and asks if you want to save it as a Smart prop. Click Yes to continue.
22. To test the figure, delete the existing ring from the left hand. Apply a pose to Jessi, and then add the engagement ring from the library. When you zoom in to the left hand with the Left Hand Camera, you should see the ring.

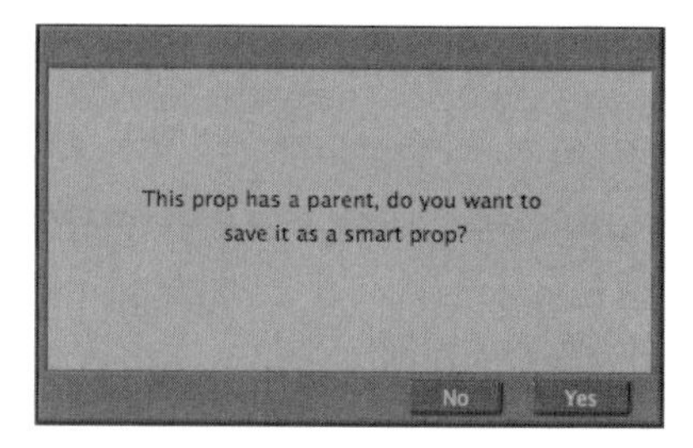

FIGURE 12.15 Since the ring is set as a child of the left ring finger, you're asked if you want to save the prop as a Smart prop.

Creating Conforming Clothing

One of the most common questions asked by people who are new to Poser is, "How do I make my own clothing?" The good news is that I'm going to show you where to begin. The bad news is that I can't address everything involved.

You're about to embark on a long, technical journey that will take time and a lot of practice to master. To put it succinctly, the hardest and most tedious part of creating Conforming clothing is getting it to work. If you take it one step at a time, you'll eventually find it easier and easier to create your own clothing.

Before I get into the steps that add a grouped model into the Poser library as a posable figure, I must stress one very important point: The steps that you are learning in this chapter are only the very beginning of a long road of modeling discovery. You must overcome many intricacies and technicalities to make Conforming clothing work well. Many things can also go wrong, and it is hard to anticipate all the possibilities you could encounter along the way.

What I give you here is a starting point. For additional information beyond that which you will learn in this chapter, I suggest going to the various Poser forums around the Internet, including the ones at Renderosity.com, RuntimeDNA.com, and http://artzone.daz3d.com.

Making a CR2 File

You've already discovered that you must divide a clothing object into body part groups before you make it a posable figure. But that's not all you have to do. Poser doesn't know where the joints are in that clothing, or how to bend, twist, and rotate the joints, without specific information—information that is contained in a CR2 library file.

A CR2 file (which is the extension for files saved in the Figures Library, for example, mySweater.cr2) contains the information that turns your grouped clothing object into a piece of clothing that bends and moves. Basically, the CR2 tells Poser what body parts your clothing object has, where and how they bend, and what textures or materials each polygon in the object uses.

It's very difficult to create a CR2 for a totally original figure, such as a human character. Poser has the Group Editor to help you create groups, the Setup Room to help you create bones that move the groups, and the Joint Parameters panel to help you specify how those joints move. However, when it comes to setting up all of the parameters for your model, you're facing a very tedious process.

When creating a figure that is compatible with Poser, there are two methods you can use. In one, you begin by creating a text file that lists each body part in a hierarchical list. Each body part is preceded by a number that lists the level in the hierarchy where they belong. At the end of each line is a three-letter designation (such as xyz), which defines the order in which the joints bend, twist, and rotate. You save this text file with a PHI extension. After this process is done, you use the File > Convert Hierarchy File menu command to convert the file to a Poser figure. The final step is to use the Joint Editor to configure joint parameters that define how the joints bend, move, and twist. This is without a doubt the most difficult and time-consuming process of figure creation, and it is typically used when creating a totally original figure rather than clothing for an already existing figure. The other method you can use is the Setup Room, taking the bone structure from the model the clothing is to work with and assigning that structure to those clothes.

For a complete description of creating a PHI file and turning it into a CR2 Character Library file, refer to the section "Tutorial: Advanced Figure Creation," of the Poser Tutorial Manual, furnished in PDF format with Poser 8.

Because it's difficult to create joints from scratch and because the clothing must bend almost identically with the original figure, most clothing modelers use the information from the original character when they create a CR2 for their clothing. That way, the clothing will bend and move exactly the same way that the original character does. It's much less tedious work. Reusing the information from the original figure is also the best option from a technical standpoint.

As you have already discovered, you divide Conforming clothing models into the same body part groups that are used in the human figure. That is the first step of the process. After you add groups to a clothing model, you have to tell Poser how those groups are connected. There are basically two ways to accomplish this:

- Use a copy of the original character's CR2 file as a donor to create a CR2 for your clothing, as described in Tutorial 12.4.
- Use the Setup Room to apply bones from the original figure to your clothing. This effectively accomplishes the same thing as editing the CR2 file in a text editor, but it gives you a visual indication of the bone structure and also allows you to add additional bones.

It is common practice for clothing creators to derive their own CR2 files from information contained in the original figure's CR2 file. Although you can technically use the CR2 from clothing made by others, that data is copyrighted by the original creator. It would be illegal for you to use the data without permission from the creator or creators of the clothing. Their clothing items contain custom variations of joint parameters that they worked very hard to create. If you want to use their work for your own projects, contact the original developer and ask permission first.

Removing Morphs from a CR2

When you use a donor CR2 or use the Setup Room to transfer bone and joint information to your own model, your clothing inherits the joint parameters from the donor object. That is exactly what you want to happen. What presents a bit of a problem, though, is that clothing also inherits the material and morph information from the donor object.

At first glance, you'll see the morph dials in the Parameters panel, and you'll be delighted that the morph information appears in your clothing. However, when you try to adjust the morph dials you won't see anything happen. You see, for morphs to work, they must be copied between geometry objects that have exactly the same number of polygons, and the vertices that make up those polygons must be listed in exactly the same order. In other words, the geometry must be identical in its construction and in the order in which the OBJ file lists all of the vertices in the geometry.

The geometry of the donor object is guaranteed to be different from your clothing. As a result, the morph information from the original donor object does nothing but add extra and unnecessary overhead to your clothing object. It makes the file size much larger than it has to be due to thousands of extra lines of text. So the best thing to do is remove the morph information before you use the donor file for one or more articles of clothing. There are two ways that you can do this.

- Open the Parameters panel. Start with the head, and locate the morphs in the selected body part. Poser does not allow you to delete the dials in the Transform category because they are necessary for posing and scaling the figure. Morphs usually appear beneath the category named Morphs. When you click the arrow at the right of a morph dial, choose Delete Morph from the menu that appears, as shown in Figure 12.16. After you delete all of the morphs, click the Add to Library icon at the bottom of your current Character Library. Enter a new name for the figure, and use this figure as your donor CR2 whenever you create clothing for this character. For example, if you remove the morphs from Jessi, save the new version to the Figures Library as JessiBlank. Use this clean version as a source CR2 each time you create clothing for Jessi.
- You can also delete morphs in the Hierarchy Editor. Choose Window > Hierarchy Editor to open the Hierarchy panel. Verify that the Show All Parameters option is checked. Morph parameter dials have a little dial icon displayed to the left of the dial name. Take care not to delete the standard dials that are required to pose or translate your figure or body parts (Taper, Scale, xScale, yScale, zScale, xRotate, yRotate, zRotate, xTran, yTran, zTran, Twist, Side-Side, Bend, Up-Down, and so on). What you do want to delete are morphs that change the appearance of the figure.

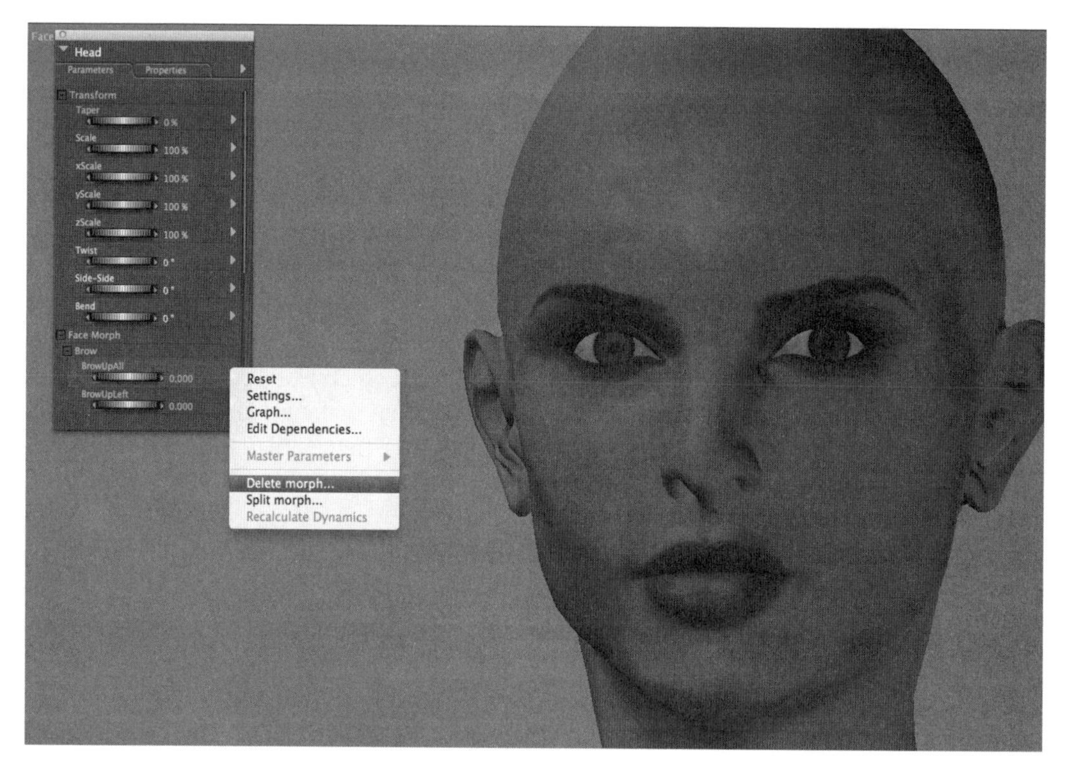

FIGURE 12.16 You can delete morphs from each body part using the Parameters panel.

- Open the figure's uncompressed CR2 (not the CRZ file) in Morph Manager 4.0, a free PC-only utility that you can download at www.morphography.uk.vu/dlutility.html. If a body part contains morphs, you will see a plus sign beside the body part. Expand the tree to reveal the morph names, which are preceded by the letter M, as shown in Figure 12.17. (Do not remove the other joint parameters that are preceded with the letter C.) To delete a morph, click the morph name, and press the Delete key on your keyboard. Click OK when Morph Manager asks if you are sure you want to delete the morph. Complete this process until all morphs are removed, and then click the Save File button. Save the CR2 under a new file name, such as JessiBlank.

After you remove the morphs from your donor figure, be sure to save a copy to your Figures Library. Assign a different name so that you don't overwrite the original version that includes the morphs.

FIGURE 12.17 The Morph Manager 4.0 interface.

If you remove the morphs from Jessi.CR2 using the Delete Morph command in the Parameters panel, make sure that you have the Use File Compression option unchecked in the Misc tab of the General Preferences dialog box before you save the unmorphed version to the library. This will save the file as an editable CR2 instead of a compressed CRZ file.

Tutorial 12.4 Using a Donor CR2

As already mentioned, it is common practice to use joint parameter information from a posable figure's CR2 file when you design clothing for that figure. Those who design original figures (such as Jessi, James, Victoria 3, Apollo Maximus, LaRoo, and so on) realize that it is common practice for clothing designers to use the joint information from the original character. In most cases, you usually don't have to ask permission. When in doubt, though, it won't hurt to ask the individual or company if it's okay to use the CR2 from a character when you create clothing for it. It's just good practice to never assume.

On the other hand, it is an entirely different story when you use information from a similar piece of clothing that someone else has created for the same character.

It is entirely possible that the clothing has custom joint parameters, morphs, or other configurations that are copyrighted by the original creator and that you don't, by default, have the permission to duplicate. It's good, sound, professional practice to be respectful of the work of others from not only a moral perspective, but a legal one as well. If you don't have written permission to use joint parameters or morph information from clothing that has been created by others, don't use it. Use the information from the original character instead. Table 12.2 provides figure and character information at a glance.

TABLE 12.2 Figure Types and Their Locations

Content Type	Conforming Props
File Extensions	CR2, CRZ (Compressed)
Path to Geometry Files	:Runtime:Geometries:(Folder Name)
Path to Texture Files	:Runtime:Texture:(Folder Name)
Path to Library Files	:Runtime:Character:(Folder Name)

Your content can be placed beneath any Runtime folder that you choose, as long as you begin the file paths in your CR2 with `:Runtime` as shown. Your custom folder can be named as you choose. Most content creators include their artist name or the product name within their folder names.

That being said, it is relatively easy to convert a figure's CR2 to a clothing CR2. Simply follow these steps:

1. Save the geometry and texture files in the locations shown in Table 12.2. You can locate the files in any Runtime folder, as long as the folders beneath the Runtime folder are as shown in the table.
2. For purposes of this tutorial, you'll find three OBJ files in the Chapter12 folder on the book's DVD. The files are named JessiConfSkirt.obj, JessiPants.obj, and JessiTShirt.obj. Copy them to the Downloads\Runtime\Geometries\PracticalPoser8 folder. If you haven't created this path yet, please do so now.
3. If you have not already done so, remove the morphs from the Jessi.CR2 object using the Delete Morph commands in the Parameters panel or by using Morph Manager.

4. Save the unmorphed version as JessiBlank.CR2. This is massively important so that you don't lose the original Jessi file. You might also want to make a copy of the Jessi.png thumbnail and save it (the file name must be the same as the new CR2) so that the library item will have a thumbnail associated with it.
5. Open the JessiBlank.CR2 file in a text editor that can handle very large files (Microsoft Word, WordPad, or similar text editor capable of handling large files if necessary).

Some CR2 files can be hundreds or even over a thousand pages long, especially when morphs are included. Windows users will find this far too large for Notepad, but WordPad is capable of handling larger CR2 files.

6. You'll work on the t-shirt in this tutorial. The t-shirt is named JessiTShirt.obj. The paths in the CR2 should look as shown in Figure 12.18. Notice that the edited path does not begin with the Downloads folder, and that it does begin with the Runtime folder. This ensures that the path will work in any Runtime in which the files are placed. Edit the paths to the OBJ file so that the file points to the object you want to make posable, and remove the reference to the PMD file (the external binary morph file). Figure 12.18 shows both references in the CR2 file before and after they are edited.

First Reference Before Editing:

```
{
version
    {
    number 6
    }
morphBinaryFile :Runtime:Libraries:character:Jessi:Jessi.pmd
figureResFile :Runtime:Libraries:character:Jessi:Jessi.obj
actor BODY:1
```

First Reference After Editing:

```
{
version
    {
    number 6
    }
figureResFile :Runtime:Geometries:PracticalPoser6:JessiTShirt.obj
actor BODY:1
```

Second Reference Before Editing:

```
    }
morphBinaryFile :Runtime:Libraries:character:Jessi:Jessi.pmd
figureResFile :Runtime:Libraries:character:Jessi:Jessi.obj
actor BODY:1
    {
```

Second Reference After Editing:

```
    }
figureResFile :Runtime:Geometries:PracticalPoser6:JessiTShirt.obj
actor BODY:1
    {
```

FIGURE 12.18 Edit both references to the OBJ file and remove the references to the PMD file.

7. Save your edited CR2 in the Figures Library in the same Runtime in which you saved your OBJ file. For example, I saved my OBJ files to the Downloads\Runtime\Geometries\PracticalPoser8 folder or into the appropriate PracticalPoser8 folder in your main library if you created the folders there. You must also save the CR2 to the Downloads\ Runtime Library. Create a folder in your Downloads\Runtime\Libraries\Character folder named PracticalPoser8, and save the edited CR2 as JessiTShirt.CR2.

Some text editors may enter a TXT extension after the file name when you save it. After you save your edited CR2, verify that the file name is JessiTShirt.CR2 and not JessiTShirt.CR2.TXT or JessiTShirt.TXT.

Tutorial 12.5 Using the Setup Room

The Setup Room is likely one of the most confusing rooms for most users. In actuality, it really isn't that difficult to use. This tutorial will give you the basic steps involved to convert a grouped clothing model into Conforming clothing using the Setup Room. After you complete this tutorial, you should have the basic knowledge required to make your clothing posable. However, you'll also need to remove some extraneous information from the CR2 file if you intend to share it with others.

One of three things can happen when you click the Setup tab to enter the Setup Room:

- If your scene is empty or if you select an item that is not a figure or prop when you enter the Setup Room, Poser informs you that you must have a prop or figure selected in order to enter the Setup Room. Choose OK to close the dialog box so that you can select the proper item.
- If you select a figure that is already grouped and boned (such as a posable figure or Conforming clothing), when you click the Setup tab, you may receive a message that the figure contains morph targets and that changing groups in the Setup Room could make morphs unusable. Choose OK to continue if you simply want to modify the bones or joints for the figure. When you enter the Setup Room, you'll see the figure in its default position. And, as you roll over portions of the model, the associated bone will be revealed. An example is shown in Figure 12.19, where Jessi is shown in Outline display mode so that you can see the bone element more easily.

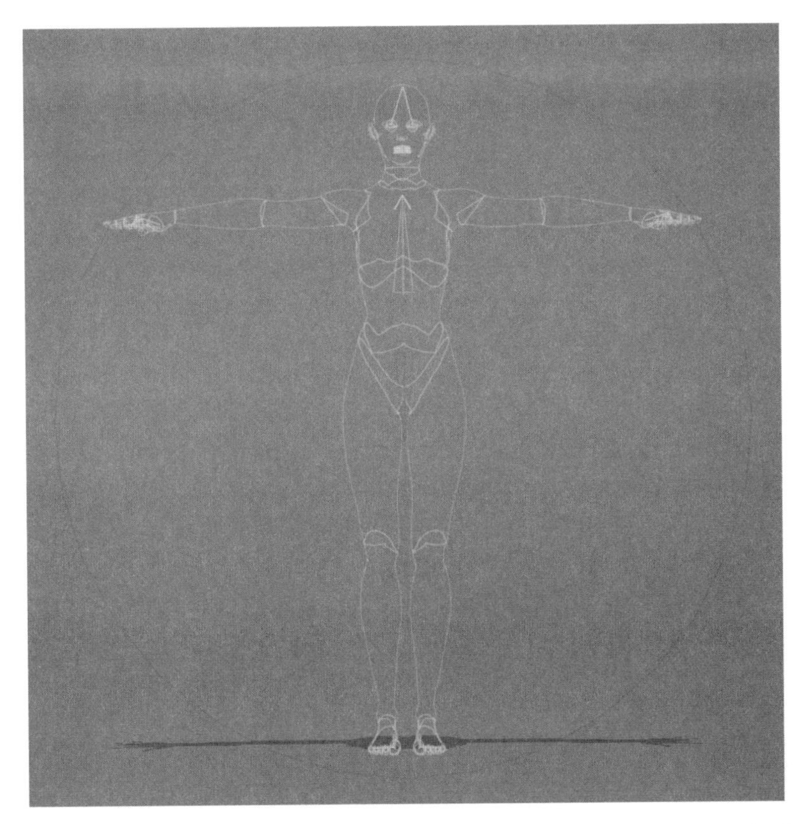

FIGURE 12.19 The bone element is revealed when you move your cursor over the body part.

It is common practice to save geometry files to one of the `Runtime: Geometries` *subfolders. If you use the Setup Room to make your geometry posable, Poser 8 automatically saves an OBJ file in the same location as the CR2 file and references that location in the CR2. You will have to edit the CR2 if you want to point to an OBJ file in the Geometries folder.*

- If you select a prop or an OBJ that you have recently imported into Poser, Poser informs you that your prop will be converted into a figure when you enter the Pose Room. The process to convert the figure is described in this tutorial.

In this tutorial, you will apply the joint parameters from the JessiBlank.CR2 file that has had the morph information removed. You will apply the joint parameters to the JessiPants.obj file, which should be located in the Downloads\Runtime\Geometries\PracticalPoser8 folder.

To turn the JessiPants.obj file into Conforming clothing using the Setup Room, follow these steps:

1. Use the File > Import > Wavefront OBJ menu command to import the JessiPants.obj file into an empty Poser scene. When the Import Options dialog box appears, do not check any options. After you locate and select the file, the pants will appear in the center of the stage.
2. With the pants selected as the current object, click the Setup tab to enter the Setup Room. Poser displays a message that your currently selected prop will be turned into a figure if you continue. Click OK to enter the Setup Room.

Some of the newer figures that are out (remember, Jessi is from Poser 6, so she has been around the proverbial 3D block a few times now) come furnished with a DEV rig (DEVeloper's Rig) that you can use as a donor CR2 for clothing creation.

3. Double-click the JessiBlank CR2 library thumbnail. You will see bones appear on the figure, as shown in Figure 12.20.

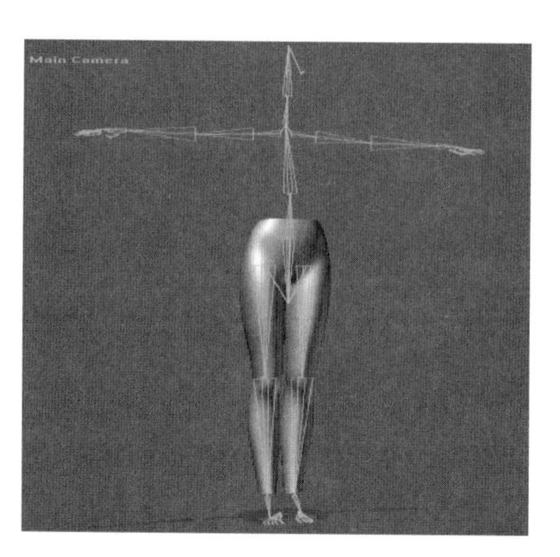

FIGURE 12.20 Apply the JessiBlank CR2 to the pants in the Setup Room. The bones appear on the figure.

4. Return to the Pose Room. You'll notice that your pants are now posable, except the legs are bent a little bit. You should turn off IK, zero the pose, and then memorize that pose before you save the pants to the library.

To do this, follow the next steps.

- First, choose Figure > Use Inverse Kinematics, and make sure that no options are checked (on).
- Next, choose Window > Joint Editor to open the Joint Editor panel. Click any body part on the pants, and then click the Zero Figure button in the Joint Editor. The pants should go back to the default position.
- To memorize the zero pose for the pants, choose Edit > Memorize > Figure. You won't notice any visible confirmation, but you can now save a preliminary copy of the pants to your library.

5. If you don't want shadows to appear in the library thumbnail, choose Display > Ground Shadows to uncheck the Shadow option if necessary. Position the camera to display the scene as you want your library thumbnail to appear.
6. Backtrack to the top level of the Poser Library, and then navigate to the Downloads > Figures > PracticalPoser8 Library. Click the Add to Library icon located at the bottom of the Library panel. Your pants will appear in the library, and a miniaturized version of your Preview window will appear as the thumbnail.

Cleaning Up the CR2

Although the clothing you have made is now posable, you are not necessarily finished. There are some items that you will definitely have to clean up in the CR2 using either a text editor or a free CR2 editing program. Highly recommended is John Stalling's CR2 Editor, version 1.51, which displays the CR2 for JessiPants in Figure 12.21. You can download this file from www.morphography.uk.vu/dlutility.html (the same site that also provides Morph Manager 4.0, mentioned earlier).

Common issues that you will have to clean up are the following:

- If the hip (on a male or female) and the chest (on a female) of your clothing disappear and display the hip and chest of the figure instead, your CR2 contains alternate geometry parts that must be removed. Adult male and female Poser figures are often modeled with body parts that you can swap, depending on whether you want to show or hide the genitalia. There are lines in the CR2 that call other pieces of geometry when this is true. You have to remove those lines from the CR2. Use CR2 Editor to search for the string `alternateGeom`. You will probably find one or two sections that reference it, and you'll have to remove it from the CR2. Figure 12.22 shows one such reference.

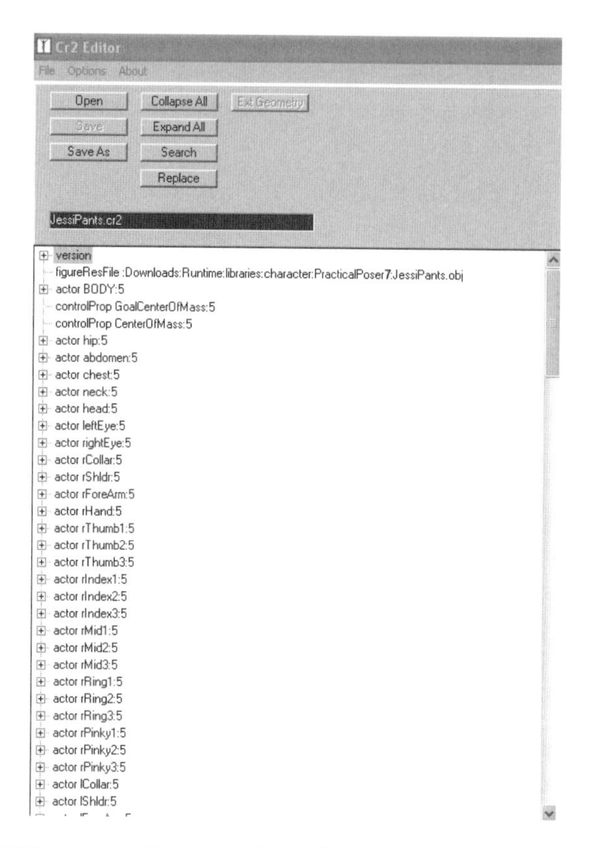

FIGURE 12.21 You can either edit your CR2 in a text editor or in a program such as John Stalling's CR2 Editor.

- Each body part in the CR2 is followed by a colon (:), which is then followed by a number, depending on the number of figures that you opened in your scene before you created the figure. For example, you'll see lines that start with `actor hip:5` or `actor BODY:5`. It is common practice to have this last number be the number 1, so you'll want to search and replace all instances of `:5` with `:1`.
- Remove extra body parts that aren't needed. The general rule of thumb is to start with the hip and work your way through all parts you need, plus one. So, for example, your pair of pants has abdomen, hip, left and right thigh, and left and right shin sections. You want to keep all of those parts, plus chest (one higher than the abdomen) and the left and right feet (one lower than the left and right shins). Delete all other parts because they aren't necessary; they will only add extra weight to your file.

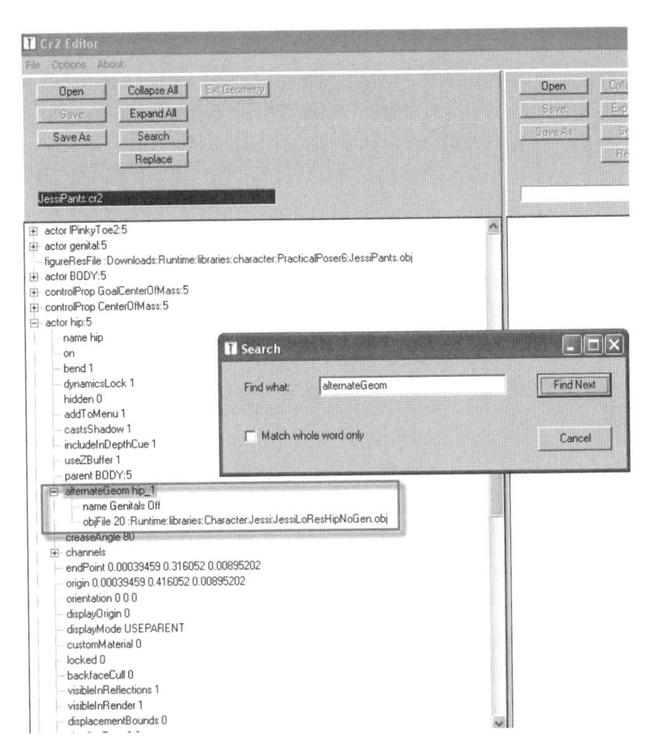

FIGURE 12.22 Remove alternate geometry references from the CR2.

- Remove extra materials that aren't needed. You'll find the materials listed toward the end of the CR2 file. The only materials that are needed are the Pants material and the Preview material. All of the other materials (Body, BottomEyelashes, TeethTop, and so on through Toenails) can be deleted because they are not a part of the Pants geometry. One easy way to clean up a CR2 is to start with the Blank.CR2 and remove all materials except for the preview material. All figures need a preview material, but make sure that it does not have any texture maps associated with it. Some Python scripts search for "Preview" as a placeholder to automatically add new materials to your figures and props. After you remove the materials, save the revised CR2 to your library under a different name, and use it as a donor CR2 for future projects.
- And now for the not-so-good news: You may have to tweak the joint parameters. You might have faces that fly away when you pose the figure or parts that don't bend right when you conform the clothing to the figure. You may have to use the Joint Editor to tweak the joint parameters. Because there are so many different things that can happen with joint parameters, I advise you to seek

assistance from the experts in the Poser community. There are several forums online at Renderosity, DAZ3D, and the Art Zone online community that are frequented by some of the best Poser content creators and who are more than happy to assist with questions and problems.

A Short Re-Pose

No matter how you look at it, it's a lot of work modeling, UV mapping, texturing, grouping, and rigging your Poser figures. In fact, I'm sweating and out of breath just from writing that sentence! But if you take the time to practice, it can be an extremely rewarding endeavor. Along with learning something that is both artistic and technical—that ol' left brain/right brain thing—you are combining the satisfaction of creating your own Poser content and enhancing your artwork with new skills and experiences. The skills you have practiced over these past few chapters are only the start of your journey. And now you know how all those modelers and Poser content providers do it.

And speaking of doing it, in the next chapter you're going to be doing it again—working with bone structures and rigging your Poser figures.

13 Joint Parameters and Dependencies

In This Chapter:

- Adding Bones to a Figure: An Overview
- Tutorial 13.1: Adding Upper Bones
- The Joint Editor
- Adjusting Joint Parameters for Clothing
- Setting Dependencies
- Tutorial 13.2: Adding a Basic Joint Dependency
- Tutorial 13.3: Making a Dependency Affect Another Object
- Tutorial 13.4: Using the Master Parameter Graph Area

"Computing is not about computers any more. It is about living."

—Nicholas Negroponte

What does that quote have to do with anything in this book, let alone in this chapter? Let's think about that for a moment. As any painter or animator does, we Poserators work to create a semblance of reality in our images or animations. When we boot up our computers and open Poser, we are transported into another world where we spend our time manipulating pixels to look like something we, and others, can relate to. It doesn't matter if it's a fantasy scene, a sci-fi image, or the frame for a comic book, we need to create a semblance of reality. If something isn't quite right, we know it. We actually can sense it. Getting back to Poser, itself, the way in which a model is set up and the way in which it moves is massively important. This means that, as you begin to work with a model's joints and setting the parameters for the mesh, you need to think about how the bones will affect the overall mesh. A poorly arranged bone structure can cause the mesh to pinch.

Adding Bones to a Figure: An Overview

Before I show you how to tweak joint parameters for clothing, you'll need a quick overview of how a figure is boned and rigged. In the following sections, you'll see how a model is brought into Poser and turned into a figure. In reality, the process to bone and rig a figure is long and tedious and will result in a lot of pulled hairs. However, if you want to get the most out of Poser, you'll eventually learn how to model, rig, and clothe your own figures. There is a lot of satisfaction in reaching this particular finish line.

Tutorial 13.1 Adding Upper Bones

Take any of the Poser figures—James, Jessi, Alyson, Ryan, and so on—and export it as an OBJ file. When you export it, make sure to turn the Ground Visibility option off; you don't want to save the Ground plane with the figure. When you export the model, all figure information will be removed, including groups and the bones, and the model will be one big mesh.

To prepare the model for the Setup Room, I grouped it similarly to the G2 versions of James, Jessi, Miki, Koji, Kelvin, and Olivia. These figures don't use a buttocks group between the hip and thighs (such as was used in DAZ's Millennium 3 figures). In addition, the chest includes the female breasts instead of having them in each of the collar groups. Refer to the Poser reference manual or Chapter 11 of this book for more information about naming conventions for each group.

After you import the figure, you can enter the Setup Room to create the bones for it. Make sure that your figure is selected, and then click the Setup tab. Poser informs you that your current prop will turn into a figure after you enter the Setup Room and asks if you want to continue. Choose OK to enter the Setup Room.

Remember, an imported OBJ file is seen as a prop.

When working in the Setup Room, you'll probably find it easier if you change to Outline mode (to view the model as an outline) and change to the Front Camera.

Once in the Setup Room, you'll need to add a bone for each group in your model. Each body part requires that you assign two names in the Properties panel: the internal name (which is referenced by Poser to make the figure pose properly) and the external name (which is a more user-friendly name that appears to the user in menus). The internal name of the bone must match the group name in your model; otherwise, Poser won't know which polygons to assign to which bone. Although you can include extra bones in your model (more about that later), you can't leave any polygons that are not assigned to a bone.

To create a bone structure, or skeleton, follow these steps.

- Choose the Bone tool from the Direct Manipulation icons. This is the button that looks like a sailboat, between the Grouping tool and the Magnifier, as shown in Figure 13.1.

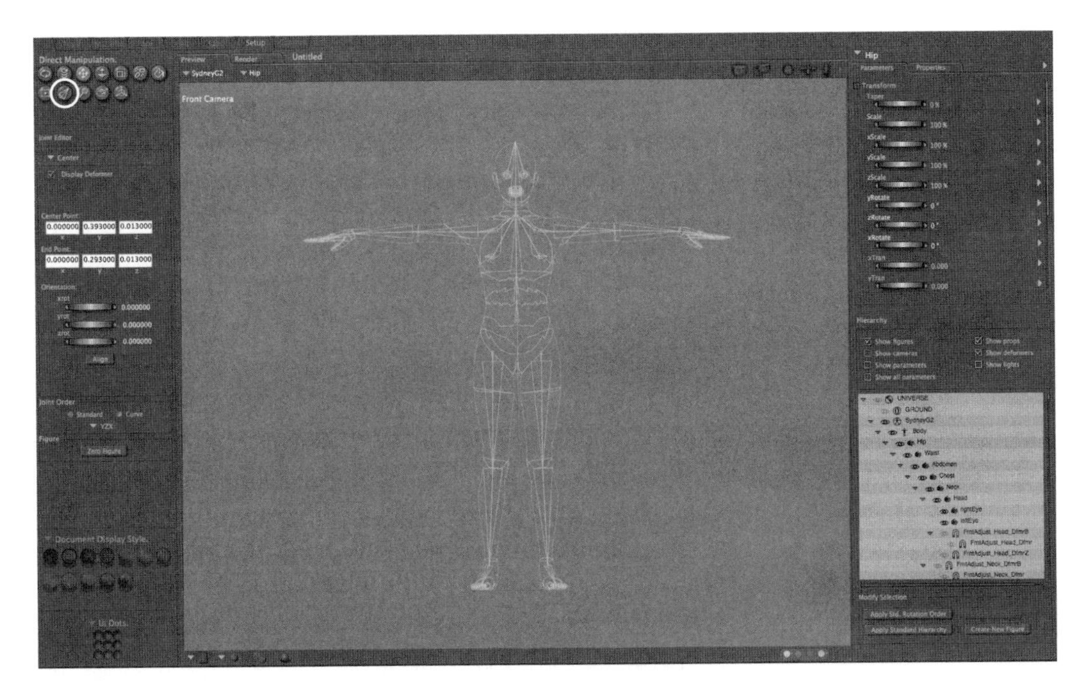

FIGURE 13.1 The Setup Room's Bone tool.

- Start by clicking the pelvic region (for the hip), and click again at the start of the abdomen. This is the start and end of the hip bone. Now, do one of two things: Either click anywhere in another portion of the Preview window to tell Poser you're finished creating that bone, or hit Return. The latter is the most effective method. Then click and drag to set the next bone. You will do this for the abdomen, chest, neck, and head. Make sure to extend the head bone slightly beyond the top of the head to ensure that all polygons are included. Then click toward the right eye to add a bone for it.

As you create new bones, you will see the previously added bones snap to connect with it. This means that, if you start the new bone too far away from the previous bone, that previous bone will lengthen in a way you probably don't want it to. And if you click too close to the end point of the previous bone, you will actually "grab" that bone and stretch it out. So the trick is to end the bone before the end of the body group, then click on the starting point of the next body group to create the new bone. This way, the previous bone will snap to the position you want it, and your bone structure will work the way you want it to.

- The Setup Room always connects a new bone to the bone that is currently selected. To add the left eye, you have to click on the Head bone again. Then add the bone for the left eye. You should now have a straight line of bones from the hip to the head and two branches that connect to the right and left eyes.
- Now you'll go back and name the bones that you've created. Click the hip bone, and open the Properties panel. Enter **hip** in the Internal Name field. Click up the hierarchy chain, adding internal names for the abdomen, chest, neck, head, rightEye, and leftEye. Take care to use the correct names and capitalization, as Poser expects certain naming conventions to make the figure work properly. Refer to Chapter 11 for more information about group naming conventions.
- Now go back and add the Name fields. Add the same name in the Name field as you did in the Internal Name field, and press the Enter key to set the name.
- Save your project. Poser will replace the external Name field with the default external names that it normally uses (such as Hip for hip, Chest for chest, and so on). Your project should look similar to what was shown in Figure 13.1.
- Return to the Setup Room after you save your file. To add the bones for the right arm, first click the Chest bone. Add four additional bones, and name them rCollar, rShldr, rForeArm, and rHand, respectively (watch the capitalization, these are standard group names).
- Click the Chest bone again to add four bones for the left arm. Name them lCollar, lShldr, lForeArm, and lHand, respectively. Figure 13.2 shows the additional progress. You can save your file again to update your changes.

Adding the Finger Bones

Depending on how your arms are positioned, you'll find it easier to use either the Top Camera or the Right or Left Camera to add your finger bones. It is usually easiest to use the Top Camera to initially add the bones and the Side Camera to refine the positioning of the bones. You add each finger one at a time, starting from the hand.

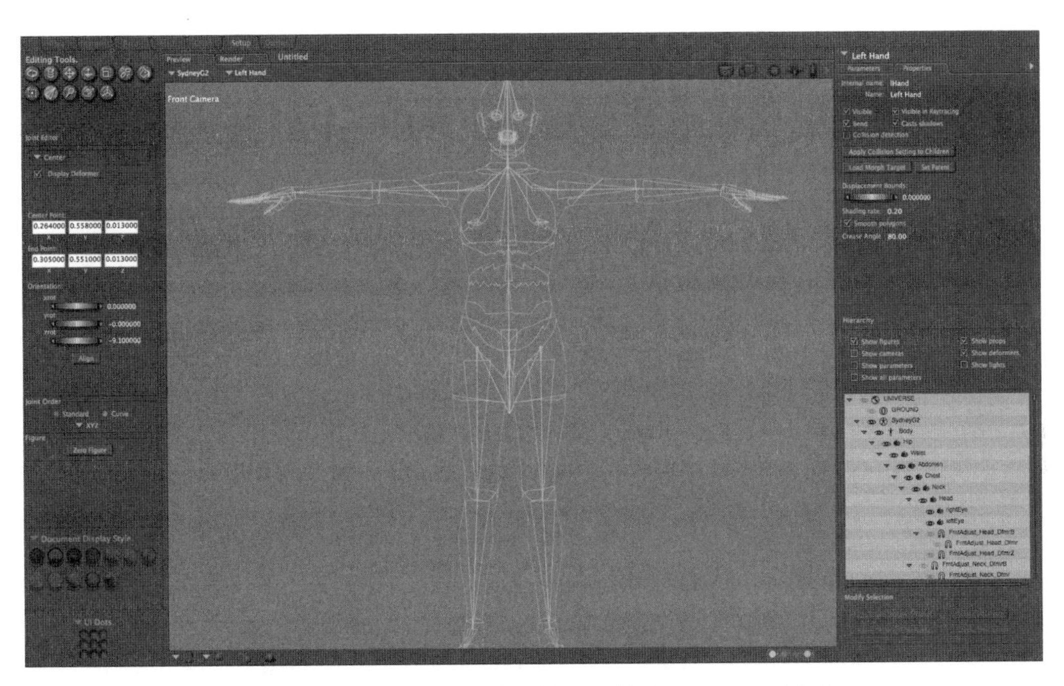

FIGURE 13.2 Bones for the right and left arms are added.

Select the hand, and add the pinky segments, calling them rPinky1 (closest to the hand), rPinky2 (middle joint), and rPinky3 (the tip of the finger). The third segment should extend beyond the fingertip just a bit.

Select the hand again, and add the rRing1, rRing2, and rRing3 segments. Continue in this manner until all finger bones are added. For the middle finger, name them rMid1, rMid2, and rMid3. The index finger segments are named rIndex1, rIndex2, and rIndex3. Finally, the thumb segments are named rThumb1, rThumb2, and rThumb3. Note that the finger names always begin with a lowercase r or l, and segment 1 is always the segment that is closest to the hand. When your groups are finished, they'll look something like the example shown in Figure 13.3, which shows the left hand bones as displayed through the Left Hand Camera. Don't forget to repeat the entire process for the fingers on the right hand!

After you add and tweak all of the bones, choose the Window > Hierarchy Editor menu command. Verify that all of your bones are connected in the right order. You will see all of the bones originating from the hip just as you created them. Figure 13.4 shows a portion of the bone structure in the Hierarchy Editor.

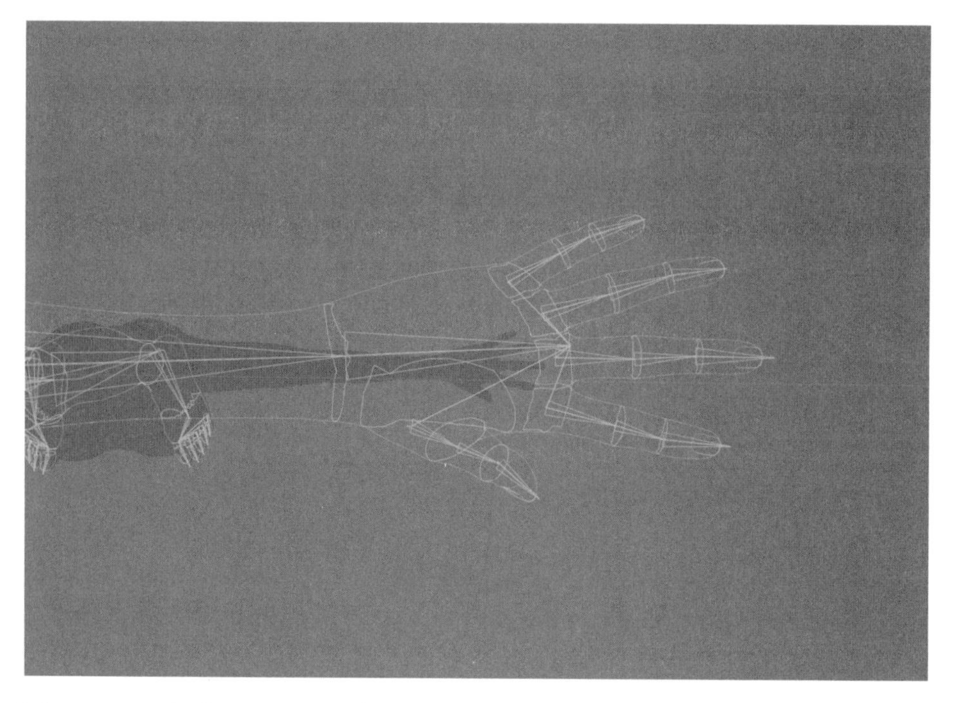

FIGURE 13.3 The bone structure for the left hand. Notice how the last bones in the chain extend beyond the fingertips in order to make sure the entire mesh is selected.

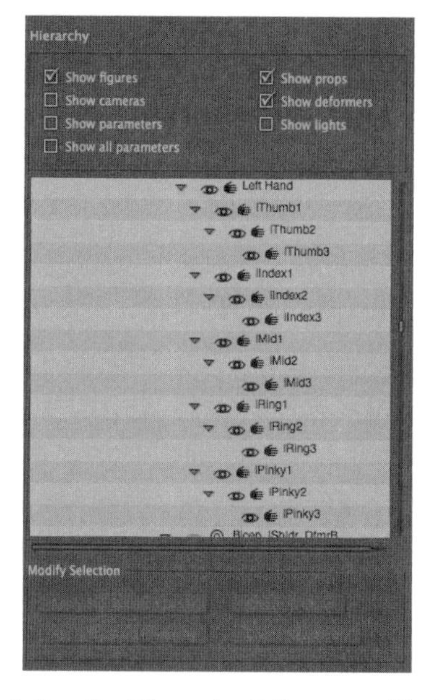

FIGURE 13.4 Use the Hierarchy Editor to verify that all your bones are connected to each other in the correct order.

THE JOINT EDITOR

By this time, you're probably thrilled that you have a figure that has moving body parts. However, you have no doubt discovered that when you try to move the body parts, the figure doesn't pose very well. Body parts collapse on each other. Things fold where they shouldn't. Limbs crinkle like bent straws or fly away in mid air. The reason is because you have to work on the joint parameters. This long and tedious process can make or break a posable figure.

Joint parameters are not an easy topic to cover in a single chapter in a book. Nor are they an easy topic to cover generically because each body shape will require different joint parameters. To step you through the complete setup and rigging of a figure could take a whole book unto itself. But Phil Cooke (known as PhilC in the Poser community) has done a great job with a series of video tutorials that are located at www.philc.net/rigging1.php and www.philc.net/joint_parameters_1.php. They can help you immensely if character rigging and the subsequent setting of join parameters are something you want to pursue. In the interim, I'll give you a dose of what setting the joint parameters is like.

To open the Joint Editor, choose Window > Joint Editor. The Joint Editor shown in Figure 13.5 opens, and the options that you see will vary, depending on the body part that you have selected.

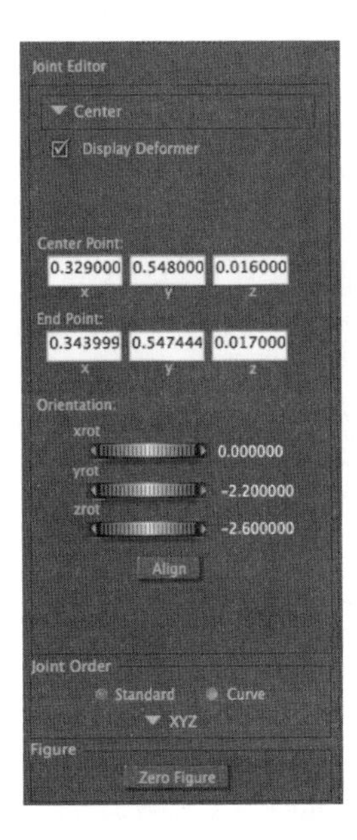

FIGURE 13.5 Use the Joint Editor to fine-tune the joint parameters of your figure.

Don't let all of these settings and controls intimidate you. I'll explain each of them in the order you'll probably need to use them. And, if you're rigging an original figure, you'll need to be familiar with all of the settings. After you complete the rigging of your figure, save it to your Figures Library. You can then use those joint parameters as a starting point for your clothing and just tweak some settings here and there. I will explain which settings you'll probably need to tweak so that your clothing works properly.

SETTING JOINT ORDERS

The first joint parameter that you will have to set is the joint order. It is good practice to set all of the joint orders before you leave the Setup Room. Doing so afterward may result in errors when you try to alter the rotation orders; while the rotation order does get altered in the selected body part, the changes may not occur in the corresponding lines in its parent.

Joint order settings apply to each body part in your figure. You'll find this setting at the bottom of the Joint Editor, as shown in Figure 13.6.

FIGURE 13.6 The Joint Order settings for the selected bone are located at the bottom of the Joint Editor.

Basically, the joint order tells Poser which axis is responsible for twisting the body part, which axis is the most important rotation axis, and which is left over. The Joint Order settings should be selected with the following points in mind:

- The first letter will always be the axis on which the joint twists, and it is also the main axis of the body part (also called the Twist axis). In other words, it follows the axis on which the bone lies. For example, the forearm bone runs horizontally along the X axis, so you assign X as the first letter in the joint order. The shin bone runs vertically along the Y axis, so you place Y as the first letter in the joint order.
- After you determine the first letter in the joint order, the last letter should be the most important rotation of the body part. (The remaining of the three letters appears in the middle.) For the forearm, the next most important rotation axis is the bend, which happens on the Y (or up and down) axis. So now you know that the first letter for the forearm is X, and the last letter is Y. So the

proper joint order assignment for the forearm is XZY: It twists on the X axis, the least used axis is Z (side to side), and the Y axis is the most used as it gives the bend parameters.

- There are two types of joint orders. *Standard* joint orders are used for most applications. *Curve* joint orders are used only for long, thin tails. They allow the tail to bend in a curve. To see the difference, you can create a long, thin multi-segmented cylinder that has at least four segments. Configure one segment with Standard joint orders, and the remainder with the Curve joint orders. When you bend the standard segment, you'll see a definite angle. When you bend the curved segment you will see a more natural curve.

To keep it simple, Table 13.1 lists the correct joint orders for the parts that are most commonly used in Poser's human figures when they are posed in the standard T position (with the palms of the hands facing downward).

TABLE 13.1 Joint Rotation Orders for Each Body Part

Part	Joint Order
Head	YZX
Neck	YZX
Chest	YZX
Collars	XYZ
Shoulders	XYZ
Forearms	XZY
Hands	XYZ
Thumb Joints	XZY
All Other Finger Joints	XYZ
Abdomen	YZX
Hip	YZX
Buttocks	YZX
Thighs	YZX
Shins	YZX
Feet	YZX
Toes	ZYX

After you set the joint rotation orders, it is a good idea to save your work. At this point, you can go to the Pose Room, open the Runtime Library of your choice, and create a new folder in the Figures Library.

Time to celebrate a little bit. You have created a posable figure. Don't celebrate too much, though. (I'm so mean!) You will find, when you try to pose your figure, there are some problems. The figure doesn't bend naturally. Parts squeeze together, or get squished, when other parts move around them. That is where joint parameters come in. So the celebration needs to be tempered for a little while longer, at which point you will be able to comfortably do the Happy Posing Dance. Now there's an interesting YouTube video waiting to happen.

Renaming Joint Parameter Dials

By default, the dials of a joint are named xRotate, yRotate, and zRotate. It will make more sense to you (and others who use your figure) to rename these dials. Most often, the dials are renamed to Twist, Bend, Side-Side, Up-Down, or Front-Back, depending on the direction that each rotation moves. To change the name, double-click on the xRotate, yRotate, or zRotate dial in the Parameters panel to open the dialog box shown in Figure 13.7. Then enter the new dial name in the Name field.

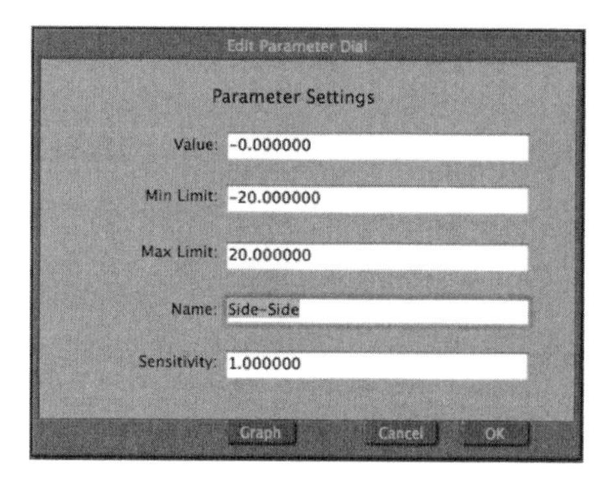

FIGURE 13.7 The Edit Parameter Dial dialog box—one that should be familiar to you by now.

Setting Joint Centers

The next step in the process is to set the joint centers for each body part. Contrary to what you might think, the joint center is not in the center of the body part. Instead, the joint center is the point around which a joint pivots in any direction. The joint center is most often near the beginning of each body part, although it may not necessarily be in the exact center. The best way to learn how a joint works is to study how your own body moves.

It's fairly easy to move the joint center. When you select a joint and have Center showing in the Joint Editor, make sure that Display Deformer is checked (near the top of the Joint Editor). The center point is displayed as three green lines, arranged in a 3D crosshair. Figure 13.8 shows the three lines slightly enhanced so that you can see them better.

FIGURE 13.8 The three intersecting lines that represent the center of the joint, which is the pivot point for all three axes of movement.

Making sure Display Deformer is active, you can move the mouse cursor over the intersection of the three lines, and the cursor turns into a bullet. At that point, you can drag the center point to place it visually at the best pivot point for the joint. Remember that the center point is common to all three axes for the joint, so try to place it accordingly. After you place the center points for all body parts, the next step is to align all of the joints. Starting with the top of the hierarchy (usually the hip), work your way through each joint in order. Click the Align button to align the axes of the center point with the movement axes of the joint. This points the axis toward the center point of the child. Then fine-tune the angle with the xrot, yrot, and zrot Orientation dials as needed. If you find that you have to rotate the alignment more than 45 degrees on any axis, you may have the joint rotation order wrong.

To test the rotations of the body part, click the part and use the rotation dials in the Parameters panel (renamed from the default xRotate, yRotate, and zRotate dials as mentioned earlier) to verify that the joints pivot from an acceptable common position.

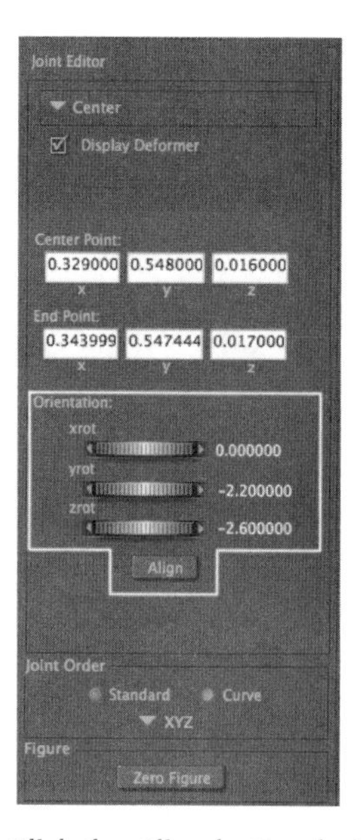

FIGURE 13.9 Click the Align button before using the rotation dials to fine-tune the center point.

Many figure creators complete this process for all joints in the figure before they work on the additional joint parameters that follow in this chapter. For body parts that have right and left counterparts, you can finish the adjustments on one side of the body and then use the Figure > Symmetry menu command to duplicate the centers on the opposite side. For example, you can set the joint centers for the right arms, hands, legs, and feet, and then use the Figure > Symmetry > Right to Left command to copy them to the left side. When Poser asks if you want to copy the joint zone's setup also (as shown in Figure 13.10), answer Yes.

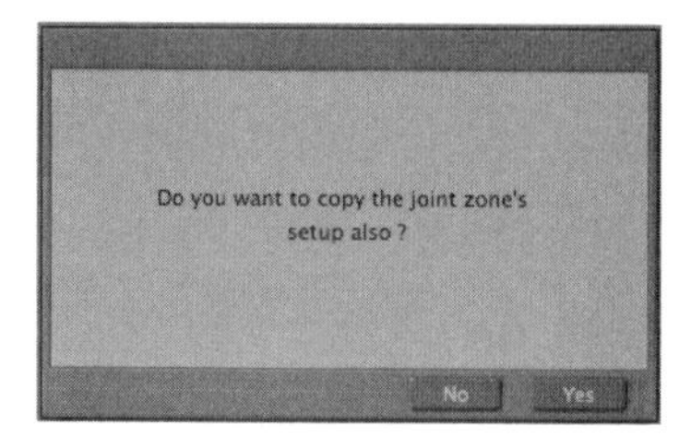

FIGURE 13.10 When using Figure > Symmetry to copy the joint setups, this message will appear asking you what you want to do.

Adjusting the Twist Axis

I mentioned earlier that the Twist axis was listed first in the joint orders. The configuration of the Twist axis differs slightly from the other two, which I will explain shortly. The Twist axis is represented by a red bar on its parent end (its starting end) and a green bar on its child end (its finishing end). The Twist bars do not necessarily have to run the entire length of the body part. Instead, you place the bars only over the portions of the body part that you want to move when you use the Twist parameter dial in the Properties panel.

Remember these key points when it comes to the Twist bars, which are illustrated in Figure 13.11.

- Any polygons above the red bar (the parent end of the Twist bar) will not move.
- Any polygons below the green bar (the child end of the Twist bar) will move completely.
- All polygons within the red and green bars will serve as the blending zone between the stationary and fully movable parts. You can also use spherical falloff zones (explained later in this chapter) to include or exclude polygons from the twisting motion.

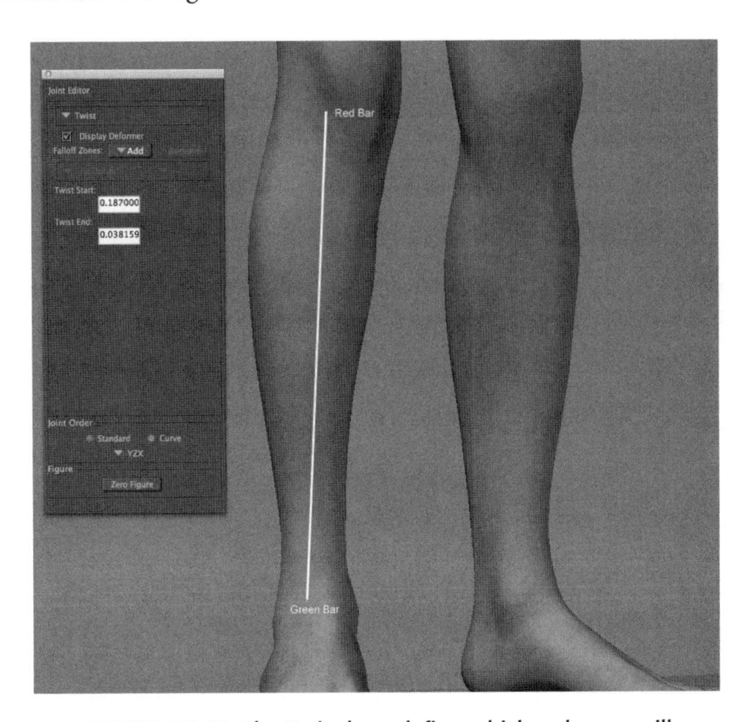

FIGURE 13.11 The Twist bars define which polygons will twist when the Twist controls are turned on.

Working with Inclusion and Exclusion Angles

So far, you've taken care of the first joint rotation: Twist. But each joint has a total of three rotations. The names of the other two rotations are usually Bend, Up-Down, Side-Side, or Front-Back. An example of the settings used for these joints is shown in Figure 13.12. Notice that the settings for these joints are much different from the Twist settings. Four arms radiate from the center point of the left wrist in Figure 13.12. Once again, these arms are enhanced so that you can view them more easily.

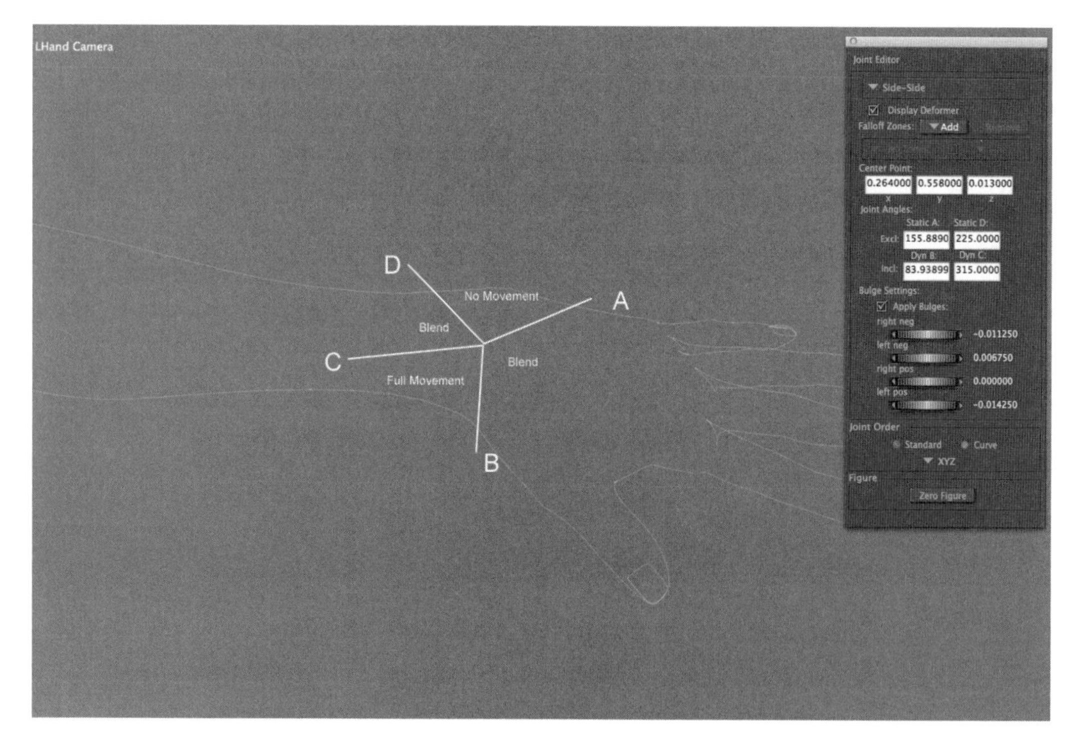

FIGURE 13.12 Four arms radiate from a center point for joints that are marked Bend, Up-Down, Side-Side, or Front-Back.

The center point in the middle of the four arms is the same center that was described in the section "Setting Joint Centers" earlier in this chapter. You may find that you have to tweak its position as you refine the remaining two joint parameters. The basic rule of thumb here is tweak and test, tweak and test, and then tweak and test some more.

As you move each arm, you'll notice the numbers changing in the Joint Angles section of the Joint Editor. If you think of the center point of the four arms as the origin of the hands of a clock, zero degrees appears at roughly the 3:00 position.

Now move your eyes counter-clockwise around the circle from the zero point while you look at the four arms in the figure and compare them to the angles in the Joint Editor. You will first come to the Static A exclusion arm (red) at 155.8890 degrees; next is the Static D arm (also red) at 225 degrees, third is the Dynamic C inclusion (green) angle at 315 degrees, and last is the Dynamic B inclusion angle (also green) at 83.93899 degrees.

When setting joints that have inclusion and exclusion angles, the following rules apply:

- Any polygons that lie between the green inclusion or Dynamic arms (marked B and C in Figure 13.12) will move completely. Their child parts will also move with them.
- Any polygons that lie between the red exclusion or Static arms (marked A and D in Figure 13.12) will not move.
- Any polygons that lie between a red arm and a green arm (area A–C and area C–D in Figure 13.12) will blend and act as transition areas between the stationary zone and the moving parts.

Using Bulge Settings

When some joints bend, you need more control over how polygons react. The most common example is when you bend a figure's forearm and you want to keep the elbow pointed. The Joint Editor has the Bulge Settings section that helps you control the shape of a joint when it bends.

For example, let's take a look at what happens to the knee of DAZ's Victoria 3 when you bend her right shin to 92 degrees. I'm using V3 because this has been fixed in Victoria 4. If you don't use the Bulge Settings options, her knee balloons out a bit too much. However, with the Apply Bulges option turned on and some small adjustments made to the Right Pos setting (–0.018) and the Left Pos setting (0.014), you see a very subtle but more believable change in the shape of her knee when it is bent. You can see this effect on the left side of Figure 13.13. To see this even more clearly, Figure 13.14 shows just how bad the knee can bulge if an extreme Bend value is applied.

While it is true that the bulge that occurs in V3 has been fixed in V4, that doesn't mean you can't use the Bulge Settings to fine-tune the Victoria 4 character. It just means that, at the outset, it's no longer necessary to worry about unsightly joint bulging when initially bending a body part.

FIGURE 13.13 When you enable the Apply Bulges option, you can control the shape of the joint as it bends.

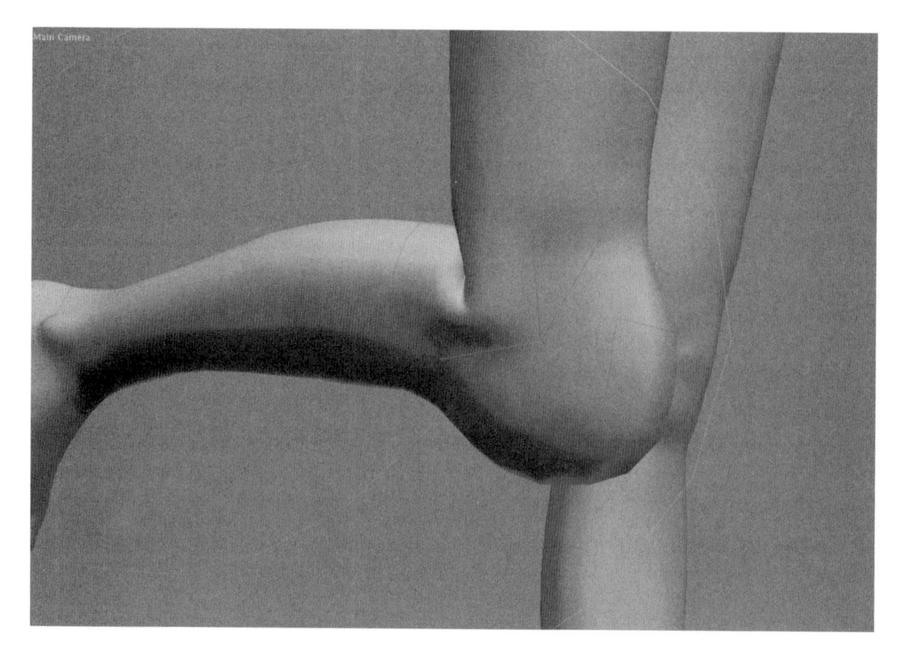

FIGURE 13.14 With Bulge Settings at extreme values, the knee looks like a gourd has been implanted.

The best way to apply bulges is to bend the limb using the Bend dial in the Parameters panel. You will probably have to scroll down in the Parameters panel to access this dial. Then, check the Apply Bulges option. Adjust the Right Pos, Left Pos, Right Neg, or Left Neg dials in the Joint Editor as necessary to get the shape you want.

ADJUSTING SPHERICAL FALLOFF ZONES

Spherical falloff zones add additional control to joints that bend. They control the area and shape of the bend, and a good use for spherical falloff zones is to control the shape of bends in the elbows, knees, or other joints when one side of the joint has to bend more than another.

Spherical falloff zones work similarly to the inclusion and exclusion angle bars. In the spherical falloff zones in Figure 13.15, note the following points:

- All polygons that lie only within a green zone will move totally.
- All polygons that lie only within a red zone will not move at all.
- All polygons that lie in the overlap of the green and red zones will become the blend zone that deforms between the stationary and moving parts.

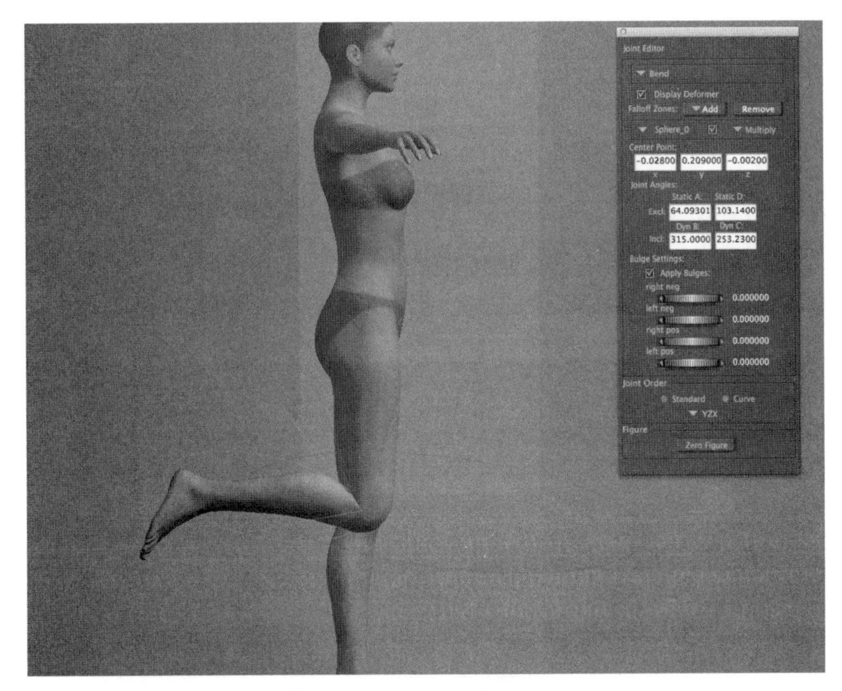

FIGURE 13.15 Spherical falloff zones allow you to further refine polygons that move and blend when a joint is bent.

Spherical falloff zones only affect the current body part and its parent. You may need to scale or rotate the spheres to get optimum results. Many find it easiest to reduce the scale of the zone, and set the x, y, and z rotation angles to zero and start from there. Children of the current body part always move with the current body part.

The areas defined by the inclusion and exclusion angle bars take precedence over the spherical falloff zones. That is, if there are polygons that fall between the green and red spherical falloff zones but that also fall outside of a red exclusion angle, they will not move. After you get this far with an original figure, there are some additional tasks that you have to complete. For example, you still have to configure the eyes and the Inverse Kinematic (IK) chains for your figure.

Adjusting Joint Parameters for Clothing

Now that you have a basic idea of the work that goes into making a posable character, you are probably thinking that it will be a chore to do the same for clothing. Fortunately, there is a solution—clothing makers typically start with the joint parameters of the figure for which the clothing is made. In fact, in the previous chapter, you learned how to use the Setup Room to apply the joint parameters of a figure to a clothing model to turn it into Conforming clothing.

To make clothing work the best it possibly can, working in the Joint Editor will have to become almost second nature to you. This is most evident when you create clothing that is not skin-tight. The looser the clothing is, the higher the chances are that you'll have to modify the joint parameters in your clothing.

Adding Bones to Clothing

Sometimes, your clothing might require additional bones to pose parts of the clothing that don't fit into standard body part names. Now that you know how to build a skeleton from scratch, it should be easy to add extra bones to clothing!

In Chapter 12, "From Modeler to the Poser Library," you learned the differences between Conforming clothing and Dynamic clothing. There is a third category of clothing that is becoming more popular in the Poser world: Hybrid clothing.

Hybrid clothing combines the best of both worlds. It is very difficult, if not impossible, to create Dynamic clothing that has a lot of modeled detail. On the other hand, it is very difficult to make Conforming clothing that flows gracefully and naturally. Hybrid clothing allows you to conform the detailed parts and make the flowing parts dynamic.

The dress shown in Figure 13.16 is a great example of how hybrid clothing can be put to good use. Two of the hardest things to make conforming are bell sleeves and long skirts. The scooped neck and puffy sleeves, along with all of the modeled lacing on the back of the dress, would also be very difficult, if not impossible, to put through the dynamic calculations required by the Cloth Room.

Looking at the dress in the Setup Room, you are now able to see the bones in the dress. The first thing that you'll notice is that all of the extraneous bones have been removed. The only bones that remain from a "normal" figure skeleton are the hip, abdomen, chest, neck, and left and right collars. In addition to those standard bones, the model has three extra groups added to the geometry: rSleeve, lSleeve, and skirt (see Figure 13.17). The polygons for the sleeves start after the sleeve puffs (which are part of the conforming collars). The skirt polygons start at about mid-hip level.

In the Setup Room, three additional bones are added to the dress. The right collar part is assigned as the parent of the rSleeve group, the left collar is the parent of the lSleeve group, and the hip is the parent of the skirt group.

You can save Hybrid clothing to the Figures Library, and you can conform the Conforming parts to the figure before you enter the Cloth Room. The Conforming parts will pose with the figure, but you'll need to create cloth simulations to pose the sleeves and skirt.

FIGURE 13.16 Many clothing items (such as this dress model) can be a challenge to convert to Conforming or Dynamic.

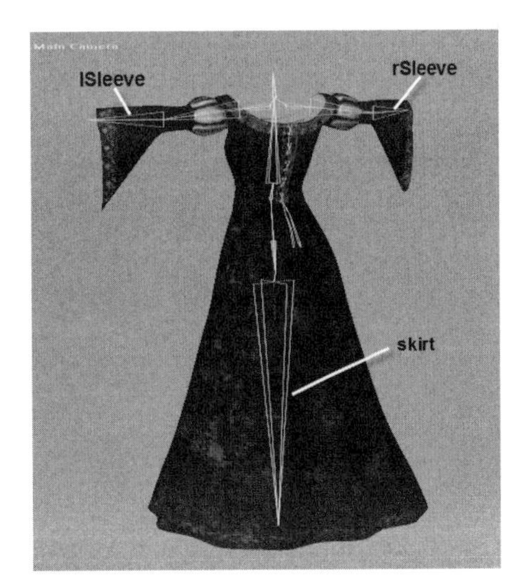

FIGURE 13.17 Three extra bones are added for each of the bell sleeves and for the skirt.

In the case of this dress, you have to create three cloth simulations:

- The first simulation is for the skirt, which should collide against the figure's legs, shoes, and any other body parts or props in your scene that will come into contact with the skirt.
- The second simulation is for the right sleeve (rSleeve), which should collide against the figure's right shoulder, forearm, and hand. You may also need to set it to collide with the skirt and any other props in the scene.
- The third simulation is for the left sleeve (lSleeve), which should collide against the figure's left shoulder, forearm, and hand, along with other items that it may come in contact with.

After you set up your cloth simulations, you can use Animation > Recalculate Dynamics > All Cloth to calculate the simulations in the order in which you created them.

Joint rotation orders and center points are usually inherited from the CR2 of the original figure. Both the figure and clothing should use the same center points and joint rotation orders.

Inclusion and Exclusion Angles for Clothing

When using the CR2 from a character, chances are good that you'll need to make adjustments to the inclusion and exclusion angles of your clothing to prevent poke-through issues. This is especially true for clothing that is very loose or puffy. If you find that the puffy areas of clothing don't move as they should, move the green arms outward a bit until the puffy areas are included within the movable area.

Figure 13.18 shows an example of how inclusion and exclusion angles can fix poke-throughs. On the left side of the figure, you see the underarm poking through the sleeve puff. The reason is because the green arm that is closest to the figure's chest (shown thicker and in white for clarity) is too close to the puff of the sleeve. An adjustment has been made to the green arm on the right side of the figure to resolve the problem.

Inclusion and exclusion angles can also be adjusted when clothing crinkles and bunches up too much when a joint is bent. Just remember that you should test the changes in many different poses before you consider the change final or before you apply the change to the opposite limb with the Figure > Symmetry menu command.

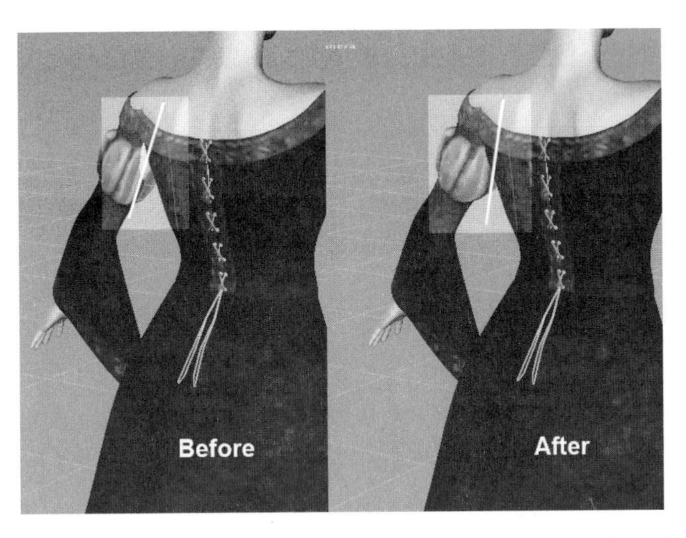

FIGURE 13.18 Adjust inclusion and exclusion angles to fix poke-through issues.

Spherical Falloff Zones for Clothing

If you apply the joint parameters from a figure to Conforming clothing made for that figure, you may see parts of the clothing spike outward when you move a body part. The usual reason is that the spherical falloff zones have to be increased in size in one or more directions to include the polygons that are not moving when you pose the body part.

The way to remedy the spikes is to first zero the pose of your figure. Then click the body part on the figure that you suspect is causing the problem. Move the offending body part in one direction only (Twist, Side-Side, Bend, Up-Down, or Front-Back) until you are able to reproduce the spike. Then increase the Scale settings of the Inner Mat Sphere (the green zone) or the Outer Mat Sphere (the red zone) until you eliminate the spike. The yScale and/or zScale settings may need adjustments for sleeves, and the xScale and/or zScale settings may need adjustment for pants. Test the other axes as well, just in case the spike was caused by a combination of more than one rotation. Use the Figure > Symmetry menu command to duplicate the settings on the opposite side of the body if necessary.

Setting Dependencies

At this stage, you have gotten a good foundation regarding bone structures and joint parameters. New to Poser 8 is the ability to create dependencies—namely, you can make each joint affect another element in the model that wouldn't normally be affected or to add features to the joint's movement, or you can make the joint affect something else in your scene. It's probably one of the most interesting of the new features, and one that has almost limitless possibilities. In this section, you will use the Andy model to learn how to create dependencies.

Before starting, you might have noticed something new in the Parameters panel as you have worked through this book. What I'm referring to is the small switch-like icon associated with some of the controls and the secondary numerics with the those parameters. Since Andy does not yet have any dependencies set, Figure 13.19 shows the switches I am talking about associated with Alyson Casual's left hand.

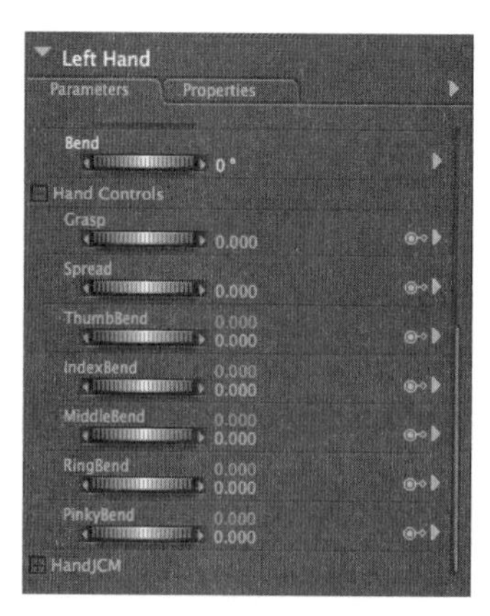

FIGURE 13.19 New icons and secondary numerics signal dependencies for a parameter.

When you click on one of those little switches, it will open the Master Parameter panel. Figure 13.20 shows the dependent parameters associated with the Grasp master parameter for the Alyson Casual model. Here, you can see that the left hand controls the bending, twisting, and other parameters of the various other joints, such as the thumb. These dependencies can be as simple or as complex as you would like, and in the next couple of tutorials, you will learn how to control single and multiple elements with one object.

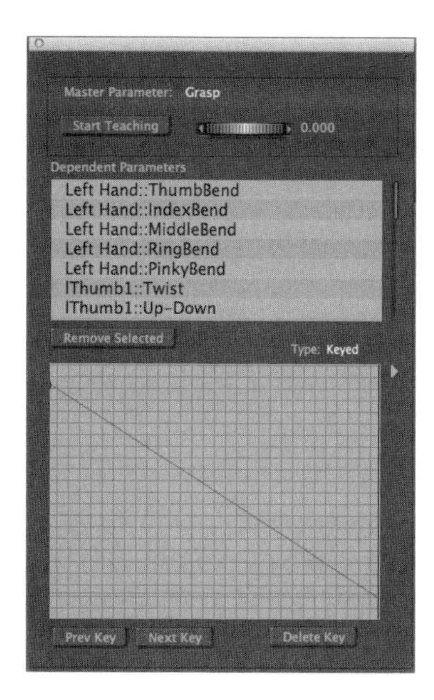

FIGURE 13.20 The Master Parameter panel.

Let's take a moment to break this window down. It's not as complicated as many, but there are still some things you should know.

- **Start Teaching:** This button tells Poser to begin "recording" the various changes you make to the selected part.
- **Numeric Dial:** Use this to control the actual movement of the selected element as well as control the changes it makes to the other model parts.
- **Dependent Parameters:** Gives you a list of the model parts that will be affected by the main part's movement.
- **Remove Selected:** Highlight an element in the Dependent Parameters list and click this button to remove it from the list.
- **Graph area:** Lets you control the response of the movement between the two keys (the 0 setting and the modified setting).
- **Prev Key:** Selects the previous key along the graph.
- **Next Key:** Selects the next key along the graph.
- **Delete Key:** Removes the currently selected key.

TUTORIAL 13.2 ADDING A BASIC JOINT DEPENDENCY

With a new scene created and Andy standing patiently for your orders, let's make him show off a little bit. With a physique like his, Andy should definitely strike a muscleman pose. So in the immortal words of Jackie Gleason, "And away we go!"

1. Select Andy's right shoulder.
2. For this project, when the shoulder twists, the head will turn, the forearm will bend, and the hand will curl inward. So click on the triangle to the right of the Twist parameter and select Edit Dependencies to open the aforementioned Master Parameter panel.
3. Click the Start Teaching button.
4. In the Master Parameters section, change the Twist value to –90, and then make the following changes to the body parts shown using the controls in the main Parameters panel. Each of these parts will be affected when the right shoulder's Twist command is changed. (Figure 13.21 shows the Twist Master Parameter panel and how it should appear at this point.)

   - **Head**: Twist = –31, Bend = 19º
   - **Neck**: Twist = –19º
   - **Right Forearm**: Bend = 72º
   - **Right Hand**: Twist = –81º, Side-Side = 78º

   Here is what has happened. You are setting the ending points first, teaching Poser that when an element (in this case the right shoulder) is moved to a specific setting, other elements will follow. Now you have to tell those elements where they are to be positioned at the start. You can't set the starting position(s) unless you first set an ending position.
5. Change the Right Shoulder Master Parameter value to 0. You will now set the starting positions of all the elements.
6. Select each element in the Dependent Parameters list and return them to their 0 (zero) positions.
7. Now that all the dependencies are set, click Stop Teaching to tell Poser you're finished making changes.

Now, close down the Master Parameter panel. Select Right Shoulder in the main Parameters panel, and use the Twist dial to move the right shoulder to the –90 value. Not only will the shoulder twist, but the forearm will bend, the hand will move inward, and the head and neck will move to look at the massive bicep.

At this point, you can change the settings for the Shoulder, setting this limit to –90 so you can't over-twist the right shoulder.

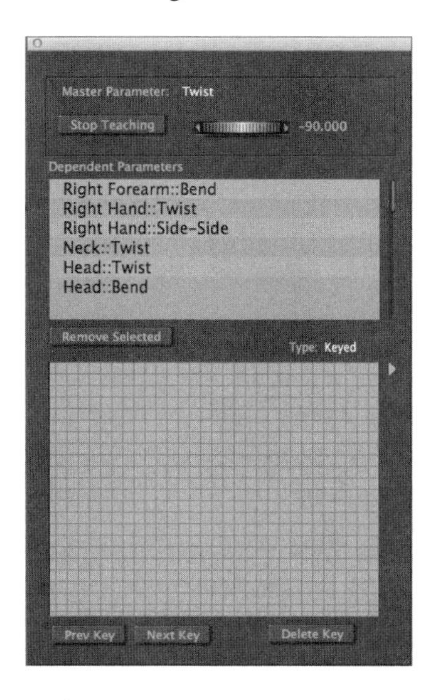

FIGURE 13.21 The Twist master parameter with the affected elements in the Dependent Parameters list.

TUTORIAL 13.3 MAKING A DEPENDENCY AFFECT ANOTHER OBJECT

Pretty nifty stuff, here. You can actually set up your own parameters that are controlled by another element in the scene. You did this in the last tutorial with one element affecting other elements in the same model. What about doing it with something else? Something like a magnet?

In this tutorial, you will add a magnet to the scene and, during the course of the shoulder twisting into a muscleman pose, you will actually make the muscle bulge. As you're probably aware, this adds to the last tutorial, so all the work you did will not be lost.

1. With the Right Shoulder selected and set to –90, add a Magnet object (Object > Create Magnet) to the body part.
2. Scale the Base to 11% and the Zone to 7%. This will make everything fit the shoulder area. But there's still some fine-tuning to do.

3. If you don't have it open already, open the Master Parameter panel for the Right Shoulder and click Start Teaching. Remember, you should be at the –90° position for the right shoulder.
4. Change the following settings for the Mag Base:

   - xRotate = 90
   - xTran = –1.171
   - yTran = 4.878
   - zTran = –0.432

5. Change the Mag Zone to the following:

   - xScale = 98%
   - yScale = 13%
   - zScale = 38%
   - yRotate = 2°

6. Now make the following change to the magnet itself:

   - xTran = –1.230

   At this point, you will have a bulging bicep like you see in Figure 13.22.

7. Now make the following changes to the Mag Zone:

   - xScale = 0%
   - yScale = 0%
   - zScale = 0%
   - xTran = –1.111
   - yTran = 4.961
   - zTran = –0.310

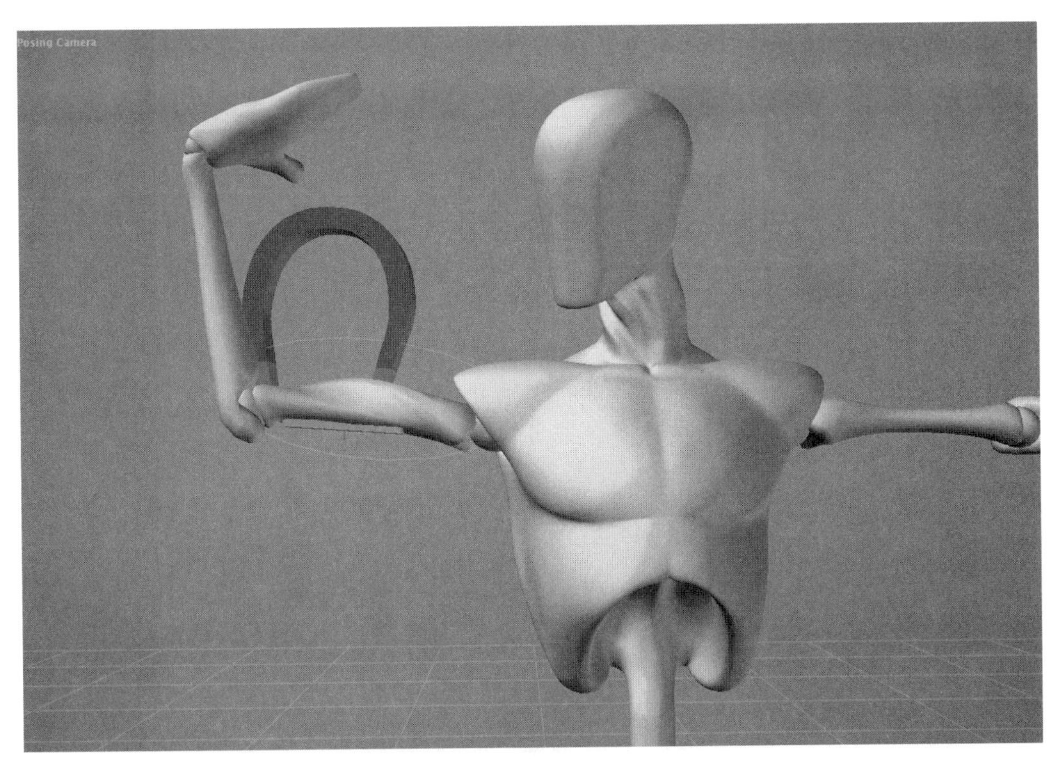

FIGURE 13.22 Andy is buff and ready for a day of sand-kicking at the beach.

8. And, finally, make the following changes to the magnet itself:

   - xScale = 100%
   - yScale = 100%
   - zScale = 100%
   - xRotate = 0°
   - yRotate = 0°
   - zRotate = 0°
   - xTran = 0
   - yTran = 0
   - zTran = 0

Click Stop Teaching, and then return to the main workspace. When you change the Twist setting for the right shoulder, not only will the arm, hand, head, and neck move as you set in the last tutorial, but the muscle will now bulge. With a little bit of thought and some foresight, you can create all new dials and parameters for almost every part of your scene.

TUTORIAL 13.4 USING THE MASTER PARAMETER GRAPH AREA

The one area that hasn't been worked with yet is the Graph area. This section of the Master Parameter panel lets you control the strength and timing for an element's movement over the course of the value changes. To see how this works, select the head and do the following:

1. From the Dependent Parameters list, choose Head: Bend. You will see a red line appear in the Graph section that goes from the top left to the bottom right (see Figure 13.23). What this shows is a smooth, even movement from the 0 point (right) to the point where Andy's looking at his bulging bicep.

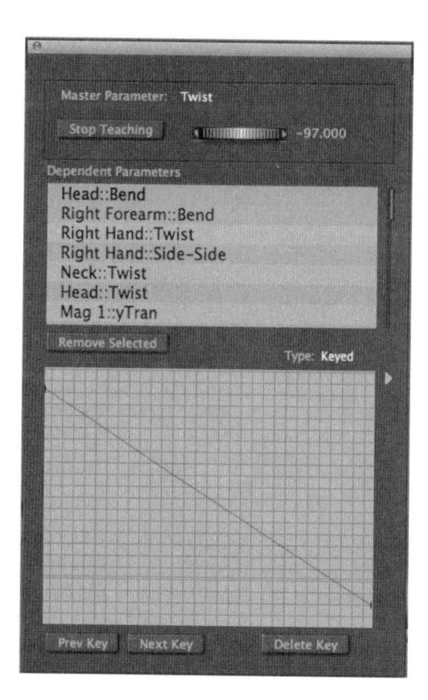

FIGURE 13.23 The graph shows how the movement of an element will occur over the course of that movement.

2. Click anywhere on the graph line, and you will create a key. This key is a point where some sort of change will occur. From that point, click and drag upward and the curve will change. What the graph line in Figure 13.24 shows is that the head will turn faster, reaching its finishing point earlier than the rest of the objects.

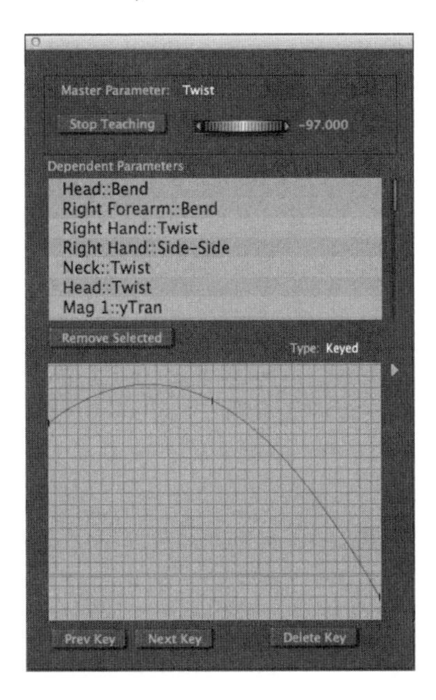

FIGURE 13.24 The graph has been modified, and the head will move to its final position earlier than before.

3. Notice, though, that the graph line curves back down. If this were an animation, the head would twist back and forth, almost like he's shaking his head no. That's not what is happening here. All this graph is showing is the time it takes to move from one position to another. So, in one sense, this downward curve means nothing. But if you're like me, this downward trend bothers my sense of balance. So click somewhere between the end point and the key you made and drag upward to straighten the graph line (see Figure 13.25). You will also need to click on the end point to finish the change.

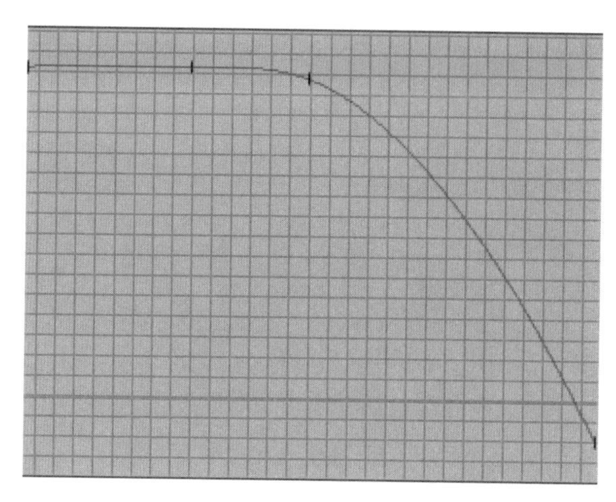

FIGURE 13.25 The modified graph shows that the head will turn faster than it originally would have.

Working with the graph is an important aspect of the Master Parameter panel, and an important part of any animation. When you initially set up a dependency for multiple elements, they all move at the same speed and same time. This looks unnatural. There's always a slight delay between the different parts. By working with the graph, you can cause the different affected elements to move in a more random manner and, in the end, look much more realistic.

A Short Re-Pose

Now you have a good base to work from when setting up a bone structure and, when you have completed that structure, to make modifications that limit each bone's effect on the mesh. You also can assign that bone structure to other elements, such as clothes, to help you save time when setting those clothes for a specific character. And, finally, you discovered one of the more powerful new features in Poser—dependencies.

In the next chapter, you'll explore an area of the program that hasn't been brought up yet—animation. So get ready to add and modify motions using controls you might have avoided up until now. Just remember: Avoidance is futile.

14 Animation Techniques

In This Chapter:

- Getting Ready to Animate
- Keyframes and Interpolation
- Tutorial 14.1: A Basic Animation
- Tutorial 14.2: Breaking Splines
- Animation Layers
- General Animation Tips
- Tutorial 14.3: The Alien Within—Creating a Creepy Animation
- Tutorial 14.4: The Rest of the Story—Animating Ryan's Reaction

"Computers have lots of memory but no imagination."

—Author Unknown

It's our imagination that drives computers around the world. Our ability to tell stories through still images or video has been enhanced by the use of computers. With Poser, you have always had the ability to create animations, but never so completely or professionally as with Poser 8. The software's animation capabilities have grown exponentially over the course of the last few releases.

In this chapter, you're going to explore the more advanced animation controls, and then look at some of the creative possibilities lying in wait for you. The object is to enable you to create sophisticated animations with a minimum of fuss.

You will find that I'm not covering the basic animation controls, but, instead, I'm delving directly into the more advanced areas of the program. If you aren't comfortable with basic animation techniques, I would suggest purchasing *Poser 8 Revealed: The Official Guide* by Kelly Murdock (Cengage Learning, 2009) and familiarizing yourself with these concepts. I will, however, define any animation-specific terms that come up during the course of the chapter just to make sure we're understanding each other. Okay, it's to make sure you understand me.

Portions of this chapter were written by Phil Cooke (PhilC at www.philc.net).

Getting Ready to Animate

The first thing you want to do is prepare your workspace. While you might be used to merely working with the Animation Drawer that, by default, is located at the bottom of the Poser workspace, to really garner the power of the program, you will want to have two extra control windows open and available at all times. Those windows are as follows:

- **Animation panel:** This is made up of three tabs: Keyframes, Layers, and Animation Sets. In order, these give you access to keyframes in your file, and layered animations that are being mixed together, and store often used animations you have created.
- **Graph panel:** This area allows you to make precise modifications to an element's animation settings.
- **Preview window:** This is the main section and is used to make your basic animation setups. You should already be familiar with this area. If not, refer to *Poser 8 Revealed* or go to Help > Poser Tutorial Manual.

All of these areas will be discussed in detail before you start animating.

Figure 14.1 shows the set up I use in order to most efficiently work with the advanced animation controls. Remember, to dock a window, you have to click the small square at the top right of the window and select Drag-Docking Enabled. When this is active, you can dock the Animation and Graph panels as you see in this image. The reason I dock them like this is to give more room to the Graph so the keyframes can be modified more easily.

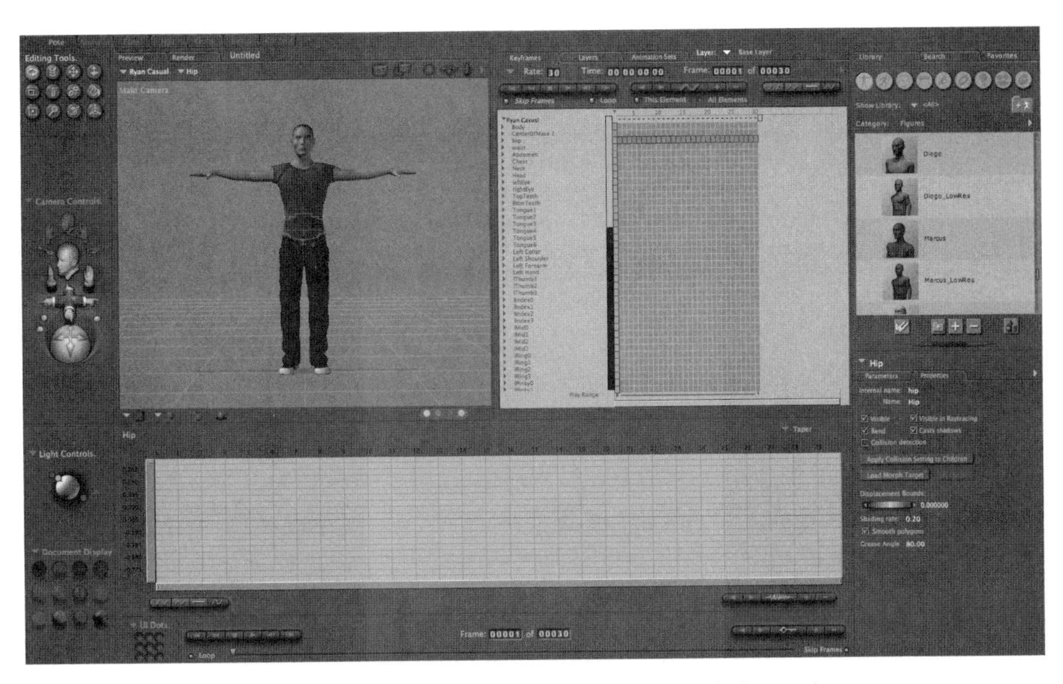

FIGURE 14.1 One example of how you can dock panels to organize your workspace when animating.

In order to open the Animation and the Graph panels, you will first need to click on the Keyframe button located in the Animation Drawer or go to Window > Animation Palette. If you want to use the quick key command to open this window, it's Shift+Ctrl/Cmd+V. To open the Graph panel, click the button with the curved line at the top center of the Animation panel (see Figure 14.2). You can also go to Window > Graph or use Shift+Ctrl/Cmd+G to open the panel.

While the Animation panel might look very complicated, it really isn't. First, let's look at the controls at your disposal.

- **Frame Rate:** Determines the number of frames per second (fps) the animation will play in. 30fps is standard for a U.S. broadcast, and 25fps is standard for PAL (European broadcasts). 24fps is the speed for high definition and for film. 15fps is the slowest frame rate and sometimes used for the web, although with broadband becoming more available, the frame rates for Flash and web animations are 24–30fps. If you create a 10-second animation at 24fps, you will have one that is 240 frames long.

- **Time:** During playback or as you move the play head along the timeline, this counter displays where in time you are within your animation.
- **Keyframe controls:** These controls frame the Graph Display button. From left to right, those controls are as follows:

  a) Previous Keyframe—Moves back along the timeline one keyframe at a time.

  b) Next Keyframe—Moves forward along the timeline one keyframe at a time.

  c) Add Keyframe (the + button)—Adds a new keyframe at the play head's position on the timeline.

  d) Remove Keyframe (the – button)—Removes a selected keyframe.

- **Current Layer:** Gives you access to any animation layers within the current animation.

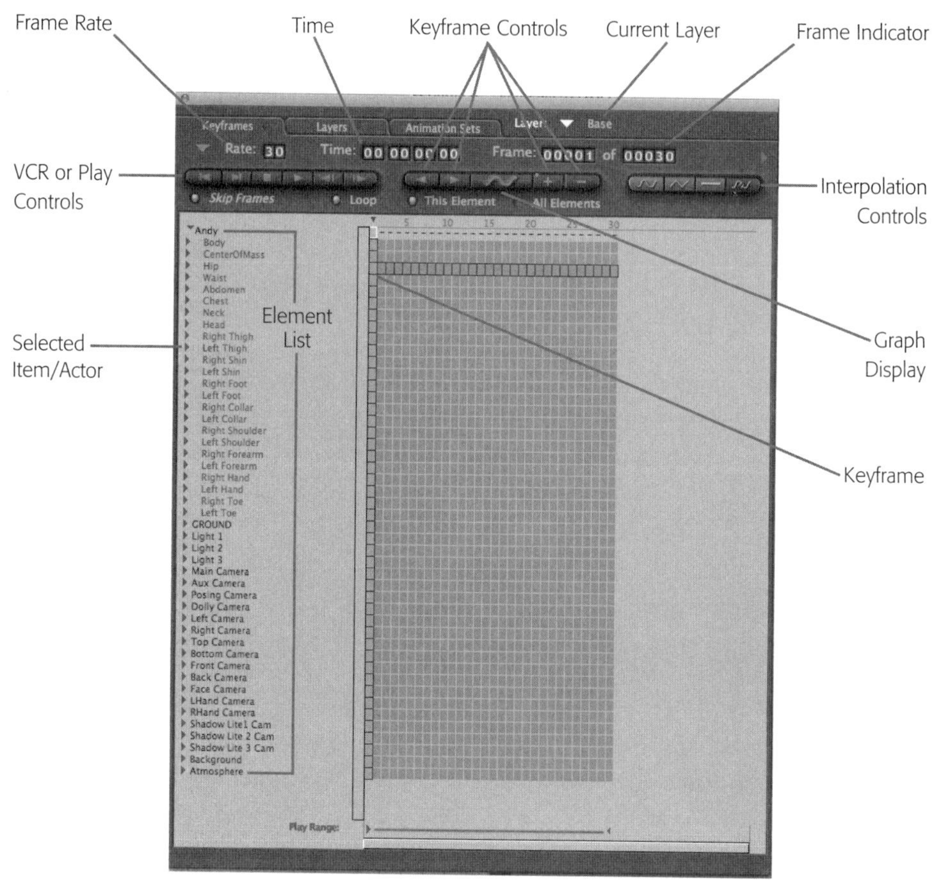

FIGURE 14.2 The Animation panel and its controls.

- **Frame Indicator:** Shows which frame you currently have selected (left number) along with the total number of frames (right number).
- **VCR/Play controls:** Standard controls that include the following (from left to right):

  a) First Frame—Takes you back to the first frame of the animation.

  b) Last Frame—Takes you to the last frame of the animation.

  c) Stop—Stops the animation playback.

  d) Play—Plays the animation within the preview window.

  e) Step Backward—Moves back one frame at a time.

  f) Step Forward—Moves forward one frame at a time.

- **Selected Item/Actor:** Shows the selected element on your model or in your scene.
- **Element List:** Lists all available model parts and elements in your scene.
- **Keyframe:** The point at which the vertical and horizontal blocks meet is the keyframe position for that current selected item.
- **Graph Display button:** The curvy line nestled between the Keyframe controls. When clicked, this opens the Graph panel (explained in the "Keyframes and Interpolation" section later in the chapter).
- **Interpolation controls:** Gives you the controls to interpolate either an element or a range of frames. From left to right, the interpolation controls are as follows:

  a) Spline

  b) Linear

  c) Constant

  d) Break Spline

What does interpolation mean? The mathematical definition, which is what I'm using here, is the calculation of the value of a function between the values already known. So, based on the method of interpolation, the calculation of movement from one point to another (or keyframe to keyframe) will determine how that movement will appear.

Keyframes and Interpolation

If you have tried any animating whatsoever, the key to animation (all puns intended) is keyframes. A *keyframe* can define a specific pose, a camera position, a lighting condition, a change in material, or any other property that is keyframeable.

For example, you can pose your figure in a specific position in the first frame of your animation, and then you can move to a frame a few seconds later to modify that position. I'll explain this by getting you to act out a real-world example. Imagine that you are standing up with your arms by your side. Now imagine yourself going through the following motions:

- Stand up with your arms by your sides. Hold that thought!
- Raise your right arm up in the air. Hold that thought!
- Lower your right arm so that you are standing as you were before. Hold that thought!
- Now sit down and imagine what you just did. You'll think of your first, second, and last thoughts in sequence and visualize the motions in between. This is exactly how Poser builds up an animation.

Tutorial 14.1 A Basic Animation

Let's take this idea and turn it into the most basic of animations. Use Andy for this tutorial.

1. At frame 1 in the Preview window, pose Andy standing with his arms by his sides. Here are the values I used for the pose you see in Figure 14.3.
   - Left Shoulder
     - Twist = 22º
     - Down-Up = –81º
   - Left Hand
     - Side-Side = 1º
     - Bend = –10
   - Right Shoulder
     - Twist = 10º
     - Up-Down = 80º
   - Right Forearm
     - Twist = –6
   - Right Hand
     - Twist = 26º
     - Bend = 7º

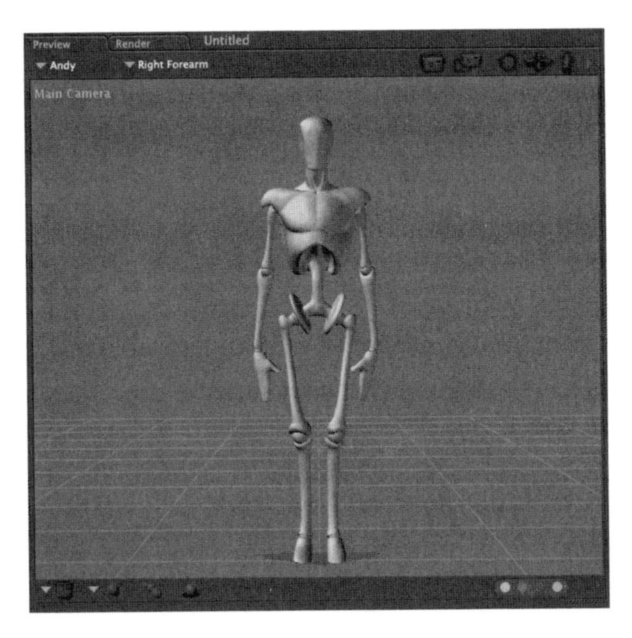

FIGURE 14.3 The starting position for Andy.

NOTE

It's important to make slight changes to each side of your models. There are always small variations to the positions of our hands, arms, and other body parts. While you can start by using the Symmetry controls to get the basic pose set up, you want to still make minor tweaks so that both sides are not mirror images of each other, thus giving your model an unnatural appearance.

2. Advance to frame 15. Make the following changes to the pose. Figure 14.4 shows the new pose.

   - Left Shoulder
   - Twist = 0º
   - Down-Up = 5º
   - Left Hand
   - Bend = 30
   - Right Shoulder
   - Twist = 10º
   - Up-Down = –7º

- Right Forearm
  - Twist = –6
  - Bend = 109°
  - Side-Side = 65°

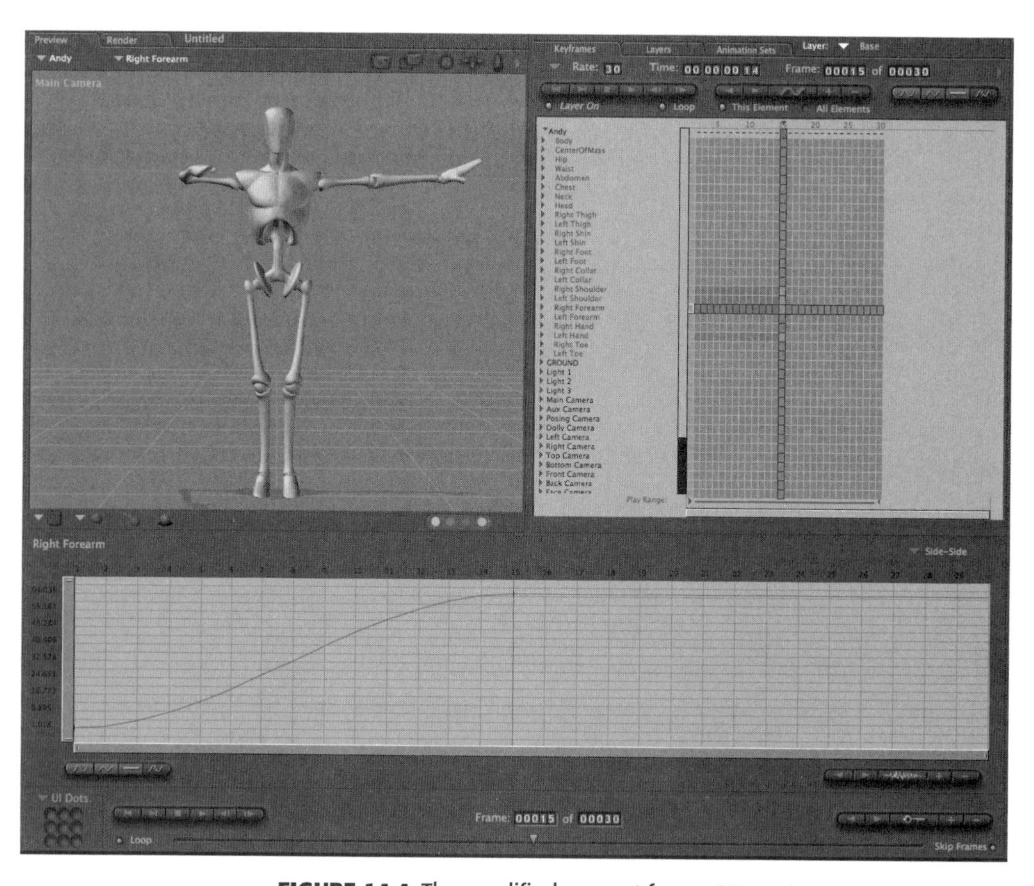

FIGURE 14.4 The modified pose at frame 15.

3. Advance to frame 30 (the final frame) and change all the values for the right and left arms back to the settings in Step 1 of this exercise. To have a little bit of fun, you could select Chest and, at frame 12 or 18 (your choice) and change the Twist to 19°. Then go to Frame 30 and make sure the Twist is still set to 0°. (It is always a good practice to double-check that your settings have not changed after making a change to another part of your timeline.) By offsetting the twisting of the torso (Chest), you get a less mechanical movement.

When animating, an easy method for resetting values or specific poses is to use Pose Dots. If, for example, you return to Frame 1 and then click on a Pose Dot, you will "record" that position. When you go to Frame 30 (in this tutorial's example), you can click that Pose Dot again to apply the pose. To learn more about Pose Dots, you can refer to the Poser Reference Manual.

4. Now click the Play button to see your animation. There's Andy doing some basic aerobics. (Even non-organic models need their exercise, y' know.)

Notice in the Animation panel that there are now horizontal green displays indicating that values have been set for the actors at the frames indicated. You'll see that frames 1, 15, and 30 are highlighted (as shown in Figure 14.5). These are the keyframes. The values of the parameters of the in-between frames are calculated by Poser using interpolation. Poser knows the start and end points and uses math to come up with the intermediate values. The Graph panel now shows these values (see Figure 14.6).

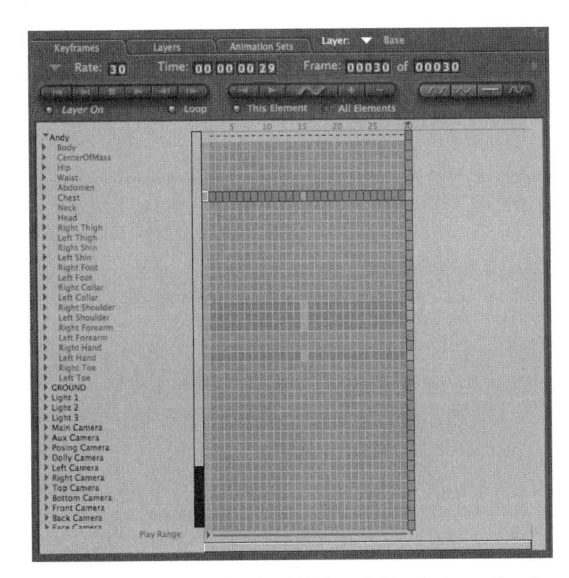

FIGURE 14.5 Notice the keyframes (the highlighted blocks) set for frames 1, 15, and 30.

Poser has three ways of doing the calculations for the interpolation. It refers to these as sections, and they may be selected using the Animation panel Interpolation controls shown in Figure 14.7. To repeat and focus on the controls for a moment, from left to right they are Spline Section, Linear Section, and Constant Section. The fourth button is Break Spline, which will be detailed in Tutorial 14.2.

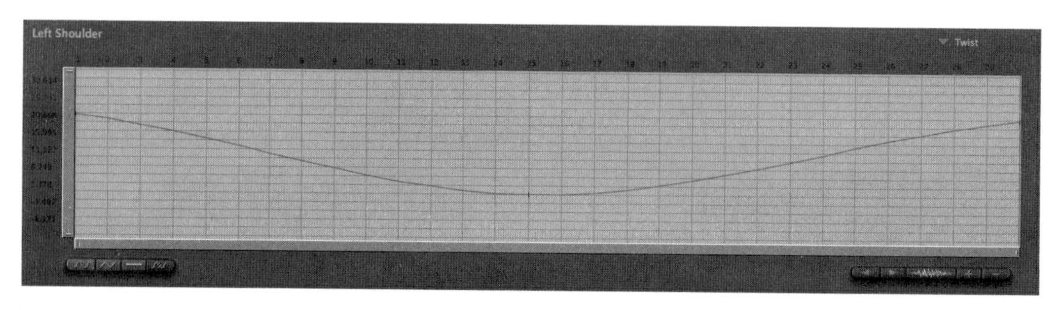

FIGURE 14.6 The Graph panel shows the spline interpolation for the animation.

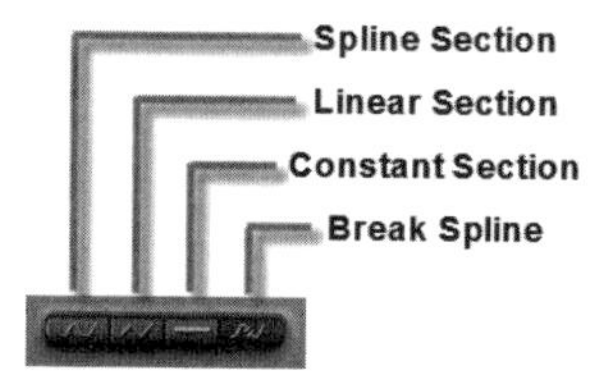

FIGURE 14.7 The Interpolation controls allow you to select how keyframes will be blended.

In order to make changes to the interpolation, select an actor and a keyframe in the Animation panel and then click one of the section buttons. The types of interpolation work as described here:

- **Spline Section**: Spline Section keyframes are colored green and are the default method of interpolation. Generally, it's how the body moves. Remember when you imagined that you stood up and raised your arm? The motion was smooth, not jerky. This interpolation method creates smooth, graceful curves, or sine waves, between your keyframes. The movement from one keyframe to the next begins slowly, accelerates in the middle, and then slows again as it reaches the next keyframe.
- **Linear Section**: Linear Section keyframes are colored orange. This interpolation method creates straight, sawtooth-like transitions between keyframes that increase or decrease at a steady rate. A project file on the DVD that accompanies this book shows how the arms respond with Linear Sections between the keyframes. Open the Chapter14\animationFiles\animation_Linear.mov file to see the example shown in Figure 14.8. Here, the motion is set to a constant velocity. There is no gradual speeding up or slowing down of the motion.

It starts at a run and keeps going at that speed until it stops. Although this is not quite so realistic for human motions, if you are just starting out with animations, it's a good method to adopt. This is because the motion before a keyframe does not affect the motion after.

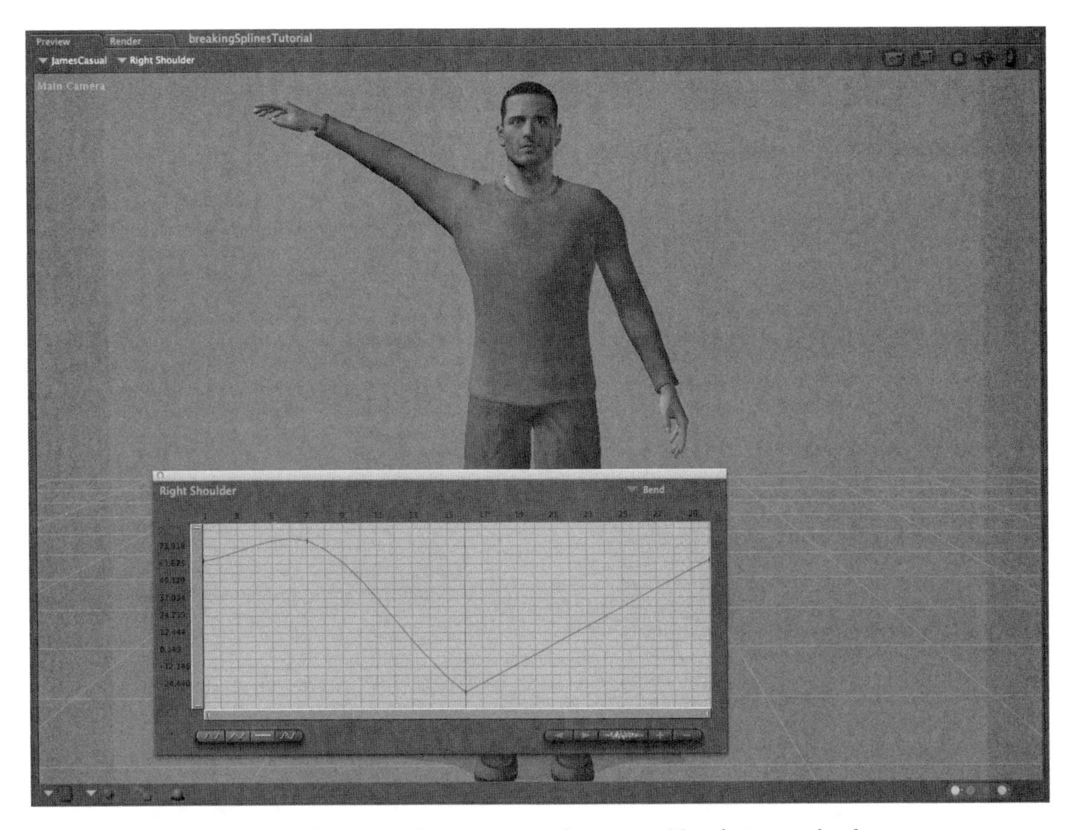

FIGURE 14.8 Linear sections create a sharp transition between keyframes.

- **Constant Section**: Constant Section keyframes are colored gray. The pose at the first keyframe does not change until it reaches the second keyframe. The change is then instantaneous, basically acting like a switch, with the value changing only at the keyframe. You can see this in the animation_Constant.mov file found in the Chapter14\animationFiles folder. You can see the spline's appearance after setting interpolation to Constant, as shown in Figure 14.9.

Take a moment to save your file. After the next tutorial, you can come back to Andy and make any modifications you would like.

FIGURE 14.9 The Constant command makes an instantaneous change that affects the element's position until the next keyframe.

Tutorial 14.2 Breaking Splines

Now let's go back to the Spline selection and consider what would happen if an extra keyframe were added at frame 7. At this point, I will use the James model as the example. Only the right arm has been animated in this file—the same animation type as you made for Andy's left arm. For this project, the object is to make James's arm relax slightly before it is raised.

1. Open the breakingSplinesTutorial.pz3 file found in the Chapter14\animationFiles folder on the DVD. Once the file opens, select Ryan's Right Shoulder and then change to Bend in the Graph panel. You see what is shown in Figure 14.10. Pay attention to frame 7 where the extra keyframe has been added.

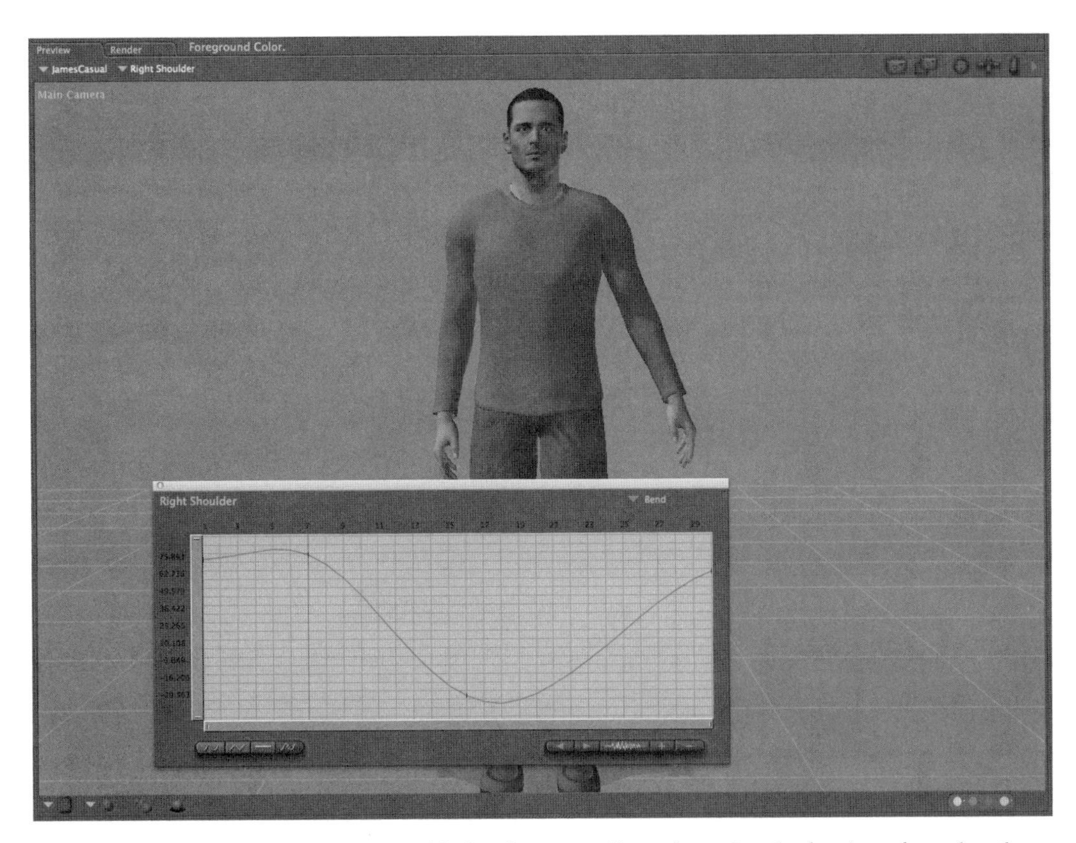

FIGURE 14.10 The extra keyframe added at frame 7 affects the spline farther into the animation.

If your spline is flat, go to the right side of the Graph panel. You will more than likely see the word Taper. Click to reveal the pop-up list and select Bend to see the correct animated element.

But now look at the graph. Frames 1 to 15 have changed. In fact, if you play the animation now, you will see James's arm disappear behind his back (actually through his side). You will also see how frames 15 to 30 have changed. Instead of the maximum amount of arm bending occurring at frame 15, it is now at frames 17 and 18, increasing the bend.

Many times, this is the one biggest problem that animators face when working in Poser—by making a change to or adding a keyframe to an element, another part of the animation dramatically flies off. There are times you'll get lucky, and the change in the animation will be slight, almost unnoticeable. But, alas, that's not the norm. By working in the Graph panel, though, and using Spline Break, you can fix problems like this very easily.

2. To break the spline, select frame 15, and then click on the Spline Break button. This probably isn't going to be a surprise to anyone, but the spline is now broken. If you look in the Keyframes panel, you'll see a black line slicing through the keyframe on frame 15 to indicate the break. Altering the bend value at frame 7 no longer has any effect on frames 15 to 30. To fine-tune this example even further, if you require frames 15 to 30 to revert to sinusoidal, just add an extra keyframe at frame 16 with the same values as frame 15. Refer to Figure 14.11 to see how your spline should now appear.

What the heck does sinusoidal *mean? Sounds like something that involves breathing or some sort of medical procedure on the sinuses. Actually, sinusoidal means having a succession of waves or curves. So when you're working with splines, the undulation of the spline is an example of being sinusoidal.*

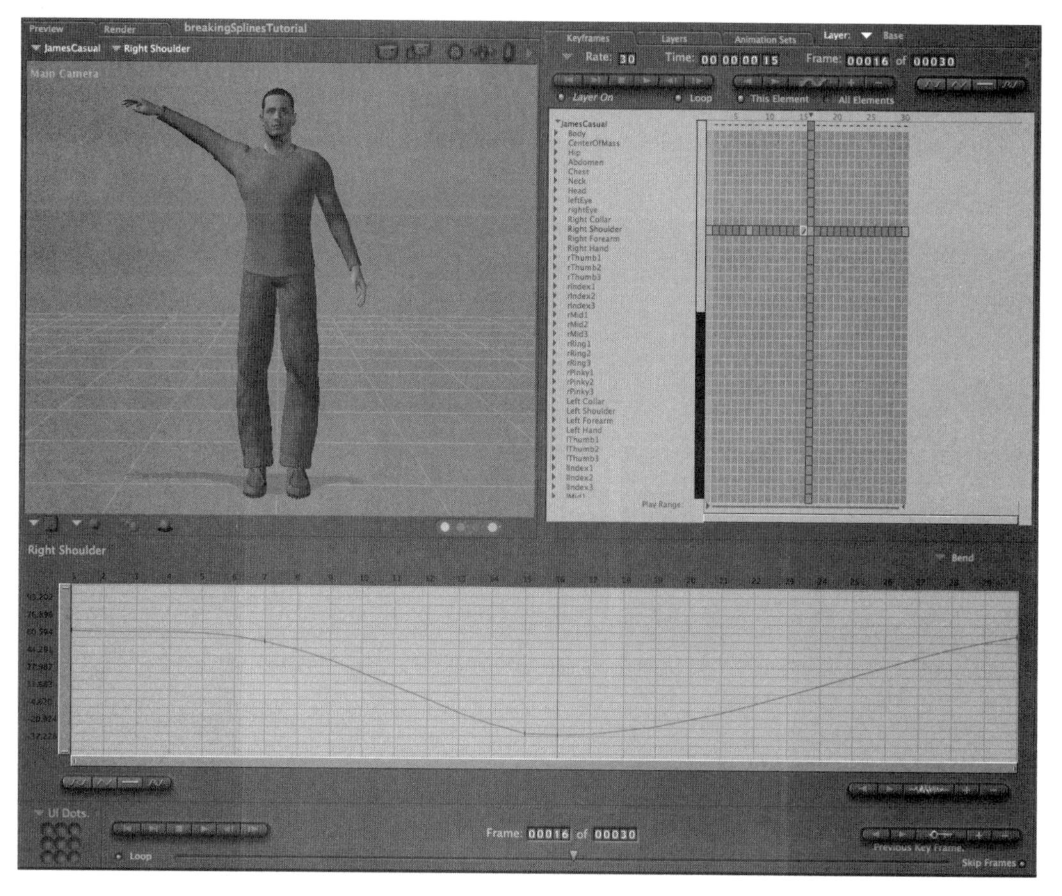

FIGURE 14.11 After adding a spline break, the section before the keyframe can be modified without affecting what happens after the keyframe.

Before breaking the spline, the right arm rises and then makes, for lack of a better term, a smooth looping motion before it begins its descent. That looping motion causes the arm to rise a bit higher than what is wanted (for this project) before it lowers. By adding the spline break, you have stopped the motion in the exact position you want it to end, and then start its return downward. It's subtle, but that is what animation is about—those subtle movements that bring a more realistic feel to the motion.

ANIMATION LAYERS

One of the niftiest features when animating in Poser is layers. The Animation Layers panel is shown in Figure 14.12 and, as you can see, looks exceptionally similar to the Keyframes panel. You can use animation layers to build your animations in pieces, meaning that you can move or hide layers without affecting content that appears in other layers. In other words, you can edit animations more freely and in a non-linear fashion, something that is not possible with a single-layer animation. Plus, when you render a layered animation, all visible layers are composited together to create a single movie.

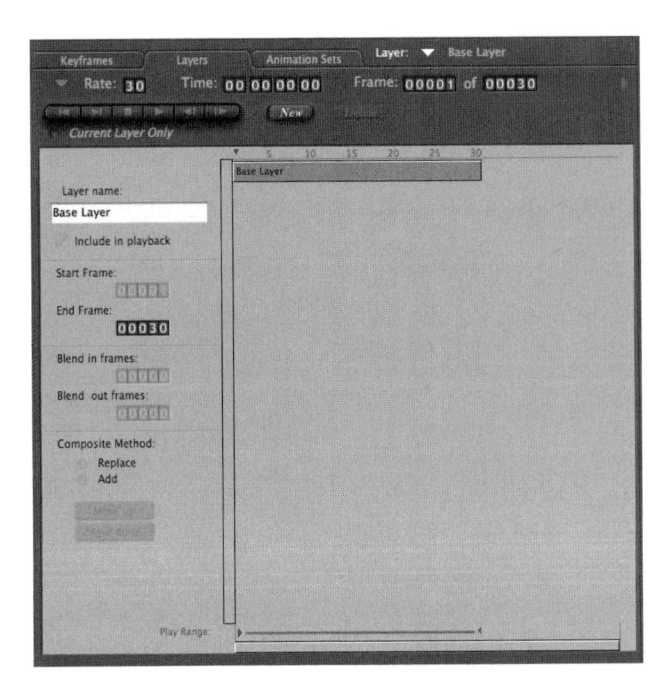

FIGURE 14.12 The Animation Layers panel.

The controls in the Layers panel assist you in creating layers in which to place additional scene elements. The Layers panel consists of the following controls:

- **New:** Click this button to create a new layer in your animation.
- **Delete:** After you select the layer you want to delete, click the Delete button.
- **Layer Name:** Enter a name for the new layer in this field.
- **Include in Playback:** When checked, this option will include playback of your layer when you preview your animation. When unchecked, the elements included in the layer will not animate.
- **Start Frame:** Enter the frame number on which the layer will start.
- **End Frame:** Enter the frame number on which the layer will end. This number cannot exceed the total number of frames in the base layer. If you need additional frames in your movie for the layer, you must add them to the base layer first.
- **Blend In Frames:** Enter the number of frames at the beginning in which the current animation layer will blend in to the underlying animation layers.
- **Blend Out Frames:** Enter the number of frames at the end in which the current animation layer will blend out to the underlying animation layers.
- **Composite Method:** The Add composite method adds new layer data to the existing underlying data. The Replace composite method replaces underlying layers with the contents of the new layer data.
- **Move Up:** Moves the animation layer up in the stack so that it takes higher precedence.
- **Move Down:** Moves the animation layer lower in the stack so that it takes less precedence.

It is also important to understand the method by which the animation layers are composited:

- **Add:** Values of each parameter are added together for all layers. If James has a shoulder bend of 5 in the base layer and a value of 10 in Layer 1, then the resulting value is 5 + 10 = 15 degrees.
- **Replace:** Parameter values of the upper layers will replace those of the lower layers. For the same example, because Layer 1 is above the base layer, the value used is 10. The 5 degrees of bend found in the base layer are ignored.

In the Layers panel, you can zero in to edit smaller sections of an animation and then blend them into the main animation. When you first view the Layers panel, it will contain just the base layer. You can, of course, change the name of this default layer in the Layer Name field. To add a new layer, click the New button. The option to rename this layer is provided with the Layer Name field.

With the new layer selected, return to the Keyframes panel. There you will find . . . nothing! The green horizontal display line has disappeared because you are now editing a new layer. The overall animation is still present, as shown by the curve in the Graph panel.

Let's continue. Back in the Layers panel, set up the layer start frame and end frame. This could be the full length of the animation (which it is by default), but that's not what you want here. Change the Start Frame value to 14 and the End Frame value to 24. The number of frames over which this animation will blend in and out respective to the base layer is set at 3. Finally, the option was selected to add this animation to the base layer. The resulting Layers panel is shown in Figure 14.13.

The animation for James's left shoulder starts at frame 16, where the Bend value is set to +56 degrees. At frame 21, the Bend value is adjusted to –79 degrees. The graph will now look as shown in Figure 14.14.

If you return to the Layers panel, you will notice that it is possible to drag Layer 1 along the time line, allowing you to freely control at which point in the animation the arm bends without destroying the other elements in your project.

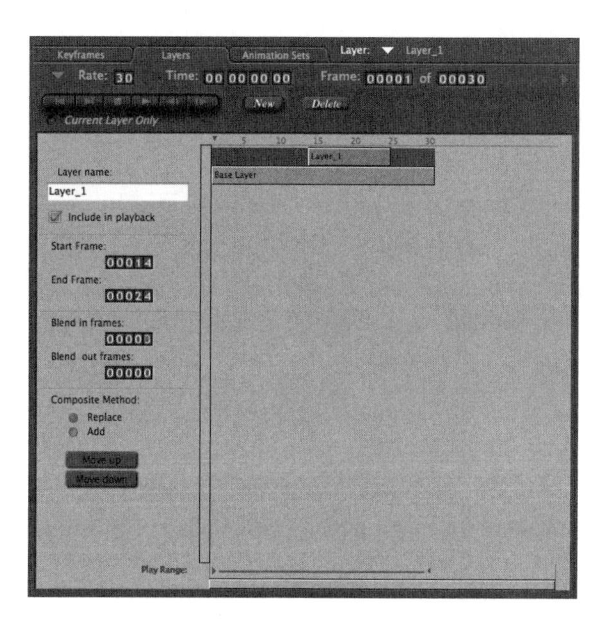

FIGURE 14.13 The new animation layer has been added and set up as needed.

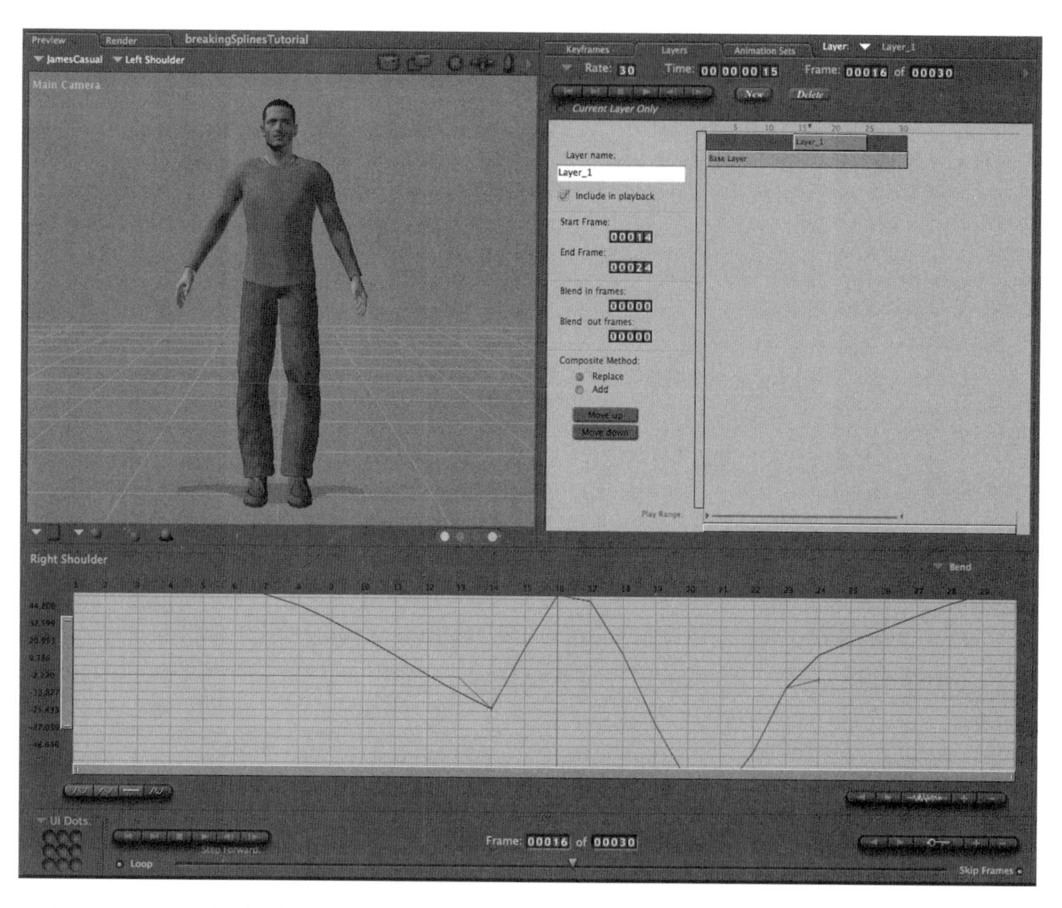

FIGURE 14.14 The look of your graph after the left shoulder Bend values have been changed.

Animation Sets

Python scripting or third-party applications use animation sets, as shown in Figure 14.15, to control animation properties. Extra attributes may be set using the Attributes button. For example, an attribute could be set to allow a script to automatically start an animation when the figure first appears in a scene.

To get to the Attributes button, open the Animation Sets panel and click the New button. You will be asked to name the new Animation Set, at which point the Attributes button will become available to you.

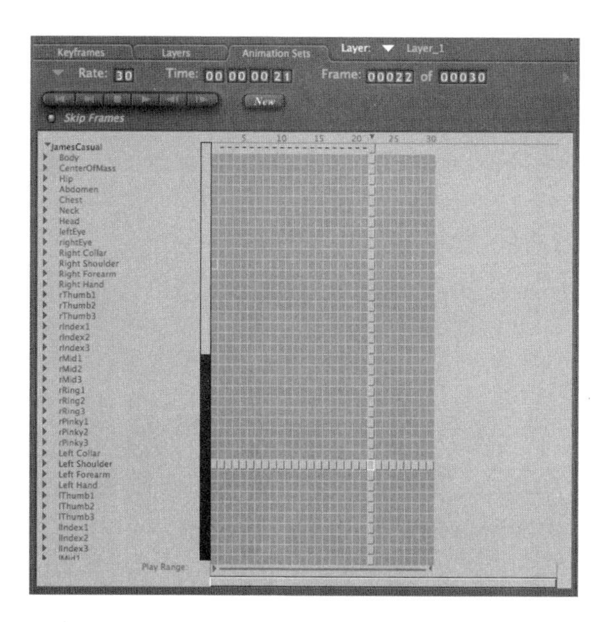

FIGURE 14.15 The Animation Sets panel allows you to control animation properties through Python scripts.

General Animation Tips

Before moving on to some formal animation tutorials, here are a few extra tips you should consider as you design your animations.

- Cut, Copy, and Paste commands may be used throughout the suite of panels. This may be facilitated by using either the Poser menu or keyboard shortcuts: Command/Ctrl+X, Command/Ctrl+C, and Command/Ctrl+V.
- You can highlight and then drag blocks of frames and keyframes. In the Graph panel, you can highlight a selection of keyframes and drag left or right to reposition them within the timeline.
- If the Ctrl/Command key is held down, you can uniformly raise or lower all of that parameter's keyframe values. An example where this is useful is when you have an animation of a figure that was made for flat shoes, but your selected figure is to wear high heels. Simply select the foot bend from the Graph panel's drop-down menu, and highlight all of the frame. Now, Ctrl-drag all the values up or down by the required amount.

- When creating animations, it's best to rough out the major movements first. Start with the hip, torso, and chest, then work down each leg, and follow this with the arms. Finally, fine-tune with animations to the hands, head, and expressions.
- Consider using images as a background for reference. This method is called Rotoscoping and is still used by the major animation film companies. The Rotoscoper Python script by PhilC (www.philc.net) provides an aid in this method.

Animation Timing

As discussed earlier in the chapter, timing is also referred to as the frame rate. You should always consider where or how your animation is going to be used because media types vary. When dealing with frame rates (fps), there are modification features you should be aware of.

The frame rate may be set in any of the Animation panel tabs. If you wanted to complete a 1-minute animation based on a frame rate of 30fps, be prepared to create a total of 1,800 frames of animation. If each frame takes five minutes to render, this will take 150 hours to complete. Some forward planning regarding render optimization may be prudent.

Animations may be retimed using the Animation > Retime Animation menu command. The Retime Animation dialog box is shown in Figure 14.16.

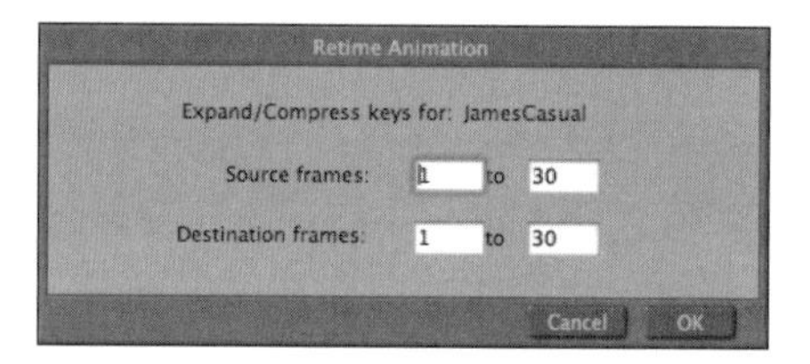

FIGURE 14.16 The Retime Animation dialog box.

On the other hand, when you resample keyframes, you increase or decrease the number of keyframes in the animation. To resample keyframes, use the Animation > Resample > Key Frames menu command. The Resample Keys dialog box shown in Figure 14.17 appears. This enables you to increase or decrease the number of keyframes in the animation. I strongly suggest that you first save your scene prior to resampling. Poser 7 does have a much improved Undo/Redo system, but there is nothing like having a backup copy just in case!

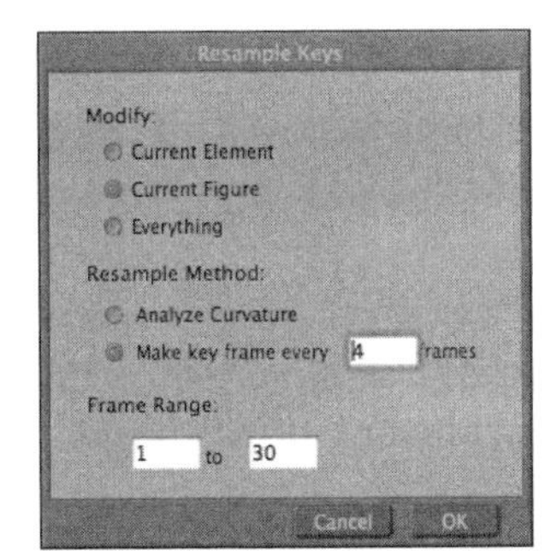

FIGURE 14.17 The Resample Keys dialog box.

LOOP INTERPOLATION

Many animations are cyclic in nature, for example, walking, running, waving an arm. Enabling Loop Interpolation from the Animation menu can help smooth out the jump from the final to the start frame and provide a continuously smooth animation.

QUATERNION INTERPOLATION

This option was deliberately left until last because it should only be used as a last resort. If your animation remains jerky even after every effort has been made to smooth it out, enable Quaternion Interpolation from the Animation menu. It will apply an algorithm to the animation in an attempt to rectify the situation.

TUTORIAL 14.3 THE ALIEN WITHIN—CREATING A CREEPY ANIMATION

Now that you have all this information, let's put it into practice. In this tutorial, you'll combine a couple of things you have worked with over the course of the book—namely, posing, using magnets, and animating those magnets to create a sci-fi type of scene. Call this a gentle homage to the *Alien* movie franchise and to the scarab beetle scene in *The Mummy* without all the blood and gore.

1. Create a new file and add Ryan_Casual to the scene.
2. Turn off Inverse Kinematics for the left and right legs and zero the figures.
3. Select Ryan's right forearm and add a magnet (Object > Create Magnet). Refer to Figure 14.18 and as you set the figure's pose.

- Right Collar
- Up-Down = 7°

- Right Shoulder
  - Twist = 29°
  - Up-Down = 72°
- Right Forearm
  - Side-Side = 6°
- Right Hand
  - Side-Side = 1°
  - Bend = 4°
  - Grasp = 13
  - Spread = –5

FIGURE 14.18 Use this image to set Ryan's pose.

4. For the last two elements (Grasp and Spread), expand the Hand Controls set to access them. After you have Ryan's arm positioned, use Figure > Symmetry > Right Arm to Left Arm menu option so the left arm's pose is the same as the right. And this is just to get into the basic position. You'll be modifying this in a few moments.
5. Next, you need to scale the Magnet, the Mag Base, and the Mag Zone values. Here are the parameters for each:

- Mag Base
  - Scale = 4%
  - zRotate = –6°
  - xTran = 1.921
- Mag Zone
- Scale = 7%
  - xScale = 22%
  - yScale = 2%
  - zScale = 27%
  - xTran = –1.929
  - yTran = 5.077
  - zTran = –0.169
- Magnet
  - yTran = 1.557

In the end, Figure 14.19 shows how the magnet should look on Ryan's arm.

6. Let's start the animation process. In the Animation Drawer, set the end frame to 75 (as shown in Figure 14.20). This will make a 2.5-second animation at 30fps.
7. With Ryan's forearm selected, make sure you're on the first frame (click the First Frame button in the VCR controls in the upper left of the Keyframes panel) in preparation to pose the arm and set up the camera.
8. Make the following position changes to the Right Shoulder and the Right Forearm values:

- Right Shoulder
  - Twist = 47°
  - Front-Back = 27°
  - Side-Side = 65°

- Right Forearm
  - Twist = 32°
  - Front-Back = 6°
  - Side-Side = 80°

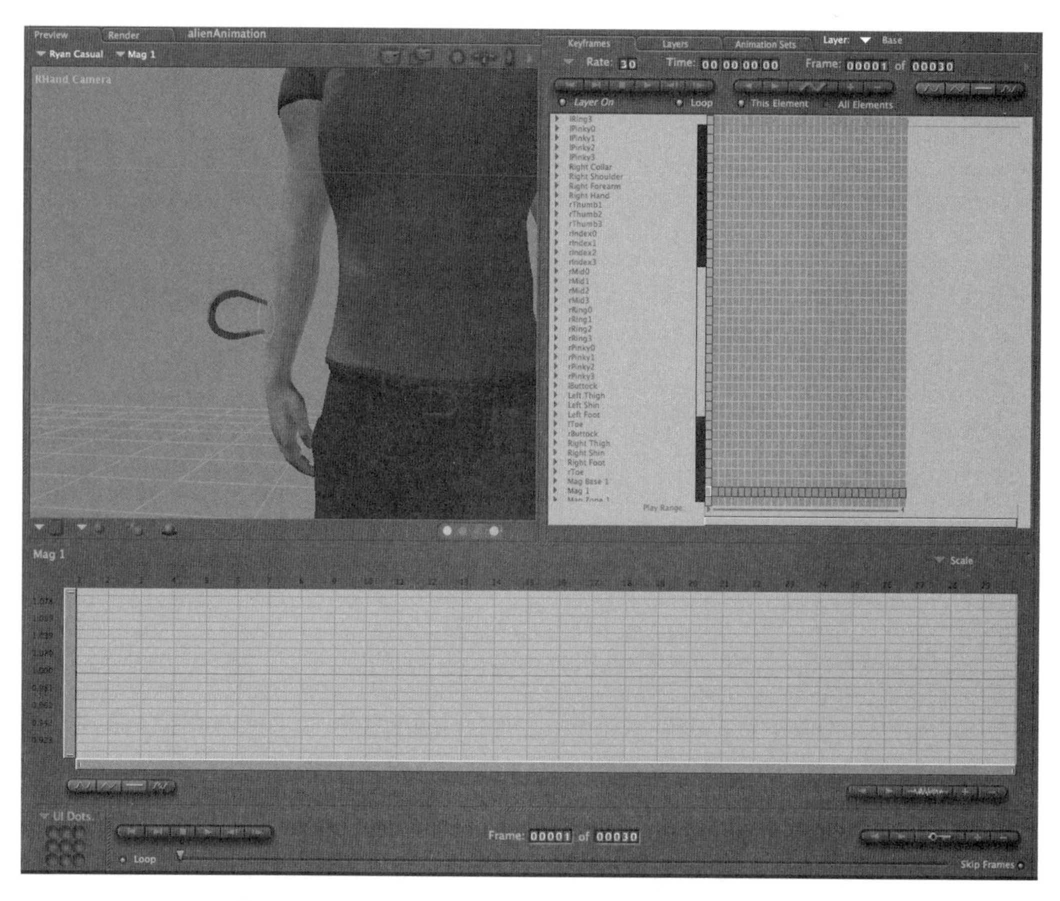

FIGURE 14.19 The magnet has been scaled for Ryan's arm and the upcoming animation.

FIGURE 14.20 The end frame has been changed to 75 in the Animation Drawer.

- Right Hand
  - Bend = –19°
  - Grasp = 0
  - ThumbBend = 20
  - IndexBend = –7
  - MiddleBend = –11
  - RingBend = –11
  - PinkyBend = –17

9. Now set up the Main Camera with the following settings. Figure 14.21 shows the way your scene should look at this point.
   - Focal = 70mm
   - DollyZ = –4.678
   - DollyY = 3.992
   - DollyX = 0.353
   - zOrbit = 8°
   - xOrbit = 12°

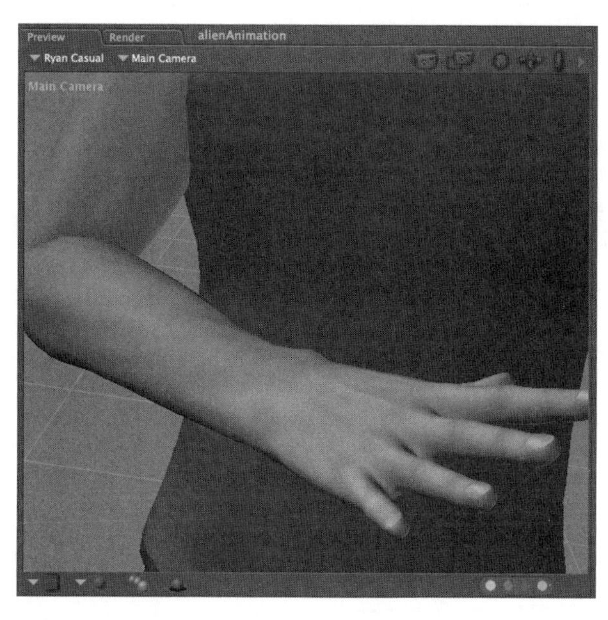

FIGURE 14.21 This is how the scene should appear after you set the various parameters.

10. You're finally at the point where you can begin the animation. Remember, this is an homage to *The Mummy* and, if modified, the *Alien* franchise. Right now, it's the scarab beetle that you're going to deal with. Type the number 10 into the left frame field so the counter reads Frame 10 of 75. Select the forearm and set a new keyframe. Do this by clicking the plus (+) button immediately to the right of the Edit Keyframes button (the one with the key icon) in the Animation Drawer. If you now look at the Keyframes panel, you will see that a keyframe has been added to your scene (see Figure 14.22). Repeat this for the Magnet, the MagZone, Main Camera, and for the Right Hand options.

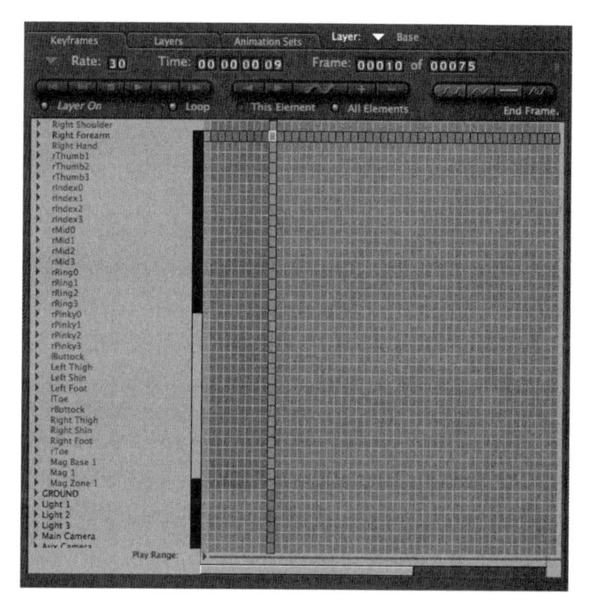

FIGURE 14.22 A keyframe added to frame 10 of the animation.

Nothing is happening yet; you have merely made it where the motion won't start at the beginning of the animation. You are, for all intents and purposes, creating some pad to give the viewer a little time to register what they are looking at.

12. Go to frame 25. This is where the first part of the movement will occur. Select the MagZone and change the yScale to 7%. A bulge will appear as the beetle or alien begins to push out. Figure 14.23 shows what this should look like.

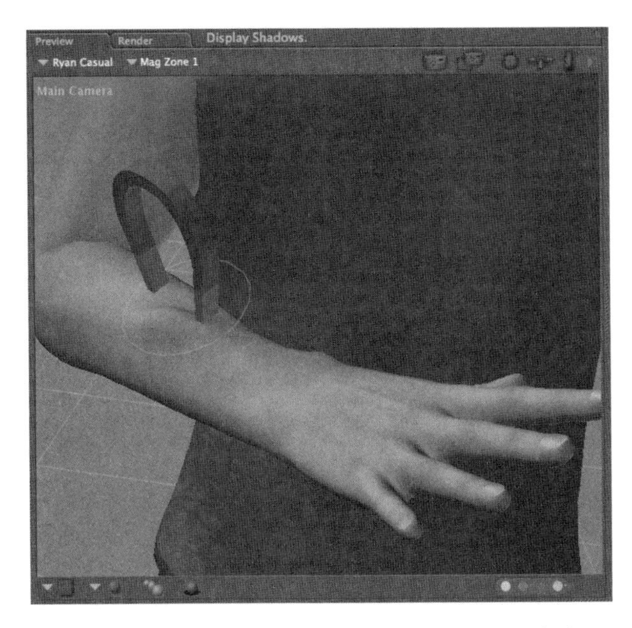

FIGURE 14.23 The alien wants to come out and play.

13. Go to frame 60. Change the Mag Zone's xTran to –1.688 and the Magnet's xTran to 2.159. The bulge in the arm will move to the bend of the arm.
14. At frame 70, change the Mag Zone's yScale back to 0 so the creature (whatever it is) descends into his arm again. At this point, as you play the animation, you'll see the creature bulge out, move across the arm, and then bury itself again.

If you have the forearm selected during playback, you'll see the magnet throughout the playback. If you want to see the animation without the magnet, select anything other than the forearm.

Tutorial 4.4 The Rest of the Story—Animating Ryan's Reaction

Okay. The magnet has been animated, but you need to do more if this scene is going to be at least a bit more realistic. At this stage, the only thing moving is the creature. But why isn't the arm and the hand reacting to what we definitely know would be a painful experience? So, let's finish the animation.

1. Let's work on the hand first. Select it, go to frame 6, and set a keyframe. Yes. This part of the animation will actually start before the creature pushes out. You need to consider a truism: For every action, there is an equal and opposite reaction. Well, the reactions would start before the creature is even seen. That's why the hand will begin moving before the creature does.
2. At frame 10, select the Main Camera and create a keyframe.
3. Go to frame 11 and make the following changes:

   - Right Hand
     - Twist = 12°
     - Bend = –33°

4. At frame 14, change the Twist setting for the Right Forearm to 31, the Right Hand's Grasp setting to 70, and Bend to –42°.
5. At frame 22, change the Right Hand's Twist to –12°.
6. Go to frame 29 and select the Right Forearm. Change the Twist setting to 43°.
7. At frame 38, set the following parameters for the Right Hand values:

   - Twist = 7°
   - Grasp = 10
   - Spread = –2
   - ThumbBend = 15

8. That will be enough to cover the time when the camera moves in to focus on the nasty beastie traveling up the poor guy's arm. So go to frame 41, the spot where the camera will lock into place. You, of course, already set the starting point, so all that needs to happen now is to set ending parameters.
9. With the Main Camera selected, make the following changes:

   - DollyZ = –5.452
   - DollyY = 3.992
   - DollyZ = 0.306
   - zOrbit = 8°
   - xOrbit = –10°
   - yOrbit = –24°

You will notice that many of the changes made at the various keyframes were subtle. Many times, the smallest of changes reap the greatest sense of realism. In the Chapter 14\animationFiles folder on the DVD, there is a file titled alienAnimation.pz3. You can use this to study the keyframing for this project—basically comparing your animation with the one I created. In addition, there is a MOV file in the same folder titled alienAnimation.mov so you can see how the animation looks at this point. Some fine-tuning is needed, but you have the base settings at this point.

A Short Re-Pose

You need to save the file you just created because it's going to be used in Chapter 16. That's where you will explore rendering and a new feature that can affect the lighting in your scenes.

At this stage, though, you should have a good understanding of animation and the need to consider small details as you are building them. While you explored keyframing in this chapter—a very tedious and time-consuming procedure—it's vital to understand this process for any animation you create. Poser allows for the use of high-end and high-quality BVH files (in this case, BioVision Hierarchy). You'll look at those and the motion controls that are built into Poser. That's all coming up in the next chapter.

15 More Animation Techniques

In This Chapter:

- Using the Walk Designer
- Tutorial 15.1: Creating a Walk-in-Place Walk Cycle
- Tutorial 15.2: Creating and Following a Walk Path
- Working in the Talk Designer
- Tutorial 15.3: Using the Talk Designer
- Biovision Hierarchy (BVH) Files
- Tutorial 15.4: Adding a BVH File to Your Figure

"Methinks that the moment my legs begin to move, my thoughts begin to flow."

—Henry David Thoreau

Poser provides a number of animation aids that help you achieve results quickly and easily. Among these aids are the Walk Designer and Talk Designer. These two features make it very easy to animate the characters in your movie projects. In addition, Poser has been able to accept BVH (Biovision Hierarchy) motion files for some time now, and with those BVH files, you can achieve amazingly realistic movements. They are, after all, what many of the "big boys" use.

In this chapter, you'll learn how to use the Walk Designer to create walk cycles that walk in place or that follow a path. You'll also learn how easy it is to use the Talk Designer to make your characters speak a few words. And you will also discover how to import BVH files for more complex animations.

Using the Walk Designer

The Walk Designer, shown in Figure 15.1, provides a quick and easy solution to making any two-legged character walk or run in a variety of ways. You can create a walk cycle that stays in place, or you can create a walk cycle that follows a path.

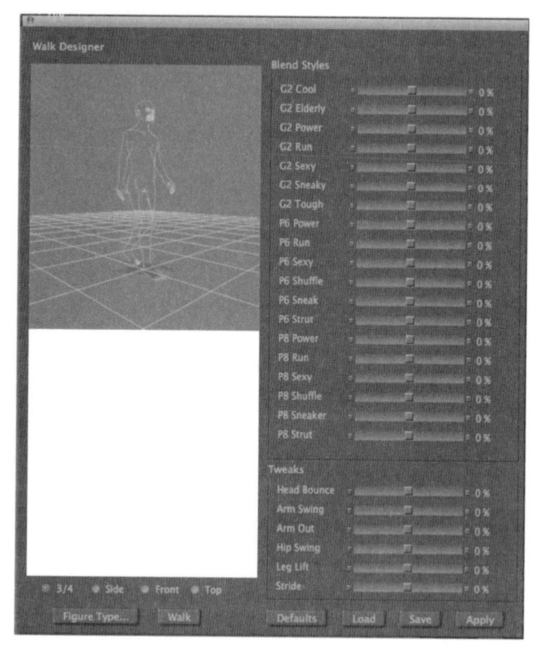

FIGURE 15.1 The Walk Designer workspace.

If you do not see all of the controls shown in Figure 15.1, click on the lower-right corner and drag outward to view the rest of them.

Here's a quick overview of the Walk Designer controls:

- **3/4, Side, Front, and Top view options:** By default, the preview area displays an outline of a figure in 3/4 view. Other options allow you to view the walk from the Side, Front, or Top.
- **Figure Type:** Click this button to preview your walk cycle with a different figure.
- **Walk:** Click this button to animate the walk cycle in the preview area.

- **Defaults:** Click this button to return the Blend Styles and Tweaks options to their zero values.
- **Load:** Click this button to load a walk cycle that you have previously saved to your hard drive.
- **Save:** Click this button to save a walk cycle to your hard drive.
- **Apply:** Click this button to apply the walk cycle to the figure that you have currently selected in your scene.

Blend Styles

The Walk Designer features a set of blend styles specifically designed for the G2 figures, as well as the P6 and P8 models. Each, as you can see, is designated with the appropriate figure type. The available Blend Styles, shown in Figure 15.2, are designed to work with both new and old Poser figures.

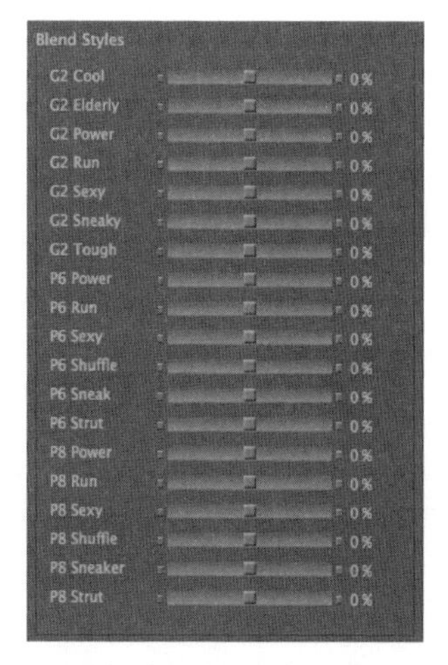

FIGURE 15.2 Blend styles add variations to walks for G2 and non-G2 figures.

As I would expect you have figured out, if you are using the G2 figures, use the blend styles that have the G2 designations. If you use other figures, such as the P6 or P8 models, you would use non-G2 blend styles. If you are used to the Walk Designer from previous versions of Poser, you'll notice there are no more P4 designations. The program is moving on.

Tweaks

The Tweaks settings are shown in Figure 15.3. These settings add more variety to the way the head, arms, hips, and legs move during your walk cycle. Head Bounce bobs the head up and down. Arm Swing exaggerates the swing of the arms during the walk. Arm Out raises the arms out toward the side. Hip Swing exaggerates the side-to-side movement of the hips. Leg Lift bends the legs more at the knees during the walk. Stride increases the length of the stride with each step.

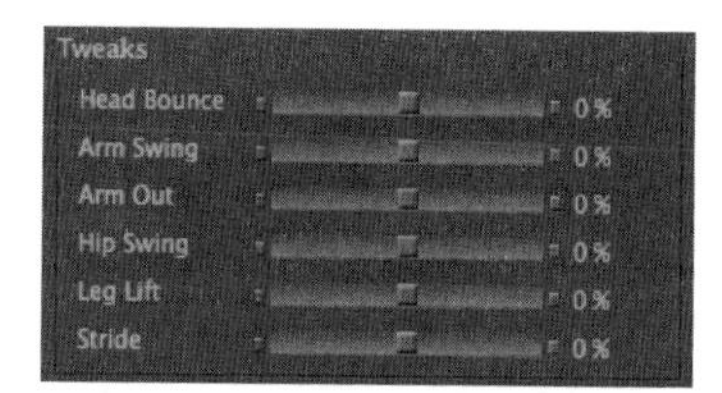

FIGURE 15.3 A close-up look at the Tweaks section of the Walk Designer window.

When using tweaks, a little goes a long way toward making your walks appear more realistic and natural. For example, start with small settings, such as 5% to 10%, and preview the change by clicking the Walk button.

Tutorial 15.1 Creating a Walk-in-Place Walk Cycle

Poser allows you to use the Walk Designer in one of two ways. You can either create a walk cycle in which the character walks in place, or you can create a walk cycle in which the figure follows a path of movement.

Walk-in-place walk cycles are excellent for use in game development where animated sprites are used to make the figure move through the game. Animated sprites are typically rendered in several directions; that is, there are walk-in-place versions of the figure walking toward the left, right, front, back, and in the various diagonal directions. Walk-in-place animations are also good to use when you want to keep your figure centered in the scene and have the scenery scrolling behind the character.

You'll create a walk cycle for Ryan Casual. So load the character, turn off Inverse Kinematics for the left and right legs, and then open the Walk Designer window.

1. Click the Walk button located immediately below the preview area. You will see the figure begin its default walk cycle. As you make changes, you will see the walk update.

2. Adjust the P8 Blend Styles as follows. You can always develop your own walk cycle after this.
   - P8 Power = 28%
   - P8 Sexy = –6%
   - P8 Shuffle = 9%
3. Add the following tweaks to hone the walk a bit further:
   - Head Bounce = 5%
   - Leg Lift = 3%
   - Stride = 17%

Figure 15.4 shows the settings used for this tutorial.

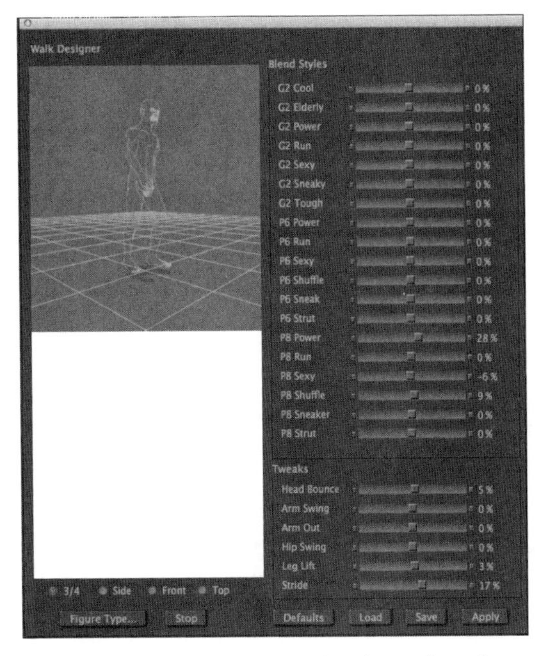

FIGURE 15.4 The settings for the walk cycle.

4. Now that you have set the walk cycle, click Stop.
5. If you like the walk you created, you can save the settings for later use by clicking the Save button. Save the file to the location you want. The saved file will have a PWK extension. You then return to the Walk Designer.

6. To apply the walk, click the Apply button, after which you'll see the Apply Walk dialog box open (shown in Figure 15.5).

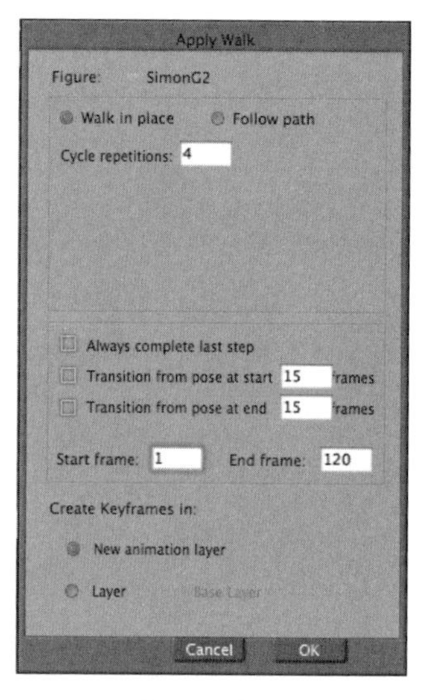

FIGURE 15.5 The Apply Walk dialog box.

7. All figures in your scene are listed in the Figure drop-down list at the top of the Apply Walk dialog box. Since there is only one figure, there's not much for you to do here but enjoy reading Ryan Casual's name. But if you had multiple models, you could choose which one you wanted this walk cycle applied to.
8. Select the Walk in Place option. Enter the number of times you want the walk cycle to repeat in the Cycle Repetitions field. The default value is 4 repetitions, so for this tutorial, you can keep it at that. What this means is, the cycle will repeat four times in the animation before either stopping or looping, depending on what you have set.
9. Verify the Start Frame and End Frame values to apply your walk cycle. By default, Poser creates a 120-frame animation (four repetitions at 30 frames per second) and starts the walk on the first frame. For this example, leave the settings at their defaults.
10. You can choose to put the keyframes of the walk cycle in a new animation layer or in the base layer. For this example, leave the setting at the default of New Animation Layer.

11. Click OK. Poser applies the walk cycle to the selected figure, which should now be posed in the first frame of the walk cycle. You can close the Walk Designer window at this point. Figure 15.6 shows an example of the walk applied to a figure.

FIGURE 15.6 The walk cycle applied to Ryan.

TUTORIAL 15.2 CREATING AND FOLLOWING A WALK PATH

What you created in the last tutorial is perfect for use in a Flash animation or a video composite. By walking in place, you would animate background and/or foreground elements in order to make it look as if the character is walking. This is what is done in video games—the character walks in place, but the images surrounding the character all move. However, this doesn't work in all animation projects you might have. Sometimes the character has to interact with objects in the scene. For that, you would need to create a walk path and have Alyson, for instance, follow it in order to navigate around the objects. This will often look more natural because shadows will be cast more realistically.

To make your characters walk through a scene, start by creating a walk path. You will then get Alyson Casual to follow that path. Start with a new scene, adding Alyson Casual to it. Turn off Inverse Kinematics, and then get started.

1. Assign the Kneeling pose you will find in the Chapter15\Original folder on the DVD. Move this folder and pose into the Poser\Poser 8\Alyson folder.
2. Choose Figure > Create Walk Path. Switch to the Top view and, upon choosing Create Walk Path, you will see a line representing the path along which Alyson will walk. There are a number of control points that, when clicked on, can modify the path's location. So you will want to take a few moments to modify the path's direction to best fit your vision for this animation. Figure 15.7 shows the created path.

FIGURE 15.7 The walk path has been created for Alyson.

You can also use the Parameters panel to adjust the rotation, scaling, or translation of the path if desired.

3. Open Walk Designer. While I went with the default settings, you should take a moment to set up a walk cycle that fits your personal tastes. Once you're ready, click Apply.
4. Select the Follow Path option. A menu will then prompt you to choose the path that you want to attach. There is currently only one path (Path 1) in the scene, which is selected by default.
5. You can optionally align the head to make it appear as though your figure is paying close attention to where she is going. The options are One Step Ahead, which makes the figure look closely toward the path; End of Path, which keeps the character's head focused on the final destination; or Next Sharp Turn, which focuses your figure's attention on the next turn he has to take. For this example, choose One Step Ahead.
6. The next set of options determines how the walk cycle starts and ends and how many frames it will require. If you check Always Complete Last Step, Poser adds enough frames so that the foot doesn't end up in mid-air at the end of the animation.
7. Choose Transition From Pose at Start and change the number of frames from the default 15 to 5. What this is going to do is allow Alyson's kneeling pose to remain and she will, over the course of five frames, stand and begin her walk. As you can tell, the number of frames you type in will determine how long it takes to go from your starting pose to the actual walk cycle. If you kept it at the default 15 frames with a 30fps file, it would take a half second to transition.
8. Poser determines the number of frames to create based on the frame rate of your animation and the length of the path. In Figure 15.8, you see that Poser has calculated that the animation will take 198 frames for Alyson to reach the end of the path. If you increase or decrease the number of frames, it will affect the length of the steps he takes, and it may not look as natural.
9. Finally, you can choose to create the walk in a new animation layer or in any other layer that exists in your animation. For this example, create the walk in a new animation layer. This makes it easier to reposition or delete the layer should you not like the results.
10. Switch back to the Main Camera view. Zoom out so you can see the entire walk path as shown in Figure 15.9.
11. Click OK to create the walk on the specified path. Then preview the motion in the Pose Room and make adjustments as necessary in the Animation panel (see Figure 15.10).

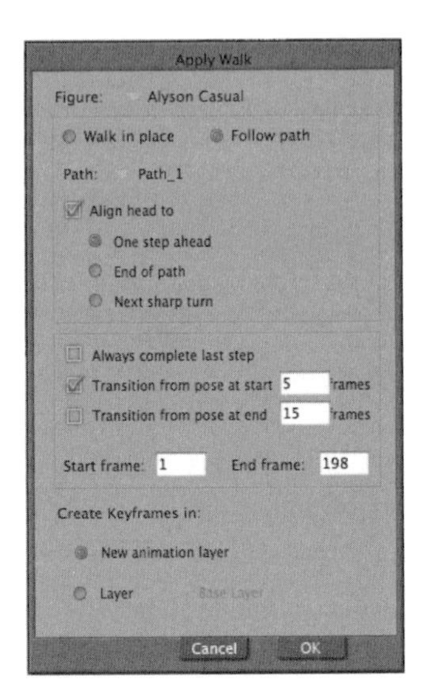

FIGURE 15.8 The Start frame and End frame fields tell you how many frames make up your animation.

FIGURE 15.9 Zooming out, you will be able to see the entire walk.

FIGURE 15.10 Alyson, although looking a bit perturbed, enjoys a walk in the digital sun.

You can save the pose and the associated walk path to the Library. Open the Poser Library of your choice, and click the Add to Library button. Poser will first present a dialog box that allows you to choose the walk path along with other elements in your scene. After you select the items, Poser asks if you want to include morph channels or body transformations with the pose. Then Poser asks if you want to save the pose as a single-frame animation or multiframe animation. Choose the latter option and enter the range of frames you want to save.

Working in the Talk Designer

One of the most exciting features is the Talk Designer, which will have your characters speaking in no time! The Talk Designer allows you to import a sound and automatically adds keyframes that move the character's mouth along with the spoken words. You can optionally type in the text of the audio file to assist Poser in determining how the words are formed.

The Talk Designer works in conjunction with an installed Viseme map. This Viseme map, which is saved in the XML format, tells Poser which morph parameters it should use when moving the mouth, face, and eyes on your figure while it speaks. In the case of Ryan Casual, the Viseme map works with the following facial morphs to create his speech. Figure 15.11 shows a list of the figures that have Viseme maps available.

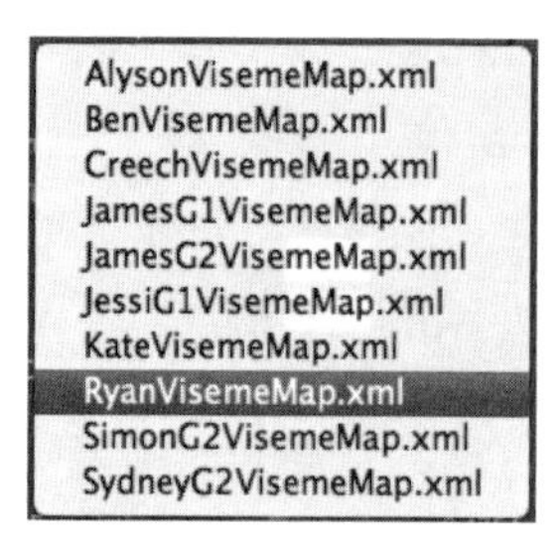

FIGURE 15.11 A list of models that have Viseme files associated with them.

In the following facial morph descriptions, uppercase letters are the hard pronunciation, and lowercase letters are the soft pronunciation of these letters.

- **MouthTH:** This facial morph is used when speaking the letters s, S, z, Z, j, J, d, G, t, k, n, and N.
- **MouthF:** This morph is used when speaking the letters F and v.
- **TongueL:** This morph is used for speaking the letters L, T, and D.
- **MouthM:** This morph is used for speaking the letters m, p, and b.
- **MouthW:** This morph is used for speaking the letters W, r, R, and u.
- **MouthE:** This morph is used for speaking the letters e, i, E, and y.
- **MouthA:** This morph is used for speaking the letters a, I, A, and H.
- **MouthCH:** This morph is used for speaking the letters c and C.
- **MouthU:** This morph is used for speaking the letters w, o, O, and U.

Go to Window > Talk Designer, and then take a moment to scan through this section explaining the different controls shown in Figure 15.12.

- **Input Files:** Click the Sound File button to load an audio file. Click the plus sign next to the Supplemental Text field to expand a box and enter the text that corresponds to the audio file, or click the button to open a ready-made text file.

If needed, you can also click the Viseme Map File button to open a custom-made Viseme map file.

- **Configuration:** This section defines the character that will be used for the speech, the number of frames required for the animation, and which layer the speech animation should appear in. You can also adjust the amount of enunciation in the animation, with higher settings producing more animated results.
- **Head Motions:** This section allows you to define the speed at which the eyes blink (in blinks per minute). The default of 12.5 bpm produces a blink every 4 to 5 seconds. You can also check or uncheck the options to create eye and head motion during speech.

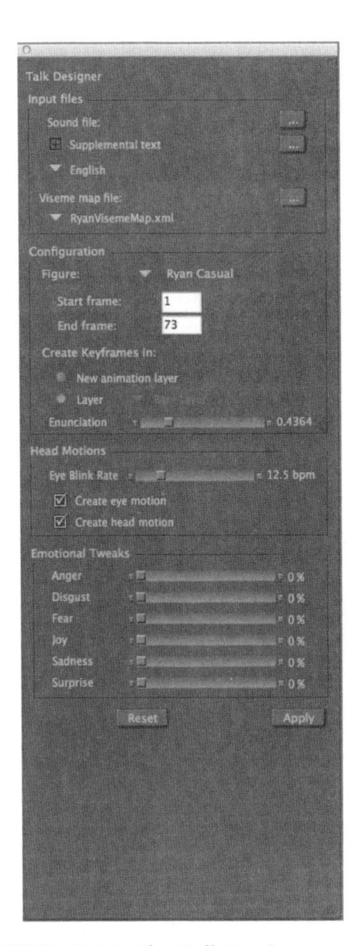

FIGURE 15.12 The Talk Designer panel.

- **Emotional Tweaks:** Sliders allow you to add emotion to the speech. Various levels or combinations of anger, disgust, fear, joy, sadness, or surprise are added to the speech. Lower settings produce milder emotion, and higher values produce very animated and over-exaggerated results that are great for 'toon work.

TUTORIAL 15.3 USING THE TALK DESIGNER

Let's turn Ryan into a Milli Vanilli wannabe and make him do some lip synching. When it comes to audio files, you can either use AIF or WAV files. No other audio file format is readable. Included on the DVD are two audio files: EasyAs123.wav and EasyToMakeUsTalk.wav. They are located in the Chapter15\audioFiles folder.

1. Place Ryan into a new scene and switch to the Face Camera.
2. Choose Window > Talk Designer. The Talk Designer panel appears.
3. Click the button to the right of the Sound File category. Load one of the two audio files mentioned in the introduction to this tutorial.
4. Click the plus sign near the Supplemental Text area to expand the text field. Enter the text that applies to the audio file that you selected. EasyAs123.wav is a man's voice saying, "It's as easy as one, two, three." EasyToMakeUsTalk.wav is a man's voice saying, "It's easy to make us talk." A sample entry is shown in Figure 15.13.

There are times when you will want to type the text phonetically rather than in the correct way. A word like "mail" might be better read using the phonetic "mayl" so the program doesn't try to add more phonemes into the mouth movement than is needed.

FIGURE 15.13 Enter the text that corresponds to the sound file you have selected.

5. After adding this text, select the Viseme map file that corresponds to the model you're using. Click the down arrow immediately under Viseme Map File and choose RyanVisemeMap.xml. The Viseme map file gives Poser the information needed to shape the model's mouth correctly to the different phonemes in your sound file. The Viseme maps are linked directly to that model's morph target setup.
6. In the Configuration section, verify that the correct figure is selected. The Start Frame and End Frame values are automatically determined by the length of the audio file and normally start at 1. If you change the start frame, make sure that you allow for the same number of frames at the end. In other words, if you instead want the voice to start at frame 250, you will need to set the end frame at 307 to accommodate the 58 frames for the talk animation.

   Another thing to be aware of is that the audio file will often be longer than the frames in your animation. Go to the Animation panel and change the animation length to match the length of the audio.
7. As has been mentioned already, you should choose to create this as a new animation layer because it is much easier to move an animation layer to a new location at some later date—if you have to, that is.
8. By default, the Enunciation value is set to 0.56, which animates the facial morphs at a natural rate. If you need more enunciation (such as when someone is yelling or surprised), increase the values accordingly. A little goes a long way, so don't overdo it! The settings in the Configuration section should now look as shown in Figure 15.14.
9. Leave the Head Motions section at their default settings. Let's move on to the Emotional Tweaks, though. Add a little bit of Joy and a little bit of Surprise to the mix. Set each of these at 5% by dragging the slider to a new value.

You cannot double-click on a numeric value in the Talk Designer to access a numeric field. You have to use the sliders to change the values.

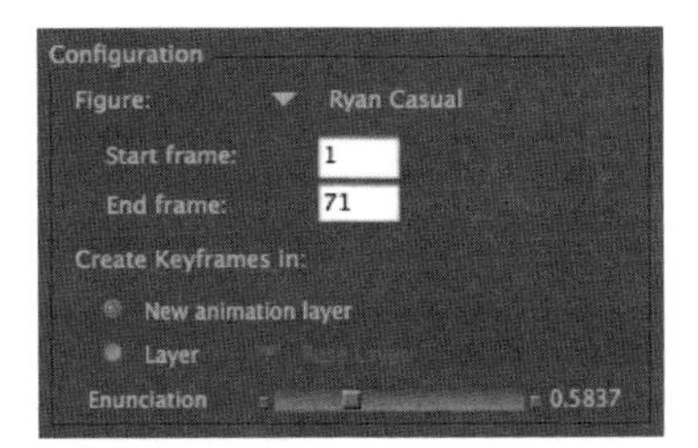

FIGURE 15.14 The Configuration settings.

10. Click Apply. After a brief wait, you should see the scene update in the preview area. When you play the scene, you should hear the audio file as well. To see the animation, you may have to choose the Display > Tracking > Full Tracking menu command if your system resources allow.

If you find that you need to tweak the animation later on, click to select the head. Then open the Graph (Window > Graph), and select the morph that you want to adjust. It is extra work to do the tweaks, but it can improve the results dramatically. And actually, due to this fact, I would advise spending the time to do this fine-tuning. While the lip synching is good, it can definitely be made better.

Biovision Hierarchy (BVH) Files

Let's get back to walking. In Chapter 14, you used keyframes to make your animations. In this section, you will use BVH motion files. These files are normally built from motion capture technology. If you have spent any time at all watching movies or the behind-the-scenes footage on DVDs, you have heard of and seen how motion capture (mocap) files are created. Poser can take advantage of these mocap files, and here's how.

There are a few websites that provide free BVH files, some of which are already set up for Poser. There are also a number that charge nominal to rather pricey fees for the files. Here are a few of them:

- *http://freemotionfiles.blogspot.com/2009/05/poser-bvh-mocap-files.html*
- *http://sites.google.com/a/cgspeed.com/cgspeed/motion-capture/cmu-bvh-conversion*
- *www.mocapdata.com*
- *www.yaodownload.com/Animation-category_Downloads_100_1.html*

A BVH file is like an OBJ file in that it is a text document that houses information that is read by the bones assigned to the mesh and tells them how to move over the course of time. The basic parts of the BVH are the joint descriptions themselves. This part is fairly easy to decipher. Then, however, comes the actual motion information—a mind-boggling series of numbers that goes on forever and ever and ever. Or, at least, it seems that way.

TUTORIAL 15.4 ADDING A BVH FILE TO YOUR FIGURE

In this tutorial, you'll use Ryan Casual again. Place him into a new scene, turn Inverse Kinematics off, and then zero the figure (all the usual stuff you have done in virtually every chapter in this book).

1. With the Ryan Casual figure selected, go to File > Import > BVH Motion. You will need to navigate to the BVH file you downloaded.
2. Upon selecting the file, the BVH Export/Import Options dialog will open (see Figure 15.15). Here, you have a couple of choices to make. Most of the time (probably 99% of time), your choices will be the same: select Scale Automatically so the BVH data will be sized to fit the Poser character, and choose Align Along the Z Axis. This is how most BVH files are set up, and unless told otherwise, these are what you should use.

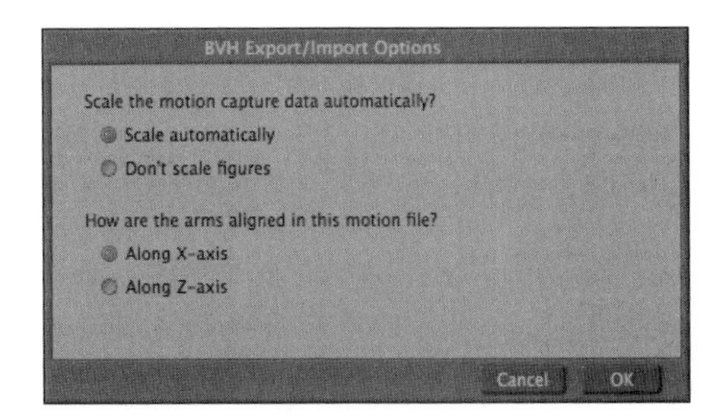

FIGURE 15.15 The BVH Export/Import Options dialog box.

3. After making your choices, you might be faced with some screens saying that some figure elements do not match with the Poser model parts. If it is a BVH file that has been modified for Poser, then just click OK on each of these screens. If it is a file that has not been converted, then you may experience problems.

PhilC makes a plug-in called BVH Helper that can help make BVH files work with Poser. You can find out more about it at www.philc.net/BVH_helper.php.

4. After you click OK, the file will begin loading. This could take a few moments, depending upon the length of the animation.

If you have had to make a number of changes to make the BVH files work, you might want to take a moment to save them so the next time you load them they work properly. To do so, merely go to File > Export > BVH Motions. As with the Import command, you will be greeted with the BVH Export/Import Options dialog. Set up the motion as necessary, and save it to whatever folder you would like.

A Short Re-Pose

You've just had a look at some of the powerful yet often overlooked animation controls in Poser. The Walk Designer and Talk Designer can help you set up basic or advanced motions, as well as lip synching, quickly and with a minimum of fuss. And with the ability to import high-end BVH files, your animations can be virtually limitless. Although there will always be some tweaking of the files needed, there are programs that can help you correct those areas where motion information doesn't match up with the Poser joint structure.

In the next chapter, you will need the file you created in Chapter 14. I'll discuss the process of rendering your files, as well as another new feature that will make your renders look amazing.

16 Rendering Options and Techniques

In This Chapter:

- Building Faster Scenes
- Rendering Environments
- Using the FireFly Renderer
- Tutorial 16.1: Render Settings and Aspect Ratios
- Indirect Lighting
- Tutorial 16.2: Setting Up and Rendering with Indirect Lighting
- Tutorial 16.3: Using the IDL Python Script
- The Sketch Designer
- Tutorial 16.4: Creating a Sketch Render

"Computers in the future may weigh no more than 1.5 tons."

—Popular Mechanics, forecasting the relentless march of science, 1949

Boy were they wrong! So was Thomas Watson, the chairman of IBM, who said, "[I] think there is a world market for five computers." In addition, back in 1977, Ken Olson, the president, chairman, and founder of Digital Equipment Corporation, said, "There is no reason anyone would want a computer in their home." After working your way through this book, you have to be amazed at the humble beginnings of computer technology. And here you come to the end of the journey in what is most definitely only the beginning of the artistic road you are travelling. In this final chapter, I'll discuss how to preserve and share the work you have created. It starts by rendering and ends with re-creation of the pixels on paper.

Throughout this book, you have explored and discovered how powerful Poser is and how much can be done with the program. All of this is far beyond what Ken Olson and Thomas Watson could have imagined, especially on a piece of equipment that can fit comfortably on a desk or on your lap. But there's one more area of the program to explore—rendering. You can work for hours on a pose or a scene and, if you have a poor render, you basically still have nothing to show for your efforts. In this chapter, you'll learn about the render controls so you can bring that scene you created to life.

Building Faster Scenes

Poser comes with two methods with which to render for final output—FireFly and Sketch. You will notice that Poser 4 rendering has been removed. Rendering in Poser 8 is much faster than in previous versions as well. But even so, high-quality renders can take a little time. But there are ways around this ongoing dilemma faced by every 3D artist, no matter what program they are using. The following considerations can help reduce rendering time considerably.

- **Polygon counts:** Use low poly-count models wherever possible. In particular, you can use low-polygon models for objects that are farther away from your camera. Many popular Poser figures come in low- and high-resolution versions.
- **Lighting considerations:** Lighting affects rendering speeds. Scenes with fewer lights render much more quickly than scenes with many lights. Rather than use several lights in a scene, consider using a single IBL light or point light, with reduced intensity, to illuminate your entire scene with a minimum amount of ambient light. Then, enhance the lighting with additional spotlights where needed for drama or composition.
- **Shadow calculations:** Lights that cast shadows take longer to render than those that don't. You can speed up renders by turning off shadows on lights that are not critical (usually only one or two lights need shadows). Also, be aware that you will use more resources when you use depth map shadows instead of ray-traced shadows. Large shadow maps eat up resources and slow down renders. If your scene does use shadow maps, you can choose to reuse them after you place your objects where you want them. You speed up the final render time when you reuse shadow maps because you don't have to recalculate them.
- **Texture sizes:** Image maps can use significant amounts of resources. Large image maps are a waste of computing power if you aren't doing close-ups. For objects that are close to the camera, such as full facial portraits, use maps that are at least equal to the size of your final render but no more than twice the size. You can use lower-resolution texture maps for objects that are farther away from the camera.

- **Using complex materials:** Complex materials can also significantly increase your render times. Lights interact with materials; so if you are using complex materials that are transparent, are reflective, scatter light, or refract light, your renders will take longer. Use less complex materials on objects that are farther away from your camera to help keep your render times as short as possible.

Rendering Environments

The Preview renderer allows you to render your Preview window using the current display mode settings and renders it to the size that you specify in the Render Dimensions dialog box (Render > Render Dimensions), up to 4096 by 4096. The Preview renderer is an excellent source for flat-shaded illustrations for things like instruction manuals and cartoon-style renders.

The settings for the Preview renderer are shown in Figure 16.1 and include the following options:

- **Display Engine:** Check the SreeD option if your graphics adapter does not support OpenGL display settings. If your graphics card does support OpenGL, check whether you want the OpenGL features to be supported by the hardware on the graphics adapter or through software.
- **Enable Hardware Shading:** If you are using OpenGL hardware rendering, check this option to see the effects of certain advanced procedural shaders in your Preview window (bump maps, displacement maps, Ambient Occlusion, and other nodes will not display). This option may slow your preview performance if there are a lot of advanced procedural shaders in your scene and will not work for more than eight lights. If your preview speed is affected, disable (uncheck) this option.
- **Optimize Simple Materials:** Check this option if you do not want Poser to generate shaders for simple materials.
- **Style Options:** These options relate to how lines, borders, and edges are displayed in the Preview window. The Silhouette Outline Width setting controls the width of outlines used in Outline display style. The Wireframe Line Edge setting controls the width of the grid lines used in Wireframe display mode. The Toon Edge Line Width setting controls the width of the Toon Outline display option. Check the Antialias option to prevent a jagged appearance on diagonal lines.
- **Transparency Display:** These options control how transparent textures are displayed in the Preview window. Choose Actual to display transparency maps exactly as they are configured by the Material Room. If you want to limit the amount of transparency, choose the Limit To option, and enter the maximum percentage that you want to display. By default, the limit is set to 90%.

- **Texture Display:** The Preview Texture Resolution setting allows you to increase or decrease the maximum texture resolution that will display in the Preview window. Higher values mean that textures are more detailed but will also consume more resources.

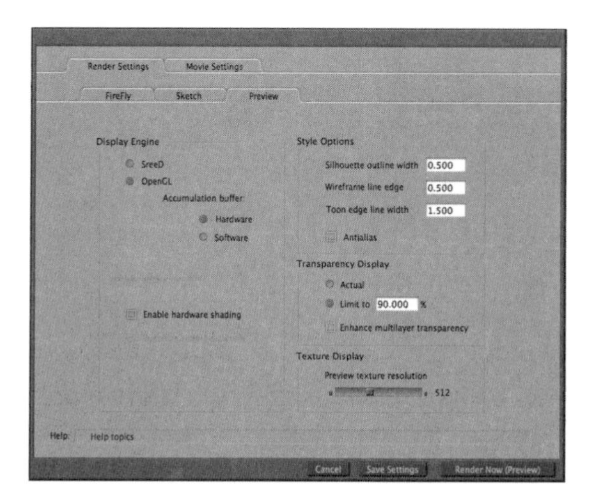

FIGURE 16.1 The Preview renderer, where you set up renders that are of preview quality rather than for final render.

After you configure your Preview renderer settings, you can click the Save Settings button to store the settings and exit the Render Settings dialog box. After you use the Render > Render Dimensions dialog box to specify your render size, you can choose Render > Render or press F9 to render your document in the current display setting.

Sketch Renderer

The Sketch renderer, shown in Figure 16.2, works in conjunction with the Sketch Designer and provides a myriad of artistic drawing and painting effects that can make your renders look hand drawn. I will be discussing the Sketch renderer near the end of the chapter, but suffice it to say this feature provides access to a number of presets that give very different render styles.

Area Renders

The Area Render feature allows you to select and render an area of your scene. It's not only useful after making some sort of change to the layout, but also when you make changes to the lighting. With the Area Render feature, you can select a small portion of your screen for rendering instead of waiting for the entire image to render again. This allows you to see the effects of your changes more quickly.

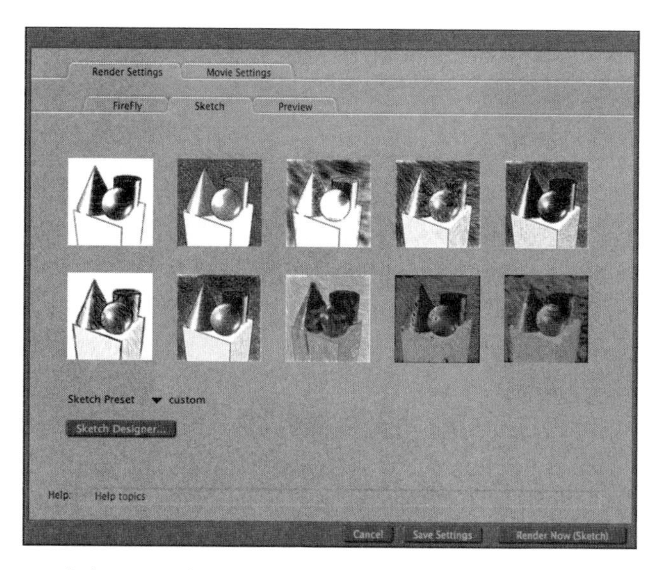

FIGURE 16.2 Hand-drawn and artistic renders can be created using the Sketch renderer.

To render a specific area in your scene, click the Area Render icon that appears at the top of the Preview window. Then click and drag to select a rectangular area in the Preview window. Release the mouse button to render the selected area. Figure 16.3 shows an area selected in the Preview window. The objects within the selected area are the only areas that will be rendered.

You can also use Area Render to assist you in rendering large images that might tax your resources. After you compose your scene and set the final render dimensions, start by selecting a rectangular area at the top of your Preview window. That section will then be rendered. When you select the Area Render icon again, click and drag across another portion of the image, making sure to overlap the sections so there are no gaps. Figure 16.4 shows how the render will be continued, with this next area being added to the first area that was rendered. Continue this process until the entire picture has been rendered.

After defining the first section of the Area Render, there is an anomaly that occurs for each subsequent section you define—you will not see a new bounding box appear as you click and drag across the next section of your image. Just know that the area you want to include in the Area Render is being set based upon where you clicked to start and where you release the mouse button at the end.

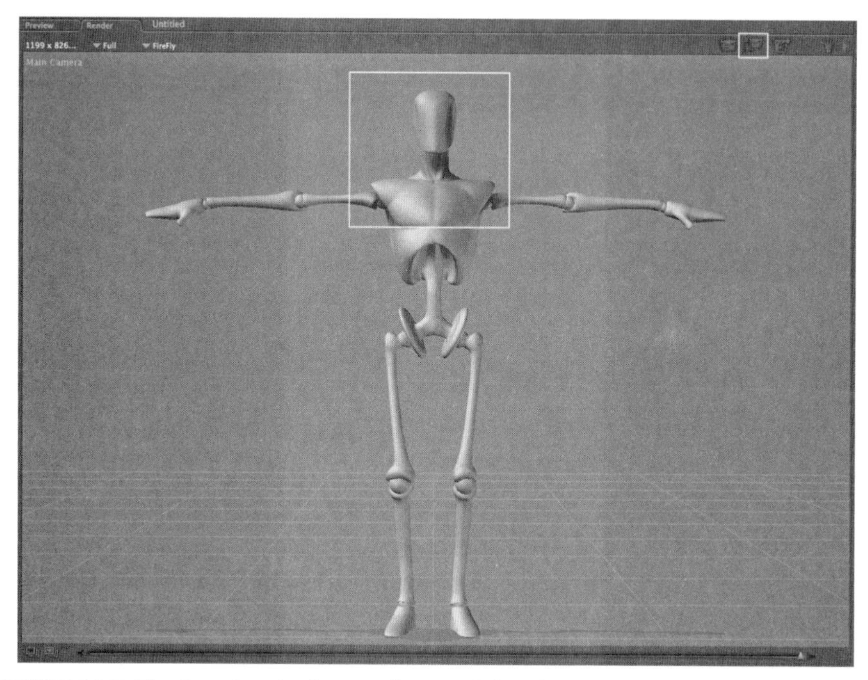

FIGURE 16.3 The Area Render icon at the top right. This gives you the ability to render a section of your scene rather than the entire scene over and over again.

FIGURE 16.4 You can create multiple area renders, each of which builds upon the next, until your entire image is rendered.

COMPARING RENDERS

The Compare Render feature allows you to compare two of your previously rendered images within the Preview window. Click the "stack of paper" icons on the bottom-left corner of the Render window. This opens a list of your most recent renders. You can configure the number of renders held in the render cache in the Document tab of the Edit > General Preferences dialog box.

The Main Render, selected from the left list as shown in Figure 16.5, is placed beside the Compare Render that you select from the right list. After you select a render from each list, you can use the Render Wipe slider at the bottom of the window to reveal the renders side by side.

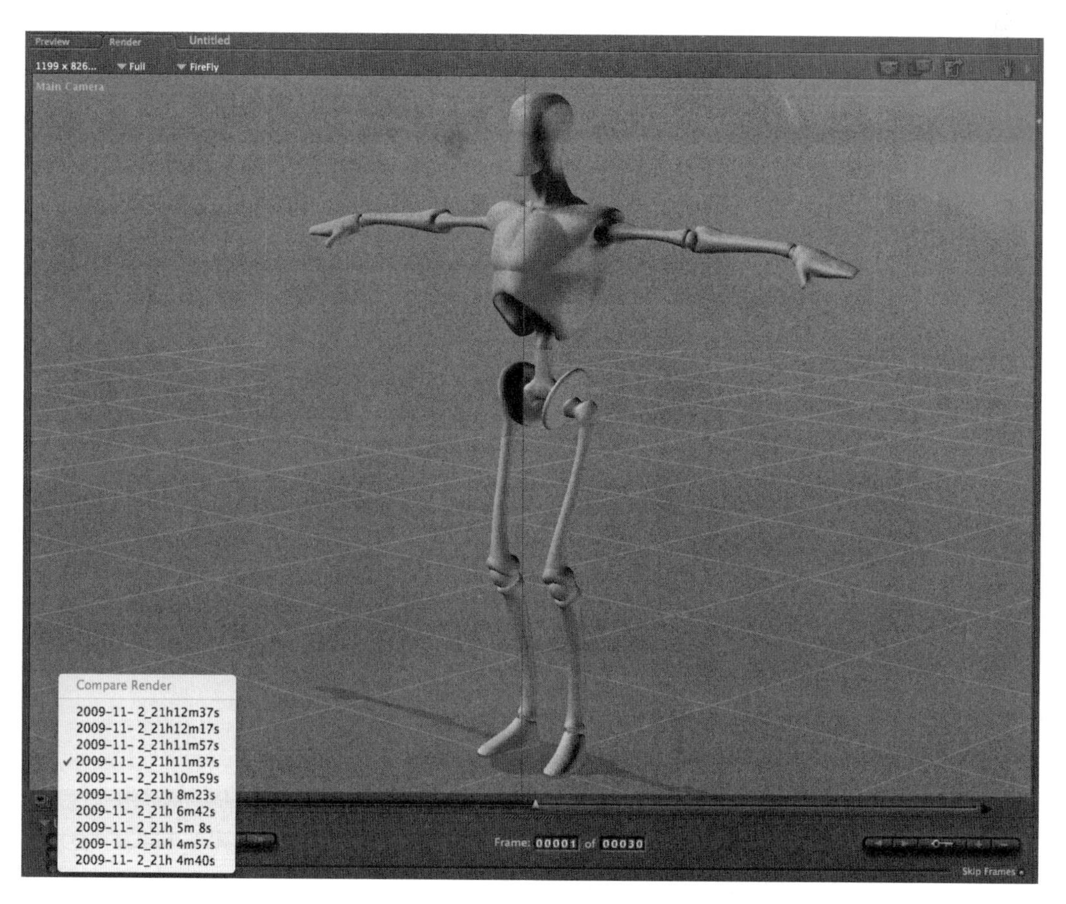

FIGURE 16.5 The Compare Render list and a comparison of two renders. Notice the black line down the middle of the image that shows where one render ends and the next begins.

Using the FireFly Renderer

Now that the overview is under your belt, let's look at how the FireFly renderer works. This is the render engine you will use most often, so it makes sense to start here. This will also lead in to one of the newest features in Poser 8—Indirect Lighting (IDL), which will be discussed in more detail in the "Indirect Lighting" section later in the chapter.

The FireFly Render engine is a very sophisticated one in relation to what you would expect from a program in Poser's price range. This engine allows for displacement mapping, enhanced reflections and shadows, atmospheric effects, depth of field (DOF), and raytracing. It's broken into two sections—Auto and Manual—giving you a full range of rendering options.

Automatic Render Settings

The Auto Settings options (see Figure 16.6) give you a visual method for defining your render parameters. The render presets on the left side are for a preview or draft quality render. They render more quickly but are not as highly detailed. As you move closer toward Final quality on the right, the renders take longer but become more realistic and detailed. As you move the arrow quality slider toward the higher quality settings, you'll notice that the settings for the various rendering parameters will change. So what exactly are these features with the strange names such as Shading Rate, Pixel Samples, and so forth? The answers are in the list that follows.

- **Min Shading Rate:** This value has to do with the micropolygon method of rendering scenes and determines how small the micropolygons will be. A shading rate of 1 means that the polygons in the object will be broken down into small pieces (micropolygons) that are equal to a single pixel of your rendered image. Draft quality renders use a Min Shading Rate of 2, whereas final quality renders use a Min Shading Rate of 0.5. Smaller values give crisper details, although your rendering time will increase. Figure 16.7 shows rendered examples of Min Shading Rates of 4, 2, 1, and 0.5.
- **Cast Shadows:** This option enables or disables the calculation of shadows for the entire render. You can disable shadow casting on a case-by-case basis for any individual object in your scene. However, if shadows are turned off here, they won't get calculated anywhere.
- **Pixel Samples:** This value is used to determine how many neighboring pixels are sampled during an antialiasing calculation. For each pixel that is being antialiased, the renderer samples a surrounding block of pixels and calculates the properties of the pixel based on the values of its neighbors. A value of 1 (which is used for draft renders) samples 1 pixel. A value of 3 (used for final renders) samples a 3x3-pixel area. Higher Pixel Samples values produce smoother images

but take longer to render. You can refer to Figure 16.7 to see the results. In this figure, you can see the differences in clarity as the Min Shading Rate is reduced because, inversely, the Pixel Samples are increased.

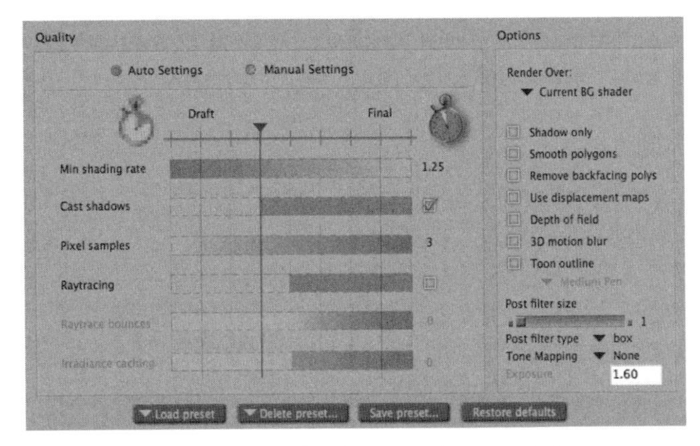

FIGURE 16.6 The Auto Settings controls.

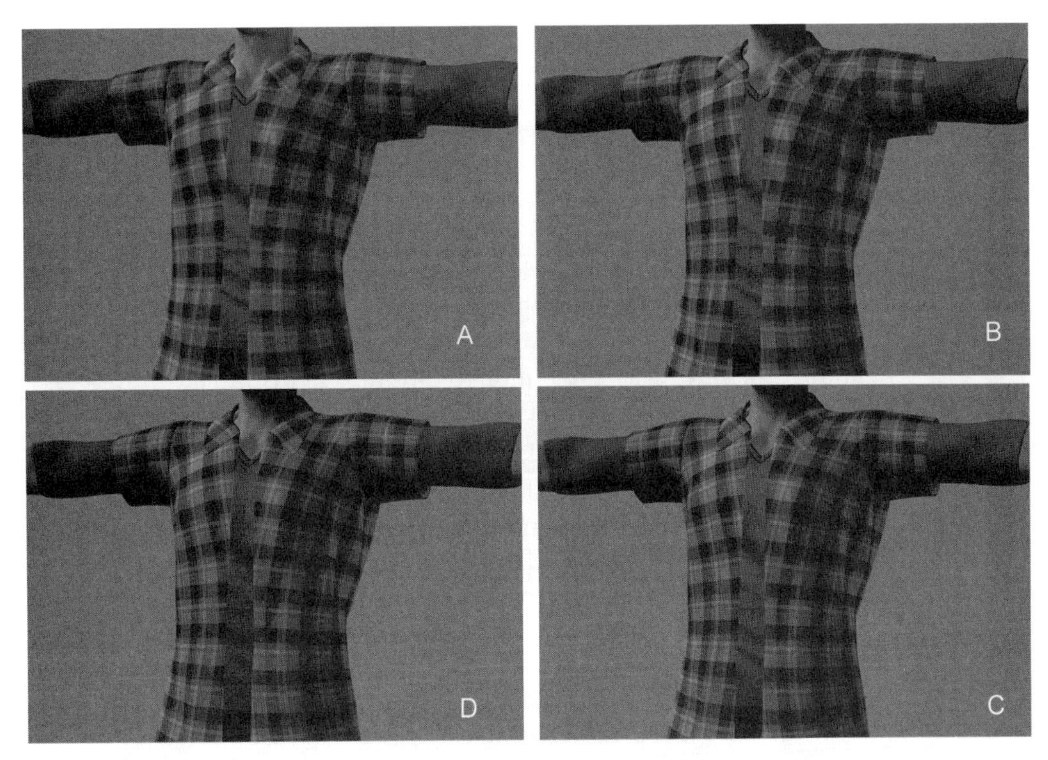

FIGURE 16.7 As the Min Shading Rate is decreased, detail is added. Here are the settings going clockwise from top left: (a) 4.00, (b) 2.00, (c) 1.00 and (d) 0.50.

- **Raytracing:** Check this option to enable or disable raytracing calculations. Some types of procedural shaders, such as the Refraction and Reflection nodes, require that raytracing be enabled in order to work. Raytracing is off for draft renders and on for final quality renders.
- **Raytrace Bounces:** When raytracing is enabled, this parameter sets the limit on how many bounces each ray of light traces through. The number you set here should be proportional to the number of raytraced reflective or refractive surfaces that appear in your scene. Higher values give more realistic reflections and refractions; however, they also eat up more of your CPU and take longer to render. A medium-quality render might use one raytrace bounce, whereas a more realistic final quality render might use a setting of 4 or higher.
- **Irradiance Caching:** This setting relates to the amount of lights and shadows that appear at any point in your scene and is most applicable to the various types of lighting nodes that you can use in your material shaders. This setting stores previous irradiance calculations that help speed up renders. Recommended settings are between 50 and 100. A higher value stores more information and helps reduce rendering time but produces less accurate irradiance.

Manual Render Settings

All of the settings that appear in the Auto Settings area also appear in the Manual Settings area. This is also where you access Indirect Lighting options, again, discussed later in this chapter. In the Manual Settings section, you can override the automatic settings to fully customize how your renders are handled. The Manual Settings area allows you to set each parameter individually. In addition to the Auto Settings already discussed, the following additional options appear in the Manual Settings area:

- **Acquire from Auto:** Click this button to copy the values from the Auto Settings area to the Manual Settings area. From there, you can manually set each attribute that was discussed in the "Automatic Render Settings" section.
- **Max Bucket Size:** If you observe the progress of a FireFly renderer, you will notice that the renderer displays one block at a time as your scene goes through the rendering process. This block of information is called a *bucket* and represents the number of pixels that are rendered at the same time. Larger bucket sizes use more of your system's resources, but they can also speed up your renders if you have the computing power to support them. If your bucket size is too large for the amount of resources you have available, you may run out of system resources. If Poser freezes during rendering, use a lower bucket size setting the next time you try to render the scene.

- **Min Displacement Bounds:** By default, FireFly looks in all directions from your geometry to determine the amount of displacement that may need to occur. The displacement bounds setting sets a limit on how far FireFly looks in each direction. When you use displacement maps, you must tell the FireFly renderer to displace the surface of an object by a value at least as high as the setting used in the displacement value set in the root node for the material. If you set the FireFly setting too high, the result will go out of the bounds of the current bucket calculation. This will cause your object to look like it has black holes or polka dots sprinkled all over it. A high value also eats up resources quickly and requires longer rendering times.
- **Indirect Light:** This feature causes Poser to render more realistic scenes based upon the natural bouncing of light off objects and how that bounced light affects the lighting of other objects in the scene.
- **Indirect Light Quality:** Determines the number of rays of light used to calculate the Indirect Lighting scheme. The higher the value, the greater the realism but at a cost to rendering speed.

Additional Rendering Options

Now let's focus on the right side of the Render Settings window. Here you have even more controls to define the quality of your renders. You can refer to Figure 16.6 as I define what each of these particular settings does.

- **Render Over:** This drop-down list allows you to choose one of several options to use as the background (BG) when rendering. The Background Color, Black, and Background Picture options render objects in your scene over a color of your choice, either black or the background picture you have loaded, respectively. The Current BG Shader option gives you the opportunity to specify a complex procedural shader as the background.
- **Shadow Only:** This option renders only the shadows that are cast by the objects in your scene. When you choose to render shadows only, all other render settings are overridden. This feature allows you to combine the shadow-only render with a render that has no shadows enabled in a graphic program. You can later use a graphic program to independently manipulate the shadows, providing very fine control without having to continually adjust and re-render different lighting settings.
- **Smooth Polygons:** The FireFly rendering engine uses polygon subdivision to smooth the polygon joints on objects. When polygon smoothing is turned on, you can improve the appearance of a low-polygon model so that it looks

smoother and softer rather than faceted. The amount of smoothing is controlled with smoothing groups or by setting a crease angle threshold in the Properties panel. The Poser 8 Reference Manual discusses this subject in Chapter 15, "Smooth Shading."

- **Remove Backfacing Polys:** This setting tells the FireFly renderer to ignore polygons that are on the backside of the object and not directly visible from the current camera position. By ignoring polygons not seen by the camera, your renders complete much more quickly. However, if your scene uses raytraced reflective materials, make sure that the backs of your objects do not show up in any reflection. Otherwise, you may get weird-looking reflections that show your objects with holes in them.
- **Use Displacement Maps:** When using displacement in your renders, check this option and set your Min Displacement Bounds setting slightly higher than the highest material displacement setting used in your scene.
- **Depth of Field:** Check this setting to calculate depth-of-field effects in your render. The depth of field is set in properties for the camera that is being used as the render view.

More information about depth of field can be found in Chapter 2, "Using Cameras."

- **3D Motion Blur:** A great way to give the impression of fast-moving objects is to blur them. This parameter enables blurring based on the rate of position change of an object from one animation frame to the next. Blurring is affected by shutter open and close times, with longer exposures (shutter open time) producing more pronounced blurring effects.
- **Toon Outline:** This is a post-render operation that draws an outline around the objects in your scene. There are nine outline styles: Thin Pen, Thin Pencil, Thin Marker, Medium Pen, Medium Pencil, Medium Marker, Thick Pen, Thick Pencil, and Thick Marker.
- **Post Filter Size:** A post-render filter smoothes, or antialiases, your render. The filter samples a group of pixels surrounding the current pixel and calculates a weighted average of the entire group to determine what that center pixel's characteristics are. Increasing the filter size increases the area used for group calculation, which in turn increases render times. Using too large a sample may cause undesirable blurring. The effect that this filter has is also dependent on the final size of your rendered output, so you may need to change this as you change the size of your final output.

- **Post Filter Type:** This defines the type of calculation the post filter uses to antialias your render. The types of post filters that FireFly supports are the following:
  - **Box:** This gives each pixel in the sample equal weight.
  - **Gaussian:** This filter varies the weight of a sample based on the distance from the center of the sample area. The Gaussian curve is sometimes called the "standard distribution curve" or the "Bell curve."
  - **Sinc:** A Sinc filter applies a declining sine wave weight to the samples based on the distance of the sample from the center. Imagine a rock falling into the water and the ripples in the surface that are created as a result. These ripples are the sine wave that will be produced—one large rise in the center with crests that decrease in amplitude the farther from the center you go.
- **Tone Mapping**: Useful for scenes incorporating high dynamic range (HDR), providing more brightness, saturation, and post-processing control for the image. The drop-down menu gives you two selections: Exponential and Hue, Saturation, Value (HSV) Exponential. The former works like film, where brighter values become less sensitive so, as the scene brightens, the more gently the change from dark to light becomes. With the latter, you create a less natural scene, but it controls the brightness levels by keeping them in a normal range rather than letting them bloom (or become too prominent).
- **Exposure:** This becomes available when HSV or Exponential tone mapping is selected. Exposure becomes the controlling element for exponential calculations.

Saving Render Settings

If you create custom rendering configurations in either the Auto or Manual Settings area, you can save and recall them whenever you need to use them. To save a render setting, click on the Save Preset button located at the bottom of the Render Settings window (see Figure 16.8). Poser will prompt you to enter a name for your render preset (see Figure 16.9).

FIGURE 16.8 The buttons to save and recall presets are located immediately under the Render Settings controls.

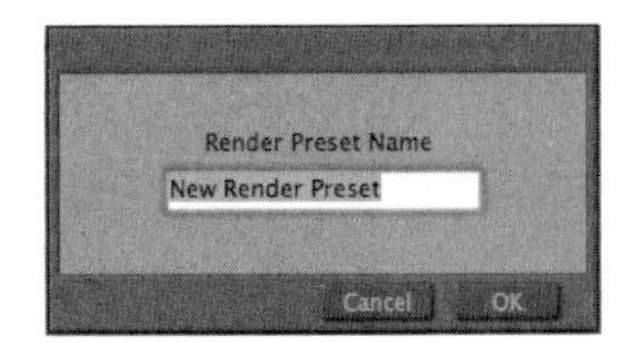

FIGURE 16.9 Name the settings you are saving for easy recall.

After you save your preset, you will be able to access it anytime by clicking the Load Preset button. You will get a drop-down list showing each of your saved settings. To restore settings to their defaults, use the Restore Defaults button.

TUTORIAL 16.1 RENDER SETTINGS AND ASPECT RATIOS

The aspect ratio of an image is simply the ratio of its width to its height. If an image is 11 inches wide by 14 inches tall, its aspect ratio is 1:1.27. (The 1.27 is derived by dividing the height by the width, which in this case is 14 divided by 11.)

As you prepare your scenes, the way in which they are framed is extremely important. The camera's position and how it captures the subject in your image helps to convey emotion, allowing the viewer to feel what you, the artist, want him to feel. Setting the correct aspect ratio literally determines your framing options. For instance, if you want to create a portrait, you would more than likely create an image that is taller than it is wide. On the other hand, if you are creating an image where the subject is looking over a wide expanse, you would set your image dimensions to be wider than tall. By default, Poser's aspect ratio is set to be more square-like (490 pixels by 500 pixels). It also has its aspect ratio locked so any change to the render dimensions will automatically remain the same. Here's how to change the defaults so you can easily set the size of the file as you need it for final output.

Let's say you need an 8x10-inch image for high-quality printing (300dpi). It is very easy to set this up in Poser:

1. Choose Render > Render Dimensions to open the Render Dimensions dialog box shown in Figure 16.10.
2. Temporarily uncheck the Constrain Aspect Ratio option until you enter the final width, height, and resolution of the image.
3. Select Render to Exact Resolution from the upper section of the Render Dimensions dialog box.

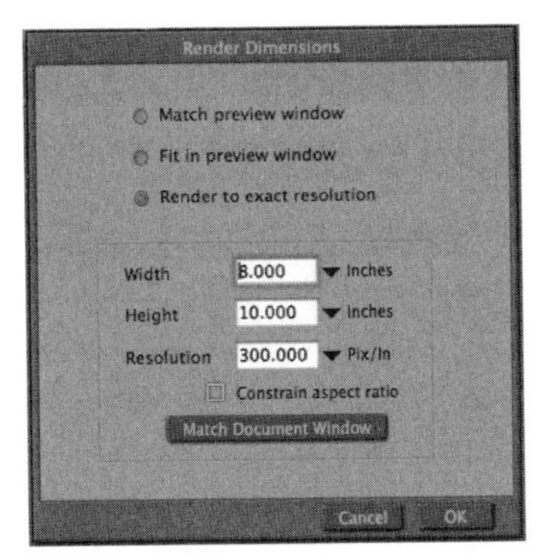

FIGURE 16.10 The Render Dimensions dialog box.

4. Enter **300** into the Resolution field, and select Pix/In from the drop-down menu. This sets the resolution at 300dpi.
5. Make sure you change from Pixels to Inches in the numeric pop-up immediately to the right of the numeric fields.
6. Next enter the dimensions into the Width and Height fields.
7. Now check the Constrain Aspect Ratio again. By doing so, you can change the Width or the Height value, and the other value will change automatically to keep the same relative proportions. Let's say that you have another frame that has the same aspect ratio as your 8x10 frame, but it is 11 inches wide instead. As long as the Constrain Aspect Ratio option is selected, you can easily get a perfect fit by simply going back into the Render Dimensions dialog box and changing the width. Your Height value will be calculated automatically for you.

PRODUCTION FRAME

To help you better position the elements in your scene, Poser has added a production frame to the Preview window. This production frame is shown as a darker gray overlay on the left and right sides of the window. So when you changed the aspect ratio of the image to 8x10 inches in Tutorial 16.1, these overlays will appear. The area between those overlays is what will actually be rendered. You can turn the Production Frame option on or off by going to Display > Production Frame > Image Output Size.

FIGURE 16.11 The production frame displayed in the Preview window.

Indirect Lighting

Indirect Lighting (IDL) is the newest addition to Poser's rendering options, and it offers probably the most realistic method for rendering in the history of the program. IDL allows global illumination and ambient occlusion, things that aren't truly possible in other versions of the program. There are two ways of working with IDL in Poser—through the Render Settings window or via a Python script where you have immense control over the output. I'll begin with the regular option and then move to the Python script.

In previous versions of Poser, the way IDL renders were accomplished was through use of Ambient Occlusion (AO) nodes. Heavy use of AO nodes. And all those AO nodes accomplished was to fake IDL. Now, we have the real thing. Many materials, though, rely on AO nodes to achieve a final realistic render, so you might want to check and disconnect any AO nodes assigned to your materials before rendering. If you don't, it can increase render times dramatically.

TUTORIAL 16.2 SETTING UP AND RENDERING WITH INDIRECT LIGHTING

For this tutorial, let's use Andy to explore working with IDL. So, create a new scene and, if you have Poser set up so Andy doesn't automatically load, place Andy in the scene.

1. Remove Lights 1 and 3 from the scene. Remember, to do this, you click on the light in the Light Controls section and click on the trash can icon, or you can go to the Parameters panel and choose the lights from the Object pop-up menu.
2. Reposition the remaining light (Light 2) in the following manner:
   - xRotate = 28°
   - yRotate = –31°
   - zRotate = 8°

   This will position the light as you see in Figure 16.12.

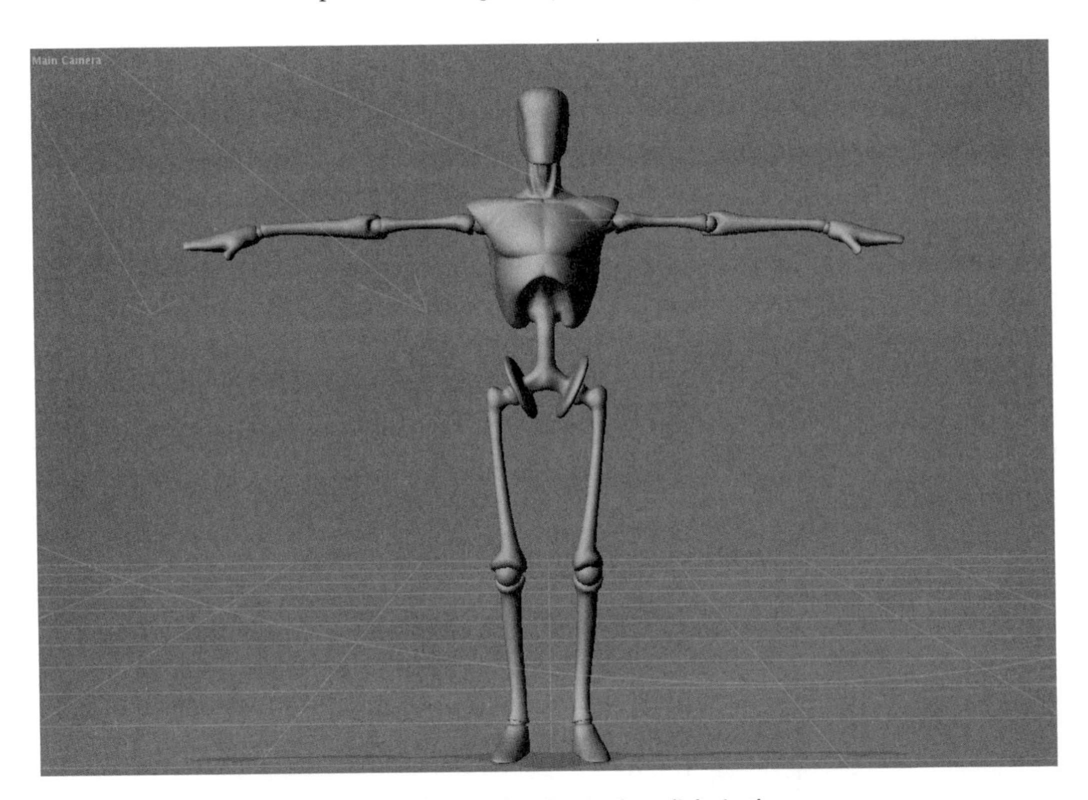

FIGURE 16.12 The position for the lone light in the scene.

3. Go to Render Settings and, with Auto Settings selected, move the Quality slider to its highest setting and click Render Now. You will get an image like the one shown in Figure 16.13, with deep shadows that block out some details in the image.

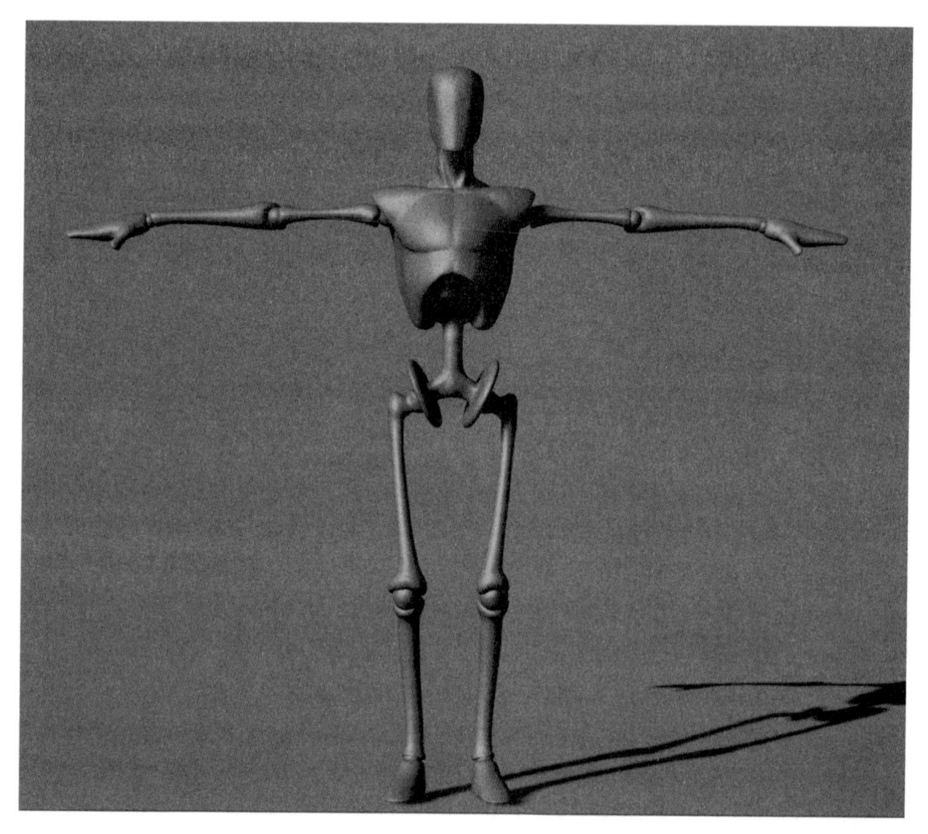

FIGURE 16.13 Dark shadows permeate this image, blocking many details on the model.

4. Return to the Render Settings window and switch to Manual Settings. In this panel, select Indirect Light, which automatically turns on raytracing. When you render the scene, it will render in two parts. First, you will see the figure in black with red points dotting the sections of the model(s) in your scene. These red points are indications of Poser figuring out the bounce of light and how that light will affect those areas not directly in its light, namely, the indirect lighting in the scene. The second pass then renders the image. You'll see that your shadows are not so overpowering, and your render looks much more realistic (as shown in Figure 16.14).

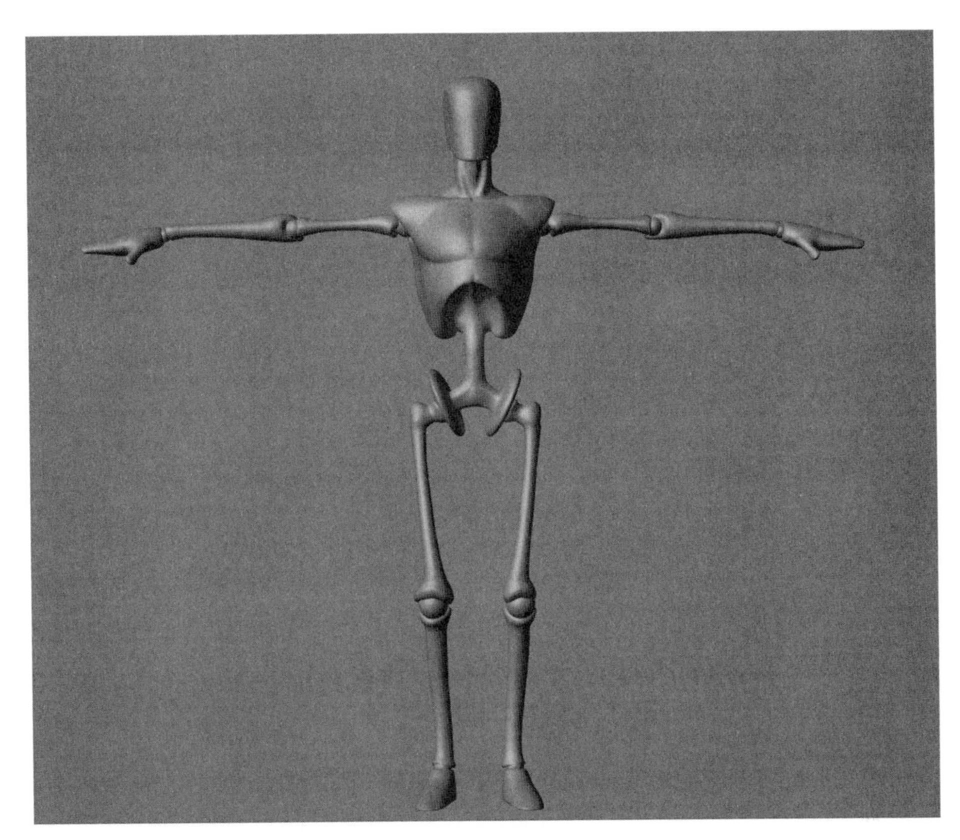

FIGURE 16.14 Shadows are much more realistic when indirect lighting is used.

Using indirect lighting can often cause your renders to take a long time to complete. Here are some tips for reducing render times. First, if you can, reduce the image size. But this isn't always possible. However, you can also change the number of raytrace bounces to somewhere between 2 and 4. This makes it so Poser doesn't have as much information to calculate. Turn off Visible in Raytracing if you're using transmapped hair props. And, finally, as mentioned earlier, turn off/disconnect all AO nodes.

To really take advantage of IDL, you need other objects in the scene. Remember, IDL calculates how light bounces off of other objects and how that light would affect those other objects in the scene. This will be demonstrated in Tutorial 16.3.

This is a very straightforward method for using IDL. But what can IDL do to enhance an outdoor scene—something with clouds and sky and outdoorsy-type lighting? That's what I'll discuss in the next tutorial.

Tutorial 16.3 Using the IDL Python Script

If you have any building models in your Props Library, place it into a new scene. Or go to Renderosity.com or RuntimeDNA.com and search for free building props. I'm going to use one of the Dystopia City Blocks for this project. (Go to www.team-dystopia.com or do a search for dystopia at Daz3D.com—they're free for the taking!) I am also using a free prop called the Environment Sphere from Bagginsbill (http://sites.google.com/site/bagginsbill/free-stuff/environment-sphere). Then, go to the Chapter 16 folder on the book's DVD and add the envMap_Clouds.jpg, .tif, and .hdr images to your Textures folder. Once you have everything, you're ready to use IDL in an outdoor scene, as well as learn about the IDL Python script.

1. Remove Lights 1 and 2 from the scene and set the power of Light 2 to 80%. You don't want to do IBL with a light at full power because it can overlight the scene.
2. Set the light to the following position:
   - xRotate = 92°
   - yRotate = –72°
   - zRotate = –84°
3. Select the Main Camera and change Focal to 24 so you can see more of the building. Then change the camera's position to the following:
   - DollyZ = -2.750
   - DollyY = 4.396
   - DollyX = 0.886
   - xOrbit = 32°
   - yOrbit = –46°

   Your scene will now look like the one in Figure 16.15.
4. Go to Props > EnvSphere and load the EnvHemisphere. This is the object that light will bounce off of in the IDL render.

FIGURE 16.15 The scene after the camera has been moved into position.

5. With the EnvHemisphere selected, go to the Material Room. You will see a node titled Panoramic Image. Click the None button in the Image_Source field and add the envMap_Clouds.hdr file. If for some reason this file is not accepted, use one of the other file formats I supplied. Now your scene should look like Figure 16.16.
6. Now that the scene is created, let's get ready to render. Go to Scripts > Partners > Dimension3D > Render FireFly to open the D3D Render FireFly window (see Figure 16.17). This window has all of the controls located in the Render Settings window, but instead of having to go through two different screens, you can access all the controls in this one window.

You might be asking at this point, "If the Render FireFly Python script gives you access to all the render controls, why should I even go into the Render Settings window?" The answer is, you don't need to. This comes down to personal preference. Choose the render options method you prefer and use that. The outcome will be the same.

FIGURE 16.16 The clouds image is added to the scene.

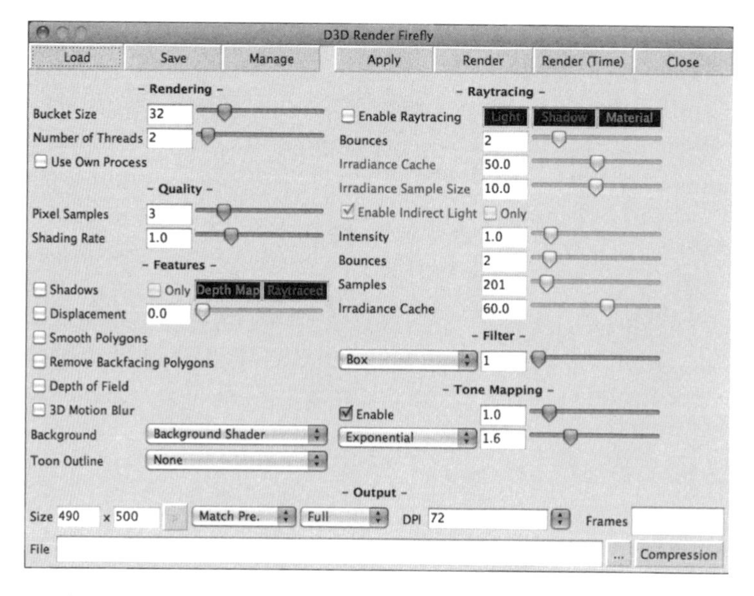

FIGURE 16.17 The D3D Render FireFly window, accessed from the Scripts drop-down menu.

While the settings I am using in this section work for this particular image, there are no set numbers I can give you that work for every image you make. Changes in the image files you use for the dome, the models you use, and the light color you choose for the light all affect the scene.

It's important to remind you that as I go through these various projects, you should also be trying different settings in order to both practice using the controls and the effects, as well as to help you cement the controls and their uses in your mind. By merely copying what I am doing, you can lose sight of what the outcome is supposed to be. Images you create are the output of your vision, so play with the numbers to make each scene your own.

7. Use the settings you see in Figure 16.18 for this particular scene. Changes you make to controls such as Number of Threads and Bounces can affect the length of the render. You can, of course, save your settings by clicking the Save button.
8. Click the Render button. You can see the result not only in Figure 16.19 but also in the color section of this book. Save this file so you can use it in the next section.

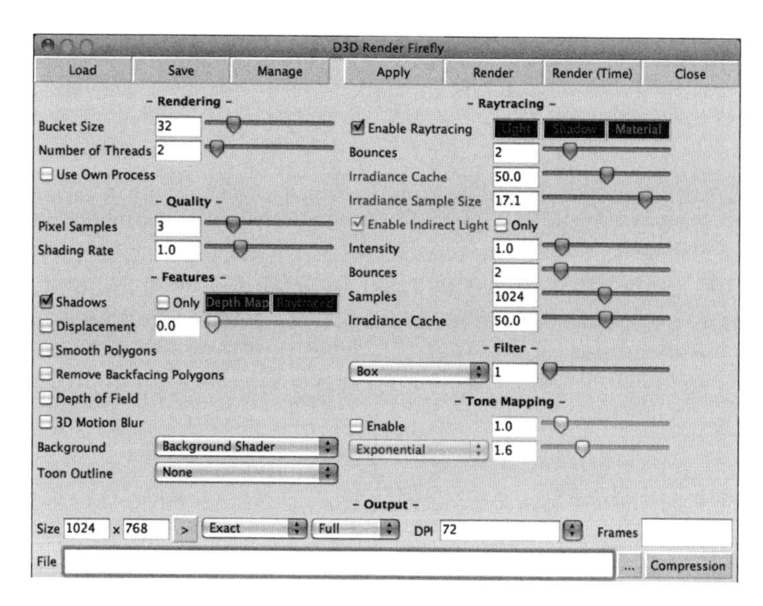

FIGURE 16.18 Use the settings shown here for the initial rendering.

FIGURE16.19 The building rendered with IDL. Look at the color section to see more detail and to compare IDL with non-IDL rendering.

The Sketch Designer

One of the most under-utilized features of Poser is its ability to create sketch renders—renders that make the image look hand drawn. There is a small group out there that has used Poser for online comics and that has used this feature, but for the most part, many users don't access this rendering feature. Earlier in the chapter, I made quick reference to the Sketch Designer, but here I'll walk through actually using it.

You have a few presets that quickly get you up and running. These presets, shown in Figure 16.20, are as follows (from left to right):

- Pencil and Ink
- ScratchBoard
- StrokedBg
- Sketchy

- Soft Charcoal
- LooseSketch
- Colored pencil
- Smoothy
- Silky
- Pastel

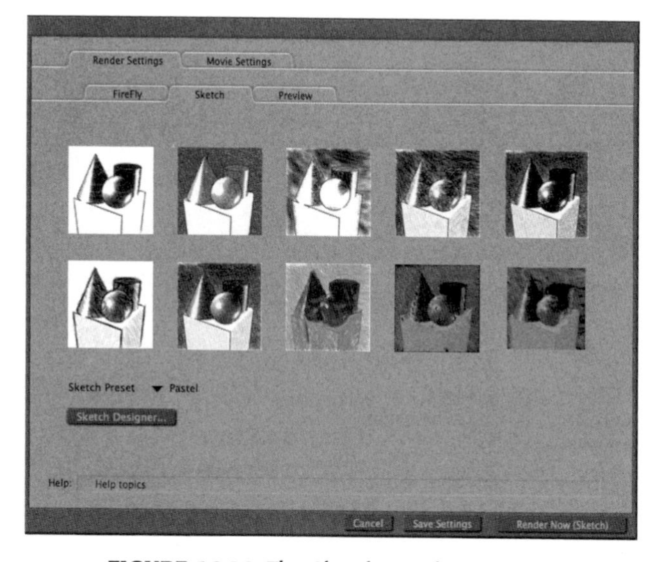

FIGURE 16.20 The Sketch Render window.

Each of these presets give you a basic look that is okay, but usually are not exactly what you would want. You also have access to more presets by clicking on the Sketch Preset pop-up menu just above the Sketch Designer button.

If you access the Sketch Designer window (shown in Figure 16.21) via the Sketch Designer button, you have access to all the controls that let you modify the look of the sketches that are created.

In addition, after you get your settings the way you want them, you can save them not only to reuse for other Poser scenes, but you can also export the settings as a TXT file usable in the Corel Painter program (www.corel.com).

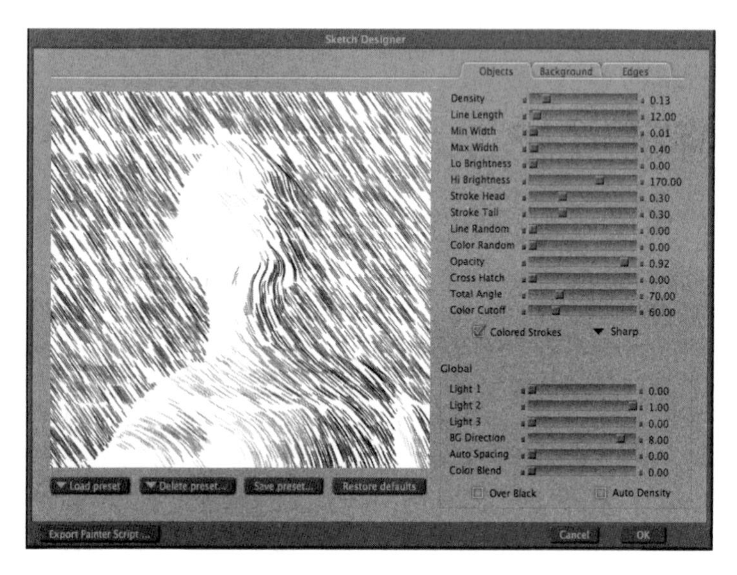

FIGURE 16.21 The Sketch Designer window, where you have full control over the final look of the sketch.

TUTORIAL 16.4 CREATING A SKETCH RENDER

Time to try gettin' sketchy with it. Poser, that is. Open the scene you created in the last tutorial and add the Andrea mannequin figure to the scene.

1. Reposition Andrea in the following manner:

   - yRotate = –62°
   - x Rotate = 8°
   - zRotate = 11°
   - xTran = –4.395
   - yTran = –3.440
   - zTran = 2.047

   Change the Twist setting for the Neck to 27° and the Head's Twist and Bend settings to 27° and –9°, respectively. And while you have the head selected, change the Facial Features to 1.000 so she has a face. Figure 16.22 shows the scene that has now been set up.

2. Open the Render Settings window, click the Sketch tab and enter the Sketch Designer.
3. Select Colored Pencil from the Load Preset button.

FIGURE 16.22 The scene with Andrea added to it.

4. Click the Edges tab and make the following changes:
   - Density = 1.00
   - Line Length = 30
   - Minimum Width = 10
5. Change the Density to 0.10.
6. Under the Objects tab, change Density and Crosshatch to 1.00.
7. Click OK. The Sketch Designer window will close, returning you to the main Render Options window. Click Render Now to render the file.

This creates a hand-drawn and colored image, with the crosshatch adding a bit more detail to Andrea. And there's an outline surrounding the elements in the picture, adding to the impression of the file having been created by hand. Figure 16.23 shows the sketched image and, again, you can see the color version in the color section.

FIGURE 16.23 The scene using modified sketch settings.

A Short Re-Pose

And there you go. You now have the knowledge to take your images to new levels of quality, whether you're going for photorealistic or something that can be used for online comics and print. Through the course of this book you have learned about the updated and new features in Poser 8. From the updated graphical user interface to the additional Python scripts, I'm sure you will agree that Poser 8 has moved into an entirely new realm of creative possibilities.

Your journey is not yet complete. On the following pages are appendixes that go beyond what was mentioned in the book. And as you practice and use either your own models or models created by third-party vendors, I look forward to seeing what you have created through your postings on the numerous galleries, like Renderosity.com, RuntimeDNA.com and deviantART.com, just to name a few.

A Content Providers

Over the years, a lot of people have provided their talents making content for Poser. Following is a comprehensive list of sites that either sell or give away Poser content. Sites are accurate at the time of this writing.

Content Paradise—www.contentparadise.com

You can also click on the Content tab in your Poser 8 workspace to access Content Paradise. Once at the site, you can choose from hundreds of models provided by various Poser users around the world. There are literally dozens of providers who create content for sale on this site, so take some time to look at all the high-quality products.

DAZ3D—www.daz3d.com

Creators of the most popular male and female models for Poser—Michael 4 and Victoria 4 (along with their hybrids, such as The Freak, The Guy, The Girl, and Aiko). DAZ3D also features excellent clothing, props, and accessories that are created by some of the top artists in the Poser community. Forums and galleries are also featured content of the site, as are various contests throughout the year.

RuntimeDNA—www.runtimedna.com

Created and run by renowned texture artist Syyd Raven and content creator Colm Jackson, this is one of the premiere Poser locations on the Internet. RuntimeDNA creates some of the base content that comes with Poser. Also includes forums and member galleries and a comprehensive store filled with Poser content.

Renderosity.com—www.renderosity.com

The granddaddy of online content providers and one of the largest online art communities, Renderosity features thousands of Poser items for free or for purchase. The site hosts numerous forums and member galleries focusing on 2D and 3D graphics programs.

3D Commune—www.3dcommune.com

Artist community that features member-built models and textures for Poser. Also includes forums, contests, galleries, and free content.

3D Universe—www.3duniverse.co.za

Creators of extremely high-quality 'toon characters. While many of the items are sold at DAZ3D, there are many upgrades and freebies available on this site that enhance their models.

Digital Babes—www.digitalbabes.jp

Run by Kozaburo Yoshimura, one of the most highly regarded hair creators in the Poser community. He provides his models for free, and you can download additional hair models from his site that are made to fit the DAZ3D characters, as well as Poser 6/7/8 characters.

Illusions Designs—http://illusions-designs.net/

Original morphs and textures, models, and props for your content library.

Meshbox—www.meshbox.com

Creators of 'toon figures and elegant sets for Poser.

Netherworks Studios—www.netherworks-studios.com

Offers Poser characters, Python scripts, clothing morph kits, and many useful freebies.

PhilC Designs—www.philc.net/index.php

A long-time member of the Poser community who creates high-quality clothing, utilities, and Poser-related tutorials.

PoserPros—http://proserpros.daz3d.com

Poser Pros is not as active an online community as it used to be, but it still has a lot of information in its forums that can be of help as you delve further into Poser's capabilities.

Art Zone—http://artzone.daz3d.com

Owned and operated by DAZ3D, this site features forums and a store filled with high-quality Poser content by some of the top digital artists in the community.

Poserworks—www.poserworks.com

Offers a wide selection of Poser items ranging from aliens and robots to animal, human, medical, and cartoon content. Also includes a large variety of props and sets.

PoserWorld—www.poserworld.com

Offers a large supply of clothing and textures for Poser and DAZ3D figures for a monthly, annual, or lifetime subscription fee. You can also purchase the items individually.

Sanctum Art—www.sanctumart.com

Home for the unique and bizarre in fantasy and sci-fi Poser content. All materials are extremely high quality.

Sixus 1 Media—www.sixus1.com

The creator of Alpha Man, Betaboy, and other figures for Poser. They also provide content at Content Paradise and Renderosity.

The Forge—www.poseamation.com

The creators of PoseAmation, a set of motion capture files compatible with Poser. The product line includes animation packs that allow you to add walks, runs, battles, and other actions into your Poser animations. They also sell through Content Paradise.

Vanishing Point—www.vanishingpoint.biz

This company provides vehicles, robots, environments, and props for Poser.

Zygote—www.zygote.com

Creators of professional-quality 3D models for the commercial, broadcast, biomedical, multimedia, and game industries. You can find Zygote's biomedical models on its sister site, 3DSCI (www.3dscience.com). Many of the models are perfect for medical and forensic illustration and animation—but they will cost you a pretty penny.

B Supported File Types

The following information briefly describes the types of files you are most likely to encounter when you purchase Poser content.

BUM files: Bump map files (companion textures that give some content a bumpy appearance) that are required for older versions of Poser. Since the Poser 4 render engine has been removed, BUM files are not supported fully in Poser 8. You can use them in the Gradient Bump channel in the Material Room, but the result is not that noticeable. I would suggest using a different file format if you are going to use an image to create your bump maps.

CM2 (CMZ when compressed): Camera files that are installed and saved into the Runtime\Libraries\Cameras folder and found in the Cameras Library.

COLLADA/RWY: Collada stands for COLLAborative Design Activity. In the past couple of years, this has become an extremely popular 3D file format that is supported by not only most of the 3D applications (Maya, Max, Cinema 4D, LightWave, and others) but also Photoshop CS4. The format was originally created by Sony Computer Entertainment for the PlayStation 3 and PlayStation Portable.

CR2 (CRZ when compressed): Posable or Conforming figure files. The files are installed and saved into the Runtime\Libraries\Characters folder, and are found in the Figures Library.

FC2 (FCZ when compressed): Face poses, which are a special type of pose that manipulates the morphs associated with the head of a figure. The head of the figure must have the same morph targets that are controlled by the face pose to have any effect on the head mesh. These files are installed and saved into the Runtime\Libraries\Face folder, and you will find them in the Expressions Library.

HD2 (HDZ when compressed): Hand poses that are installed and saved into the Runtime\Libraries\Hand folder. You will find them in the Hands Library.

HR2 (HRZ when compressed): Hair objects that are installed and saved into the Runtime\Libraries\Hair folder. You will find them in the Hair Library.

LT2 (LTZ when compressed): Light sets that are installed and saved into the Runtime\Libraries\Light folder. You will find them in the Lights Library.

MC6 (MCZ when compressed): Material Collection files that are compatible with Poser 6 and later versions. They are installed and saved to the Runtime\Materials folder, and you will find them in the Materials Library.

MT5 (MZ5 when compressed): A single material file that is installed and saved to the Runtime\Materials folder. You will find it in the Materials Library.

MTL: Material files that are generated when you export or save an OBJ file. These are not Poser-compatible files, but they are sometimes required to define material assignments in other 3D programs. You will sometimes see them saved with OBJ files.

OBJ (OBZ when compressed): A Wavefront Object geometry file that is associated with a library item. Poser 4 and earlier versions generate an accompanying RSR file the first time the object file is used. OBJ files are most commonly found in the Runtime\Geometries folder, but you can also find them in the Figures Library in the same folder as the CR2.

PMD: External morph data files. When you save an object or project that contains morph data, Poser saves all of the morphs in a separate file, in the same directory as the saved file. Character files (such as CR2/CRZ files) make reference to these external morphs, so if you move them to a different location, you will have to edit the referencing file.

Content developers should deselect the option to save external binary morphs in the General Preferences dialog box to maintain compatibility with older Poser versions.

PP2 (PPZ when compressed): Prop files that can serve a variety of functions. Prop files can be scenery, jewelry, figure add-ons, furniture, or other content that is not posable. Dynamic clothing is also saved as a prop file. With Poser 6 and later versions, you can also find Conforming clothing with this extension. Prop files are installed into the Runtime\Libraries\Props folder and can be found in the Props Library.

PY: These files are Python scripts, usable with Poser Pro Pack and later versions of Poser. They are installed to the Runtime\Python folder.

PZ2 (P2Z when compressed): Pose files that can also serve a variety of purposes. Pose files began as files that, when applied, posed an object in various positions. Later, they came to be used for poses that changed the materials applied to an object (MAT poses), poses that set existing morphs to change the appearance of an object (MOR poses), or pose files that show or hide various body parts in your figures or clothing. Later, poses were used to add external morphs to a character or remove them from a character (INJ or REM poses). Pose files are installed into the Runtime\Libraries\Pose folder and can be found in the Poses Library.

RSR: These files are no longer supported in Poser 8, but I would be remiss if I didn't bring them up because many of you will probably have RSR files in your libraries. You will have to convert those RSR files to PNG files in order for Poser 8 to recognize them. To convert these files, you will need P3DO Explorer (which only works with one folder at a time) or RSR2PNG (a free utility in the Renderosity marketplace). If you are working on a Mac, there is also a utility called RSRConverter, which can be downloaded from http://sourceforge.net/projects/macposerutils/.

C Frequently Asked Questions

No matter how long you have used Poser (or any program, for that matter), there are questions that come up. You can forget about a feature you don't use very often, and then you have to wrack your brain to remember where it's located or how to make it work. Following is a list of frequently asked questions (FAQs) that can help you through those brain-wrinkling moments.

General Interface Questions

Q: *I set my General Preferences to customize my startup settings, but now my Preview window is stuck near the top of the screen when I open Poser. How do I get it back?*

A: Go back to the General Preferences dialog box (Edit > General Preferences, or on the Mac, go to Poser > Preferences), and reconfigure Poser to start up in factory state in both the Document and Interface tabs. Restart Poser again to get your Preview window back. Then, you can reconfigure your startup preferences again.

Q: *I know I can change the background color of the Poser interface. Can I change the color of the fonts or the font that is used?*

A: Neither the font nor the font color can be changed at the present time.

Q: *I have two monitors. If I put some items on the second monitor, can I save my interface settings that way?*

A: Yes. For example, if the Preview and Render windows are on your second monitor when you close Poser, they will open up in the same position when you next open Poser, providing that you selected the Launch To Previous State option in the General Preferences dialog box.

Building Scenes

Q: *What are the Editing Tools at the left of the screen used for?*

A: The Editing Tools, from left to right, are used as described in the following list. To show or hide them, choose Window > Editing Tools. Note that the Editing Tools vary slightly from room to room.

- **Rotate**: Rotates a figure, body part, or prop.
- **Twist**: Twists a figure, body part, or prop. The same as using the Twist dial in the Parameters panel.
- **Translate/Pull**: Moves a figure up, down, left, or right.
- **Translate In/Out**: Moves a figure forward or backward.
- **Scale**: Increases or decreases the size of a figure or body part.
- **Taper**: Tapers a body part. Select the Taper tool, and then drag over a body part to taper it. Drag left to increase the size of the outermost end of the chain, or drag right to decrease the size.
- **Chain Break**: The Chain Break tool allows you to prevent parts from moving when you pose other parts. For example, if you don't want the shoulders to move when you pose the forearm and hands, you can apply a chain break to the shoulders. Click the Chain Break tool to select it, and then click the figure where you want to break the chain. Click the Chain Break icon again with the Chain Break tool to remove it.
- **Color**: Allows you to change the color of an item in your Preview window or the background color of the Poser interface. Click the Color tool, and then click the object you want to change. A color picker then allows you to choose a color. Continue in this manner until you change the colors that you want to change, and then click the Color tool again to turn it off.
- **Grouping Tool**: Allows you to create groups in your objects and assign polygons to them. The Grouping tool is covered in Chapter 11, "Groups and Materials for Models."
- **View Magnifier**: Allows you to zoom in to an area in the Preview window. Select the View Magnifier, and then draw a rectangle around the area you want to view more closely.
- **Morphing Tool**: Allows you to visually adjust morph settings of a figure by sculpting changes.
- **Direct Manipulation**: Allows you to rotate, twist, or bend body parts using one tool. Three circles represent the axes that will be affected by the tool. Drag the yellow square along the axes that you want to change to rotate, twist, or bend the part.

Q: *How about the Parameter dials? What do they do?*

A: The Parameter dials can help you pose a character, but they also contain several other dials that help you personalize your figures.

Q: *What are Memory Dots used for?*

A: There are actually three kinds of dots: UI Dots, Camera Dots, and Pose Dots. Click the down arrow near the label to choose between them. Choose Window > Memory Dots to show or hide the dots. Memory Dots allow you to store settings for poses, user interface, and cameras so that you can go back to them later. For example, if you create a pose that you like but want to experiment a little further in case you can make improvements, click one of the Pose Dots to store the pose in one of nine dots. When a dot contains information, it will change color; a gray dot is empty. Experiment a bit, and then click the same dot again to return to the saved pose for more experimentation. You can also store interface settings or camera positions in a similar manner. Pose Dots and Camera Dots are saved until you begin a new project or close Poser. Interface Dots are saved between projects, but you lose them when you close Poser.

Q: *How is the Pose Memory Dots option different from using the Edit > Memorize and Edit > Restore menu commands?*

A: You can use the Pose Dots to memorize up to nine poses that are specific to your current scene. A good use for Pose Dots is to save incremental poses while you experiment on additional versions. This way you can experiment with slight changes to a pose as you perfect it and decide which version you like best. The Edit > Memorize and Edit > Restore commands allow you to save more than just a pose. It also stores Morph Dial settings in addition to pose information. You can memorize and restore position, scale, morphs, parameters, materials, parent/child relationships, and so on for the entire scene (All), an entire figure, or an element (body part, prop, single camera, or single light).

Q: *When I create a new scene, my figure appears all gray. How do I change that?*

A: To change the way items are displayed, you use the Display > Document Style, Display > Figure Style, or Display > Element Style commands. Alternatively, you can use the Document Style, Figure Style, or Element Style controls in your Poser interface. If you do not see the controls on your screen, choose Window > Preview Styles to display them.

You can actually display the contents of the entire Preview window, a single figure, or a part of a figure in one of 12 different styles, as follows:

- To display everything in your Preview window in the same style, choose Display > Document Style, and then select the display mode you want to use.
- To display one figure in your Preview window in a selected style, click the figure you want to change, and choose Display > Figure Style. Select the display mode you want to use. You can also choose Use Document Style to use the same display mode that you selected for the entire document.
- To display part of a figure in a selected style, click the part you want to change. Choose Display > Element Style, and select the display mode you want to use. You can also choose Use Figure Style to use the same display mode as the figure that contains the selected part.

Q: *When I add a second figure to the scene, it merges into the first one. How do I prevent that?*

A: You can move the character with the Translate tools. You might find it easier, however, to select the figure's body or hip, and use the xTran, yTran, or zTran dials in the Parameters panel to move the figure.

Q: *How do I remove a figure or prop from a scene?*

A: Select the figure or object that you want to delete (either by clicking or by using the Select Figure menu in the Preview window), and press the Delete key.

Q: *I changed a lot of morph dials on my figure, and I'm not happy with the results. Is there a quick way to remove all of the body morphs and start all over?*

A: If you don't want to lose your pose, save the pose to the library first. Select the figure, and choose Edit > Restore > Figure. All morphs will be reset, and the figure returns to its default pose. After that, you can reapply the pose that you saved in the library.

Q: *Is there a quick way to remove all of the face morph settings and start all over?*

A: You can actually select any morphed part on a figure and return it to its default state. Click to select the face (or any other body part), and choose Edit > Restore > Element. The selected body part returns to its default state.

Q: *Some adult figures are anatomically correct. Sometimes it shows through the clothing. How do I fix that?*

A: You can hide the offending parts with the Figure > Genitalia command.

Q: *Can I make figures of different ages in Poser?*

A: The Figure > Figure Height command changes body proportions. This feature offers the ability to scale the model to something closer to the average height for a baby, toddler, child, juvenile, adolescent, ideal adult (the default size of the base models you add to the scene), fashion model, and heroic model. The feature also scales body parts (arms, legs, stomach, and so on) to resemble the way they actually look for that age group. However, the Figure Height option only controls the scale of the model's body parts from the neck down, so you have to scale and modify the head after you assign a figure height. After setting the figure height, you will still want to tweak the morphs associated with the model to make the figure look more realistic. (Remember, Figure Height only provides an approximation of a body height/age.) It's often best to use the built-in Ben and Kate models or just purchase models that fit the age requirements for your scene from a third-party vendor.

Q: *Is there a way to copy one side of my figure's pose to the other side so that the left and right sides are symmetric?*

A: Yes, indeed there is! You can pose all or part of a figure the same as the other side, or even swap sides, with the options in the Figure > Symmetry command:

- **Left to Right**: Applies the poses on the figure's left side to the right side to make the sides mirror each other.
- **Right to Left**: Applies the poses on the figure's right side to the left side to make the sides mirror each other.
- **Swap Right and Left**: Simultaneously applies the pose from the left side to the right, and from the right side to the left.
- **Left Arm to Right Arm**: Applies the poses on the figure's left arm to the right arm to make the arms mirror each other.
- **Right Arm to Left Arm**: Applies the poses on the figure's right arm to the left arm to make the arms mirror each other.
- **Swap Right and Left Arms**: Simultaneously applies the pose from the left arm to the right, and from the right arm to the left.
- **Left Leg to Right Leg**: Applies the poses on the figure's left leg to the right leg to make the legs mirror each other.
- **Right Leg to Left Leg**: Applies the poses on the figure's right leg to the left leg to make the legs mirror each other.
- **Swap Right and Left Legs**: Simultaneously applies the pose from the left leg to the right, and from the right leg to the left.
- **Straighten Torso**: Straightens the torso as it relates to the position of the body.

Q: *If I try to pose a body part with the Editing Tools, the pose gets way out of whack and the figure looks like a pretzel. How can I prevent that?*

A: There are actually a couple of different commands in Poser that can help you with that problem:

- **Turn Limits On:** The main figures that you use in Poser have limits on the joints. That is, there are predetermined settings that specify how far a joint is allowed to bend, move sideways, or twist. By default, Poser doesn't use these limits, and what happens is that joints very often get posed far beyond the limits that are humanly possible. However, when you enable the Figure > Use Limits option, Poser does not pose joints any farther than the set limits. This option helps you create poses that are more realistic.
- **Use Auto Balancing:** The Auto Balance feature helps you achieve realistic poses. Basically, this feature adjusts poses to keep the figure as close as possible to the center of its weight distribution, which Poser calculates based on the shape of the body. Therefore, with Auto Balancing, a figure should automatically balance itself to respond to poses that are unnatural for a figure. To enable or disable Auto Balancing, choose the Figure > Auto Balance command. When there is a check beside the command, it is enabled.

Q: *When I load a figure from the library, its feet don't always line up with the default ground of my scene. How do I get my figure to drop to the default ground level of my scene?*

A: The Figure > Drop to Floor command drops your figure to ground level, which is at the 0 coordinate of the Y (up and down) axis. However, sometimes you might have props or scenery in your Preview window that places "ground level" above or below the 0 coordinate. In that case, you will need to select the Hip or Body of your figure, and move the yTran parameter dial up or down until your figure is placed correctly.

One of the most common mistakes made by new users of Poser is that figures hover over the ground. This is because in some cases, you need to make adjustments to the pose. The point closest to the ground makes contact with the ground when you use the Drop to Floor command. If, for example, the foot is bent, you may need to adjust the position of the feet so that they do not appear as though your figure is floating above the ground.

The best way to make these adjustments is to put your Document Display style to Outline mode (Display > Document Style > Outline) and to use one of the orthogonal cameras (Left, Right, Top, Bottom, Front, or Back) so that you are not viewing your scene at an angle while you fix the feet.

Q: *I have several objects in a scene. Sometimes when I want to pose or move a figure or object, I accidentally move another one by mistake. Is there any way to prevent that?*

A: There are several ways that you can control this. After you get a figure or other item posed the way you like, you can prevent further changes using any of the following methods:

- **Hide the figure:** You can hide the figure from view by using the Figure > Hide Figure command. Click the figure you want to hide, and then choose the command. Continue in this manner until you hide all the figures that interfere with the parts you want to edit. To unhide all hidden figures, choose Figure > Show All Figures. You can also use the Hierarchy Editor (Window > Hierarchy Editor) to unhide selected figures. Simply click on the eye icon of a figure or part name to unhide it.
- **Lock the figure:** Choose the figure that you want to protect. Then choose the Figure > Lock Figure command. This will lock the figure in place and prevent you from moving the figure or changing its pose.
- **Lock a body part or prop:** If you want to prevent changes to a single body part or a prop, choose Object > Lock Actor. This will cause a body part to stay in place in relation to its parent. In other words, you can lock the position of a forearm in relation to the upper arm, but if you move the upper arm, the forearm will move accordingly.
- **Lock the hands:** Hands are the most time-consuming to pose, especially if you've posed them around an object. You can use the Figure > Lock Hand Parts command to lock a hand into position. This will prevent changes in hand and finger positions while you work with other areas in your Poser scene.
- **Use the Chain Break tool:** The Chain Break tool, which displays a link on its icon, allows you to prevent movements of body parts below a specified level in the hierarchy. For example, if you want to pose the lower portions of an arm but leave the shoulder in place, you can put a chain break at the shoulder before you move the lower portions. For the Chain Break tool to work, you have to turn Inverse Kinematics off with the Figure > Use Inverse Kinematics command. Further information about the Chain Break tool can be found in the Poser 8 Reference Manual.

Q: *Can I raise or lower the level of the ground plane of my scene?*

A: No, you can only move the ground left, right, forward, or back. As an alternative, you can use the Square, Square Hi-Res, or One-Sided Square props that are found in the Props > Primitives Library. Scale the square prop to the desired size, and then adjust the yTran setting to raise or lower the prop.

Q: *Can I make a figure hold something (like a ball), so that when I move the hand, the ball moves with it?*

A: Yes. Using the ball as an example, here are the steps:

1. Use the Editing Tools or the xTran, yTran, and zTran dials in the Parameters panel to position the ball in your figure's hand.
2. Pose the fingers around the ball. You will probably get better results by using the dials in the Parameters panel rather than trying to pose them with the Editing Tools.
3. Select the ball as the current figure.
4. Choose Object > Change Parent. Select the appropriate hand (right or left, depending on which hand is holding the ball) as the parent to the ball. Now whenever you move the hand, the ball follows. You can still move the ball, but its relation as a child to the hand will remain until you "unparent" it. To "unparent" the ball, select it, choose Object > Change Parent, and choose UNIVERSE (the first object in the hierarchy) as the parent.

Cameras

Q: *How do I use the camera controls?*

A: The Camera Controls allow you to select cameras for various purposes or to move them so that you can get a better view of the items in your Poser document. The controls serve the following functions:

- **Camera Selection Menu:** Click the Camera Selection menu to display a list of cameras to choose from.
- **Face Camera:** The Face Camera is good to use when you are creating a face expression or using Face Morph dials to create a unique character. The camera remains fixed on the character's face, even as you zoom in, out, or rotate the camera view.
- **Right Hand and Left Hand Cameras:** These cameras keep the designated hand in view, even while zooming in or out or rotating the camera. Their purpose is to keep the camera centered around the hand while you pose it—most especially while posing a hand to hold another object.
- **Animating On/Off:** When you are posing body parts or props for the purposes of animation, you sometimes have a need to adjust cameras so that you can get a better view of things. However, each time you move a camera in a frame of an animation, it adds a keyframe that keeps track of the position change. As a result, you may accidentally add animation keyframes without intending to do so. One way to prevent this from happening is to turn camera animating off. To turn camera animation off, click the key icon to turn it red. Click it again to resume camera animation.

- **Flyaround View**: Click this icon to get a 360-degree flyaround view of your scene. Click again to turn the Flyaround view off.
- **Select Camera**: The mouse displays a double-arrow cursor when you are able to select a camera. To advance forward in the list, click the icon at its right side, or drag the mouse to the right to advance quickly. To move backward in the list, click the left side of the icon, or drag your mouse toward the left. Click to cycle through the various camera views.

Starting from the Main camera, the icons appear in the following order:

- **Move Y and Z**: Your mouse cursor displays arrows when you position it over this control. Click and drag left or right to move the camera along the Z (forward/backward) plane. Drag up or down to move the camera along the Y (up/down) plane.
- **Move X and Y**: Your mouse cursor displays arrows when you position it over this control. Click and drag left or right to move the camera along the X (left/right) plane. Click and drag up or down to move the camera along the Y (up/down) plane.
- **Camera Plane**: Click and drag left or right to move the camera along the X (left/right) axis, or up or down to move the camera along the Z (forward or back) axis.
- **Scale**: Click and drag left to increase the scale of the camera. This "zooms in" to the scene without affecting focal or perspective settings. Click and drag right to decrease the scale of the camera, which "zooms out" without affecting focal or perspective settings.
- **Roll**: Click and drag toward the left to roll the camera clockwise. Click and drag toward the right to roll the camera counterclockwise.
- **Focal Length**: Click and drag toward the left to decrease the camera's focal length; click and drag toward the right to increase the focal length.
- **Trackball**: Click the trackball to give the current camera focus. You can move the trackball at any incremental angle to change the view. Drag the trackball up to look above a scene, down to look below a scene, and left or right to view the scene from either side.

Q: *Can I make cameras always look at an object, even when I move the object?*

A: If you want to make a camera follow an object, first select the camera, and then choose Object > Point At. When the Hierarchy panel comes up, choose the item or body part that you want the camera to follow.

You can also make objects follow the camera. For example, you can make eyes always look toward a camera as you position it. To do so, select the object (such as the left eye or right eye), choose Object > Point At, and then choose the camera that you want the object to follow.

Note, however, that if you try to make the head follow a camera, the top of the head points to the camera rather than the front of the head.

Lights and Shadows

Q: *How does a light probe work?*

A: The purpose of a light probe is to simulate the lighting conditions in a photograph or movie. Imagine the light probe as an invisible hemisphere that surrounds your scene.

The area in the center of the light probe is the area of the hemisphere that is directly overhead at the highest part of the hemisphere. The outer edges of the light probe are the lowest parts of the hemisphere, which encircle the scene at floor height. The top of the light probe determines the lighting conditions at the back of your scene. The bottom of the light probe determines the lighting conditions at the front of your scene.

Q: *Can I use an AVI or MOV file for an image-based light probe?*

A: Yes. One way to accomplish this is to set up your IBL light in the Material Room first, using the IBL wacro. During this process, the wacro will prompt you to select an image. After this process is complete, your IBL light will be configured properly. All you have to do afterward is disconnect the Image Map node and replace it with a Movie node (New Node > 2D Textures > Movie).

Q: *Can I make a light that looks something like a movie being projected onto a screen?*

A: Yes. After you create a spotlight, go to the Material Room, and change the color of the light to white. Then attach an Image Map node (New Node > 2D Textures > Image Map) or a Movie node (New Node > 2D Textures > Movie) to the Diffuse channel. Check the Auto Fit option in the Image Map node to fit the image in the spotlight.

Face Room

Q: *If I apply the Face Room head to the figure so that the original head gets replaced, how do I get the old head back?*

A: The Edit > Restore > Element command won't work if you apply a Face Room head to your figure. To restore the original head, return to the Face Room. Click the Reset Face Room button that appears below the Face Sculpting area. Click the Apply to Figure button in the Actions area. When you return to the Pose Room, the default head should appear on your figure.

Q: *I used the Face Room to create a face morph. But when I go back to the Pose Room and dial the Face Room morph to 1, the eyes look funny. What happened?*

A: When you use the Face Room to spawn morph targets for a face, it also spawns morph targets for the Left Eye and Right Eye. They also have to be set to 1 to restore the entire face to the shape you created in the Face Room.

Q: *Are there other programs available that work like the Face Room so that I can use them on other figures?*

A: The code used in the Face Room module was licensed by efrontier from Singular Inversions, the makers of FaceGen Modeler and FaceGen Customizer. You can learn more about these packages at www.facegen.com.

Hair Room

Q: *When I save my hair projects to the library, you can't see the hair in the thumbnails. How do I get the hair to show up?*

A: The thumbnails in the Poser library are saved in PNG format and measure 91×91 pixels. Some people render a scene and save it as a PNG file with a transparent background. The transparent background is important for the thumbnail to display properly. After rendering, resize the PNG file to 91 x 91 pixels, and assign the same prefix as the library item. For example, if you have a hair file named JonisHair.HR2, name the PNG file JonisHair.PNG.

Q: *How do I get rid of bald spots in Dynamic hair?*

A: "Bald spots" are less prominent if you use the proper lighting in conjunction with the Opaque in Shadows option in the hair material. Go to the Material Room, and select one of the hair sections. Verify that the Opaque in Shadow option is checked in the hair material. If that does not resolve the problem, adjust the lighting so that some lighting comes from above the head so that shadows are generated. Finally, if you still see bald spots, you can increase the hair density a little bit at a time until the baldness is less obvious.

UV Mapping

Q: *You've shown how to map skirts, pants, and shirts. What about dresses?*

A: For the most part, you've learned the basic techniques for dresses already. Think of a dress as nothing more than a shirt and a skirt combined. If desired, you can then stitch the shirt and dress together at the waist, and relax it.

Q: *What about organic models, such as humans or animals? How do you map those?*

A: Break it down into pieces. For example, you can detach the head from the body and map it in cylindrical mode. The eyes, of course, are spherical. The teeth are arranged in the mouth in a shape of a "C," which is basically half of a cylinder. The tongue can either be two planes (top and bottom) or cylindrical with a seam along the bottom of the tongue.

Now, what about the body? Take the hands and feet away from the remainder of the body for a moment. What basically remains is something similar to the shirt and pants that you learned how to map in this book! Go one step further than the pants, however, and join the vertices in the center, near where the groin is. Then, relax the two sides until the vertices that you joined are blended together.

As for the hands and feet, all you have to do is divide the hands in half as if you're slicing the top away from the bottom—one side of the hand shows the palm and underside of the fingers, whereas the other side of the hand shows the tops of the hands. Split the feet in half so that one view shows the top, and the other half shows the sole of the foot. After you break it into individual sections like this, UV-mapping a human becomes predictable and methodical.

Q: *Sometimes after I relax things in UVMapper, there is still a little bit of distortion. Can I eliminate it entirely?*

A: It depends on the software you use and how skilled you are in using it. One thing that was not covered in this book was the Interactive Mapping mode in UVMapper Professional. When you choose Interactive mode, you can move or rotate a spherical, planar, or cylindrical indicator to align the UV map more accurately with your models. The texture map updates in real time while you make the adjustments.

There are also additional UV-mapping programs that have more advanced mapping and relaxing features in addition to features that allow you to paint directly on the 3D models. However, they are also much more expensive than UVMapper Professional. If you are interested in researching them further, go to www.righthemisphere.com for information about Deep Paint 3D and Deep UV or www.maxon.net for information about Maxon Body Paint.

Materials

Q: *What is a gather node?*

A: A gather node is a very powerful and complex procedural shader that allows you to create materials that actually accumulate light from their surroundings. This works well for simulating the reflected light interacting between two objects that are close to each other (think "radiosity-effects") or even simulating a glowing object. The effect is perfect for creating a light saber or bioluminescent sea creature.

You will need to use the FireFly rendering engine to take advantage of the gather node. You will also need to make sure you have raytracing enabled. Using the gather node will increase your rendering times significantly.

Q: *What is up with my displacement? Why does it have black spots? Something very wrong happened here!*

A: When your Displacement Bounds are too small, you may find that your materials develop black "specks," or even what appear to be large black "holes" in unexpected places. This happens because the displacement on the material is too large to be contained within the current boundary.

Here's what happens: The render engine begins by assuming that every pixel in the image is black, or zero (R=0, G=0, B=0), until calculated otherwise by the interaction of light with the various material properties of objects visible at that pixel. When the displacement calculation overflows the current displacement boundary, the tips of the displaced mesh move outside the current render bucket. Once outside the current bucket, the color at that point remains unknown, or uncalculated, and therefore stays zero, its default value.

Whenever you use displacement, make sure that you set the Min Displacement Bounds settings for the FireFly render engine. The Min Displacement Bounds should be large enough to handle the largest displacement of all the materials in your current scene. Also, keep in mind that using displacement in your materials will take longer to render. Setting the Min Displacement Bounds too high may have a negative impact on rendering performance. As a rule, set the Min Displacement Bounds to be roughly twice the largest displacement of any of your material.

Q: *Can I create water that actually looks like water?*

A: I found a really nice tutorial online that does a wonderful job explaining the aspects you should consider when creating a realistic water material. Stuart Runham's Water Tutorial can be found here: www.stu-runham.co.uk/water.htm. While it was written in the days of Poser 5, it is still a viable tutorial, as it utilizes Poser's texture nodes.

Q: *I want to make a mirrored surface; what do I need to do?*

A: The quickest way to create a true reflective material is to use the Material Room wacro Add Reflection. After the reflection node has been added, you can tweak parameters to accommodate your lighting conditions.

Remember to enable raytracing, and pay attention to the number of ray bounces you have configured. More bounces will yield a more realistic mirror but will also slow down the render considerably. A Ray Bounce setting as low as 2 may be sufficient to create a convincing mirror material.

Q: *What's the quickest way to create a displacement map?*

A: If you are using a simple image-based texture, the quickest way to create a displacement map is to tie the texture map that you use for your Diffuse channel into the Displacement channel as well.

If you want a bit more control, you can create a grayscale copy of the same map you are using for your Diffusion channel and use that instead. For the purposes of creating a displacement map, you are only interested in the brightness component of the texture, so the color data is extraneous. After you have your grayscale image, you can edit it using your favorite image editing program to maximize the range of brightness to give you the widest possible range of displacement at render time.

If you are using a procedural shader to drive the Diffusion channel of your root material node, you can tie that node into the Displacement channel of the root node as well.

Don't forget that you can always include additional shader nodes to create more interesting and natural displacement effects, regardless of if you are using a procedural shader or image-based texture map to drive your Displacement channel. For example, you can add a Noise node to create some random bumps to bias the value of your existing Displacement output—essentially creating bumps within bumps.

The white values of your displacement map or procedural shader will create a larger displacement than black areas, with absolute black areas not being displaced at all and absolute white areas being displaced the maximum amount.

Q: *Can I create glowing objects?*

A: Yes! See the gather node answer.

Additionally, if you are not averse to some post-processing work, there is a tutorial available online written by Jim Harnock that shows how you can create a halo around your glowing objects. The tutorial can be found at www.castleposer.co.uk/articles/shader_gather.html and www.castleposer.co.uk/articles/shader_gather2.html.

Q: *How can I make fur without using Poser Hair?*

A: A quick technique to simulate the look of fur is to use displacement at render time. With Poser 8, all you need to do is add a Noise node and attach its output into the displacement parameter's input on the root node. After you have your Noise node attached, make sure you also set your Min Displacement Bounds and enable the use of displacement maps in the FireFly render engine's parameter palette.

Q: *What the heck is a node mask, and why should I use one?*

A: A node mask is simply a template that defines where on your object a certain node will have its effect. It's rather like using a stencil to control where paint goes on. Instead of paint, however, the Node Mask determines where a particular node will apply its effects to the object. You can download a free tutorial from http://heromorph.com/hmdownload/index.php?main_page=product_info&products_id=219 to help you create a node mask.

RENDERING

Q: *How can I speed up my renders?*

A: There are a few things you can do to help speed up your renders:

- Use smaller texture map images.
- Use low poly figures whenever possible.
- Use less complex procedural shaders and materials for objects that are not critical to your design.
- If you aren't using a true reflective material, try enabling the Remove Back Facing Polygons option.
- Decrease the pixel samples.
- Increase the Minimum Shading Rate.
- Don't use Texture Filtering.
- Use reflection maps rather than raytraced reflections.
- Disable raytracing.
- Don't use Ambient Occlusion.
- Disable shadows on lights that are not the primary light sources for your scene.
- Reduce the complexity of as many textures in your scene as you can.
- Reuse texture and shadow maps whenever possible.
- Keep your hard drives defragmented.
- Don't run other applications.

Q: *FireFly looks like it has stopped rendering and/or stops responding while rendering. How can I fix this?*

A: If you find that your Poser "goes out to lunch" when you try to render, you can do a few immediate things to help speed it up:

- Reduce shadow map sizes.
- Reduce the Render Bucket size.
- Reduce the number of pixel samples.
- Increase the shading rate.
- Disable shadows on noncritical lights.

Q: *My objects have black holes where I don't expect them. Why?*

A: If you are using displacement, you may need to increase your Min Displacement Bounds. If you aren't using displacement but have overlapping or closely positioned object surfaces, you may need to enable displacement on the material that is having problems to lift the surface of the object a bit. If you need to do this, remember to enable displacement mapping in the Render window.

If you don't have overlapping object surfaces, increasing the Shadow Min Bias on your light(s) might fix the problem.

If the holes are all facing away from the camera, you may have enabled the Remove Backfacing Polygons option.

Q: *Everything gets puffy when I render it! Help!*

A: If you have enabled smooth polygons in the object's properties, you may find that your object bloats at render time. This happens because the object's polygons are not specifically optimized for Poser or polygon smoothing algorithms. For an object to accommodate smoothing on selective polygon intersections, the object must be created with very small polygons right at the joints where smoothing is not desired. Those smaller polygons in the corners, or joints, will make the smoothed corner appear crisper and less bloated.

In other cases, not all the joints on an object are actually "welded" together. This will keep the edges of the object crisp; however, unwelded edges may also affect how seamless and procedural textures appear. Welding or not welding edges of objects when they are created should be evaluated on a case-by-case basis depending on the type of object, the morphs that are typically applied to the object and the complexity and types of materials that object is usually mapped with.

Q: *What's the quickest way to set up a material that uses refraction?*

A: The quickest way to set up a material that uses refraction is to use the Add Refraction wacro. This will create a new Refraction node, which plugs into the Refraction Color channel of the root node. Make sure you set the Transparency, Translucence Value, and Transparency Edge values, and enable Raytracing. You'll have to use the FireFly rendering engine, too.

Q: *Can Poser 8 load texture files larger than 4096 pixels?*

A: Yes! Unlike previous versions of Poser, Poser 8 now allows you to load image maps that are larger than 4096 pixels.

Index

Numbers

A

B

C

D

E

F

G

H

I

J

K

L

M

N

O

T

License Agreement/Notice of Limited Warranty